FRANCE

The Bordas/Helm Guide

Director:
Pierre CABANNE

Photographs by
Hervé Bordas
and Philippe Houdebine

Translated by
Michael Jacobson and
Gela Jacobson
in collaboration with
Ruth Hemingway

CHRISTOPHER HELM
London

© Bordas, Paris, 1976
© 1988 Christopher Helm (Publishers) Ltd, English Translation
Christopher Helm (Publishers) Ltd, Imperial House,
21–25 North Street, Bromley, Kent BR1 1SD
This translation based on the 12th edition

ISBN 0–7470–1607–0

A CIP catalogue record for this book
is available from the British Library

Iconography Ph. Hervé Bordas © Photeb
except p. 129, Bayeux. Ph. © Luc Joubert
p. 182, Epinal, Ph. Jeanbor. © Photeb
p. 318, Saint-Savin. Ph. © Robert Thuillier
Cartography © Bordas

Printer industria gráfica, sa   Barcelona
D.L.: B. 1645-1988

Typeset in Great Britain by Butler & Tanner, Frome, Somerset
Printed and bound in Spain

A Traveller's
Guide to France

This is the first English-language edition of the leading French guide designed specifically for people discovering France by road. It describes more than 3,500 towns, historic buildings, localities or individual sights of particular interest. Whatever your inclination – sandy beaches, mountains, fishing, water sports, fine arts, archaeology, Roman remains, lovely châteaux, venerable churches, forests, superb food and wine – no other guidebook offers you so much information about the whole country, complete with an abundance of full-colour photographs, within one volume. Nor does any other give you so much help in planning your itineraries: a grid-map on pp. 10–11 refers you to the page numbers (12–101) of the areas of France on which you wish to concentrate. Within each of these large detailed maps (linked one to the other by arrowed numbers at each edge), every place outlined in yellow is the subject of a separate entry in the extensive A-to-Z section (pp. 105–361), likewise shown in bold type within the text and index. Special sights are shown in red, and all other places printed on the maps, in light type, are also duly mentioned under the nearest appropriate A-Z entry. (To make the maps easier to read, minor roads and unimportant places not mentioned in the text have been omitted from them.)

This system is reinforced by the Index, which is in two parts. The first lists every town, locality and named site in the maps. The second part groups sights into various different categories (e.g. châteaux and forts, abbeys and churches, mountain features, and so on) – so, if you wanted to spend a week visiting castles, for instance, your planning would be simple. As in the main text, all places are listed with the page number of the map concerned and a grid reference (letter and figure), indicating the map square within which to find them.

Keeping in the Mood

As befits France's most comprehensive guide of its type, we have set out to retain as much as feasible of its original French flavour. First, in the maps and text, names are not invariably translated into their English equivalents, because we took the view that the French version is what you'll actually *see* on signposts, terminal information boards, and so on. (By the same token, although putting accents on capital letters is normally a solecism in French, we have done so as an aid to pronunciation.) Secondly, we have also preserved much of the French emphasis as regards subject-matter. To give an example: if the A-Z entries appear to give considerable weight to local churches and other religious buildings, this does not merely echo French people's deep interest in the subject but also, above all, reflects the unrivalled wealth and variety of France's church history and architecture.

Yet that is only one of an almost infinite range of possibilities now open to you. The simple fact remains that, when you use this guidebook, you will be seeing France as the French themselves see it.

Bon voyage!

When was it?

Approximate centuries of various historical or architectural periods mentioned frequently in the A-Z text:

Baroque 17–18c.
Carolingian Late 8c to latter half of 10c.
Classical If not referring to Graeco-Roman antiquity, applies (architecturally) to the post-Renaissance period – late-17 but mainly 18c.
Feudal Principally 12–13c (but can also cover a century or so on either side).
Gallo-Roman 1c BC to 4c AD.
Gothic Broadly, from 12c up to the Renaissance in 15–16c. Within this period, individual developments were: **Gothic Rayonnant**, late-13 and 14c. **Gothic Flamboyant**, 15c. (So-called 'primitive' or early Gothic was confined to 12c.)
Megalithic The era of menhirs, dolmens and so on. Thought to be mainly around 2,000 BC, but perhaps stretching back as early as 4,000 BC.

Merovingian The first dynasty of Frankish kings, from mid-5c until succeeded by 'Pépin le Bref' of the Carolingians in the year 751.
Neo-Gothic, etc. 19c. (Embraces so-called 'troubadour' fashion, also applicable to literature and the arts, manifested by liberal echoes of medieval and Gothic styles, which became popular after the restoration of the French monarchy from 1815.)
Paleo-Christian Roughly, end of 2c to end of 4c.
Renaissance In French terms, specifically, dates from early years of 16c.
Rococo 18c.
Romanesque 11–12c. (In English church architecture, it is usually known as Norman.)
Visigoth 5c.

Some Personalities

A brief guide to a few of the names which crop up a number of times throughout the A-Z section – historic figures who are immediately familiar to French people (some habitually just by their surnames), but who may be rather less familiar to other nations.

Agrippa d'Aubigné
Writer, poet and warrior (1552–1630), comrade-in-arms of France's King Henri IV. Grandfather of Mme. de Maintenon, mistress and then wife of Louis XIV.
Frédéric Auguste Bartholdi
Sculptor (1834–1904) who created the Lion of Belfort; also responsible for New York's Statue of Liberty.
Jean Bullant
16th-century architect (d. 1578); worked for Catherine de Medici.
Philibert Delorme
Also a 16th-century architect (d. 1570), regarded as the most important of his day. Works included the Château des Tuileries in Paris.
Du Guesclin
14th-century military hero (d. 1380); as Constable of France, from 1370, he waged a highly effective guerrilla war against the English forces in the country. (See entry for Dinan, p. 176.)
Fénelon
Forward-looking writer and prelate (1651–1715), so far ahead of his time – both in his extraordinarily eloquent preaching and in his political thinking – that he may justly be regarded as one of the catalysts for the Age of Reason and the democratic stirrings which led to the French Revolution. Although out of favour with Louis XIV, he ended his days unharmed as Archbishop of Cambrai.
Jean Goujon
16th-century sculptor and architect, leading light of the Renaissance in France; partly responsible for the Louvre in Paris.
Le Nôtre
Garden designer and architect (1613–1700). The many great gardens he created included those of Versailles and Vaux-le-Vicomte. These are 'French-style', i.e. formal gardens, as distinct from the 'English-style' landscape gardens of his

slightly later English counterpart, 'Capability' Brown.
Le Vau
Architect (1612–1670) responsible for the main lines of the Palace of Versailles. His previous works included the château de Vaux-le-Vicomte and the famous building across the river from the Louvre, in Paris, which became the Institute (under whose dome the French Academicians hold their public sessions).
Mansart (F. and J. H.)
François Mansart (1598–1666), a superb Classical architect who built numerous churches and also perfected the form of roof named after him (in English, 'mansard'). His great-nephew, Jules Hardouin (1646–1708), who added Mansart to his surname, became Louis XIV's principal architect. Besides enlarging the Palace of Versailles (e.g. the Hall of Mirrors), Hardouin-Mansart's many other works included the Grand Trianon, the mighty Place Vendôme in Paris, and the chapel of the Invalides, with its famous dome.
Pierre Puget
Sculptor who swam against the artistic current of his day (1620–1694) by espousing realism and the baroque. Many religious works; also famed group-statue of the Greek athlete Milo of Crotona, a pupil of Pythagoras, in the Louvre.
Sully
Minister and former comrade-in-arms of Henri IV (1560–1641). A Protestant, he not only put the country's finances in order but was also responsible for giving France roads, canals and many other improvements.
Vauban
Marshal of France (1633–1707), with a genius for military architecture. He improved the country's defences by the construction of new fortifications, or the strengthening of existing ones, almost beyond number – right round the French coast and along every frontier. Personally directed

several sieges for Louis XIV in the Low Countries. (He is also credited with invention of the socket-bayonet.)

Eugène Viollet-le-Duc
19th-century architect who restored an enormous number of historic medieval buildings throughout France – notably various cathedrals, Notre Dame in Paris, and the walled city of Carcassonne. In his writings, he played a leading role in promoting the use of metal in architecture.

Some Definitions

As a result of France's unsurpassed architectural, geographical and historical wealth, certain descriptive words or phrases – sometimes rather esoteric – tend to occur quite frequently in the A-Z entries. Since it would have been too space-consuming to explain them each time, here is a list of the main ones.

Ambulatory A sheltered walkway, such as a cloister.

Barbican A tower or other defensive structure attached to a gate or bridge.

Bartizan A small projection from a building, such as a turret, where sentries can be stationed.

Bastide Small fortified towns or villages, mostly on hill-tops, built in 13–14 c: latterly, very much a feature of the 100 Years' War in Guyenne and Gascony, with English and French bastides strategically interspersed and often eyeing each other angrily across a valley. All were built round a similar rectangular or square lay-out and were intended to be self-supporting and, to some extent, self-governing.

Belvedere A structure that affords a magnificent view of the surrounding area.

Calefactory The room in a monastery where the inmates warmed themselves.

Calvary An open-air representation of the crucifixion of Christ.

Cathar Member of a Roman Catholic sect with nonconformist views (e.g. refusing to accept the Church's hierarchical system) which swept French Catalonia – that is, mainly Languedoc-Roussillon – from 12 c. Although the Cathars had a spiritual purity which many would regard as admirable nowadays, they were branded as heretics and bloodily massacred throughout first half of 13 c. (Also known as Albigensians, from town of Albi.)

Causse Name given to the limestone plateaus, often very extensive, of the Massif Central (notably Auvergne) and Aquitaine (the Quercy).

Cirque Natural bowl or large hollow in mountainous areas – equivalent to a corrie or cwm.

Concretions Irregular crystalline or mineral formations precipitated from sedimentary rock (particularly in prehistoric caves) – sometimes turning into fantastic animals or other weird-and-wonderful shapes.

Corbels/corbelling An architectural support angling up from a wall to hold up, for example, a roof.

Corniche A road above a coast or along a gorge or steep valley, especially one cut into the side of a cliff.

Cornière Name often given incorrectly to covered arcade skirting central square of a bastide. Properly speaking, the cornières are *angles* which form narrow passageways (*cf* the 'valley' of adjoining roofs).

Crenellated Having battlements – toothlike parapets or walls, with gaps.

Cromlech A circle of prehistoric monoliths

Cryptoporticos An enclosed gallery having, at the side, walls with openings instead of columns.

Defile A narrow passage or gorge.

Dolmen A prehistoric monument shaped like a table, with one flat slab supported by two pillars.

Enceinte A line of fortifications enclosing a castle or town.

Étang Same as a lake (although, according to one strict dictionary definition, an 'étang' is a natural or artificial stretch of *stagnant* water). For everyday purposes, however, the only reason confusion may arise is variation in local usage: water shown on maps as Lake X may be known to the people living in the area as Étang X (and vice-versa, of course).

Félibrige Literary school founded in 1854 (and still very much alive) to restore the use of the ancient Provençal language. Results are exhibited in quite a few museums in S. of France. Someone writing prose or poetry in Provençal (which is a 'cousin' of Catalan) may be termed a *félibre*.

Grotto Broadly the same as cave – but can range all the way from some small prehistoric or troglodytic dwelling to a mighty underground chamber of the kind explored by pot-holers.

Historiated capitals As the term implies, they 'tell a story' – usually biblical or other religious scenes, but can also be of animals, folk art, even caricatures of local personalities. Besides the upper part of columns or piers, ornamentation of this nature may be found as well on hanging keystones, etc. For an excellent example, see photograph on p. 209. (Also pp. 121, 180, 313, 340).

Lapidary (*museum*) Principally sculptures in stone, but may also embrace stone inscriptions, even Roman mosaics and the like.

Lauze Kind of flat roofing stone usually found only in southern France. May also be used for flagstones.

Machicolated/Machicolation Describes projecting parapets or galleries (supported on corbels) at top of early castle walls, with holes in the floor through which missiles or boiling oil could be dropped on attackers.

Maquis French Resistance, underground forces.

Menhir A solitary monolith, usually dating from prehistoric times.

Oppidum Ancient Roman fortified town, especially those which are the site of excavations. Correctly, 'fortified place built on a height'.

Pelota A ball-game, of Basque origin, resembling fives or Jai Alai, using a basket catching and throwing device.

Puy The former cone of a small extinct volcano (applied above all to those in the Auvergne).

Retable Usually a sculpted or painted screen-like decoration, either above or – mostly – at the back

of an altar (*cf* a reredos). But can also describe an ornamented frame for panels carved or painted with religious scenes (not necessarily near the altar).

Son et lumière A dramatic spectacle, presented after dark, involving lighting effects or natural features of the country or chosen building and an appropriate theme illustrated by spoken words and by music.

Treasure (*church*) Not only gold and silver plate, jewelled chalices, etc., but also may include (for instance) rare old vestments and reliquaries.

Viewing tables/panoramic tables Invaluable sight-seeing aids on high places: metal plates, rather like a protractor, with lines or arrows pointing in exact direction of places of particular interest in the distance. Usually with coin-in-the-slot telescopes or binoculars alongside.

Troglodytic Cave-dwelling.

Tympanum Recessed space between the cornices of a triangular pediment or – on most occasions in this guide – between the arch and lintel of a church portal, frequently lending itself to sculpture or other decoration. (For good examples, see photos on pp. 131 and 215.)

ABBREVIATIONS

aka = Also known as	Goth. = Gothic	Prehist. = Prehistory/prehistoric
Alt. = Altitude	Hist. = History/historical	Rec. = Recommended
Blvd. = Boulevard	Hr./hrs. = Hour/hours	Reg. = Region/regional
Cath. = Cathedral	Inf. = Information	Ren. = Renaissance
c = Century	Int. = Interior/internal	r. = right
Ch. = Château (named)	l. = left	R. = River (named)
cl. = Closed	Mt./mts. = Mount/mountain(s)	S.I. = Syndicat d'Initiative
Contemp. = Contemporary	Mus. = Musée/museum	Trad. = Traditional/traditions(s)
Exc. = Except	Natnl. = National	v.a. = Visitors admitted
Ext. = Exterior/external	n.v.a. = No visitors admitted	
Fmr. = Former	Pop. = Population	

Days of week: Mon./Tues./Wed./Thurs./Fri./Sat./Sun.
Months: Jan./Feb./Mar./Apr./May/June/July/Aug./Sept./Oct./Nov./Dec.
Compass directions: E = East. W = West. S = South. N = North. (And in combination, eg. NW = North-West)

Châteaux. Some are feudal fortresses, but because of their later transformation into elegant residences (internally, anyway), are not described as castles but simply by the generic term 'château'.

Convent. Not only for nuns, as often supposed, but can also be for monks (i.e. as well as monasteries). Depending on the religious order, one distinction often accepted is that, broadly speaking, a convent inhabited by monks would be within a town.

D roads. Such is the speed and extent of road improvement in France that you may well find that, since the maps in this guide were prepared, some D roads have already been upgraded to the N category (though usually under the same number). Another point to watch is that a road's number will often change when it crosses a Departmental boundary.

V.a. It may be assumed that all museums are open to the public, so 'visitors admitted' is cited only when it is necessary to add a note of restricted hours or periods of closure. If no 'v.a.' or other qualifications are shown, it is implicit that the museum will normally be open seven days a week.

MEASUREMENTS

As a rough rule-of-thumb ...

1 kilometre = $\frac{5}{8}$ of a mile
To translate kilometres into miles, therefore, multiply by five and divide by eight.

(i.e. 8 km = 5 miles;   100 km = 62.5 miles)

1 metre = 39 in ($3\frac{1}{4}$ ft)

To translate metres into yards, multiply by 13 and divide by 12. Into feet, multiply by 13 and divide by 4.

(i.e. 30 metres = $32\frac{1}{2}$ yards or $97\frac{1}{2}$ ft
100 metres = $108\frac{1}{3}$ yards or 325 ft)

CONTENTS

Where does that car come from?

In France: the last two figures on a number plate correspond with those of the Department where the vehicle is registered, as shown below. 'Collecting' as many as possible, seen on the road during your journey, is a popular family competition – and a good way of keeping children from getting bored.

From elsewhere: Letters showing the country of origin should be displayed in a small oval sign on the back of the vehicle (see list of some of the main ones, on the right).

French cars

01	Ain	48	Lozère
02	Aisne	49	Maine
03	Allier	50	Manche
04	Alpes-de-Hte-Provence	51	Marne
05	Alpes (Hautes)	52	Marne (Haute)
06	Alpes-Maritimes	53	Mayenne
07	Ardèche	54	Meurthe-et-Moselle
08	Ardennes	55	Meuse
09	Ariège	56	Morbihan
10	Aube	57	Moselle
11	Aude	58	Nièvre
12	Aveyron	59	Nord
13	Bouches-du-Rhône	60	Oise
14	Calvados	61	Orne
15	Cantal	62	Pas-de-Calais
16	Charente	63	Puy-de-Dôme
17	Charente-Maritime	64	Pyrénées-Atlantiques
18	Cher	65	Pyrénées (Hautes)
19	Corrèze	66	Pyrénées-Orientales
2A	Corsica (South)	67	Rhin (Bas)
2B	Corsica (North)	68	Rhin (Haut)
21	Côte-d'Or	69	Rhône
22	Côtes-du-Nord	70	Saône (Haute)
23	Creuse	71	Saône-et-Loire
24	Dordogne	72	Sarthe
25	Doubs	73	Savoie
26	Drôme	74	Savoie (Haute)
27	Eure	75	Paris
28	Eure-et-Loir	76	Seine-Maritime
29	Finistère	77	Seine-et-Marne
30	Gard	78	Yvelines
31	Garonne (Haute)	79	Sèvres (Deux)
32	Gers	80	Somme
33	Gironde	81	Tarn
34	Hérault	82	Tarn-et-Garonne
35	Ille-et-Vilaine	83	Var
36	Indre	84	Vaucluse
37	Indre-et-Loir	85	Vendée
38	Isère	86	Vienne
39	Jura	87	Vienne (Haute)
40	Landes	88	Vosges
41	Loir-et-Cher	89	Yonne
42	Loire	90	Territoire-de-Belfort
43	Loire (Haute)	91	Essonne
44	Loire Atlantique	92	Hauts-de-Seine
45	Loiret	93	Seine-Saint-Denis
46	Lot	94	Val-de-Marne
47	Lot-et-Garonne	95	Val-d'Oise

Other countries

A	Austria
AL	Albania
AND	Andorra
AUS	Australia
B	Belgium
BG	Bulgaria
BR	Brazil
C	Cuba
CDN	Canada
CH	Switzerland
CS	Czechoslovakia
D	West Germany
DDR	East Germany
DK	Denmark
DZ	Algeria
E	Spain
ET	Egypt
FL	Lichtenstein
GB	Great Britain
GBA	Alderney
GBG	Guernsey
GBJ	Jersey
GBM	Isle of Man
GBZ	Gibraltar
GR	Greece
H	Hungary
I	Italy
IL	Israel
IND	India
IR	Iran
IRL	Ireland
J	Japan
L	Luxembourg
MA	Morocco
MC	Monaco
MEX	Mexico
N	Norway
NL	Netherlands
P	Portugal
PE	Peru
PL	Poland
R	Rumania
RA	Argentina
RCH	Chile
RL	Lebanon
RM	Madagascar
S	Sweden
SF	Finland
SN	Senegal
SU	Soviet Union
TN	Tunisia
TR	Turkey
U	Uruguay
USA	United States
V	Vatican City
YU	Yugoslavia
ZA	South Africa

Some vehicles in France have special registration letters. Among those seen most frequently are: **CD** – Diplomatic Corps (in yellow on green background). **TT** – Temporary transit (in white on red background). **W** - Vehicles on road in course of sale or repair.

Legenda - Légende - Legend

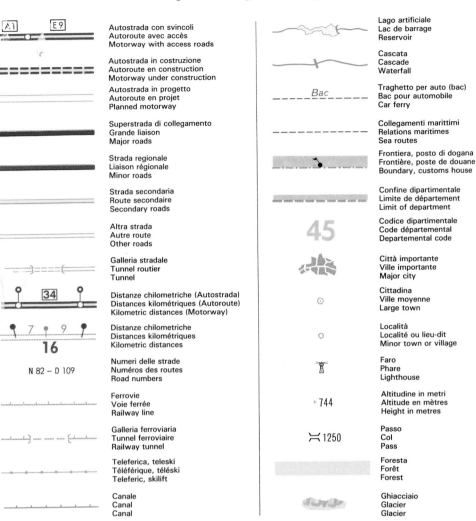

A.1 **E 9**	Autostrada con svincoli Autoroute avec accès Motorway with access roads
	Autostrada in costruzione Autoroute en construction Motorway under construction
	Autostrada in progetto Autoroute en projet Planned motorway
	Superstrada di collegamento Grande liaison Major roads
	Strada regionale Liaison régionale Minor roads
	Strada secondaria Route secondaire Secondary roads
	Altra strada Autre route Other roads
	Galleria stradale Tunnel routier Tunnel
34	Distanze chilometriche (Autostrada) Distances kilométriques (Autoroute) Kilometric distances (Motorway)
7 9 **16**	Distanze chilometriche Distances kilométriques Kilometric distances
N 82 – D 109	Numeri delle strade Numéros des routes Road numbers
	Ferrovie Voie ferrée Railway line
	Galleria ferroviaria Tunnel ferroviaire Railway tunnel
	Teleferica, teleski Téléférique, téléski Teleferic, skilift
	Canale Canal Canal

	Lago artificiale Lac de barrage Reservoir
	Cascata Cascade Waterfall
Bac	Traghetto per auto (bac) Bac pour automobile Car ferry
	Collegamenti marittimi Relations maritimes Sea routes
	Frontiera, posto di dogana Frontière, poste de douane Boundary, customs house
	Confine dipartimentale Limite de département Limit of department
45	Codice dipartimentale Code départemental Departemental code
	Città importante Ville importante Major city
⊙	Cittadina Ville moyenne Large town
○	Località Localité ou lieu-dit Minor town or village
⌶	Faro Phare Lighthouse
· 744	Altitudine in metri Altitude en mètres Height in metres
⤫ 1250	Passo Col Pass
	Foresta Forêt Forest
	Ghiacciaio Glacier Glacier

Simboli turistici (eccetto nelle città)
Symboles touristiques (excepté dans les villes)
Signs for tourists (except in towns)

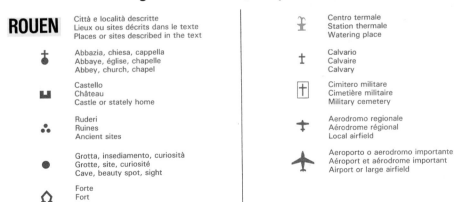

ROUEN	Città e località descritte Lieux ou sites décrits dans le texte Places or sites described in the text
☥	Abbazia, chiesa, cappella Abbaye, église, chapelle Abbey, church, chapel
⊔	Castello Château Castle or stately home
∴	Ruderi Ruines Ancient sites
●	Grotta, insediamento, curiosità Grotte, site, curiosité Cave, beauty spot, sight
Ω	Forte Fort Fort

♀	Centro termale Station thermale Watering place
†	Calvario Calvaire Calvary
⊞	Cimitero militare Cimetière militaire Military cemetery
✈	Aerodromo regionale Aérodrome régional Local airfield
✈	Aeroporto o aerodromo importante Aéroport et aérodrome important Airport or large airfield

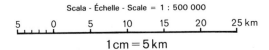

Scala - Échelle - Scale = 1 : 500 000

5   0   5   10   15   20   25 km

1cm = 5km

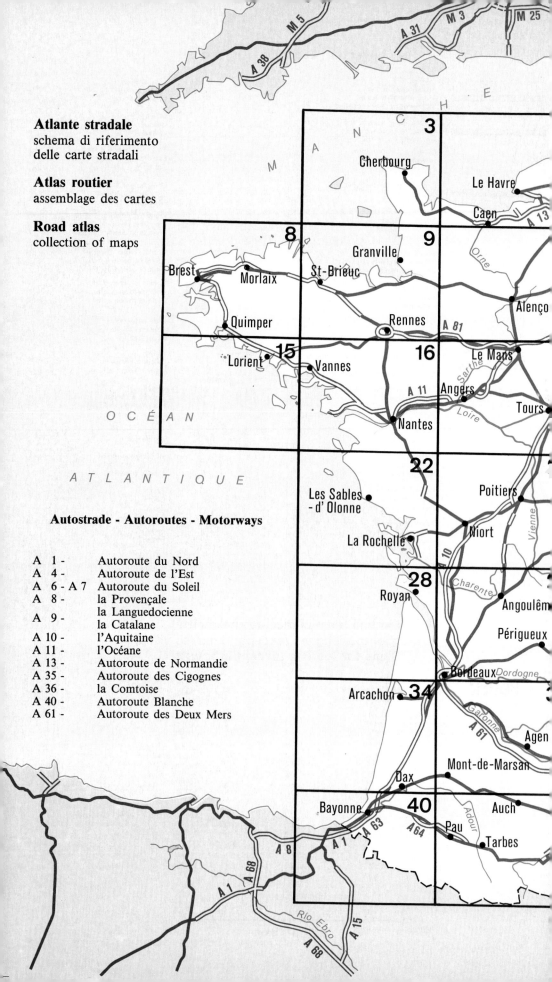

Atlante stradale
schema di riferimento
delle carte stradali

Atlas routier
assemblage des cartes

Road atlas
collection of maps

Autostrade - Autoroutes - Motorways

A 1 -	Autoroute du Nord
A 4 -	Autoroute de l'Est
A 6 - A 7	Autoroute du Soleil
A 8 -	la Provençale
A 9 -	la Languedocienne
	la Catalane
A 10 -	l'Aquitaine
A 11 -	l'Océane
A 13 -	Autoroute de Normandie
A 35 -	Autoroute des Cigognes
A 36 -	la Comtoise
A 40 -	Autoroute Blanche
A 61 -	Autoroute des Deux Mers

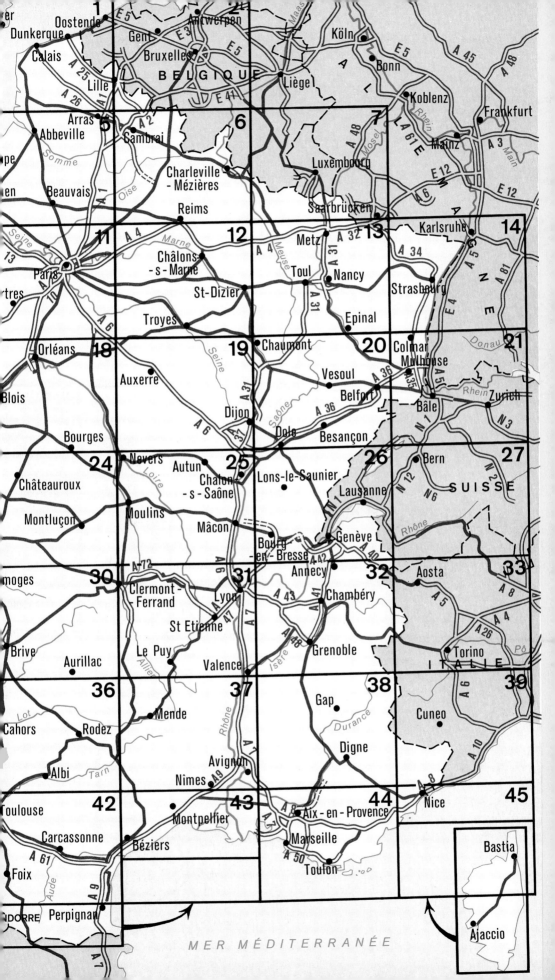

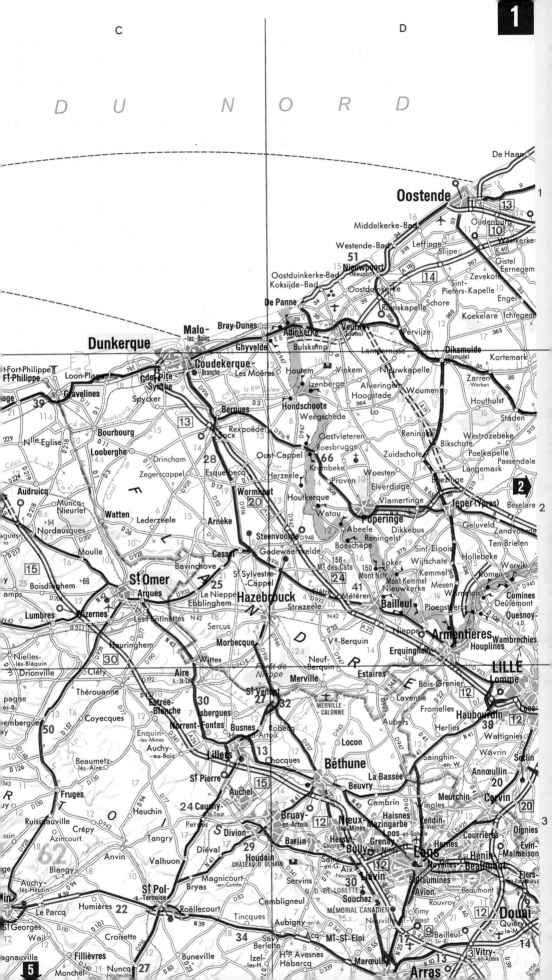

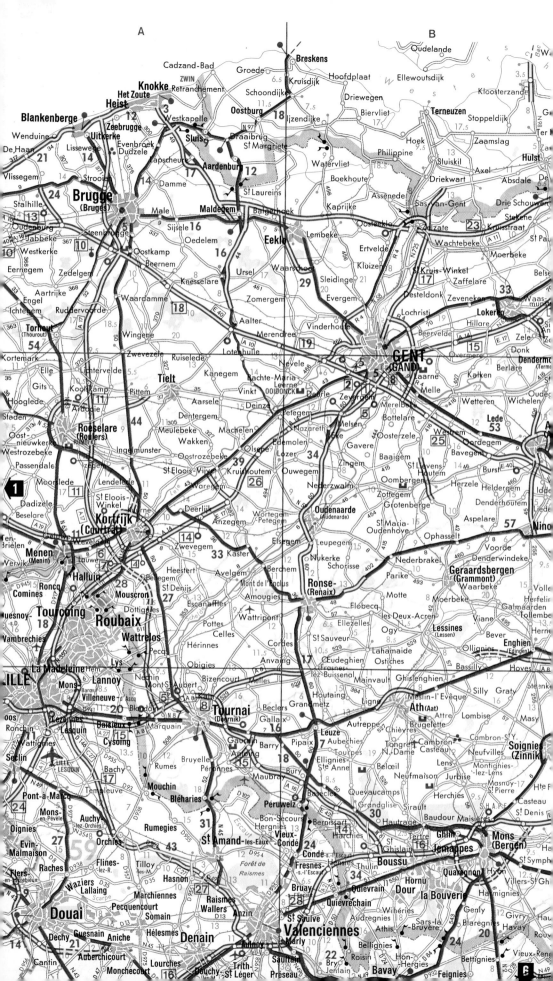

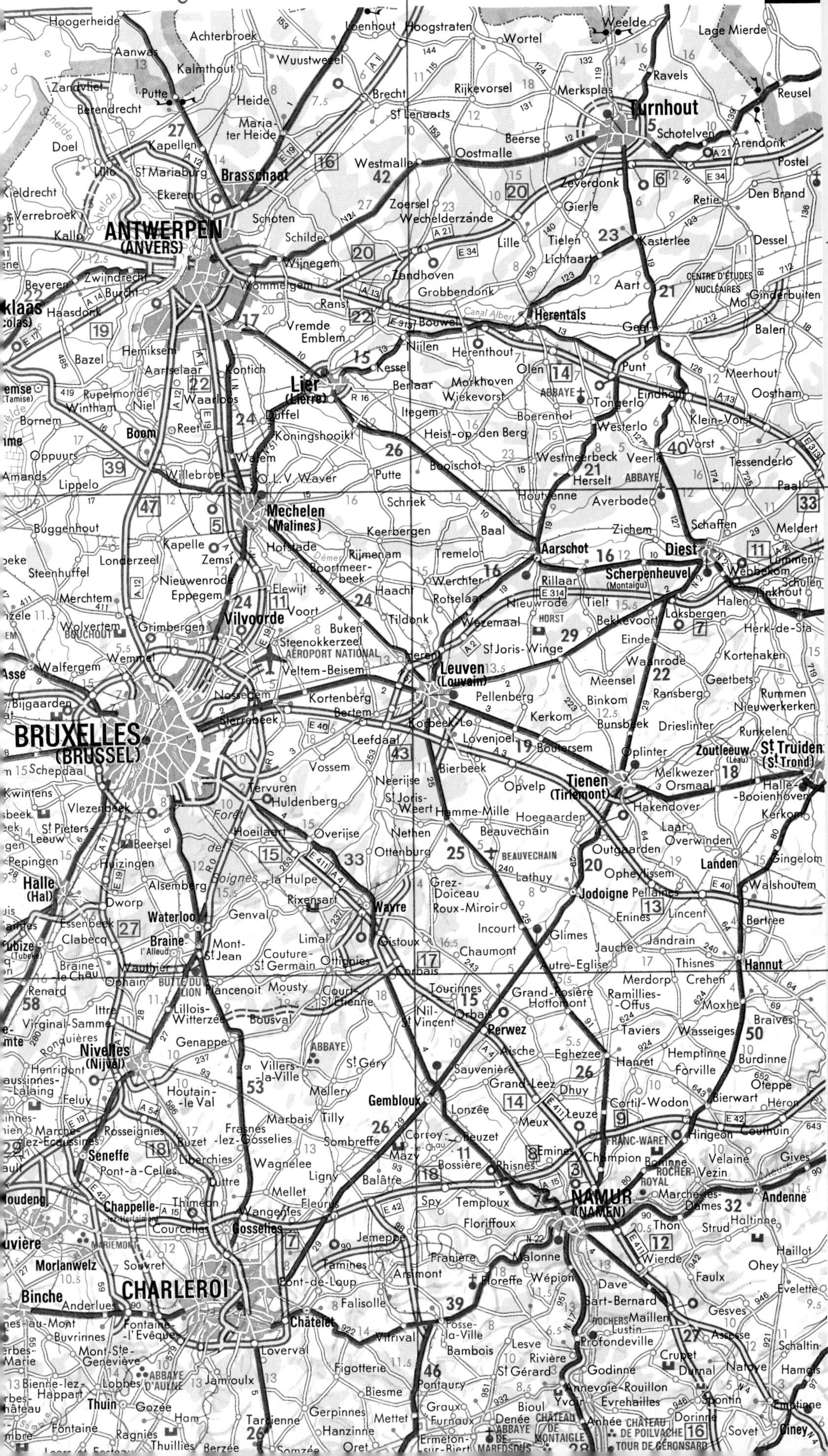
C
D
1
2
3
Hoogerheide
Achterbroek
Aanwas
Kalmthout
Zandvliet
Putte
Berendrecht
Heide
Maria-ter Heide
Doel
Kapellen
Lillo
St Mariaburg
Brasschaat
Kieldrecht
Ekeren
Verrebroek
Schoten
Kallo
ANTWERPEN
(ANVERS)
Schilde
Wijnegem
Beveren
Zwijndrecht
Burcht
Wommelgem
Haasdonk
Ranst
Vremde
Emblem
Bazel
Hemiksem
Aartselaar
Kontich
Rupelmonde
Wintham
Niel
Waarloos
Lier
(Lierre)
Bornem
Boom
Reet
Duffel
Koningshooikt
Oppuurs
Walem
Lippelo
Willebroek
O.L.V. Waver
Mechelen
(Malines)
Buggenhout
Kapelle
Zemst
Hofstade
Londerzeel
Steenhuffel
Nieuwenrode
Eppegem
Elewijt
Merchtem
Vilvoorde
Voort
Wolvertem
Grimbergen
Buken
Steenokkerzeel
AÉROPORT NATIONAL
Wemmel
Walfergem
Asse
Veltem-Beisem
Bijgaarden
Nossegem
Kortenberg
Bertem
BRUXELLES
(BRUSSEL)
Sterrebeek
Schepdaal
Tervuren
Huldenberg
Kwintens
Vlezenbeek
St Pieters-Leeuw
Beersel
Hoeilaart
Overijse
Pepingen
Huizingen
Halle
(Hal)
Alsemberg
Forêt de Soignes
La Hulpe
Rixensart
Dworp
Waterloo
Genval
Essenbeek
Clabecq
Braine-l'Alleud
Mont-St Jean
Limal
Couture-St Germain
Ottignies
Braine-le-Château
Wauthier
Ophain
BUTTE DU LION
Plancenoit
Mousty
Court-St Etienne
Renard
Ittre
Lillois-Witterzée
Bousval
Virginal-Samme
Ronquières
Genappe
Nivelles
(Nijvel)
Henripont
Villers-la-Ville
ABBAYE
St Géry
Feluy
Houtain-le Val
Mellery
Marbais
Tilly
Frasnes-lez-Gosselies
Buzet
Rosseignies
Seneffe
Liberchies
Sombreffe
Pont-à-Celles
Wagnelee
Ligny
Luttre
Mellet
Fleurus
Chappelle-lez-Herlaimont
Thiméon
Wangenies
Courcelles
Gosselies
MARIEMONT
Souvret
Morlanwelz
CHARLEROI
Binche
Anderlues
Fontaine-l'Évêque
Châtelet
Buvrinnes
Mont-Ste-Geneviève
Loverval
ABBAYE D'AULNE
Jamioulx
Lobbes
Thuin
Gozée
Ham
Tarcienne
Ragnies
Thuillies
Berzée
Fontaine
Loenhout
Hoogstraten
Wuustwezel
Wortel
Brecht
Rijkevorsel
Merksplas
St Lenaarts
Westmalle
Oostmalle
Beerse
Zoersel
Wechelderzande
Lille
Zandhoven
Grobbendonk
Bouwel
Nijlen
Kessel
Herenthout
Berlaar
Morkhoven
Wiekevorst
Itegem
Heist-op-den Berg
Putte
Booischot
Schriek
Keerbergen
Baal
Rijmenam
Boortmeer-beek
Tremelo
Werchter
Haacht
Rotselaar
Tildonk
Wezemaal
Herent
Leuven
(Louvain)
Pellenberg
Korbeek-Lo
Lovenjoel
Leefdaal
Vossem
Neerijse
St Joris-Weert
Bierbeek
Hamme-Mille
Nethen
Ottenburg
Grez-Doiceau
Roux-Miroir
Wavre
Gistoux
Incourt
Chaumont
Corbais
Tourinnes
Orbais
Nil-St Vincent
Perwez
Sauvenière
Gembloux
Lonzée
Grand-Leez
Corroy-le-Château
Beuzet
Mazy
Bossière
Balâtre
Spy
Temploux
Floriffoux
Jemeppe
Tamines
Arsimont
Pont-de-Loup
Falisolle
Franière
Malonne
Floreffe
Wépion
Vitrival
Fosse-la-Ville
Bambois
Figotterie
Biesme
Pontaury
Graux
Furnaux
Mettet
Gerpinnes
Hanzinne
Weelde
Lage Mierde
Ravels
Turnhout
Reusel
Schotelven
Arendonk
Postel
Zeverdonk
Gierle
Retie
Den Brand
Kasterlee
Dessel
Tielen
Lichtaart
Aart
CENTRE D'ÉTUDES NUCLÉAIRES
Mol
Ginderbuiten
Herentals
Canal Albert
Geel
Balen
Olen
Punt
Meerhout
ABBAYE
Tongerlo
Eindhout
Oostham
Boerenhol
Westerlo
Klein-Vorst
Vorst
Westmeerbeck
Veerle
Herselt
Tessenderlo
Paal
Houtvenne
Averbode
Schaffen
Meldert
Zichem
Aarschot
Diest
Lummen
Scherpenheuvel
(Montaigu)
Rillaar
Webbekom
Schulen
Linkhout
Nieuwrode
Tielt
Halen
HORST
Bekkevoort
Loksbergen
Herk-de-Sta
Einde
St Joris-Winge
Waanrode
Kortenaken
Meensel
Geetbets
Binkom
Ransberg
Rummen
Kerkom
Bunsbeek
Drieslinter
Nieuwerkerken
Boutersem
Runkelen
Oplinter
Zoutleeuw
(Léau)
St Truiden
(St Trond)
Tienen
(Tirlemont)
Melkwezer
Orsmaal
Halle-Booienhoven
Opvelp
Hakendover
Hoegaarden
Laar
Beauvechain
Overwinden
BEAUVECHAIN
Outgaarden
Landen
Gingelom
Lathuy
Opheylissem
Jodoigne
Pellaines
Walshoutem
Enines
Lincent
Glimes
Bertree
Jandrain
Jauche
Thisnes
Autre-Eglise
Hannut
Merdorp
Crehen
Grand-Rosière
Hottomont
Ramillies-Offus
Moxhe
Braives
Taviers
Wasseiges
Aische
Eghezee
Hanret
Hemptinne
Burdinne
Forville
Oteppe
Dhuy
Cortil-Wodon
Bierwart
Héron
Leuze
Meux
Hingeon
Couthuin
FRANC-WARET
Emines
Champion
Bonnine
Velaine
Gives
Rhisnes
ROCHER ROYAL
Vezin
NAMUR
(NAMEN)
Marche-les-Dames
Andenne
Thon
Haltinne
Strud
Wierde
Haillot
Ohey
Faulx
Dave
Evelette
Sart-Bernard
Gesves
ROCHERS
Lustin
Maillen
Assesse
Profondeville
Lesve
Rivière
Crupet
Schaltin
St Gérard
Godinne
Durnal
Natoye
Hamois
Annevoie-Rouillon
Spontin
Biou
Yvoir
Evrehailles
Emptinne
Denée
ABBAYE DE MAREDSOUS
CHÂTEAU DE MONTAIGLE
Anhée
CHÂTEAU DE POILVACHE
TOUR DE GÉRONSARD
Dorinne
Sovet
Ciney
Ermeton-sur-Biert

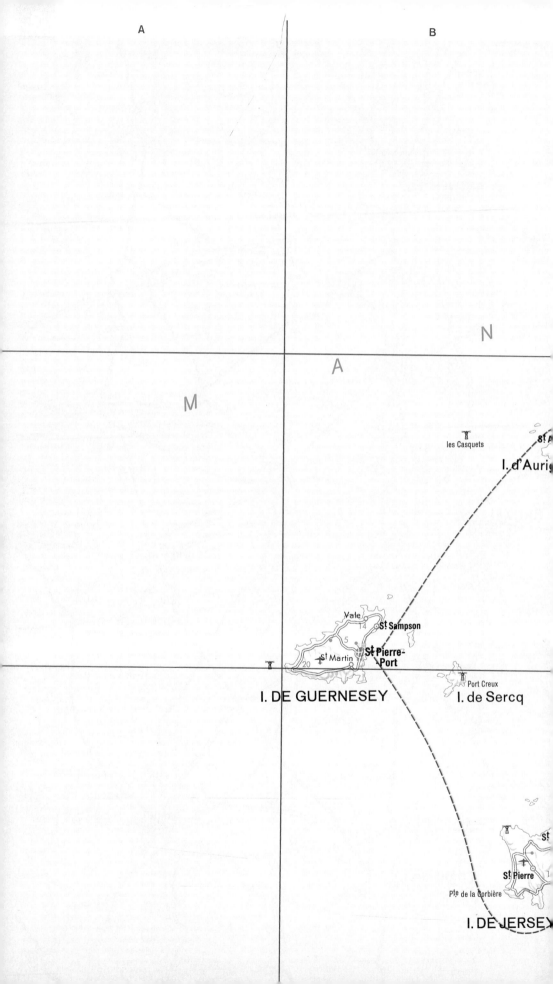

A

B

N

A

M

les Casquets

Sᵗ A

I. d'Auri

Vale

14 ᵒSᵗ Sampson

5

Sᵗ Pierre-
Port

Sᵗ Martin

20

I. DE GUERNESEY

Port Creux

I. de Sercq

Sᵗ

Sᵗ Pierre

Pᵗᵉ de la Corbière

I. DE JERSEY

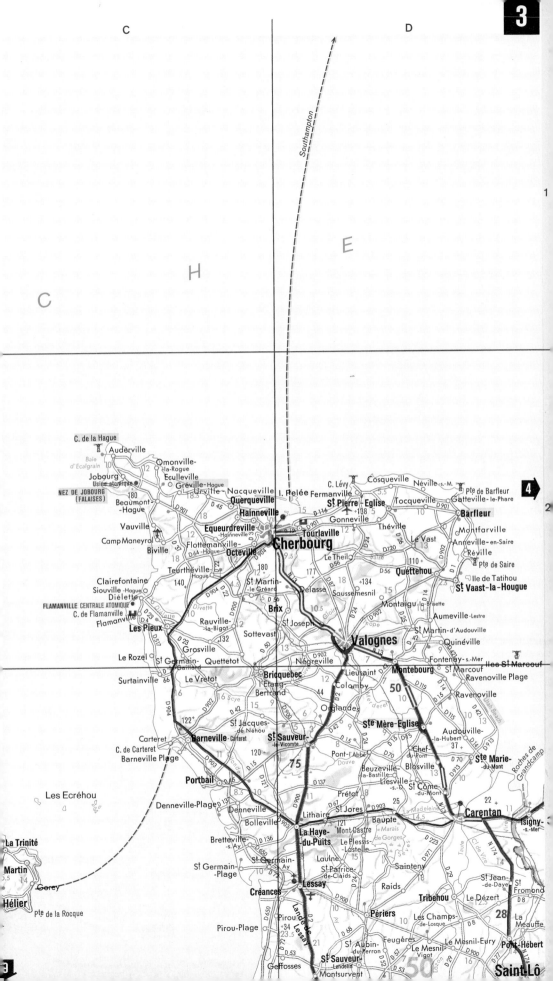

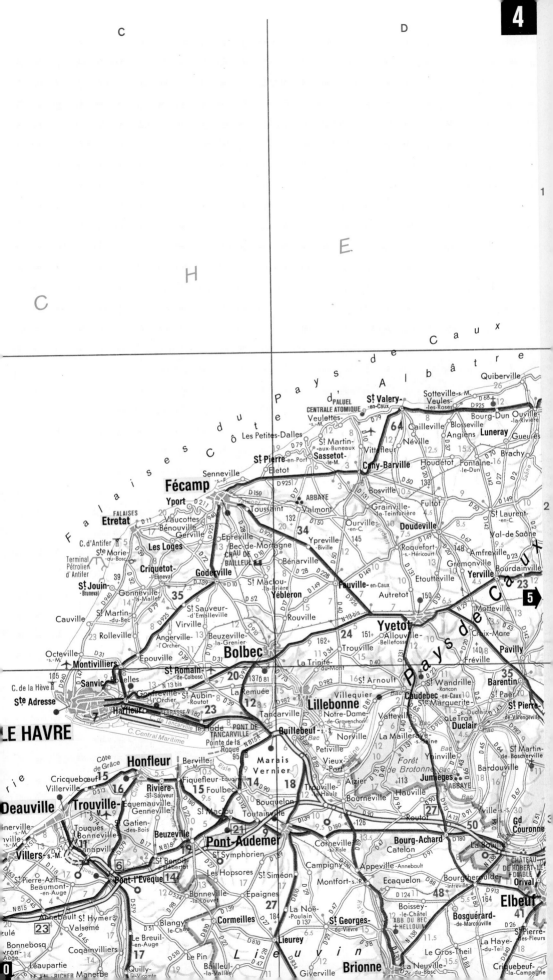

AMIENS

Arras

Albert

Péronne

Doullens

Bapaume

Ham

Roye

Noyon

Montdidier

Breteuil

Clermont

Beauvais

Compiègne

Fillièvres · Nuncq · Hautecôte · Bunéville · Izel-les-H. · Hte Avesnes · Habarcq · Marœuil · Vitry-en-Artois · Lécluse · Écourt-St-Quentin

Regnauville · Monchel-s.-Canche · Frévent · Étrée-Wamin · Liencourt · Avesnes-le-Comte · Wanquetin · Dainville · Tilloy-les-Mofflaines · Monchy-le-Preux · Étaing

Abroye · Monchel · 138 · Frévent · Gd Rullecourt · Beaumetz-les-Loges · Wailly · Beaurains · Vis-en-Artois

Auxi-le-Chau · Bonnières · Sombrin · N25 · Ransart · Boiry-St-Martin · Boyelles · Croisilles · Inchy-en-Artois

Frohen-le-Grand · Bouquemaison · Lucheux · Monchy-au-Bois · Courcelles-le-Comte · Lagnicourt-Marcel · Boursies

Maizicourt · Barly · Mondicourt · Pommier · Fonquevillers · Bucquoy · Achiet-le-Gd · Beugny · Hermies · Vélu · Bertincourt

Occoches · Pas-en-Artois · Souastre · Mailly-Maillet · Puisieux · Miraumont · Bapaume · Le Transloy · Metz-en-Couture

Beaumetz · Candas · Fieffes-Montrelet · Authie · Marieux · Acheux-en-Amiénois · Beaumont-Hamel · Le Sars · Pozières · Longueval · Étricourt-Manancourt · Fins · Nurlu

Bernaville · Fienvillers · Beauval · Beauquesne · Puchevillers · Hédauville · MÉMORIAL BRITANNIQUE · Bouzincourt · Combles · Moislains

Domart-en-Ponthieu · La Vicogne · Toutencourt · Warloy-Baillon · Vadencourt · Albert · Maricourt · Bouchavesnes-Bergen · Cléry-s.

Berteaucourt-les-Dames · Canaples · Havernas · Talmas · Rubempré · Béhencourt · Morlancourt · Péronne · Herbécourt · Doingt · Hancourt

Vignacourt · Villers-Bocage · Rainneville · Franvillers · Bray-s.-S. · Méricourt · Dompierre-Becquincourt · Barleux · Estrées-Mons

St-Sauveur · Querrieu · Corbie · Sailly-Laurette · Proyart · Villers-Carbonnel · Athies

Picquigny · Daours · Fouilloy · Warfusée-Abancourt · Foucaucourt-en-S. · Marchélepot · Brie

Longueau · MÉMORIAL AUSTRALIEN · Villers-Bretonneux · Harbonnières · Chaulnes · Omiécourt · Pargny · Croix-Moligneaux

Boves · St Fuscien · Sains-en-A. · Domart-la-Luce · Caix · Rosières-en-Santerre · Maucourt · Morchain · Matigny

Dury · Cottenchy · Thennes · Demuin · Beaucourt-en-Santerre · Le Quesnel · Vrély · Hattencourt · Nesle · Hombleux

Moreuil · Plessier-Rozainvillers · Liancourt-Fosse · Marche-Allouarde · Esmery-Hallon

Ailly-s.-N. · Mailly-Rainéval · La Neuville-Sire-Bernard · Hangest-en-Santerre · Bouchoir · Fresnoy-lès-R. · Andechy · Carrépuis · Ercheu · Fréniches

Chaussoy-Epagny · Pierrepont-sur-Avre · Davenescourt · Roye · Champien · Beaulieu-les-Fontaines · Guiscard

Sourdon · Grivesnes · Guerbigny · Marquivillers · Amy · Frétoy-le-Ch. · Bussy

Folleville · Coullemelle · Fontaine-s.-s.-M. · Boulogne-la-Grasse · Roye-sur-Matz · Dives

Tartigny · Welles-Pérennes · Rollot · Conchy-les-Pots · Lassigny · Thiescourt · Noyon

Hardivillers · Mory · Crèvecœur-le-Pt · Tricot · Cuvilly · Ressons-sur-Matz · Ribécourt · Carlepont

Viefvillers · Francastel · Ansauvillers · Quinquempoix · Maignelay-Montigny · Méry-la-Bataille · St-Martin-aux-Bois · Elincourt-Ste-Marguerite

Froissy · Wavignies · Thieux · Ravenel · Gournay-sur-Aronde · Chevincourt · Villiers-s.-C. · Giraumont · Ollencourt

Luchy · Noyers-St-Martin · Reuil-sur-Brèche · Saint-Just-en-Chaussée · Montiers · Laneuvilleroy · Monchy-Humières · Longueil-Annel · Choisy-au-Bac

Haudivillers · Fournival · Bulles · Argenlieu · Erquinvillers · Rémy · Marguy-lès-C. · Berneuil-s.-A. · Attichy

Tillé · BEAUVAIS-TILLÉ · Fouquerolles · Rémérangles · Étouy · Bailleul-le-Soc · Estrées-St-Denis · Compiègne · Vieux-Moulin · Trosly-Breuil

Allonne · Bresles · Rue-St-Pierre · Fitz-James · Grandfresnoy · Longueil-Ste-Marie · Lacroix-St-Ouen · Chelles

Warluis · Hermes · St Aubin-sous-Erquery · Catenoy · Bazicourt · CHAMPLIEU · St-Jean-aux-Bois · Pierrefonds · Mortefontaine

Noailles · Mouy · Rantigny · Liancourt · Sacy-le-Gd · Chevrières · Verberie · Béthisy-St-Pierre · Morienval

Bonvillers · Bury · Rieux · Pontpoint · Néry · Bonneuil-en-Valois

Ste Geneviève · Ully-St-Georges · Rousseloy · Cires-lès-Mello · Pont-Ste Maxence · Villeneuve-sur-Verberie · Raray · Haramont

Méru · Ercuis · Montataire · Creil · Nogent · Forêt d'Halatte · Rully · Crépy-en-Valois

Puiseux-le-Hauberger · Neuilly-en-Thelle · Précy-s. · St Leu-d'Esserent · Senlis

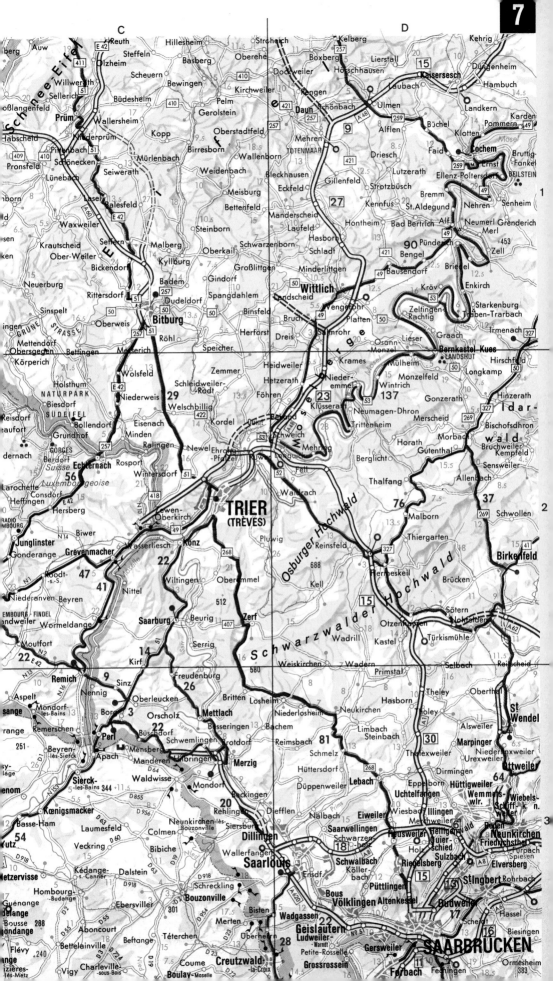

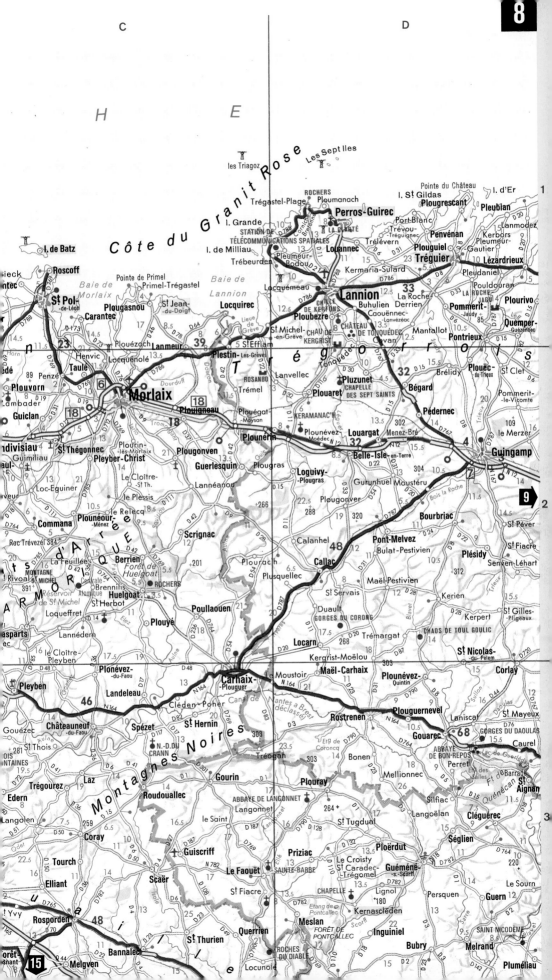

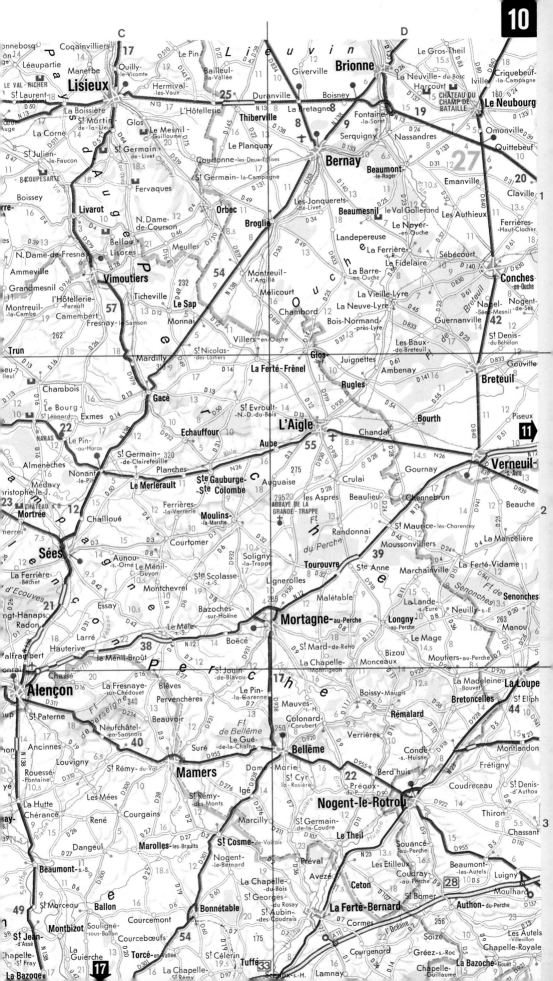

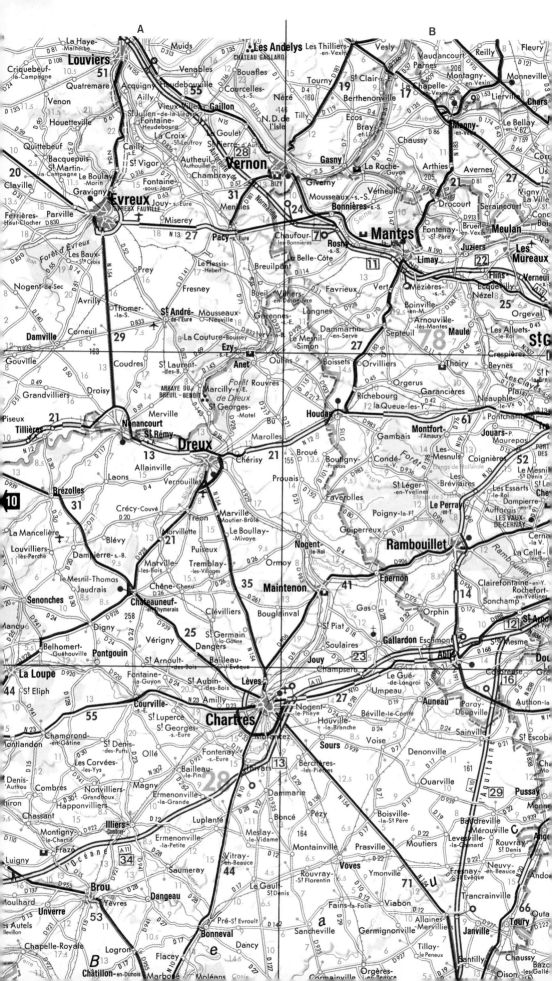

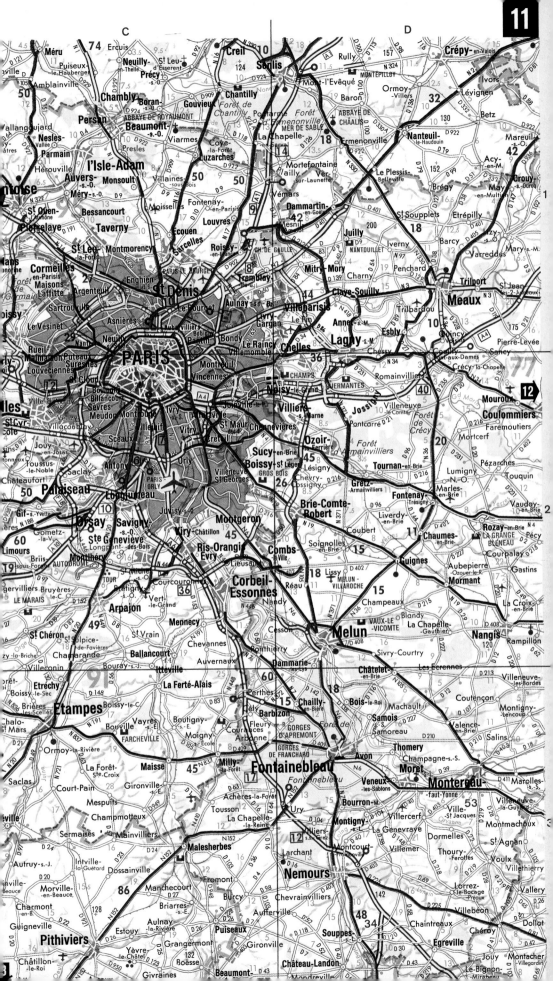

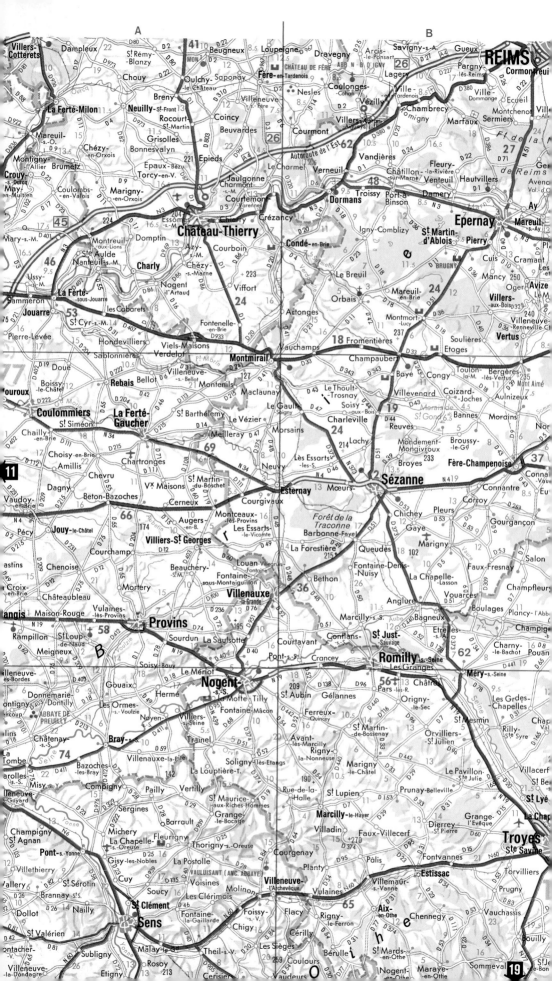

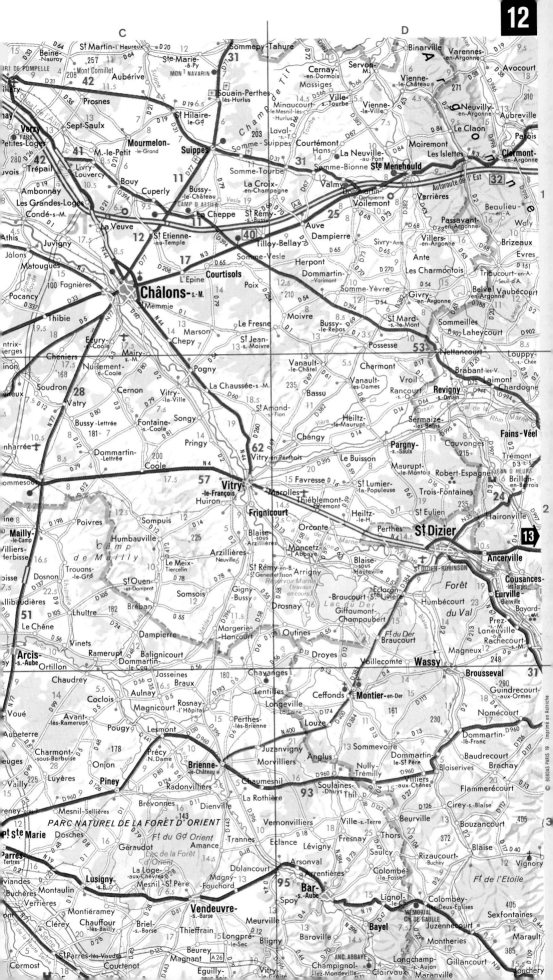

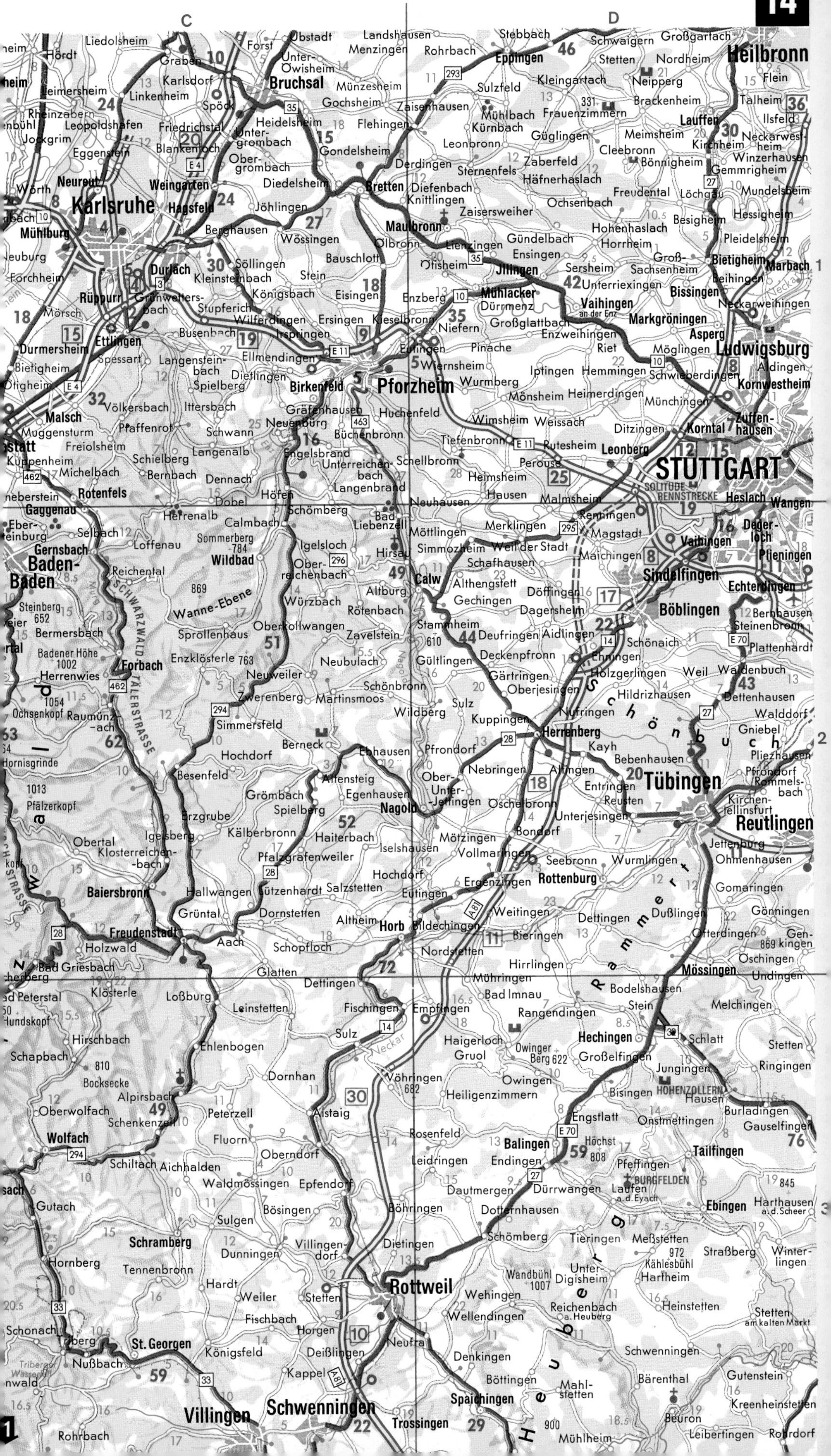

Heilbronn

Karlsruhe

Bruchsal

Pforzheim

STUTTGART

Ludwigsburg

Leonberg

Böblingen

Sindelfingen

Tübingen

Reutlingen

Baden-Baden

Gernsbach

Forbach

Freudenstadt

Baiersbronn

Wolfach

Schramberg

St. Georgen

Villingen Schwenningen

Rottweil

Balingen

Mössingen

Hechingen

Horb

Nagold

Calw

Wildbad

Herrenalb

Durlach

Ettlingen

Malsch

Rastatt

Gaggenau

Rotenfels

Birkenfeld

Herrenberg

Rottenburg

Spaichingen

Trossingen

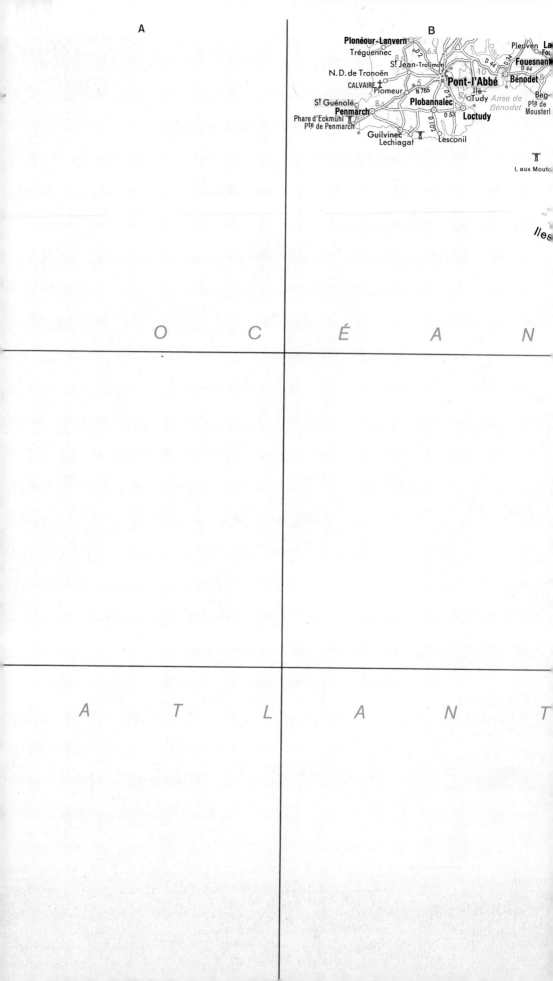

A

B

Plonéour-Lanvern
Tréguennec
St Jean-Trolimon
N. D. de Tronoën
CALVAIRE
Plomeur
St Guénolé
Penmarch
Phare d'Eckmühl
Pte de Penmarch
Guilvinec
Lechiagat
Lesconil

Pont-l'Abbé
Plobannalec
Île-Tudy
Loctudy

Pleuven
Fou
Fouesnan
D 44
Bénodet

Beg
Pte de
Mousterl

Anse de
Bénodet

D 2
D 44
D 53
D 1010
N 785

I. aux Mouto

Îles

O   C   É   A   N

A   T   L   A   N   T

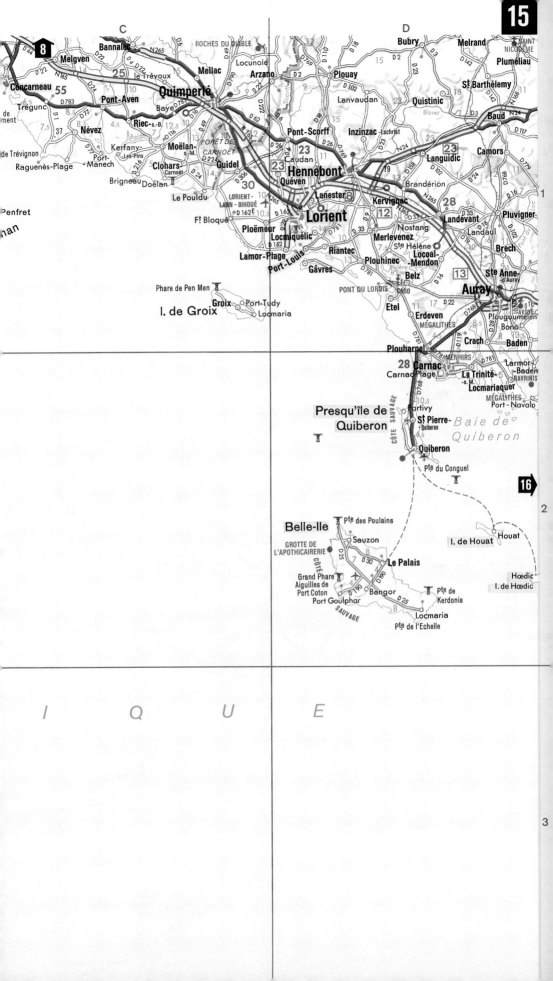

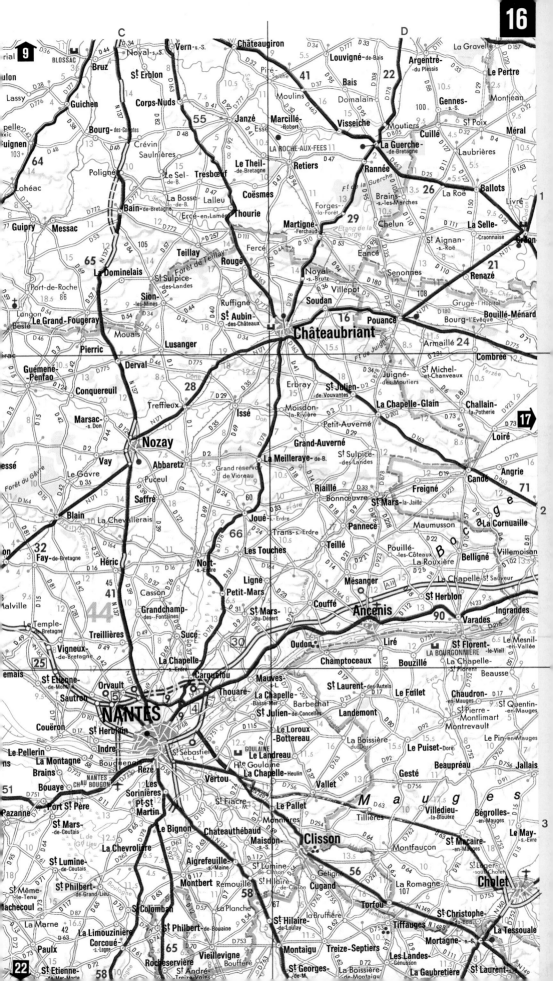

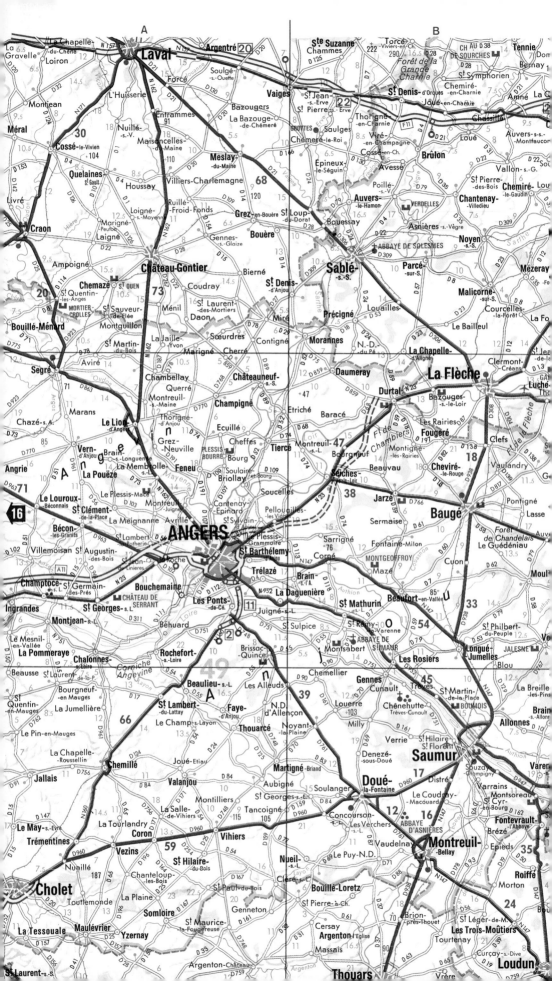

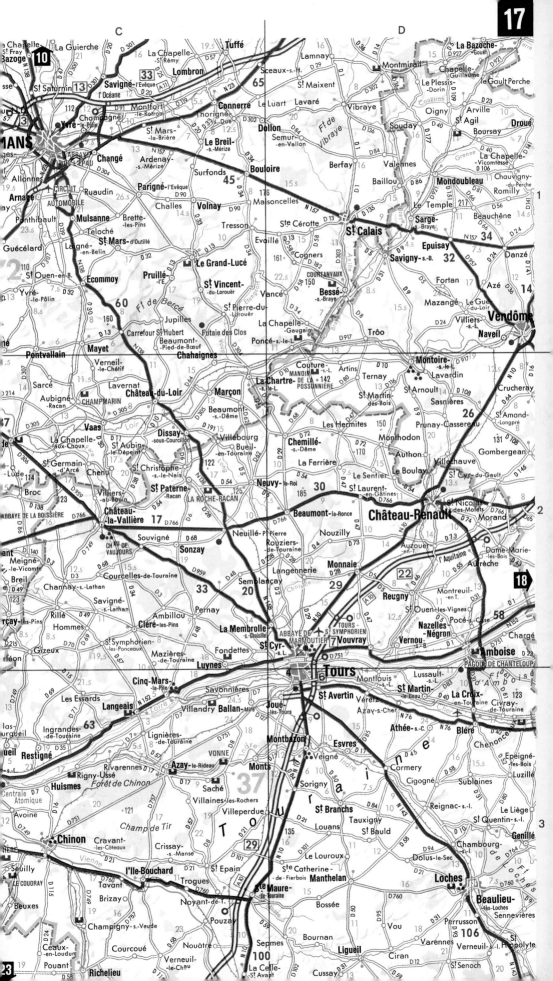

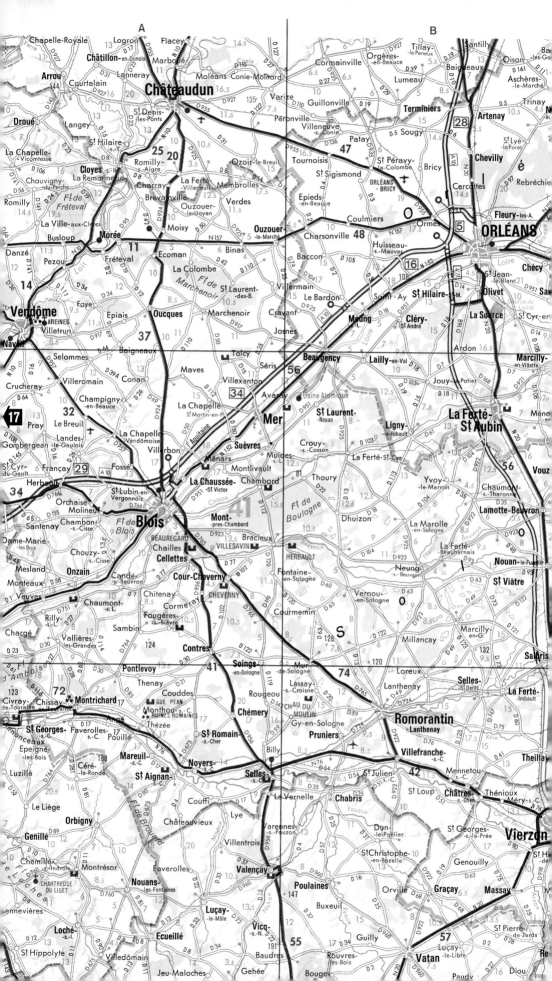

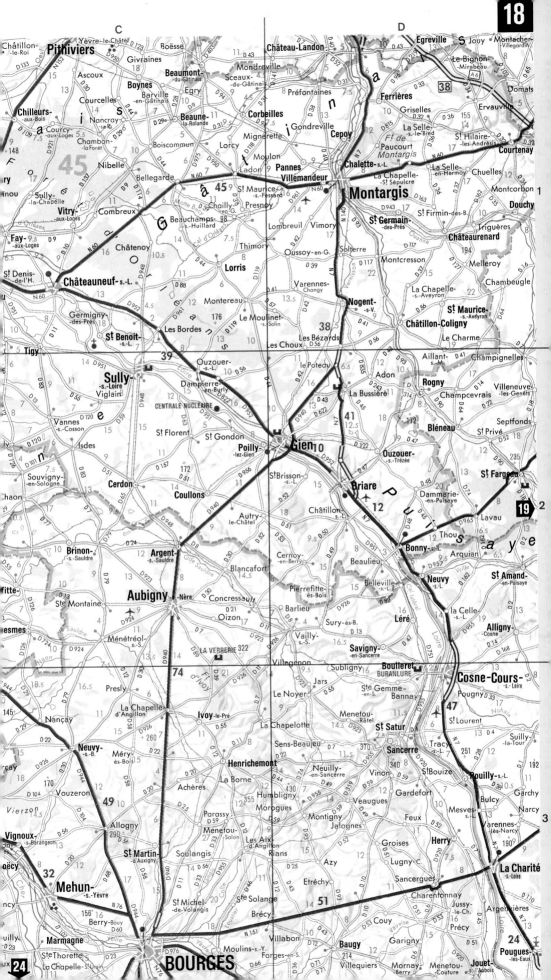

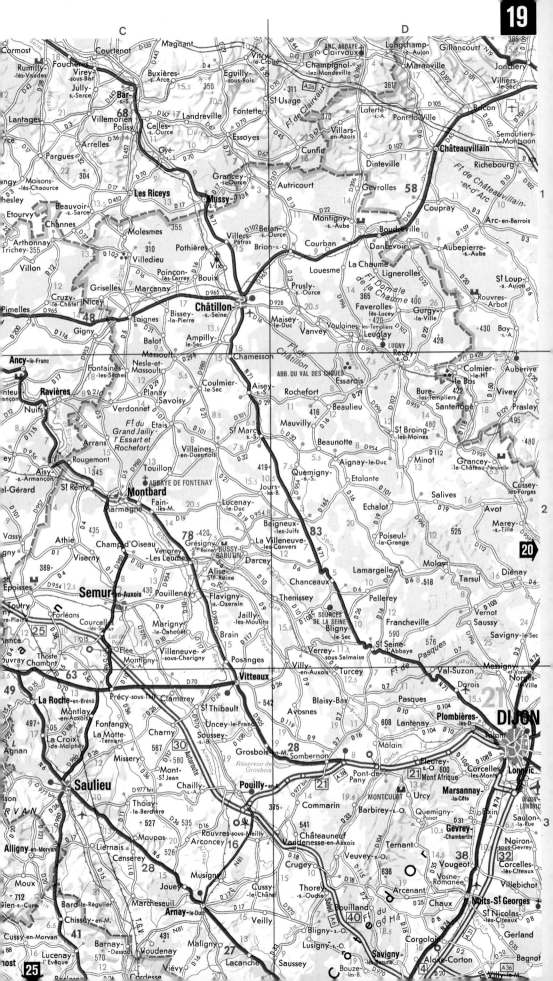

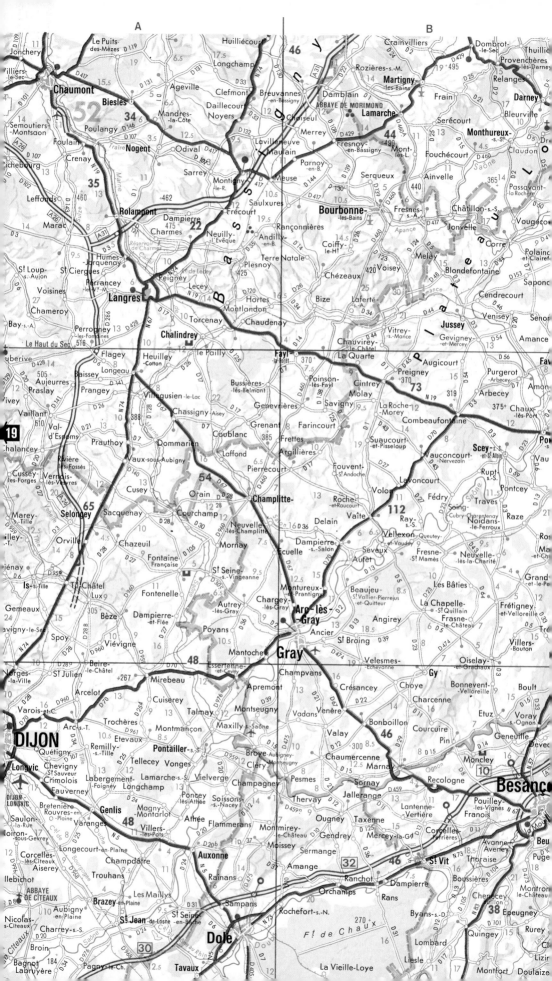

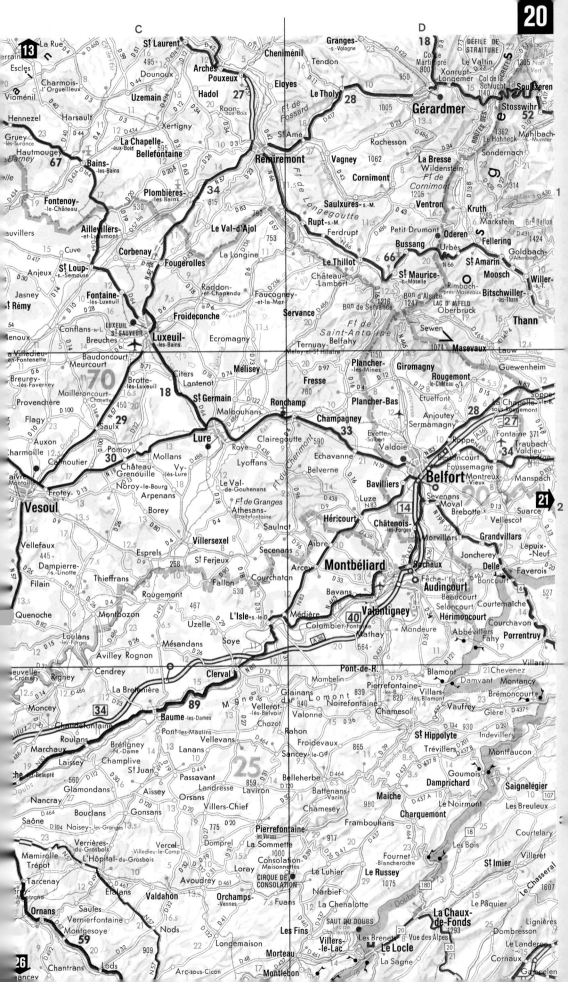

C · D

Villingen Schwenningen Spaichingen Mahlstetten 900 Beuron Kreenheinstetten Leibertingen Rohrdorf

Rohrbach Pfaffenweiler Marbach 22 Trossingen Schura Rietheim Mühlheim Fridingen Worndorf Messkirch 311

Vöhrenbach Tannheim Bad Dürrheim A 86 6 Öfingen Tuttlingen Nendingen Neuhausen 24 Krumbach Sauldorf 313

Urach Biesingen 927 Möhringen Liptingen Schwackenreute Mahlspüren Sentenhart

Hammereisenbach-Bregenbach Waldau Wolferdingen 5 11 Immendingen Emmingen 24 23 Schwackenreute

Eisenbach Donaueschingen Hüfingen Pfohren Geisingen 28 311 Mauenheim Rorgenwies A 81 E 70 Eigeltingen 22 Stockach

Neustadt Bräunlingen Unterbränd Behla Aulfingen Fürstenberg 31 28 Engen Aach Volkertshausen Orsingen 13 Espasingen Ludwigshafen 31

Titisee 35 Röfenbach Kappel Döggingen 20 Blumberg Achdorf Welschingen Tengen Hegau Mühlhausen Hohenstoffeln 844 Binningen Riedheim Hilzingen 14 Mögglingen 11 Bodman Liggeringen 39

Holzschlag 315 Löffingen Ewattingen Münchingen Fützen 12 Randen Singen Radolfzell Allensbach 21 Dettingen

Glashütte Bonndorf 36 Wellendingen Weizen Bargen 17 Beggingen Merishausen Schleitheim Mauchen 14 Schaffhausen 21 Gottmadingen Rielasingen Bankholzen Moos Niederzell Iznang Horn Reichenau

Schluchsee Rothaus Grafenhausen Schönenbach Birkendorf Höchenschwand Amrigschwand Obermettingen Ober-Eggingen Hallau Neunkirch 39 Rheinfall Neuhausen Feuerthalen Basadingen Stein am Rh. Ohningen Steckborn Arenenberg 46 Mammern Hörhausen Raperswilen

Berau Aichen Detzeln Tiengen 314 Horheim Wilchingen 13 Jestetten Dettighofen Rheinau Benken Trüllikon Unterstammheim Wagenhausen 13 Müllheim 42 Engwilen Marstetten

Waldshut Gurtweil Unterlauchringen Erzingen 33 Grießen 23 Marthalen Gisenhard Oberstammheim Hüttwilen Pfyn N7 Eschikofen Hüttlingen Amlikon Weinfelden

Koblenz Leuggern 7 Zurzach Lienheim Hohentengen Rafz Ellikon Großandelfingen Thalheim Altikon Uesslingen Frauenfeld Märwil

Döttingen 18 Rekingen Kaiserstuhl Weiach Eglisau Flaach Henggart E 70 Ellikon Seuzach Attikon Gerlikon Matzingen Lommis Affeltrangen

Mönthal Brugg 13 Tegerfelden Rümikon 30 Siglistorf Stadel Glattfelden Hettlingen Wiesendangen 28 Elgg Aadorf 31 Wängi Bettwiesen

Wildegg Wettingen Würenlos Niederweningen Bülach Embrach Pfungen 7 Winterthur Oberschlatt Ifwil Sirnach 27 Wil E 17

Baden Killwangen Weiningen Rümlang Adlikon Dielsdorf Niederglatt Kloten Bassersdorf Kempthal Weisslingen 25 Turbenthal Balterswil Rickenbach Kirchberg

Mellingen Dietikon Bellikon Schlieren Kloten Wallisellen Nagelswangen Rumikon Wila Tablet Fischingen Steinen Gähwil Bäzenheid 21

Lenzburg 19 Gösliken Wohlen Birmensdorf Dübendorf Pfäffikon Saland Bauma Mühlrüti 1133 Bütschwil Mosnang

Seon Villmergen Bremgarten Stallikon Kilchbg. Maur ZÜRICH Witikon Gutenswil Uster Steg Krinau

Hallwil 39 Oberlunkhofen Adliswil Forch Wetzikon Grüningen Hinwil Girenbad Gibswil Kreuzegg 1265 Wald Walde Ricken

Boswil Langnau Thalwil Esslingen Uetikon Hombrechtikon Rüti Eschenbach Rüeterswil Uznach 25 Rieden

Muri Affoltern Meilen Mönchaltorf Feldbach Schmerikon Kaltbrunn Starrberg Schmitten

Geltwil Mühlau Kappel Horgen Hausen Wädenswil Stäfa Uerikon Rapperswil Lachen 15 Tuggen 9 Schänis

Beromünster Hochdorf Sins Zug Schönenberg Hütten Richterswil 4 Ober 1098 Siebnen Buttikon Reichenburg Unterbilten Niederurnen

Sursee 50 Eich 23 Sempach Gisikon Root 6 Cham Baar Menzingen Biberbrugg Egg Sattelegg 1190 Willerzell Vorderthal Näfels

Nottwil Neuenkirch Rothenburg Küssnacht Immensee Walchwil Unterägeri Oberägeri Einsiedeln Rothenthurm Euthal Innerthal 2135 Brünnelistock

Ruswil Ebikon Adligenswil Arth Goldau Sattel Alpthal Ruti Studen 2096 Fluhberg Netstal

Wolhusen Emmenbrücke Luzern Horw Weggis Rigi 1665 Vitznau Gersau Brunnen Ried Weglosen 2282 Drusberg Eggstöcke 2459 Glärnisch 2918

A

B

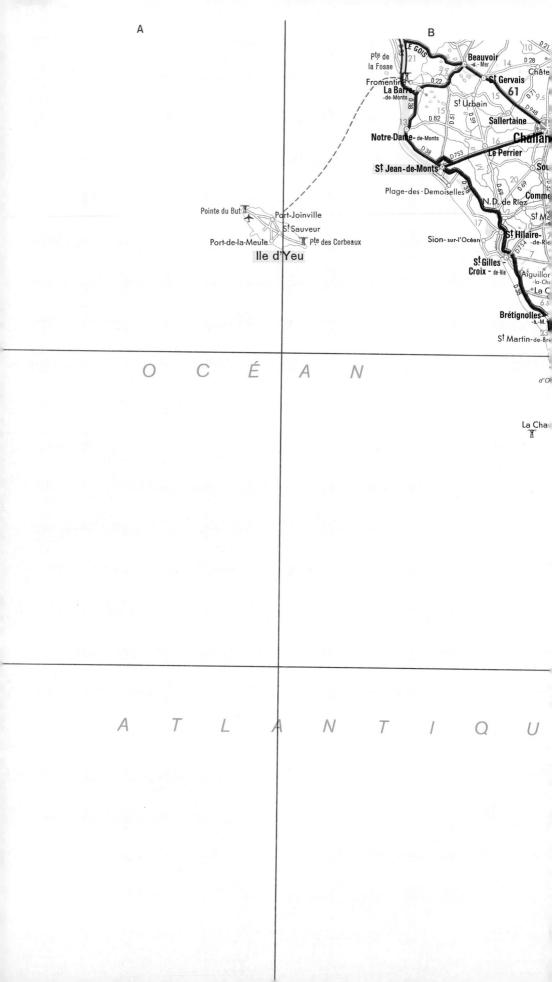

LE GOIS

pte de
la Fosse

Beauvoir
-s.- Mer

14

Châte

D 28

Fromentine

St Gervais

61

D 22

D 21

10

D 948

9.5

La Barre
-de-Monts

St Urbain

D 38

D 82

15

D 59

D 51

Sallertaine

16

Challan

Notre-Dame- de-Monts

Le Perrier

D 38

D 753

St Jean-de-Monts

Sou

20

Plage-des-Demoiselles

N.D. de Riez

Comme

D 59

17

N.D. de Riez

St Ma

Pointe du But

Port-Joinville

Sion- sur-l'Océan

St Hilaire-
-de-Ri

D 754

7

St Sauveur

St Gilles -
Croix - de-Vie

Port-de-la-Meule

pte des Corbeaux

Aiguillor
-la-Ch

Ile d'Yeu

La C

D 38

6.5

Brétignolles-
-s.- M.

St Martin-de-Br

23

O   C   É   A   N

d'O

La Cha

A   T   L   A   N   T   I   Q   U

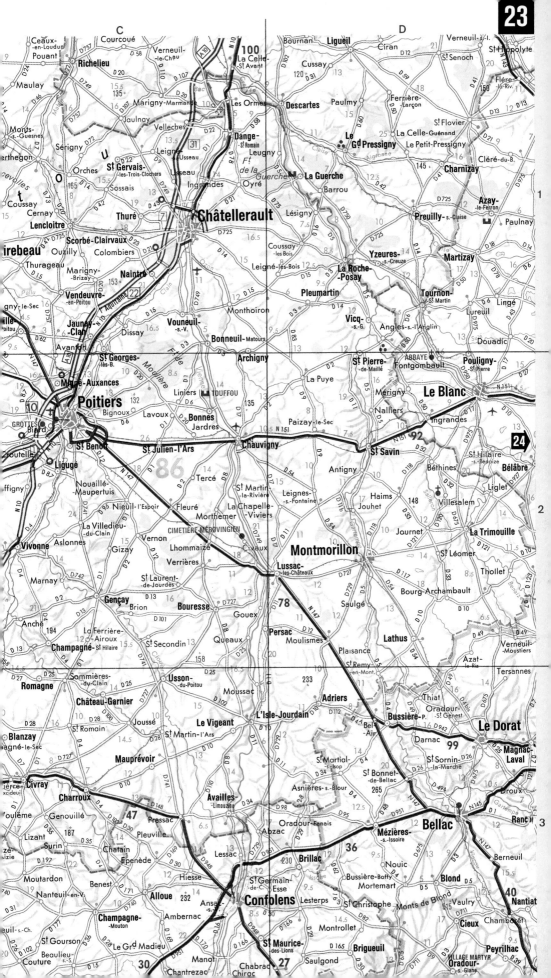

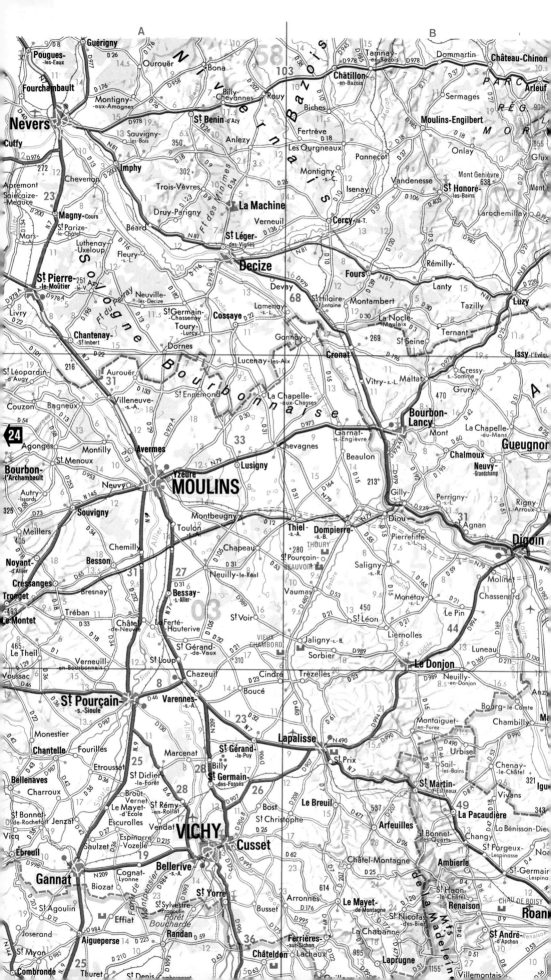

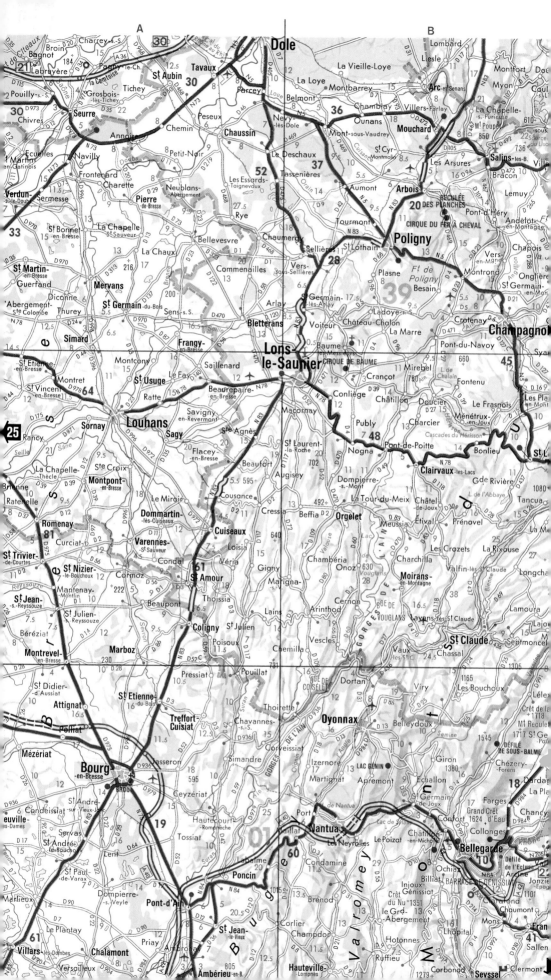

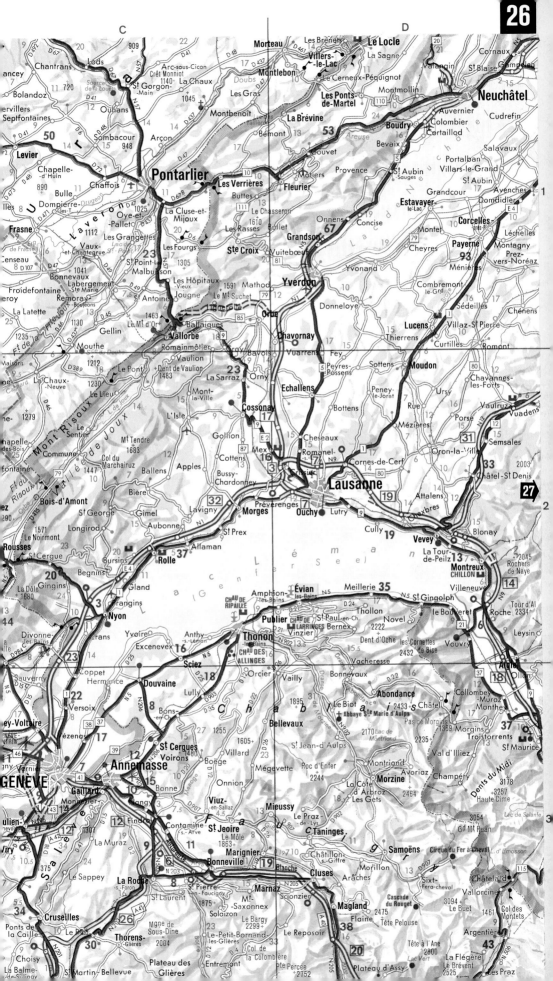

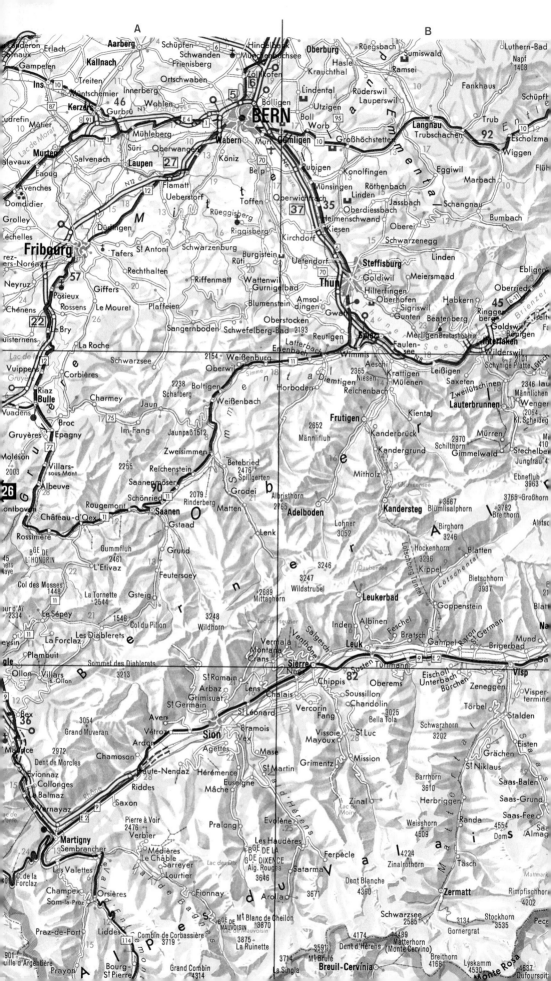

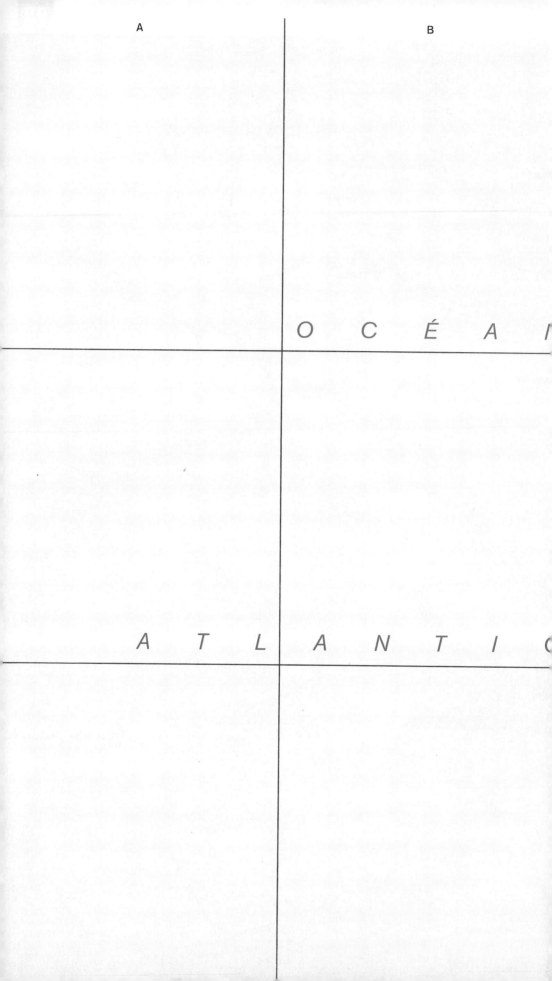

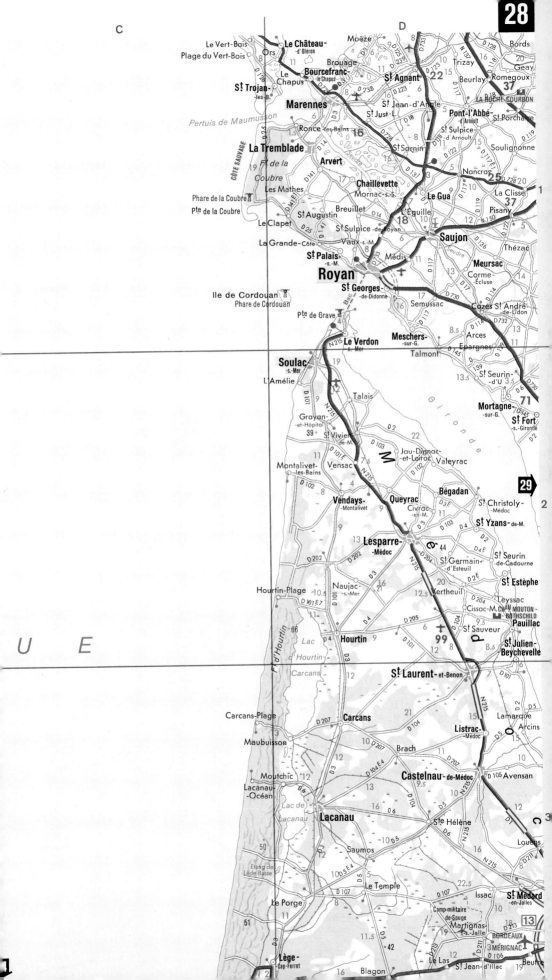

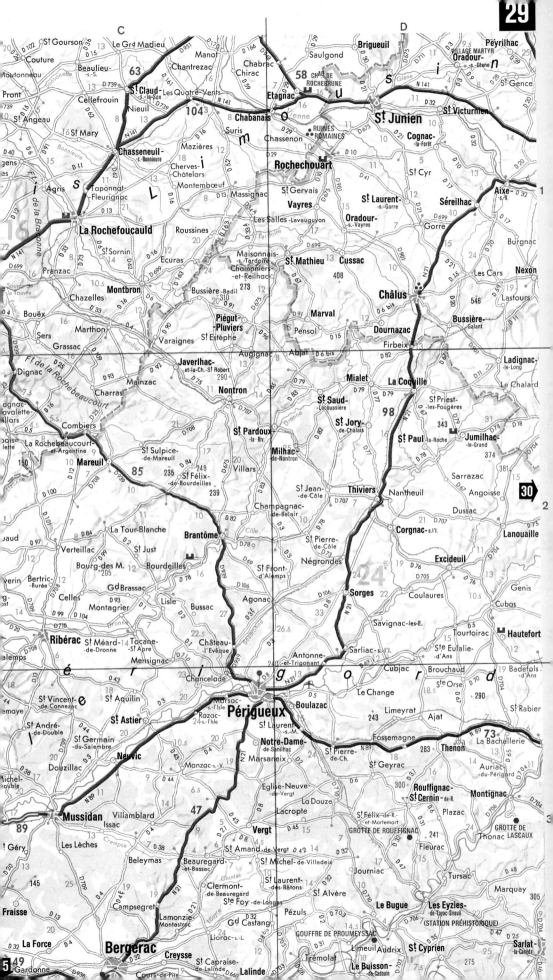

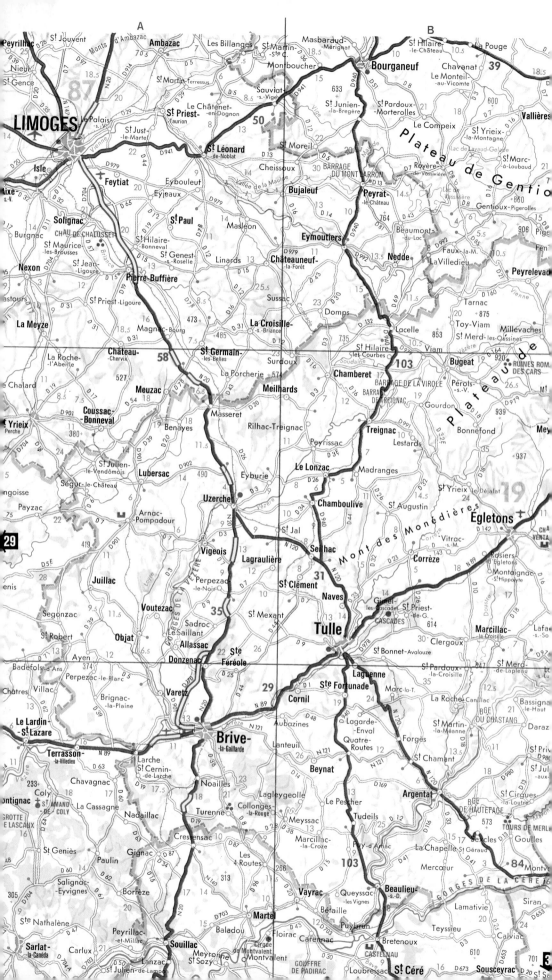

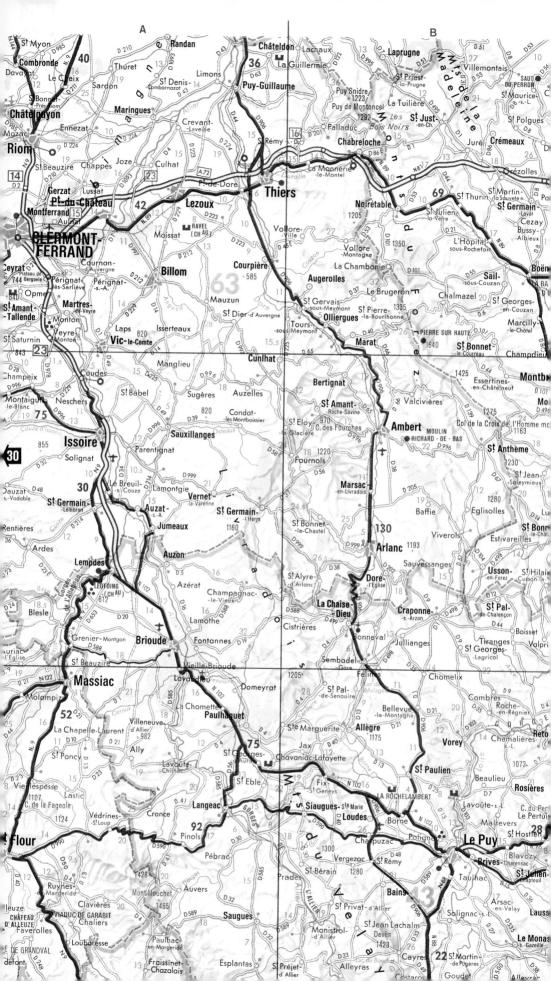

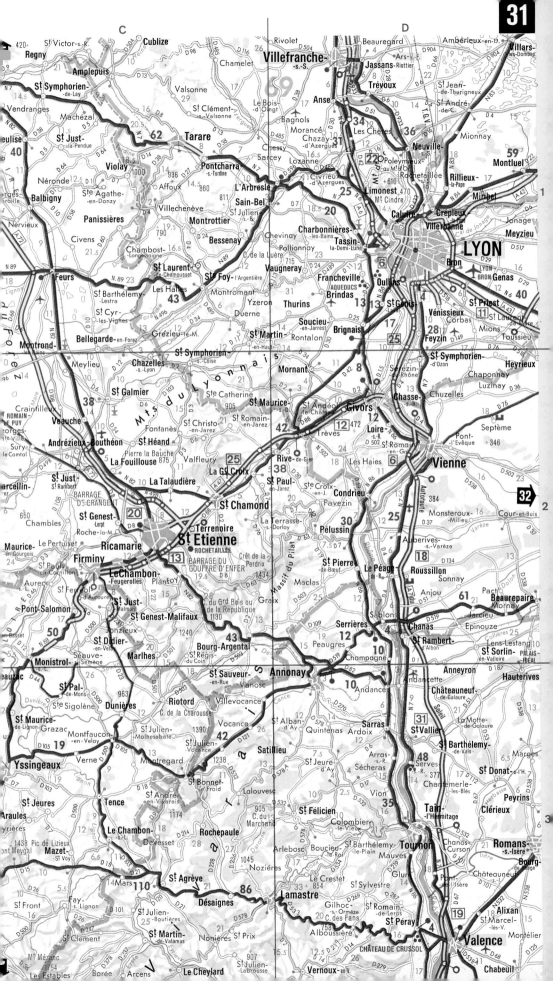

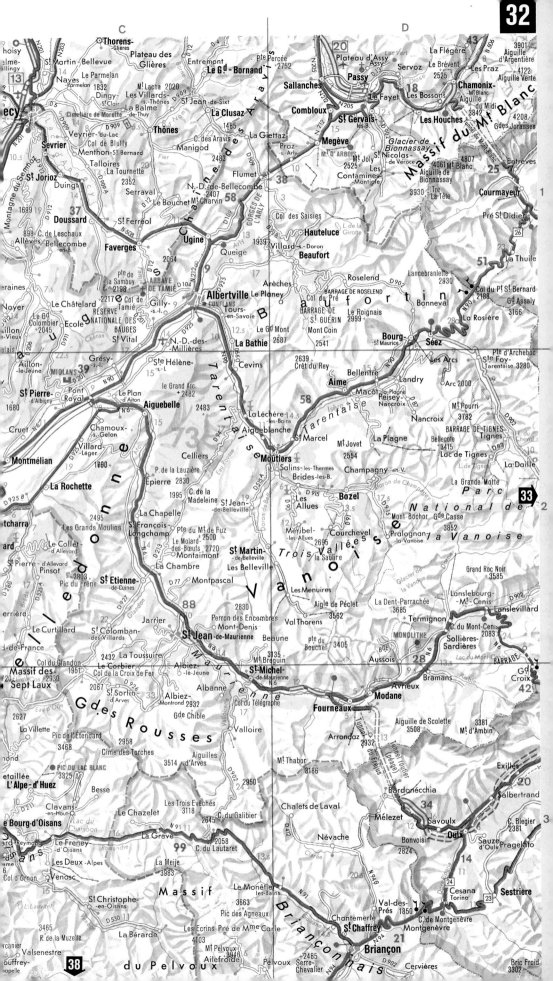

33

Carcóforo · Rimella · Fobello · Massiola · Gravellona · Toce · Baveno · Isole Borromee · Laveno · Cittiglio · Brenta · Ganna · Porto Cérésio · Viggiù · Stabio

Madonna d. Ferrate · Rimasco · Ferrera · Omegna · Quarna · Mottarone · Stresa · Gignese · Reno · Orino · Brinzio · Bisuschio · Induno · Olona

Cravagliana · Corte · Césara · Armeno · Belgirate · Vezzo · Arolo · S. Andrea · Campo d. Fiori Rasa 1226 · Varese

Bocciolèto · Vocca · Varallo · SACRO MONTE · Civiasco · Pettenasco · Massino · Lesa · Ispra · Cadrezzate · Cassinetta · Azzate · Malnate · Solbiate

Balmúccia · Rocca Pietra · Cast. di Gavala 1827 · Alzo · Orta · Pisano · Méina · Angera · Comábbio · Mornago · Castronno · Solbiate · Tradate

Scopa · Scopello · Piode · M. Barone 2044 · Póstua · Quarona · Invório · Arona · Angera · Mercallo · Vergiate · Besnate · Cairate

Andorno · Pettinengo · Borgoséssia · Grignasco · Maggiora · Boca · Gozzano · Paruzzaro · Gattico · Castelletto s. Ticino · Golasecca · Somma Lombardo · Casorate Sempione · Gallarate · Busto Arsizio · Legnano

Biella · Gattinara · Romagnano Séssia · Ghemme · Fara Novarese · Cávaglio d'Agogna · Suno · Marano Ticino · Aeroporto d. Malpensa · Busto Garolfo

Biella · Cossato · Lenta · Badia di Dulzago · Momo · Galdina · Castano Primo · Buscate · Turbigo · Inveruno · Magenta

Vercelli · NOVARA · Galliate · Trecate · Cerano · Cassolnovo · Vigévano · Mortara · Gambolò

Santhià · S. Germano Vercelli · Vercelli · Asigliano · Pezzana · Róbbio · Nicorvo · Parona · Gambolò

Trino · Trino · Palazzolo Vercelli · Morano Po · Bálzola · Terranova · Cándia Lomellina · Valle · Lomello · Valéggio · Ferrera

Casale Monferrato · Borgo S. Martino · Ticineto · Bózzole · Torre Beretti · Mede · Mezzana Bigli

Alessándria · Felizzano · Spinetta · MARENGO · S. Giuliano Nuovo · Pozzolo Form.

Asti · Castello di Annone · Másio · Oviglio · Bergamasco · Borgoratto · Casal Cermelli · Bosco Marengo · A 7

A

B

O C É A N

A T L A N T I Q U

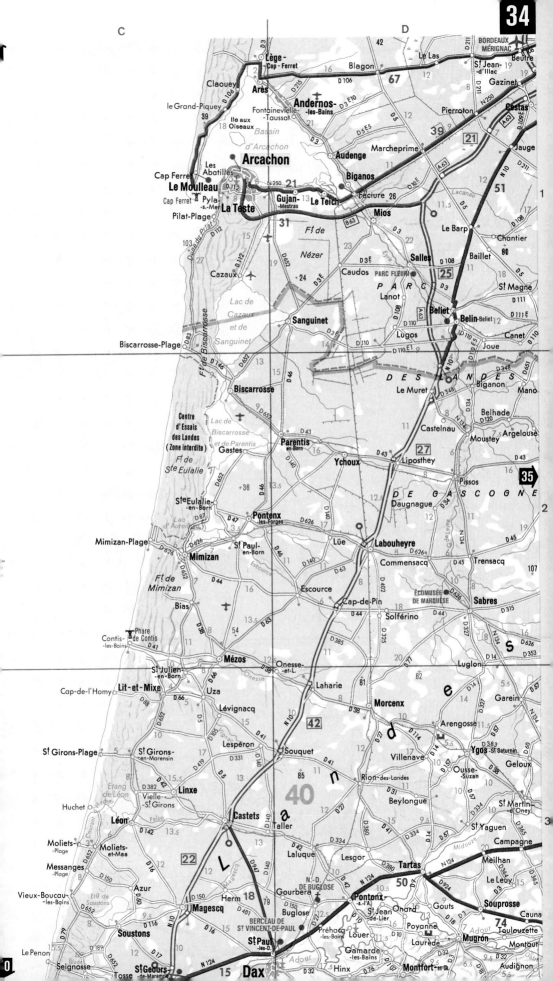

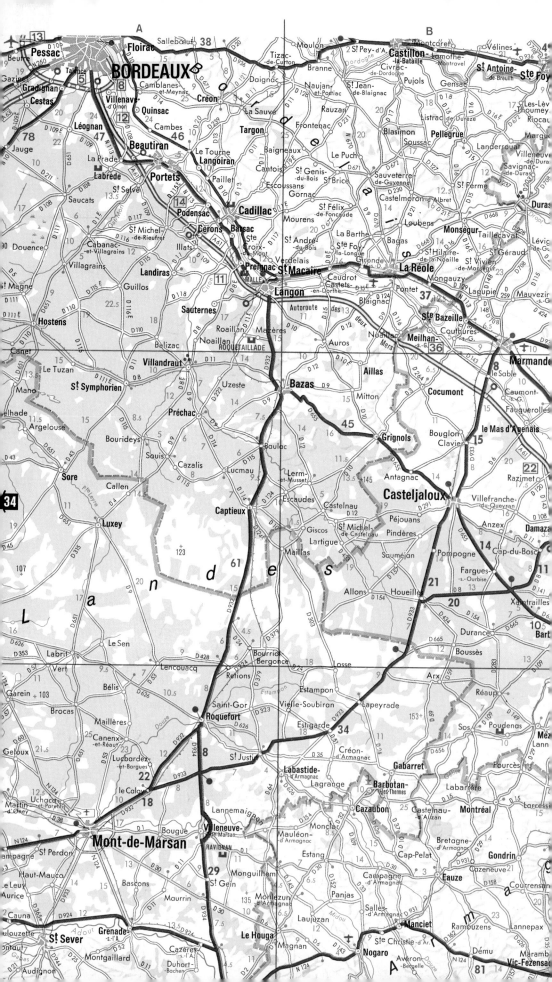

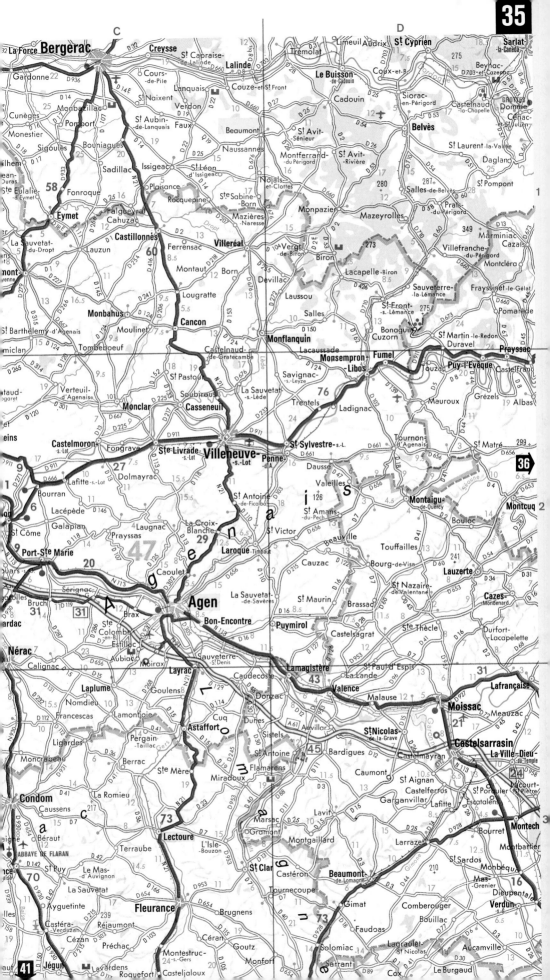

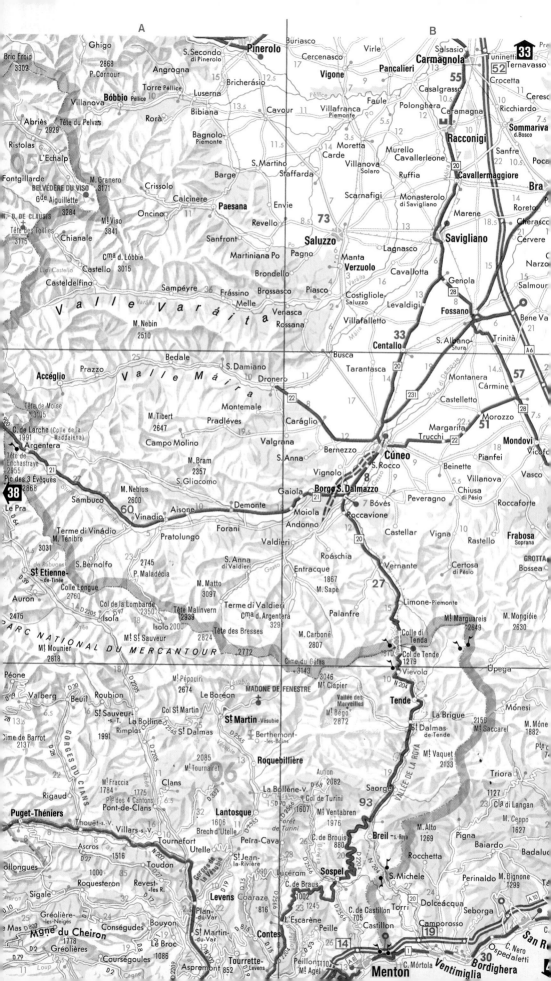

C | D

Soustons · St Paul-les-D · Gamarde-les-Bains · Montfort-en-Ch. · Audignon · Dumes

15 Dax · Hinx · St Aubin · Doazit

St Geours-de-Marempe · Saubusse · Tercis-les-Bains · Ozourt · Baigts · Castelnau-Chalosse · Donzacq · Gaujacq · Hagetmau

St Vincent-de-Tyrosse · Josse · St Lon-les-Mines · Clermont · Pomarez · Brassempouy · Monségur

Benesse-Maremne · Orx · St Jean-de-Marsacq · Cagnotte · Benesse-lès-Dax · Estibeaux · Arsague · Amou · Nassiet · Castaignos-Souuens · Monget

Orx · Saubrigues · St Martin-de-Hinx · St Etienne-d'Orthe · Pouillon · Habas · Tilh · Sault-de-Navailles · Monségur

St André-de-Seignanx · Port-de-Lanne · Bélus · Ossages · Puyoô-Bellocq-Ramous · Hagetaubin

Peyrehorade · 64 · Baigts-de-Béarn · Orthez 11

Quartier Neuf · St Laurent-de-Gosse · Sames · Guiche · Sorde-l'Abbaye · Bellocq · Bérenx · Castétis · Arthez-de-Béarn · Arance · Lacq · Artix

Biarrotte · Bidache · St Dos · Carresse-Cassaber · Salies-de-Béarn · 14 · Argagnon · Maslacq · Mourenx · Noguères

Bardos · Came · Escos · Oraàs · I'Hôpital-d'Orion · Laà-Mondrans · Lagor · Ville-Neuve

Mouguerre · Urt · Labastide-Clairence · Bergouey-Viellenave · Sauveterre-de-Béarn · Laas · Narp · Loubieng · Abos

Briscous · Arraute-Charitte · Ilharre · Auteviulle-St-M.-B. · Osserain-Rivareyte · Narp · Viellesègure · Lahourcade

Hasparren · Isturits · Béguios · Aïcirits · Domezain-Berraute · Rivehaute · Nabas · Bastanès · Monein

La Place · St Esteben · Méharin · St Palais · Aroue-Ithorots-Olhaiby · Undurein · Gurs · Navarrenx · Lucq-de-Béarn

Cambo-les-B. · Hélette · Iholdy · Uhart-Mixe · Lohitzun-Oyhercq · Moncayolle-Larroy-Mendibieu · I'Hôpital-St-Blaise · Saucède · Cardesse · Verdets

Artzamendi 926 · Irissarry · Larceveau-Arros-Cibits · Musculdy · Chéraute · Orin · Oloron-Ste Marie

Bidarray · Ossès · Jaxu · Lacarre · C. d'Osquich · Garaybie · Mauléon-Licharre · Gotein-Libarrenx · Barcus · Agnos · Val-du-Gave-d'Aspe · Eysus

Gorramendi 1080 · St Just-Ibarre · Trois-Villes · Esquiule · Féas · Asasp-Arros · St Christau

ya del Baztán · St Jean-le-V. · Hosta · Ft des · Lanne · Aramits · Lurbe-St Christau · Issor

St Etienne-de-Baïgorry · St Jean-Pied-de-Port · Mendive · P. de Zaboze 1188 · Tardets-Sorholus · Montory · Arette · Escot · 55

Banca · Arneguy · Valcarlos · Esterençuby · Arbailles · P. des Vautours 1078 · Laguinge-Restoue · Lacarry-Arhan-Charitte-le-H. · Sarrance

Les Aldudes · Urepel · Onzanzurrieta · Roncesvalles · Pic Occabé 1456 · Pic des Escaliers 1478 · Licq-Athérey · Ste Engrâce · Bedous · Accous

Espinal · Viscarret · Burguete 75 · Orbara · Orbaiceta · Pantano de Irabia · FORÊT D'IRATY 1656 · Larrau 1559 · GORGES DE KAKOUETTA · GOUFFRE DE LA PIERRE St MARTIN · Pic d'Anie 2504 · Lescun

Mezquíriz · Garralda · Villanueva de Aézcoa · Sierra de Abodi · Port de Larrau 1573 · Portillo de Eraice 1578 · N134

Puerto Erro · Arive · Garayoa · 1499 · Alto Laza · Venta de Arracos · Meseta de los Tres Reyes 2434

Arrieta · Aburrea Baja · Aburrea Alta · Ochagavía · Uztárroz · P. de Labigouer 2175

Oróz-Betelu · Jaurrieta · Escároz · Oronz · Isaba · Urzainqui · Forca 2390 · Visaurin 2669

Azparren · Esparza del Salazar · Sarries · Igal · Roncal · Garde · 2020 · de Estanes

Arce · Muniain · Elcoaz · Ibilcieta · Vidangoz · Siresa · 1785

Aoiz · Arangozqui · Ayechu · Izal · Adoain · Güesa · Iciz · Garde · Ansó · Hecho · Urdués · Aragüés del Puerto

Eparaz · Guindano · Gallues · Uscarrés · Ustés · Burgui · Jasa

Villaveta · Aós · Murillo · Zabalza · Imirizaldu · Navascués · Salvatierra de Esca · Embún

Artaiz · Ardanaz · Turrillas · Sansoáin · Iso · Bigüezal · Villarreal de la Canal · Sigüés · Asoberal · Biniés

Indurain · Ripodas · San Vicente · Domeño · SIERRA DE LEIRE · MON. DE SAN SALVADOR DE LEYRE · Salvatierra

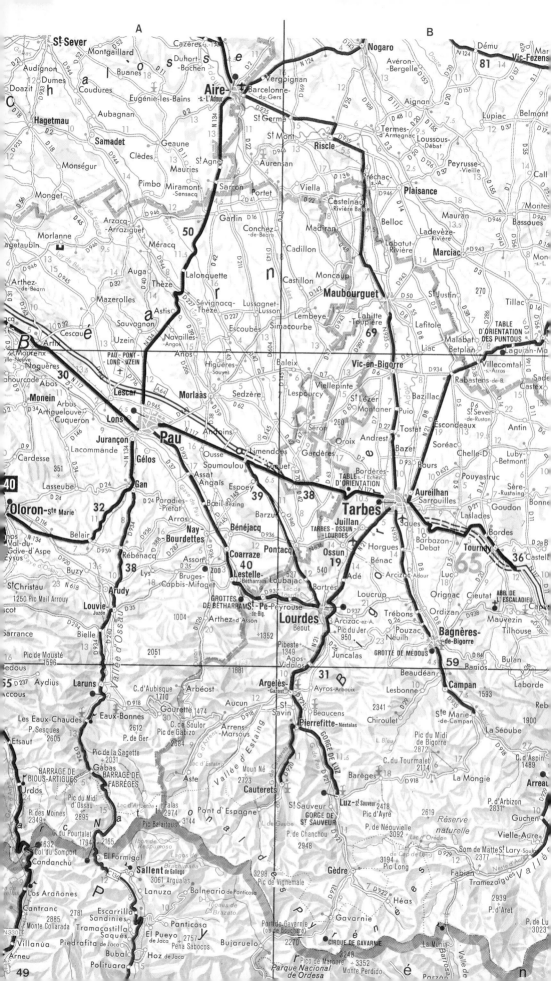

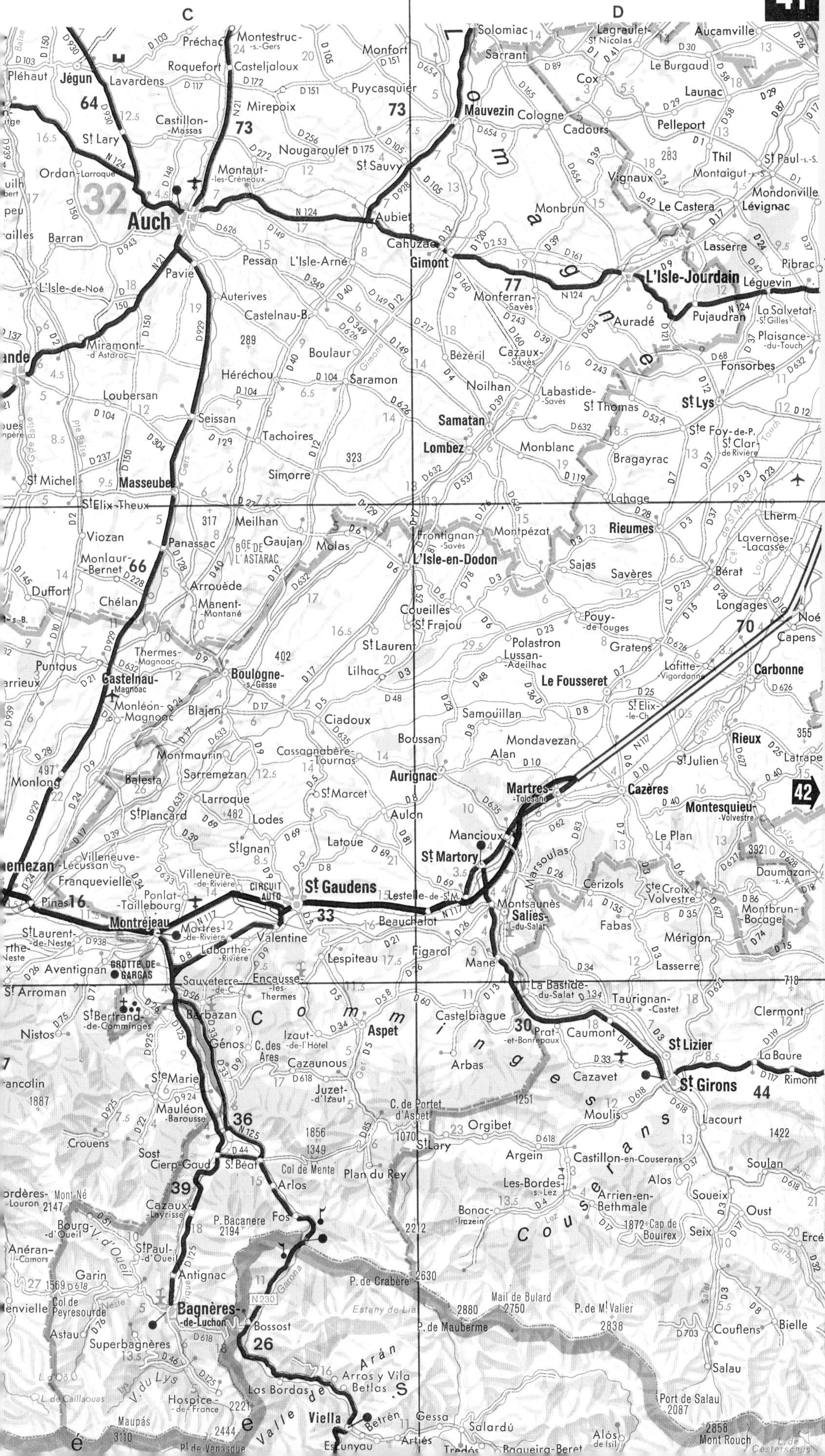
C
D
Solomiac
Préchac
Montestruc-s.-Gers
Monfort
Lagraulet-St Nicolas
Aucamville
Sarrant
Roquefort
Casteljaloux
Le Burgaud
Pléhaut
Jégun
Lavardens
Cox
Launac
Mirepoix
Puycasquier
Castillon-Massas
Mauvezin
Cologne
Cadours
Pelleport
St Lary
Nougaroulet
St Sauvy
Thil
St Paul-s.-S.
Ordan-Larroque
Montaut-les-Créneaux
Montaigut-s.-S.
Vignaux
Mondonville
Auch
Aubiet
Monbrun
Le Castera
Lévignac
Barran
Cahuzac
Lasserre
Gimont
Pibrac
Pavie
Pessan
L'Isle-Arné
L'Isle-Jourdain
Léguevin
L'Isle-de-Noé
Auterives
Monferran-Savès
Pujaudran
La Salvetat-St-Gilles
Castelnau-B.
Auradé
Plaisance-du-Touch
Miramont-d'Astarac
Boulaur
Bézéril
Cazaux-Savès
Fonsorbes
Héréchou
Saramon
Noilhan
Labastide-Savès
Loubersan
St Thomas
St Lys
Seissan
Samatan
Ste Foy-de-P.
Tachoires
Lombez
Monblanc
St Clar-de-Rivière
Bragayrac
Simorre
St Michel
Masseube
Lahage
St Elix-Theux
Meilhan
Lherm
Rieumes
Viozan
Panassac
Gaujan
Molas
Frontignan-Savès
Montpézat
Lavernose-Lacasse
Monlaur-Bernet
BGE DE L'ASTARAC
L'Isle-en-Dodon
Sajas
Bérat
Duffort
Arrouède
Savères
Chélan
Manent-Montané
Coueilles
Longages
St Frajou
Pouy-de-Touges
Noé
Capens
Thermes-Magnoac
St Laurent
Polastron
Gratens
Puntous
Castelnau-Magnoac
Boulogne-s.-Gesse
Lilhac
Lussan-Adeilhac
Le Fousseret
Lafitte-Vigordane
Carbonne
Monléon-Magnoac
Blajan
Ciadoux
Samouillan
St Elix-le-Ch.
Rieux
Boussan
Mondavezan
Montmaurin
Cassagnabère-Tournas
Alan
St Julien
Latrape
Monlong
Balesta
Sarremezan
Aurignac
Martres-Tolosane
Cazères
Montesquieu-Volvestre
42
St Marcet
Larroque
St Plancard
Lodes
Aulon
Latoue
Mancioux
Le Plan
St Martory
St Ignan
Villeneuve-Lécussan
Marsoulas
Daumazan-s.-A.
Franquevielle
Villeneure-de-Rivière
CIRCUIT AUTO
St Gaudens
Cérizols
Ste Croix-Volvestre
Pinas
Ponlat-Taillebourg
Lestelle-de-St M.
Montsaunès
Salies-du-Salat
Montbrun-Bocage
Montréjeau
Mazères-de-Rivière
Valentine
Beauchalot
Fabas
Mérigon
St Laurent-de-Neste
Labarthe-Rivière
Figarol
Aventignan
GROTTE DE GARGAS
Lespiteau
Mane
Lasserre
Sauveterre-de-C.
Encausse-les-Thermes
La Bastide-du-Salat
St Arroman
Taurignan-Castet
Clermont
St Bertrand-de-Comminges
Barbazan
Castelbiague
Nistos
Izaut-de-l'Hôtel
Aspet
Prat-et-Bonrepaux
Caumont
St Lizier
Génos
C. des Ares
Arbas
La Baure
Cazaunous
Cazavet
St Girons
Rimont
Ste Marie
Juzet-d'Izaut
C. de Portet d'Aspet
Moulis
Lacourt
Mauléon-Barousse
Orgibet
Crouens
St Lary
Argein
Castillon-en-Couserans
Soulan
Sost
Cierp-Gaud
St Béat
Col de Mente
Plan du Rey
Arlos
Les Bordes-s.-Lez
Alos
Arrien-en-Bethmale
Soueix
Oust
Mont Né
Cazaux-Layrisse
P. Bacanere
Fos
Bonac-Irazein
Seix
Ercé
Bourg-d'Oueil
St Paul-d'Oueil
Cap de Bouirex
Antignac
Garin
P. de Crabère
Col de Peyresourde
Bagnères-de-Luchon
Mail de Bulard
P. de Mt Valier
Estany de Lia
Astau
Superbagnères
Bossost
P. de Mauberme
Couflens
Bielle
Salau
Arros y Vila
Betlas
Las Bordas
Hospice-de-France
Port de Salau
Viella
Betrén
Gessa
Salardú
Mont Rouch
Artiés
Escunyau
Tredós
Baqueira-Beret
Alós de Isil
Maupás
P. de Venasque
V. du Lys
L. de Caillaouas
Lomagne
Comminges
Couserans
Valle de Arán

Le Travet · St Jean-de-Jeannes · Belmont-s.-R. · Gissac · Camarès · Montagnol · Le Clapier · Ceilhes-de-Rocozels
St Sever-du-Moustier · Mounès-Prohencoux · Fayet · Cenomes · Montagnac
St Pierre-de-Trivisy · Le Masnau-Massuguiès · Brusque · Tauriac-de-Camarès · Avène
Montredon-Labessonnie · Lacaze · CH AU Viane · Moulin-Mage · Arnac-s.-Dourdou · Mélagues · Truscas
Vabre · Espérausses · Lacaune · La Trivalle · Nages · Plaisance · Le Bouquet-d'Orb · Graissessac
Lacrouzette · Ferrières · Castelnau-de-Brassac · BGE DE LADUZAS · Murat-s.-Vèbre · St Gervais-s.-Mare · La Tour-s.-Orb
Roquecourbe · Brassac · Lamontélarié · La Salvetat-s-A. · Cambon-et-Salvergues · Parc Naturel du Caroux · Bédarieux
Castres · Boissezon · St-Salvy-de-la-B. · Le Bez · BGE DE LA RAVIEGE · Fraisse-s-A. · Villemagne · Lamalou-les-B. · Hérépian
Noailhac · Le Rialet · Anglès · Le Soulié · C. du Cabaretou · Olargues · Le Poujol-s-Orb · Villemagne
La Fontasse · Le Vintrou · Rouairoux · St Pons · Riols · St Etienne-d'Albagnan · Vieussan · Roquebrun · St Nazaire-de-Ladarez
Mazamet · Aussillon · St Amans-Soult · Labastide-Rouairoux · Courniou · Berlou · St Geniès-le-Bas
St Amans · Lacabarède · Albine · Pic de Nore · Peyrefiche · Rieussec · St Jean-de-Minervois · Assignan · Pierrerue · St Chinian · Cessenon · Murviel-les-Béziers
Pradelles-Cabardès · Lespinassière · Ferrals-les-Montagnes · Villespassans · Cébazan · Cazouls-lès-Béziers
Cuxac-Cabardès · Mas-Cabardès · Citou · St Julien-de-M. · Minerve · Cesseras · Aigues-Vives · Azillanet · Cruzy · Puisserguier · Lignan · Maureilhan
Lastours · Cabrespine · Caunes-Minervois · Siran · Bize-Minervois · Quarante · Capestang · Montady
Limousis · GROTTE · La Livinière · Pouzols-M. · Ouveillan · OPPIDUM D'ENSERUNE · Nissan-lez-Ensérune
Villeneuve-Minervois · Peyriac-Minervois · Rieux-Minervois · Azille · Olonzac · Ventenac-d'Aude · Sallèles-d'Aude · Cuxac-d'Aude · Lespignan
Villegailhenc · Villegly · Conques-s.-Orbiel · Laure-M. · Homps · Roubia · St Marcel-sur-A. · Coursan · Fleury
Pezens · Laredorte · Marcorignan · Salles-d'Aude · Vinassan
Carcassonne · CITÉ · Trèbes · Puichéric · Lézignan-c. · Villedaigne · Narbonne · St Pierre-s.-Mer
Marseillette · St Couat-d' · Moux · Bizanet · Montagne de la Clape · Narbonne-Plage
Lavalette · Barbaira · Capendu · Ornaisons · CHAPELLE DES AUZILS
Palaja · Fontcouverte · Ferrals-les-Corbières · Ste Marie · ABBAYE DE FONTFROIDE · Bages · Gruissan · Gruissan-Plage
Leuc · Monze · Fabrezan · St Laurent-de-la-Cabrerisse · Montséret · Peyriac-de-Mer
Rouffiac-d'Aude · Villefloure · Montlaur · Thézan-des- · Donos · Portel-des- · Sigean
Pomas · Ladern-s.-Lauquet · Mas-des-Cours · Serviès-en-Val · Lagrasse · Talairan · Coustouge
St Hilaire · Labastide-en-Val · St Pierre-des-Champs · Port-la-Nouvelle
Buc · Caunette-s.-Lauquet · Villerouge-Termenès · Albas · Durban-Corbières
Villardebelle · Vignevieille · CH AU DE TERNES · Villeneuve-les-Corbières · Fraissé-des-Corbières · Les Cabanes de Fitou
Alet-les-Bains · Montjoi · Mouthoumet · Davejean · St Jean-de-Barrou · Les Cabanes-de-Lapalme · La Franqui-Plage · Cap Leucate
Valmigère · Arques · Laroque-de-Fa · Maisons · Leucate · Leucate-Plage
Serres · Auriac · Tuchan · Opoul-Périllos · Port-Leucate
Rennes-les-Bains · Massac · Soulatgé · CH AU DE PEYREPERTUSE · Paziols · Vingrau · FORT · Port-Barcarès · Grau-St Ange
Bugarach · Cubières-s.-Cinoble · GORGES DE GALAMUS · CH AU DE QUERIBUS · Padern · Salses · LYDIA · Le Barcarès
St Louis-et-Parahou · Caudiès-de-Fenouillèdes · St Paul-de-Fenouillet · Maury · Tautavel · Rivesaltes · St Laurent-de-la-Salanque
Puilaurens · Fenouillèdes · Estagel · Baixas · Pia · Bompas · Ste Marie
Gincla · Montfort-s.-Boulzane · Rabouillet · Ansignan · Latour-de-France · PERPIGNAN-RIVESALTES · Canet-en-Roussillon-S. N.
Sournia · Trévillach · Perpignan

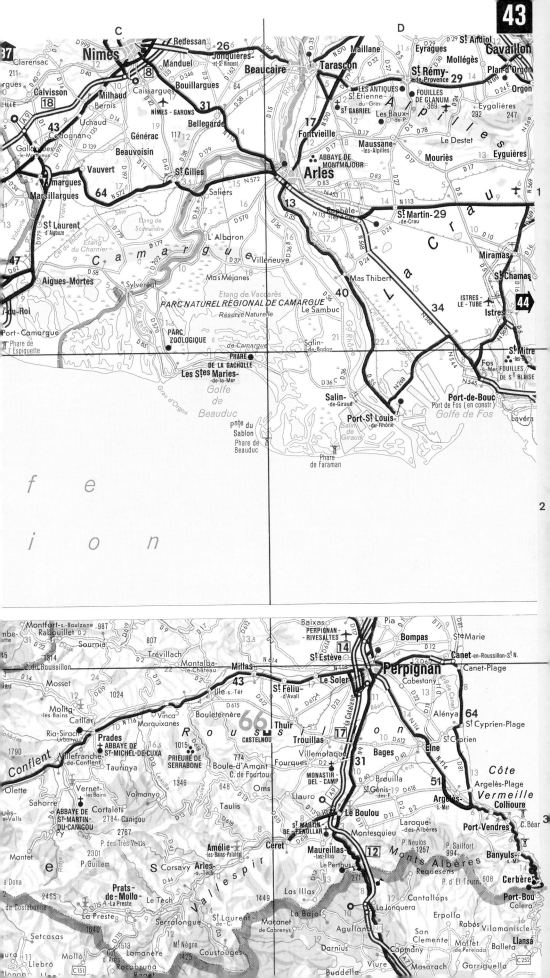

Roumoules · Riez · La Foux · La Foux · Valderoure · Thorenc · D 79
Montagnac-Montpezat · Les Salles-s.-V. · La Palud-s.-V. · Rougon · C. de Luens 1054 · Le Logis-du-Pin · Andon · N 85 · D 81 · St Lambert
Aiguines · Trigance · La Bastide · C. de Valferrière 1715 · Mgne de Lachens 1642 · Escragnolles · St Vallier-de-Thiey
Bauduen · Plan de Canjuers · La Barre · Comps-s.-A. · Mons · Brovès · Cabris
Baudinard-s.-Verdon · 1141 · CAMP MILITAIRE DE CANJUERS · Seillans · St Cézaire-s.-Siagne
Régusse · Moissac-Bellevue · Vérignon · 1130 · 1086 · Fayence · Callian · BARRAGE DE St CASSIEN · Tanneron
Montmeyan · Aups · Montferrat · Ampus · Bargemon · Mont Vinaigre · Pic de l'Ours 28 · Esterel
Barjols · Salernes · Villecroze · Lentier · Callas · Bagnols-en-Forêt · 352 · 373 · 28
Châteauvert · Cotignac · Draguignan · Flayosc · Trans-en-Provence · La Motte · Le Muy · 12 · Mont Vinaigre · Valescure · Agay
Correns · Entrecasteaux · Lorgues · Les Arcs · 301 · Puget-s.-Argens · Roquebrune-s.-Argens · Fréjus · St Raphaël · Boulouris · C. du Dramont
Carcès · ABBAYE DU THORONET · Le Thoronet · Taradeau · Vidauban · 34 · 19 · St Aygulf · G. de Fréjus
Le Val · Vins-s.-Caramy · Cabasse · Les Muraires · Le Cannet-des-Maures · C. de Grattelloup 225 · 354 · 29 · Les Issambres · Val d'Esquières
Brignoles · Flassans-s.-Issole · Le Luc · 83 · Plan-de-la-Tour · Ste Maxime
La Celle · Besse-s.-I. · Gonfaron · Les Mayons · Beauvallon · Port-Grimaud · G. de St Tropez · St Tropez · Plage de Tahiti · Plage de Pampelonne
Rocbaron · Carnoules · Pignans · N.DAME DES ANGES · La Sauvette 780 · Grimaud · La Foux · Gassin · Ramatuelle · C. Camarat
Puget-Ville · 52 · Collobrières · CHARTREUSE DE LA VERNE 648 · Cogolin · 5 · C. Cartaya
Cuers · Pierrefeu-du-Var · Massif des Maures · La Môle · La Croix-Valmer · C. Lardier
Solliès-Pont · Laquina 599 · 46 · 528 · Cavalaire-s.-M. · C. Cartaya
Farlède · La Crau · La Londe-les-Maures · Bormes · 56 · Rayol-Canadel-s.-M. · Cavalière
TOULON · La Garde · 18 · Hyères · Port-de-Miramar · Cabasson · Le Lavandou · C. Nègre
Carqueiranne · 23 · Hyères-Plage · FORT DE BRÉGANÇON · C. Bénat · Rade de Bormes
G. de Giens · La Capte · Iles d'Hyères · I. du Levant · Phare du Titan
Giens · Port-Cros · Le Grand Avis · Héliopolis
Presqu'île de Giens · Porquerolles · I. de Port-Cros
Phare du Grand-Ribaud · I. de Porquerolles · PARC DE PORT-CROS
Cap d'Arme

MÉDITERRANÉE

45

C
D

1

M É D I T E R R A N É E

2

3

CORSICA
Schaal 1 : 600 000

10 km
10
5
0
5
10

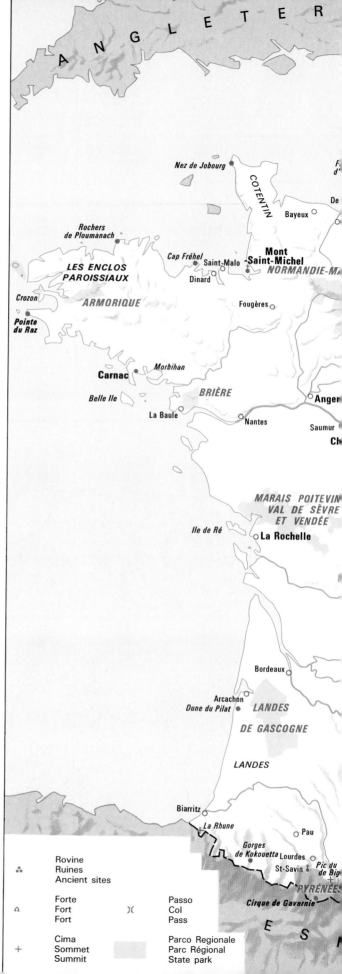

La Francia turistica

Una scelta delle città e dei siti turisticamente più importanti.

La France touristique

Une sélection des villes et sites les plus importants sur le plan touristique.

France and tourism

A selection of the most important cities and sites from the tourist point of view.

Rouen	Città turistica importante Ville touristique importante Major tourist city
Ventoux	Curiosità naturale importante Curiosité naturelle importante Important natural attractions
○	Città turistica Ville touristique Tourist city
⊔	Castello Château Castle or stately home
‡	Abbazia Abbaye Abbey
●	Curiosità Curiosité Sites of local interest
	Parco Nationale Parc National National park

⁂	Rovine Ruines Ancient sites		
⋒	Forte Fort Fort	)(	Passo Col Pass
+	Cima Sommet Summit		Parco Regionale Parc Régional State park

Map labels

ANGLETERR

Nez de Jobourg
COTENTIN
De
Bayeux
F.
d'
Rochers de Ploumanach
Cap Fréhel
Saint-Malo
Mont Saint-Michel
NORMANDIE-M.
Dinard
LES ENCLOS PAROISSIAUX
Crozon
ARMORIQUE
Fougères
Pointe du Raz
Morbihan
Carnac
BRIÈRE
Anger
Belle Ile
La Baule
Nantes
Saumur
Ch
MARAIS POITEVIN VAL DE SÈVRE ET VENDÉE
Ile de Ré
La Rochelle
Bordeaux
Arcachon
Dune du Pilat
LANDES DE GASCOGNE
LANDES
Biarritz
La Rhune
Pau
Gorges de Kokouetta
Lourdes
St-Savin
Pic du de Big
PYRÉNÉES
Cirque de Gavarnie
ES

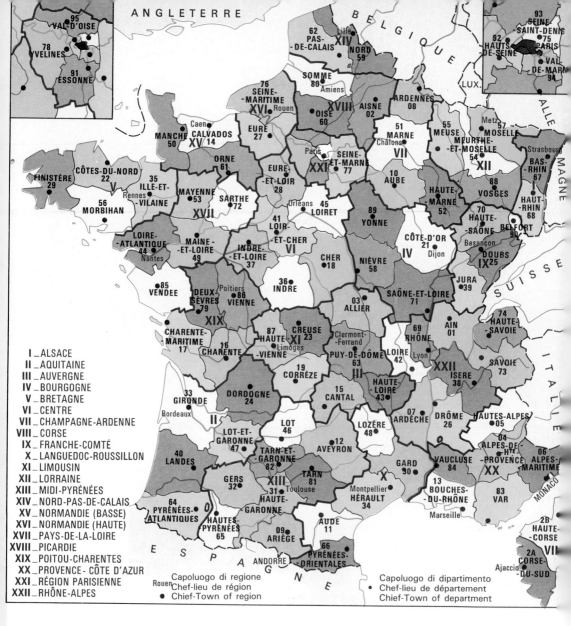

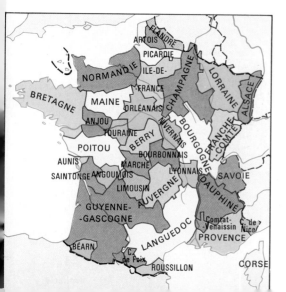

La Francia dipartimentale e le sue regioni amministrative
La France départementale avec ses régions administratives
The "départements" and the administrative regions of France

La Francia delle province

La cartina qui a fianco mostra le province francesi secondo la ripartizione del 1789. Oggi, i confini geografici non sono più così rigidi.

La France des Provinces

La carte ci-contre présente les provinces françaises, telles qu'elles se répartissaient en 1789.
De nos jours, les limites géographiques ne sont plus aussi rigoureuses.

The French provinces

This map presents the French provinces as they were defined in 1789.
Nowadays, the geographical borders are not as strict.

France, A to Z

Abbeville
80 – Somme   5 – B 1
Ch. de Bagatelle, elegant mid-18c 'folly' (v.a. daily exc. Tues. during summer), fine panelling. Former collegiate church of St. Vulfran, 15–16c, richly sculpted façade; leaves of main doors were the work of Picardy's once-famed trough-makers. Mus. Boucher de Perthes (prehistory, paintings, etc.).
Vicinity ● **Baie de Somme*** and Vimeu region ● To SW, Mill of *St. Maxent*.

Aber-Wrac'h (L')
29N – Finistère   8 – B 1
Fishing village and seaside resort in wild country at mouth of Aber-Wrac'h estuary. Boating centre, sailing schools. Remains of 16c Franciscan convent, Notre-Dame-des-Anges. Many islands, reefs.
Vicinity ● 7 km SE, *Ch. de Kerou-artz*, 17c, beautiful terraced gardens (v.a.). ● Recommended excursions: to W. Ste. Marguerite peninsula; to N, *Phare de la Vierge* (at 75 m., the tallest lighthouse in Europe); to NE, sandbanks of St. Michel, etc., one of the wildest stretches of the 'Côte des Abers' – literally, Coast of the River Mouths, see **St. Renan***.

ABBEYS (route of the Norman Abbeys)
76 – Seine-Maritime   5 – A3–4 – D 3
From Rouen, take D982 through Forêt de la Roumare to *St. Martin-de-Boscherville* (11 km); abbey church of St. Georges is notable example of 12c Norman Romanesque; apply at presbytery to see chapter-house, dating from 1170. D982 continues via *Duclair*, where church combines Romanesque (11c nave), Goth. (14c choir) and Ren. (side door). After 4.5 km, l. on to D143 for 3.5 km to **Jumièges***. Return to D982 and carry on NNW, until turning r. on to little road leading to Benedictine abbey of **St. Wandrille***.

St. Martin de Boscherville
The chapter-house opens on to the cloisters through three arches, resting on clustered columns with historiated capitals.

Abondance
74 – Haute-Savoie   26 – D 3
Summer and winter resort. The church, once part of 13c abbey, has 14c cloister decorated with late-15c frescos (restored); 17c abbey buildings surrounding it on three sides contain a mus. of religious art.
Vicinity ● 11.5 km E, via La Chap-elle-d'Abondance, dominated by the Cornettes de Bise (2,438 m.) is *Châtel-d'Abondance*, winter sports centre; in summer, cable car to Super-Châtel, chair-lift to summit of Morclan (1,970 m.), vast panorama; from there you can get to the *Pas de Morgins* (1,375 m., on Franco-Swiss frontier), then *Morgins*, in a superb setting.

Agde
34 – Hérault   43 – A 2
St. Étienne cathedral (late-12c), formerly fortified, in black lava. Agde mus. (cl. Tues.), local arts and traditions, period décors. Also museum for objects recovered from undersea expeditions; Greek, Italic and Roman amphorae. Traditional jousts, first week Aug.
Vicinity ● 7 km SE, *Cap d'Agde*, residential and holiday New Town, with marina; internatl. naturist centre; most unusual beach of black sand (Grande Conque); out to sea, fort of Brescou. ● 4 km SW, *La Tamarissière* and *Grau-d'Agde*,

Agde: *the black lava bulk of St. Étienne cathedral, with its two huge square towers and still showing traces of its former fortifications, rises impressively over the Quai de l'Hérault.*

L'Aigle: *Gothic Flamboyant tower of St. Martin church, richly embellished with gargoyles, etc.*

AIGUEBELETTE (lake of)
73 – Savoie   32 – B 2
Running 4 km N to S, dominated by Mt. de l'Épine, the lake is full of fish (pike, perch, trout, etc.) and has several summer resorts around its 17 km banks: *St. Alban*, Lépin-le-Lac, *Aiguebelette*, La Combe-du-Lac.
Vicinity ● To W, Col de la Crusille (582 m.) towards *St. Genix*. ● To E, Col de l'Épine (fine panorama). ● To S, Mont Grelle.

fishing village; Agenouillade chapel, 17c, surrounded by pines.

Agen
47 – Lot-et-Garonne   35 – C 2
The mus. (cl. Tues.), housed in four 16–17c buildings, boasts five Goyas, archaeological collections (prehist., Middle Ages), 17–20c

paintings, and a 1c BC Greek marble, the 'Venus du Mas'. St. Caprais cathedral (Romanesque transept and choir, Gothic nave, 16c vaulting) has Romanesque historiated capitals.
Vicinity ● 9 km SW, *Aubiac*: noteworthy 12c Romanesque church; the square choir, flanked by three

apsidioles, is surmounted by a tower, also square, forming a lantern. ● At nearby *Estillac*, the 13–16c castle is an imposing example of military architecture; in the grounds is cenotaph with recumbent effigy of Blaise de Montluc, famed 16c French field-marshal. Castle interior has vaulted kitchens and period apartments (v.a. Sun. p.m., July 1 to Nov. 1, or on request). ● 9 km S, *Moirax*, Romanesque church with square choir under a dome.

Aigle (L')
61 – Orne   10 – D 2
The Gothic Flamboyant church of St. Martin, 15–16c, richly sculptured and with a square Romanesque tower, is flanked by a 12c clock tower. The late-17c château, by Hardouin-Mansart, houses waxworks mus., 'June '44', commemorating the battle for Normandy.
Vicinity ● Forêt de la Trappe and *Abbaye de la Grande Trappe* (Trappist abbey), services open to public. ● *Haras du Pin* (v.a.), France's best-known stud farm.

Aigues-Mortes
30 – Gard   43 – C 1
Amid the solitude of the lakes and saltpans which separate it from the sea, the town and its ramparts – with 20 towers and 10 gates – provide a striking echo of the Middle Ages. The walls are more than 1,500 m. in length. The town, laid out in chequer-board pattern, is entered via the Gardette gate. The Tour de Constance (v.a.), a fine cylindrical keep, crowned by a watchtower, includes a Salle des Gardes and, above it, a Salle des Chevaliers, former prison; fine panorama. The town's different gates lead directly

Agen: *the Romanesque apse is one of St. Caprais cathedral's most remarkable features. Grafted on to it are three Gothic Rayonnant chapels, the middle one sculpted with a blind arcade.*

to the countryside, from where you get superb views of the ramparts.
Vicinity ● 3.5 km N, Carbonnière tower, 13c. ● To SW, *Le Grau-du-Roi*, colourful and lively fishing village, and **La Grande Motte***. ● To E, the **Camargue*** and road to **Stes-Maries-de-la-Mer***.

of 15c château. ● *Breteuil-sur-Noye*, 16c and 18c remains of former abbey. ● To W, *Conty*, Gothic Flamboyant church.

Aime
73 – Savoie   32 – D 2
Former basilica of St. Martin (11–

region' (open Shrove Tues., and Suns. from mid-Feb. to Easter, then daily to Nov. 30). Flanked by pepper-pot towers, a postern-gate and moat, the 14c octagonal enceinte retains its 'feel' of a medieval fortress; within it, an elegant building with Gothic Flamboyant showing first Renaissance refinements. Fine views from ramparts. Interior has Ren. oratory.
Vicinity ● 4.5 km NW, *Drevant*, Roman remains (theatre, temple, baths); excavations.

Aire-sur-l'Adour
40 – Landes   41 – A 1
On the borders of the Chalosse and Armagnac regions, this little town is renowned in France for its (wintertime) goose and duck liver markets. Former cathedral, 15–18c, with 18c furnishings.
Outskirts ● 2 km S, Mas-d'Aire: Ste. Quitterie church, Goth. portal (The Last Judgment); int. has historiated capitals; in crypt, fine Merovingian sarcophagus in white marble, said to be of (14c) Ste. Quitterie herself.

Aire-sur-la-Lys
62 – Pas-de-Calais   1 – C 3
Former fortress, 17–18c. St. Pierre, Gothic and Renaissance (pilgrimage to Notre-Dame-Panetière). St. Jacques, 17c. Old houses.

Aix-en-Provence
13 – Bouches-du-Rhône   44 – A 1
The old quarter of this remarkable town, famed for its associations with art, has retained both its nobility and elegance. The Cours

Ainay-le-Vieil: *in the medieval château, an elegant Renaissance staircase tower.*

Aigues-Mortes: *the imposing Tour de Constance, reached from the ramparts. In earlier times, it served as a lighthouse.*

Ailly-sur-Noye
80 – Somme   5 – C 2
The 19c church contains 15c tomb, in slaty schist, with recumbent effigies of the royal Jean de Luxembourg (d. 1466) and his wife, plus 'mourners'. 16c polychrome Ecce Homo.
Vicinity ● To S, *Folleville*: superb Goth. Flamboyant decoration in church; tombs with reclining effigies of Raoul de Lannoy and his wife (early 16c) and with kneeling effigies of François de Lannoy and wife (16c); numerous works of art; ruins

12c), now housing lapidary mus., is a good example of pre-Romanesque and Romanesque architecture in Savoie; interior still has traces of a Gallo-Roman edifice and of a 5–6c church with crypt from same period. Pierre Borrione archaeological and mineralogical mus., chapel of St. Sigismond.
Vicinity ● 19 km S, **La Plagne***. Fine walking country.

Ainay-le-Vieil (Château)
18 – Cher   24 – C 2
The 'Carcassonne of the Berry

Aix-en-Provence: *in the Cours Mirabeau, shaded by plane-trees and lined with fine old mansions, is a fountain of warm water – 34 deg. C. – which was familiar to the Romans. Right: the Château de Vauvenargues, facing the Montagne Ste. Victoire, was Picasso's home.*

Mirabeau, shaded by plane-trees and lined with superb 18c aristocratic mansions, is its principal thoroughfare.

● St. Jean-de-Malte quarter: charming Place des Quatre-Dauphins, with fountain and old mansions; 13–14c church of St. Jean-de-Malte (numerous 17c paintings). Former Priory of the Order of Malta now houses the rich Granet mus. (cl. Tues.): notable archaeological collection (from Celto-Ligurian fortified town of Entremont, N of Aix) and galleries for paintings of many schools – Italian, Dutch (Rembrandt), Flemish (Rubens, Frans Hals, Van Dyck), 18–19c French (Ingres, Géricault, Delacroix, Granet), and a Salle Cézanne. Paul Arbaud mus. (cl. Sun. and all Oct.) specialises in folklore, Provençal paintings, earthenware and work of Provençal language preservation society.

● Cathedral quarter: 13–14c St. Sauveur cath. is renowned for its early-16c carved panels and Nicholas Froment's 'Buisson ardent' triptych (1476), one of the masterpieces of the Provençal school; 5c octagonal baptistry – its eight columns with Romanesque Corinthian capitals; lovely 12c Romanesque cloisters. Former archbishop's palace, a superb 17–18c mansion, now houses tapestry mus. Partly 17c town hall is flanked by clock tower and old town gate, early-16c. Rue Gaston-de-Saporta: 18c mansions, including Hôtel d'Estienne de St. Jean, housing Vieil-Aix (Old Aix) mus. (cl. Mon. and all Oct.).

● Madeleine quarter: 17c church of Ste. Marie-Madeleine, aka Church of the Preachers, boasts renowned *Annonciation* panel from 15c Provençal school. Superb late-17c Hôtel Boyer d'Eguilles houses natural hist. mus. (cl. weekends). Crescent-shaped Place Albertas,

with fountain, lined by 18c mansions (floodlit in summer).

● Pavillon de Vendôme, charming 18c 'folly' turned into mus., still has its period lay-out and décor (cl. Tues.). To N, Avenue Paul Cézanne, Pavillon Paul Cézanne and studio of the great artist (cl. Tues.). At W exit from town, Fondation Vasarely, designed to the artist's own plans (1973–76); mus. and study centre.

Vicinity ● 6 km SW, *Les Milles*: 18c Ch. de Lenfant, in fine park. ● 3 km N, *Oppidum d'Entremont*, capital of the Salii, destroyed 123 BC; archaeological digs have recovered remarkable sculptures, now in Granet mus. (cl. Tues.).

● *Montsagne Ste. Victoire* circuit, via Route Paul Cézanne; after 6 km, *Le Tholonet*, 18c château of Galliffet (military) family. Passing Cézanne's stele and medallion, route continues towards *Puyloubier* (Foreign Legion mus.), from where you can climb in four hrs. (blue markers) to the *Montagne Ste. Victoire*, via the Pic des Mouches and ridges until reaching hermitage of St. Ser. At *Pourrières*, take road N to Puits-de-Rians (7 km) and get back to *Aix* through *Vauvenargues*: the impressive 16–17c château here belonged to Picasso – his tomb is on the terrace (private). *Ste. Victoire* itself can be scaled by many different paths, as far up as the Croix de Provence (945 m., beautiful view).

Aix-les-Bains
73 – Savoie   32 – B 1
Famed spa and holiday centre on shores of the Lac du Bourget. Town hall is in early 16c château; museum within 2c remains of Roman temple to Diana. The Arch of Campanus, 3c or 4c, was a tomb. Remains of Roman baths amid the 19–20c natnl. thermal baths; huge grottoes (v.a. in summer). Docteur Faure

mus., Villa des Chimères (cl. Tues. in summer; open Wed. only Oct.– Apr.): fine group of works by Rodin, Jongkind, Boudin, Monticelli, Carpeaux, Corot, Degas, Cézanne – Impressionists and contemporaries (Bonnard).

Vicinity ● 2 km S, Tresserve, on ridge of hills overlooking the lake. ● To E, *Mont Revard*, 22 km by road. ● To N, *Gorges du Sierroz* (v.a. in summer), picturesque tour on foot; a gallery leads to subterranean cascade of *Grésy*.

Ajaccio
2A – Corsica   45 – C 3
On N shore of 14 km wide gulf ringed by mountains, Ajaccio is the 'imperial town', Napoleon's birthplace. Maison Bonaparte, where he was born, is natnl. mus. (cl. Sun. p.m. and Mon. a.m.). Also Napoleonic mus. on first floor of town hall (cl. Sun.). Mus. Fesch, many Italian paintings from 14c to 18c: Botticelli, Titian, Veronese, etc. The Palais Fesch, site of the mus., also contains imperial chapel, with burial vault of Bonaparte family in crypt. On the Place de Gaulle, equestrian statue of Napoleon, surrounded by his four brothers. The port, dominated by 16c citadel (n.v.a.) offers many good views of the gulf. Cathedral is a domed building in 16c Venetian style. Place d'Austerlitz: grotto and monument to Napoleon.

Vicinity ● 12 km W, along N bank of gulf (several fine beaches), *Pointe de la Parata* – a rocky cape, 60 m. high and crowned by a tower, offering vast panorama. Opposite: *Iles Sanguinaires*. ● 13 km N, late 19c *Ch. de la Punta* has 18c paintings and furniture; panorama. ● *Chiavari*, 17 km S by road hugging *Gulf of Ajaccio*; picturesque route and superb views: *Porticcio* beach, *Pointe de Sette Nave*, and *Chiavari* harbour, lying under village of *Coti-*

Chiavari (again, splendid view over gulf).

Albert
80 – Somme　　　　　5 – D 1
Basilica of Notre-Dame-de-Brebières, late 19c–20c; 70 m. steeple topped by gilded Virgin. Throughout region, numerous World War I monuments and cemeteries.
Vicinity ● To NE, *Pozières*: British military cemetery for 14,960 of the men known killed in first Battle of the Somme, 1916. ● To N, near *Thiepval,* British memorial and Anglo-French cemetery; at *Beaumont-Hamel,* Newfoundland commemorative park (some original trenches have been preserved). ● 11 km E, British cemetery and monument at *Longueval.*

Albertville
See **Conflans***　　　　32 – C 1

Albi
81 – Tarn　　　　　36 – B 3
Among all French towns of artistic interest, this is one of the loveliest. ● Ste. Cécile cathedral, like an enormous rose-pink brick 'galleon' dominating old quarter of the town above R. *Tarn*, is magnificent example of middle Goth., late 13c-early 14c, crowned by a 78 m. fortified tower. Entry to it, in contrast, is through a very elaborate Goth. Flamboyant porch, early 16c, known as the 'Baldaquin'. Inside, the building is divided by a superb stone rood-screen, biggest in France (dating from about 1500), whose central door leads into the chapter choir (pay to enter); with double

row of carved wood stalls on each side, the choir is ringed by very richly sculpted stone screen; outside, polychrome statues of prophets and Old Testament figures; to rear of façade behind main altar, a huge mural, *The Last Judgment* (late 15c); side-chapels and vaults also richly decorated. (Guided tours of interior every evening during summer.) ● Former archbishop's palace, Palais de la Berbie, impressive 13–18c fortress, contains 13c chapel (with 17c paintings) and the Toulouse-Lautrec mus. (cl. Tues.), which has more than 600 works by the great painter (born at Albi in the Hôtel du Bosc – v.a.); the mus. also has galleries of contemporary art. Terraced gardens above the Tarn (views over river, Madeleine district, Pont-Vieux and Pont du 22 Août, from where you get a superb sight of the cathedral and town, highlighted in summer by a Son et Lumière). ● Collegiate church of St. Salvi, 12–15c, has Romanesque capitals and 13c galleried cloisters. Maison Enjalbert, in wood and brick, 15c; Hôtel Reynès (or Maison des Viguiers – House of the Provosts), in brick and stone Toulousain Ren. style. Mus. Lapérouse.

Alençon
61 – Orne　　　　　10 – C 3
Church of Notre-Dame, 15–18c, has fine early 16c Gothic Flamboyant porch, richly decorated, and 16c stained-glass windows. Maison d'Ozé, 15c. Mus. des Beaux Arts et de la Dentelle (fine arts and lace): French paintings, 17–19c, also Dutch; collection of European lace (cl. Mon.). Mus. of Alençon lace (cl. Sun. and Mon.). Near lawcourts, remains of 14–15c château. Lace-

making school: exhibition and sale rooms (cl. Sun. and Mon. during winter).
Vicinity ● To SE, *Fôret de Perseigne* (picturesque Vallée d'Enfer). ● To N, *Fôret d'Ecouves* (**Sees***). ● To SW, the *'Alpes Mancelles',* via *Mont des Avaloirs* and the eye-catching Corniche du Pail, *St. Céneri-le-Gérei* (Romanesque church, 12c and 15c frescos; old bridge), and *St. Léonard-des-Bois,* within ring of rocky escarpments.

Aleria
2B – Corsica　　　　45 – C 2
Site of an Ancient Greek, then Roman town, whose successive foundations have now been uncovered for all to see. The Jérôme Carcopino museum, in the fort of Matra (v.a.), exhibits objects recovered from the site – one of prime importance for Mediterranean as well as Corsican art and history.
Vicinity ● To N, *Étang de Diana* (island of Roman oyster-shells). ● To NW, *Gorges de Tavignano* (see **Corte***). ● To W, towards *Ghisoni* and **Vivario***, the *Fium Orbo* gorges and *Défilé de l'Inzecca.* ● To S, *Ghisonaccia,* main town of Corsica's fertile eastern plain; *Prunelli-di-Fiumorbo* (perched high, good view), and *Pietrapola,* spa.

Alès
30 – Gard　　　　　37 – B 3
Large-scale urbanisation has transformed the town by destroying the old slums behind former cathedral. Beautiful Bosquet gardens around fort built by Vauban (military engineer and field-marshal under

Albi: *Ste. Cécile cathedral rises above the town like a mighty galleon in rose-pink brick – sailing to war, in effect, for the bloody 13c crusade in the region against the 'Albigensian heresy', the Cathars. The rich ornamentation and whiteness of the Baldaquin are in striking contrast.*

Alise Ste. Reine: *remains of the double line of fortifications which Vercingetorix built round Alésia, in a vain bid to defy Caesar.*

Louis XIV). Town museum is in Ch. du Colombier (cl. Tues.).
Vicinity ● 11 km NE, *Ch. de Rousson,* early 17c, at Salindres. (v.a., July and Aug.; otherwise, on request, Easter to Nov.). ● 16 km SW, **Mas Soubeyran***, Protestant mus. du Désert; 3 km to NW, in the Cévennes natnl park near *Mialet,* the Trabuc-Mialet grottoes (illuminated path).

Alise Ste. Reine
21 – Côte d'Or   19 – C 2
Excavations have shown that the plateau atop Mt. Auxois (428 m.) was probable site of Alésia, fortified town where Julius Caesar defeated the great Gallic chief, Vercingetorix, in 52 BC. A colossal statue of the chief now looms over the plateau, along with remains of the Gallic fortifications, Gallo-Roman

houses and shops, and a Christian basilica, 5–8c, with its necropolis. St. Léger church. Ste. Reine fountain. Excavations, Gallic village of Encuriot. Finds are exhibited at Alésia mus. (open Easter to Nov. 2).
Vicinity ● 5 km N, Ch. de **Bussy-Rabutin***. ● 8 km SE, **Flavigny-sur-Ozerain***.

Allevard
38 – Isère   32 – C 2
Spa town in beautiful Alpine setting, alt. 475 m.: thermal baths, casino, magnificent park; Mus. Joseph Laforge (mineralogy, folk arts, religious art).
Vicinity ● 11 km NE, Carthusian monastery of St. Hugon, 17c, picturesque ruins in lovely forest setting (private); also the monks' four forges. ● To E, road to Le Collet, via D525 and D109, superb views; *Le Collet d'Allevard* (1,450 m.), winter sports centre. ● 11.5 km W, Brame-Farine, long 1,210 m.-high ridge between *Bréda* and *Grésivaudan* valleys, magnificent panorama. ● 17 km S, *Le Curtillard,* summer resort and winter sports at 1,012 m.; *Fond-de-France,* 1,105 m. (chalet-hotel); 3½-hour climb up path to *Sept-Laux* (2,187 m.), wild plateau with nine lakes; the *Allevard* and *Sept-Laux* massifs offer many different excursions or climbs.

(The) ALPILLES
13 – Bouches-du-Rhône   43 – D 1
This limestone chain, in the heart of Provence between **Avignon*** and **Arles***, has a rich variety of historic buildings and sights of interest. Two good itineraries: (1) From **St. Rémy***, W to *St. Étienne-du-Grès,* the charming Romanesque chapel of **St Gabriel*** and *Fontvieille* (see abbey of **Montmajour***); to S, impressive remains of Gallo-Roman aqueducts of Barbegal and Meunerie; through *Maussane* to **Les Baux***; then take the beautiful D 5 across the *Alpilles,* passing *Les Antiques* and *Glanum*

before getting back to **St. Rémy***. (2). From *Maussane,* continue E on D78 to *Le Destet,* whence D24 leads (via the Mas de Montfort) to superbly situated hillside village of *Eygalières,* much haunted by artists; chapels of St. Laurent and Les Pénitents; Bruno Isnard family's country house; 1.5 km to N, Mas de la Brune, Ren. building; 1 km E, typically Provençal chapel of St. Sixte, 12c. surrounded by cypresses; continue on D24 to *Orgon* (14c church, with 17c chapels), dominated by ruins of château and chapel of Notre-Dame-de-Beauregard; magnificent panorama.

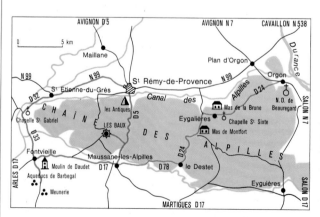

Alouettes (Mont des)
85 – Vendée   22 – D 1

One of the highest hills in the Gatine region; wide panorama; three windmills, calvary and neo-Goth. chapel in 'troubadour' style (1823). Among the highspots of local royalist rebellion at end of 18c.
Vicinity ● 2.5 km S, *Les Herbiers,* in a hilly part of the Bocage (the local area of mixed woodland and pasturage), 15c St. Pierre priory church, in granite; 7 km SW, La Grènetière, former Notre Dame abbey, founded 12c, traces of church and monastic buildings (remains of Romanesque covered cloister gallery, chapter-house, monks' dormitory, fortified towers, etc.). ● 10 km E, Ch. du Puy-du-Fou, late 16c, Son et Lumière.

Alpe d'Huez (L')
38 – Isère   32 – C 3

At 1,860 m. alt., this summer resort and winter sports mecca is world-renowned for its exceptional sun-shine and the beauty of its setting. Also an important mountaineering centre, notably for climbs in the *Grandes-Rousses* massif.
Vicinity ● *Pic du Lac Blanc,* vast panorama, by cable-car (3,350 m.); Lac Blanc by chair-lift, half-an-hour on foot to Dôme des Petites-Rousses (lovely view). ● From Oz (830 m.) climb to the *Pic de L'Et-endard* (3,468 m.). ● Numerous tours from **Le Bourg-d'Oisans***.

Amance
54 – Meurthe-et-Moselle 13 – C 2

Between the Petit-Mont d'Amance (379 m.) to the W and the Grand-Mont d'Amance (410 m.) to E. Elegant 15c church. Wide views from the Grand-Mont.
Outskirts ● 1 km S, Laître-sous-Amance, interesting 16c church, with earlier Romanesque parts.

Ambazac
87 – Haute-Vienne   24 – A 3

The church, 12c and 15c, owns two masterpieces: a late 12c reliquary in the form of a church, made of copperware decorated with enamel and precious stones, and a 12c Byzantine dalmatic (special ec-clesiastical vestment). Apply at presbytery to see.
Vicinity ● 6 km N, *St Sylvestre*: in church, 13c reliquary of St. Junien, in silver gilt, and 15c master-reli-quary of St. Étienne-de-Muret, in chased silver; 2 km to NE, ruins of Grandmont abbey. ● 13 km NW, *Compreignac*: the church, 12c and 15c, is a prime example of the for-tified churches of Limousin region. ● Excursions recommended to the

Monts d'Ambazac, to NW (lovely views).

Ambert
63 – Puy-de-Dôme   31 – B 2

Late 15c church, 15–16c houses, rotunda-shaped town hall.
Vicinity ● 4 km E, in Val de Laga: *Moulin Richard de Bas,* mill where paper is still made by hand (v.a.); mus. of history of paper. ● Excur-sions recommended over *Livradois* and *Forez* mountains, particularly to *Valcivières,* in ring of wooded mountains dotted with lively streams. To **Montbrison*** via *Col de la Croix-de-l'Homme-Mort* (pass at 1,163 m. alt.): superb view over *Bassin du Forez*, the *Monts du Lyon-nais,* the *Massif du Pilat* and the *Cévennes.* ● 16 km S, *Arlanc,* Mus. de la Dentelle, collection of hand-made lace.

Ambialet
81 – Tarn   36 – C 3

Unusually situated village, built along a rocky spit formed by one of the R. *Tarn's* meandering twists and turns. On ridge above it are ruins of château, Romanesque church and, at top, former monastery of Notre-Dame-de-l'Oder.
Vicinity ● Descent of the *Tarn* from Ambialet to **Albi*** (29 km) is par-ticularly picturesque. ● Up-stream from Ambialet, peninsula and village of Courris.

Ambierle
42 – Loire   25 – B 3

Late-15c church has a remarkable triptych of same period, sculpted and painted (at Beaune) in Flemish style, decorating the main altar; also 15c stalls and stained-glass windows. Mus. Alice Taverne (cl. Tues.), devoted to peasant and artisan life of nearby Feurs region.
Vicinity ● Worth trip to Côte Roan-naise (rosé wines): 6 km S, *St. Haon-le-Châtel,* old fortified township, 15c and Ren. houses; in church, 12–17c, furnishings typical of the region, folk-art statues, etc.; *Renai-son, St. André-d'Apchon* (16c church with Ren. stained-glass windows). ● To N, *La Pacaudière,* 16c Petit-Louvre was one-time coaching inn; 1 km to W, Crozet, fmr. fortified township, with 12c keep and 14–15c and Ren. houses.

Amboise
37 – Indre-et-Loire   17 – D 2

The château here was one of the finest and oldest royal residences in the Loire valley (v.a., Son et Lumière in summer). Flanked by the enormous Tour des Minimes, inside which is unusual spiral ramp enabling horsemen to ride up direct into main castle. Royal apartments, late 15c, include council chamber and, below, guardroom. Fine view over R. Loire from terrace. Late 15c chapel of St. Hubert, jewel of Goth.

Ambialet: *this old fortified village, nestling under the slopes of a steep ridge, stretches along a rocky spit formed by one of the meandering River Tarn's tightest bends.*

Flamboyant art; Leonardo da Vinci believed buried there; superbly sculpted porch. ● In town, unusual vaults known as 'Caesar's granaries' under former Minimes convent. Church of St. Denis in 12c Angevin Romanesque style (historiated capitals). In early 16c Hôtel Joyeuse, museum devoted to postal service – records of postmasters, mail-coaches, etc. On Promenade du Mail, intriguing monumental fountain (1968) by painter Max Ernst.
Outskirts ● Rue Victor Hugo, 600 m. from château, the Clos Lucé, 15c manor house where Leonardo spent his last years and died in 1519

sculptures, notably renowned 'Beau Dieu d'Amiens', over main door, and statues of prophets and Apostles; l. door is devoted to St. Firmin and r. door to episodes from life of the Virgin; pier on door of S transept bears celebrated 'Gilded Virgin'; the nave, 145 m. long, is one of highest in France (42.30 m.); see above all the 110 magnificent 16c carved stalls and 15–16c choir screen. ● In 17c Hôtel des Trésoriers de France, museum of local art and regional history. Mus. de Picardie: archaeology; early local paintings (15–16c); Dutch and Flemish (Frans Hals, Van Goyen, Teniers); French 18c (Fragonard, Hubert

Amboise: *rising high over the town on the banks of the Loire, the Renaissance château and its enormous Tour des Minimes, enclosing a spiral ramp.* ◄

There are 149 steps to the top of the Chanteloup pagoda, 3 km from the château, but the view makes the effort worth while. ▲

(v.a., cl. Jan.); exhibition of 40 models of his inventions, constructed from his own plans. ● 3 km SW, *Pagode de Chanteloup*, then-fashionable 'chinoiserie' built in 1775 by Duc de Choiseul, Louis XV's Foreign Minister. The six-storey, 44 m. pagoda is all that remains of his estate. From its top, good views of *Loire* valley and the *Fôret d'Amboise* (20 sq. miles).

Amiens
80 – Somme   5 – C 2
Capital of Picardy, famed above all for its cathedral. But don't miss the 'hortillonages', marshland market gardens drained by little canals which feed the many arms of R. *Somme* and *Avre*; vegetables, fruit and flowers are also transported by barge along these canals; waterside market. ● Notre Dame, 13–15c, is one of the finest Goth. cathedrals; façade has exceptional number of

Robert, Boucher, Chardin), 19c (Delacroix, Géricault) and 20c. ● 15–16c churches of St. Leu and St. Rémy (imposing mausoleum of 17c High Constable). Exhibition centre, display of historic costumes, in 17–18c house. Former Premonstrant abbey (order of regular canons), elegant stone and brick buildings around classic 17c cloisters. Maison du Sagittaire (1591), sumptuously decorated, old bailiff's court, in Gothic Flamboyant style adorned with Renaissance medallions. ● La Hotoie zoological park, laid out in 17c.

Ancenis
44 – Loire-Atlantique   16 – D 2
Picturesque little town, with old houses (Rue du Château, Rue des Tonneliers, Basse-Grande-Rue, Place des Halles). 15–16c château with 17c pavilions (v.a. July-Aug.). *Vicinity* ● 3 km S, *Liré*: mus.

Joachim du Bellay; Muscadet vineyards. 9 km to W, *Champtoceaux*, exceptional site overlooking R. *Loire* and its islands; lovely view from Promenade du Champalud, behind church. ● 9 km W, *Oudon*, fine 14–15c keep.

Ancy-le-Franc
89 – Yonne   19 – C 2
One of Burgundy's loveliest Renaissance châteaux, built in 1555 to plans of Italian architect Sebastiano Serlio and comprising four blocks linked by corner pavilions. Square internal courtyard embellished with composite pilasters framing niches and black marble plaques. Richness and refinement of the apartments reflects influence of Italian-inspired second Renaissance (v.a. Apr. 1–Nov. 1).

Andelys (Les)
See **Château-Gaillard***   5 – A 3

Andilly-en-Bassigny
52 – Haute-Marne   20 – A 1
Important Gallo-Roman site (v.a. during summer). Excavations have uncovered a 1–2c 'mansion' – combining post-house and religious and leisure facilities, inc. baths. Many finds also from Merovingian necropolis, inc. weapons and tools, etc., displayed in local museum.

Andlau
67 – Bas-Rhin   14 – A 3
Typical Alsace village; old houses. 17c church; Romanesque porch decorated with bizarre early sculptures: Creation and earthly Paradise; above these, Christ between St. Peter and St. Paul, with hunting scenes. Church's Romanesque interior was updated to 17c, but crypt remains 11c. Monastery buildings, 17–18c.
Vicinity ● 9 km W, the *Hohwald*, holiday area amid magnificent forests, via wooded gorge of the Andlau (D425). ● To SW, worth going up the Ungersberg (901 m.) for view.

Andorra
Principality of **Andorra**   43 – A 3
From France, you enter Andorra from the N20, over the *Port d'Envalira* (2,407 m., vast panorama). The Envalira refuge hut is starting-point for numerous excursions to Cirque des Pessons, studded with 42 lakes and innumerable torrents. Les Pessons ridge (2,500–2,800 m.). ● Many excursions also from *Soldeu* (winter sports centre, chair- and ski-lifts). Sant Bartomeu is typical of Andorra's little Romanesque chapels; interior contains unusual examples of folk art. The road runs through Valira de l'Orien to 11c chapel of *Sant Joan de Casellas*, on a bluff above the river; int. has interesting works of art. Next, *Canillo*: chapel of Notre-Dame-de-Méritxell, 13-18c, with Baroque retable and folkish Virgin of Méritxell. Road now climbs above gorge of Valira into green basin of *Encamp*. ● In the capital, Romanesque church and 16c Casa de la Vall (House of the Valley), seat of the Government (cl. Sun. p.m.). Excursions recommended to *Ordino* (old houses), via gorges of Sant Antoni and *La Massana*, and to La Cortinada (Romanesque church of San Marti, rebuilt in 17–18c); *El Serrat* is starting-point for some good mountain climbs. From Andorra-la-Vella, road runs S to *Santa Coloma*: noteworthy pre-Romanesque church, with cylindrical steeple (interior has a 12c Virgin of the Cures); then to *Sant*

Juliá de Lória, before reaching Spanish frontier.

Anduze
30 – Gard   37 – B 3
One-time fortress, with tortuous narrow streets. Clock tower (1320). Château, 16–17c. Park of former convent of the Cordeliers (rare trees, magnificent bamboos).
Vicinity ● 2 km N, Parc de Prafrance (v.a. Easter to Nov. 1): rare trees, lotus ponds, magnificent alley of bamboos and sequoias, 400 m. long. ● 8 km NW, Le Désert museum at **Mas Soubeyran***.

Anet (Château)
28 – Eure-et-Loire   11 – A 2
Of the superb Ren. château built by 16c royal architect Philibert Delorme for Henri II's favourite, Diane de Poitiers, all that remain are: monumental gateway, surmounted by reproduction of Benvenuto Cellini's *Diane couchée* (Reclining Diana – original in the Louvre); front entrance; chapel with bas-reliefs by 16c sculptor Jean Goujon; and some buildings of same period (cl. Tues.). Funerary chapel contains Diane de Poitiers' magnificent tomb in black and white marble.

Angers
49 – Maine-et-Loire   17 – A 2
Old capital of Anjou; town of artistic interest, with several important museums, churches and historic buildings. ● The most notable is the château, an enormous fedual structure flanked by 17 round towers, which dominates R. *Maine* and surrounding old quarter (v.a.); château houses tapestry mus., richest in world. Round internal courtyard are royal apartments and early 15c chapel of Ste. Geneviève (noteworthy figured vaulting and sculpted keystones). Galérie de l'Apocalypse was built (1952) to display the famed tapestry of that name, masterpiece of medieval craftsmanship. 15, 16 and 17c tapestries displayed in Governor's house (15–18c). ● St. Maurice cathedral, 12–13c, fine nave (largest of any French cath.); notable group of stained-glass windows, from late 12c. Between cath. and château, the Cité quarter: to r., around Place du Ralliement, old houses. ● In Ren. Hôtel Pincé, mus. Turpin de Crissé: archaeology, Renaissance art, notable Chinese and Japanese collection (prints, bronzes and ceramics). 15c Maison d'Adam, in wood and brick, with sculpted corbels. Parts of former bishop's palace are 11–12c; opposite, two

timbered houses, 15 and 16c. Old houses in Rues de l'Oisellerie, St. Laud, des Poëliers, David d'Angers. Inside 13c abbey church of Toussaint, restored, the Galérie David d'Angers has works by the world-renowned Angers-born sculptor (cl. Mon.). Mus. des Beaux-Arts in late 15c Barrault house: primitives, 18–19c paintings and sculpture, objets d'art (cl. Mon.). Church of St. Serge has choir in early 13c Goth. Angevin style. ● On r. bank of R. Maine: Hôpital St. Jean, 12–13c, among finest hospices of Middle Ages, now housing Mus. Jean Lurçat; in the great hall for the sick is the *Chant du Monde,* series of 10 tapestries by Lurçat (executed between 1957 and 1965), together forming group 80 m. long; see also cloisters with 12c and Ren. galleries, and unusual 17c pharmacy (cl. Mon.). Wine museum in cellar of old St. Jean granaries. The Doutre quarter still has several timber-framed houses, particularly around late 12c Trinité church (fine Romanesque doors). Steps lead down to crypt of former abbey church. Place de la Laiterie has 15–18c mansions.
Vicinity ● 6 km S, *Les Ponts-de-Cé,* 12 and 15c church. five-sided keep of a 15c castle; 9 km to SE, Ch. de **Brissac***. ● 16.5 km SW, Ch. de

Amiens: *one of the many fine sculptures to be seen in the cathedral. This one, by the choir, depicts the martyrdom of St. Firmin (late 15c).*

Angers: *two of the feudal castle's 17 towers.* ▲
The 15c Maison d'Adam ▼

Angoulême: *cathedral of St. Pierre (originally 12c.).* ▼

Serrant*. ● 16.5 km NW, *Le Plessis-Macé,* 15c château (v.a.), with towered walls surrounding elegant Ren. residence; chapel is a masterpiece of Goth. Flamboyant style.

Angoulême
16 – Charente   29 – B 1
Lying on a large promontory, the town looks over an immense landscape, seen ideally from a stroll round the ramparts (still almost unbroken, except for their round towers and bastions). Early 12c cathedral of St. Pierre, with Romanesque facade much restored in 19c, with blind arcades and medallions displaying 75 statues and bas-reliefs. Former bishop's palace, 12–15c, houses town museum (ethnography, paintings). Of the Count of Angoulême's old château, only two towers remain: the Tour Lusignan (late 13c) and Tour de Valois (late 15c). Old Angoulême is picturesque: Rues de Beaulieu, du Soleil, de Turenne, François I. Mus. of Charente archaeological society. A Natnl. Centre for Comic Strips and Picture Books is to be installed in a renovated one-time factory (Champigneule).
Vicinity ● 5 km SE, via *Puymoyen* (13c church), excursion recommended in little Eaux-Claires valley, fringed by cliffs riddled with grottoes. ● 9 km E, via *Touvre* (Romanesque church) to *sources of* R. Touvre (impressive 'abyss'). ● 4 km W, St. Michel d'Entraygues, fine Romanesque octagonal church, with dome and eight apsidioles. ● 8 km SW, remains of abbey of *La Couronne* (private – but free access to ruins of noteworthy abbey church, 12–13c). ● 17 km N, via *Montignac* to *St. Amant-de-Boixe:* interesting early 14c murals in church (Romanesque nave, Gothic choir). ● 22 km NE, via the *Forêt de Braconne,* to the huge quadrilateral *Ch. de la Roche-foucauld,* 12–16c; from courtyard, the two Renaissance wings boast three floors of elegant covered galleries and a remarkable stairway (v.a.). To S, valley of R. *Tardoire* has numerous grottoes and natural curiosities, notably the Grottoes of Rangogne (v.a.). 11 km NE of *La Rochefoucauld,* at *Chasseneuil,* is important memorial to the French Resistance (cemetery and crypt).

Anjony (Château)
15 – Cantal   30 – C 3
Looming over vale of Tournemire, this château is a stout, square 15c keep, with towers at each corner (v.a. Easter to Nov. 1, p.m. only). Salle des Preux, entirely painted with frescos illustrating knightly legends. Late 15c chapel, with frescos of scenes of the Passion.
Vicinity ● 1 km E, *Tournemire,* Interesting works of art in church. ● 4 km W, *St. Cernin-du-Cantal,* Romanesque church with 15c panelling.

Annecy
74 – Haute-Savoie   32 – C 1
The town, at N end of Lake of Annecy, is dominated by its château, an imposing fortress (12–17c). In Nemours building, archaeological and Alpine natural history museum. Conservatoire d'Art et d'Histoire de la Haute-Savoie (library and paintings on Alpinism and Mont Blanc). In old Annecy, very picturesque arcaded streets, canals, historic houses. St Pierre cathedral formerly a 16c Franciscan church. Palais de l'Isle, group of 12–16c buildings, on island in Canal du Thiou. The Pont des Amours spans charming Canal du Vassé. Terraced public garden fringing the lake; opposite, Île des Cygnes. Beach (boat hire, etc.). 1 km to S, new Monastery of the Visitation and basilica of St. François de Sales (1930); reliquaries of the saint and of Ste. Jeanne de Chantal; Salesian mus.; wide view.
Vicinity ● 11.5 km W, *Gorges du Fier* and 13–15c *Ch. de Montrottier* (v.a. Easter to mid-Oct.), large collection of weapons, ceramics, sculptures, etc. ● 17 km SW, *Rumilly,* many 16–17c mansions and old town houses, 16c bridge; 1 km to E, 13c chapel of Notre-Dame-de-l'Aumone, remains of a priory ● Via D41 to S, circuit of the *Semnoz*: Route des Crêtes (ridges) offers magnificent panoramas, particularly to crest of Chatillon (1,704 m.). ● 14 km NE, *Thorens-Glières,* 15c château (v.a. Apr. 1–Sept. 30); collection of pictures and objets d'art, Salesian mementoes; 1.5 km away is chapel on site of château where St. François de Sales was born in 1567; by a forest road, *Plateau des Glières,* entrenched camp of French Resistance fighters, defended against the Germans in March 1944; imposing memorial by Gilioli (1973). ● 9 km SE, via lovely D909 lake road, *Menthon-St. Bernard,* under 13-15c château, and *Talloires,* pleasant summer resort, where former 11c Benedictine abbey has been turned into hotel.

Annonay
07 – Ardèche   31 – D 3
Area round château, original gates,
narrow streets and old houses are
well worth seeing. César Filhol mus.
devoted to adjoining Vivarais
region: archaeology, local ethnography (also mementoes of
Montgolfier brothers, balloon
pioneers). Along R. Deûme, stretch
of narrow rocky passages once
occupied by succession of weavers'
workshops.
Vicinity ● 8 km ENE, *Champagne*,
remarkable two-domed Romanesque church; sculpted tympanum
over W door. ● 15 km NE *Serrières-
sur-Rhône*: picturesque old quarter
in amphitheatre form, under hill
with fine view; unusual Mus. des
Mariniers du Rhône et de la Batellerie (Rhône bargees and their
craft).

Antibes
06 – Alpes-Maritimes   45 – A 1
Charming old town, with very
colourful narrow streets, market,
harbour, château and ramparts
above the sea. St. Roch cove
(marina) lies under the imposing
late 16c Fort Carré. Ch. Grimaldi,
austere 16c fortress with 14c square
tower, now houses Picasso mus. (cl.

tibes, via La Salis beach and Pointe
Bacon (lovely view); wide panorama from La Garoupe lighthouse; 13–14c chapel; Thuret villa
and botanic garden (Provençal
centre for agronomic research) has
rare, exotic essences (garden open
daily, exc. Sun.). Batterie du Grillon
contains naval and Napoleonic
mus.; coast road leads finally to
Juan-les-Pins* and *Golfe-Juan*.

Apt
84 – Vaucluse   38 – A 3
Church of Ste. Anne, late 12c and
14c, once a cathedral; two crypts,
7c and 12c, church treasure and
numerous works of art. Fine 18c
mansion has mus. (cl. Tues. and
Sun.) with large collection of pharmacy jars and earthenware, also
archaeology and religious art.
Vicinity ● To SE, *Saignon* (Romanesque church); former abbey of St.
Eusèbe (Romanesque chapel);
valley of the *Coulon* and Grand-
Lubéron (1,125 m., two-hour
climb). ● To S, on way to **Lubéron***
park and mountain ridge on scenic
D 113: after 7.5 km, *Buoux*; 2 km
on, ruins of old *Fort de Buoux,*
remains of priory of St. Symphorien. ● 9 km N, *St. Saturnin-d'Apt,*

Anjony: *massive 15c keep built on
a rock over the little valley of
Tournemire.*

Les Planches (v.a. Apr. to end of
Oct.); to S, *Cirque du Fer à Cheval*;
old-looking little village of La
Châtelaine, below ruins of 11c
castle.

Arcachon
33 – Gironde   34 – C 1
Seaside and health resort on S shore
of the *Bassin d'Arcachon*. The
summer town includes fine esplanade along sea (casino, aquarium);
above it, the winter town comprises
villas and chalets scattered through

Annecy: *the old houses at the foot
of the château, reflected in the
gentle waters of the Canal du
Thiou.* ◄

Antibes: *the old quarter around
the church and the château.*▼

Tues. and in Nov.) – exceptional
group of works by the great artist;
also local archaeology and contemporary art. Adjoining château is
17c church, formerly a cathedral,
still with some Romanesque parts;
interior has interesting *Retable du
Rosaire* (Retable of the Rosary)
from early 16c Nice school. Behind
church and château, Promenade
Amiral de Grasse runs along the
ramparts, giving superb views over
coast, **Nice*** and summits of the
Alps.
Vicinity ● Round-trip, *Cap d'An-*

ruins of château (Romanesque
chapel).

Arbois
39 – Jura   26 – B 1
Pasteur's childhood home (cl.
Tues.). Church of St. Just, Romanesque with earlier parts. Mus. Sarret
de Grozon in 18c mansion (decorative arts). Wine mus. in town
hall.
Vicinity ● To SE, *Reculée des Planches,* grandiose half-moon of
pointed rocks; below them, R. *Cuis-
ance* has its source in grottoes of

Arcachon: *the Dune du Pilat, highest sand dune in Europe.* ▲

Lac de Cazaux et de Sanguinet, covering more than 22 sq. miles. ◄

Ch. de Vieuzac, 16c keep; to S, Ch. d'Ourout, 15–16c.
Vicinity ● Recommended 'valley tour' via *St. Savin* and *Pierrefitte-Nestalas*, returning through *Beaucens* and Préchac. At *St. Savin*, 3 km S, former 12c Benedictine abbey church, fortified in 14c, has Romanesque door and sculpted tympanum; small museum of religious art in chapter-house; vast panorama from terrace. ● 12 km SW, *Arrens*, one of the gateways to *Pyrenees Natnl. Park*: 15c church with crenellated walls; 500 m. away, 18c chapel of Pouey-Laün; interior has rich carved wood decoration. Excursions recommended in upper valley of Arrens; magnificent mountain views of *Balaïtous* (3,146 m.) and Lake Néous glacier.

forest. To E, fishing port. To W, Péreire park and Abatilles beach.
Vicinity ● Trip round the bay; you can get to *Cap Ferret* either by boat (40 min. crossing) or by road (63 km) through *Andernos* and *Arès*. ● To S, via *Le Moulleau* and *Pyla-sur-Mer*, the coast road leads (9 km) to foot of the great *Dune du Pilat* – at 105 m., highest sand dune in Europe (climbable, but arduous!) ● 18 km S, Cazaux, village of forest resin tappers, to N of *Étang* (or Lac) *de Cazaux et de Sanguinet* (boat hire, sailing, swimming, fishing, camping). ● *Parc des Landes de Gascogne* nature reserve covers some 800 sq. miles between Arcachon and **Mont-de-Marsan*** (see also **Sabres***). ● Trips through typical Landes scenery along D 83 to *Biscarrosse-Plage*, D 652 via *Sanguinet*, then D 46 to *Parentis-en-Born* and *Étang* (or *Lac*) *de Biscarrosse*.

Arc-et-Senans
25 – Doubs   26 – B 1
One of the most original architectural groupings of the 18c. The Royal Saltworks of Chaux was con-

ceived by Louis XVI's architect, Claude-Nicolas Ledoux, as a 'model industrial village'. Only a part was completed, 1775–79. The monumental entrance is flanked by a half-circle of buildings for the workers and clerks; at the centre, the director's pavilion and the salt pavilions.
Vicinity ● To NE, *Forêt de Chaux* (nearly 80 sq. miles); two roads across it from the village, W and E.

Arch (Les)
73 – Savoie   32 – D 2
Large winter sports complex, recently established and an interesting example of contemporary mountain architecture (reached from *Bourg-St. Maurice*); several successively higher stations between valley of the Isère and Mt. Pourri.
Vicinity ● 11 km N, from *Bourg-St, Maurice*, Fort de la Plate (1,995 m., belvedere, vast panorama).

Argelès-Gazost
65 – Hautes-Pyrénées   41 – B 3
Spa and holiday resort. The old town, climbing around the Tour Mendaigne, is picturesque. To N,

Arc-et-Senans: *salt pavilion – the beauty of its stone enhanced by architectural originality.*

Argelès-Gazost: *the nearby little town of St. Savin, now a pleasant holiday spot, was formerly an important religious centre in the region and still has an interesting abbey church.*

Argentan
61 – Orne   10 – B 2
Church of St. Germain, 15–17c, features two towers, 17c and Ren.; fine 15c lateral porch. Former 14c castle with two square towers; 12c keep (good view). Church of St. Martin in early 16c Gothic Flamboyant style. At Benedictine abbey, exhibition and demonstration of Argentan lace-making, exclusive to the monks.
Vicinity ● 9 km W, Écouché (noteworthy Ren. church); valley of R. *Orne* towards *Putanges*, picturesque scenery. ● 14 km E, *Haras du Pin*, château and 18c stables (v.a.). ● 10 km S, *St. Christophe-le-Jajolet* (pilgrimage last Sun. in July, blessing of motor cars); 1 km to S, Ch. de Sassy, 18c, with three-stage terracing.

Argentat
19 – Corrèze   30 – B 3
Terraced old township above R. *Dordogne*. The Escondamine quarter is picturesque. On quay along river, old terraced houses with wooden balconies.
Vicinity ● 6 km NW, *St. Chamant*, church with Romanesque portal and 15c steeple with wood platform. ● *Gorges de la Dordogne*, Ch. du Gibanel, 13–19c (hotel); 13 km NE, *Barrage de Chastang*, dam 85 m. high and 300 m. wide. ● 8 km SE, *Barrage de Hautefage*; the R. *Maronne* forms a big, winding reservoir, 7 km long. 13 km to E, amid bushy vegetation within a tight loop of the Maronne, the 12–15c *Tours de Merle* form an extraordinary group of ruins, in a superb location (v.a., Son et Lumière

during summer); from D13, view plunges down to distant horizon.

Argentière
74 – Haute-Savoie   26 – D 3
Holiday centre, winter sports and mountaineering.
Vicinity ● 4 km NE, Le Tour, departure-point for cable car to the Col (pass) of Balme, on Franco-Swiss frontier; first to Charamillon (1,850 m.), then to the pass (2,190 m., vast panorama). ● Cable car from Lognan to the Croix de Lognan (1,972 m.), from where another cable car leaves for the Aiguille des Grands-Montets (3,260 m.); splendid panorama. ● 11 km to N, by N506 and a savage gorge, *Col des Montets* (1,461 m.); then down through Eau-Noire valley to *Vallorcine* and the frontier.

Argenton-sur-Creuse
36 – Indre   24 – A 2
Banks of R. *Creuse* are picturesque, with old slate-covered houses, sporting timbered loggias and balconies; good view of them from the Pont-Vieux. 15-16c chapel of St. Benoît (also fine view) and chapel of Notre Dame, 15c, are worth seeing.
Vicinity ● 2 km N, *St. Marcel*, on site of a Gallo-Roman town, of which several remains have been uncovered (baths, amphitheatre, nymphaeum, etc.). Church, 12 and 14c, and 16–17c murals. Argentomagus exhibition galleries (prehist., Gallo-Roman art).

Argent-sur-Sauldre
18 – Cher   18 – C 2
15c château with stout round towers.
Vicinity ● 8 km SE, *Blancafort*: 15c château in brick, with square keep, 17c pavilions, gardens in formal French style (v.a. Apr. 1–Oct. 30).

Arlempdes
43 – Haute-Loire   37 – B 1
Unusual fortified village, dominated by ruins of feudal castle, 12–15c, above wild gorges of R. *Loire* on last stretch towards its source. Small Romanesque church, portal with small columns, belfry wall with four arcades.

Arles
13 – Bouches-du-Rhône   43 – D 1
One of France's richest towns for Roman and medieval remains. ● Place de la République (Roman obelisk in centre) is lined by the imposing late 17c town hall, with belfry from 1555, by a museum of pagan art (very rich in Gallo-Roman antiquities), and by church of St. Trophime (11, 12, 14 and 15c), with classically-inspired monu-

Argent-sur-Sauldre: *the splendid-looking red-brick château at Blancafort, with its pepper-pot towers and surrounding gardens laid out in the formal French style.*

Arles: *the two-storey octagonal belfry above the centre of St. Honorat church is the most unusual Romanesque tower in Provence.* ◄

The Arena – still used for spectacles. ▲

mental portal which is among the masterpieces of Romanesque art; the lofty (20 m.), narrow interior contains numerous works of art. The cloisters (entry, Rue du Cloître): N and E galleries are second half 12c Romanesque, their corner pillars carved in relief with statues of Apostles, also classically inspired; superb historiated capitals; the S and W galleries are 14c Goth. ● Arlaten mus., founded by Provençal poet Mistral in fine early 16c Hôtel de Laval-Castellane, specialises in art and Provençal ethnography and literature; chapel houses Fernand Benoît mus. of Christian art (large collection of sarcophagi), with steps down to Roman cryptoporticus (110 m. long, 76 m. wide). Réattu mus., in old Grand Priory of Malta, has interesting range of 17 and 18c paintings and galleries of contemporary art (exceptional group of 57 sketches and gouaches by Picasso), also section of photographic art. ● Nearby, the baths of Constantine, aka the Palais de la Trouille, offer impressive early 14c remains. The early 3c amphitheatre, the Arena, whose tiers covered 130,000 sq. ft., could hold 26,000 spectators; in Middle Ages, it was transformed into a fortified village, of which three towers remain. The original theatre was nearly 104 m. in diameter; most of it is in ruins, exc. for two fine Corinthian columns, with their entablature, and the orchestra. Blvd. Émile Combes has considerable remains of 1c BC Roman ramparts. An avenue of tombs is all that survives

of the once-vast Gallo-Roman and Christian necropolis of Alyscamps; it leads via two chapels – of St. Accurse (16c) and Les Porcelets (late 15c) – to church of St. Honorat (12c, with 15–17c chapels). ● In the Trinquetaille district, on r. bank of R. Rhône, vestiges of a late 1c Roman business quarter.
Vicinity ● 4 km NE, Abbey of **Montmajour*** and the **Alpilles***. ● To SE, huge plain of the *Crau*. ● To SW, **St. Gilles*** and the **Camargue***. 11.5 km on D570, Mas du Pont-de-Rousty, Camargue mus.

Arles-sur-Tech
66 – Pyrénées Orientales 43 – C 3
11c abbey church of Ste. Marie is among oldest churches in Roussillon region. The portal belonged to an earlier, 9c church; 11c sculptures on façade; 4c sarcophagus known as the 'holy tomb'; church interior has mid-17c retable and two 15c reliquaries, busts in silver (apply at sacristy to see). 13c Goth. cloisters, with stylised leaf-work on capitals.
Vicinity ● 7.5 km SW, Montferrer, Romanesque church; lovely views

of the *Vallespir* and Mt. **Canigou***.
● To SW, the D115 runs along R. *Tech* via the Pas du Loup to the upper Vallespir; *Serralongue,* Romanesque church (door with iron braces and inscribed bolt); from the Pas du Loup, 9 km to S, the D3 runs to *St. Laurent-de-Cerdans,* then *Coustouges:* mid-12c Romanesque church, noteworthy sculpted portal; 2 km to S, chapel of Notre-Dame-du-Pardon (1966).

Armorique
(Regional nature reserve of‡)
See: **Brasparts***, **Huelgoat***, **Mennez-Hom***, **Crozon***, **Ouessant***.

Arnay-le-Duc
21 – Côte-d'Or 19 – C 3
Ancient township on promontory over little R. *Arroux.* Church of St. Laurent, 15–16c, coffered ceiling; nave with barrel vaulting (in style of 16c royal architect Philibert Delorme). Behind the apse, 15c Tour de la Motte-Forte. Old houses (Manoir de Sully, 16c).
Vicinity ● 7 km W, Roman spring of Maizières (spa).

ARMAND (swallow-hole)
48 – Lozère 37 – A 2
One of the most extraordinary sites in the Causses (v.a. Palm Sunday to Sept.). Discovered in 1897, the hole is 200 m. deep; a funicular now takes you to the bottom. In the main chamber, the 'virgin forest' is formed by more than 400 stalagmites, one of which is 30 m. in height.

Arques-la-Bataille
76 – Seine-Maritime   5 – A 2
Church, in Goth. Flamboyant style, has a magnificent rood-screen (1540) and highly figured stone choir-screen. On narrow promontory, ruins of former castle of the Dukes of Normandy, remains of chapel and 13c keep.
Vicinity • Forest of Arques, to NE, fine beech-groves; monument commemorating 1589 Battle of Arques.

Arras
62 – Pas-de-Calais   5 – D 1
The Grand Place and the Place des Héros, or 'Petite Place', form a remarkable group of 17c Flemish architecture 15c town hall and its 16c belfry were rebuilt after World War I. Abbey of St. Vaast is biggest 18c monastic complex in France; the abbey church, now a cathedral, possesses many works of art. Abbey buildings also house fine arts mus. (cl. Tues.), from which you can see the small cloisters, called the 'Cour du Puits' (well court), and the large cloisters (Romanesque and Goth. galleries, sculptures and tapestries). Salle des Mays de Notre Dame, 17–18c: Italian, Dutch, Flemish and French paintings, 16–18c; two superb triptychs by 16c Flemish master Jean Bellegambe; on second floor, neo-classic and Romantic painting. Mus. de la Résistance et de la Déportation, Palais St. Vaast. See also the Ostel des Poissonniers (1710), the 17c citadel and lower town (interesting example of 18c town planning), for which Place Victor Hugo is focal point.
Vicinity • 13 km N, **Notre-Dame-de-Lorette***. • 10 km N, *Vimy* Ridge, Canadian memorial.

Arreau
65 – Hautes-Pyrénées   41 – B 3

Main town of the Aure valley. 15–16c houses – notably 16c timber-framed Maison Valencia Labat, aka House of the Lilies (Lys). Churches of Notre Dame, 15–16c, and St. Exupère (Romanesque portal with sculpted capitals and 11c tower).
Vicinity • Worth visiting: the Rocher de Hillère (rock-climbing school), the Hourquette D'Arreau, Jézeau (12 and 16c church with interesting works of art). • To S, the D929 climbs up the high *Vallée de la Neste d'Aure* – part of the *Parc National des Pyrénées Occidentales* (national park) – via Cadéac-les-Bains (16c church, Romanesque door), *St. Lary* (winter sports centre) and *Tramezaïgues* to *Fabian*. 14 km to NW of Fabian, the *Lac de Cap-de-Long* (alt. 2,160 m.), in grandiose setting dominated by Mt. *Néouvielle* (3,092 m.); tours, with guides, in surrounding nature reserve (*Réserve naturelle de Néouvielle*).

Arromanches-les-Bains
14 – Calvados   4 – B 3
Fishing village and seaside resort, famed as site of the vast Mulberry harbour, altogether 12 km in length, built for Normandy landings. From D-Day on June 6, 1944, it was this artificial port, a few vestiges of which can still be seen, that enabled the Allies to land more than a million soldiers, as well as 20,000 tons of supplies a day. Permanent D-Day exhibition (open daily).

Ars-sur-Formans
01 – Ain   25 – D 3
Popular pilgrimage (particularly in early Aug.) to the 'Curé d'Ars', one-

time village priest St. Jean-Baptiste-Marie Vianney (d. 1859). His presbytery (v.a.) and his modest country church have been kept unchanged. Now adjoining latter is a pretentious basilica, in rotunda form, with the saint's reliquary in gilded bronze. Huge underground basilica in concrete (1959–61).
Vicinity • 8 km NW, 17c Ch. de

Arras: *the town hall's belfry, 75 m. in height, houses a world-famed carillon.*

Fléchères (v.a. in summer) – fine furniture, painted ceilings.

Asnières
92 – Hauts-de-Seine   11 – C 1
Dog cemetery on Ile des Ravageurs, in mid-Seine: more than 100,000 animals buried there (cl. Sun. a.m.).
Vicinity • Ch. de St. Ouen (cl. a.m. and Tues.) is rare example of early 19c Restoration architecture. • At Courbevoie, Roybet-Fould mus. (open p.m. only, Wed., Thurs., Sat., Sun.) has collection of antique dolls and works by 19c sculptor Carpeaux.

Asnières-sur-Vègre
72 – Sarthe   17 – B 1
Charming village on r. bank of little R. *Vègre*, crossed by a 14c humped-back bridge. 11c Romanesque church has valuable group of murals from 12c, early 13c and 14c. (Life of Christ, Virgin and Child, singular vision of Hell.)
Vicinity • 3 km N, on road to Poillé, somewhat feudal-looking Ch. de Verdelles, late 15-early 16c (v.a.). • To SW, Abbey of **Solesmes***.

Assy (Plateau)
74 – Haute-Savoie   32 – D 1
Climatotherapeutic centre in gran-

Assy: *this huge mosaic by Fernand Léger is among many modern works in the church of Notre-Dame-de-Toute-Grâce.*

Aubigny-sur-Nère: part of
château built by the Stuarts on
banks of the R. Nère.

diose country at 1,032 m. alt.
Church of Notre Dame-de-Toute-
Grâce (1950) was one of the first
testifying to the renaissance of
religious art in modern times; built
by the architect Novarina, it has a
huge tapestry by Lurçat in the choir
and works by Rouault, Chagall,
Bonnard, Matisse, etc., with a huge
mosaic by Fernand Léger on the
façade.
Vicinity ● Excursion recommended
to the *Lac Vert* (1,368 m.).

Aubenas
07 – Ardèche   37 – C 1
The château is a massive fortress,
flanked by four towers and keep,
dating from 12 to 15c, renovated
17–18c; Renaissance internal courtyard is lined by openwork galleries;
elegant 18c panelling in the salons
(now town hall). Former chapel of
St. Benoît, 18c hexagonal building,
guards tomb of leading 15–16c military man, Marshal Ornano, and his
wife.
Vicinity ● Upper valley of R.
Ardèche to NW, via Labégude (see
Val-les-Bains*), *Thueyts* (very
beautiful setting), *Mayres* and Col
de la Chavade. ● To S, the middle
valley, towards **Vallon-Pont-d'Arc***
via *Vogüé, Balazuc* and **Ruoms***. ●
17 km SE, *Villeneuve-de-Berg,*
former stronghold, old houses,
mansions with Renaissance turrets;
4 km to N, Olivier de Serres
museum at Domaine du Pradel;

7 km to N, *Mirabel,* fortified village
with keep, walls and towers,
huddled at foot of rock cliff.

Aubeterre-sur-Dronne
16 – Charente   29 – B 2
Alba terra, 'white earth', was the
original name of this ancient little
township, with narrow, steep-
sloping streets, clinging to a chalk
cliff above valley of R. *Dronne.*
Good view from ruins of 14–15c
château. Unusual monolithic 12c
church of St. Jean, carved into the
rock; 6c hermitage, necropolis with
sepulchres also dug into rock. 12c
church of St. Jacques has good
Romanesque facade and historiated capitals.
Vicinity ● 4 km S, *Bonnes*, on the
river: 16c château; 12, 14 and 15c
church (with 12c font). 5 km to S,
St. Aulaye, above the Dronne: 12c
Romanesque church; large fairs.

Aubigny-sur-Nère
18 – Cher   18 – C 2
15–16c château of the Stuarts (now
town hall) is surrounded by 17c
gardens, adorned with bowers and
green arbours. Works of art in
church of St. Martin (12, 13 and
15c) include wands of office. Early
16c timber-framed houses.
Vicinity ● 11 km SE, on edge of a
lake, *Ch. de la Verrerie*, 15–16c (cl.
Jan.); picturesque turreted entry
pavilion, elegant Renaissance
arcaded gallery, 15c chapel.

Aubrac
12 – Aveyron   36 – D 1
Little summer resort, good for
excursions. Remains of one-time
'house' of the mounted monks who,
in 12c, escorted pilgrims on their
way to and from Santiago de Compostela.
Vicinity ● To NE, *Nasbinals*
(Romanesque church), *St. Urcize*
(church with 12c ambulatory, 13–

14c nave). 22.5 km to N, *Chaudes-
Aigues,* spa, ancient hot water
system; Goth. Flamboyant and
Ren. church. ● Excellent excursions
in the *Massif de l'Aubrac.* ● To SW,
beautiful country towards R. *Lot*
and **Espalion***. ● To E, via *Lac des
Salhiens* and the *Cascade de Déroc*
(waterfall), then to SE, highly picturesque route over Col de *Bon-
necombe* to *St. Germain-du-
Teil* and *La Canourgue* (see
Marvejols*).

Aubusson
23 – Creuse   30 – C 1
Home of French tapestry, in picturesque setting in narrow valley of
R. *Creuse.* Jean Lurçat artistic and
cultural centre; departmental tapestry mus.; 15c Maison du Vieux
Tapissier (reconstruction of workshop, with demonstrations of tapestry weaving).
Vicinity ● 10 km S. *Felletin*: granite-
built township, also a tapestry
centre, still has several 16c houses.
Churches of Le Moûtier (12–15c)
and Notre-Dame du-Château (15–
16c). Excursion recommended in
valley of the Creuse; the D 23 leads
to vast plateau of **Millevaches***
(981 m.), with immense panoramas.

Auch
32 – Gers   41 – C 1
Monumental staircase with 200
steps, dominated by statue of d'Ar-
tagnan, links the lower town, on R.
Gers, to upper town crowned by
Ste. Marie cathedral (late 15c, 16–
17c). In cathedral choir, remarkable
group of 113 sculpted stalls,
regarded as finest in France; early
17c choir screen in stone and
marble. Early 16c stone sculpture
of the Entombment (unusually,
with 12 figures); Renaissance
stained-glass windows in apsidal
chapels. In old quarter below
cathedral, the narrow streets, called

Auch: the town, an important crossroads in Roman times, is built in
amphitheatre form above the R. Gers, in the heart of Gascony. In the
background, the cathedral of Ste. Marie.

'pousterles', are lined with ancient houses. Mus. des Jacobins in former convent: archaeology, folk arts and traditions, and important collection of S. American art (pre-Columbian and colonial).

Vicinity ● 24 km SW, *Mirande* has delightful fine arts mus: Dutch, Flemish and French paintings, 18–19c. ● 18 km NW, *Jegun,* Romanesque and Gothic church; 5 km to E, *Lavardens,* fortified village on an outcrop, point of which is occupied by large 16–17c château (v.a.). ● 25 km E, *Gimont,* old bastide (fortified township).

Audierne
29S – Finistère   8 – B 3
Large fishing village on estuary of R. *Goyen,* in lovely setting. 'La Chaumière', reconstruction of interior of 17–18c Breton home (v.a. June to mid-Sept.).

Vicinity ● 4.5 km W, early 16c chapel of *St. Tugen,* noteworthy furnishing; the D 784 continues across bare heathlands in direction of *Plogoff, Cléden-Cap-Sizun* (interesting church) and the Pointe du **Raz***. ● The *Baie d'Audierne* stretches in long arc to SE. Fine churches at *Plouhinec* and *Plozévet.* ● 6 km NE, old township of *Pont-Croix*: church of Notre-Dame-de-Roscudon, beautiful 13c nave and superb 67 m. stone steeple (Breton Pardon, Aug. 15).

Aulnay-de-Saintonge
17 – Charente-Maritime   23 – A 3
12c church, surrounded by country graveyard, is a masterpiece of Romanesque Poitevin art. The apse, under slender steeple, is the most harmonious portion. Note, too, sculpted decoration on portals

Aulnay: *capital above one of the columns of the south transept door.*

and on windows of central apse. Historiated capitals.
Vicinity ● 7 km NW, Ch. de **Dampierre-sur-Boutonne***.

Aulus-les-Bains
09 – Ariège   42 – A 3
Spa and winter sports centre, in a verdant setting surrounded by magnificent wooded slopes.

Vicinity ● Excursions recommended to the cascades of Arse and Fouillet, the Tuc de Caïzardé, lakes of Le Garbet and Bassiès, etc. ● From valley of R. *Garbet* to *Ercé* (worth going to top of Géou, 1,669 m., magnificent panorama); thence to *Oust* – where road forks r. to *Soueix* and l. to **Seix*** and valley of R. *Salat.*

Auray
56 – Morbihan   15 – D 1
Ancient town. St. Goustan quarter, on l. bank of R. Loch, looks unchanged from the past: 15c houses, church of St. Goustan with 16c porch. On r. bank, church of St. Gildas has odd mixture of Goth. and Ren. styles. Chapel of the Père Éternel, 17c. Fine views from Promenade du Loch.

Vicinity ● 4 km SE, *St. Avoye*, picturesque hamlet; mid-15c chapel has remarkable mid-16c timbering and Ren. carved wooden roodscreen; site has a melancholic, wild grandeur. ● 13.5 km S, *Locmariaquer*, renowned megaliths of the Table des Marchands and the Mener-Hroëch (Fairy's Stone), a giant menhir of 20.3 m., now broken. Boat trips round Golfe du **Morbihan*** and to R. d'Auray. ● 14 km W, *Belz*; 1.5 km to W, part-Romanesque chapel of *St. Cado*, at end of peninsula into the *Rivière d'Étel.*

Aurillac
15 – Cantal   30 – C 3
The old quarter, around town hall, has some interesting houses (e.g. 16c Maison des Consuls, Rue du Collège). Former abbey church of St. Géraud, 14–15c, rebuilt in Goth. style, 17 and 19c. In 15c chapel of St. Géraud, Romanesque capitals and shrine of the saint. Ch. St. Étienne (technical college) has 11c keep, 16–17c buildings and fine view from terrace. Local museums cl. Sun. a.m. and Tues.: Mus. du Vieil-Aurillac (Gallo-Roman finds, religious art), mus. Hippolyte de Parieu (paintings) and Mus. Jean-Baptiste Rames (reg. geology, archaeology).

Vicinity ● To NE, superb scenic route along D 17, climbing up valley of R. *Jordanne* and *Val de Mandailles,* via Belliac, *Lascelle*

Aurillac: *the Puy Mary, from one of the green valleys typical of once-volcanic Auvegne.*

(12c church), Mandailles (in ring of pastures and forests) and the Pas de Peyrol. Climb to top of *Puy Mary* (1,787 m.), half-an-hour; viewing table, wide panorama.

Autun
71 – Saône-et-Loire   25 – C1
St. Lazare cathedral, 12c, is one of the most notable Romanesque religious edifices; above main door, tympanum of the Last Judgment, outstanding example of Burgundian version of Romanesque monumental sculpture; the artist was Gislebertus, also responsible for the capitals and the transept's N portal; in third chapel to N is the *Martyre de St. Symphorien* by Ingres (1834). Mus. Rolin (cl. Tues.) has collection of Gallo-Roman and medieval archaeology (including Romanesque statues from demolished tomb of St. Lazare); above all, it possesses the celebrated *Tentation d'Eve*, masterpiece of Romanesque sculpture originally in the cathedral, and one of the finest works of 15c French painting, the *Nativité* by the Maître de Moulins. Lapidary museum in former chapel of St. Nicholas, 12c; also natural history museum. Ruins of Roman theatre. The Arroux and St. André gates, both 3c, were part of the Roman ramparts, of which fragments remain.

Vicinity ● 16.5 km NE, *Sully*: 16c château, with its gardens and out-

Autun: *below the cathedral of St. Lazare, the town still shows remarkable signs of its past – Roman remains mingling freely with historic buildings from the Middle Ages.*

buildings, is magnificent example of Burgundian Ren. (v.a. March to Nov.). In forest to S, picturesque ruins of 13c Val-St. Benoît (15c chapel). ● Outing recommended from Autun to **Château-Chinon***, via the rock-strewn, wooded gorges of the Canche, the forest of St. Prix and *Arleuf.*

Auvers-sur-Oise
95 – Val d'Oise   11 – C 1
This typical little Ile-de-France village, now otherwise fairly unprepossessing, owes its reputation to such artists as Cézanne, Pissarro and, above all, Van Gogh, who settled here in May 1890, two months before committing suicide, and now lies in the local cemetery alongside his brother Théo. In the Place de la Mairie is the former Auberge Ravoux, since renamed after Van Gogh, where he died on July 27, 1890. In village, statue of the painter by Zadkine (1961).

Auxerre
89 – Yonne   19 – B 1
St. Étienne cathedral, 13–16c, in Goth. style as adapted within Champagne region, has three beautiful sculpted portals (see especially the bas-reliefs on the piers); interior, partic. the choir, has a perfect harmony of line; superb 13c stained-glass windows; in 11c crypt, fresco from same period, *Christ à cheval* (on horseback). Former abbey church of St. Germain, 13–14c (cl. Tues.) has 9c crypt with murals on life of St. Étienne believed to be among oldest in France (painted about year 850). Mus. d'Art et d'Histoire in the abbey buildings. Mus. Leblanc-Duvernoy: early paintings, sculpture, tapestries. Paul Bert Con-

Auxerre: *the cathedral of St. Etienne, renowned for its sculptures and stained glass.*

servatoire de la Nature and natural history museum. Mus. of local geology. Old houses in Rue de l'Horloge, Place Charles Surugue, Place Robillard, Rue de Paris, Rue Sous-Murs, Rue Joubert. 17c Maison du Coche d'Eau is now regional centre of folk arts and crafts (cl. Tues.).
Vicinity ● To S, **Gy-l'Eveque***; **Escolives-Ste. Camille***. ● To SE, *St. Bris-le-Vineux,* 13c and Ren. church; one-time Templars' house, 12c. Amid vines and cherry trees, pretty villages on R. *Yonne,* Vincelottes and *Vincelles. Cravant* (see **Vermenton***) at confluence of the Yonne and R. *Cure,* 15c and Ren. church. Follow l. bank of Yonne to *Mailly-le-Château* (Goth. church); cross river by 15c bridge towards *Rochers du Saussois* (rock-climbing school); then to *Châtel-Censoir* (collegiate church of St. Potentien, fine 11c Romanesque choir, two

Ren. portals, early Romanesque capitals, 13c sacristy, 12c chapter-house). Ch. de Faulin, 14–15c, perimeter walls with towers and moat. **Clamecy***.

Auxonne
21 – Côte d'Or   20 – A 3
Ancient stronghold on R. *Saône.* 13–14c church, in Burgundian Goth. style, has Romanesque tower and Renaissance porch. Former arsenal, late 17c (now covered market). On Place d'Armes, Gothic town hall, in late 15c brick; in centre, statue of Napoleon, who was garrisoned at Auxonne as young lieutenant of artillery (1788–91). Mus. Bonaparte (open p.m. in summer, exc. Thurs.). Five large towers of 15–16c château.
Vicinity ● 18 km SW, *St. Jean-de-Losne:* 15–16c church with interesting portal; majestic early 17c pulpit in red marble, adorned with sculptures. ● 13.5 km ENE, *Montmirey-le-Château,* vast ruins of feudal castle destroyed end of 15c. 7 km to N. *Pesmes:* noteworthy church, 13–14c; contains chapel with sumptuous Ren. décor and tomb of 16c Andelot brothers, with figures; chapel of Holy Sepulchre also richly sculpted.

Auzon
43 – Haute-Loire   31 – A 2
Once-fortified township on rocky spur. Romanesque church has large arcaded porch, known as a 'ganivelle', with stairways on each side and historiated capitals; interior has wooden gallery and 14c chapel on two levels, decorated with unusual paintings. In upper chapel, dedicated to St. Michael and all the Angels, frescos of great iconographic rarity.

Avallon
89 – Yonne   19 – B 2

Built on a granite promontory, this formerly fortified town seems little changed from the past. Church of St. Lazare, in mid-12c Burgundian Romanesque style, has two portals with richly sculpted arching; main door is mutilated but still has a pillar statue (of a prophet). The Porte d'Horloge (clock gate), surmounted by 15c tower, was part of the old castle; to one side is turret leading to 15c Salle des Échevins (magistrates). Interesting old houses, 15c salt loft. Panorama from Promenade des Petits-Terraux. Tour of the ramparts. Town mus.: archaeology, 19–20c paintings. Good view of town from Parc des Chaumes, 500 m. to E.
Vicinity ● Valley of R. *Cousin,* running W to E from *Pontaubert* (Burgundian Romanesque church) to *Cussy-les-Forges.* ● To SE on D 10, country church at Marrault. ● To S, excursions in **Morvan*** nature reserve and to **Quarré-les-Tombes*** and Abbey of *La Pierre-qui-Vire.* ● To NW, valley of R. *Cure,* grottoes of *Arcy-sur-Cure* (v.a. Palm Sunday to Oct.), **Vermenton***, *Cravant.* Manoir de Chastenay, large collection of paintings on wood (v.a. in summer, cl. Sun. a.m.). ● To NE, *Montréal,* fortified township on isolated hillock; fine 12c church (magnificent 16c carved stalls, big English retable in alabaster, 15c).

Avesnes-sur-Helpe
59 – nord   6 – B 1

One-time stronghold rising above l. bank of R. *Helpe.* The Grande Place is lined by old houses with high slate roofs; 18c town hall in blue stone of Tournai; 16c collegiate church of St. Nicolas. Maroilles cheese is made throughout region; particular local cheese speciality is the Boulette d'Avesnes.
Vicinity ● To E, valley of the *Helpe,* **Liessies***. ● To W, *Forêt de Mormal,* **Le Quesnoy***.

Avignon
84 – Vaucluse   37 – D 3

The Palace of the Popes, both fortress and residence, is the largest of the many historic buildings in Avignon – one of the most beautiful cities of artistic interest in all of France. The building actually comprises two palaces; to N is that of Pope Benedict [Benoît] XII (or Old Palace), mid-14c, and to S, more ostentatious, that of his successor Clement VI (or New Palace). Between the two is main courtyard, where the Festival of Avignon's principal productions are performed (v.a.). In Old Palace, the Consistory wing contains Grande

Avallon: *one of many old houses to be found throughout the town.*

Salle of the Consistory (18c tapestries) and, above it, the 48 m. long Grand Tinel, or Salle des Festins, with frescos – originally on main door of cathedral – by 14c Siennese artist Simone Martini; the two superposed chapels of Tour St. Jean are also decorated with 14c frescos, while others adorn the Pope's Chamber, in Tour des Arges, and the Chambre du Cerf, in Tour de la Garde-Robe – charming pictures of birds, squirrels, vines, hunting and fishing scenes, fruit harvesting, etc. In New Palace, the Clémentine or Grand Chapel (with nave 15 m. broad and 19 m. high) is linked by Grand Staircase to Salle of the Grande Audience, 52 m. long and divided into two naves. ● The building overlooks huge square, bordered by the Hôtel des Monnaies (with richly decorated 17c façade) and the Petit Palais, mus. of early

Mediterranean art (cl. Tues.); magnificent salons of this 14–16c former archbishop's palace now display 12–14c sculptures from Avignon area, examples of Siennese, Florentine, Venetian and Lombard schools, and works from 15c Avignon school. Cathedral of Notre-Dame-des-Doms, Romanesque refashioned in 14, 15 and 17c, has early 14c tomb of Cahors-born Pope John [Jean] XXII in sacristy. The cathedral stands on Rocher des Doms, which is laid out as gardens and has magnificent view over R. *Rhône*, **Villeneuve-lès-Avignon***, the **Alpilles***, **Mt. Ventoux***, etc. On river, remains of 12c Pont St. Bénézet, the celebrated 'Pont d'Avignon'.
● Several churches worth seeing: St. Agricol, 14c, fine Ren. retable. St. Pierre, 14–16c, doors with carved Ren. leaves; in choir, paintings surrounded by beautiful 17c panelling. St. Symphorien, 17c, with 15c façade. St. Didier, 14c, in southern Goth. style; interior has important retable of Notre-Dame-du-Spasme, late 15c, one of first Ren. works in France; also 14c frescos in chapel opposite entrance. Chapel of the Pénitents Noirs, 18c façade, richly decorated.
● Old parts of Avignon have large number of notable mansions, especially in Banasterie quarter behind Notre-Dame-des-Doms: Rue du Four (No. 5, late 17c Hôtel de Galléans), Rue Arnaud de Fabre, Rue de la Croix, Rue de la Banasterie (No. 13, late 17c Hôtel Palun, aka Hôt. de Chateaublanc), Rue Peyrolerie. In market quarter (Halles): Rue du Vieux-Sextier (Louis XV façades), Rue Rouge and Place du Change. St. Didier quarter: Rue du Roi-René (No. 7, early 17c Hôtel de Berton de Crillon, and several others equally

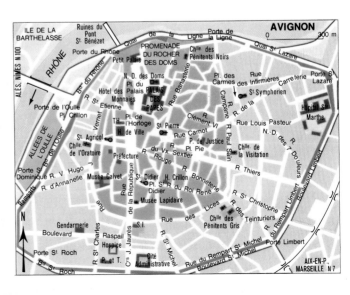

Avignon: *the 14th-century Palace of the Popes, one of the most instantly recognisable buildings in the world.*

fine), Rue de la Masse. Les Cordeliers quarter: Rue des Teinturiers, where water-mills once turned under plane-trees in the tiny R. *Sorgue*, Rue des Lices, Rue des Trois-Faucons. Beyond St. Agricol: many 17–18c mansions, Rue de la Petite Fusterie. Rue Joseph Vernet is also lined with fine mansions of same period; Hôtel de Villeneuve-Martignon houses Mus. Calvet, one of richest in France (cl. Tues.): collection of wrought iron, Greek antiquities, galleries of 16–19c painting, Flemish, Dutch, Italian and French (notably Vernet, David, Chassériau, Géricault), also contemporary art. Lapidary mus. in former chapel of Jesuit college, 17c. Mus. Théodore Aubanel (Provençal literature). Mus. Requien (natural history). Mus. Vouland (18c decorative arts).
Vicinity ● 2.5 km NW, over Ile de la Barthelasse, **Villeneuve-lès-Avignon*** and Les Angles (good view).

Avioth
55 – Meuse   7–A 3
This little frontier village has superb 14–15c church, with very delicate sculpted décor; in choir is pyramidal tabernacle and throne of the Madonna, from same period. Beside church is small 15c hexagonal monument, the *Recevresse*, unique in France – designed to receive pilgrims' offerings.

Avranches
50 – Manche   9 – D 2
Main sight is Jardin des Plantes (botanical gardens, open daily); from terrace (viewing table), splendid panorama of Bay of Mont St. Michel; fine view also from the 'Platform' in Place Daniel Huet. In

old bishop's palace, Mus. de l'Avranchin (folk arts and trad.), with noteworthy collection of Mont St. Michel manuscripts, 8–15c. At exit from town on N 176, grandiose monument to General Patton and US Third Army.

Ax-les-Thermes
09 – Ariège   42 – B 3
Spa in a deep mountain valley, centre for summer excursions; also for winter sports, thanks to installations on plateau of *Le Saquet*, off N 20 to S (inc. cable-car and chairlift). From plateau, climb of about 1 hr to top of *Tute de l'Ours*, 2,259 m., vast panorama.
Vicinity ● To N, Col and Signal de Chioula (1,507 m., fine view); through Col de Marmare (1,360 m.), you reach Route des Corniches, very twisting but picturesque; over to NE, via Col des Sept Frères, *Gorges du Rebenty*. To SE, via Orgeix and *Orlu*, hydro-electric power station and former forge, dominated by impressive Groles waterfall, 300 m. in height; path leads to *Lac de Naguilles* and Orlu-Naguilles dam, in lovely setting. ● To S, the N 20 follows gorges of R. *Ariège* to *Mérens-les-Vals*, then climbs in hairpin bends – passing near the Bezines cascades – up to *L'Hospitalet-près-l'Andorre* (1,436 m.). From there, road continues along river for a while, then leaves it for another winding climb up to *Col de Puymorens* (1,915 m.), big winter sports centre. N 20 now makes sweeping descent to *Porte-Puymorens*, starting-point for climbs of the *Pic Carlit* (2,931 m.).

Azay-le-Ferron (Château)
36 – Indre   23 – D1
Surrounded by formal gardens, 15–

18c château contains wide range of furniture and decoration from 16 to 19c. (v.a. April 1–Sept. 30, daily exc. Tues. Oct. and Mar., open Wed., Sat., and public holidays. Nov. 1 to Feb. 28, open Wed., weekends and public holidays).
Vicinity ● 12 km SE, **Mézières-en-Brenne***. ● 12 km W, *Preuilly-sur-Claise*, 11–12c Romanesque church, 16–17c mansions; on hillock, ruins of château and 12c collegiate church of St. Melaine. At Boussay, 4 km to SW, 17–18c château with 15c towers (v.a. grounds only).

Azay-le-Rideau (Château)
37 – Indre-et-Loire   17 – C 3
This gorgeous château, in a delightful green setting lapped by waters of R. *Indre*, was built early 16c in a style still Goth. and feudal, but has fine apartments furnished and decorated to Ren. taste. (v.a., Son et Lumière in summer). Church of St. Symphorien, 12 and 16c, has unusually marked Carolingian façade, adorned with 14 early statuettes arranged on two levels.
Vicinity ● 6.5 km E, *Ch. de Saché*, 16c renovated 18c (v.a., but cl. Dec.-Jan., also cl. Wed., Oct. 1–Mar. 14); Balzac wrote several of his novels here; you can see his room and small mus. devoted to him. 4 km to NE, charming Manor of *Vonne*, late 16c, with high slate roofs and sculpted dormer-windows. ● 6.5 km SE, *Villaines-les-Rochers*, picturesque village of basket-makers (exhibitions, visits to workrooms).

● **Azay-le-Rideau:** *the nearby Château de Saché, where Balzac lived and worked.*

B

Baccarat
54 – Meurthe-et-Moselle 13 – D 3
World-famed glassworks, founded 1764. Mus. du Cristal, historic and modern pieces (v.a. summer, p.m. Rest of year, opening hrs. vary). Church (1957) is highly original example of contemporary religious art. Tour des Voués, 14c.

Bagnères-de-Bigorre
65 – Hautes-Pyrénées 41 – B 2
Spa and summer resort. Old town has retained its original character, notably Rue des Thermes (remains of late 12c cloister, 17c marble house), Rue de l'Horloge (Tour des Jacobins, 15c), Rue and Place du Vieux-Moulin ('Jeanne d'Albret's house', Ren.). Church of St. Vincent, 15–16c. Salies mus.: historic paintings, pottery, natural history. Mus. du Vieux-Moulin: regional ethnography.
Vicinity ● Excursion to Mt. Bédat (863 m., 1 hr. climb): panoramic table, fine view, Bédat grottoes. ● 13 km NE, fmr. *Abbaye de l'Escaladieu*: 12c church, renovated 17c, partly ruined; late 12c chapterhouse; 3.5 km to E, *Ch. de Mauvezin*, 13–14c: fmr. fortress of Gaston Phébus, in superb setting (v.a. May 1–Sept. 30); 'Escolo Phébus' mus. in the keep. ● 2 km S, in grounds of château of Médous, *Grotte de Médous*, boasting one of richest concretions in Pyrenees (v.a. Apr.–Oct.); road continues to *Beaudéan* (16c church), *Campan* (16c church, int. with fine 18c panelling) and *Ste. Marie-de-Campan*, where D918 divides: SE, via Payolle marble quarries, to *Col d'Aspin* (1,489 m., viewing table) and **Arreau***; SW, to *La Mongie* (1,800 m.), winter sports centre in vast amphitheatre, and *Col du Tourmalet* (2,115 m.), where side road (toll, open July–Sept.) leads up to *Pic du Midi de Bigorre*, with TV relay tower on summit (2,865 m.); on a terrace below are the Observatory and Inst. of Global Physics of the Pic du Midi (v.a. in groups).

Bagnères-de-Luchon (or Luchon)
31 – Haute-Garonne 41 – C 3
Spa and summer resort. The 600 m.-long Allées d'Etigny form its main thoroughfare and, in S, lead into Parc des Quinconces. The old quarter, round the neo-Romanesque church, has kept its Pyrenean village character. Hôtel Lassus-

Nestier (18c) houses an interesting reg. mus. (Gallo-Roman collection, Pyrenean mountaineering). From its terrace (780 m.), magnificent view over town and valley.
Vicinity ● Luchon is a well-known excursion centre. ● 1.5 km E, Montauban: 13c church with Romanesque crypt; magnificent cascades. ● 6 km NW, St. Aventin: unusual late 11c church with two square belfries; main door has historiated capitals and carved tympanum; int. contains Romanesque font, 12c screen, 13c retable, 16c crucifixion, etc. ● 18 km SW, via *Vallées de la Pique* and *du Lys, Superbagnères* (1,800 m.): well-known winter sports resort; magnificent view, recommended excursions to lakes of Espingo and Oô (beautiful setting). ● 10.5 km SE, *Hospice de France* (1,385 m.), via *Pique* valley and l'Hospice road; excursions to passes of *Vénasque* (2,448 m.) and La Picarde. ● *Val d'Aran*: round trip of about 60 km to SE, partly in Spain, via Col du Portillon, *Bosost* (Romanesque church), *Viella*: main town of the Aran valley, linked to Catalonia by the Bonaigue pass (2,072 m.) and 5 km-long Viella tunnel.

Bagnoles-de-l'Orne
61 – Orne 10 – B 2
With Tessé-la-Madeleine, forms an important spa in rocky, wooded Vée valley.
Vicinity ● Attractive walks in Vée gorges, to rocks of 'Saut du Capucin' (follow arrows), to old Janolin refuge hut (232 m.) which overlooks R. Vée in a beautiful park, etc. ● To NW, *Forêt d'Andaine* in Parc Naturel Régional Normandie-Maine. ● 3 km S, *Couterne*, château in pink brick, 16c, enlarged 18c, surrounded by water (n.v.a.). ● 17 km SW, castle at **Lassay***.

Bagnols-sur-Cèze
30 – Gard 37 – D 3
Léon Alègre mus. (cl. Tues.). Adèle and Georges Besson collection of contemp. paintings (many works stolen in 1972). Also galleries for works by young artists and 19c paintings from Lyons region. Sculptures. Local archaeology in Maison Jourdan, on Avignon road. To S, interesting modern housing development.
Vicinity ● 6 km E, atomic research station at *Marcoule* (information centre). ● 17 km NW, *Gourdargues*, remains of Romanesque abbey, chapel and church; 12c parish church; springs; magnificent *Cèze* gorges on *Barjac* road.

Bailleul
59 – Nord 1 – D 2
Town was destroyed during World War I, but its belfry (fine view), churches, lace-making school and Flemish-style yellow brick houses have since been rebuilt. Benoît De Puydt mus.: many ceramics, also Flemish tapestries, decorative art.
Vicinity ● *Mont Noir* (6 km N).

Balleroy (Château)
14 – Calvados 4 – A 3
Attractive Louis XIII-style building set among magnificent flower-beds and avenues of trees (v.a. March–Oct., cl. Wed.). Richly decorated int. In its outbuildings is the only hot air balloon mus. in world (château is owned by a famed enthusiast and collector, the US publisher Malcolm Forbes).

Bandol
83 – Var 44 – B 2
Pleasant seaside resort in a bay, at foot of wooded hills. Opposite is island of *Bendor* (motorboat service

---

BAIE DE SOMME
80 – Somme 5 – B 1
Area of vast sandbanks, known locally as 'Molières' (best seen at low tide, though only covered completely by spring tides), which provide a refuge for seabirds and grazing for salt-meadow sheep. Fishing from footpaths between channels. Wildfowling by boat or from hides along banks. ● Bay can be crossed on foot from **St. Valery-sur-Somme*** to Le Crotoy at low tide (3 km in a straight line, about 1 hr.'s walk). ● Many species of marsh and sea birds in *Marquenterre* nature reserve, on edge of bay, to W of **Rue***. They can be watched from numerous hides dotted around surrounding area of dunes and salt-meadows.

every 30 mins.), private property, tourist, cultural and sports centre; maritime and wine museums
Vicinity ● 4 km SE, *Sanary-sur-Mer, Le Brusc*, in magnificent setting to S of Sanary bay; important motorboating centre on island of *Les Embiez*. ● 7.5 km N, *La Cadière-d'Azur*, old Provençal village perched on top of a steep hill; interesting Penitent chapels (18c works of art and church furniture); 2 km to NE, Le Castellet, unusual fortified village on a rocky peak, magnificent view. ● 9 km NW, *St. Cyr,* seaside resort; 2 km on, *Les Lecques*, Tauroentum museum (1c mosaics, Greek and Roman artefacts, sigillated pottery); 7 km to W, *La Ciotat*, important ship-building centre.

Banyuls-sur-Mer
66 – Pyrénées-Orientales 43 – D 3
Fishing village and seaside resort. The fishermen's tiny, brightly-painted houses clamber up the steep slopes of Point Doune. Aquarium at Arago laboratory (v.a. Thurs.); collection of Mediterranean fauna. A breakwater links village to Grosse island (memorial to the dead by Maillol) and divides the marina in two. World-famed Banyuls wine.
Vicinity ● Recommended excursions to NW to **Collioure*** via Route des Crêtes (ridges) and Balcon de Madeloc. ● 3.5 km SW, through Puig-del-Mas, is farmhouse of sculptor Maillol (d. 1944); over his grave is statue entitled *La Méditerranée*. ● To S, the N114 winds round coast, high above Cape Rederis, Cape Peyrefite and its beach, and Cape Canadell, and then drops down to *Cerbère* and *Port-Bou* (French and Spanish customs).

Barbezieux-Saint-Hilaire
16 – Charente 29 – B 2
Church of St. Mathias (11c nave, 18c façade) and mid-15c château, which now houses mus. and theatre, add to provincial charm of this little city of the Saintonge region.
Vicinity ● 15 km E, *Blanzac*: 12–13c church with elegantly sculpted façade and main door; 3 km to N, *Manoir du Maine-Giraud*, home of poet Alfred de Vigny (mus.); 9 km E of *Blanzac*, recommended excursion to abbey of Puyperoux: Romanesque abbey church boasts numerous historiated capitals; lovers of the unusual should visit *Ch. de la Mercerie* (15 km to NE), begun in 1930 as a – very free! – copy of Versailles' Grand Trianon; this vast structure, which groups together a number of buildings of differing decorative and furnishing styles (v.a., p.m.), stands in 1,000-

---

BALLON D'ALSACE
68 – Haut-Rhin, 88 – Vosges, 90 – Territoire de Belfort 20 – D 1
Most picturesque route is along N 465 from **Belfort***, which zigzags up *Savoureuse* valley via *Giromagny*, first through impressive, wooded, rocky country, then across broad meadows. From Col du Ballon (1,178 m.), there is a 10 min. climb to *Ballon d'Alsace* (1,242 m.), from which view is breath-taking. Two routes down: 1) continuing N along N465 to *St. Maurice-de-Moselle*. 2) turning SE along D466, past lakes of *Alfeld*, one of the most beautiful in Vosges, and Sewen, to Kirchberg (Romanesque church), Niederbruck (monumental *Virgin and Child* by Bourdelle) and *Masevaux*.

---

acre grounds, which include an arboretum. ● 29 km SE, *Montmoreau-St. Cybard*: 15c château (12c Romanesque chapel) and 12c Romanesque church with unusual nave, dome and multifoil door.

Barbizon
77 – Seine-et-Marne 11 – D 3
Formerly village of painters of Barbizon school, from 1830 to 1850, now a residential and tourist town. Homes of Millet and Théodore Rousseau, latter housing municipal mus. of Barbizon School (cl. Tues.) – without interest except for the almost unchanged settings. *Père Ganne* inn, int. originally decorated by numerous artists (cl. Tues.).
Vicinity ● **Fontainebleau*** can be reached through lovely forest of Bas-Bréau (9 km). ● 4 km N, *Chailly-en-Bière*, 13–14c church; Millet, who painted his world-famed *Angelus* near Chailly, and Théodore Rousseau are buried here. ● 6 km W, *Fleury-en-Bière*, 16c brick and stone château, flanked by an imposing tower, surrounded by a moat (v.a. to grounds on request); Romanesque church.

Barcelonnette
04 – Alpes-de-Haute-Provence 38 – D 2
Set among mountains, at an alt. of 1,133 m., town retains many traces of its original fortifications. Place Manuel, Cardinalis tower, 15c belfry. In Chabrand mus.: examples of every species of European bird. Magnificent villas of the 'Barcelonnettes' (inhabitants of town who made their fortune in Mexico).
Vicinity ● *Le Sauze*, 4 km to SE, summer resort and winter sports centre of *Super-Sauze* (1,500 m.). ● *Col d'Allos*, to S, via Le Fau bridge and Malune gorges; road climbs up through dark forests to refuge hut (2,220 m., viewing table) and *Col d'Allos* (2,250 m.), then down again in hairpin bends (v. picturesque) to La Foux (1 km beyond, Romanesque church of Notre-Dame-de-

---

Valvert), and *Allos*, and finally runs alongside R. *Verdon* to 17c fortified town of *Colmars*, now a summer resort and winter sports centre (1,259 m.). ● *Col de la Cayolle* (2,326 m.), to SE, via *Bachelard* valley and *Fours*; from pass, road drops through *Var* valley to *Entraunes, St.-Martin-d'Entraunes* (1,055 m.), interesting church) and *Guillaumes*, in easy reach of winter sports centre of *Valberg* (1,700 m.).

Barèges
65 – Hautes-Pyrénées 41 – B 3
Well-known spa and winter sports centre, 1,240 m. alt., on Tourmalet road. Well-equipped with cable cars, chair-lifts and rack railways to carry visitors high into surrounding mountains.
Vicinity ● To S, Pic d'Ayré (2,148 m.), access by funicular. ● To E, La Laquette (1,715 m.), by cable car. ● 11 km E, *Col du Tourmalet* (2,115 m.), highest pass in Pyrenees; 5.5 km N, *Pic du Midi de Bigorre* (See **Bagnères-de-Bigorre***). ● 7.5 km SW, **Luz-St. Sauveur***.

Barfleur
50 – Manche 3 – D 2
Fishing port and seaside resort, its granite houses ringed round a cove, on a rocky, wild, windswept coast at NE tip of Cotentin peninsula; 17c church.
Vicinity ● 4 km N, *Pointe de Barfleur, Gatteville* lighthouse. ● To S, *Réville*, Romanesque and Goth. Flamboyant church, on mound in centre of country graveyard; *St. Vaast-la-Hougue*, fishing village on a spit between two bays: a breakwater links beach to fort of La Hougue, designed by Vauban (17c French military genius).

Bar-le-Duc
55 – Meuse 13 – A 2
Busy town famed for its currant jams, with many notable monuments to its past. Upper town, which has kept its original character, is dominated by 16–17c

Château-Neuf containing Counting House and town mus. (cl. Tues.): pottery, natural sciences. In Rue des Ducs-de-Bar, mansions of nobility with sculpted façades. In lower town lies old quarter of Le Bourg; Rue du Bourg boasts numerous 17–18c houses, 13–14c church of Notre-Dame. Gilles de Trêves college: courtyard is surrounded by imposing 16–17c buildings, including a Ren. gallery. 14–15c church of St. Antoine, partly built over a canal; int. contains 14–15c frescos. 14c church of St. Étienne is proud possessor of Ligier Richier's masterpiece, the impressive *Squelette* (skeleton), above mausoleum containing René de Chalon's heart (mid-16c).
Vicinity ● The road from *Bar-le-Duc* to **Verdun*** played a crucial role in World War I. ● 16 km SE, *Ligny-en-Barrois*: tiny, ancient city, whose mid-18c Dauphine gate is sole relic of improvements made by King Stanislas of Poland, Duke of Lorraine; in 12–17c church of Notre-Dame, chapel of the blessed Pierre de Luxembourg (d. 1387); Luxembourg tower (v.a.).

Barles
04 – Alpes-de-Haute-Provence   38 – C 2
Little hillside village, on road between **Digne*** and *Seyne* through *Bléone* and *Bès* valleys. The *Clues de Barles*, to S of village, are narrow, wild ravines whose vertical, rocky walls loom over road and stream; ravine of the *Clue de Verdaches* between Barles and Verdaches is greener.
Vicinity ● To NE, *Seyne-les-Alpes*, Romanesque church (Goth. doors), one of most impressive in region; citadel is characteristic of 17c military architecture.

Barneville-Carteret
50 – Manche   3 – C 3
Carteret, tiny port on Gerfleur estuary; attractive beach. Rec. excsn. along cliff path round *Cap de Carteret* – schistous cliffs, with lighthouse and corniche path; viewing point at Biard rock (panoramic table). *Barneville* has late 11c Romanesque church with 15c machicolated tower.
Vicinity ● 1.5 km S, *Barneville-plage*. ● 8.5 km SE, *Portbail*; 150 m. from 11c church of Notre-Dame are remains of a hexagonal 6–7c Paleo-Christian baptistry.

Barr
67 – Bas-Rhin   14 – A 3
Mid-18c Folie Marco still has its original décor, in which are exhibited collections of antique furniture, pottery, Alsace porcelain, pewterware, etc. (cl. Tues. in

Barneville-Carteret: *shale cliffs loom over the beach; fine views from clifftop path, the Sentier des Douaniers.*

summer; rest of year, opening hrs. vary). Place de l'Hôtel-de-Ville, typical Alsace architecture.
Vicinity ● Ruins of med. castles of Andlau and Spesbourg to W, and of Lansberg to NW. ● 3 km NW, mid-18c Ch. de Truttenhausen.

Barre-des-Cévennes
48 – Lozère   37 – B 2
Picturesque village. 12c priory church of L'Assomption-Notre-Dame, on former Roman site. Feudal castle. Fine view.
Vicinity ● Rec. trips to **Corniche des Cévennes*** and Valfrancesque, or 'French valley', an unusual area – blackish schist, but nevertheless richly green; R. Gardon du Mialet, which flows through it, is bounded by mountains of Chaîne française to NW and Serre de Lansuscle to SE.

Bar-sur-Aube
10 – Aube   12 – D 3
Two churches recommended: St. Pierre, in Burgundy's early Goth. style, late 12c, with 14c timbered gallery used as covered market; St. Maclou, late 12–15c (deconsecrated). In hospital chapel, early 16c sculpture of Childhood of the Virgin, Champagne school.
Vicinity ● To SE, *Bayel,* church contains two masterpieces of sculpture of Champagne school: an early 14c Virgin and Child, and early 16c *Pietà* by the Master of La Ste. Marthe; the glassworks, founded 1666, are worth visiting. 6.5 km to S, *Clairvaux*, former abbey, now a local detention centre; v.a. only to Ste. Anne's chapel and to see 18c façade of main courtyard. ● To E, **Colombey-les-Deux-Églises***: General de Gaulle, who died at 'La

Boisserie' (v.a.), is buried in cemetery; a huge Cross of Lorraine (44 m.), in pink granite, stands nearby; recommended excursion in upper valley of R. *Blaise*, from *Juzennecourt* to *Doulevant-le-Château* ● To W, *Parc Naturel de la Forêt d'Orient* (see **Brienne-le-Château***).

Bassoues
32 – Gers   41 – B 1
The magnificent 14c square keep, 38 m. high, of fmr. fortress of archbishops of Auch dominates the tiny village, which stands on a hillside. One of best preserved in the Midi, its refined construction and well-equipped int. betoken a real concern for comfort (v.a.); beautiful halls with ribbed vaulting. From top, fine view over Pyrenees. 14c church of Notre-Dame. Old timbered covered market, ancient houses. In cemetery, basilica of St. Fris (or Pris), 16c, rebuilt end of 19c; beneath the choir, a vast crypt houses the saint's sarcophagus.

Bastia
2b – Corsica   45 – A 2
Bustling town, economic centre of Corsica. The 300 m.-long Place St. Nicolas runs along the New Port (statue of Napoleon). The Old Port is overlooked by the old town, with its narrow, winding lanes. 17c church of St. Jean Baptiste and early 17c chapel of the Conception – both magnificently decorated in 18c – are its main sights. To S, the citadel stands on steep promontory; in fmr. Genoese Governors' Palace (14–16c), mus. of Corsican ethnography: folk history, arts and traditions; geology and botany (v.a. Nov.–Easter, cl. Sun.); memorial to

Bastia: *the picturesque Old Port; the vast façade of the church of St. Jean Baptiste towers over the houses and narrow lanes.*

Les Baux de Provence: *one of the most impressive sites in Provence. Ruins and barren rock blend into each other.* ▲

Local mansions display many features of Renaissance art, e.g. this staircase decorated with quadrifoil motifs. ▼

two Corsican regiments. In apse of 17c Cath. of Ste. Marie, 15c chapel of Ste. Croix, decorated with gilded Louis XV stucco-work, housing the *Christ des Miracles*. Bastia-Plage, 6 km to S, is a large tourist complex. *Vicinity* ● Departure point for **Cap Corse***, to N. ● To W, **St. Florent***, via *Col de Teghime* and *Patrimonio*, surrounded by vineyards. ● To SW, via *Défilé de Lancone, Murato*, tiny Pisan polychrome church of San Michele. ● To S, Romanesque church of **La Canonica***.

Bastia d'Urfé (Château)
42 – Loire   31 – B 1
The most outstanding Ren. building in the *Forez* (cl. Tues.). Overlooking main courtyard, two-storey sculpted and decorated gallery in Italian style. At ground level in main building, strange rococo 'grotto' covered with polychrome pebble-work, with mythological figures in relief. In chapel, coffered ceiling, decorated with biblical scenes. On first floor, beautiful painted ceilings, 16–17c furniture and tapestries.
Vicinity ● 4 km S of *Boën*, late 16c Ch. de Goutelas, on terrace overlooking the *Forez* plain (v.a. to exterior of château only).

Bastide-Puylaurent (La)
48 – Lozère   37 – B i
Summer resort in lush setting.
Vicinity ● 8 km E by D4 along Cévennes ridge through magnificent countryside, *St. Laurent les-Bains*, small spa at 850 m. alt.; rec. visit to Trappist monastery of Notre-Dame-des-Neiges in natural amphitheatre in mountains, modern buildings (v.a., p.m.; cl. Sun.).

Batz (Island)
see **Roscoff***   8 – C 1

Baule (La)
44 – Loire-Atlantique   16 – B 2
One of the most popular of Atlantic beaches; hotels and villas line the esplanade. The new town of La Baule-les-Pins lies among the magnificent pine forests of the Bois d'Amour.
Vicinity ● 3 km W, *Le Pouliguen*, quayside lined with picturesque old houses, beach; at 2.5 km, Pen-Château point: Grand-Côte corniche road leads to *Batz-sur-Mer*, fmr. salt-marsh workers' town at foot of jagged cliffs, whose 15–16c granite church of St. Guénolé is dominated by 60 m. tower; ruins of 15-16c chapel of Notre-Dame-du-

Bavay: *the atmosphere of the Roman city is best evoked by the cryptoporticos which supported the shopping arcades.*

Joyeuse-Garde. ● 4 km S, Paradou; 2 km to S, remains of castle of St. Martin-de-Castillon, and chapel of St. Jean. ● To NNE and NE, the **Alpilles***, **St. Rémy-de-Provence***, Eygalières, charming old village.

Bavay
59 – Nord   **2 – B 3**
Archaeological digs have uncovered remains of Roman town of Bagacum: a large mid-2c group of buildings enclosed by rectangular wall bordered by shops with cryptoporticos. Site mus. (cl. Tues.).

Bayeux
14 – Calvados   **4 – A 3**
The 13c Cath. of Notre Dame is one of the finest examples of Norman Goth.; spires of the towers along the façade are 75 m. high, the central tower is 80 m.; 11c crypt, 12–13c treasury and chapter-house (v.a.). Fmr. 18c seminary, now Centre Guillaume-le-Conquérant (William the Conqueror), contains famed late-11c *Tapisserie de la Reine Mathilde*; in reality, a piece of embroidery, 48 m. long by 51 cm. wide, which depicts conquest of England by the Normans (v.a.). Fmr. bishop's palace houses Baron Gérard mus. (archaeology, paintings, tapestries, lace); fmr. Ren. octagonal chapel with particularly fine ceiling. Interesting old houses: 15–17c Governor's House (the most noteworthy), 14c mansion (Tourist Office), 15–16c Argouges house. Memorial mus. of World War II battle for Normandy.
Vicinity ● 3 km N, Vaux-sur-Aure; 4 km to NW, once fortified manor house at Argouges, remains of ram-

Mûrier; to NW, *Le Croisic* has number of fine 17–18c houses, especially along the quayside: the tiny 16c Ch. d'Aiguillon houses town hall and naval mus.; attractive granite, late-15c church of Notre-Dame-de-Pitié; corniche road around *Pointe du Croisic*. ● From Saillé, to NW, D92 crosses salt marshes to *La Turballe*, a lively sardine port.

Baume-les-Messieurs (Abbey)
39 – Jura   **26 – B 1**
The abbey, founded 6c, still retains among its 15–16c buildings a magnificent 12c Romanesque abbey church with 15c façade embellished with statues of Burgundy school; 12–13c nave, partly paved with tombstones; 13–15c choir with high altar surrounded by magnificent Flemish sculpted and painted panelled retable. Chalon chapel to l. of choir: remarkable 15c stone statue of St. Peter, Chalon family tombs. Mus. of folk art and traditions.
Vicinity ● 3 km S, *Cirque de Baume*; (v.a. to grottoes, in magnificent amphitheatre with sheer cliffs.

Baux-de-Provence (Les)
13 – Bouches-du-Rhône   **43 – D 1**
The town, now ruined, lies on a bare promontory in the **Alpilles***, 900 m. long by 200 m. wide (magnificent view). Numerous Ren. houses, esp. Manville mansion (town hall and hist. mus.) in Grande-Rue, Porcelet mansion in Place de l'Église (mus. of contemp. art), 14c Tour de Brau mansion (lapidary mus.), etc. In Jean de Brion mansion, mus. of Fondation Louis Jou (book designer). In 13–15c church of St. Vincent. Christmas Eve brings celebration of picturesque shepherds'

festival, at which a lamb is offered up. Opposite it lies 17c chapel of the Pénitents Blancs. Plan du Château is dominated by weird ruins of med. castle (enormous 13c keep, numerous towers, Ste. Catherine's chapel, etc.). On a rock, unusual relief sculpture of the Three Marys (les Trimaïë). Below Les Baux, rocky gorge of Enfer valley, grotto of the Fairies and Portalet rocks, ancient troglodytic dwellings. In tiny Fontaine valley, elegant Ren.-style pavilion which once belonged to Queen Jeanne of Navarre.
Vicinity ● 9 km SW, *Fontvieille* and Alphonse Daudet's mill (see abbey of **Montmajour***); 2 km to S, Roman aqueducts of Barbegal and Meunerie. ● 4 km S, *Maussane*; 6 km to SE, *Mouriès* and castle of

Bayeux: *the famed 'tapestry' is a veritable 'strip cartoon'; the English are depicted with moustaches, the Normans as clean-shaven.*

Bazas: *Roquetaillade castle, built 14c, redesigned 19c.*

cloister with soaring arcades. The quarter surrounding it contains a number of interesting streets with old houses. The busiest is Rue du Pont-Neuf, edged with low arcades. From St. Esprit bridge, over R. *Adour*, there is magnificent view of town and its quays. Two mus. rec.: Basque mus. (cl. Sun. and public hols.), in 16c house, is fascinating reg. mus. – period décors and reconstructions of artisans' shops, rooms devoted to Basque dancing, theatre, pelota, trads. and customs; Bonnat mus. (cl. Tues.) is especially devoted to works collected by the painter (e.g. Murillo, van Dyck, Rubens, Rembrandt, El Greco, Géricault, Ingres, Barye, Degas, Goya, etc.). Rec. walk along ramparts.

Vicinity ● 6 km NW, *Barre de l'Adour*, modified 1967 by construction of 1,100 m. jetty on N edge of river-mouth; road continues along coast towards **Biarritz*** via wood and lake of Chiberta and Chambre d'Amour beach. ● 7 km SE, Croix de Mouguerre (panoramic table, fine view); from *Mouguerre*, winding Napoleonic Route des Cîmes affords magnificent views over Pyrenees (see **Hasparren***).

Beaucaire: *all that remains of the castle is the keep.*

parts and moat, attractive late 15c Ren. building. ● 1.5 km SW, *St. Loup-Hors*, 12–14c church, magnificent Romanesque tower. ● 9 km S, *Abbaye de Mondaye*, founded early 12c, 17–18c building; 18c church possesses one of Normandy's very few Classical ornamented interiors (v.a.).

Bayonne
64 – Pyrénées-Atlantiques 40 – C 1
Once fortified town on R. *Adour*, Bayonne still has its quays, old streets and ramparts. 13–14c Cath. of Ste. Marie, one of most beautiful in SW (19c spires), has mid-13c

Bazas
33 – Gironde   35 – B 2
Built high on promontory above the valley, town is dominated by imposing 13–14c Cath. of St. Jean Baptiste; noteworthy 13c sculpted doorways. 15–16c arcaded houses border Place de la République. Fine view of Beuve valley from terraced

garden on ramparts of former archbishop's palace.
Vicinity ● 11 km NW, at *Mazères*, *Ch. de Roquetaillade*, early 14c, restored unusually in med. style by Viollet-le-Duc (v.a. in Easter holidays and June 15–Oct. 15; out of season, Suns. and public hols.). ● 10 km W, *Uzeste*, interesting Goth. church with sculpted doorway; int. contains mutilated tomb of Pope Clement V (d. 1314); 5 km to NW, *Villandraut*, impressive ruins of 14c fortress. ● To SW, *Ciron* valley and gorges, ruins of numerous châteaux; canoe trips down R. Ciron from *Beaulac* to *Villandraut*.

Beaugency: *nuclear power station of St. Laurent-des-Eaux, on an artificial island.*

Beaucaire
30 – Gard   **43 – D 1**
The 13–14c fortress and its magnificent triangular buttressed keep stand on a steep escarpment overlooking the Rhône; fine view (v.a.). Ext. of early 18c church of Notre-Dame-des-Pommiers has sculpted Romanesque frieze portraying two scenes from the Passion. Vinhassa municipal mus. (archaeology, local folk arts and traditions).

Beaugency
45 – Loiret   **18 – B 1**
Attractive little town on R. *Loire*. Picturesque bridge with 22 arches. The old quarter evokes memories of provincial towns of long ago and boasts 11c keep (or Caesar's tower), 15c Dunois château (regional museum of folk arts and traditions), 16c St. Firmin tower, fmr. 12c abbey church of Notre-Dame, 12c Templars' mansion with Romanesque façade, Rue du Puits-de-l'Ange and 16c town hall. Beside the river, 18c abbey buildings; terrace of Le Petit-Mail.
Vicinity ● 7 km NE, *Meung-sur-Loire*; 17–18c château with some 13c parts (v.a. April–Oct., and weekends Nov.–Mar.), and attractive 11–13c church of St. Liphard; old houses; beaches along R. Loire. ● 9 km SW, *St. Laurent-des-Eaux*, nuclear power station. ● 16 km W, Ch. de **Talcy***.

Beaulieu-sur-Dordogne
19 – Corrèze   **30 – B 3**
Fmr. Benedictine abbey church of St. Pierre, in Limousin Romanesque style, has carved doorway which is one of greatest masterpieces of Languedoc Romanesque sculpture (Last Judgment on tympanum); int. contains 18c stalls and rich treasure. 12 and 15c Penitent chapel. 14 and 15c houses.
Vicinity ● 8 km S, *Bretenoux*; Ch. de Castelnau, 2 km to SW, is one of finest medieval fortresses (cl. Tues.); 62 m. high keep, 14–15c perimeter walls, 17c main building; at foot of castle, church of Prudhomat. ● To E, picturesque, wild *Gorges de la Cère*.

Beaumont-du-Périgord
24 – Dordogne   **35 – C 1**
13c bastide with central square partly surrounded by 'cornières', remains of ramparts (fortified double gate). Late 13c fortified church flanked by four towers, with parapet walk.
Vicinity ● 3 km N, 16c *Ch. de Bannes*, flanked by impressive towers; entry via a drawbridge and small crenellated, machicolated for-

Beaulieu-sur-Dordogne: *tympanum of south doorway of St. Pierre; Christ in Majesty welcomes the chosen on Judgment Day.*

tified tower (n.v.a.); in guardroom, magnificent Ren. fireplace; so-called Henri IV's Room (murals). ● 7 km NW, *Couze et St. Front*: 11–12c churches, troglodytic dwellings; 3 km to W, Goth. and Ren. *Ch. de Lanquais*: interesting Louis XIII period furniture (v.a. Easter–Nov. 1, cl. Tues.).

Beaune
21 – Côte-d'Or   **25 – D 1**
Town of considerable artistic interest, enclosed by ramparts flanked by huge towers. Mid-15c Hospice (v.a.) is striking example of Flemish Goth. architecture and ornamentation; most important elements are main courtyard, with its well, wooden galleries and vast expanses of polychrome glazed tiles, huge hospital ward (72 m. long), kitchen (guided tour), and 18c dispensary. It possesses one of the masterpieces of 15c Flemish art: polyptych of the *Jugement dernier* (Last Judgment) by Rogier van der Weyden. Marey and Beaux-Arts museum in town hall: 17c Italian and French paintings; Fondation Marey (inventor of chronophotography) (v.a. Easter–Nov.). Collegiate church of Notre-Dame, in Burgundian Romanesque style, 15c murals; in choir, magnificent 15c Flemish tapestries depicting life of the Virgin (v.a. Palm Sunday–Dec.). In former mansion of Dukes of Burgundy, impressive wine museum. Numerous 15 and 16c mansions and houses in old town.
Vicinity ● 6 km S, Archeodrome on A6. ● Rec. excursion through vineyards of 'la Côte' to SSW, along N74 and D973, Pommard, *Volnay, Meursault*, Chassagne-Montrachet, etc.; 5 km to W, *Ch. de la Rochepot*

Beaune: *main courtyard of the world-famed Hospice, run by nuns, has remained virtually unchanged since its foundation.*

(v.a. Mar.–Nov., cl. Tues.); built 12c, reconstructed 15c, restored 19c, flanked by towers with glazed tiles in mosaic form. ● 18 km ENE, *Abbaye de Cîteaux* (see **Nuits-St. Georges***).

Beauregard (Château)
41 – Loir-et-Cher 18 – A 2
Built 16c, reconstructed and enlarged 17c (v.a.; cl. Wed. Oct. 1–Mar. 31), it is famed for its magnificent early 17c gallery containing portraits of 363 historic figures. Panelling painted with emblems and devices, ceiling with decorated beams, Delftware floor tiles. Grelots Room is entirely lined with 16c sculpted and gilded wood panelling and paintings on wood. Beautiful coffered ceiling.
Vicinity ● 12.5 km SW, **Fougères-sur-Bièvre***.

Beauvais
60 – Oise 5 – C 3
Magnificent Cath. of St. Pierre, of which only 13–14c choir, the highest ever to be constructed (48.20 m. to vaulting), was completed, dominates the town, rebuilt since World War II; Goth. Flamboyant façades of transept are richly ornamented; int. has 13, 14 and 16c stained glass windows and rich treasure. The old cath., or Basse Œuvre, adjoins transept. Natnl. tapestry gallery. Fmr. episcopal palace, late 15c (huge fortified door), houses law courts and reg. mus. (cl. Tues.), containing important collections of regional sculpted wood and stone, local tapestries and ceramics (16–17c glazed earthenware), 16–19c Italian and French paintings, Art Nouveau and Art Deco. Romanesque and Goth. church of St. Étienne, to S of town, has beautiful Goth. Flamboyant choir; 16c glassware.
Vicinity ● *Epte* and *Thérain* valleys.

Bec-Hellouin (Le) (Abbey)
27 – Eure 4 – D 3
The impressive 15c St. Nicolas tower rises above this Benedictine abbey, founded 11c (v.a.); 17c cloister and refectory; imposing main staircase. In town, 14 and 16c church contains many 17c stone statues. Abbey church museum (history of the car).

Bego (Mont)
See: **Merveilles (Les)***
(Valley) 39 – B 3

Belfort
90 – Territoire de Belfort 20 – D 2
The town, through which flows R. Savoureuse, and whose old quarter, late 18c town hall and 18c church of St. Christophe are well worth visiting, is dominated by Bartholdi's world-famed red sandstone *Lion de Belfort*, 22 m. long by 11 m. high, resting against the citadel rock; panorama; art and hist. mus. (cl. Tues.): collection of Alsace numismatics, engravings by Dürer. At NE end of town, entrenched camp of Le Vallon, fortified walls, flanked by forts of La Justice and La Miotte (panorama).
Vicinity ● 7.5 km NW, lake and sailing centre of Bas-Evette, near *Evette-Salbert*.

Bellegarde-sur-Valserine
01 – Ain 26 – B 3
Important excursion centre.
Vicinity ● *Valserine* valley, 3.5 km NW, strange 'Valserine sink', chalk dam in which the river has cut deep holes and gullies; 15 km N, at *Chézery*, entrance to *Défilé de Sous-Balme*, impressive, wild gorge; 12 km to N, *Lelex* is a winter sports centre and summer resort (898 m.), beyond which road climbs up to *Col de la Faucille* (1,323 m.) via *Mijoux*; magnificent views of **Mont-Blanc*** range. ● To S, 14 km, via *Billiat*: *Barrage de Génissiat*, masterpiece of modern technology, built 1937–1947 (v.a. to power station by permission of Rhône water authority). ● 12 km E, *Défilé de l'Écluse*, magnificent valley between *Grand Crêt d'Eau* (1,624 m.) and Vuache mountain (1,111 m.).

Bellême
61 – Orne 10 – D 3
Picturesque cluster of old houses on a rocky outcrop; 15c fortified gateway, known as 'Le Porche', flanked by two towers, is all that remains of 15c castle; Rue Ville-Close is lined with 17 and 18c mansions (no. 26, Bansard des Bois mansion). Richly decorated 17c church of St. Sauveur.
Vicinity ● Rec. visits in Perche reg. to **Mortagne-au-Perche*** and **Nogent-le-Rotrou***. ● To NW, *Forêt de Bellême* (Étang de la Herse, Chêne de l'École, 16c Ch. des Feugerets, etc.). ● To SE, *St. Cyr-la-Rosière*, remarkable 17c Entombment of Christ in polychrome terracotta in church; 500 m. to S, 15–16c med.-looking L'Angenardière manor; 1 km to E, Ste. Gauburge,

BELLE-ILE-EN-MER
56 – Morbihan 15 – D 2
Largest of the Breton islands. Small fortified town of *Le Palais* is dominated by imposing late 16c citadel, whose walls were strengthened by Vauban; int. houses hist. mus. 1 km SE, Ramonette beach. 6.5 km NW, *Sauzon*, attractive fishing port. Rec. excursions: from Sauzon, 2 km to NW, *Pointe des Poulains*, Fort Sarah Bernhardt, fine view; 2.5 km to SW, *Grotte de l'Apothicairerie*, one of Brittany's most extraordinary natural sights. *Grand-Phare, Aiguilles de Port-Coton*; to S, v. picturesque *Port-de-Goulphar*; beach and cliffs at Port-Donnant; extremely wild and beautiful area.

Belfort: *the famed lion, in red sandstone from the Vosges, rests against the rock. It commemorates the town's valiant stand against the Prussians in 1870.*

BELVAL (Forest)
08 – Ardennes   6 – D 3
S of **Sedan***; reached via Belval-Bois-des-Dames, 2,700-acre safari park, dotted with lakes; 6.5 km-long circuit by car. Four optional stopping places, partic. on embankment of the Grand-Étang; two observation towers; bison, elk, deer, wild boar, wild sheep, mallards, herons, etc. (Open during school hols.)

Goth. church converted into mus. of regional folk arts and traditions (v.a. in summer). ● 8 km NE, *Colonard-Corubert*, 15c Le Courboyer manor, in white stone, flanked by huge round tower and number of watchtowers; one of most typical 'Percheron manors'.

Belley
01 – Ain   32 – B 1
Former capital of Bugey region. St. Jean Cath., mid-19c neo-Goth. exc. for early 15c choir; interior has 14 and 15c rose windows. Episcopal palace by Soufflot (1775).
Vicinity ● 8.5 km S, Pierre-Châtel fort on 180 m.-high rock overlooking R. Rhône (n.v.a.); magnificent Pierre-Châtel gorge (N521B); *Yenne* has interesting church with 12c façade; sculpted doorway and corbels; Goth. stalls in wood carved with arms of Duchy of Savoy.

Belvès
24 – Dordogne   35 – D 1
Picturesque old town on hill overlooking Nauze valley. 14 and 16c church, 15c belfry, and old timbered covered market. Many Goth. and Ren. houses.

Bénévent-l'Abbaye
23 – Creuse   24 – B 3
Remarkable mid-12c Romanesque former abbey church, crowned by domes and two steeples. 14 and 15c remains of abbey.
Vicinity ● 6 km N, *La Grand-Bourg*: 12 and 16c church with external pulpit; over N doorway, sculpted capitals forming a frieze; interior has interesting works of art; treasure (reliquaries). ● To SE, Puy de Goth (541 m.), fine view.

Bergerac
24 – Dordogne   29 – C 3
Peyrarède mansion houses unique tobacco mus. and mus. of urban hist. (cl. Sun. a.m., Mon. and public hols.). Tobacco mus. contains fascinating collections devoted to history, cultivation, trade and use of 'Nicot's weed'.
Vicinity ● 7 km E, Ch. de Grateloup. ● 3 km NW, Ch. de Guarrigue, strange Goth. and Ren. pastiche of a building constructed

in late 19c by the actor Mounet-Sully, now a hotel. ● 6 km S, *Ch. de Monbazillac*: magnificent 16c building in middle of vineyards, flanked by four towers and crowned by machicolations, above which rise tiers of lovely sculpted dormer windows (v.a.).

Bergues
59 – Nord   1 – C 2
Picturesque Flemish city, enclosed by 17c ramparts surrounded by water, which retains the character of a fortified town. A 54 m.-high belfry (rebuilt after 1944) towers over Grand-Place. 17c former pawnshop now houses museum (15–17c Flemish and French paintings, Georges de la Tour). Impressive remains of 11c abbey of St. Winoc. Enormous 18c door and two towers.
Vicinity ● 13 km E, *Hondschoote*, Spanish Ren. town hall (1606); hall-church; at 500 m., 'Nordmolen', one of oldest windmills in Europe (12c); picturesque 'moëres' (marshes) alongside *Canal de la basse Colme* as far as village of *Moëres* (NW of *Hondschoote*).

Bernay
27 – Eure   10 – D 1
14–15c church of Ste. Croix, int.

contains interesting works of art. 15c basilica of Notre-Dame-de-la Couture. Town hall, post office and law courts now occupy 17c fmr. abbey with church dating from 11c; reg. mus. in abbot's house, walls of which are a checkerwork of brick and stone. Interesting old houses, 15 and 16c hospice chapel.
Vicinity ● 11 km SW, 18c château at *Broglie* (n.v.a.). ● 13 km SE, 17c château at *Beaumesnil*, one of Normandy's most impressive (v.a., p.m. May–Sept.). ● To E, *Beaumont-le-Roger*, 14, 15 and 16c church; ruins of priory of the Trinity and 13c church (v.a.). ● 11 km NE, *Nassandres* (chapel of St. Éloi).

Besançon
25 – Doubs   20 – B 3
Capital of the Franche-Comté, within loop of R. *Doubs*, dominated in N. by defensive walls of Fort Griffon and in SE by the citadel, one of Vauban's masterworks, towering 118 m. above river (v.a., cl. Tues.). Reg. folk mus., Mus. de la Résistance et de la Déportation, and mus. of natural history and African art. 12–14c Cath. of St. Jean, of off-centre design, contains celebrated early 16c *Vierge aux Saints* by Fra Bartolommeo. ● 2c Roman Porte Noire leads to Castan square (Roman remains). Grande-Rue: No. 138, birthplace of Victor Hugo; imposing mid-16c Ren. Granvelle palace, with square arcaded int. courtyard (town hist. mus.; cl. Tues.); attractive 16, 17 and 18c houses. The prefecture, fmr. Hôtel des Intendants, is one of loveliest of late 18c neo-Classical buildings. Hôpital St. Jacques, magnificent 18c screen, elegant Louis XV-style chapel. ● Fine arts mus., recently modernised, is one

Besançon: *Victor Hugo called it the 'old Spanish town'. Despite modern change, it retains many traces of its past glories. The round towers of the Rivotte gate can be seen on the left.*

Beynac: *with its sheer walls towering over the valley, the castle commands one of the most striking vistas in the Périgord. View from nearby La Roque-Gageac (above), where the Dordogne winds lazily between green banks.*

of richest in France: archaeology, paintings of Flemish, German (Cranach), Italian (Tintoretto, Titian, Bellini), and 17 and 18c French schools; impressive collection of works by Fragonard, Boucher, Hubert Robert; 19c gallery: Courbet, Ingres, sketches by David and Géricault; galleries of Impressionist (Renoir) and contemp. works (Bonnard, Matisse, Picasso, Van Dongen, Marquet, etc.); collection of sketches (cl. Tues.). ● 17c houses line Quai Vauban. Across Battant bridge (fine view), on r. bank of *Doubs*, is Battant quarter, bristling with fortifications by Vauban; 18c church of Ste. Madeleine; behind Griffon gate, picturesque Promenade des Glacis. Also on r. bank, casino and La Mouillère salt baths. *Vicinity* ● To E, Brégille plateau (fine view of Besançon), by funicular. ● 3.5 km SE, chapel of Les Buis (panorama). ● 4.5 km S and 30 mins. walk, *Beure* and Bout-du-Monde, strange semicircle of rocks; remains of abbey of Gouailles, founded 12c. ● 13 km N, *Voray-sur-l'Ognon*, impressive 18c church. ● To NE, *Fôret de Chailluz*.

Béziers: *the Orb, spanned by the Pont-Vieux, flows peacefully below the town, dominated by the old cathedral of St. Nazaire. Béziers is an important centre for the local wine trade.*

Besse et St. Anastaise
63 – Puy-de-Dôme   30 – D 2
Picturesque old town whose narrow streets are lined by houses of black lava; the butchers' shops of the Rue de la Boucherie still have their stone counters. 15–16c building with turret staircases and carved doors, known as Queen Margot's house (wife of Henri IV). Church of St. André, fmr. collegiate chapel with 11c Romanesque nave and unusual historiated capitals. 15c belfry.
Vicinity ● *Super-Besse* is a winter sports centre at 1,300 m. alt., in Cirque de la Biche. ● *Lac Pavin*; *Lac de Bourdouze* (1,170 m.); and *Lac de Montcineyre* beneath peak of Montcineyre (1,333 m.). ● 8 km NE, *Grottes de Jonas*, ancient troglodytic dwellings; stairways link different levels; unusual spiral staircase, late 15c rustic murals in chapel.

Bétharram (Notre-Dame-de-)
64 – Pyrénées-Atlantiques 41 – A 2
At *Lestelle-Bétharram*. 17c church
(noteworthy period decoration) is
important pilgrimage centre. 17c
convent and modern chapel of St.
Michel Garricoïts, containing the
saint's shrine.
Vicinity ● To SE, *Grottes de Bétharram* (v.a. in summer); from upper
rooms, 270 steps lead down 80 m. to
lower rooms and an underground
river (300 m. boat trip).

Béthune
62 – Pas-de-Calais 1 – D 3
Former Vauban-inspired fortified
town. 14c main square and belfry.

Beynac-et-Cazenac
24 – Dordogne 35 – D 1
Beynac is dominated by a sheer cliff,
rising 150 m. above R. *Dordogne*,
on which stands imposing 13, 14
and 15c castle (v.a. Mar.–Nov.);
13–14c chapel (parish church). On
opposite bank, 15–16c manor of
Fayrac.
Vicinity ● 3 km S, 13, 14 and 15c
ruins of *Ch. de Castelnaud*. ● 2 km
SE, 18c Ch de Marqueyssac. To
SW, on l. bank of *Dordogne*,
Ch. des Milandes, Ren. with 15c
chapel, where Josephine Baker
lived with her intnl. community of
children.

Bèze
21 – Côte-d'Or 20 – A 2
13c fortified town. Former abbey
church, rebuilt 18c, retains only the
transept surmounted by a steeple of
the original Romanesque building.
13c house with façade adorned with
ogival bays.
Vicinity ● 11 km NE, *Fontaine-
Française*, perfect example of a
Classical château (v.a. p.m. in
summer, cl. Tues. and Thurs.);
beautiful formal gardens, large
park.

Béziers
34 – Hérault 43 – A 2
Allées Paul Ricquet form heart of
the town, ending in front of the
theatre, one of the rare examples
of Restoration architecture (1844).
Picturesque Plateau des Poètes,
public garden containing fountain
depicting a Titan. Old town (interesting old houses) is dominated by
13–14c cath. of St. Nazaire; fortified
W façade opens on to terrace with
fine view; Romanesque crypt. Lapidary mus. in 14c cloister. Beaux-
Arts mus.: 14–19c Italian, German
and French paintings. Mus. du
Biterrois (hist. and cultivation of
the vine, archaeology and natural

hist.). Church of St. Jacques, interesting Classically-inspired Romanesque apse.
Vicinity ● 15 km SE, *Valras-Plage;*
● *13 km W,* **Ensérune***.

Biarritz
64 – Pyrénées-Atlantiques 40 – B 1
A walk along the beaches will show
visitors all the best-known features
of Biarritz, from the Côte and Plage
des Basques, rocky cove of Port-
Vieux, the esplanade (maritime
mus., aquarium), Rocher de la
Vierge, and plateau of L'Atalaye, to
fishing port and the Grande Plage
(casinos), which extends NE as far
as the Hôtel du Palais (on site of
Napoleon III's summer residence)
and St. Martin's point (lighthouse).
The old village, clustered round
mid-16c country church of St.
Martin, is still picturesque in parts.
Son et Lumière in summer.
Vicinity ● To S. along Ave.
Kennedy and Ave. du Bois-de-
Boulogne, Mouriscot lake (or Lac
de la Négresse), surrounded by
woods and lawns. ● 7 km NE, via
La Chambre d'Amour and Chib-
erta forest, *Barre de l'Adour* (see
Bayonne*). ● 8 km E, **Bayonne*** via
Anglet (13c church). ● 8.5 km SE,
Arcangues: 16c church, Basque int.
with carved wooden galleries, 18c
ornamentation in choir. ● To SW,
along coast road, *Bidart*, (5 km to
E, *Arbonne*, typical Basque village),
Guéthary (17c church of St.
Nicolas) and **St. Jean-de-Luz***.

Bienassis (Château)
22 – Côtes-du-Nord 9 – B 2
Magnificent 16–17c rose-coloured
granite building (v.a. in summer, cl.
Sun.). Entry through turreted
doorway in crenellated wall flanked
by two gatehouses. Exquisitely-
furnished apartments.

Vicinity ● To W, *Val-André* (2 km -
long beach), point at *Pléneuf, Île de
Verdelet*. To N, coast and promontory of *Erquy*, magnificent cliffs
of purple sandstone.

Billom
63 – Puy-de-Dôme 31 – A 1
This little town had its own university from 13 to 15c. On l. bank of
R. Angaud, closed quarter around
church of St. Cerneuf, whose late
13c vaulted choir (one of oldest in
Auvergne) is built over a late 11c
crypt; interesting works of art (12c
screen, tombs). Numerous old
houses in Rue des Boucheries.
Also rec.: 16c magistrates' house,
chapter-house, belfry, etc.
Vicinity ● 6 km NNE, Glaine-
Montaigut, 11c Romanesque
church; choir has beautiful capitals.
● 10 km SE, 12–16c castle at
Mauzun: fine view from its impressive ruins, bristling with 14 towers
(v.a.).

Biot
06 – Alpes-Maritimes 45 – A 1
In church, two retables by 15c local
early masters. 2 km outside town,
Mas St. André: Fernand Léger mus.
(cl. Tues.); 400 sq. m. polychrome
mosaic on façade; int. has range of
the great artist's work: paintings,
tapestries, sculptures, ceramics,
etc.; on terrace: group in polychrome ceramic entitled *Le Jardin
des Enfants*. Tiny local history
museum (v.a. Thurs., Sat. and Sun.
p.m.; cl. Nov., Dec.).
Vicinity ● 9 km W, *Valbonne*, built
on rectangular grid pattern, with
central square lined by arcades. ●
3 km NW, 11c Notre-Dame-de-
Brusc, built over Paleo-Christian
sanctuary whose baptistry has been
excavated; archaeological digs have

*Biot: on the façade of the Fernand Léger museum is a huge mosaic on
the theme of sport, its brilliant colours in striking contrast to the
austerity of the countryside.*

uncovered prehistoric remains and a Roman necropolis.

Biron (Castle)
24 – Dordogne   35 – D 1
The castle, an impressive, complex building, dates from various periods between 11–12c and 18c; standing on a 236 m. rock, it commands a breathtaking view (v.a., cl. Tues. exc. during July and Aug.). Most of the towers and fortified walls are 15c, living quarters are 17 and 18c Ren. Two-storey 15 and 16c chapel (carved monumental tombs); lower storey serves as parish church.
Vicinity ● Recommended excursions, via *Lacapelle-Biron* (4 km S) to gorges of Gavaudun.

Biville
50 – Manche   3 – C 2
Village stands on plateau overlooking wild shoreline of *Vauville* cove. In church, marble sarcophagus of the blessed Thomas Hélie (d. 1257), pilgrimage centre.
Vicinity ● 14 km S, tiny port of *Diélette*; 2.5 km to S, *Flamainville*: mid-17c château comprises imposing collection of granite buildings surrounding a courtyard; v.a. only to the park, which is dotted with ornamental lakes; recommended excursion along *Cap de Flamainville*, fine view from clifftop.

Blasimon
33 – Gironde   35 – B 1
The 12–13c fmr. abbey church of St. Nicolas has noteworthy Romanesque façade surmounted by wall-belfry; main doorway, also Romanesque, is one of loveliest in reg.; its pointed arches are decorated with sculpted figures representing a hunting scene, angels holding the instruments of the Passion, and the Vices and Virtues, all of a subtle elegance; ruins of mid-12c chapter-house and of cloister. Municipal mus. (paleontology, archaeology).
Vicinity ● 2 km N, mill of Labarthe, fortified 14c, in picturesque site. ● 6.5 km S, *Sauveterre-de-Guyenne*, typical late 13c bastide with four fortified gates and huge central square with 'cornières'.

Blaye
33 – Gironde   29 – A 3
To W of town, on R. Gironde, the 17c citadel stands on a clifftop plateau; entry via two huge gates. A veritable township in itself, its sights include Town Major's house (mus. of local hist. and art), ruins of a Goth. fortress, Place d'Armes, 17c Franciscan convent, Aiguillette

Blois: *the great staircase in the château's François I wing is decorated with the French royal salamanders and monograms.*

tower (panorama), etc. Facing citadel, forts of Pâté (on islet) and Médoc (17c).
Vicinity ● 14 km SE, picturesque *Bourg*, on edge of cliff above R. *Dordogne*; upper town, originally fortified, is dominated by castle of 17c citadel; to E, from terrace of Le District, magnificent panorama of confluence of Dordogne and Garonne (viewing table); 2.5 km downstream, Bec d'Ambès, oil port; 6 km E of *Bourg*, prehistoric grotto of Pair-non-Pair (v.a.).

Blesle
43 – Haut-Loire   31 – A 2
One of most picturesque cities in Auvergne. In 10–11c Romanesque former abbey church of St. Pierre, interesting treasure, 14c belfry of St. Martin; remains of outer walls and 13c keep; former abbey courtyard (now town hall square) is surrounded by 15c buildings (one-time canonesses' houses); town hall is in 13c abbot's house.
Vicinity ● Gorges de l'Allagnon (Babory 'organ pipes') to N as far

as *Lempdes* (Romanesque church), ruins of *Ch. de Léotoing* (fine view).

Blois
41 – Loir-et-Cher   18 – A 2
The château, dominating R. *Loire*, was built in four main stages: 13c, 15c, Ren., 17c (v.a., Son et Lumière Apr.–Sept.). Entry into main courtyard is through late 15c Louis XII wing, in brick and stone; in N corner, vast 13c Salle des États joins Louis XII to 16c François I wing, which is richly sculpted and decorated and famed for its elegantly sculpted open staircase enclosed in an octagonal tower. At W end, mid-17c Gaston d'Orléans wing, in Classical style. Early 16c St. Calais chapel is linked to Louis XII wing by so-called Charles d'Orléans gallery. Attractive view of town from Le Foix terrace. On first floor of François I wing are the queen's apartments and on second, those of Henri III where the Duc de Guise was assassinated in 1588; ground floor houses town archaeological mus. (objects from local digs). On first floor of Louis XII wing, fine arts mus., Dutch and Italian paintings, decorative arts. ● Town is rich in historic buildings: fmr. abbey church of St. Nicolas, Romanesque and Goth.; cath. of St. Louis, rebuilt 18c in Goth. style (under choir: 10–11c crypt). Fmr. archbishop's palace (18c) now houses town hall, whose gardens cover two long terraces. Old town clusters around Place de l'Ave Maria; its streets are lined with 15 and 16c houses. Two beautiful Ren. mansions in Rue St. Honoré: early 16c Alluye mansion with remarkable int. courtyard, and early 16c Denis-Dupont mansion. Robert-Houdin mus. is devoted to the world-famed Blois-born illusionist, Houdini (v.a.). ● On l. bank of *Loire*, St. Saturnien cemetery, with early 16c galleries and lapidary museum 500 m. upstream from new bridge over *Loire* is a 600-acre lake with big water sports complex.
Vicinity ● To SE, châteaux of **Beauregard***, **Cheverny***, *Villesavin*, *Herbault*. ● To E, Ch. de **Chambord***. ● To NE, châteaux of **Menars*** and **Talcy***.

Bonaguil (Castle)
47 – Lot-et-Garonne   35 – D 1
The impressive remains of this formidable fortress are a unique example of late 15–early 16c military architecture. The castle (v.a. Mar.–Oct., floodlit in summer) has 350 m. perimeter wall with 13 towers, and 13c keep. It was designed to facilitate artillery fire. Archaeological and iconographic mus.

Bonifacio
2A – Corsica   45 – D 2

The old town, or upper town, perched on a steep fortified headland, is criss-crossed by tiny streets lined with tall houses joined by flying-buttresses, which often rise abruptly over the sea. 12–13c church of Ste. Marie-Majeure, Count Cattacciolo's house (Ren. door) and, opposite, Passano house, where Napoleon lived (1795). Citadel, on W tip of cape, is occupied by Foreign Legion (n.v.a.). Church of st. Dominique is in 13–14c S. Goth. style (guided tour). An old paved ramp leads down to the port; standing back from the headland, in narrow inlet, is most typical quarter of Bonifacio – La Marine; mus. with aquaria built in natural grotto.

Vicinity ● Tour of marine grottoes (45 min.), esp. grotto of Sdragonato. ● Rec. excursions to *Ermitage de la Trinité* (6 km NW), *Cap Pertusato* (5 km to S, 45 min. walk), signal station and lighthouse, marvellous view of Bonifacio and Straits of Sardinia. ● Year-round daily boat service to Sardinia.

Boquen (Abbey)
22 – Côtes-du-Nord   9 – B 3

Founded 12c on N edge of *Forêt de Boquen*, reoccupied by monks in 1936; v.a. to Romanesque abbey church, 72 m. long, with 14c choir; ruins of 12c chapter-house.

Bordeaux
33 – Gironde   29 – A 3

Capital of Aquitaine. ● The heart of the town is the Place de la Comédie with its late 18c neo-Classical Grand-Théâtre, among finest of its kind. To l., Cours du 30 Juillet and Esplanade des Quinconces with enormous monument to the Girondins in centre; on E terrace, 21 m.-high rostral columns. To r., along Quai Maréchal-Lyautey, is Place de la Bourse, magnificent ensemble of 18c buildings; interesting museum. ● Next to mainly Goth. 14–15c cath. of St. André (beautiful 13c sculpted Porte Royale) is 15c Tour Pey-Berland, 48 m. high. Behind cath., imposing late 18c town hall, former Rohan palace; wings overlooking garden house: to S, reg. mus. (prehist. and Gallo-Roman archaeology); to N, fine arts mus., Flemish, Dutch, Italian (Veronese, Titian, etc.) and French paintings (esp. 19c: Delacroix, Redon, Renoir, etc.); two large 20c collections: Marquet and Lhote; works by Matisse, Soutine, Bissière, Zadkine, Despiau. Natnl. Centre Jean Moulin (resistance and deportation). Natural hist. mus. in 18c Lisleferme mansion. Mus. of decorative arts in 18c Lalande

mansion: marvellous furniture, miniatures, pottery, gold and silver plate, and ironwork, in beautiful rooms (cl. Tues.). ● Principal churches: late 12c St. Seurin, with 11c porch and 11c crypt (apply to sacristan), contains large lapidary collection; 15c St. Michel (beneath bell tower: strange mummies' cave) (n.v.a); 12–13c Ste. Croix, original Romanesque façade, etc. ● Also ruins of the Gallien palace, really the remains of 3c Roman amphitheatre; and, at beginning of Rue St. James, 13–14c Porte de la Grosse Cloche (tiny Goth. church of St. Éloi).

Vicinity ● Tour of the *Médoc*, to NW, on l. bank of R. *Gironde*, world-famed vineyards (magnificent red wines) and chateaux: neo-Classical *Ch. Margaux*, whose apartments still have their original Empire-style décor and furnishings (v.a. by permission only), mid-18c *Ch. Beychevelle*, amid terraced gardens (v.a. by permission); fascinating wine mus. at 15 and 17–18c Ch. Mouton-Rothschild, at *Pauillac* (v.a. by permission only); recommended Romanesque churches at *Vertheuil*, with three naves under 15c ribbed vaulting and two steeples, beautiful

Bonifacio: *strung out along a sheer limestone cliff, the old houses often jut precariously over the sea.*

Bordeaux: *the cathedral, its flying-buttresses bristling with pinnacle turrets, is a masterpiece of Gothic architecture.*

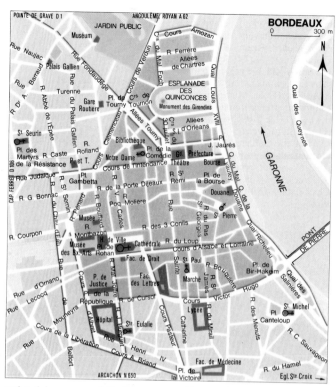

BORDEAUX

0   300 m

Bort-les-Orgues: *columns of basalt, like organ pipes.*

sculpted doorway, and *St. Laurent-de-Médoc.*

Bormes-les-Mimosas
83 – Var   44 – C 2

Built in a natural amphitheatre at foot of Massif des Maures, this picturesque flower-filled old village has narrow streets intersected by postern-gates and arches. The Montée Belle-Vue leads up to terrace of 12–13c former castle of the lords of Fos, from which the view is magnificent. Cazin mus. (late 19c paintings, two casts by Rodin).
Vicinity ● 9.5 km , *Fort de Brégançon*, French President's summer residence. ● To N, **Collobrières***, via Dom natnl. forest and Col de Babaou. ● To E, a tiny road, the Corniche des Crêtes, links Bormes, via Col de Caguo-Ven, to Col de Canadel (15 km E) in heart of *Massif des Maures.*

Bort-les-Orgues
19 – Corrèze   30 – C 2

On r. bank of R. *Dordogne*, dominated, 3 km downstream, by the 'organ-pipes' of Bort, name given to enormous colonnades of phonolitic rock, 80 to 100 m. high. Many grottoes in area. 2 km upstream: Bort dam, 120 m. high, across the river. In summer, boat trip to Ch. de **Val***.

Vicinity ● To SE *Gorges de la Rhue*; via Cournilloux (24 km from Bort), Gabacut waterfalls. ● To SW, via *Champagnac*, and, l. before Serandon, picturesque Route des Ajustants follows gorges of *Dordogne*, rejoins D 682, crosses Dordogne by St. Projet bridge and ends at **Mauriac***. ● 8 km W, *site de St. Nazaire*; on rocky outcrop, statue of the saint and a calvary look down

on confluence of Dordogne and R. Diège; fine view.

Bouges (Château)
36 – Indre   24 – B 1

Berry's mid-18c answer to the Petit Trianon (at Versailles), surrounded by park and formal gardens, houses collection of 18c furniture which includes some extremely valuable pieces (daily July 1–Sept. 30; Nov. 1–Mar. 30, Wed. p.m., Sat. and Sun.; Apr. 1–June 30 and Oct., cl. Tues.). In 18c outbuildings, large stables: collection of saddles, harnessing, and 1900 veteran cars.
Vicinity ● 12 km SW, *Levroux*, 13c collegiate church of St. Sylvain, built on Gallo-Roman ruins, 15c timbered houses (carved figures).

Boulogne-Billancourt
92 – Hauts-de-Seine   11 – C 3

Unusual Albert Kahn gardens (Vosges forest, English landscape garden, Japanese garden, French formal garden, orchard, rose garden, v.a.). *Île St. Germain* partly converted into public garden. Paul Landowski garden-mus. Paul Marmottan Napoleonic library (small mus.). Municipal mus. in town hall.

Boulogne-sur-Mer
62 – Pas-de-Calais   1 – B 2

France's premier fishing port, also a commercial port. Upper town is bounded on all four sides by ramparts, broken by four gates flanked by towers. In centre, Place Godefroy de Bouillon, 18c town hall, 18c Androuins mansion and Goth.

Bormes-les-Mimosas: *typical Provençal village, lying between the forest of Dom and the sea*

belfry. 12c castle (n.v.a.). In basilica of Notre-Dame, 11c crypt (well-known pilgrimage to the Virgin). Mus. (most important collection of Greek vases after the Louvre's). A second mus. (reg. art, pottery, Eskimo masks) is being set up in castle. Natnl. maritime centre also planned. Tour of harbour installations.
Vicinity ● Follow *Côte d'Opale* corniche road to **Calais*** via capes *Gris-Nez* and *Blanc-Nez*. ● 5 km N, Colonne de la Grande-Armée, 53 m. (1841). ● 5 km S, 18c château of Pont-de-Briques, where Napoleon once lived (small museum).

Bourbon-Lancy
71 – Saône-et-Loire   25 – B 2
Spa. The old town climbs up a hillside. Old houses, clock gate and tower; in 11–12c church of St. Nazaire, small museum of local antiquities.
Vicinity ● 7 km E, Signal de *Mont*; good view from observation point (472 m.). ● 6 km S, château at St. Aubin-sur-Loire, noble example of Classical style from second half of 18c (v.a. July–Sept. 1, p.m., cl. Tues.); beautiful apartments, exquisitely decorated and furnished (tapestries, panelling); imposing outbuildings.

Bourbon-l'Archambault
03 – Allier   24 – D 2
Spa, well-known since ancient times. Impressive ruins of castle, rebuilt 14c: to N, three fine round towers (of 24), connected by a curtain, and, to S, huge Quiquengrogne tower capped by modern belfry. 12c Romanesque church of St. Georges, enlarged 15 and 19c; 15 and 16c capitals and statues. Unusual 14c fortified mill beside pond. Augustin Barnard mus. (collection of pharmacy jars, prehistory and ethnography).
Vicinity ● 9 km E, *St Menoux*: 12c former abbey church is one of most beautiful in region ● 10 km SW, *Ygrande*: 12c church, lovely stone steeple.

Bourboule (La)
63 – Puy-de-Dôme   30 – D 2
Spa and winter sports centre at 850 m. alt., in upper *Dordogne* valley (Massif du Sancy, see **Le Mont-Dore***). Fenêstre park. 'Fairy Rock' (fine view of town and surrounding area). Good excursion centre.
Vicinity ● 7 km N, via Murat-le-Quaire, then footpath, *Banne d'Ordanche* (1,515 m.), magnificent views of volcanoes of Auvergne and valley of *Dordogne*. ● 2.5 km E, then footpaths, cascades of La Vernière and Le Plat à Barbe. ● 4.5 km SE, then footpath, Vendeix Rock

(1,130 m.), magnificent panorama. ● 7 km S, marked footpaths, Charlannes plateau (1,250 m.), views of Dore and Cantal mountains.

Bourdeilles (Castle)
24 – Dordogne   29 – C 2
Perched on a steep promontory, it consists of two completely separate buildings: one 14c, enclosed by fortified perimeter wall, over which towers 34 m.-high octagonal keep; the other Ren., whose int. boasts marble dining hall and sumptuously decorated gold room (cl. Tues., otherwise daily July–Aug.).
Vicinity ● *Dronne* valley. ● 5 km W, late 16c. Ch. de Maroitte; 4.5 km SW, **Grand-Brassac***.

Bourg-d'Oisans (Le)
38 – Isère   32 – C 3
Main town of Oisans region. Excellent excursion centre.
Vicinity ● 14 km NE, **L'Alpe d'Huez***. ● To E, Route des Grands Cols (high passes), round *Grandes Rousses* mountains, via *Châmbon* dam (315-acre lake) across R. *Romanche*, imposing structure 90 m. high by 294 m. long (1927–1935); Malaval combe, a long ravine through which flows R. *Romanche* (torrents, occasional glimpses of glaciers); *La Grave*, leading mountaineering centre at foot of mt. *Meije* (12c church, surrounded by cemetery, 17c chapel of Pénitents Blancs); **Col du Lautaret***, 2,058 m.; via *Col du Galibier*, **St. Michel-de-Maurienne***, **St. Jean-de-Maurienne***, then via passes of *Croix-de-Fer* and *Glandon* to *Rochetaillée*. ● To SE, **St. Christophe-en-Oisans***, *La Bérarde*.

Bourg-en-Bresse
01 – Ain   26 – A 3
Church and monastery of *Brou*, in outskirts of town, along N 75, were built in 16c. The church is perfect jewel of stonecarvers' art: choir, lined by 74 stalls in carved oak, with brilliantly coloured stained-glass windows, is separated from nave by richly decorated rood-screen in Goth. Flamboyant style; it houses extravagantly decorated tombs of Philibert le Beau, Duke of Savoy, his wife, Margaret of Austria, and his mother, Margaret of Bourbon; on altar, huge 16c Flemish alabaster retable of *Sept Joies de la Vierge* (Seven Joys of the Virgin).

Boulogne: *a view of one of France's busiest ports.*

Bourdeilles: *a Gothic bridge spans the Dronne below the castle.*

Monastery buildings spread out around three cloisters: reg. mus. (re-creation of local house, furniture, handicrafts, folklore, contemp. art).
Vicinity ● Along N 83, to S, through the *Dombes*, dotted with lakes, *St. Paul-de-Varax* (Romanesque church, charming 15c brick manor-house), *Villars-les-Dombes* (reg. nature reserve and zoo park); 7 km from St. Paul: Trappist monastery of Notre-Dame-des-Dombes.

Bourges
18 – Cher   18 – C 3
One of the most important cities of artistic interest in France. Façade of 13c cath. of St. Étienne offers you choice of five doorways which – especially the centre one – rank among the masterpieces of Goth. sculpture; inside, warm blues and reds of 13c stained-glass windows form exceptionally beautiful patterns; in late 12c crypt (cl. Sun. a.m. and Tues.), fragments of 13c rood-screen and 15c marble recumbent figure of Duke of Berry, 14c stain-ed-glass windows. Jacques Coeur mansion (v.a., cl. Tues.) is one of most notable Goth. civil buildings of 15c. Cujas mansion, charming early 16c Ren. building, houses Berry reg. mus. (archaeology, folk arts and trad.). Late 15c Lallemant mansion (elegantly decorated Ren. façade) houses archaeology and decorative art, dolls and toys. Also rec., magistrate's house, fmr. town hall and many old houses in Place Gordaine, Rues Mirebeau and Pel-voysin (Pelvoysin house, Caisse d'Epargne – savings bank – Goth. façade), Rue des Arènes which leads to 13c St. Pierre-le-Guillard (15c chapel). Gabriel Foucher mus. (natural history).
Vicinity ● 16 km NW, *Mehun-sur-Yèvre*, ruins of Duke John of Berry's 14c château (small mus.); 11 and 12c Romanesque collegiate church. ● 12 km SE, *Plaimpied*, fmr. abbey, Romanesque church (fine historiated capitals), 15c monastery buildings; 10 km to S, ruins of early 15c castle of Bois-Sir-Amé, home of Agnès Sorel (Charles VII's beautiful mistress).

Bourg-en-Bresse: *this graceful statuette is one of ten Sybils or virtues on the tomb of Philippe le Beau in the church at Brou.*▲

Bucolic scene in the Dombes zoological park ▲ ▲

Bourgonnière (Chateau)
49 – Maine-et-Loire   16 – D 2
Built 19c in large park; only a cyl-indrical tower and a machicolated keep remain of 15c castle. Chapel (v.a.) is an elegant Ren. building, with turrets; ext. is decorated with shells and taus; charming, delicately sculpted doorway; inside, nave with star-shaped vaulting, with hanging keystones and sculpted coats of arms; noteworthy early 16c Ren. retables in Italian manner: seign-eurial pews decorated with bizarre grotesques.
Vicinity ● To SW, near *Bouzillé*, Ch. de la Mauvaisinière, in Louis XIII style, encircled by moat.

Bourg-St. Andéol
07 – Ardèche   37 – D 2
Noteworthy Romanesque church contains sarcophagus of 3c martyr, St. Andéol, sculpted in 12c. Chapel of St. Polycarpe, beside the church, is Merovingian crypt of a long-lost church. Remains of Goth. and mid-16c Ren. Nicolaï mansion. A boarding school now occupies fmr. palace of bishops of Viviers, lovely early 16c Goth. façade overlooking R. *Rhône*. In hospice, fmr. convent, 15 and 17c cloisters, and richly dec-orated late 16c chapel. 10 km to SW, Tournes fountain, topped by huge 2c bas-relief of Mithras.

Bournazel (Château)
12 – Aveyron   36 – C 2
Magnificent Ren. building (v.a. to ext. only). Three 15c towers frame its remarkable façade, along which Doric and Ionic columns are super-posed. N wing dates from first half of Ren., E wing from second half. Classically-inspired ornamental sculpture is of finest quality.

Boussac
23 – Creuse   24 – C-2
Standing on rocky promontory, 15–

Bourget (Le)
93 – Seine-St. Denis   11 – C 1
The airport has been closed to com-mercial traffic since 1977. Terminal building houses v. large Mus. of Air and Space (cl. Mon.), whose col-lections illustrate history of aero-nautics and conquest of space from beginnings of aviation to days of Mirage jet and Ariane space rocket. Many spacecraft (Sputnik, Soyuz, etc.) are on show in huge Hall of Space. In old village, tiny fmr. country church of St. Nicolas.

Bourget-du-Lac (Le)
73 – Savoie   32 – B 1
On lake of same name: beach, watersports. 13 and 15c church with Carolingian crypt; round choir, fine 13c stone sculpted frieze, repre-senting scenes from the Gospels. 15c priory castle with two-storey cloister gallery, park in Italian style.
Vicinity ● Trip round *Lac du Bourget* via Abbey of **Hautecombe***, *Conjux,* Savières canal, **Aix-les-Bains***. ● To NE, *Yenne* via Col du Chat (see **Belley***).

BRAMABIAU
30 – Gard 37 – A 3
R. Bonheur, which rises at foot of Mt. *Aigoual*, buries itself in the causse and, after running underground for 700 m., gushes out in fantastically-shaped rocky amphitheatre, known as the Alcove. The sound it makes is reminiscent of roaring of a bull: 'bramabiau', the bellowing bull (v.a. Easter–mid. Oct., depending on water-level).

Bourges: *a picture of harmony – the soaring turrets and graceful flying-buttresses of the magnificent cathedral.*

16c castle is flanked by imposing towers, from which there is a wide view; int. (v.a.) contains large guardroom with monumental fireplace; interesting tapestries and furniture, 13–15c church, picturesque view from Petite-Creuse bridge.
Vicinity ● 6 km S, Pierres-Jaumâtres, enormous granitic blocks in fantastic shapes, 595 m. up on summit of Mt. Barlot, in barren countryside; 5 km to S, *Toulx-Ste. Croix*, on granite hill, 655 m. alt.; wide panorama; remains of

oppidum and successive perimeter walls; village is v. picturesque; 12c Romanesque granite church with isolated belfry-porch, containing sarcophagi; 23 m. radio relay tower (well worth ascending for magnificent view from top).

Bozouls
12 – Aveyron 36 – D 2
The 'Bozouls hole', a deep canyon dug by R. Dourdou in the red sandstone, is one of most extraordinary sites in the Causses. Town still looks as it did in Middle Ages. 12c

BRÉHAT (Island)
22 – Côtes-du-Nord 9 – A 1
10 min. boat trip from *Pointe de l'Arcouest*. This 'island of flowers and pink rocks' has very jagged coastline; cliffs and rocks of pink granite contrast with Mediterranean vegetation. Town of Bréhat has an interesting Goth. church. Phare du Paon ('Peacock Lighthouse') rises above extraordinary, chaotic piles of pink rocks. Boat trip round island strongly recommended.

Romanesque church with 15 and 16c chapels. Old houses on cliff edge.

Brantôme
24 – Dordogne 29 – C 2
Standing on island formed by two arms of R. *Dronne*, this is one of the loveliest towns in the Périgord. Isolated Romanesque belfry towers over former Benedictine abbey, rebuilt 18c (superb staircase – curious museum of mediumistic paintings by Fernand Desmoulin). The many grottoes, in cliffs behind, often have finely carved interiors. 12 and 13c church; remains of cloisters (delightful late 15c gallery) and chapter-house. At end of Promenade des Terrasses, Ren. pavilion adjoining 16c elbow bridge, from which there is splendid view of the abbey.
Vicinity ● 11 km SW, castle at **Bourdeilles***. ● 1 km E, Pierre-Levée dolmen. ● 12 km NE via *Champagnac-de-Belair*, *Villars;* 4 km to NE, lovely grottoes with concretions, and prehist. paintings and carvings (v.a. in summer); 1 km to NW of *Villars*, Ren. Ch. de Puyguilhem, finely sculpted decoration (v.a. daily, July–Aug.; rest of year, cl. Tues.). ● 8 km E of *Villars*, *St. Jean-de-Côle*, late 11c Romanesque church (Romanesque historiated capitals, 16c panelling and choirstalls). ● 22 km N, *Nontron*: picturesque town standing on steep promontory, from which there is fine view; in vicinity, St. Estèphe rocking stone, Saut du Chalard, etc.

Brasparts
29S – Finistère 8 – C 2
Numerous parish buildings. Mid-16c church with Ren. porch embellished with statues. Calvary.
Vicinity ● 6 km N, *Montagne St. Michel* (380 m. alt.), fine view of *Monts d'Arrée* and *Montagnes Noires;* **Parc Naturel Régional d'Armorique*** covers 270 sq. miles; park hq at Domaine de Menez-Meur (reception and inf. centre, v.a.); Centre for Rural Techniques and Trads., and centre for Apiculture at *St. Rivoal;* 9.5 km NE of Montagne St. Michel, the sharp schist needles of *Roc Trévezel* (wide view); W of Montagne St. Michel, *Le Faou* road, one of loveliest in Brittany, crosses *Monts d'Arrée* via *St. Rivoal, Forêt du Cranou* and *Rumengol* (pardons to Our-Lady-of-All-the-Cures on Trinity Sun. and Aug. 15).

Bressuire
79 – Deux-Sèvres 23 – A1
Romanesque church of Notre-Dame, with late 16c Goth. choir, magnificent 56 m.-high Ren. steeple, small municipal mus. Ruins

of castle (v.a.), perched on a rocky outcrop, comprise two perimeter walls, a barbican and numerous 11–15c towers; 15c inner wall encloses ruins of living quarters overlooked by tower of the Treasury.
Vicinity ● 17 km N, *Argenton-Château*, church with Romanesque doorway, adorned with sculpted vaulting; 2.5 km to NE, ruins of 15c pink granite château of *Ébaupinay*.

Brest
29N – Finistère   8 – B 2
France's premier naval port; its rade (shipping roads) and surrounding coast are among loveliest

nou has one of loveliest churches in reg. (early 17c); beautifully sculpted Ren. N side door.

Briançon
05 – Hautes-Alpes   32 – D 3
Highest city in Europe. Upper town, fmr. stronghold at 1,326 m. alt., enclosed by Vauban's ramparts, has remained unchanged since 17c. Between Pignerol and Embrun gates: network of narrow streets, bisected by Grand-Rue, with stream called the 'gargouille' running down middle. Church of Notre-Dame, also by Vauban, is part of town's defensive system;

which road divides at Esteyère fork: to E, **Château-Queyras***, *Guil* valley and *Queyras* park; to SW, narrow gorges of R. *Guil*, or Queyras combe, *Guillestre* and **Mont-Dauphin***.

Brie-Comte-Robert
77 – Seine-et-Marne   11 – D 2
13c church of St. Étienne, renovated 15 and 16c: 13c stained-glass windows (in 15 and 16c apse); 13c tomb in N side aisle). Old hospital (chapel has Goth. façade). Castle ruins.
Vicinity ● 8 km NW, Ch. de **Gros-Bois***.

Briançon: *the towers of the church of Notre-Dame rise above Europe's highest city. In the background are the breathtaking, snow-capped peaks of the Alps.*

in world. Old town was destroyed in 1944. Castle, a strongly fortified 12–14–16c building, looms over town and port; keep and naval mus. (ship models, paintings) (v.a. to both, cl. Tues.). Cours Dajot and Kennedy garden, laid out on Vauban's ramparts (panoramic table, fine view). Fine Arts mus. (cl. Tues., Sun. a.m. and public hols.): 17–18c Italian school, late 18–19c neo-Classical paintings, Pont-Aven school and Symbolism. V.a. to old part of Penfeld arsenal and Lannion naval base. 14c La Motte-Tanguy tower: town history museum.
Vicinity ● Brest is rec. excursion centre for its *goulet* and *rade*, *Conquet* estuary (24 km W) and *Pointe St. Mathieu* (ruins of huge 13c abbey church, 14c doorway and chapel of Notre-Dame-des-Grâces), *Léon* coast (W–N), *Élorn* river basin and its noteworthy religious monuments, *Monts d'Arrée* (to E), etc. ● 8 km N, *Goues-*

behind, viewing table. Imposing citadel or castle fort (guided tour); on upper platform, colossal statue of *La France* by Bourdelle.
Vicinity ● 6 km W, *Serre-Chevalier-Chantemerle*, major winter sports centre (cable car, well-equipped sports centre, mountaineering school, etc.); upper resort of Serre-Chevalier is at 2,483 m., panoramic table, magnificent view. ● To NW. via *Guisane* valley and *Le Monétier-les-Bains,* **Col du Lautaret***. ● To N, lovely *Clarée* valley as far as *chalets de Laval* via *Névache* (15c church). ● 12 km NE, *Montgenèvre*, winter sports resort below *Col de Montgenèvre* (1,854 m.), cable-car to Chalvet ridge (2,630 m.); beyond pass, French and Italian customs posts. ● 21.5 km SE, via Cerveyrette gorge and *Cervières, Col d'Izoard* (2,340 m., viewing table); after mountain pass, road crosses Casse Déserte, vast amphitheatre of reddish rocks, to *Arvieux*, after

Brienne-le-Château
10 – Aube   12 – C 3
Late 18c château is elegant and sober in style (psychotherapy centre, n.v.a.). In fmr. Franciscan convent, once a military academy where Napoleon was a student (1779–1784), Napoleonic museum.
Vicinity ● 2.5 km S, Brienne-la-Vieille, church with 12c nave, 16c choir and transept; Romanesque doorway. ● To N, *Rosnay-l'Hôpital*, lovely 12 and 16c church with 16c crypt, statues and stained-glass windows. ● To S, *Forêt d'Orient*, reg. nature reserve, dotted with numerous pools and dams; large artificial lake of Seine Reservoir (fishing, beach, water sports) has bird sanctuary on its NW bank; beautiful oak, beech and hornbeam woods; in old provincial house, tourist inf. centre; St. Charles pavilion, nature studies centre; sailing bases at *Mesnil-St. Père* (sailing school, beach, harbour instal-

Brière: *one of the thatched cottages typical of this somewhat uncommon region.*

BRIÉRE (Parc régional)
44 – Loire-Atlantique   16 – A 2 – 16 – B 2
One of France's most picturesque regions: 1,700 sq. miles of marshes, meadows and peat bogs – including more than 57 sq. miles for *La Grande Brière* – with a few scattered villages built on small granitic islands and linked by 100 km of canals. From **Guérande***, D51 leads to *St. Lyphard* and *La-Chapelle-des-Marais*, from where D50 to SE crosses *Grande Brière* via Camerun (typical habitat), Kerfeuille; *St. Joachim* on narrow island of Pendille is joined by 1 km road to island of Fedrun, perfect example of ring-shaped village. Ecological mus. at Kerhinet. Boat trips on canals.

lations, etc.); equestrian centre at Montreuil-sur-Barse.

Brignoles
83 – Var   44 – C 2
Ruined castle of Counts of Provence dominates old quarter with its narrow, winding streets. Church of St. Sauveur in 15–16c Provençal Goth. style (beautiful Romanesque doorway). Local mus. exhibits 3c Gayole sarcophagus, oldest Christian monument of ancient Gaul yet found.

Brignoles: *a bauxite quarry in the typically Provençal hills surrounding this local wine-growing centre.*

Vicinity ● 2.5 km SW, fmr. abbey of *La Celle*, of which only Romanesque church (circa 1200) and 17c monastery buildings still stand; remains of chapter-house, cloisters, refectory, etc. ● 13 km SW, *Montagne de la Loube*, picturesque climb, fine view; reached by private road from *La Roquebrussanne* road.

Brigue (La)
06 – Alpes-Maritimes   39 – B 3
Attractive Alpine township with narrow streets lined by houses of local greenish stone. Early 13c church of St. Martin, with Lombard-style belfry, has, in Lascaris chapel, early 16c retable of Notre-Dame-des-Neiges, with rococo frame, *retable de la Nativité* by Louis Brea, and several other works of art.
Vicinity ● 5 km NE, Notre-Dame-des-Fontaines: built at 866 m. alt., above seven intermittent springs; int. of chapel is entirely decorated with murals by late 15c Jean Canavesio which represent, in vividly expressionist style, scenes from Life and Passion of Christ in period costumes (key at Auberge St. Martin, Place de l'Église).

Brionne
27 – Eure   10 – D 1
Standing in shadow of ruins of typically Norman 12c square keep, 14–15c church contains remarkable works of art from abbey of **Le Bec-Hellouin***.
Vicinity ● 6 km SE, *Harcourt*, 14c feudal castle surrounded by moat, renovated 17c, arboretum (v.a., p.m., summer season, cl. Tues.), conifers and exotic species.

Brioude
43 – Haute-Loire   31 – A 2
Basilica of St. Julien is one of Auvergne's finest Romanesque churches; inside, nave and side aisles have fine historiated capitals; 12c murals, in a chapel in gallery, in l. side aisle; 15c leprous Christ and 16c Virgin in childbirth.
Vicinity ● 9 km SE, *Lavaudieu*: church (14c frescos in nave) and 12c Romanesque two-tiered cloister are all that remain of fmr. Benedictine abbey; in refectory, 13c fresco and interesting works of art.

Brissac (Château)
49 – Maine-et-Loire   17 – A2
At *Brissac-Quincé*. Magnificent early 17c building, among most beautiful châteaux in Anjou (v.a. throughout most of the year, cl. Tues.). E wing, two 15c machicolated towers, also has tall Henri IV-styled domed pavilion, with Ren.

Brissac: *home of the Maréchal de Cossé, 16th-century military chief who was made Duc de Brissac.*

decorations. Inside, large apartments furnished according to 16c taste, many works of art.

Brive-la-Gaillarde
19 – Corrèze   30 – A 3
Old town is encircled by boulevards which have replaced original ramparts. Church of St. Martin, Romanesque with lovely 14c nave. Ernest Rupin mus. (cl. Sun.): prehist., Gallo-Roman and medieval archaeology; 16–19c paintings; local handicrafts. Labenche mansion is elegant Ren. building.
Vicinity • 1.5 km and 5.5 km S, grottoes of St. Anthony of Padua (church and pilgrimage) and Lamouroux. • 13 km E, *Aubazine*, 12c Romanesque church; inside, 13c tomb of St. Étienne d'Obazine (local 12c saint who founded abbey on site) and 12c cupboard, one of oldest pieces of furniture in France; 16–17c monastery build-

ings (orphanage). • 11.5 km N, *Donzenac*: Romanesque church; inside, valuable works of art (13c reliquary, 13c enamelled pyxis, etc.); 6 km to NW, *Allassac*: 12c fortified church, 11 and 12c Caesar's Tower; remains of perimeter walls.

Brouage
17 – Charente-Maritime   28 – D 1
This small town surrounded by ramparts in manner of Vauban, known familiarly as 'the Aigues-Mortes of the Saintes region', was formerly a prosperous port; nowadays, it is surrounded by marshes and pastures (Son et Lumière in summer). Rec. tour of perimeter walls (apply to Tourist Office for guide), flanked by seven bastions. See also Governor's House, powder magazine, late 17c grocery shop, church of St. Pierre, etc.
Vicinity • To NE, *Moèze*, in cemetery, unusual Ren. 'hosanna cross', known as 'temple of Moèze'.

Bruniquel
82 – Tarn-et-Garonne   36 – A 3
Picturesque old town encircling 12–14c castle, said to have been founded in 6c by a Visigoth princess, Brunhilda, which stands on edge of cliff overlooking R. *Aveyron*. To r., a huge building houses 12c chapel; main living quarters inc. charming Ren. sculpted Italian-inspired gallery, with magnificent view.
Vicinity • 5 km NE, *Penne*, its old houses overlooked by huge limestone rock crowned by ruins of fortress; standing on narrow isthmus between r. bank of *Aveyron* and ravine of 'Cap de Biaou' (Bull's Head), this is one of most unusual of southern villages. D 115 continues through *Gorges de l'Aveyron*,

first on r. bank of river, then on l., to *St. Antonin-Noble-Val*, whose town hall is one of rare examples of 12c Romanesque civil architecture; interesting old houses (Amour house, 18c Vaissière or Sonnets mansion) and unusual tannery quarter; 4 km to NE, *Grotte du Bosc* (v.a.); D 658 follows *Aveyron* to E of *St. Antonin*, first to Varen, a medieval town whose old half-timbered houses cluster round Romanesque church and tiny 14–15c priory castle, then to *Laguépie*, at confluence of R. *Viaur* and *Aveyron*.

Bugue (Le)
24 – Dordogne   29 – D 3
On r. bank of R. *Vézère*. Grotto of Bara-Bahau (v.a. Palm Sun.–Sept. 30 and Suns. in Oct.), prehist. drawings.
Vicinity • 3 km S, *Gouffre de Proumeyssac*, 50 m. deep, fine concretions (v.a. as above). • Numerous excursions in Vézère and Dordogne valleys.

Bussière (Château)
45 – Loiret   18 – D 2
Surrounded on three sides by huge moat opening on to a large lake, this 16c brick building (v.a. Mar. 15–Nov. 15, cl. Tues.; rest of year, v.a. Sun. and hols.) houses freshwater fishing mus.; unchanged linen room and kitchen still have their original equipment and utensils; in outbuildings, vaulted cellars contain aquaria full of river and lake fish.
Vicinity • 12 km NE, *Châtillon-Coligny*, on R. Loing; three tiers of terraces, 16c orangery and a monumental well attributed to Jean Goujon are all that remain of château; in church, interesting 17c paintings. • 11 km E, *Rogny*, seven 17c locks.

Bussy-Rabutin (Château)
21 – Côte-d'Or   19 – C 2
Magnificent 16–17c building flanked by towers (v.a. Apr. 1–Sept. 30, cl. Tues.). Apartments still have their 17c mythological or allegorical decorations: Salle des Devises, Salon des Grands Hommes de Guerre; Mme. de Sévigné's bedchamber hung with 36 portraits of women, inc. many royal mistresses; Dorée tower (large collection of 17c paintings), library-gallery (many portraits). Large 85-acre park in form of amphitheatre; gardens are ornamented with fountains, lakes, statues, etc.
Vicinity • Recommended excursions to **Alise-Ste. Reine*** (Alesia) and **Flavigny-sur-Ozerain***.

Bruniquel: *from the ruins of the castle, perched on the edge of a rocky cliff 100 m. above the Aveyron, the view is stunning.*

C

Cabourg
14 – Calvados   4 – B 3
One of the most elegant beaches of the 'Côte Fleurie'. The town stretches out in fan-shape from Place du Casino, with Promenade Marcel Proust as a splendid embankment along the shore.
Vicinity ● R. *Dives* separates Cabourg from *Dives-sur-Mer* (14–15c church, fine timbered covered market, 15–16c). ● Between Cabourg and **Deauville***, beaches of *Houlgate* (trips to Vaches-Noires cliffs), *Villers-sur-Mer*, Blonville-sur-Mer, Bénerville-sur-Mer (cliffs).

Cadillac
33 – Gironde   35 – A 1
13c rectangular bastide on r. bank of R. *Garonne*. Château of Dukes of Épernon, late 16-early 17c, mentioned in 1630 as among most beautiful in France: interior has fine painted ceilings and sculpted monumental fireplaces in multicoloured marble (v.a., cl. Mon.). Church of St. Blaise, 15c; on r., funerary chapel (1606) of Épernon family, whose sumptuous mausoleum was destroyed during the French Revolution.
Vicinity ● 6 km NE, impressive remains of Ch. de Benauge (12, 15, 17 and 18c).

Cadouin
24 – Dordogne   35 – D 1
Mid-12c church, in Romanesque style imported from Poitiers region, is all that remains of famed Cistercian abbey, founded in 1116, where pilgrims came to venerate a 'holy shroud' (declared false in 1934). Late 15–16c cloisters, elegantly decorated, fine sculpted doors and keystones. Mus. de Pélerinage (religious art).
Vicinity ● 6 km SW, *St. Avit-Sénieur*, splendid 12–13c fortified church.

Caen
14 – Calvados   4 – B 3
The moated castle, restored from heavy damage of World War II, is a vast, powerful fortress, 11, 14 and 15c. Within its walls: 12–15c chapel of St. Georges; Echiquier (exchequer) de Normandie and fmr. 12–13c keep; old Governor's House with Mus. des Beaux-Arts and Mus. de Normandie (cl. Tues). The fine arts mus. has early Flemish and Italian works, 16–17c Italian and 17–18c French paintings and rich collection of contemporary art (Van Dongen, Villon, Vasarely, Clavé, etc.); also pottery, enamel, ivory, large print-room with 50,000 engravings. Latter mus. contains fascinating Norman costumes.
● Caen's churches are its main glory. Late 11c Abbaye aux Dames, or Trinity church, and 11c Abbaye aux Hommes, or church of St. Étienne (apse on three levels, with 13–14c flying buttresses) are outstanding examples of Romanesque art; the latter's 18c monastery buildings (now town hall) have fine panelling and Messager collection of Norman costumes (v.a.). In church of St. Pierre, 13–16c, under 13–14c tower, the 16c apse is among masterpieces of Norman Ren. In church of St. Sauveur, two coupled naves, 14 and 15c, have polygonal apses, one Goth. Flamboyant, the other Ren. Picturesque remains include Vieux-St. Étienne, 13–15c, in garden setting; St. Nicolas, late 11c Romanesque, surrounded by pretty graveyard; 17c Notre Dame de la Gloriette, fmr. Jesuit church. ● To W side of St. Pierre church is lovely Ren. building, Hôtel d'Escoville, with superbly sculpted internal courtyard. Interesting 18c houses in Vieux-St. Sauveur quarter; 17c Hôtel de Colomby, 6 Rue des Cordeliers; 14–16c Maison des Quatrans. 31 Rue de la Géôle; timbered houses, Rue St. Pierre.
Vicinity ● 10 km NNE, towards *Ouistreham* (interesting church): Ch. de Bénouville, impressive 18c building by Louis XVI's architect, Ledoux (n.v.a.). ● 4.5 km NW,

Caen: *the apse of the Abbaye aux Hommes, an outstanding feat of Romanesque art, now adjoins the town hall gardens.*

Abbey of *Ardenne*, church, lodge and 13c barn. ● 10 km NW, Ch. de *Lasson*, Ren., elegantly sculpted facade (v.a. by permission only); 3 km to N, *Thaon*, deconsecrated 11c Romanesque church in setting of trees and bubbling waters; interesting capitals in nave (v.a.); 2 km away, Ch. de **Fontaine-Henry***. ● 13 km N, *La Délivrande*, 19c neo-Goth. basilica of Notre Dame (popular pilgrimage centre); then through **Courseulles*** to D-Day beaches.

Cagnes-sur-Mer
06 – Alpes-Maritimes   45 – A 1
The old town, built on a very steep, conical little hill, is dominated by the museum, former 14–17c château of the Grimaldis, with charming patio and galleries on two floors (cl. Tues. and Oct. 15 to Nov. 15). Mus. de l'Olivier is on ground floor and rooms for modern Mediterranean art above it. In 1st floor Salles des Fêtes, monumental stucco fireplace and, on ceiling, 17c trompe l'oeil, *La Chute de Phaéton*. Lane to E leads to Domaine des Colettes and Renoir's home (cl. a.m. and Tues.). You can visit olive grove where the great artist painted many pictures; his studio, with personal belongings, has been kept unchanged.

Cahors
46 – Lot   36 – A 2
The old town, between Blvd. Gambetta and R. *Lot*, is picturesque. St. Étienne cathedral is among the most original of SW France's domed churches; Romanesque nave enlarged by Goth. chapels built in 13c but with 14c façades; Romanesque N portal has tympanum of the Ascension, 12c masterpiece from sculpture workshops of Languedoc region; 14c paintings on first dome and choir. To S of cathedral, early 16c cloisters and former archdeaconry of St. Jean, 16c (noteworthy façade over courtyard). Early 16c Hôtel de Roaldès; 12–13c Goth. church of St. Urcisse (Romanesque capitals). Many old houses in surrounding quarter and that of Les Badernes, to S, notably in Rues du Dr. Bergounioux, de Lastié, Nationale; likewise, in Soubirous quarter to N, in Rues du Château-du-Roi, des Soubirous, St. Barthélemy. 16c church of St. Barthélemy has belfry in brick and stone. 14c Palais Duèze, surmounted by Tour Jean XXII (named after 14c Pope born at Cahors). 15c barbican and Tour St. Jean, aka 'Hanged Men's Tower'. Town mus. (v.a. Easter to Sept.): prehist., Romanesque and Goth. sculpture, paintings, etc. Pont

Cahors: *the Pont Valentré – three machicolated towers and seven spans over the Lot.*

Calvi: *on a rocky promontory, the ramparts of the Genoese citadel, or Upper Town.*

Valentré, superb 14c fortified bridge, is remarkable example of medieval military architecture.
Vicinity ● Excursions recommended in valleys of the *Lot* and R. *Célé*, to NE; see **St. Cirq-Lapopie***, grotto of **Peche-Merle***, and **Luzech*** to W of Cahors.

Cajarc
46 – Lot 36 – B 2
Old township in ring of reddish cliffs. Remains of 13–14c castle. Old houses. 700 m. to N, the Cogne falls.
Vicinity ● 4 km S, unusual Anthouy chasm; 3km to S, Oule chasm. ● 13 km SW, on l. bank of the Lot, *Cénevières*; 13, 15 and 16c château rises sheer above the river.

Calacuccia
2B – Corsica 45 – B 3
Township in central bowl of Niolo region, surrounded by chestnut groves. Church of St. Pierre-et-Paul (strikingly realistic carved wooden Christ), old houses and typical alleys.
Vicinity ● To NE, trip round lake formed by Calacuccia dam, on R. *Golo*, to mouth of narrow pass of *Scala di Santa Regina*. ● To NW, *Monte Cinto* (2,710 m.), island's highest peak. ● To SW, *Forêt de Valdo-Niello* (from forest hut of Popajo, path up to lake of Nico, 1,743 m.); Vergio pass.

Calais
62 – Pas-de-Calais 1 – B 2
Calais-Nord, port town rebuilt after World War II, comprises harbour, docks and new town dominated by mid-16c citadel. To S, industrial town of St. Pierre, or Calais-Sud, centres round Place du Soldat-Inconnu (Unknown Soldier), site of Rodin's world-famed group sculpture, *Les Bour-*

geois de Calais (1895). Beach claimed to be one of the best in north of France. Mus. des Beaux-Arts et de la Dentelle (cl. Tues.): contemporary sculpture – Rodin, Zadkine, G. Richier, Maillol; also European ceramics and rich collection of lace.
Vicinity ● Along coast road of *Côte d'Opale* to **Boulogne***, via capes of *Blanc-Nez* and *Gris-Nez*. ● 10 km S, forest of *Guînes* (19,400 acres).

Calvi
2B – Corsica 45 – B 3
The citadel, or Upper Town, with 13–16c ramparts, stands on rocky promontory jutting out to sea; lovely view from N corner; 16c church of St. Jean Baptiste, at top, contains many works of art. Late 15c oratory of St. Antoine is treasure-house of religious art from surrounding Balagne region: sacred

objects from 15 to 18c inc. superb collection of liturgical vestments. In Lower Town, the Marine quarter offers lively, colourful spectacle, with its open-air cafés on quays planted with palm-trees and its port and marina. 14c chapel of Ste. Marie still has traces of 4c Paleo-Christian basilica.
Vicinity ● By sea, Grotto of the Veaux-Marins (3hr. round trip); **Porto*** (all day), revealing the extraordinarily jagged coast, with its myriad gulfs and capes. ● 6 km SW, *Madona della Serra* chapel, wide panorama. ● 18 km SE, forest and *Cirque de Bonifato*. ● To E, many churches of *Balagne* region: *Calenzana* (18c fmr. collegiate church, on site of Romanesque predecessor); Ste. Restitute (4c sarcophagus, 15c frescos); *Montemaggiore*, big baroque church (good views) and Romanesque church of St. Rainier, in black and white granite; through-

Cambrai: *lofty baroque façade of the Grand Seminary chapel, with statue in front of the enlightened writer and priest, Fénelon.*

out the round trip, superb views over *Gulf of Calvi*; see also tiny village of *Sant' Antonino*, perched high up, and picturesque village of *Corbara*, spreading in fan-shape on mountain slopes (remains of Guido and Corbara castles). From **L'Ile-Rousse***, you can return to Calvi on coast road through *Algajola*, fmr. fortified village, under powerful 17c citadel (very good beach).

Camaret-sur-Mer
29 – Finistère   8 – A 2
Magnificently situated on tip of Crozon peninsula. The port is protected by natural dike, Le Sillon, 600 m. long, on which stands early 16c chapel of Notre Dame-de-Rocamadour; naval mus. in late 17c polygonal tower built by Vauban. *Vicinity* ● 2 km W, Pointe du Toulinguet, unusual reddish rocks. ● 1 km W, Lagadyar lines (143 white quartzite menhirs). ● 3 km SW, *Pointe de Pen-Hir*, impressive point 70 m. high; from below it, isolated line of rocks, the *Tas-de-Pois.* ● To NE, fortified peninsula of *Roscanvel* protects the sea approaches to **Brest***; superb view from *Pointe des Espagnols* at N end.

Cambo-les-Bains
64 – Pyrénées-Atlantiques 40 – C 2
R. Nive divides lower town, still largely rural, from residential upper town. On **Bayonne*** road, sumptuous Villa Arnaga, built by playwright Edmond Rostand in Basque style, is now mus. (v.a. in summer season); superb formal gardens. *Vicinity* ● 5.5 km W, *Espelette*, typically Basque church and cemetery; 5.5 km to SW, *Aïnhoa*, lovely 17c houses. ● 4.5 km S, *Itxassou*, equally typical, at mouth of narrow defile called Pas de Roland; road continues to *Louhossoa* (Basque church) and *Bidarray*, in mountain bowl; picturesque 13c bridge, grotto. To S, road forks r. to *St. Étienne-de-Baïgorry*, l. to **St. Jean-Pied-de-Port***.

Cambrai
59 – Nord   6 – A 1
In 18c Notre Dame cathedral is tomb of Fénelon, great liberal preacher and forward-looking writer who ended his days as archbishop of Cambrai in 1715. Chapel of Grand Seminary, former chapel of Jesuit college, raises lofty, very ornate baroque façade over Place St. Sepulcre. Church of St. Géry has superb Ren. rood-screen in red and black marble, with bas-reliefs and statues. 'Entombment of Christ' by Rubens. 17–18c mansions; to r. of cath., late-16c timbered 'Spanish

CAMARGUE (Parc Naturel Régional)
13 – Bouches-du-Rhône   43 – C 1
Covering nearly 330 sq. miles, made up of the Grande Camargue, island formed by *Rhône* delta and the big *Étang de Vaccarès*, and the Petite Camargue to W. Absolute bird paradise; also home of the 'manades', troops of wild horses watched over by mounted 'gardians' (cowboys of the Camargue). About two-fifths of area is cultivated (particularly rice-paddies); further 37,000 acres around Étang de Vaccarès are botanical and zoological reserve (restricted to specialists and research workers). Several round-trips: ● From **Arles***, via *Albaron* and *Méjanes* (horse-breeding centre, arenas; livery stables in village). From **Stes. Maries-de-la-Mer***, via sea dike (poor road surface) to Gacholle lighthouse and *Salin-de-Badon*; then N along lake to *Villeneuve*, whence back to *Méjanes* and *Albaron*. ● Another route from *Albaron* to **Stes. Maries*** is S along lake via Mas de Cacharel. ● From **Stes. Maries*** to **Aigues-Mortes***, take either N570, past Pont de Gau *parc zoologique*, or D38 past Grand Radeau and Bac du Sauvage to D85, leading to *Sylvéréal* on the *Petit-Rhône*. It's on l. bank of river here, between D85 and N570, that Carmargue's traditional way of life is best preserved.

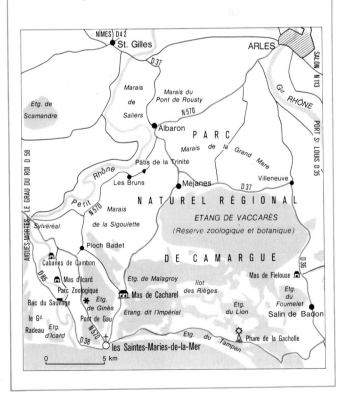

house'. Town mus.: 16–20c paintings, including Veronese, Rubens, Ingres; medieval sculptures; local archaeology. Early 17c Notre Dame Gate and late–14c Paris Gate. 16c citadel, enlarged by Vauban; fine 30-acre public garden.

Vicinity ● 12 km S, remains of Abbey de Vaucelles (12, 13 and 17c).

Cancale
35 – Ille-et-Vilaine   9 – C 2
Fishing village famed for its oysters. Huge panorama from tower of St. Méen church (viewing table). Maison des Bois Sculptés (v.a. in summer): simple wood carvings of allegorical or folk groups by 19c local priest.

Vicinity ● 2 km N, *Pointe du Grouin*: immense panorama, all the way from coast of the *Cotentin* (Cherbourg peninsula) over to *Cap Fréhel* in W.

Cannes
06 – Alpes-Maritimes   45 – A 1
Cannes lies in a privileged situation along seashore, edged by world-famed Blvd. de la Croisette, with its grand hotels and luxury shops. The port lies under the old town, which stretches up slopes of the Mont-Chevalier, the 'Suquet'. Flower market is among Côte d'Azur's most picturesque. Super-Cannes, to E side of town, has observatory (lift inside) with views over whole coast and inland to foothills of Alps. In Le Suquet, works of art in 16–17c church of Notre Dame-de-l'Espérance. Behind it, Tour du Suquet, former watchtower alongside premises of Mus. de la Castre (cl. Mon.) – Mediterranean, Middle East and S. Pacific archaeology and ethnography, pre-Columbian ceramics, 16–19c and Provençal paintings.
Vicinity ● Boat trips to **Iles de Lérins*** (Son et Lumière in summer).

Canonica (La)
2B – Corsica   45 – B 2
The island's largest Romanesque church, early 12c; its rectangular body, in polychrome marble, is divided into three naves – in v. bare style, though sculpted decoration of W door is influenced by Romanesque art of northern Italy. 50 m. to S are foundations of 4–5c Paleo-Christian cath. and baptistry; symbolic mosaics, small mus. 500 m. to W, Romanesque church of San Parteo; early 11c apse is remarkably sculpted. Remains of earlier Paleo-Christian church and necropolis were uncovered in 1957–58.

CANIGOU (Route and Peak)
66 – Pyrénées-Orientales   43 – C 3
Getting to the top of Le Canigou, an isolated, pyramidal mountain 2,785 m. high, is among the most striking climbs in the Pyrenees, taking about a day. Most people start from *Vernet-les-Bains* (2.5 km from Abbey of **St. Martin-du-Canigou***). The road up from *Vernet* to the chalet-hôtel of *Les Cortalets* (2,175 m.) is practicable only in summer and difficult even then: 21 km of narrow, stiff slopes and hairpin bends. Jeeps can be hired from *Prades* or *Vernet* – or from the Col de Millères (850 m.), whence road climbs Escala de l'Ours, corniche along the Taurinya gorges, then over Forêt de Balatg (forest hut at 1,600 m.). From Les Cortalets chalet-hôtel, ascent of Canigou is completed on foot: several paths up to summit, from where panorama is superb – over Pyrenees, all of Roussillon and as far N as the Cévennes.

CAP CORSE
2B – Corsica   45 – A 2
120 km round-trip, mostly narrow coast road: **Bastia***; *Erbalunga* (at nearby Castello, 9c church, Santa Maria della Nevi, with 14c frescos); *Rogliano* (remains of three castles, convent, fortified towers); *Ersa*, where branch N to *Barcaggio* and tip of the cape. Back S through *Centuri*, painted houses, roofs of green rock (serpentine); *Pino* (baroque church); *Marinca* (interesting churches at nearby Canari: Santa Maria, late 12c, and St. François); *Nonza* (extensive view from tower); and **St. Florent***.

Cancale: *this craggy little island, just off the Pointe du Grouin, is a bird sanctuary.*

La Canonica: *the rectangular church, stark but elegant. In the foreground, foundations of a much older cathedral and baptistry.*

Carcassonne: *with its two sets of walls and 50 towers, the Cité (old city) is truly unique.*

Carcassonne
11 – Aude   42 – C 2

The old city (Cité) of Carcassonne is biggest medieval fortress surviving in Europe, restored by top 19c French architect, Viollet-le-Duc. Successively Roman, Visigoth (5c) and feudal (12–13c), it has two elliptical sets of walls, with 50 towers, two barbicans and Count of Toulouse's castle (v.a. inner walls, castle and lapidary mus.). City is floodlit every evening, but its special illumination on July 14 is breath-taking. St. Nazaire basilica has late-11c Romanesque nave, 13–14c Goth. transept and choir bedecked with 22 statues, and 14–15c stained-glass windows famed for their gorgeously warm colours; also tombstone of Simon de Montfort, who led the savage Albigensian crusade (against the Cathars) and was killed while besieging Toulouse in 1218. A walk along the *lices*, grass stretches between the double walls, gives you better idea of city's formidable defensive system and opens up wide views over surrounding countryside.

● The lower town, at foot of city, was founded in 1247 by France's King Louis IX (St. Louis) on fortified grid pattern, with central square and two huge churches: St. Vincent, in southern Goth. style, completed in early 14c, and late-13c cathedral of St. Michael (rich church treasure, v.a. in summer). Fine arts mus., Dutch and French paintings, 17–19c.

Vicinity ● 16 km N, *Lastours*, jagged ruins of châteaux on four crests of same ridge. ● 18 km S, *St. Hilaire-de-l'Aude*, late 12–13c abbey church with 11c sarcophagus of the saint and elegant 14c cloisters. ● 27.5 km E, *Moux*, in pretty setting, chapel and tomb of playwright Henry Bataille (d. 1922), with reproduction of Ligier Richier's masterly 16c sculpture of a skeleton (original at Bar-le-Duc). ● Trip through *Montagne Noire*, mountain range to NW, via *Montolieu* (huge Goth. church), *Saissac* (remains of 14c château, fine view of Pyrenees) and the *Bassins de Lampy* (see **Sorèze***); good walks in Ramondens and La Loubatière forests. ● To S, trip along upper valley of R. *Aude*, through **Limoux***, *Alet-les-Bains*, *Couiza*, **Quillan***, the gorges of *Pierre-Lys*, *St. Georges* and the *Aude*.

Carennac
46 – Lot   30 – B 3

This very picturesque village is grouped round an old Benedictine abbey where Fénelon lived for much of his earlier career (see entry for Cambrai). 12c Romanesque church has doorway with fine sculpted tympanum and early 16c 'Entombment of Christ' (below). The cloisters have one Romanesque and three Gothic galleries.

Carennac: *part of the church's expressive 'Entombment of Christ', dating from the early 16c.*

Carnac
56 – Morbihan   15 – D 2

Rising in middle of wild moorland, the unique megalithic Lines of Carnac are made up of three main groups: the Ménec Line (the most impressive, with 1,099 menhirs) and those of Kermario (1,029 menhirs) and Kerlescan (594). Below a chapel, the St. Michel tumulus caps several funerary chambers (v.a. in summer season). In town, 12c church has porch surmounted by unusual stone canopy. Mus. Miln-Le Rouzic (cl. Tues. between Nov. and Apr.) is regarded as best in unusual 18c synagogue (v.a.), oldest in France: sanctuary, oven for making unleavened bread, pool for ritual washing. Sobirats mus. of decorative arts in 18c mansion; lapidary mus. in 17c fmr. chapel of the Visitation. Fine arts mus., interesting 17–18–19c paintings (cl. Wed.); on ground-floor, Venaissin-period mus. To S of town, imposing Hôtel-Dieu (mid-18c hospital); façade with sculpted pediment, crowned by balusters and flame ornaments; pharmacy (cl. weekends) has large collection of 16–17c pharmacy jars and pottery; elegant

Carnac: *the significance of the megalithic lines remains a mystery, though it seems likely they were associated with sun worship.*

world for megalithic period, tracing mankind's evolution from about 450,000 BC to late Middle Ages.
Vicinity ● Carnac-Plage. To N, abbeys of St. Michel and Ste. Anne de Kergonan (Gregorian chants). ● 4 km E, *La Trinité-sur-Mer*, fishing and holiday village, beach. ● Between *Plouharnel* and *Erdeven*, to NW, dolmens and megaliths.

Carpentras
84 – Vaucluse   38 – A 3

Main town of old Comtat (county) of Venaissin, which belonged to Papacy for more than five centuries. Wealth of fine historic buildings. ● In centre, Place du Palais, former cathedral of St. Siffrein, 15–16c, in southern Goth. style; chapel with relics of the saint; in choir, 15c stained glass and monumental gilded wood aureole. ● Façade of Palais de Justice (lawcourts), formerly bishop's palace, is smaller-scale version of Farnese palace in Rome; interior has beautiful rooms with 17c decoration; in courtyard, Roman triumphal arch. Most chapel with noteworthy liturgical furnishings. To N, handsome gate, Porte d'Orange, survives from medieval ramparts. ● Local speciality: caramel sweets called 'berlingots'.
Vicinity ● 14 km N, *Dentelles de Montmirail*, unusual jagged chalk ridges; to N, *Beaumes-de-Venise*, dessert wines, 10c chapel.

Carrouges (Château)
61 – Orne   10 – B 2

Huge quadrilateral château, 15–16–17c, surrounded by moat and flanked by towers and 14c keep; constructed of red brick framed in granite; in heart of regional wildlife park. (v.a., cl. Tues.) Sumptuous state rooms, monumental staircase (portrait gallery), beautiful granite fireplaces. 16c little château ('chatelet') has exhibition of lower Normandy arts and crafts.

Cassel
59 – Nord   1 – C 2

Typically Flemish old town, at top of Mt. Cassel. The Grand Place is surrounded by gabled houses, notably late-18c Hôtel d'Halluin and 16–17c Hôtel de la Noble Cour (mus. of art, history and folklore – Flemish furniture, earthenware, documentation on historic archers' fraternities). On château heights, monument to the three battles of Cassel, equestrian statue of Marshal Foch, viewing table and reconstructed 18c windmill; vast panorama over the 'pays plat' (flat country).
Vicinity ● 8 km E, *Steenwoorde*: main square with painted houses; two well-preserved windmills. ● 13 km NW, *Esquelbec*, 17c brick château and 16c hall church, with unusual confessionals.

Cassis
13 – Bouches-du-Rhône   44 – B 2

Very lively Provençal fishing port, at head of a bay ringed by mountains. The old town, built to 18c regular lay-out, is very picturesque. Town museum.
Vicinity ● La Ciotat (see **Bandol***), via Corniche des Crêtes road (14 km), a route offering wonderful views. ● Highly recommended excursion by boat to the *calanques* (deep creeks); paths lead (green markers) to those of Port-Miou, Port-Pin and En-Vau, under shadow of grandiose cliffs.

Castellane
04 – Alpes-de-Haute-Provence
                    38 – D 3

Typically Provençal little village on the Route Napoléon. It is dominated by the 'Roc', a huge cliff with peak from which you get superb

Carpentras: *Romanesque chapel of Notre Dame-d'Aubune, at nearby Beaumes-de-Venise.*

Cassis: *the jagged cliffs of En-Vau, most beautiful of the calanques, can be reached on foot, via a forest path, as well as by boat.*

view. Path behind the church runs along remains of medieval walls (14c buttressed tower) to 17c chapel of Notre Dame-du-Roc: bird's eye view over Castellane and surrounding region. *Vicinity* ● 6.5 km NE, *Barrage de Castillon* (dam), on R. *Verdon*. ● To NE, via Col de Toutes-Aures and Les Scaffarels, on route of the pass of *La Colle St. Michel*, to large, picturesque township of *Annot*; numerous rocks eroded into bizarre shapes. ● To SW, gorges of the **Verdon***. ● 18 km NW, *Senez*: former cathedral is noteworthy example of Provençal Romanesque; nave contains superb group of 11 tapestries, 17c.

Castillon-en-Couserans
09 – Ariège   **41 – D 3**
Good excursion centre. Village is dominated by pine-covered hillock whence path laid out as Stations of the Cross leads to fortified Romanesque chapel of St. Pierre (fine

sculpted portal with small marble columns). *Vicinity* ● 1 km N, Audressein: unusual Gothic church of Notre Dame-de-Tramezaygues, 14–15–16c, with bell-tower, arcaded wall and three-door porch; decorated with 15–16c frescos. ● To S, via *Bordes-sur-Lez* and *Arrien*: valley of Bethmale, one of the Pyrenean valleys where old traditions are still most closely observed (above all, don't miss the August 15 public holiday at Ayet); road climbs up valley as far as Bethmale lake, angler's paradise, amid magnificent mountain scenery. ● From *Bordes-sur-Lez*, below peak of the Midi de Bordes (1,785 m.), the D4 takes you SE to high *Vallée du Lez* as far as Sentein: 15–16c church with Romanesque tower and remains of fortified walls.

Castres
81 – Tarn   **42 – C 1**
The town has two focal points of

interest: banks of R. *Agout*, with authentic old houses (floodlit in summer), and the Goya mus (v.a.), devoted to Spanish painting from primitives to 20c, in town hall built by Mansart mid-17c – one-time bishop's palace, fronted by formal gardens, which also houses Jaurès mus. The Goya mus. possesses two special works by the great Spanish master, a self-portrait and his biggest painting, *La Junte des Philippines*, as well as the bulk of his engravings. Other Spanish artists exhibited inc. Borrassa, Luis de Moralès, Ribera, Valdès Léal, Coello, Murillo, Fortuny, Madrazo, Clavé. Also Flemish tapestries, regional archaeology. *Vicinity* ● 6 km SW, former charterhouse of Saix, 16c, behind fortified walls.

Castries (Château)
34 – Hérault   **43 – B 1**
Imposing 16–17c château, surrounded by formal gardens attributed to Le Nôtre (v.a., cl. Mon. end of Mar. to mid-Dec.; otherwise, v.a. weekends only, Dec. 15 to Apr. 1). In Ren. wing, huge États du Languedoc room, 32 m. long (magnificent carpets, large collection of porcelain and antique bookbindings). Sumptuous reception rooms. Aqueduct 7 km away brings in water from Fontgrand springs.

Cateau (Le)
59 – Nord   **6 – A 1**
Palais Fénelon, former residence of the archbishops of Cambrai (1772), is now home of Henri Matisse mus. (cl. Mon. and Tues., hrs. vary). The great artist was born in this town, and works on show include a self-portrait (1918), *Fenêtre à Tahiti* (1936), sculptures and drawings. Town hall has 18c belfry. Church of St. Martin, old Benedictine abbey church, 17c, with richly decorated baroque façade.

Caudebec-en-Caux
76 – Seine-Maritime   **4 – D 3**
Church of Notre Dame, in 15–16c Flamboyant style, is crowned by superb 54 m. spire; in chapel of the Virgin, 4.30 m. hanging keystone. Interesting 15c. houses. Also 13c house of the Templars (Musée du Vieux-Caudebec). *Vicinity* ● 12 km N, *Yvetot*, unusual round modern church, with huge stained-glass frame in place of normal walls (1955).

Cauterets
65 – Hautes-Pyrénées   **41 – B 3**
Ringed by high, snow-covered peaks: spa and winter sports centre. Casino. Thermal baths of Pauze-Vieux; 1.5 km away, spa establishment of La Raillère (1,053 m.)

and Les Griffons; from there, 3.8 km farther on, baths of Le Bois, at 1,147 m.

Vicinity • Excursions rec. to *Pont d'Espagne* and the *Lac de Gaube*, to SW; also, to NW, Turon de Sacca, cable-car service in two sections, then third section to *Soum de Monné*, at 2,724 m. To W, summit of Péguère (2,552 m., magnificent panorama); to E, Riou pass (1,949 m., viewing table); to SE, via *Lac de Gaube*, Baysselance refuge, to foot of the *Vignemale*, the Gave (mountain torrent) of Ossoue and *Gavarnie* (see **Luz-St. Sauveur***).

Cavaillon
84 – Vaucluse   38 – A 3
Typically Provençal little town, famed for its melons. Principal sight: the synagogue, 1772–74, with panelling, wrought-iron and Louis XV-style decorated plaster-work – overall effect being very characteristic of Comtadin art in 18c (see entry for Carpentras). Small Judeo-Comtadin mus. (cl. Tues.). 12–13c church of St. Véran, in purest Provençal Romanesque style, extended in 14 and 18c; int. adorned with panelling and 17c paintings; Romanesque cloister. Archaeological mus. in chapel of fmr. hospital (lapidary exhibits, terracotta vases, Gallo-Roman medals). Remains of finely decorated Roman triumphal arch. Extensive views from calvary of St. Jacques chapel – 12c, renovated 16–17c. Remains of Roman oppidum.

Vicinity • Good centre for excsns. to the **Lubéron***.

Caylus
82 – Tarn-et-Garonne   36 – B 2
Small town in amphitheatre layout, under remains of 14–15c château. In 14c church, big Christ in wood by Zadkine (1954). Many old houses along the Grande Rue.

Vicinity • 7 km SE, *Abbaye de Beaulieu*: admirable Cistercian abbey, in pure mid-12c style, with its adjoining buildings, now home of centre of contemp. art (exhibitions in summer); 3 km to N, *Ch. de Cornusson*: enormous early 16c fortress, with double walls and moats, is flanked by four corner towers and a keep (n.v.a.).

Céret
66 – Pyrénées-Orientales 43 – D 3
Mus. of modern art (cl. Tues.) testifies to frequent stays at Céret of sevl. leading contemp. artists – notably Picasso (fine group of ceramics and two paintings), Matisse, Max Jacob, Marquet, Juan Gris, Chagall, Derain, Dufy, Manolo, Masson, etc. 18c church with three domes. Traces of fmr. ramparts.

Vicinity • 8 km SW, *Amélie-les-*

Bains, spa in lush green setting. Excursions recommended to: Mondony gorges; Palalda (typical Catalan village, 12c Romanesque church); Montbolo (alt. 576 m., above valley of R. *Tech*, panorama, Romanesque church); Montalba, in superb setting above wild ravines and gorges of the Terme. • 8.5 km S, Fontfrède peak (1,094 m.), wide views over Catalonia, on both French and Spanish sides. • 8.5 km NE, *Le Boulou*: church has Romanesque portal, 17c retable and 12c historiated capitals; 3 km to S, *St. Martin-de-Fenollar*: church, known as the 'Mahut', boasts very original early-12c Romanesque murals (key at neighbouring house), painted in very primitive style, on coloured backgrounds, and depicting scenes from the Life of Jesus (inc. partic. unusual Nativity).

Cerisy-la-Forêt
50 – Manche   4 – A 3
11c abbey church is among most beautiful Romanesque edifices in Normandy (v.a., Son et Lumière in summer). Choir has 44 early-15c stalls, 18c lectern, 15–16c statues; monastery buildings include mid-13c lodgings and elegant 15c chapel.

Vicinity • To SE, Cerisy forest. 6 km NE, at *Littry-la-Mine*: odd little museum from former local coal-mine.

Châalis (Abbey) – **Fontaine-Châalis**
60 – Oise   11 – D 1
Ruins of 13c abbey church and the Abbot's chapel, built in imitation of the Ste. Chapelle in Paris (vaulting decorated with 16c paintings), are all that remain of Cistercian abbey founded in 12c. Main 18c abbey building is now mus., with fine collections of antiquities, paintings and objets d'art, chiefly Italian Ren. period; also French 18c school and mementoes of Jean-Jacques Rousseau (v.a. Mar. to end of Oct. on Sun. and p.m. Mon., Wed. and Sat.).

Vicinity • In *Forêt d'Ermenonville*, lakes, *Mer de Sable* (Sea of Sand, leisure park) and Jean Richard zoo (open Apr. to Nov.). To S, château and park of **Ermenonville***.

Chablis
89 – Yonne   19 – B 1
Vineyard capital of Lower Burgundy (world-famed white wines). Early-13c church of St. Martin; on side door, 13c strap hinges and horseshoes in votive offering to St. Martin. Old streets and houses; former chapel of 13c Hôtel-Dieu (hospital), wine cellar.

Vicinity • To SW, *Courgis*: 16c murals in church. • To N, *Ligny-le-Chatel* (see **Pontigny***). • To SE, lovely valley of the *Serein* (see **Noyers***).

Chabotterie (Château)
85 – Vendée   22 – C 1
In heart of the Bocage (mixed woodland and pasture-land of the Vendée region), this typical fortified manor – late 16c-early 17c – is where François de Charette, a leader of the local royalist uprising after the French Revolution, was captured and held prisoner before being shot. Military mus. on Vendéen wars.

Chaise-Dieu (La)
43 – Haute-Loire   31 – B 2
From alt. of more than 1,000 m., imposing 14c abbey church of St. Robert dominates the township, spreading up the slopes below it. Most notable part of the church is the monks' choir (cl. Tues. from Nov. 1 to June 1), with its 156 sculpted stalls, from late 14c, and tomb of Pope Clement VI (d. 1352); on N choir screen is renowned 15c fresco, *La Danse Macabre*; 15c rood screen with three blind arcades and monumental organ-chest, supported by four caryatids; near the apse, mid-14c Clémentine tower; remains of 14c cloister (reached through Salle de l'Écho).

Vicinity • 19 km E, *Craponne-sur-Arzon*: 16c church, interesting works of art; 9 km to N, *Suc de Medeyrolles*, extensive views over *Auvergne* and the *Forez*.

Chalon-sur-Saône
71 – Saône-et-Loire   25 – D 1
Niepce mus., in 18c mansion (cl. Tues.), has rich photographic collection. Denon mus., in 18c ex-convent, has prehist., Gallo-

CÉVENNES (Corniche)
48 – Lozère, 30 – Gard   37 – B 3
To S of **Florac***, follow N107 for 5.5 km, then on to D583 for *St. Laurent-de-Trèves* and the Col du Rey (992 m.), where fork r. on to D9. This is the spectacular road known as the Corniche des Cévennes, which, after the Col de Faïsses (1,026m), crosses the Hospitalet causse and continues to *Le Pompidou* and St. Roman-de-Tousque, picturesque village in really beautiful setting (700 m. alt.). The route takes you through several passes before descending in hairpin bends, through pine forests, to *St. Jean-du-Gard*.

Châalis: *the impressive remains of the abbey church give some idea of the splendid early 13c construction for which the Cistercians first adopted the Gothic style.*

Cauterets: *the 42-acre Lac de Gaube, at an altitude of 1,728 m., in a wild valley at the foot of the Vignemale massif.*

Chablis: *this little town, with its colourful markets and world-famed white wines, is the 'Golden Gate' into Burgundy.*

Chalon-sur-Saône: *an old well, with elegant wrought-iron work, in St. Vincent's cloisters.*

Châlus: *the crossbow bolt which killed Richard the Lion Heart was fired from here.*

CHALAIN (Lake)
39 – Jura   26 – B 2
Largest and most beautiful lake in the region, surrounded by steep cliffs; its waters feed the R. *Ain* through the Bief d'Oeuf. Remains from a village built on piles, discovered in the lake, are exhibited at the museum in **Lons-le-Saunier***.
Vicinity ● To SE, lakes of Chambly and Le Val, *Cascades du Hérisson* (particularly L'Éventail and the Grand Saut), Aigle mountain, La Motte and Narlay lakes.

Roman and medieval collection, also galleries with 16, 17 and 19c paintings. Fmr. St. Vincent cathedral, 12–15c, with 14–15c cloister. Maison des Vins, centre for local wines. Beautiful rose-garden in St. Nicolas leisure area.
Vicinity ● To N, **Côte de Beaune*** and Côte de Nuits (see **Nuits-St. Georges***). ● To S, **Tournus***, **Mâcon*** and the Beaujolais (see **Villefranche-sur-Saône***).

Châlons-sur-Marne
51 – Marne   12 – C 1
St. Étienne cathedral, dating from second half of 13c, has admirable 13, 14 and 16c stained-glass windows. Notre Dame-en-Vaux is one of Champagne region's most beautiful 12c churches, with beautiful 16c stained glass. Destroyed in 18c, the cloisters have been partly reconstructed in museum which also has many capitals and pillar-statues from the old site. Two other interesting churches: St. Loup, 15c, and St. Alpin, 12c and 16c. Town mus.: local sculptures, large col-

lection of Hindu divinities, 16–17c. Mus. Garinet in charming 18c

Chambéry: *one of the four big bronze elephants from the town's extraordinary fountain.*

mansion, also housing Goethe-Schiller museum.
Vicinity ● 8 km NE, Notre Dame de l'Épine*.

Châlus
87 – Haute-Vienne   29 – D 1
Still looming over the town are remains of enormous keep of late-11c castle where Richard the Lion Heart met his end (v.a. daily Apr. 1 to June 30; Suns. and public hols., July 1 to Sept. 15; daily, Sept. 16– Mar. 31, by arrangement).
Vicinity ● 8.5 km NW, Ch. de Brie, 15c; int. has fine Louis XVI furnishing (v.a. Sun., p.m., Apr. to Oct.). ● 6.5 km SW, *Dournazac*: domed Romanesque church and remains of priory; 2 km to NW, in vale of the Petite-Dronne, 12 and 15c Ch. de Montbrun, with towers and large square keep (v.a.).

Chambéry
73 – Savoie   32 – B 2
Capital of the Savoie, dominated by ducal château – 14–15c, enlarged in 18c (v.a., but cl. Sun. a.m. June 15 to Sept. 15 and Sat. p.m. Sept. 16 to June 14). Goth. Ste. Chapelle (16c stained glass), carillon concerts, 14c Trésorerie tower. Surrounding quarter is interesting, notably the 'allées' – passages running between many streets, forming picturesque labyrinths. Unusual Fountain of the Elephants, town's most popular monument, was erected (mid-19c) in memory of Count de Boigne, who lived in India. Savoie mus. (cl. Tues.) in old Franciscan convent.

Fine arts mus. (also cl. Tues.): French school, Dutch, and partic. Italian works, 15–18c. – one of largest collections in France, in this field. St. François-de-Sales cathedral, 15–16c; rich church treasure. Fine mansions, Rue Croix d'Or. To N, at top of Lemenc hill, 15c. St. Pierre-de-Lemenc; in crypt, hexagonal Carolingian baptistry, with six ancient columns.
Vicinity ● 2 km S, Les Charmettes, delightful 17c property where Jean-Jacques Rousseau lived as guest of Baroness de Warens (v.a., cl. Tues.). ● Wine road.

Chambord (Château)
41 – Loir-et-Cher   18 – A 2
Largest of the Loire châteaux and undoubtedly the most imposing in its forest setting – a 13,750-acre national hunting reserve, of which more than 1,500 acres are open to the public. The building, from early 16c, is on feudal lines, with central keep, four round towers and outer wall; but Ren. decorative richness turned it into sumptuous royal residence. Within the keep is magnificent double staircase, crowned by a 32 m. lantern, which rises above roof terraces bristling with more than 360 chimneys, dormer windows and sculpted pinnacle turrets. (v.a.; Son et Lumière every evening, June 1–Sept. 30; also Fri., Sat., Sun. and public holidays, Apr.–May.) Louis XIV's apartments are on first floor of keep; king's room and adjoining salons decorated with tapestries, furniture, portraits, etc. François I apartments, in NE tower, and adjoining part of main building are in course of renovation.

Chambord: *largest of the Loire châteaux, crowned by an extraordinary mass of chimneys, dormer windows and turrets – architecturally, as rich as they are varied.*

Chamonix-Mont Blanc
74 – Haute-Savoie   32 – D 1
Leading winter sports and mountaineering centre on both banks of R. *Arve*, in centre of valley dominated by the chain of the Aiguilles, crowned by Europe's highest mountain, Mont Blanc (4,807 m.).
Vicinity ● By rack-railway, 20-min. climb to Montenvers (1,909 m.): viewing table, small zoo for mountain animals; wide view over Mer de Glace (Sea of Ice), with funicular down to grotto of same. ● Planpaz (2,000 m., magnificent view of *Mont Blanc massif*) and the *Brévent* (2,525 m.), extraordinary trip through the skies by cable-car. ● *La Flégère*, by cable-car (1,930 m., view over *Mont Blanc massif*); cable service reaches alt. of 2,390 m., ascending to foot of the Aiguilles-Rouges. ● The *Aiguille du Midi* cable-car route, highest in the world, runs via the Plan de l'Aiguille, where you change into another cabin which takes you to 3,790 m. alt. in a single swoop; from the arrival platform, lift ascends to final point, 3,842 m., from where you get absolutely unsurpassed panorama of *Mont Blanc massif*. Passage leads to Vallée Blanche cable-car, which runs to Pointe Helbronner, at 3,452 m.; finally, Col du Géant cable-car down to *Courmayeur*, in Italy. ● Lower chalet of *Les Bossons*; from village of that name, outpost of *Chamonix* (1,012 m.), cable-car climbs to 1,400 m. – visit to Grotte de Glace (cave of ice) is rec. *Les Houches*: Bellevue cable-car climbs to Plateau of Bellevue (1,790 m., panorama), departure-point for the Col de Voza-Prarion cable-car (see **St. Gervais***). ● *Mont Blanc Tunnel*: from *Chamonix* by expressway to Les Pèlerins (1,274 m.), from where access road to the tunnel branches off; the 11.6 km road tunnel (toll) is longest of its kind in the world, emerging on Italian soil at alt. of 1,381 m.

Champagnole
39 – Jura   26 – B 1
Holiday resort, excursion centre.
Vicinity ● To N, forests of La Fresse and *La Joux*, France's most beautiful fir plantation (President fir, 230 years old; viewing points, marked route). ● To NE, Mièges valley, strange fortified village of *Nozeroy* (16c church, clocktower, ruins of medieval castle); to S, source of R. Ain (resurgence) and Saut mill; Romanesque and Goth. church at Sirod; *Ain* water sink. ● To SE, *Syam* mill, Langouette gorges. ● To S and SW, area of lakes via Lemme valley (see lake of **Chalain***).

Chamonix: *the Aiguille du Midi cable-car service, highest in the world, soars across splendid panoramas to an altitude of 3,842 m., opposite the Mont Blanc massif.*

Champ-de-Bataille (Château)
27 – Eure   10 – D 1
One of the most remarkable
châteaux in Normandy. It consists
of two huge twin buildings (17c)
linked by porticos. Beautiful apartments (furniture, objets d'art, etc.;
v.a. Apr. 15–Dec. 11, cl. Tues.).
Vicinity • *Le Neubourg* (16c church)
has given its name to a flat plain,
dotted with interesting country
churches and châteaux. • 25 km N,
Bourg-Achard. • 18 km NNW,
Boissy-le-Châtel (Ch. de *Tilly*). •
15 km NW, **Brionne***; *Harcourt*
(medieval castle, rebuilt 17c; arboretum).

Champlitte
70 – Haute-Sâone   20 – A 2
Late 18c Classical-style church; int.
has 15c Burgundian statues. In
castle, Albert Demard reg. mus. of
folk arts and trads. (v.a. exc. Tues
and Sun. a.m.): remarkable reconstructions of peasant homes, games
and pastimes, country medicine,
magic). 16c and 17c houses.

Champs (Château)
77 – Seine-et-Marne   11 – D 2
This sober, elegant late-17c building, home of Mme. de Pompadour,
possesses a remarkable suite of
sumptuous 18c apartments, arranged around a huge oval room
which occupies centre of château.
The park is one of loveliest of 17c
formal gardens (v.a., cl. Tues.).
Vicinity • *Chelles*, prehistoric site,
ancient Merovingian capital;
Alfred Bonno museum.

Chamrousse
38 – Isère   32 – B 3
Large winter sports resort (1968
Olympic Games), rising in four
stages from 1,450 to 2,255 m.;
highest stage is upper resort at head
of Croix de Chamrousse cable-car
(wide view).
Vicinity • To W, *Uriage*, spa, surrounded by wooded mountains, via
forests of Prémol and St. Martin;
Grenoble*.

Chantilly (Château)
60 – Oise   11 – C 1
So-called Petit-Château, below the
neo-Ren. château built at end of 19c
by Daumet for the Duc d'Aumale,
is all that remains of the 16c buildings. They are surrounded by ornamental lakes and reached via a large
terrace. • The château houses
Condé mus., with remarkable collections of paintings (Provençal
early masters, Fra Angelico,
Clouet, Raphael, Poussin,
Veronese, Reynolds, Lancret, Delacroix, Ingres, etc.) (v.a., cl. Tues.);
esp. rec. are main gallery, Clouet
room (16c portraits), Santuario
(two Raphaels, Filippino Lippi,

Chantilly: *the pseudo-Renaissance building encloses Jean Bullant's Petit-Château, reflected in the waters of the lake.*

and 40 miniatures by Fouquet),
Gem room (pink diamond) and
Tribune (Perugino, Watteau, Van
Dyck, Botticelli, Fra Angelico,
Poussin). • In Petit-Château, sumptuous 18c white and gold apartments of Duc de Bourbon (so-called
Monkey drawing-room, huge
gallery aka Galerie des Actions de
Monsieur le Prince). Library contains 13,000 rare works inc. some
500 manuscripts and the world-
famed *Très Riches Heures du duc de
Berry*. In chapel, altar sculpted by
Jean Goujon. • In park, landscape
garden and Jeu de Paume mus. (mid
18c); small garden called 'La Cabot-
ière', charming house aka Maison
de Sylvie (1648), late 18c Hamlet is
earlier than that at Trianon. • Not
far from château stands one of masterpieces of 18c architecture: the
Grandes Écuries (stable buildings),
which overlook world-famed Chantilly race course and house mus.
dedicated to the horse (v.a., Apr.–
Oct.)
Vicinity • To S, *Forêt de Chantilly*
(5,190 acres) contains lovely Com-
melles lakes and Queen Blanche's
castle, in troubadour style (1826). •
10 km E, **Senlis***. • 4 km N, **St. Leu-
d'Esserent***.

Chaource
10 – Aube   19 – C 1
13–14c church contains a noteworthy 'Entombment' (1515) with
eight figures, characteristic of 16c
school of Troyes, and numerous
16–17c statues or works of art.
Unusual old houses with wooden
pillars.
Vicinity • 15 km N, via forest of
Aumont, *L'Isle-Aumont*, church
with two naves, one 12–13c, other
15–16c, 10c Carolingian choir; 5–
9c sculpted sarcophagi from nearby
necropolis; 15–16c folk-art statues.
• 11.5 km NE, *Rumilly-lès-Vaudes*:

in 16c church, 16c retable of the
Passion, in stone; Ch. des Tourelles;
16c manorhouse in stone and wood.

Chapelle-d'Angillon (La)
18 – Cher   18 – C 3
Castle of Béthune (v.a., cl. Sun.
a.m. from Palm Sunday to Oct.) still
has 15–16c buildings and an 11c
keep.
Vicinity • 7.5 km S, via forest of St.
Palais, ruins of abbey of Loroy; 13c
abbey church, 17c monastery buildings and cloister. • 11 km SE, *Henrichemont*, built 1608 on grid
pattern, has large central square
from which radiate eight straight
streets; 4 km to SE, *La Borne*, centre
for Grès pottery (exhibition workshops); to S, along D.46, *Morogues*
and Romanesque *Ch. de Maupas*
(see **Sancerre***). • 21 km W,
Nançay, radioastronomic research
centre: huge radio telescope (v.a. on
request; an esplanade open to
public has explanatory panels).

Chapelle-en-Vercors (La)
26 – Drôme   32 – A 3
Burnt down during the fighting
between the Germans and the
Vercors Resistance in 1944, the
town has been rebuilt. Recommended excursion centre for
Vercors massif and *Forêt de Lente*.
Vicinity • 5 km N, *Les Baraques-en-
Vercors*, impressive ravine of
Grands Goulets via D518 winding
round mountainside. • 9 km S,
Grotte de la Luire, geological curiosity (Decombaz hall, 80 m. high
cavity leading into a swallowhole
through which flows R. Vernaison)
and shrine to the Resistance: the
Germans murdered the Resistance
fighters here in 1944; D518 continues to *Col du Rousset* (1,411 m.)
across magnificent, wild countryside; after Rousset tunnel, road
zigzags down to *Chamaloc* and **Die***

basin. ● To W, *Forêt de Lente* (see **Vassieux-en-Vercors***).

Charavines-les-Bains
38 – Isère   32 – B 2
Holiday resort at 800 m. S of *Lac de Paladru* (975 acres, 5.5 km long), very rich in fish, in superb setting.
Vicinity ● At Grands-Roseaux and La Neyre, remains of lake dwellings. ● Beaches on S tip of lake. ● Trip round lake via Pagetière, W bank, *Paladru* and hamlet of Coletière. ● 4 km NW, remains of charterhouse of Silve-Bénite, founded 12c, ruins of main cloister and former prior's house.

Charité-sur-Loire (La)
58 – Nièvre   18 – D 3
This little town on R. *Loire* still has remains of Romanesque abbey church of Ste. Croix-Notre-Dame (11–12c): choir is extremely lofty (unusual historiated capitals of Byzantine inspiration); transept and square belfry with blocked-up Romanesque main doorway, sculpted tympanum; in monastery enclosure, ruins of abbey buildings: 15c main abbey living-quarters, early 16c prior's house, etc. Municipal mus. (archaeology, decorative arts, 1880–1930). Many old houses. Rec. walk around ramparts. Unusual humpbacked stone bridge with 10 arches, spanning R. *Loire*.

Charleville-Mézières
08 – Ardennes   6 – D 2
Mézières has a beautiful church in Goth. Flamboyant style, the basilica of Notre Dame-de-l'Esp-érance (pilgrimage to the Black Virgin), and remains of 14 and 16c ramparts. Centre of Charleville is 17c Place Ducale, 23 brick and stone pavilions above an arcaded gallery; the old mill, fmr. communal mill (1626), houses Ardenne mus. and Arthur Rimbaud mus. (the poet's birthplace is at 12 Rue Thiers). Wildlife park. Fine view from Olympe hill (205 m. alt.).
Vicinity ● Trip round valley of R. *Meuse*, to N; from *Charleville*, D1 follows *Meuse* along r. bank via *Nouzonville* and *Braux*, where road crosses river; strange rocks of Quatre-Fils-Aymon loom over *Château-Regnault; Monthermé* has 12–15c fortified church (Romanesque font, 16c frescos); numerous unusual rock formations in area: Sept-Heures rock (2 km N), Longue-Roche (2.5 km NNW), Sept-Villages rock and Roma rock (3 and 4 km S); from *Monthermé* to Belgian frontier, to E, D31 follows magnificent wooded valley of R. *Semoy*; returning to *Monthermé*, take D1., which follows *Meuse* to N towards *Laifour*, facing Laifour rocks, at foot of vast rocky wall of the *Dames de Meuse* rising abruptly above the river – an impressive, grandiose landscape. Road continues to *Revin* and **Rocroi***.

Charlieu
42 – Loire   25 – C 3
The remains of the Benedictine abbey are well worth visiting (v.a.; cl. Tues. from Apr. 1 to Sept. 30; cl. Tues, Wed. and annual holiday from Oct. 1 to Mar. 31); see especially main door of abbey church, a masterpiece of 12c Burgundian Romanesque sculpture and, below porch, 11c doorway with sculpted tympanum; also rec., late 15c cloister, chapterhouse, chapel and 16c abbot's house, etc. Cordeliers cloister, a late 14-15c trapezoidal-shaped building, lies 500 m. W. Many old houses (13c Armagnacs house, 16c 'English' house).
Vicinity ● The Brionnais reg. has many Romanesque churches in lovely warm golden stone; to NW, *Iguerande*, early 12c (panorama); *Semur-en-Brionnais*: church in style of Cluny, beautiful belfry, St. Hugues castle (9c keep); *Anzy-le-Duc*, one of most beautiful churches in reg., sculpted doorway, polygonal bell-tower with triple-tiered bays; to NE, *Bois-Ste. Marie*, 12c church with cupola and square belfry; *Châteauneuf-sur-Sornin*: château, partly 16c, in wooded setting, mid.-12c Romanesque church. ● 12 km W, *La Bénissons-Dieu* remains of 12c and Goth. Cistercian abbey. ● 22 km NNE, *La Clayette*: 14c castle, greatly restored, still has its outbuildings flanked by a fortified postern-gate; in chapel, 15–16c frescos (v.a. on request); to SE, mt. Dun (708 m.), fine view, remains of oppidum.

Charroux
86 – Vienne   23 – C 3
Numerous remains of St. Sauveur abbey, founded in reign of Charlemagne, notably magnificent 11c Romanesque central lantern-tower

La Charité-sur-Loire: *Notre-Dame, a remarkable example of Burgundian Romanesque architecture.*

Charroux: *at Civray, the façade of St. Nicolas, on traditional regional themes.*

Chartres: *the spires of the cathedral soar high above the town. One of the late 12c pillar-statues on the royal portal. The Annunciation and the Visitation on the lefthand door of the north portal.*

of abbey church (v.a.). A 15c building contains collection of 13c sculptures, mostly from main doorway of abbey, and two 13 and 14c reliquaries.
Vicinity ● 11 km W, *Civray*; 12c Romanesque church of St. Nicolas; sculpted décors of façade and apse are outstanding; 15 and 16c houses.

Chartres
28 – Eure-et-Loire   11 – A 3
Notre Dame cathedral is supreme masterpiece of early 13c Goth. art; only the façade is largely Romanesque, from second half of 12c; its triple portal, aka 'Portail Royal', devoted to the glorification of

Christ, and whose recessed pillar-statues are world-famed, is one of the loveliest examples of Romanesque art. The two façades of the transept each offer a triple portal decorated with sculptures: those on the N portal are devoted to the Old Testament (circa 1230), those of the S (1225–1250) to the New Testament. Inside, the 12–13c stained-glass windows are exceptionally beautiful; partic. rec. are the two rose-windows in the transept and that of the façade. The choir screen, in 16c sculpted stone, illustrates scenes from the Life of Christ and that of the Virgin, in 41 groups of some 200 figures. 14c St. Piat chapel

houses the church treasure (Intnl. Stained-glass Window Centre opened in 1980). 11c crypt, largest in France, encloses a second, 9c crypt (v.a.). ● In fmr. episcopal palace, which still has its state rooms, Beaux-Arts mus. (cl. Tues.), collection of 12 Anet enamels by Léonard Limosin (mid-16c), tapestries, picture galleries: Zurbaran, Teniers, 18c French school (Chardin, Fragonard). Arms and armour, large collection of objects and documents from the Pacific. Contemporary art, 15 canvases and African sculptures by Vlaminck. Opposite N porch of cath., canon's house (13c windows); Rue du Car-

dinal Pie, fmr. chapter-house store-rooms, aka Loëns cellars, with three 13c naves. ● Chartres boasts many old houses: 35, Rue des Écuyers, unusual 'Queen Berthe's staircase', elegant 16c turret with carved beams; 12, Rue des Grenets, 15c Caige mansion; 10, Rue Noël-Ballay, Ren. Claude Huvé house; Rue du Cheval-Blanc: Collin d'Harleville and Champrond mansions (16c). ● Churches of St. Aignan (16c), St. Pierre (12–13c), with 10–11c square tower and remarkable series of 14 and 16c stained-glass windows. Behind 12c church of St. André (deconsecrated), on r. bank of R. Eure, strange old streets of La Tannerie and La Foulerie, lined by wash-houses and picturesque old houses. ● Lovers of the unusual should visit Raymond Isidore's eccentric house, called 'Picassiette', beside cemetery of St. Chéron.
Vicinity ● 1.5 km SE, 11c church of St. Martin-au-Val, remains of Merovingian sanctuary in crypt. ● To NE, *Eure* valley, fresh and green, via *Lèves, Jouy, St. Piat* (interesting churches) and Ch. de **Maintenon***. To S, *Beauce* plain, towards **Illiers-Combray*** and **Châteaudun***.

Château-Arnoux
04 – Alpes-de-Haute-Provence   38 – C 3
Town is dominated by picturesque late-14c castle. 17c church.
Vicinity ● 4 km SW, St. Auban: viewing-point belonging to E.D.F. (natnl. electricity service), on R. *Durance*, overlooks L'Escale water-works, moving barrage bridge and 445 m. embankment; 6.5 km to S, unusual rock formation called 'Pénitents des *Mées*'. ● Near *Peyruis* (10 km SW), 11c Romanesque church of St. Donat. ● To SE, N85 follows lovely *Bléone* valley via *Malijai* (on Alpine Route Napoléon) towards **Digne***.

Châteaubriant
44 – Loire-Atlantique   16 – D 1
Ruins of medieval fortress, or Vieux-Château (13c door, 12–13c chapel, late 15c main building), are dominated by a huge square keep. Ren. Château-Neuf is linked by an arcaded gallery, in brick, to an elegant square pavilion with two-tiered arcades; it houses the law court and library (v.a.). Late-11c church of St. Jean-de-Béré has red sandstone or 'roussard' transept crossing.
Vicinity ● 1.5 km E, on road to **Laval***, natnl. monument to those who were shot or massacred during the Resistance. ● 16 km E, *Pouancé*, ruins of 13 and 14c castle, flanked by 11 towers, dominating lake of St. Aubin; to SE, lake of Tressé.

Château-Chalon
39 – Jura   26 – B 1
Village built like an eyrie on rocky escarpment, in midst of the vines which have made its reputation (world-famed 'yellow wine'). Old gateway, remains of castle. Country church. Panorama.
Vicinity ● 6 km E, impressive viewing-point over *Ladoye* basin.

Château-Chinon
58 – Nièvre   19 – B 3
Main tourist centre of **Morvan*** reg., which one can view from Le Calvaire (609 m. alt.), built on remains of Gallic oppidum and former medieval castle. Folklore and Costume museum.
Vicinity ● To S, towards *Mt. Beuvray* (remains of ancient Gallic oppidum of Bibracte, fine view), through *Arleuf* and *St. Prix* (round trip, *Haut Folin*, forest road); *Mt. Prénelay* (source of R. *Yonne*). ● 19 km E, *Anost* (interesting church); at 1.5 km, viewing-point of Notre Dame-de-L'Aillant, magnificent panorama. ● 22 km NE, **Settons*** reservoir, via D37. ● 18 km N, lake and dam of *Pannesière-Chaumard*, on R. *Yonne*.

Châteaudun
28 – Eure-et-Loir   18 – A 1
Built 12–16c, the château looks like a fortress from outside, but inside is a purportedly refined aristocratic dwelling (v.a., cl. public hols.). 12c cylindrical keep, 46 m. high, and Ste. Chapelle, in mid-16c Goth. Flamboyant style (noteworthy 15c statues from Loire workshops). Old town, at foot of château, has three outstanding churches: 12–13c St. Valérien, 12c Romanesque La Madeleine, 11–15c St. Jean-de-la-Chaîne, also Notre Dame-du-Champdé, of which only the elegantly sculpted late-15c façade remains. Municipal mus.: note-worthy ornithological collection, also Egyptology, Indian art.
Vicinity ● 7 km E, Lutz-en-Dunois, Romanesque church decorated with 12–13c murals. ● 14 km N, *Bonneval*, fmr. fortified town on R. *Loir*, fmr. abbey of St. Florentin (v.a. to ext. only), ruins of late 12c abbey church; church of Notre Dame, 13c Goth. ● Rec. trip along *Loir* valley, to SW, esp. from *Cloyes-sur-le-Loir*, to **Vendôme***.

Château-Gaillard
27 – Eure   5 – A 3
Its impressive ruins dominate the Seine and *Les Andelys*, esp. Le Petit-Andely. Impregnable stronghold, built late-12c by Richard the Lion Heart, it consists of two fortified walls surrounding a squat cylindrical keep; it is separated from the plateau by huge moat defended by casemates cut out of the rock; the second wall, or exterior wall, is also surrounded by moat and flanked by triangular outwork (v.a. Mar. 15–Oct. 15, cl. Tues. and Wed. a.m.). Dramatic view. Le Grand-Andely has a lovely Goth. church whose façade with three doorways is flanked by two towers; interior mixes Goth., Goth. Flamboyant and Ren. styles; attractive Ren. organ-chest in sculpted oak, 16c. stained-glass windows, 15c. choir stalls and statues.

Château-Gaillard: *the ruins of this impressive fortress, built in the late 12c by Richard the Lion Heart, dominate Les Andelys and the harmonious curve of the Seine.*

Château-Gontier
53 – Mayenne   17 – A 1
Old town, rising in tiers above r. bank of R. *Mayenne*, is dominated by 11–12c Romanesque church of St. Jean (remains of 12c murals). Fine view from Promenade du Bout-du-Monde. Interesting 16, 17 and 18c mansions. Museum.
Vicinity • 7 km SW, on *Chemazé* road, 15–16c Ch. de *St. Ouen*, flanked by magnificent square tower (n.v.a.). • To S, between *Jaille-Yvon* and *Chambellay*, Ch. du Percher, elegant late-15c building, with unusual turret staircase, early 16c chapel (n.v.a.); 15, 17 and 19c Ch. du Bois-Montbourcher, on edge of large lake.

Châteauneuf-du-Faou
29S – Finistère   8 – C 3
Excursion centre for *Montagnes Noires*, anglers' paradise (salmon and pike).
Vicinity • From *Laz* (8 km S), follow ridge road (D41): magnificent views. • 9.5 km E, near *Spézet*, chapel *Notre-Dame-du-Crann* (1535), lovely 16c stained-glass windows. • To S, forest of Laz and regional forest of Trévarez en St. Goazec, 185-acre park, marked paths through woods, rhododendron plantations, azaleas, etc.

Château-Queyras
05 – Hautes-Alpes   38 – D 1
In centre of Queyras national park, where big effort is under way to develop area as winter sports centre. Dominated by Queyras fort (v.a. in summer) – built 13c (magnificent 16 m.-high keep), strengthened by Vauban and again in 19c – the town is divided into two separate quarters, one at foot of fort, other on bank of R. *Guil*.
Vicinity • To S, 11 km road to summit of Le Bucher (2,260 m., viewing table). • 11 km SE, via Ville-Vieille (16c church) and *Molines-en-Queyras*, picturesque old village (winter sports), **St. Véran***. • To NE, via *Aiguilles*, pretty holiday resort and winter sports centre (Vieux-Queyras mus.), and *Guil* valley, *Abriès* (Romanesque church, Penitents chapel) and *L'Echalp* (1,677 m.); a narrow, extremely steep road leads to viewing-point in bowl of *Mt. Viso* (2,127 m.), magnificent panorama. • To N, Col d'*Izoard*, towards **Briançon***. • To SW, via *Guil* valley, *Guillestre* and **Mt. Dauphin***.

Châteauroux
36 – Indre   24 – B 1
Church of St. Martial (13c choir,

15c nave, Ren. belfry), Bertrand mus. (cl. Mon.) and fmr. 13c Franciscan church (occasional exhibitions) are town's principal sights; mus. houses Napoleonic and archaeological collections, and paintings or souvenirs of local personalities (e.g. George Sand), two galleries are devoted to region's traditional way of life.
Vicinity • 2 km on r. bank of R. *Indre*, *Déols*; only the lovely Romanesque belfry remains of once-flourishing abbey, founded 10c; 12 and 15c church has two Merovingian crypts (5c tomb of St. Ludre). • To S, lovely forest of Châteauroux, follow arrows.

Château-Thierry
02 – Aisne   12 – A 1
La Fontaine's birthplace is a charming 16c mansion transformed into a mus. Impressive remains of castle, whose ramparts stand proudly on a hilltop (fine view); 14c St. Jean gate, to E, is framed by two huge towers. A little lower down, St. Pierre gate, also flanked by towers. In Grande Rue and Rue du Château, 17c houses. 15–16c Balhan tower.
Vicinity • 4 km W, American memorial for Hill 204. • 10 km to NW, vast American cemetery of *Bois-Bellau* (2,300 graves) and German cemetery. • To SW, banks of R. *Marne*, which curve gently between Château-Thierry and *La Ferté-sous-Jouarre*, across attractive, lush countryside (see **Jouarre***).

Châtelguyon
63 – Puy-de-Dôme   30 – D 1
Well-known spa. Place Brosson separates thermal quarter (casino, thermal baths, park, sporting facilities) from old town, which stands on hill dominated by a calvary (fine view).
Vicinity • Prades valley to NNW, Sans-Souci valley to W, and Enval gorges to S, are all pleasant walks. • 3 km W, 13, 14 and 15c castle of Chazeron (v.a. p.m. May–Sept. 1.). • 7 km to WSW, *Volvic* and picturesque ruins of Ch. de Tournoël (see **Riom***). • 7 km NE, *Ch. de Davayat*, manorhouse dating from reign of Louis XIII, surrounded by formal gardens; interesting collections inside (v.a.); in village, magnificent 4.66 m.-high menhir.

Châtellerault
86 – Vienne   23 – C 1
Small mus. in Descartes' house, 16c (162, Rue Bourbon). Only a turreted building remains of fmr. castle (mus.). Henri IV bridge, with two towers and nine arches, in stone,

dating from early 17c.
Vicinity • 10 km W, Ch. de *Scorbé-Clairvaux*, late 15 and 16c, surrounded by a moat and with vast 17c outbuildings, an orangery and dovecote. • Recommended excursions to N and to SE, in valleys of R. *Gartempe* and the *Vienne*.

Châtel-Montagne
03 – Allier   25 – B 3
Majestic church in pure 12c Auvergnat Romanesque style, built of granite; notable two-tiered porch with three rows of semicircular bays. 15c houses with turrets.
Vicinity • Climb to top of Puy du Roc (644 m.) is rec.: magnificent view. • 6 km S, *Le Mayet-de-Montagne*: excursion centre for *Mts. de la Madeleine*, area of gorse, heathland and forests.

Châtillon-sur-Indre
36 – Indre   24 – A 1
Church of Notre Dame, fmr. 11–12c collegiate church; Romanesque porch has unusual historiated capitals. Cylindrical 11c keep and a 15c building are all that remains of castle. Leisure amenities.
Vicinity • 13 km SE, *Palluau-sur-Indre*, impressive 12 and 15c castle (v.a. in summer; cl. Tues. out of season); Philippe Auguste tower and chapel decorated with 15c frescos; in fmr. church of St. Laurent, 12c murals (well-known Virgin and Child); 4 km to SE, *St. Genou*, noteworthy 12–13c church, old abbey church, with choir in purest local Romanesque style; 8 km to E, 15–16c *Ch. d'Argy* (v.a.), huge square keep flanked by turrets; int. courtyard is surrounded by an elegant two-tiered gallery dating from late 15c.

Châtillon-sur-Seine
21 – Côte-d'Or   19 – C 1
Main attraction of this little old town is in local archaeology mus. (v.a.), housed in Ren. Philandrier mansion – the magnificent Vix vase (1.65 m., 208 kg.), dating from 6 BC, discovered in 1953 at Mt. Lassois; without doubt, it originates from a Greek workshop in S. Italy and is one of the masterpieces of the Ancient World; the 'Vix treasure' also includes jewellery, parts of chariots, numerous gold and bronze objects, etc. Church of St. Vorles is one of the most important examples of early Romanesque art, from end of 10c. 500 m. to E, source of R. Douix in picturesque site.
Vicinity • 7 km N, Mt. Lassois, St. Marcel, tiny 12c Romanesque church; the 'Vix treasure' was discovered at foot of the hill. • 15 km

N, *Mussy-sur-Seine*, interesting 13 and 15c church; inside, lovely 13c tomb, 14–15c statues and early–16c Pietà; town hall in fmr. 15 and 18c château belonging to bishops of Langres; small mus. to the Resistance. ● To SE, lovely forest of *Châtillon* (32 sq. miles); ruins of Cistercian *Abbaye du Val des Choues*, founded late 12c (v.a.).

Châtre (La)
36 – Indre   24 – B 2
Climbing up the slopes on r. bank of R. *Indre*, this small town has picturesque old quarters, whose

cl. Tues. and Wed.) and contains small mus.; 2km to NW, in church at *Vic*, remarkable early-12c Romanesque frescos; George Sand described the landscapes and communities of *Indre* valley in her novels; to NE of Nohant, Chanteloube wood, setting for her 'La Mare au Diable'. ● 25 km NE, *Lignières*, lovely 17c château built by a leading architect of the day, François Le Vau (v.a. to ext. only). ● 17 km E, *Châteaumeillant*, lovely Romanesque church of St. Genès, dating from first half of 12c; 5.5 km to NE, St. Jeanvrin, Romanesque

cre: 11–12c circular church, modelled on Church of the Holy Sepulchre in Jerusalem.

Chaumont
52 – Haute-Marne   20 – A 1
Town stands on edge of steep-sloped plateau between two valleys. Magnificent viaduct. 13 and 16c Church of St. Jean Baptiste; inside, interesting works of art (late 15c Entombment with 11 very realistic figures. Old town is well worth strolling through for its old houses, narrow streets and picturesque corners. Law courts still have

Chaumont-sur-Loire: *the 100-year-old cedars in the park are one of the château's main features.*

CHAUSEY (Islands)
50 – Manche   9 – C 1
Boat service from **Granville*** during season (16 km in 1 hr.). Granitic archipelago, with more than 300 tiny islands at low tide. Only the main island is inhabited (55 inhabitants); village consists of some houses, harbour, school and fishermen's chapel. On far tip of island, disused fort and a lighthouse. Ruins of Franciscan convent founded in 14c.

square 12c keep of castle of Counts of Champagne, aka Hautefeuille tower. It contains lapidary and archaeology mus.

Chaumont-sur-Loire (Château)
41 – Loir-et-Cher   18 – A 2
On r. bank of R. *Loire*, château looks like an imposing fortress flanked by four huge machicolated towers. Main building in W and mid.-late 16c Amboise tower belong to late Goth. period, buildings in S and E, together with three remaining towers and the chapel are all Ren. (v.a.). Apartments include bedchambers of Diane de Poitiers and Catherine de Médici. Enormous stables.

houses, especially, those of the tanners, still look as they did in olden times. In 15c castle-keep, George Sand and Vallée Noire mus. (v.a.).
Vicinity ● 9 km NW, *Sarzay*, imposing 13c castle flanked by four round machicolated towers (v.a. Apr. 1–Sept. 30). ● 6 km N; Nohant-Vic; château in which George Sand lived is unchanged (cl. Tues., Apr. 1–Sept. 30; rest of year,

church, mid.-16c tomb of François de Blanchefort with weeping figures. ● 10 km SE, La Motte-Feuilly; in 15–16c church, tomb of Charlotte d'Albret (d. 1514), wife of Caesar Borgia, who lived in the 14–15c castle (which has round towers topped by wooden hoardings and a hexagonal keep). ● 14.5 km S, *Ste. Sévère-sur-Indre*, formerly fortified town, 18c château, remains of 13c keep. ● 18 km W, *Neuvy-St. Sépul-*

Chauvigny
86 – Vienne   23 – C 2
Dominated by a rocky promontory on which stand the imposing ruins of five medieval castles – the baronial castle (12c keep), the 13 and 15c Harcourt castle, the 12 and 15c

Montléon castle, and the Gouzon castle with its Flins tower – this picturesque little city contains, in upper town, one of the most noteworthy examples of the Poitou Romanesque school: the 12c church of St. Pierre, with an admirable apse and, inside, renowned historiated capitals, graphically realistic. In lower town, 11–12c Romanesque church of Notre Dame.

Vicinity ● 7.5 km NW, via *Bonnes* (two Romanesque churches), 12, 13 and 16c *Ch. de Touffou*, on terrace overlooking R. *Vienne* (v.a. in summer); inside, Four Seasons room, decorated with 16c frescos. ● 18 km S, *Civaux*, on r. bank of *Vienne*, 12c church, with 11c apse, in middle of a Merovingian cemetery.

Chavaniac-Lafayette (Château)
43 – Haute-Loire   31 – A 3
This beautiful early 18c building was birthplace of Marie-Joseph La Fayette (1757). It houses museum devoted to this great general and to the American War of Independence (cl. Wed.).

Chemin des Dames
See **Laon***.   6 – B 3

Chenonceaux (Château)
37 – Indre-et-Loire   17 – D 3
The most beautiful of all the Loire châteaux; built on R. *Cher* (v.a.; Son et Lumière and boat trips on *Cher* in summer). On r. bank, framed by Diane de Poitiers' garden to l. and Catherine de Médici's to r., are a 15c cylindrical keep and Bohier's early 16c château. The long gallery leading from S. façade of Bohier's château is the work of best-known 16c royal architect, Philibert Delorme; 60 m. in length, its two storeys rest on a five-arched bridge which spans the *Cher*. Interior is exquisitely decorated and furnished in Ren. style.

Vicinity ● 9.5 km E, on R. *Cher*, *Montrichard*: Nanteuil quarter (Romanesque and Goth. church) has many old houses (16c Ave Maria house, with three gables, 15c chancellery, etc.); 12–15c church of Ste. Croix; fortified castle, above town, has powerful 12c keep (v.a. in summer); 7 km to SE, ruins of abbey of Aiguevive, 12c church (n.v.a.); 10 km to E of *Montrichard*, Ch. du **Gué-Péan***.

Cherbourg
50 – Manche   3 – C 2
Commercial port, Chantereyne marina and naval dockyard. Trinity church, in 15–16c Goth. Flamboyant style, dominates the huge Place Napoléon, which has statue of the Emperor. Thomas Henry mus. of painting has large collection of work of J-F. Millet (portraits). Emmanuel Liais park contains unusual trees and exotic plants; mus. of natural history, ethnography and prehistory. In Roule fort (fine view), mus. of the Liberation (map room).

Vicinity ● To NW, capes of *Querqueville* and *Urville-Nacqueville*, whose charming 16c manorhouse (v.a., cl. Tues. and Fri.) stands in a romantic setting. ● To E, Ren. Ch. de *Tourlaville*, surrounded by a moat; v.a. daily to park only, containing many rare species; 6 km to E, not far from airfield, gallery tomb: impressive megalithic monument (16 m. long).

Cheverny (Château)
41 – Loir-et-Cher   18 – A 2
Built in 17c Classical style, the richness of its decoration contrasts with simplicity of its ext.: a rectangular main building linked by two wings to two enormous square pavilions (v.a.). The apartments are sumptuously decorated and furnished, esp. the king's apartments on the first floor, reached by magnificent stone staircase; main element of apartments is the royal bedchamber. In outbuildings, Cheverny hunting museum (2,500 trophies). Formal gardens leading into park. Ch. de Troussay, 16c, houses small regional museum.

Vicinity ● 9 km NE, Ch. de *Villesavin* (v.a., cl. Dec. 20–Jan. 20), charming Ren. building dating from 1537; 4.5 km to E, *Ch. d'Herbault*, Ren., rebuilt 19c; the chequerboard pattern of the bricks contrasts with the white tufa and grey slate of the roofs (n.v.a.); 3 km to S, *Fontaine-en-Sologne*, 12c church.

Chevreuse
78 – Yvelines   11 – B 2
Ruins of castle of La Madeleine and imposing 12c keep (v.a.) dominate the town, whose church has 12c Romanesque belfry. Place des Halles still looks like a village square.

Vicinity ● Chevreuse valley is good for excursions. ● To N, Rhodon

Chauvigny: *St. Pierre's Romanesque belfry towers over the fortified castles; the upper town lies on a rocky spur.*

Chenonceaux: *this priceless jewel of the Renaissance adds still further to the natural beauty of its setting.*

Cherbourg: reconstructed after the 1939–1945 war, the port provides anchorage for both pleasure boats and trawlers.

in ruins; the middle castle, including clock pavilion (12–14c), 35 m. high, which houses Joan of Arc mus.; and remains of 12–14–15c royal lodgings (Son et Lumière, Jun. 15–Aug. 15), flanked by 12c Treasury tower. Coudray castle, to W, with enormous towers (Boissy tower, Moulin tower), dominated by a 13c cylindrical keep aka Coudray tower, 25 m. high. Fine view of Chinon and R. *Vienne* valley from S. curtains of castle. ● Old town, very picturesque, is crossed from W to E by Rue Voltaire, intersected by narrow alleys and lined by lovely 15, 16 and 17c houses; in 15–16c States-General mansion, Vieux-Chinon museum. Grand Carroi, surrounded by old 15c houses with half-timbering and tall gables (see in particular the Red House, in brick and wood), was heart of city in medieval times. Church of St. Maurice has nave in pure 12c Anjou style. From Grand-Carroi, continuing eastwards, you come to St. Étienne, in 15c. Goth. Flamboyant style, then to St. Mexme, of which only 10c nave and 11c narthex, framed by two towers, remain. On

valley leads to *St. Lambert* and Port-Royal des Champs. ● To W, **Dampierre*** and upper *Yvette* valley (Levis-St. Nom, Notre Dame-de-la-Roche, etc.); to SW of **Dampierre***, the **Vaux de Cernay***. ● To SW, Louise XIII-style Ch. de Breteuil, surrounded by magnificent gardens; botanical tours of park (cl. Sun.). History recaptured by means of waxwork figures. ● To E, St. Rémy-lès-Chevreuse, *Yvette* valley Mérantaise valley, *Gif*, Bures, *Orsay*.

Cheylade
15 – Cantal   30 – D 3
The nave and side aisles of 16c church are covered with wainscoting (18c) made up of 1,428 tiny oak panels decorated with flowers and animals.
Vicinity ● 5 km NW, *Apchon*, framed by two volcanic dykes, one of which is crowned by impressive ruins of castle; fine view over Cheylade valley and *Puy Mary*; 5.5 km to S, chapel of Font-Sainte, at 1,250 m. alt. (solemn processions and pilgrimages in summer); 6 km to N of *Apchon*, *Riom-ès-Montagnes*, old township, seat of fmr. abbey, of which all that remains is church of St. Georges, Romanesque with 11–12c cupola, 13c porch and 14c belfry; esp. rec. is ext. decoration of apse; 3 km to NW, 19c Ch. de St. Angeau, with 15c tower; 2 km to E, little lakes of Bondes and Roussilhou.

Chinon
37 – Indre-et-Loire   17 – C 3
The castle (v.a., cl. Dec. and Jan.), whose imposing remains stretch for 400 m. along the steep promontory

which dominates the town, consists of three fortresses, separated by deep moats: St. Georges fort, to E,

Cheverny: externally, this is the most sober of the Loire châteaux; inside, though its boasts sumptuous apartments.

Chevreuse: the ruins of La Madeleine castle and its rectangular keep; there is a magnificent view from the terrace.

Chinon: *the town, which stretches along the banks of the Vienne in a superb setting, is dominated by the remains of three separate fortresses, dating from 12th to 15th centuries, which together form a 10-acre defensive network.*

hillside, 6, 10 and 12c troglodytic chapel of Ste. Radegonde; mural dating from 1200, representing a royal hunt. Museum of local folk art and tradition.
Vicinity ● 7 km SW, near *Seuilly, Manoir de La Devinière*, birthplace of Rabelais (small mus.); 2 km to SW, *Ch. du Coudray*, early 15c (n.v.a.); all around is 'Rabelais country', a smiling, gently undulating landscape in which the writer set the main action of both Gargantua and Pantagruel. ● 8 km to NW, *Avoine*; on l. bank of Loire, 4 km to N, *Centrale Atomique d'Avione-Chinon*, brought into service in 1962 by the E.D.F., the first nuclear power station in France designed for industrial production of electrical energy; mus. viewing-point (models and plans), from which one can see the whole installation; v.a. on request. ● 8 km E, *Cravant-les-Coteaux*: 10–11–12c church (Merovingian pillars, Carolingian nave), deconsecrated, now contains archaeological museum.

Cholet
49 – Maine-et-Loire 16 – D 3
In town centre, Place Travot is lined by theatre, town hall and late-19c neo-Goth. church of Notre Dame. Museum of history and of Vendée wars in the 1790s. Art museum contains number of interesting canvases, inc. those of Pierre-Charles Trémolières, born in Cholet (18c). Le Mail garden covers terrace and gardens of former château, overlooking Moine valley.
Vicinity ● 1 km to NW, Lavau wood and Ch. de Bois-Landry. ● Pierre-du-Diable (1 km SW), Poch-etière menhir (3 km SE), Grand-Champ menhir and Guil-au-Boin dolmen (2 km W). ● 4 km SE, Ribou dam, beach, swimming pool, water sports, etc. ● 10 km SW, *Mortagne-sur-Sèvre*, remains of ramparts with terraced gardens, ruins of 14–15c castle (Treasury tower); 6 km to SE, *St. Laurent-sur-Sèvre*: the (modern) basilica contains tombs of St. Grignion de Montfort (d. 1716) and Sister Marie-Louise de Jésus. ● 9.5 km NW, *Bégrolles-en-Mauges*; 1 km to N, former Benedictine abbey of Belle-Fontaine, founded 11c, occupied by Trappist monks: Ren. abbot's house, 19c neo-Goth. church. ● D572 crosses *Mauges* country.

Clairvaux-les-Lacs
39 – Jura 26 – B 2
Holiday resort. In church, beautiful 15c carved choir stalls and noteworthy 17c paintings.
Vicinity ● 300 m. to S, large lake of Clairvaux, beach, boat hire; small lake, at foot of Rochette hill (611 m.), on which stand ruins of medieval fortress. ● 5 km NW, *Pont-de-Poitte* and Saut-de-la-Saisse. ● 11 km NE, *Bonlieu* and its lake, surrounded by pine forests; to N, waterfalls, *Cascades du Hérisson*; recommended excursions in lake region (see lake of **Chalain***).

Clamecy
58 – Nièvre 19 – A 2
Old town merits a prolonged stroll; picturesque streets, lined by houses from 15c (Maison du Tisserand) and 16c (Hôtel de Bellegarde, housing mus.: 3c coins, pottery, old paintings [Claude Lorrain], local ethnology). These old streets lie round 13–14c church of St. Martin (lovely Goth. Flamboyant façade). Ugly Bethlehem church (1927), in reinforced concrete, is reminder of the days when Clamecy gave refuge to Bethlehem's bishop when that town was occupied by the Turks (12–13c).
Vicinity ● 16 km SW along D33, *Varzy*, lovely Goth. church; interior has triptych of Ste. Eugénie (1537); old houses (15c Guiton house, 15–16c magistrates' house, etc.). Municipal museum.

Clécy
14 – Calvados 10 – B 1
This large town is main excursion centre for 'Suisse Normande' region, full of picturesque sites.
Vicinity ● Rec. walks: to N, 16c manorhouse of Placy, small mus.; Pain de Sucre (panorama); to SE, Faverie cross, view of Parcs rocks, banks of R. *Orne* and Vey bridge, L'Éminence (panorama), St. Clair hill, etc. ● To SE, via *Pont-d'Ouilly*, is strange *Roche d'Oëtre* in magnificent setting; this is most 'mountainous' landscape in the 'Suisse Normande'; from *Roche d'Oëtre*, follow *Orne* valley as far as *Forêt-*

> **CLAPS (Le)**
> **26 – Drôme** 38 – A 1
> On leaving *Luc-en-Diois* (see **Die***), road passes under Le Claps viaduct, a metal construction, 210m, long, 60m. high, and reaches the site of Le Claps, a fantastic rocky scree traversed by R. *Drôme*; then road continues along corniche slopes above site, providing magnificent views.

Auvray bridge. ● To N, **Thury-Harcourt***. ● To W, Ch. de **Pontécoulant***.

Clères (Château, Zoological Park)
76 – Seine-Maritime 5 – A 2
13–14c château, with 12c keep, restored 19c, is surrounded by a beautiful zoological park; in partic., enormous aviaries. Automobile mus. (v.a. daily in summer; hrs. vary out of season) has comprehensive collection of working models (oldest dating from 1876). Vehicles or machines which took part in the battle for Normandy. Bocasse fun fair.

Clermont-en-Argonne
55 – Meuse 12 – D 1
16c church of St. Didier, with two Ren. doorways. 16c. Ste. Anne's chapel, on a hill overlooking *Forêt de l'Argonne*, has interesting 16c sepulchre; panorama; viewing-table.
Vicinity ● 6 km W, *Les Islettes* from where D2, to S, runs along *Biesme* valley (aka Route de la Haute-Chevauchée) to hermitage of St. Rouin (chapel in lovely setting in Beaulieu wood), near sources of R. *Biesme*, which form an attractive chaplet of lakes. ● Excursion centre for *Forêt d'Argonne*, to N.

Clermont-Ferrand
63 – Puy-de-Dôme 31 – A 1
Capital of the Auvergne; the old town, between cathedral and Notre Dame-du-Port, still looks as it did in days gone by; old 16, 17 and 18c houses: Rue du Port, Rue Pascal, Place and Rue du Terrail, Rue des Chaussetiers (No. 3: early 16c Savaron house, courtyard with turret staircase and three Goth. galleries. In Rue des Gras, No. 34, Hôtel Fontfreyde, aka 'The Architects' House', 16c, is occupied by Ranquet mus. (local hist. and art, souvenirs of Pascal, who was born in town). Cath. of Notre Dame, built 13–14c in black Volvic stone, is most beautiful Goth. building in Auvergne (the two steeples and the façade, though, are late 19c); inside, 13 and 15c frescos; see also the upper stained-glass windows of apse and Goth. Rayonnant chapels. Notre Dame-du-Port is an outstanding example of 12c Auvergnat Romanesque architecture; the apse

is particularly fine; massive and squat, it contains magnificent historiated capitals; in 11c crypt, highly venerated Black Virgin. In Bargoin museum, fine collections of archaeology, sculpture and painting, mainly 18 and 19c.: Boucher, Chassériau, Gustave Doré, Chinard, Bartholdi, C. Claudel. Nudes, contemp. art. Worth seeing in N. district of town are strange petrifactive springs of St. Alyre.
Vicinity ● 2 km, *Montferrand*: built to a square plan, with two right-angled axes, which end at the four gates in the surrounding wall, this little medieval-looking town has a number of fine Goth. and Ren. houses; 13 and 14c church of Notre Dame-de-Prospérité; int. has 17c carved wooden panelling. ● 15 km N, **Riom***. ● Rec. tour of the Puys, to NNW (see **Puy-de-Dome***). ● 12 km S, via *Plateau de Gergovie*, viewing-table and monument commemorating Vercingetorix's victory over Julius Caesar (52 BC); magnificent panorama (700 m. alt.); picturesque village of *Opme* is dominated by fmr. castle of Dauphins of the Auvergne, in 12 and 13c black lava, flanked by three round towers and a square keep, modified and enlarged 18c, magnificent gardens on two-tiered terraces (v.a., cl. Wed., July 1–Sept. 30. Rest of year, on request); 2 km away,

Clermont-Ferrand: *Amboise fountain, with Gothic architecture and Renaissance décor.*

Chanonat: 18c château of La Batisse still has two 15c towers; interesting furnishings (v.a. daily May 1–Sept. 30; Sat. and Sun. p.m., Oct. 1–Apr. 30); lovely formal gardens.

Clermont-l'Hérault
34 – Hérault 43 – A 1
Old town dominated by ruins of medieval castle with keep and round towers. 13–14c Goth. church of St. Paul, fortified apse and façade. In lower town, fmr. church of St. Dominique, late 16c.
Vicinity ● 2.5 km N, Lacoste, under hill of Belbézé (calvary, fine view); 1 km away, ruins of abbey of Cornils. ● 9 km N, then 40 mins. walk, Deux-Vierges peak (535 m. alt.), St. Fulcran chapel, fine view. ● 8 km W, corrie of **Mourèze***.

Cléry-St. André
45 – Loiret 18 – B 1
Basilica of Notre Dame, in Goth. Flamboyant style, is outstanding; inside, tomb of Louis XI (d. 1483), surmounted by a statue of the king, depicted in kneeling position. Lovely Ren. St. Jacques chapel, richly sculpted, and Dunois-Longueville chapel with Dunois tomb (d. 1468).

Clisson
44 – Loire-Atlantique 16 – D 3
Impressive ruins of castle (v.a., cl. Tues., Son et Lumière). 13–14c E part is entered via an enormous 15c doorway, surmounted by machicolations; W part dates from 15c. On r. bank of R. Sèvre, 12–13c church and district of La Trinité. Fine view of castle and surrounding area from viaduct crossing R. Moine (Poitiers road).
Vicinity ● 19 km SE, ruins of castle of **Tiffauges***.

Cluny
71 – Saône-et-Loire 25 – D 2
Of what used to be one of the most influential abbeys in Christendom (now an Arts and Crafts school), there remains only a 14c Goth. façade, some enormous 18c buildings, a 13c flour-mill converted into a lapidary museum (magnificent Romanesque capitals), some lapidary remains of the abbey and 14c Moulin tower. (v.a., cl. Tues.; audiovisual commentaries in summer.) 11–12c abbey church of St. Pierre and St. Paul, the largest church in the world before St. Peter's in Rome was built, has also been mutilated; only r. arm of Romanesque main transept remains, along with two apsidal chapels, octagonal, 62 m.-high Holy Water belfry, and Bourbon chapel, a finely decorated Goth. jewel. 15c abbot's palace contains

Ochier museum (variable opening hrs.), which has lapidary room and galleries of paintings and decorative arts, tapestries, pottery, etc. St. Marcel has magnificent octagonal Romanesque mid-12c belfry with a steeple. 13c Notre Dame is surrounded by Romanesque and Goth. houses.

Vicinity • 10 km N, *Taizé*: Protestant monastic community, with an ecumenical attitude to religion; 12c Romanesque church, Church of the Reconciliation (1962) shared by Roman Catholics and Protestants alike; nearby, Orthodox church;

(Christ in Majesty, 12c, 4 m. high); Berzé-le-Châtel has ruins of enormous feudal castle. • 11 km S, Ch. de St. Point, home of poet, Lamartine (see **Mâcon***).

Cognac
16 – Charente   29 – A 1
Old town, on banks of R. Charente, has many old streets and houses, especially Grande-Rue, Rue des Cordeliers, Rue Magdeleine, Rue de l'Isle d'Or (lovely 16–17c mansions), Rue Saulnier, Rue de Lusignan, etc. Church of St. Leger has Romanesque façade with big 15c

noteworthy Romanesque church of Châtres, surmounted by four majestic cupolas, and Ch. de Garde-Épée, with 17c fortified wall and monumental gate. • 8 km E, Bourg-Charente, Romanesque church with three cupolas; recommended execution in winding valley of R. *Charente*, to E, via abbey of Bassac: 13c church, in local Romanesque style, has magnificent 12c belfry; inside, impressive monks' choir, with rich stone and marble decorations; carved wooden choir stalls from early 17c.

Collioure
66 – Pyrénées-Orientales 43 – D 3
Very picturesque fishing port, much beloved of painters, built around a bay at foot of steep cliffs. Old fortified town lies between church, Miradou fort and castle; Moure quarter is bisected by narrow streets lined by old houses. Overlooking bay on rocky escarpment is royal castle or Templars castle, built 12–14c, reinforced in 16 and 17c. Collioure's defensive system also includes St. Elmo's fort, to SE (n.v.a.), and Miradou fort, to N (military base, entry forbidden). Church of Notre Dame-des-Anges and the port together form a setting which is justly famed. The brick-built church, flanked by a round tower, contains many 17–18c gilded and sculpted retables in Catalan baroque style.

Vicinity • 4 km S, late 12c hermitage of Notre Dame-de-Consolation, fine view; via footpath, ruins of 13c abbey of Valbonne. • St. Elmo's fort dominates winding road (N114) which leads down to *Port-Vendres*, from which a tiny corniche road leads to *Cape Béar* and *Fort Béar*, 4 km to E (magnificent views). • Recommended drive from Collioure to **Banyuls*** via Route des Crêtes and Balcon de Madeloc (15km along D86); magnificent panoramic views.

Cluny: *the Holy Water and Clock belfries are among the few remains of the original huge Romanesque abbey.*

3.5 km to N, *Cormatin*: the château, built in 17c in Ren. style, with courtyard enclosed by two wings (v.a. Sat. and Sun. during May and June; daily, July 1–Oct. 30), has an exceptionally richly decorated interior: panelling, ceilings, furniture, 16–19c paintings. • 10 km NE, Blanot, picturesque medieval village, old houses built of lava, grottoes; 4 km to N, Mt. St. Romain (579 m.), fine view. • 12 km SE, Berzé-la-Ville, in early 12c fmr. chapel of château of Les Moines, Romanesque murals

rose-window. Former Valois château, where François I was born, has interesting remains of 13, 15 and 16c castle (v.a.; cl. Sat. and Sun. out of season). Opposite, early-16c gate of St. Jacques, flanked by two large towers. On edge of town hall park, Cognac mus. contains interesting collections of paintings and decorative arts. Galleries devoted to viticulture, distillation, cooperage and sales of Cognac brandy.

Vicinity • 4 km E, St. Brice, 10–11c church, 14c castle; 1.5 km to NE,

Collobrières
83 – Var   44 – C 2
Old town, built on a hill dominated by remains of 12–16c church. Old houses.

Vicinity • 12 km E, *Chartreuse de la Verne*, in wooded, wild setting (v.a., cl. Tues.), noteworthy group of monastic buildings, dating from 12 to 18c, currently being restored. • To N, via *Col de la Fourche* (536 m.), chapel of *Notre Dame-des-Anges* (779 m.), highest point in *Maures* range; 10c sanctuary is flanked by dormitories for pilgrims and a small cloister; fine view; forest road leads to *Gonfaron*, 11 km to N. • To S, towards **Le Lavandou***, via *Massif des Maures*: really lovely route.

Collioure: *a typical Western Mediterranean town, with its church, old quarter and fort.*

Collonges
19 – Corrèze   30 – A 3
Nicknamed 'The Red' (Collonges La Rouge) because of its brilliant red sandstone buildings, this tiny old town has retained much of its medieval character. It is well-worth taking time to stroll along its narrow, badly paved streets, lined by 15, 16 and 17c houses. Romanesque church with exquisite Limousin Romanesque tympanum and belfry. 15c town gates.
Vicinity ● 10 km W, *Turenne*; its old 15–16c houses are dominated by highly impressive ruins of castle, with two 13 and 14c towers.

Colmar
68 – Haute-Rhin   21 – A 1
One of most noteworthy towns of artistic interest in France. Its old houses, with timber frames or with sculpted or painted façades, its monuments and its mus. form an exceptionally interesting ensemble. Unterlinden mus. (v.a., cl. Tues., Nov.–Mar.), in fmr. Dominican convent, is one of richest in France, with outstanding Rhenish early masters, and world-famed *Issenheim altarpiece* by Matthias Grünewald (early 16c), Romanesque and Goth. lapidary collections, arms, furniture, and decorative arts. Folk art, Alsace trads. Contemp. art: Braque, Rouault, de Staël, Mathieu, Bonnard, Dubuffet, Clavé, etc. ● In middle of old quarter, many typical houses, two churches: St. Martin known locally as the Cathedral, 13–

14c; and 13–15c Dominican church, in yellow sandstone, built in Rhenish Goth. style with 14c cloister; inside has 14c stained-glass windows and *Vierge au buisson de roses*, masterpiece by 15c local artist, Schongauer; Bartholdi mus. See also Rue des Têtes, Maison des Têtes aka *Kopfhaus*, Colmar's most beautiful early 17c Ren. house. ● Old Customs House is centre of tanners' quarter, recently restored, where gentle stroll is highly rec. through Place du Marché-aux-Fruits, Grande-Rue (17c House of the Arcades), Rue des Tanneurs on R. Lauch, Quai de la Poissonerie, Rue St. Jean, etc. The quays along R. Lauch, between St. Pierre bridge and Rue de Turenne, are nicknamed 'Little Venice'. Krutenau quarter, once fortified island, is home of local market gardeners (floodlit in summer); Rue de Turenne is lined by beautiful 16–18c houses; Rue de la Poissonerie, by old bargees' house. ● In Aug., Alsace wine fair. In autumn, Sauerkraut festival.

Combourg (Château)
35 – Ille-et-Vilaine   9 – C 2
Superb feudal castle, 11, 14 and 15c, where Chateaubriand (d. 1848) spent part of his childhood, raises its imposing towers alongside a lake (v.a., cl. Tues. Mar. 1–Nov. 30). Small mus. devoted to the writer (who was also one-time French ambassador in London).

Commercy
55 – Meuse   13 – A 2
Magnificent 18c château overlooking courtyard lined by out-

Collonges: *fortified church, with square belfry below two-tiered octagonal section.*

Colmar: *houses with gables, corbelling and carved beams – epitome of Alsace.*

Compiègne: *the town hall, a fine example of Gothic Flamboyant civil architecture.*
On the edge of a forest of beech and oak, the Gallo-Roman ruins of Champlieu.◄

buildings which open on to the Fer-à-Cheval (horseshoe), a huge Classical hemicycle. Museum (in town hall): interesting collection of ceramics and of French and foreign ivories (16–19c). *Local speciality:* Madeleine cakes.
Vicinity ● Excursion in Meuse valley, to N, *Lérouville* and *Sampigny*, as far as **St. Mihiel***.

Compiègne
60 – Oise   5 – D 3
Rebuilt 18c, the château covers more than five acres of triangular-shaped ground in middle of large park (v.a. daily July–Aug.; Sun. and public hols. from Easter to Nov. 11). It contains three mus.: State Apartments, beautifully decorated and furnished in reign of Louis XVI

and during the Empire; Second Empire mus., evoking the life, customs, art and taste of reign of Napoleon III; Automobile and Tourism mus. (cl. Sat., Sun. and Tues.) in fmr. kitchens and adjacent courtyard. ● In town, see town hall, in early-16c Goth. Flamboyant style; mus. of historic figurines (100,000 individual pieces depicting

Concarneau: *these big blue nets evoke the bustle of the fishing port, in contrast with the silence of the adjoining Ville-Close, behind its 14th-century ramparts.*

different historical events) installed 1984 in fmr. Hôtel de la Cloche; and Vivenel mus., in early-19c Hôtel de Songeons (largest collection of Greek vases after Louvre's).

Vicinity • *Forêt de Compiègne*, bounded by three rivers, crisscrossed by marked paths, and extended by *Forêts de Laigue* and *Ourscamp*, covers 56 sq. miles; 6.2 km to NNE, *Clairière de l'Armstice*, commemorative stone, statue of Marshal Foch (reconstructed), railway carriage in which armistice was signed on Nov. 11, 1918 (v.a.); to E and SE, *Vieux-Moulin* (fmr. woodcutters' village), hills of St. Marc (130m.) and *St. Pierre* (141 m.), lakes of St. Pierre, *St. Jean-aux-Bois* (early 13c church, late-12c chapter-house, 16c door), 2c Gallo-Roman ruins of *Champlieu*, etc.

Concarneau
29S – Finistère   15 – C 1
The Ville-Close (enclosed town) is one of Brittany's most unusual sites. Built on 300 m.-long island, surrounded by granite ramparts flanked by 15c towers, reconstructed by Vauban, it is linked to Place Jean Jaurès by a bridge (floodlit in summer); inside, v. picturesque fishing mus. Rec. tour of ramparts. Port is v. lively, esp. during fish auctions and when boats leave or return.

Vicinity • Rec. trips to *Îles de Glénan* (large yachting centre) via daily boat service in summer.

Condé-en-Brie (Château)
02 – Aisne   12 – B 1
Built 12c, rebuilt 17–18c, (v.a.; cl. Tues.); inside, dining-room and music-room, both with trompe-l'oeil paintings, huge Louis XV drawing-room decorated by Oudry, wood panelling, furnishings and numerous objets d'art, 18c paintings; Richelieu's room; studios used by Watteau and Oudry.

Vicinity • 11 km NE, *Dormans*: church with Roman and Goth. remains; Louis XIII-style château, flanked by two feudal towers; in park, pseudo-Goth. Interesting chapel, commemorating the two battles of the Marne; crypt and charnel-house; fine view from tower.

Condom
32 – Gers   35 – C 3
Former cathedral, in early 16c southern Goth. style, has Goth. Flamboyant doorway. Old bishop's palace has a beautiful 16c Goth. Flamboyant cloister; on first floor, Armagnac museum, viticultural ethnography. Picturesque streets, 16–17c mansions.

Vicinity • 8 km S, *Abbaye de Flaran*,

church with three naves and dry-stone cloister (mid-12c) (v.a. during summer season). • 4 km W, **Larressingle***; 11 km to W, *Montréal*, early-14c church, containing fragment of 3c Roman mosaic; ruins of Romanesque church of St. Pierre-de-Genens; 2 km to SW, *Séviac*, noteworthy remains of sumptuous Gallo-Roman villa; beautiful mosaics. • 12km E, *La Romieu*, old fortified town, Goth. church with two towers, 14c frescos.

Conflans
73 – Savoie   32 – C 1
Suburb of *Albertville*, one of most unusual sites in Savoie. Perched on

Condé-en-Brie: *the château, dating from the 12th century, has beautiful Louis XV apartments, installed six centuries later.*

a rocky outcrop, this one time military township is criss-crossed by narrow, steep streets lined by old houses linked by arcades. Savoie and Tarine gates are linked by Grande-Rue (Rue Gabriel Pelouze), in which are 15c Ramus tower, early 18c church and 16c Red House, in brick (local mus.: reconstruction of old interiors, art and folklore). On La Roche terrace, overlooking valley, Saracen tower with fine view.

Vicinity • 11km E, fort of Le Mont (1,120 m., wide panorama). • 10 km NE, beyond *Ugine*, *Gorges de l'Arly*. • 12.5 km W, via *Col de Tamié* (908 m.), *Abbaye de Tamié*; 17c church is divided in three: lay brothers' choir, monks' choir, sep-

arated by carved wooden rood-screen, and sanctuary.

Confolens
16 – Charente   23 – C 3
Picturesque old town huddles round confluence of R. Vienne and the Goire; attractive views from Pont-Neuf, esp. of 15c Pont-Vieux, formerly fortified, which straddles Vienne. Alleyways lined by old houses, 15c timber-framed buildings, 17–18c mansions (Rue du Soleil, Rue des Francs-Maçons). Former priory church of St. Barthélemy: 11c Romanesque façade and nave. In Aug., International Folklore Festival.

Vicinity • 22 km SW, *Cellefrouin*, lovely 11c Romanesque abbey church of St. Pierre; in neighbouring cemetery, Romanesque graveyard lantern. • 4.5 km N, *St. Germain-de-Confolens*, in picturesque site; ruins of med. château, Romanesque church; 22 km to N, *L'Isle-Jourdain*, rising in tiers above R. Vienne. • 22 km NW, abbey of La Réau (v.a. Mar. 1–Sept. 30; cl. Tues.): 12–13c abbey church, 12c chapter-house, 17–18c convent buildings.

Conques
12 – Aveyron   36 – C 1
Old fortified town, medieval in character, lies in an amphitheatre in magnificent site on r. bank of R.

CONSOLATION (Cirque – Bowl)
25 – Doubs   20 – C 3
One of the loveliest sites in Jura, more than 300 m. deep, source of R. *Dessoubre* and the Lançot. Notre Dame-de-Consolation, former 17c Franciscan monastery (now a small seminary), has interesting Jesuit-style chapel (interior contains beautiful mausoleum in red and white marble). On promontory between blind valleys of two rivers, viewpoint of Le Prêtre rock: marvellous view over the bowl.

Ouche. Many old houses with lauze roofs (circa 1500, Ch. de Humières) and traces of fortifications, of which only three gates remain. Mid-11c– late 12c Ste. Foy is one of most beautiful Romanesque churches in France; tympanum of main doorway, representing the Last Judgment (circa 1140), is one of masterpieces of Romanesque sculpture of S of France (doorway and façade floodlit in summer); int. of church is vast but harmoniously proportioned; in only remaining gallery of cloisters, small lapidary museum. Alongside, treasury, outstanding collection of 9–11c gold and silver plate: renowned *Majesté de Ste. Foy*, late 9c reliquary statue, 5c head, Pépin reliquary (circa year 1000), late 11c reliquary known as 'Bégon lantern', etc.

Corbeil-Essonnes
91 – Essonne 11 – C 2
12 and 14c cathedral of St. Spire contains many works of art, inc. 14c recumbent figure of Count Haymon, and 17c funerary monument of Jacques Bourgoin.
Vicinity ● To N, forest of Sénart (6,500 acres); at La Faisanderie, old hunting lodge dating from time of Louis XVI, national contemporary sculpture park; elegant 18c white and gold panelling of church at Brunoy is worth seeing.

Corbie
80 – Somme 5 – C 2
Monastery, founded 657, was one of most important in Middle Ages. Of church of St. Pierre, built in Gothic style between 16 and 17c, only the nave remains, containing numerous works of art and some of the abbey's treasure. Fmr. 13c

collegiate church of St. Étienne has sculpted doorway: on tympanum, 'Coronation of the Virgin'.
Vicinity ● Many vestiges of 1914–1918 war; to S, Australian and Canadian memorial of *Villers-Bretonneux*.

Corbigny
58 – Nièvre 19 – B 3
Mid-16c Goth. Flamboyant church of Ste. Seine and fmr. Benedictine abbey, rebuilt 18c.
Vicinity ● 13 km N, via Monceau-le-Comte, Réconfort abbey, founded 13c, rebuilt 18c, beautiful park (n.v.a.).

Cordes
81 – Tarn 36 – B 3
Fortified town, built pyramid-fashion on conical hill overlooking *Cérou* valley. Its steeply-sloping streets, fortified gates and old

Conques: *on the road to Santiago de Compostela, this little town was a centre for pilgrimages to Ste. Foy.* ▲

One of the statues of the saint. ◄

houses are very picturesque. Rue Droite: see 14c Master of the Horse's house (Grand-Écuyer), with sculpted façade decorated with people and animals, 14c Master of the Royal Hunt's house (Grand-Veneur), and Master Falconner's house (Grand-Fauconnier), with lovely 14c façade, now housing town hall, also Yves Brayer gallery (paintings, watercolours, illustrated books). 14 and 15c church. 14c covered market still has its timbered roof resting on 24 octagonal stone pillars. Charles Portal museum (regional history). From La Bride terrace, fine view of Cérou valley.
Vicinity ● 15.5 km E, *Monestiès-sur-Cérou*: chapel of St. Jacques hospital houses numerous 15c sculptures, esp, an Entombment of Christ with 11 figures and a Pietà with eight.

Corps
38 – Isère 38 – B 1
Old town, on Alpine highway called Route Napoléon. Recommended excursion centre.
Vicinity ● 15 km N, via *La Salette*, **Notre Dame-de-la-Salette***. ● 4.5 km W, at entrance to canyon containing R. *Drac, Le Sautet* arched dam: a bridge of daring construction (single arch with span of 86 m.) crosses R. *Drac*; rec. tour of lake (35 km round-trip). ● *Le Dévoluy*, to S, via Le Sautet dam: beyond La Posterle, road and torrent run between high limestone

cliffs; from Les Payas, one can climb mt. *Obiou* (2,790 m.), highest point in Dévoluy reg. (fine view; difficult climb, only for experienced hikers); road then follows R. Souloise through narrow gorge and reaches *St. Disdier*, amid lush pastureland; on r. slope of valley, 13c chapel aka 'La Mère Église'; from *St. Étienne-en-Dévoluy*, in tiny cultivated valley surrounded by cliffs, one can get to new resort of *Super-Dévoluy*, a good excursion centre. ● *Le Valgaudemar*: 10 km to SE, on **Gap*** road, beyond *St. Firmin*, take r. bank of R. *Séveraisse*, road cut deep into crystalline schistous rocks; villages are esp. picturesque; from *La Chapelle-en-Valgaudemar* (climbing centre), a tiny road leads to chalet-hôtel of Le Gioberney, in magnificent setting (1,650 m.).

Corte
2B – Corsica   45 – B 2
Built on steep hill, town is dominated by huge 15c citadel: you can get impressive view of it from belvedere opposite old castle (to which n.v.a.); in opposite direction, view takes in old quarter and confluence of R. *Tavignano* and *Restonica*. At foot of citadel, Palais National, Place Gaffori, centre of old town, and 17c church of the Annunciation.
Vicinity ● 2.5 km E, 9 and 10c church and baptistry of St. Jean, noteworthy example of pre-Romanesque art. ● SW, *Gorges de la Restonica* may be followed by car (15 km). ● To W, along footpaths, *Gorges du Tavignano* (6½ hr. walk as far as Col de la Rinella, 1,522 m. alt.). ● To E, *Castagniccia* (see **Piedicroce***). ● To SE, towards **Aleria***, valley and *Gorges de Tavignano*. ● 18 km S, towards **Vizzavona***, via *Venaco, Vivario*, unusual village overlooking rocky bowl full of forests and torrents, ruins of Genoese fort; important tourist centre; to SE, *Ghisoni* and *Défilé de l'Inzecca* towards *Ghisonaccia* (see **Aleria***).

Côte-St. André (La)
38 – Isère   32 – A 2
Birthplace of Hector Berlioz has been turned into mus. (v.a., cl. Mon. and Jan.). Huge 16c covered market. 12–15c church and 17c château (now a high-school).
Vicinity ● 8 km S, remains of castle at Bressieux, standing in isolation on a hillock and dominated by tower from which there is magnificent view; 10 km to SW, at Marnans: interesting Romanesque church.

Coucy-le-Château
02 – Aisne   6 – A 3
Once-fortified town built on prom-

ontory, on edge of which stand the impressive ruins of castle of lords of Coucy, one of most remarkable from Middle Ages (v.a.; cl. Tues. and Wed.). 13c town wall still has its three gates, inc. beautiful Laon gate; Soissons gate has small history museum. 12–14c church.
Vicinity ● To N, *Forêts de Coucy* and *St. Gobain* (see **La Fère***).

Coulommiers
77 – Seine-et-Marne   12 – A 2
The moat, 25 m. wide, surrounds rectangle where 17c château once stood. Now only the two entry lodges and vast park, Parc des Capucins, remain. Archaeology and history museum in fmr. 17c Capucin chapel. Hospital farm was 12–13c Templar commanderie.
Speciality: Brie cheese.
Vicinity ● *Grand-Morin* valley is one of most pleasant walks in this area of Ile-de-France, to E, towards *La Ferté-Gaucher*; to NW and W, towards **Meaux***. ● To N and NE, *Petit-Morin* valley (see **Jouarre***).

Courchevel
73 – Savoie   32 – D 2
A complex of three winter sports resorts: Courchevel-1550, Courchevel-1650-Moriond, and Courchevel-1850, largest in *Trois-Vallées* reg. (see **Moûtiers-Tarentaise***). International-class hotel and sporting facilities. Cable-cars of Les Verdons (2,072 m.) and La Saulire (2,693 m.) link Courchevel to Méribel; fine views.

Courseulles-sur-Mer
14 – Calvados   4 – B 3
Seaside resort at mouth of R. *Seulles*.

Vicinity ● Ch. de **Fontaine-Henry*** (S) and Ch. de **Creully*** (SW). ● To SE, towards *Riva-Bella*, coast is full of tiny, low rocks; *Bernières-sur-Mer* (Romanesque and Goth. church, 13c belfry), *St. Aubin-sur-Mer, Langrune-sur-Mer, Luc-sur-Mer, Lion-sur-Mer* (Haut-Lion has château with elegant Ren. pavilion). *Riva-Bella* and *Ouistreham* (church characterised by Norman Romanesque and Goth. styles; lovely Romanesque façade).

Courtanvaux (Château)
72 – Sarthe   17 – D 1
1.5 km to NW of *Bessé-sur-Braye*. Beautiful 15–16c building, on large terrace, with monumental Ren. postern-gate, flanked by two richly sculpted round towers with dormer windows; int. terraced courtyard, rising above the valley, and Goth. chapel form an elegant ensemble; main building, aka 'Grand Château', contains, on first floor, magnificent suite of salons decorated in 19c; souvenirs of King of Rome (Napoleon's son, who died in his early 20s) and of Montesquieu family (v.a. in summer).

Court d'Aron (La) (Château)
85 – Vendée   22 – C 2
Rebuilt 19c in Ren. style, it contains noteworthy art collections: prehist., Greek, Roman and medieval archaeology, medals, enamels and ivories from Middle Ages and Ren., 16c Flanders tapestries (Triomphe des Dieux, after Jules Romain). 17c monumental fireplaces. Funerary statue of Suzanne Tiraqueau (d. 1627), paintings, sculptures, etc. (v.a. Apr. 1–Sept. 30).

Cordes: perched above the Cérou valley, this little town, with its steep streets and beautiful Gothic houses, has scarcely changed since the Middle Ages.

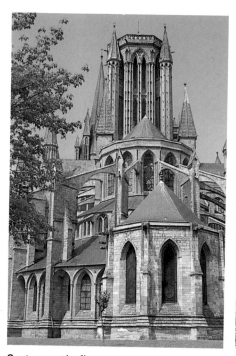

Coutances: *the fine octagonal lantern-tower dominates the apse of the cathedral.*

La Couvertoirade: *the north tower of the 14th-century ramparts, erected by the Knights Hospitalers.*

Coutances
50 – Manche   9 – D 1

Notre-Dame cathedral, a masterpiece of 13c Norman Goth. architecture, dominates town with its two towering steeples (77 m.); above transept crossing is 57 m.-high octagonal lantern-tower, known as 'Le Plomb'. 15–16c church of St. Pierre also has huge octagonal Ren. lantern; 16–17c St. Nicolas has 18c tower. Public garden, designed in style of 17c formal gardens, on tiered terraces, leads into a small wood. Municipal art mus. (early paintings, Norman pottery). 13c aqueduct.

Vicinity ● 12 km W, *Coutainville*, seaside resort, lovely sandy beach. ● 10.5 km SW, *Regnéville-sur-Mer*, small port and seaside resort, ruins of 13c castle.

Couvertoirade (La)
12 – Aveyron   37 – A 3

Standing in solitary splendour on arid **Larzac*** causse, this strange town belonged first to the Templars (12c) and then to the Knights Hospitalers of St. John of Jerusalem (14c), who surrounded it with a strongly fortified perimeter wall flanked by four round towers, each with two gateways. Fortress church, castle ruins, 15 and 16c half-ruined houses may seem out of place but are undeniably fascinating for their unusual architectural features. To S, Signal de la Couvertoirade, fine view of the Causses.

Crémieu
38 – Isère   32 – A 1

Old town, between hospital and royal castle (v.a.), still has its narrow streets and many old houses. Town hall is in fmr. Augustinian priory (cloisters), dating from 16–17c. See also 15c Augustinian church which has interesting furnishings. The town still has three gates from its old perimeter wall. 14c market hall is covered by an enormous lauze roof. Good view from clock tower.

Vicinity ● Unusual rocky range around town, known as 'Île Crémieu'; to N, Amby gorges between *Hières* and *Optevoz*; grottoes of *La Balme* are well worth visiting. ● Throughout region, numerous châteaux and manors, majority of them to SW: Mallein, Bienassis, Montiracle, Poisieu, remains of Ch. de Ville, etc.

CRÊTES (Route)
68 – Haut-Rhin, 88 – Vosges   21 – A 1
                                    20 – D 1   13 – D 3

This magnificent 77 km route along mountain ridges (of immense strategic importance in 1914–1918) has become one of the Vosges' greatest tourist attractions; it stretches from *Col du Bonhomme* to *Cernay*. First, through Col de Luschpach (panorama) and Col du Calvaire, or Luschpach Calvary. To E, *Lac Blanc* dam (1,054 m.); Belmont observatory (1,272 m.), *Lac Noir* dam (954 m.), *Col de la Schlucht* (see **Gérardmer***). Mt. *Hohneck*, highest point at 1,362 m., viewing table – magnificent panorama of upper Vosges range. Road now crosses miles of pastures before climbing again up side of mt. Rainkopf; magnificent view of upper Thur valley and lake at *Wildenstein*. Cols of Herrenberg and Hahnenbrunnen (panorama). *Le Markstein*, 1,200 m. alt., is well-known summer and winter sports resort (panorama). Route continues above Thur valley, passing below *Grand Ballon*, or Ballon de **Guebwiller***; finally, after skirting foot of ruined castle of Freundstein, D431 reaches mt. **Hartmannswillerkopf*** or **'Vieil-Armand'**, and zigzags down into *Cernay* (in July, Festival of the Storks).

Crépy-en-Valois
60 – Oise   5 – D 3
Tiny old town whose mus. (Valois and Archery), in former Valois château, is the main sight. It contains some 150 statues of religious art, mainly 13–18c, reg. and pop. in nature (v.a., cl. Tues., Mar. 20–Nov. 1). Church of St. Denis, Romanesque nave and 16c choir, ruins of abbey of St. Arnould (12, 13 and 14c). Church of St. Thomas: only 12c façade remains standing. Interesting old houses.
Vicinity ● Recommended excursion in valley of R. *Automne*.

Crest
26 – Drôme   37 – D 1
Once-fortified town, at foot of rocky escarpment on which stands huge rectangular 12c keep, 45 m. high (v.a.): panorama. Old town is a maze of unusual vaulted passageways and 'violes' (alleyways),

with many old houses.
Vicinity ● To SE, lovely *Forêt de Saou*, in deep amphitheatre. ● To E, *Drôme* valley (recommended excursion) via *Aouste-sur-Sye, Saillans* (Romanesque church), Pontaix and ravine of Pontaix, **Die***; from *Saillans*, narrow but picturesque D156 leads, to S, via. *Col de la Chaudière* (1,067 m.) to *Bourdeaux* and *Dieulefit*.

Creully (Château)
14 – Calvados   4 – B 3
15c main building, flanked by 16c turret, is adjoined by square keep (v.a.).
Vicinity ● Fmr. prior of *St. Gabriel* (v.a.), founded 11c, comprises numerous buildings and monumental 12c gateway; huge vaulted refectory and prior's rooms; remains (11–12c choir) of fmr. chapel. 1 km to SW, Ch. de *Brécy*, mid-17c, with decorated monu-

mental portal; beautiful terraced gardens (v.a., p.m. mid-Apr–Nov. 1, cl. Wed.; rest of year, on request).

Creusot (Le)
71 – Saône-et-Loire   25 – C 1
One of most important metal-working centres in Europe. 18c Ch. de la Verrerie houses ecological museum for area; its collections illustrate diversity of reg. artistic and industrial products (cl. Mon.).
Vicinity ● To S, large expanses of Torcy lakes (beach, water sports). ● 18 km NE, near *Couches*, 15c castle of Marguerite of Burgundy, dominated by a keep and 10 and 13c machicolated towers; chapel (v.a. July 1–Aug. 31. Rest of year, on request).

Crozon
29S – Finistère   8 – B 2
In centre of Crozon peninsula. Church has magnificent 16c polychrome retable.
Vicinity ● To S, *Grottes Marines de Morgat* (sea caves) and *Cap de la Chèvre* (vast panorama); 2 km to N, beach of La Palue. ● To W, *Pointe de Dinan*, and 'castle' of Dinan, enormous mass of rocks joined to point by a natural arch. ● To NW, **Camaret-sur-Mer***.

Culan (Château)
18 – Cher   24 – C 2
This impressive 14 and 15c castle, standing on a rock overlooking the gorges of R. *Arnon*, has three big towers topped by round wooden 'hoardings' (v.a., cl. Wed. and Feb.). In apartments, beautiful 15–16c furnishings and magnificent 15, 16 and 17c tapestries. From terrace, fine view of *Arnon* valley.

Culan: *this huge medieval fortress, flanked by three enormous round towers, dominates the Arnon gorges.*

Cunault: *on the tympanum above the main door of the church is this Virgin and Child, supported by two adoring angels (early 13c).*

Cunault
49 – Maine-et-Loire   17 – B 3
11–13c church is one of the most noteworthy and unusual Romanesque buildings in Loire valley; beautiful belfry; fortified W façade has doorway with 13c Adoration of the Virgin; interior has 223 sculpted capitals, 12c, forming an exceptionally harmonious series: fragments of 15c murals.
Vicinity ● 1 km NE, *Trèves*, Romanesque church, 15c keep. ● 3 km NW, *Gennes*, 12, 13 and 14c church of St. Vétérin, with wooden porch; fmr. church of St. Eusèbe, 11–12c, pre-Romanesque traces in 15c nave; 7 km NW, on edge of R. Loire, fmr. *Abbaye de Saint-Maur* (now a school), founded 6c (12c chapel and 17c buildings); 2 km to SW, 15c castle of *Montsabert*.

D

Dabo
57 – Moselle   14 – A 2
Summer resort, good excursion centre, surrounded by 50 sq. miles of forests. Unusual sandstone Rock of Dabo (664 m.) has chapel on top; viewing table, fine panorama.
Vicinity ● NE, Nutzkopf Rock (515 m.), extensive view, and Grossthal gorges; higher up, lushly green and wooded valley of the Zorn. ● To E, valley of the Mossig leads to *Wasselonne*, under ruins of stout feudal castle. ● To S, waterfall and castle of *Nideck*; keep and one 13–14c tower of the castle still stand, in attractive setting; the waterfall tumbles over a high ledge of porphyry; lovely wide views from belvedere. 9 km to S, Niederhaslach (near *Oberhaslach*): 13–14c church, elegant sculpted Goth. portal (tympanum and statuary); interior has late 18c stalls and 13–14c stained-glass windows.

Dampierre (Château)
78 – Yvelines   11 – B 2
Brick and stone château, built by Mansart in 17c, is approached by monumental gate and huge main courtyard (v.a., cl. Tues., Apr. 1 to Oct. 15). The 18c apartments owe their often excessive luxury and surfeit of decoration to 19c tastes. In Salles des Fêtes, an Ingres painting, the *Age d'Or* (1843–49).
Vicinity ● Excursions recommended in upper valley of the Yvette (see **Chevreuse***); to W, Levis-St. Nom, 15c church with 16c door; interesting old statues. 5 km away, fmr. priory of Notre Dame-de-la-Roche (now horticultural college) has chapel containing the oldest stalls in France (13c). Also worth visit is 16c church at *Mesnil-St. Denis*. ● To S, **Vaux de Cernay***.

Dampierre-sur-Boutonne (Château)
17 – Charente-Maritime   23 – A 3
Among the loveliest Ren. châteaux in Saintonge reg.: early-16c, with two very big machicolated towers. Façade is adorned with two superposed galleries separated by a sculpted frieze; the upper gallery has sculpted coffered ceiling with hanging keystones. Flemish tapestries and furniture in apartments. On island site. (V.a. daily, June 1 to Sept. 30; otherwise Sun. and public holidays.)
Vicinity ● 7 km SE **Aulnay-de-Saintonge***.

Dax
40 – Landes   34 – C 3
R. Adour divides town in two: on r. bank, Sablar district; on l. bank, the old town, still with part of its Gallo-Roman walls. Notre Dame cath, in Classical style, late 17–18c; 13c Apostles door has been re-erected in l. arm of the transept. Hôtel St. Martin d'Aġes, 17c, houses Borda museum: local arts and traditions. Hot water fountain – portico with three arcades above the basin – fed by a spring with a flow of 520,000 gallons per 24 hours of water with a temperature of 64 deg. C. (147 deg. F.).
Vicinity ● *St. Paul-lès-Dax* (in church, 12c apse; exterior has unusual 11c Romanesque frieze). 6 km to NE, commune of *St Vincent de Paul*, where the saint was born in 1581: little farm of Ranquine has been turned into chapel; oak tree from where the saint guarded his flock; church in neo-Byzantine style (1864). 5 km to N, *Notre Dame-de-Buglose*: in church, much-venerated 15c stone Virgin; 'miracle' spring; chapel where St. Vincent de Paul celebrated mass (it was restored and transformed into local Landais style in 1966). ● Excursions recommended in Landes forest to N. and NW: *Étang de Soustons, Seignosse, Étang Blanc*, etc.

Deauville
14 – Calvados   4 – C 3
The Normandy resort most famed for its brilliant international way of life. Its terraced flower gardens, broad walks (the 'planches'), casino and great hotels, the Normandy and Royal, are renowned worldwide. The beach stretches for 3 km from the Port-Deauville marina to the cliffs of *Bénerville-sur-Mer*.
Vicinity ● To SW, Mt. Canisy (good view, golf course, remains of 17c Ch. de Lassay). ● To S, St. Arnoult (remains of 11–15c church). ● To E, *Trouville*, on r. bank of R. *Touques* – a quieter and more homely resort than its neighbour, but with a lovely 1 km beach, lined by Promenade des Planches, and fine views over coast from the corniche road. Very lively port (picturesque fish market, morning auctions).

Demoiselles (Les) (Grotto)
34 – Hérault   37 – B 3
6 km from *Ganges*. From the terrace at the site (good view), a funicular takes you right to the grotto (v.a. daily), enormous excavation with a central chamber, known as 'The Cathedral', which is 48 m. high and covered with concretions, glowing from their very transparency. Stairs lead to the bottom where a giant stalagmite has formed into a statue shape, 'Virgin and Child'.

Demoiselles Coiffées
See **Theus***   38 – C 2

Die
26 – Drôme   38 – A 1
Little town famed for its 'Clairette', mildly sparkling white wine. Fmr. Notre Dame cath., 12, 13 and 17c, is entered through belfry-porch

Dieppe: seaside resort, fishing port and commercial centre, with a long maritime history. Its quays are always busy – particulary the Quai Henri IV, above,

Dijon: *on the façade of the Hôtel Aubriot, a line of arched double arcades.*

The Bar tower and Bellegarde staircase in the former palace of the Dukes of Burgundy.

The powerful statue of Moses on the well in the 14c charterhouse of Champmol.

(Romanesque door). Interesting old houses (partic. Hôtel de Fontgalland, Place de l'Horloge). Lawcourts and town hall are in fmr. bishop's palace; fine 12c mosaic in chapel. St. Marcel gate, remnant of Roman triumphal arch, forms part of the ramparts, of which some sections to N are from 3c. Late-18c mansion houses a museum.
Vicinity ● 3 km SE, Sallières baths, 3 km farther on, fmr. abbey of Valcroissant (large 12c remains). Sources of the Rays (4.5 km, then path) in picturesque setting (lovely waterfall). ● To N, magnificent country of the *Vercors* and *Forêt de Lente* (see La Chapelle-en-Vercors* and Vassieux-en-Vercors*). ● To SE, via *Châtillon-en-Diois*, two possible tours: (1) From Menée, valley and bowl of *Archiane*, magnificent escarpments in amphitheatre form, then climb to top of Dôme du Glandasse (2,045 m., huge panorama); or (2) via Gas gorges (smooth walls, 100 m. high) to *Glandage* and *Lus-la-Croix-Haute* (1,030 m.), pleasant holiday resort. ● To SE, *Luc-en-Diois* (picturesque lavender fair, Sept. 19) and Claps*.

Dieppe
76 – Seine-Maritime 5 – A 2
Fishing port and seaside resort. The old town is squeezed between the docks and 16–17c château which overlooks beach and houses very interesting museum: unusual collection of 16–17c charts, Flemish, Dutch and French Impressionist paintings, ivories, Braque engravings. St. Jacques church, 13–14c, with 1524 frieze and other works

of art; oratory of ship-owner Jehan Ango (d. 1551) is sumptuously decorated. St. Rémy church, 16–17c, Ren. decoration in apse chapels.
Vicinity ● To S, **Arques-la-Bataille***. ● 2 km to W, on Route de Pourville, open-air military mus., souvenirs of Dieppe raid of August 19, 1942. 8 km away, *Manoir d'Ango* at **Varengeville-sur-Mer***.

Digne
04 – Alpes-de-Haute-Provence
38 – C 3
Lower town is crossed by Blvd. Gassendi, which has town mus. and culminates in unusual Grand Fountain. Fmr. cath., early-13c Notre Dame-du-Bourg basilica, is among most imposing Romanesque churches in Provence. Upper town, with narrow winding streets, is dominated by late-15c St. Jérôme cath., with 16–17c bell tower.
Vicinity ● 3.5 km SE, Baths of Digne, at 650 m. alt., in picturesque gorge. ● 6 km NW, Courbons, unusual ruined village, wonderful view over *Alpes de Provence*. ● To NE, grandiose, wild upper valley of the Bléone. ● 14 km S, via *Châteauredon*, the R. *Asse* valley forms the picturesque *Clue de Chabrières*, between steep limestone cliffs, in direction of *Barrême*.

Dijon
21 — Côte-d'Or 19 – D 3
Capital of Burgundy and town of outstanding artistic interest. ● Palace of the Dukes and États of Burgundy, one-time residence of

the Dukes of Valois, is composite 14, 15 and 17c historic building now housing town hall and mus. Of original medieval constructions, all that remain are two towers: 14c Tour de Bar and 15c Tour de Philippe le Bon (fine view from top); all the rest, designed by Mansart, is 17c. Exceptionally rich fine arts mus. (cl. Tues.) embraces various parts of the palace on Cour de Bar: the ducal kitchens, Tour de Bar, 'Chapel of the Élus' and big Goth. hall known as Salle des Gardes, in which are magnificent sculpted tombs of two royal Dukes of Burgundy, Philippe le Hardi (d. 1404) and his son Jean Sans Peur (d. 1419); also 15–16c tapestries and renowned gilded, carved wooden retables, shutters painted by Broederlam, late 14c, and best contemp. art collection in Burgundy. ● Other mus. inc.: in 17c mansions, Magnin mus., furniture and paintings, 16–19c.; archaeology in old Benedictine abbey of St. Bénigne, 13–14c; Burgundian life in fmr. Bernardine convent (17c cloister); natural history mus. and Arquebuse botanical garden; Mus. Rude in fmr. church of St. Étienne, 15–17c. ● City's main churches are: 13c cath. of St. Bénigne, with 10c crypt (v.a.); St. Michel, 16c, superb Ren. façade, among loveliest of all French churches; Notre Dame, in Burgundian Goth. style, three-bay monumental porch and façade displaying two tiers of blind arcades with small columns; 12c St. Philibert (exhibitions, concerts). ● Old quarter: (1). From Place Rude, with fountain, you reach various streets with mansions dating between 13 and 18c: Rue des Forges (No. 34,

Hôtel Chambellan, 15c; No. 40, Hôtel Aubriot, noteworthy 13c façade, with 17c door; No. 38, mid-16c Maison Milsand, richly decorated façade); Rue Verrerie, Rue de la Chouette (No. 8, Hôtel de Vogüe, early 17c); Rue Chaudronnerie (No. 8, Maison des Cariatides, 1603); Rue Vannerie. Rue de la Préfecture is lined almost entirely by 18c mansions. (2). Place Bossuet, surrounded by 17-18c parliamentary buildings; in centre, 15c church of St. Jean; Place des Cordeliers (typically Burgundian houses); Rue Charrue; Rue Berbisey, etc. The lawcourts, fmr. Parliament of Burgundy: fine example of Ren. architecture, notably the 16c façade; interior includes St. Esprit chapel, which has fine sculpted screen and early-16c Golden Room, with coffered ceiling, carved and gilded. Ave. Albert I takes you to charterhouse of Champnol, founded 1383; portal of the long-vanished church is adorned with five most expressive late-15c statues: the Virgin, Philippe le Hardi, his wife and their patron saints; in the courtyard, famed for its vigorous realism, the Moses Well (*Puits de Moïse*), masterpiece by Claus Sluter (completed 1395–1404).
Vicinity ● 1.5 km W, big artificial lake, created in 1964 (water sports, beach); 2 km W, *Talant*: 13c church;

Fontaines-lès-Dijon, late-14c church. ● 13 km NW, Val Suzon (see **St. Seine-l'Abbaye***). ● To S, Côte de Nuits, famed wine reg., via *Fixin, Gevrey-Chambertin, Vougeot* (see **Nuits-St. Georges***). ● To SW, *Ch. de Commarin*, late-14, 17 and 18c (v.a. Apr. 1–Nov. 1, cl. Tues.). ● 13.5 km SSE, via *Fauverney*: 12–13c church at *Rouvres-en-Plaine* has three magnificent statues of 15c Burgundian school.

Dinan
22 – Côtes-du-Nord   9 – B 2
The old town, ringed by ramparts, with its narrow streets and houses jostling each other, offers a perfect example of Breton cities of bygone days (see partic. Place des Merciers, Rue de l'Apport, and steep-sloping Rue du Jerzual, lined by overhanging 15–16c shops). 14–15c château houses mus. of local history and ethnography (cl. Tues.). St. Sauveur church is part-Romanesque (façade and r. side of nave) and partly late-15c Goth. Flamboyant, under mid-16c tower; in l. arm of transept. cenotaph holding heart of locally-born military leader Bertrand Du Guesclin, 14c Constable of France, who waged successful guerrilla war against the English before his death in 1380; behind the apse, terraced garden (lovely view over valley of R. *Rance*).

Dinan: *the ghost of Du Guesclin still seems to haunt the old streets of this little Breton city.*

Vicinity ● Boat trip down R. *Rance*, from Dinan to **Dinard*** and **St. Malo*** (daily in summer). ● Round-trip of the Rance, by car or on foot along l. bank (D12): *Plouër, La Richardais, Barrage de l'usine marémotrice* (dam of tidal power station), *St. Jouan-des-Guérets, La Vicomté*. ● 1 km SE, Léhon, under remains of feudal castle; 14–15c church (tomb statues, 13–14–15c); remains of 17c cloister. ● Pleasant walks in little valley of the Argentel, to N. ● 8.5 km NW, ruins of Temple of Mars.

Dinard
35 – Ille-et-Vilaine   9 – B 2
Popular seaside resort opposite St. Malo, on other side of Rance estuary. From St. Énogat plage (beach) to the Pointe de la Vicomte, beautiful walk via the Pointe des Étêtés (view of the islands and coast), main beach (casino, causeway, promenade), Pointe du Moulinet (views from Cap Fréhel to St. Malo and Rance estuary), Promenade du Clair de Lune (illuminations and music during summer season), Le Prieuré beach, La Vicomté (rampart walk; out to sea, panorama over the roads, R. *Rance* and tidal power station). Marine museum and aquarium.
Vicinity ● Boat trip or round-journey by road from Dinard to **Dinan***, via the *Rance* and dam for tidal power station, is not to be missed. ● The many renowned beaches along the *Côte d'Émeraude* include: *Lancieux, St. Briac, St. Lunaire* (very picturesque Pointe du Décollé, superb site, wide views, and typically Breton old village), and St. Énogat.

Dol-de-Bretagne
35 – Ille-et-Vilaine   9 – C 2
One-time episcopal city, dominated

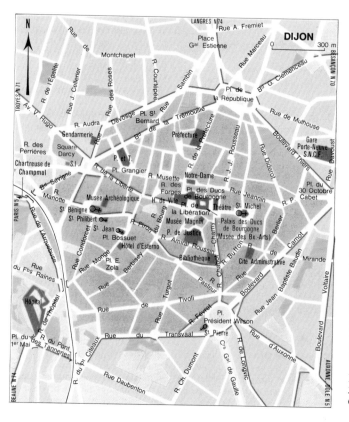

by 12–13c St. Samson cath., in granite; S part includes huge 14c porch; interior has Ren. tomb of Bishop Thomas James. Old houses in Grande Rue (see Romanesque Maison des Plaids). Mus. in 16c house known as the Treasury (Trésorerie) has exceptional collection of Breton saints, in wood, from 13 to 18c.
Vicinity ● 2 km S, *Menhir du Champ-Dolent*, 9 m. tall, among the most impressive in Brittany. ● 12 km SE, via *La Boussac*, Ch. de Landal, impressive feudal structure beside lake, ringed by ramparts, with towers (v.a. to main courtyard and ramparts). ● 3 km N, *Mont-Dol*, granite rise 65 m. high, said to be site of the legendary battle between St. Michael and Satan; Notre Dame-de-l'Espérance chapel and tower (fine panorama).

Dole
39 – Jura   20 – A 3
Characteristic Franche-Comté town, rich in historic old buildings. 16c Notre Dame basilica, in Goth. Flamboyant style, is dominated by square belfry, 74 m. high; int. has numerous works of arts. At 43 Rue Pasteur, birthplace of the great scientist, with mus. (v.a.): includes reconstruction of workroom Pasteur's father used as a tanner. Several old houses in same street. Hôtel-Dieu (early hospital), noteworthy 17c edifice; cloister has two floors of arcaded galleries. Picturesque Tanneaux (tanners) quarter along canal, numerous old houses. 7, Rue du Mont-Roland, fmr. Hôtel de Froissard, from Louis XIII period (17c); late–16c college of the Arc, with chapel dating from 1601 – its porch an outstanding example of Ren. sculptured decoration. Fine arts mus. in 18c. officers' mess of former barracks (French, Dutch, Italian paintings).
Vicinity ● to E, forest of *Chaux*.

Domme
24 Dordogne   36 – A 1
On steep promontory soaring above valley of R. *Dordogne*, this gorgeous old township – a one-time bastide – still has its 13c ramparts and many old houses along its narrow streets. Also two early gates, Porte Delbos, 13–14c, and Porte des Tours, 13c, as well as 14c timbered market-hall and Governor's Mansion, flanked by round tower. Entry to grottoes (v.a. during summer season) is under the covered market. Paul-Reclus mus. Wide-sweeping views from the terrace and public garden.
Vicinity ● 2 km NE, monolithic church of Caudon, hollowed out of rock. ● 10 km N, **Sarlat-la-Canéda***.

Domrémy-la-Pucelle
88 – Vosges   13 – B 3
Joan of Arc's birthplace; small mus.

Dole: *the unusual courtyard of the Hôtel-Dieu, with its balustraded balconies.*

Renovated village church still has font where Joan was baptised (1412). 1.5 km to S, pretentious late-19c basilica backs on to the Bois-Chenu, where Joan heard her voices; fine view over valley of R. *Meuse*.
Vicinity ● 5.5 km N, *Goussaincourt*, interesting mus. devoted to peasant life in Joan of Arc's day. 5 km to N, late-16c *Ch. de Montbras*, machicolated and flanked by towers, but with richly adorned Ren. façade; int. is tastefully furnished (v.a.). 10 km away, *Vaucouleurs*; it was

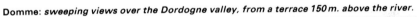

Domme: *sweeping views over the Dordogne valley, from a terrace 150 m. above the river.*

through the France gate of this ancient little town that Joan set out on the fateful journey that was to end on the stake at Rouen in 1431. Remains of castle of the Sire de Baudricourt and late-13c chapel; small mus. devoted to Joan of Arc and local hist.; 6 km away, remains of 14–15c *Ch. de Gombervaux*.

Dorat (Le)
87 – Haute-Vienne   23 – D 3
Collegiate church of St. Pierre is fine Romanesque edifice, in grey granite, with 60 m.-high belfry; 11c crypt. Porte aux Bergères (gate) and remains of 15c ramparts.
Vicinity • To NW, valley of the Brame: see especially the torrents and waterfalls of the Saut-de-Brame. • 7 km E, *Magnac-Laval*: 12c church (Whit Monday, unusual Procession of the Nine Leagues). • 12 km S, *Bellac*, church with two naves, Romanesque and Goth.; 11 km to SW, remains of Ch. de *Mortemart*; 12 and 16c church.

Douai
59 – Nord   2 – A 3
The Grande Place, or Place d'Armes (fountains), is town centre; soaring over it is superb 14–15c belfry of the town hall, int. of which is worth a visit. See also mid-18c Maison du Dauphin, church of Notre Dame (13–14–15c), and Valenciennes gate (15 and 18c). St. Pierre church, 16–18c, has huge choir, once reserved for canons and Members of Parliament. Old Carthusian convent, 16–18c, now houses mus. (cl. Tues.): notable groups of paintings from northern schools, inc. Jean Bellegambe's famed *Polyptique d'Anchin*, and late 16–17c Dutch and Flemish, as well as Italian (two masterpieces – Veronese's *The Venetian Woman* and Carracci's *The Flagellation*); also French pictures (17–18–19c), earthenware and objets d'art.
Vicinity • 14 km NE, *Flines-lès-Raches*: 13c Goth. church with 12c square tower; 9 km to E, *Marchiennes*: monumental entrance and one 18c building from one-time Benedictine abbey; 6 km to SW, *Pecquencourt*: remains (two pavilions) of abbey of Anchin. • To S, Sensée lakes (fishing, wild-fowling, canoeing), *Lécluse* and *Aubigny-au-Bac*.

Douarnenez
29S – Finistère   8 – B 3
Archetypal Breton fishing port, always lively and colourful at periods when the fishermen are leaving or returning. To N, New Port, reserved for trawlers; to S, Rosmeur harbour, for the sardine boats. To W, Blvd. Jean Richepin follows ledge along coast, skirting

Douai: *in traditional procession through the town, the lofty figures of 'Jacquot', 'Fillion' and 'Binbin', all in 18c costume.*

Les Dames beach and leading to a point, separated by narrows from the little island of Tristan (lighthouse).
Vicinity • *Tréboul*, on l. bank of Pouldavid estuary, is very popular seaside resort as well as fishing port; beautiful *Sables-Blancs* beach; 3 km to NW, Pointe du Leydé. • 1 km SE, Ploaré, 16–17c church with magnificent 65 m. belfry, 16c. • 10 km E, **Locronan***. • 16 km SE, via Le Juch (interesting church), *Guengat* has church with fine 15–16c stained-glass windows, rich church treasure.

Doullens
80 – Somme   5 – C 1
Characteristic 18c town of Picardy region. 16c château within 17c citadel, in brick. Former town hall, with square brick belfry dating from 1406, is topped by slate belltower. Notre Dame church in 15–

16c Goth. Flamboyant style. Nave and part of transept (all that remains) from church of St. Pierre, 13c. Lombart mus.: 18–19c pictures and local hist. Mus. Foch in town hall (inc. conference room where he was appointed as sole C-in-C of Allied armies in 1918).
Vicinity • 7 km NE, *Lucheux*, castle built on spur (v.a.), sizeable remains from 12 and 16c, reached via Bourg gate; see also the Haut-Bois gate, with machicolated archway, remains of Leaded Tower and 12c keep. St. Léger church, 12c, has some of the oldest ribbed vaults in north of France, also capitals decorated with picturesque scenes ('The Seven Deadly Sins').

Dourdan
91 – Essonne   11 – B 2
Town has kept its provincial charm. Early 13c castle, with towers and large moat, is dominated by power-

Douarnenez: *one of Brittany's busiest ports; the Rosmeur harbour's fish auction is a spectacle not to be missed.*

ful keep (v.a.); small mus. St. Germain church, 12–13c, enlarged in 15–16c. Covered market, 13c.
Vicinity ● 12 km NE, via *St. Chéron*, late 18c *Ch. du Marais*, surrounded by gardens (v.a., p.m. in summer season: mus. and gardens). ● 8 km NW, *St. Arnoult-en-Yvelines*, Romanesque and Ren. church; 4 km NE, *Rochefort-en-Yvelines*, 12 c Romanesque church and ruins of 11c castle.

Draguignan
83 – Var   44 – C 1
Winding narrow streets of the old town encircle small hill crowned by Tour de l'Horloge, late-17c clock tower. Picturesque Place du Marché, with two fountains, shaded by superb plane trees; Place aux Herbes has Roman gate – surviving, with Portaiguières gate, from medieval ramparts. New town extends from foot of old quarter. Municipal mus. in fmr. Ursuline

16c church of *Les Arcs*, with fine gold-based retable attributed to Louis Brea (from Nice family of painters, 15–16c); 4 km to E, Ste. Roseline chapel, splendidly sculpted 17c stalls and retable; modern stained-glass, Diego Giacometti furniture (private property, v.a.). ● 35 km W, through *Flayosc* and *Salernes*, village of *Cotignac*, under cliff riddled with caves; 15 km to W, *Barjols*, old township laid out in tiers.

Dreux
28 – Eure-et-Loir   11 – A 2
Standing high over town is imposing belfry, Goth. and Ren., richly sculpted, crowned by 18c campanile (stairway with 142 steps). St. Pierre church, 13–15–16c, beautiful 15–16c stained-glass windows. Marcel Dessal mus. (Romanesque capitals, decorative arts, paintings, inc. Monet). On hillside to NW, in middle of park, St. Louis royal chapel, mid-19c, in

Dunkerque
59 – Nord   1 – C 1
Former stronghold, now in three sections: the town proper, dominated by fmr. bell-tower of St. Éloi, in 15c brick; lower town, to S; and citadel quarter to NW, its boundary marked out by moat of one-time ramparts. In centre of town, the Place Jean Bart – site of the belfry and church of St. Éloi (Goth., with five naves) – is lined by brick houses rebuilt after last world war. Fine arts mus. (Dutch, Flemish and Italian paintings, model ships). Outstanding mus. of contemporary art, in garden of sculptures by Féraud, Arman, César, Dodeigne; interior (cl. Tues.) has works by Miró, Hartung, Soulages, Vasarely, Warhol, Magnelli, etc. Tours of the port, by motor-launch (embark Place du Minck) or by car (inf. from port or SI). Fine view over port from terrace of weather station, at entrance to Watier lock.

Draguignan: *orchards in flower. From the bright colours of the typically Provençal countryside round the little town, it is evident that one is getting near the Côte d'Azur.*

convent, 17c, summer residence of bishops of Fréjus: 17–18c paintings and regional archaeology. Mus. of guns and gunners at artillery school. Lovely Allées d'Azémar (*bust of Clémenceau*, by Rodin).
Vicinity ● 1 km NW, Fairy Stone, imposing dolmen consisting of three upright stones and one lying flat. ● 1.5 km SW, St. Hermentaire hermitage, Romanesque chapel, remains of Gallo-Roman baths. ● 4.5 km S, *Trans*, superb waterfalls of the *Nartuby*; 5.5 km to S, early

'troubadour' style; the crypt (v.a.) contains monumental tombs, with recumbent figures, of the Orléans family: stained-glass by Ingres.
Vicinity ● 16 km NE, Ch. d'**Anet*** 21 km E, ancient little town of *Houdan*; enormous 12c keep (Son et Lumière in summer); Goth. church with Ren. apse (int. has unusual mural painted 1582); 15–16c timber-framed houses.

Duclair
See **Abbeys*** (Norman)   4 – D 3

Vicinity ● 1 km NE, *Malo-les-Bains*, v. popular seaside resort; fine sandy beach stretching for 15 km to *Bray-Dunes*; on the causeway, inscribed column commemorating Dunkirk evacuation in 1940.

Dun-sur-Meuse
55 – Meuse   7 – A 3
Perched on steep little hill over valley of R. *Meuse*. 14–15c church of Notre Dame; int. has good works of art. On l. bank of river, Vert lake (beach, canoeing, camping).

E

Eaux-Chaudes (Les)
64 – Pyrénées-Atlantiques 41 – A 3
Spa 4 km S of *Laruns*, in wild gorge with mountain torrent, *Gave d'Ossau*, running through it.
Vicinity • 8 km NE, *Les Eaux-Bonnes*, summer resort and spa. • Excursion reccommended to *Lac d'Artouste* by cable-car: from Artouste electricity generating station to La Sagette (1,950 m.), then by railway along ledge above Souséou mt. torrent to dam of Artouste lake at 2,000 m., amid grandiose scenery. • Climbs to summits of *Midi d'Ossau* (2,885 m.), to S, and of *Balaïtous* (3,146 m.), to SE, both of which are in *Parc National des Pyrénées Occidentales* (national park). • To S, N134 follows valley of the *Ossau* (very typical of Béarn region). 8 km to S, *Gabas*; road continues to pass, *Col du Pourtalet* (1,792 m.), then enters Spain.

Ebersmunster
67 – Bas-Rhin 14 – A 3
The former abbey church, rebuilt in 18c, is unusual example of baroque architecture; the white and pink edifice is surmounted by three onion-shaped belfries; the huge, luminous interior is adorned with paintings, fine 18c furnishing, stalls crowned by 20 wooden statues; seven altars with carved gilded retables, including an outstanding baroque master-altar. Organ dates from 1730.

Ébreuil
03 – Allier 25 – A 3
Town on R. *Sioule*. St. Léger, former Benedictine abbey church, Romanesque and Goth., with 12 and 15c frescos. Notable reliquary of St. Léger in wood and silvered copper, 16c. In the hospice (one-time monastery buildings): collection of lace and pharmacy jars.
Vicinity • Picturesques *Gorges de la Sioule* as far as *Châteauneuf-les-Bains*, via *Chouvigny* (13c castle); gorges marked by fine pyramid-shaped granite rocks, cliffs, viewing-points. Near *Pont-de-Menat*, remains of 13c Ch. Rocher.

Écouen
95 – Val d'Oise 11 – C 1
One of Ile-de-France's loveliest Ren. châteaux; national museum of the Renaissance (cl. Tues.) Built in mid-16c, renovated a century later under France's King Henri II, it has huge main reception-room, with monumental fireplace adorned by a *Victoire* in bas-relief, after Le Rosso; also magnificent salons and galleries filled by world's first mus. devoted solely to Ren. arts: paintings, sculptures, tapestries, stained-glass on religious themes. In addition, notable displays of enamel, mainly by Léonard Limosin (16c), majolica, glassware and Teutonic plate. See also the 12 fireplaces sculpted with biblical themes. Noteworthy Ren. stained-glass windows, as well, in church of St. Acceul, 16–17c.

Écouis
27 – Eure 5 – A 3
Former collegiate church, early 14c, is veritable mus. of 14–15c Goth. sculpture: statue of Notre Dame d'Écouis, recumbent tomb figure in marble of Archbishop Jean de Marigny, Ste. Véronique, Ste. Agnès, wooden Ecce Homo.

Effiat (Château)
63 – Puy-de-Dôme 25 – A 3
Superb 17c construction (v.a. daily June–Dec.; weekends and public hols., Mar.–June; cl. Jan.–Feb.). 17c décor in Grand Salon: monumental fireplace, painted ceilings and panelling, 17–18c furniture, tapestries, portraits. Formal gardens by Le Nôtre.
Vicinity • 4 km SW, *Aigueperse*, two churches worth visiting: Ste. Chapelle, 15c, and Notre Dame, with 13c apse and transept. 3 km to W, near *Chaptuzat*, is Ch. de la Roche, planted on lofty plateau with extensive views – 12–13c fortress, enlarged and renovated 15–16c, with apartments decorated and furnished in 17c (v.a.). 5.5 km to SW from *Aigueperse*, just before *St. Myon*, fine Romanesque church, 10–12c, at Artonne.

Elne
66 – Pyrénées-Orientales 43 – D 3
Built on hill above vast panorama, Elne is divided between an upper and lower town (the latter partly enclosed by ramparts). Cathedral of St. Eulalie, 11–15c, has notable cloister in blue-veined grey marble; its S gallery has historiated capitals or others sculpted with fantastic animals, masterpieces of local Roussillon version of Romanesque sculpture. Small museum (archaeology, ceramics).
Vicinity • 7 km SE, Argelès-sur-Mer; 2.5 km to E, Argelès-Plage, part of St. Cyprien tourist complex (see **Perpignan***). 6.5 km SE, **Collioure***.

Elven (Towers)
56 – Morbihan 16 – A 1
In middle of thick forest, beside a lake, remains of 13–15c feudal fortress of Largoët-en-Elven: 15c machicolated gate and round tower; imposing late-14c octagonal keep, the tallest in France (57 m.), with granite finish; the walls are 6–9 m. thick.

Embrun
05 – Hautes-Alpes 38 – C 1
Built on high cliff of 'The Rock', a promontory over R. Durance, this one-time stronghold is still enclosed by part of its old ramparts. Fmr. Notre Dame cathedral, late 12c, is one of Dauphiné reg.'s most

Elne: *masterpieces of Catalan Romanesque art – animal sculptures on capitals in the cathedral cloister's south gallery.*

ENCLOS (Breton Parish Churches)
29N – Finistère   8 – B 2, 8 – C 2
To tour the *enclos* – the big parish churches in countryside near Brest –
one route takes you from **Landerneau*** on N 12 to *La Roche*, where
church has superb Ren. rood-screen and huge ossuary; then on to
Lampaul-Guimiliau and **Guimiliau*** (famed calvaries), **St. Thegonnec***
and *Pleyber-Christ*. ● Another route, SE from **Landerneau*** on D 764,
takes in *La Martyre*, *Ploudiry* and **Sizun***.

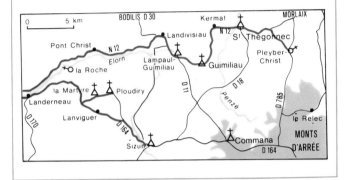

bronzes, Greek vases, reconstruction of Iberian, Greek and
Celtic sepulchres, etc., plus variegated articles from 6 to 1c BC,
together evoking the evolution of
daily life and Mediterranean art
over nearly 10 centuries.
Vicinity ● 2.5 km S, *Nissan-lez-
Enserune*, 14c church; museum,
archaeology and religious art.

Entraygues-sur-Truyère
12 – Aveyron   36 – C 1
Picturesque little medieval city, at
confluence of R. *Truyère* and the
Lot. 13c Goth. bridge. 15–16c
houses (Rue Basse, Rue du Collège,
Rue Droite) and ruins of feudal
castle.
Vicinity ● To NE, *Vallée de la
Truyère*, dams and reservoirs. ●
15 km NW, Puy de l'Arbre, view
over Cantal reg. ● To W, the D107
follows the impressive *Gorges of the
Lot*, through *Viellevie* and *Grand
Vabre*, where road continues

notable churches: on W façade,
elegant Romanesque door; on N
side, fine 12c porch, known as the
'Réal', framed by pink marble
columns, with sculpted capitals,
supported by lions (see photo).
Interior of church, with three naves
and three apses, is characterised by
alternate black and white stone;
rich church treasure. Old archbishop's palace is dominated by 12c
Brune tower (viewing table). For
unusual view of town, take a trip
along the Durance.
Vicinity ● **Serre-Ponçon*** dam.

Enghien-les-Bains
95 – Val d'Oise   11 – C 1
Pleasant spa (sulphurous waters).
The lake (canoeing) is surrounded
by lovely estates and villas. Casino.
Mineral-water plant.
Vicinity ● To N, *Montmorency*, on
hills crowned by picturesque,
rugged forest (some 13 sq. miles);
Ren. church of St. Martin (fine
stained-glass windows); small Jean-
Jacques Rousseau mus., in house
where he lived. *St. Leu-la-Forêt*;
Taverny, very beautiful 13 and 15c
church, flanked by unusual wooden
belfry, 15c; inside, has superb Ren.
sculpted stone retable and organ
loft with interesting 16c wood
panels depicting St. Barthélemy's
voyage to India. Méry-sur-Oise,
fine 16, 17 and 18c château (n.v.a.),
adjoining 15–16c church; 2 km
away, fmr. Cistercian abbey of the
Val, 12c (n.v.a.).

Ennezat
63 – Puy-de-Dôme   31 – A 1
Former collegiate church known as
'Cathedral of the Marsh', combines
Romanesque (nave, transept and

Embrun: *the columns of the cathedral's Romanesque porch rest on
lions, each holding a child or animal between its paws.*

side-aisles in arkose, a form of sandstone) and Gothic (choir, ambulatory and chapels in lava from
Volvic, 15 km to W); Romanesque
historiated capitals and 15c murals.
Vicinity ● 9 km N, *Thuret*, church in
Auvergne version of Romanesque;
interior has a Black Virgin.

Enserune (Oppidum)
34 – Hérault   42 – D 2
Important archaeological site, on
rocky spur 700 m. long; magnificent
panorama. Comprises several successive habitats from 6, 5 and 3c
BC – a veritable town, with remains
of houses with paved floors, plas-
tered and painted walls, cisterns,
sewers, etc. Mus. (v.a. daily) exhibits many of the finds: ceramics,

towards **Figeac*** or branches l. to
Conques*.

Entrevaux
**04 – Alpes-de-Haute-
Provence**   38 – D 3
This one-time stronghold, unchanged since 18c, combines with
its citadel (lovely view over R. *Var*)
to form a fine composite picture, of
austere grandeur. Town is entered
by three drawbridges; main one, to
S, is approached over a fortified
bridge. Goth. church, with single
16c nave, contains sumptuous
monumental retable, 17c, and interesting works of art.
Vicinity ● The *Gorges de Daluis*,
to NW, cut out of red schist, offer
sweeping views above ravine
through which R. *Var* flows.

Épernay
51 – Marne   12 – B 1

Capital of the Champagne vine-yards and centre for visits to the slopes planted with its world-famed vines. Houses of the principal producers (some from 18c) stretch along the Ave. de Champagne; three of these companies which organise visits enabling you to see the different processes in the making of champagne are: Moët et Chandon, Mercier (grape presses and cooperage) and Perrier Jouët; their cellars, dug out of the chalk in long tunnels often dating back to Roman times, are unforgettable. In fmr. Ch. Perrier: museums of the of secondary fermentation fundamental to the making of champagne. 7 km to W, noteworthy 12–13c church at *Damery*. ● Tour of champagne wine road, via *Montagne de Reims*, to N (see **Reims***). ● To SW, Montagne d'Épernay; *Ch. de Brugny*, 16c, renovated 18c, with superb square keep; Boursault wood; forests of Enghien and Vassy, etc. ● Tour of champagne wine areas via Côte des Blancs to S, through Cubry valley, *Pierry*, Chavot (very good viewing point), *Cuis* (Romanesque church), *Cramant, Avize, Oger* (12–13c church, panorama), *Le Mesnil-sur-Oger* (12–16c church), **Vertus***.

Quand toute sa plantation des Sablons fut en fleurs, Parmentier fit un gros bouquet et le porta à Versailles. Le roi mit une des fleurs à sa boutonnière et toute la cour en fit autant. C'était le plus bel hommage qu'on pût rendre aux efforts de Parmentier: de ce jour, la pomme de terre était acceptée sans retour.

Épinal: *one of the prints in the museum – Parmentier introduces the potato into France.*

Wife; large Gallo-Roman lapidary collection and rich group of drawings. Basilica of St. Maurice, 13–14c. Lovely views from grounds of château (65 acres). In library (cl. Sun. and Mon.), priceless illuminated manuscripts, 10 to 15c, in 18c. carved wood cabinets. Beautiful rose garden (500 varieties of roses).

Épine (Notre Dame)
51 – Marne   12 – C 1

Standing alone in the wide plain of Champagne, this imposing 15–16c Goth. church has a richly decorated Flamboyant façade, with three sculpted portals; int. has rood-screen with three arcades and two spiral staircases, 15 and 16c.

Époisses (Château)
21 – Côte d'Or   19 – C 2

The château, 14 and 16c, fortified and previously surrounded by moat, is flanked by very big outbuildings. Its chapel, dating from 12 and 15c, now serves as parish church (v.a.). Interior of château (v.a. July–Aug., cl. Tues.) has 17c décor and furniture: Grand Salon (17c portraits), room occupied by Mme. de Sévigné during stay at Époisses (painted ceiling, 16c tapestries), King's Room, etc.

Notre Dame de l'Épine: *the Gothic Flamboyant church with its two pierced spires; the right-hand spire is 55 m. tall.*

wine of Champagne, regional pre-history and archaeology, and fine arts. Church of St. Vincent-des-Vignes-Blanches (1967), designed in accordance with modern liturgical symbolism.
Vicinity ● 6 km NW, rec. visit to abbey of *Hautvillers*; in fmr. abbey church, 16–17c, interesting works of art and memorial stone to Dom Perignon (d. 1719), the monk credited with discovering the process

Épinal
88 – Vosges   13 – C 3

The Mus. International de l'Imagerie, specialising in very early forms of strip-cartoon and popular colour prints from 16c to present day, forms part of departmental mus. of the Vosges, which possesses several notable canvases, inc. two masterpieces – Rembrandt's *Portrait of an Old Woman* and Georges de la Tour's *Job Mocked by his*

Ermenonville
60 – Oise   11 – D 1

The 18c château (n.v.a.) has lovely grounds (v.a.) which were among first in France created in (English) landscaped style, with mock ruins, garden pavilions, etc. Here, for instance, you can find the Altar of Reverie, the Temple of Philosophy, Tomb of the Unknown Man, etc.; in the Isle of Poplars, cenotaph of Jean-Jacques Rousseau.
Vicinity ● To N and NW, Ermenon-

ville forest – *Mer de Sable* (Sea of Sand, leisure park), Jean Richard zoo, circus mus., abbey of **Châalis***. To S, park of Vallière (take D 607) and *Mortefontaine*.

Escolives-Ste. Camille
89 – Yonne   19 – B 2
Foundations of baths, temple and Gallo-Roman villa, 1–4c, have been excavated here, as well as remains of Merovingian cemetery (mus.). Fine church in 12c Burgundian style (sculpted capitals, superposed crypts).

Espalion
12 – Aveyron   36 – D 2
One of Aveyron region's most renowned sites. Ren. château over-looking the 13c bridge and ancient houses bordering R. *Lot* make a highly attractive picture. Mus. devoted to manners, customs and folk art of Rouergue, old name of this once separate reg. which did not become part of French kingdom until 1607. Also Joseph Vaylet mus. (Rouergue-style int.) in 15c fmr. church of St. Jean.
Vicinity ● 1 km SE, 11–12c church of Perse, in pink sandstone, has fine portal adorned with primitive sculptures. 2 km SE, Puy de Vermus (481 m.), wonderful view over *Valley of the Lot*, mts. of *Aubrac*, the *Causses*, etc.: sightseeing route from Espalion to **Entraygues-sur-Truyère***, on D120 via *Estaing*, under rock topped by 15–16c château; exceptional view from 13c bridge over *Lot*; first Sun. in July, unusual procession of St. Fleuret. Son et Lumière in summer.

Essarts (Les)
85 – Vendée   22 – D 1
Fortified entry gate leads into ruins of feudal castle (v.a.); 11c square keep has fine vaulted rooms; extensive grounds; remains of Gallo-Roman tumulus. Modern château, mid-19c, is in 'troubadour' style. In church, crypt has three 11c naves.

Étampes
91 – Essonne   11 – C 3
Notre Dame-du-Fort, from second half of 12c, is among Ile-de-France's loveliest churches; S portal (circa 1150) has pillar statues in same style as those of Chartres; interior has Romanesque capitals, 16c stained-glass windows, 11c crypt. Church of St. Gilles, 13, 15 and 16c, has 12c Romanesque façade; St. Basile, 15–16c, has fine Romanesque sculpted portal (to r., 16c mansion, Hôtel Diane de Poitiers). St. Martin, 12–13c, has a 16c leaning tower. Ren. mansion, Hôtel d'Anne de Pisseleu, and early-16c Hôtel St. Yon. Early-16c town hall has small reg. mus.: prehist. and

Espalion: *the old houses with their wooden balconies reflected in the River Lot are one of the many attractive features of this little town in the south of the Massif Central.*

Merovingian collections. Looming over town is Guinette tower, 12c fmr. royal keep, built to (rare) quatrefoil design.
Vicinity ● 3 km NE, at Morigny-Champigny, remains of Benedictine abbey of Morigny, 13 and 15c; choir now serves as parish church. 4 km away, Ch. de Jeurre; 18c garden pavilions in grounds (v.a. to these only, cl. Wed., Sat. a.m., and public hols.). ● 11 km E, *Ch. de Farcheville*, 13–15c feudal castle behind impressive rectangular fortified walls crowned by crenellated curtains (n.v.a.). ● To S, valley of the *Juine*; Ch. de *Méréville*, 17–18c, beautiful grounds (v.a. by arrangement). ● To SW, valley of the Chalouette, past lake and picturesque remains of Moulineux church, 12–13c; *Chalou-Moulineux*, Romanesque church.

Étretat
76 – Seine-Maritime   4 – C 2
One of the most extraordinary sites of the Normandy coast, above Le Havre, with white cliffs 60–80 m. tall towering over the shore. The cliff of Aval is flanked by a natural arch, the Porte d'Aval, in front of which stands the famed Needle, 70 m. high. Magnificent view from ridge of Porte d'Aval. To l. rises the Manneporte, formidable stone arch 90 m. high. Cliff and Porte d'Amont, on other side of the cove, are crowned by a chapel and memorial to French aviators Nungesser and Coli (lost while trying to fly Atlantic in 1927). Small museum.
Vicinity ● 4 km SW by footpath along cliffs or 7 km by road, *Cap d'Antifer*; vast panorama from top of lighthouse. ● 4 km NE, *Bénouville*, 'valleuses' (small dry valleys

Étretat: *the famed 70 m. Needle, in front of the cliff, seems like the advance guard for a defensive system in which the arch of the Porte d'Aval represents the fortified entrance.*

between cliffs) of St. Ange and Le Curé, Belval needle. ● 8 km SE, *Criquetot-l'Esneval*; 2 km away, 18c Ch. de Cuverville, home of the great writer André Gide (d. 1951), buried in local cemetery.

Eu
76 – Seine-Maritime   5 – A 1
12–13c church, dedicated to St. Laurent O'Toole, 12c Primate of Ireland, has several sculptures – inc. an Entombment, with eight figures, under a richly-sculpted late-15c canopy. In 12c crypt, tombs with recumbent figures of the saint and of d'Artois family, 13–15c. Late-16c château, renovated 19c, houses Louis-Philippe mus. (v.a. Apr.–Oct., cl. Tues.) – devoted not only to that monarch's turbulent reign (1830–48) but also to local ethnography and glassware. In late-16c college chapel, fmr. Jesuit house, notable 17c monumental mausoleums of the Duke of Guise, assassinated at Blois in 1588, and his wife.
Vicinity ● Beautiful *Forest of Eu* (36 sq. miles), various marked routes.

Évaux-les-Bains
23 – Creuse   24 – C 3
Spa known to the Romans (remains of antique baths), in picturesque region, the Combraille country. Romanesque church of St. Pierre and 11–12c St. Paul, with five-storey belfry porch and shingled 13c spire.
Vicinity ● 5 km W, *Chambon-sur-Voueize*: pretty little town and good centre for excursions; Romanesque bridge over R. Voueize. Fine Romanesque church of Ste. Valérie, 11–12c; int. has 15c reliquary bust and 17c choir stalls and screen in wood. To N of Chambon, Gorges of the Voueize, via cliff road. ● 17 km N, through *Budelière*, Rochebut dam on R. Cher, in midst of wooded hills.

Évian-les-Bains
74 – Haute-Savoie   26 – D 2
Wonderful position on Lac Léman (Lake of Geneva), the lake-front lined with gardens and avenues filled with flowers. Hotel and sporting facilities of highest class.
Vicinity ● 3.5 km W, *Amphion-les-Bains*, in garden near the lake, temple dedicated to poet Anna de Noailles. ● Tour of the lake (apply S.I.). ● Mountain walks and excursions; to S, 14c *Ch. de Larringes* (n.v.a.), fine view; *Bernex, Dent-d'Oche* massif.

Evisa
2A – Corsica   45 – B 3
The 'Pearl of Corsica' – village on rocky promontory between two valleys covered with chestnut trees.

Important excursion centre.
Vicinity ● Various walks. To NE, the Belvédère (impressive view over the red rocks); Aïtone torrent and mill. To W, towards *Ota*, the *Cirque de la Spelunca*, the Aïtone's narrowest defile. ● By car: to W, **Porto***; to E, via *Col de Vergio* (pass at 1,464 m. alt.), the road to **Corte*** crosses *Forest of Aïtone*, surrounded by high mountains.

Évreux
27 – Eure   11 – A 1
Though half-destroyed in 1940, town still has several important historic buildings. Notre Dame cathedral, 13–14c, has notable 16c façade and N door, and some of the loveliest 14c stained-glass windows; see also wood screens of Ren. ambulatory's chapels. In St. Taurin, fmr. abbey church, 14–15c, one of the Goth. masterpieces of goldsmith's art: reliquary of St. Taurin (much restored). Old bishop's palace, late 15c, now houses mus. (cl. Mon. and a.m. Sun.): tapestries, medieval statuary, paintings and decorative arts, 17–18–19c (works by Géricault, Boudin, Gérome); also 20c (Soulages, Debré, Tal Coat, etc.); archaeology in underground room (3c Gallo-Roman rampart). Clock tower with 44 m. belfry; walk along top of ramparts.
Vicinity ● Excursions rec. in valleys of R. *Iton*, the *Risle* and R. *Charentonne*. ● 18 km SW, *Conches-en-Ouche*, 15–16c church of St. Foy and valley of the Rouloir.

Évron
53 – Mayenne   10 – B 3
One-time abbey church, among finest Goth. buildings in western France (only one tower and the

principal nave are Romanesque); interior has 17c Aubusson tapestries and numerous works of art; chapel of Notre Dame de l'Épine, adjoining N side of choir, dates from 12c, with remains of 13c murals (poorly restored); rich church treasure includes statue of Notre Dame de l'Épine, in wood covered with silver foil, from early 13c. Huge 18c buildings of fmr. abbey.
Vicinity ● 5 km NW, Ch. du *Rocher*, 15c, one of finest in W France; Ren. eastern façade has richly sculpted décor (v.a. to ext. during summer). ● 4 km SW, early-17c Ch. de *Montecler*, with drawbridge guarded by imposing vaulted porch (n.v.a.). ● 7 km SE, **Ste. Suzanne***.

Eymoutiers
87 – Haute-Vienne   30 – B 1
Formerly enclosed town, ringed by R. *Vienne*. Romanesque and Goth. church, good group of 15c stained-glass windows. Old houses.
Vicinity ● 15 km SE, *Lacelle*, from where you climb up to Limousin plateau; after skirting 92-acre lake of *St. Hilaire-les-Courbes*, the road runs above Treignac reservoir, formed by R. *Vézère*, to the *Barrage de Vaud* (dam). 3 km to S, *Treignac* is a little town in amphitheatre layout above the *Vézère* (very picturesque valley). ● To N, excursions from *Peyrat-le-Château*: to W, *Valley of the Maulde* forms a long, winding lake behind the *Barrage du Mt. Larron*; to E, on big *Vassivière* lake (almost 4 sq. miles), beach and water sports centre; to N, *Bourganeuf*: remains of one-time Auvergne priory of Order of Malta, 12–15c church of St. Jean, Lastic tower and late-15c Zizim tower (remarkable three-storey oak struc-

Eu: *the château, then owned by the Princes of Orleans, was one of Louis-Philippe's favourite residences. Garden by Le Nôtre*

Evisa: *the village is splendidly situated on a promontory overlooking the Porto valley.*

ture); also good centre for excursions in R. *Thaurion* valley.

Eyzies-de-Tayac-Sireuil (Les)
24 – Dordogne   29 – D 3

The 'cradle of prehistory', in a grandiose site of limestone cliffs pitted with caves, above the valley of the R. *Vézère*. The village of Eyzies lies under enormous massif of rocks – halfway up which are imposing remains of castle, 10 and 11c, with square keep. Natnl. prehist. mus., in old château of Barons of Beynac, recently renovated and enlarged, is richest for prehistoric archaeology in all of France. Remains of 'Cro-Magnon man' were discovered in vicinity in 1868. On r. bank of R. Beune, Eyzies grotto in which first cave drawings were discovered.

1.5 km to S, 11–12c fortified church at Tayac; speleological mus. in local fort.

Vicinity ● *Valley of the Vézère*: 2 km NW, Grotto of the Grand Roc (stalactites, stalagmites); 5 km away, prehistoric sites, Laugerie-Basse and Laugerie-Haute (v.a.). 2 km to NW, Grotto of Carpe Diem, fine concretions (v.a.). ● 2 km SE, Grotto of the Mouthe, paintings and wall-carvings (v.a.). ● To E, on l. bank of valley of the Beune, Grotto of Font-de-Gaume: remarkable prehistoric paintings (v.a., cl. Tues.), Grotto of the Combarelles, depictions of animals on cave walls (v.a.); on r. bank, Cap-Blanc rock-shelter, famed raised relief frieze of animals (v.a., guided tour); opposite, imposing feudal

ruins of Ch. de Comarque, surrounded by trees.

Èze
06 – Alpes-Maritimes   45 – B 1

The village, clinging like eagle's nest to peak rising 427 m. above the shore, is one of the most remarkable sites on the Côte d'Azur: picturesque maze of narrow little streets, liberally dotted with arches and stairways. Remains of Ch. des Riquier. 18c church of Notre Dame-de-l'Assomption; 15c chapel of the Pénitents-Blancs. Exotic garden (v.a.), with numerous varieties of succulent plants and cacti; looming above it are ruins of former château (magnificent view). Èze village is linked to Èze-sur-Mer by zigzag path.

Évreux: *Gothic stained-glass in the cathedral apse.*

Les Eyzies: *the first discovery of prehistoric cave drawings was made in the grottoes honeycombing these steep cliffs.*

Falaise
14 – Calvados 10 – B 1
The huge 11–13c castle, which dominates the town from a rocky spur opposite *Mt. Myrrha,* is said to have been birthplace of William the Conqueror; flanked by 16 towers, it contains an impressive rectangular 12c keep linked by a curtain to early 13c Talbot tower, 35 m. high (v.a.; cl. Tues. and Sun. a.m., Easter–Sept.; cl. Mon. and Tues., Oct.–Easter). 13, 15 and 16c Trinity church, with beautiful Ren. porch. Church of St. Gervais, 11 and 13c nave, 16c choir, 12c central tower.
Vicinity ● 4 km W, Noron l'Abbaye, 13c church with Romanesque belfry, 18c château. ● 3 km N, just before *St. Pierre-Canivet,* Aubigny, 16c château (n.v.a.); in church, tomb of the Lords of Aubigny, kneeling in chronological order; 6 km to N, Mont-Joly inn, picturesque tomb of actress Marie Joly (d. 1798); Brèche du Diable,

narrow gorge in wild setting; 13c chapel of St. Quentin-de-la-Roche.

Fanjeaux
11 – Aude 42 – B 2
Old town on hilltop overlooking plain of Carcassonne; fine view. Late 13c church, recently restored (rich treasure). St. Dominic's house. On site known as Le Seignadou, in 1206, St. Dominic had the vision which led to his founding the monastery of Prouille, birthplace of Dominican order, below Fanjeaux; the church, which is the only part open to visitors, is mediocre example of late-19c Romano-Byzantine architecture
Vicinity ● 9 km E, *Montréal,* dominated by collegiate church of St. Vincent, in 14c S. Goth. style; fine view over Cévennes and Pyrenees.

Faouët (Le)
56 – Morbihan 8 – C 3
One of most characteristic sites in Brittany; its chapels and pardons attract vast crowds.
Vicinity ● *Chapelle Ste. Barbe,* in Goth Flamboyant style, 2.5 km to NE of town, in magnificent setting, dominates valley of R. Ellé; access is by a monumental Ren. staircase linked by an arch to St. Michael's oratory (pardons on last Sun. in

June and Dec. 4); early 18c fountain; under a dome, bell which pilgrims ring when offering up their prayers. ● 6.5 km NE, chapel of St. Nicolas; inside, noteworthy Ren. carved wooden rood-screen; 3 km beyond, *Priziac,* ruins of Ch. de Belair; Romanesque church, enlarged 16c; 4.5 km to E, late-16c chapel and Ren. ossuary at *Le Croisty.* ● 11 km NE, 17–18c *Abbaye de Langonnet,* 13c chapterhouse (mus. of African Missions). ● 2.5 km S, *Chapelle St. Fiacre,* late 15c, has original, typically Breton gabled belfry with two turret staircases and sculpted porch; inside, magnificent Goth. rood-screen, a delicate lacework of carved wood.

Fécamp
76 – Seine-Maritime 4 – C 2
Fishing port and seaside resort. Trinity church, in 12c Norman Goth. style, is former abbey church; exceptionally large (its nave is 127 m. long) and impressively proportioned, it contains numerous works of art. 18c monastic buildings are occupied by town hall. In Benedictine mus., in late-19c neo-Goth. Flamboyant style, interesting lapidary collections, enamels, metalwork, etc. Municipal mus., collection of Rouen pottery, porcelain and glassware, 16–18–19c paintings and drawings, objects connected with Newfoundland fishing industry.
Vicinity ● 13 km SE, *Ch. de Bailleul,* Ren., with richly carved décor (v.a. in summer). ● 15 km E, ruins of abbey at *Valmont* (v.a. in summer): abbey church still has lovely Ren. choir and chapel of the Virgin, an exquisite 16c jewel (stained-glass windows and sculptures); 15–16c castle, with 11c keep. ● 20km E, *Cany-Barville,* Ren. church (interesting works of art); moated Ch. de Cany (2 km S), in Louis XIII style (n.v.a.)

Fénelon (Chateau)
24 – Dordogne 36 – A 1
At Ste. Mondane, 3 km to SW of *St. Julien-de-Lampon.* Magnificent 15–16c fortified building, in which Fénelon (Archbishop of Cambrai under Louis XIV, and world-famed writer) was born in 1651. 17c façade with horseshoe-shaped flight of steps leading up to cloisters and courtyard, overlooked by Louis XIII-style gallery with balustrades; kitchens hewn out of the rock; beautiful apartments (v.a.).

Fénétrange
57 – Moselle 13 – D 1
Tiny old town. France gate, a remnant of 15–16c perimeter wall, is flanked by a round tower. Enormous 13–16c castle. 15c church of

Fécamp: *the Classical-style façade of Trinity church contrasts with the Gothic nave and the square lantern-tower, 64 m. high.*

St. Rémi; Goth. Flamboyant choir decorated with 18c wood panelling; unusual monumental tomb of Count Henri de Fénétrange (d. 1336).
Vicinity ● To NW of *Sarrebourg* (15 km S), on edge of forest of Hoff, natnl. cemetery for 1914–18 prisoners of war (14,000 graves).

Fère (La)
02 – Aisne　　　　6 – A 2
Once-fortified town on R. *Oise*. 13, 15 and 16c church. Jeanne d'Aboville museum (paintings by old masters from N of France).
Vicinity ● 7 km N, *Vendeuil* zoo park (v.a.). ● To S, *Forêt de St. Gobain*, very hilly, leading in SE into *Forêt de Coucy* (see **Coucy-le-Château***); *Abbaye de Prémontré*, founded 12c, 18c Classical buildings (psychiatric hospital; v.a. to ext. only); Romanesque church of *Septvaux*; remains of 14–15c fmr. abbey of *St. Nicolas-aux-Bois*; Tortoir priory in clearing on edge of lakes.

Fère-en-Tardenois
02 – Aisne　　　12 – A 1
15–16c church. 16c timber-work market-hall.
Vicinity ● 3 km N, impressive ruins of *Ch. de Fère*, dominated by huge 13c keep flanked by seven towers, bridge with five monumental arches surmounted by Ren. gallery; 15–16c château has been converted into an hotel. ● 5 km SW, *Villeneuve-sur-Fère*, birthplace of writer Paul Claudel (museum). ● 14.5 km W, *Oulchy-le-Château*, church of Notre Dame, 11c nave, 12c transept and square choir, is one of most remarkable in region; on Chalmont hill, 'Monument des Fantômes' by Landowski (Battle of the Marne). ● 4 km E, Ch. de Nesles.

Ferrette
68 – Haut-Rhin　　　21 – A 2
One of most picturesque sites in Alsatian Jura range. Upper town (old houses) is dominated by ruins of two medieval castles. Vast panorama.
Vicinity ● To E, *Oltingue*, interesting peasant museum.

Ferté-Bernard (La)
72 – Sarthe　　　10 – D 3
Built along numerous arms of R. Huisne. Picturesque old houses surround lovely 15–16c church of Notre Dame-des-Marais, whose Ren. choir is as imposing as it is harmonious; the sculpted decorations are just as refined: see, above all, vaults of 16c apsidal chapels, which are finely worked (Rosary chapel is a perfect jewel of exquisitely carved stone).

Fère-en-Tardenois: *a bridge leads to the ruined towers of the Château de Fère, the work of Jean Bullant and Jean Goujon.*

La Ferté-St. Aubin: *the 'lake road' is one of the loveliest in the Sologne region, crossing heathland and pine forests.*

Vicinity ● 8 km SE, near *Courgenard*, Ch. de Courtangis, elegant, finely decorated early-16c manor-house; in church, 16c murals depicting the tortures of hell; 7 km to SE, *Montmirail*, formerly fortified town on a hill, still has some of its ramparts, fortified gate and 15c castle. (v.a., cl. Tues., July-Aug.; Sun. only, Mar.–Oct.); Son et Lumière; 12–16c church; interior has early-17c Entombment.

Ferté-Loupière (La)
See **Joigny***.　　　19 – A 1

Ferté-Milon (La)
02 – Aisne　　　12 – A 1
Impressive remains of 13c castle dominate the town (fine views). Churches: 12c and Ren. Notre Dame, 15–16c St. Nicolas (stained-glass windows depicting the Apocalypse). Racine was born and spent his childhood here.
Vicinity ● To NNW, forest of *Villers-Cotterets*. ● To SW, *Mareuil-sur-Ourcq* and *May-en-Multien* have interesting churches.

Ferté-St. Aubin (La)
45 – Loiret　　　18 – B 2
In heart of Sologne reg. 12–16c church, imposing mid-17c château, enlarged 19c, surrounded by moat, in huge park.
Vicinity ● N 20 crosses forest dotted with lakes, with numerous 18 or 19c châteaux. ● 12.5 km S, at *Chaumont-sur-Tharonne*, tiny road leads to Montevran zoo park (v.a. Apr.–Oct.); from Chaumont, road leads 10 km SE to *Lamotte-Beuvron*, one of main venues for hunt meetings in area (16–17c château), then 7 km to S, to *Nouan-le-Fuzelier*; to W,

Figeac: *in St. Sauveur's former chapter-house, 17c carved wooden panels depicting the Passion (here, the Last Supper).*

and original example of 'Jesuit style'. 15c Carmelite house (town hall). St. Thomas' church, Romanesque and Goth. Behind cemetery, chapel of Notre Dame-des-Vertus (Romanesque main doorway, magnificent 16c wood panelling).
Vicinity ● 3.5 km SE, Tertre-Rouge zoo park (v.a.); natural sciences museum. ● 10 km E, 15c. Ch. de *Gallerande*, with four round towers and octagonal keep (n.v.a.). ● 7 km W, *Bazouges-sur-le-Loir*, early-16c château, reconstructed 17c; inside, 18c drawing-rooms; late 16c chapel (v.a. Tues., Thurs. a.m. and Sat. p.m.); 16 km to W, *Durtal*, 16–17c château (old people's home, n.v.a.), built on site of former fortress, of which only two 15c towers remain.

picturesque 'lake road' through *St. Viâtre* (interesting 13c church), *La Ferté-Beauharnais, Neung-sur-Beuvron, La Marolle, Yvoy-le-Marron*, from where you can return to *Chaumont-sur-Tharonne* or continue NW to *Ligny-le-Ribault*.

Figeac
46 – Lot   **36 – B 1**
Old town rich in attractive houses. Champollion mus. is housed in birthplace of the world-famed Egyptologist (personal souvenirs and objects belonging to Champollion, Egyptian works of art). 13–14c Mint, lapidary remains, prehist. collection. Church of St. Sauveur, Romanesque and Goth. (14–15c chapter-house, converted into chapel). Notre Dame-du-Puy, Romanesque, restored 16–17c.
Vicinity ● Valleys of R. Lot and Célé. ● 20 km SE, unusual medieval village of *Peyrusse-le-Roc*, partly ruined, remains of medieval castle. ● 22 km NE, *Maurs-la-Jolie*: in 14c church, noteworthy reliquary bust of St. Césaire, in wood cased in silver and gilded copper, a masterpiece of late-12c metalwork. ● 16 km NW, *Ch. d'Assier*, magnificent Ren. building, badly damaged 18c; only W wing remains, with its pilasters topped by composite capitals, friezes and sculpted reliefs (cl. Tues, Mar. 15–Sept. 30); elegantly decorated Ren. church.

Filitosa
2A – Corsica   **45 – D 3**
Important megalithic centre (v.a.). The oppidum, standing on natural spur, includes central cultic monument, constructed around mid-2c by the Torreans. At E and W ends are two further monuments. Numerous menhir-statues, some of them outstanding, are exhibited

near central and W monuments. Inside perimeter wall, remains of Torrean village. In hamlet of Filitosa, inf. centre and small mus. (finds from excavations).

Flaine
74 – Haute-Savoie   **26 – D 3**
Large winter sports resort, built 1968–1970 at 1,650 m. alt. Interesting modern architectural development, designed by Marcel Breuer. Huge polychrome sculpture by Vasarely. Grandes-Platières cable-car goes up to 2,447 m., and that of *Tête-Pelouse* to 2,350 m.

Flavigny-sur-Ozerain
21 – Côte-d'Or   **19 – C 2**
This most picturesque little town is magnificently situated on a wooded spur, isolated by three rivers; it is surrounded by ramparts; two 16c fortified gates, Porte du Bourg and Porte du Val. Interesting old houses. 13 and 15c church of St. Genès has many 15–16c statues, notably a beautiful early-16c stone 'Angel of the Annunciation' and, in choir, late-15c choir stalls carved with satirical or anecdotal scenes. Only Carolingian crypts, aka Ste. Reine, remain of fmr. abbey of St. Pierre (v.a.); a 10c hexagonal chapel, Notre Dame-des-Piliers, was discovered leading out of them in 1960. Local speciality: Flavigny aniseed apéritif.
Vicinity ● To N, **Alise-Ste. Reine***, **Bussy-Rabutin***. ● To W, **Semur-en-Auxois***.

Flèche (La)
72 – Sarthe   **17 – B 2**
The Military School, formerly a Jesuit college founded by France's King Henri IV, has imposing 17c buildings, main courtyard and chapel of St. Louis, an outstanding

Filitosa: *a megalithic menhir-statue of visibly human form.*

Flers-de-l'Orne
61 – Orne   **10 – A 2**
The château, surrounded by a moat and lake, includes 18c main building and late-16c wing flanked by towers; inside, town hall, library and Bocage Normand mus. (v.a., p.m., Easter–mid-Oct.): large collection of paintings, especially 19c, Corot, Boudin, Daubigny. Norman cockery. Galleries devoted to weaving. Lovely park.
Vicinity ● 3 km W, *Mt. de Cerisi*, reached by path bordered by giant rhododendrons; remains of Belle-Étoile abbey, 13c church and cloisters.

Florac
48 – Lozère   37 – A 2

At foot of cliff of *Causse Méjean*, in magnificent setting. A ruined medieval castle, flanked by two round towers, dominates the town. Rec. excursion centre for **Gorges du Tarn*** and the *Cévennes*.

Vicinity ● To NW, **Tarn*** gorges, via *Ispagnac* (Romanesque church and ruins of Benedictine fortified priory); *Molinès* and Ch. de Rocheblave (15c manor-house, crowned by machicolations); Montbrun, rising in tiers above a ravine (lower down, 16c Ch. de Charbonnière); *Castelbouc*, unusual village at foot of circle of cliffs on which stands a ruined castle (superb view from belvedere overlooking the site; Son et Lumière in summer); **Ste. Enimie***. ● To SE, towards **Barre-des-Cévennes*** and towards **Alès***, roads cross *Parc National des Cévennes*, largest and most populated French national park.

Foix
09 – Ariège   42 – A 3

On a rocky peak, dominating town, stand the three remaining towers – inc. 42 m.-high keep – of 11–12 and 15c castle of the Counts of Foix (cl. Tues. in low season), which contains a reg. mus. (prehist., folklore and ethnography). Quarter around 14c cath. of St. Volusien (Romanesque door) contains many old houses, some of which are half-timbered, in Place du Mercadal-Dutilh. *Vicinity* ● 5.5 km N, *St. Jean-de-Verges*, Romanesque church and picturesque cemetery. ● 6 km to NW, *Rivière Souterraine de Labouiche*, underground river, 2,500 m.-long boat trip (Easter–Nov. 1), highly varied concretions. ● 13 km W, via Serres-sur-Arfet and *Burret* (winding road), *Col des Marrous* (960 m.) and *Massif de l'Arize*. ● 16 km S, **Tarascon-sur-Ariège*** and grotto of **Niaux***.

Folgoët (Le)
29N – Finistère   8 – B 2

Its Sept. 7–8 pardon is famous throughout Brittany. 15c church of Notre Dame-de-Folgoët, flanked by two magnificent towers; beautiful sculpted doorways, esp. to W, 15c Apostles' door with striking granite statues; inside, Goth. Flamboyant rood-screen, in granite, is one of most important examples of 15c Breton Goth. sculpture. Behind church, Salaün fountain.

Vicinity ● 13 km N, *Brignogan-Plage*, magnificent chaotic mass of rock; 8 m.-high menhir, aka Men-Martz; 2 km to NW, Pol chapel; 5 km to SE, *Goulven*, Goth. church, lovely Ren. belfry with steeple; Créac'h-Gallic gallery tomb.

Foix: *the castle appears to blend into the surrounding mountains; its three towers are linked by a double perimeter wall.*

Fontainebleau (Palace)
77 – Seine-et-Marne   11 – D 3

Palace consists of a number of 16 and 17c buildings, in town centre (v.a., cl. Tues.). Entry is via Cheval-Blanc or Adieux courtyard (Napoleon bade farewell to the Imperial Guard here in 1814), with its famed 'Horseshoe' stairway. Tour of interior covers two parts: on first floor, Napoleon I's state apartments; Marie-Antoinette's apartments, exquisitely decorated; Diane de Poitier's gallery; royal apartments of François I, transformed by Louis XIV into sumptuous reception rooms; magnificent 30 m.-long ballroom, built during reigns of François I and Henri II, magnificently decorated by Il Primaticcio; splendid coffered ceiling by Philibert Delorme. Grandiose François I gallery, decorated with carved wood panelling surmounted by frescos and sculptures in stucco. On ground floor: private apartments of Napoleon I, Josephine and Marie-Louise; gallery known as 'Galerie des Cerfs'. Palace also contains Chinese rooms and charming Napoleon III theatre (cl.). A Napoleonic museum is being installed in Louis XV wing of Adieux courtyard. ● V.a. to gardens and park (landscape garden, carp pond, formal flower beds, King's arbour dating from about 1730, etc.). ● See also Napoleonic mus. of art and military history: large collection of uniforms, arms, equipment, Napoleonic souvenirs.

Vicinity ● 2 km E, *Avon*, picturesque church, pre-Romanesque nave and doorway with 16c wooden porch; 5.5 km to E, *Thomery* and banks of R. Seine: beaches, water

Fontainebleau: *the ballroom windows open on to flowerbeds planted under François I and re-designed under Louis XIV.*

Fontainebleau: *Napoleon took leave of his Imperial Guard at the foot of this 'Horseshoe' stairway in the Adieux courtyard.*

sports. ● 12 km NE, *Samois-sur-Seine*, on l. bank of Seine; on r. bank via ferry: Héricy, lovely 15-16c church and 17c château; water sports; from Valvins bridge, 2.5 km to S, lovely view of banks of Seine and forest of Fontainebleau. ● 10 km SE, via N5, **Moret-sur-Loing***. ● 8 km NW, **Barbizon***.

Fontaine-de-Vaucluse
See **Isle-sur-la-Sorgue (L')***.

38 – A 3

Fontaine-Henry (Château)
14 – Calvados 4 – B 3
Beautiful Ren. building (v.a., p.m., days vary). Vast slate roof covers the 'Large Pavilion', flanked by elegantly-decorated pepperpot turret; noteworthy Louis XIII and Louis XIV drawing-rooms, 13c cellars

FONTAINEBLEAU (Forest)
77 – Seine-et-Marne 11 – C 3 – 11 – D 3

It covers 96 sq. miles, of which 65 belong to the State. Traversed by numerous roads (parking permitted only at junctions, in immediate vicinity of forest roads, and in car-parks). Well-marked 'silent zones' are reserved exclusively for walkers and horse-riders. As well as arrowed footpaths, such as those of 19c 'wood genies' Dénecourt and Colinet, and recent so-called 'long-distance trails', there are tracks usable by car. Rock-climbing schools also operate in the forest. So-called Round Route gives easy access to most important areas. Main itineraries: ● Solle heights and Dénecourt tower: in Fontainebleau, follow Louis-Philippe and Gros-Fouteau roads, from which branches, to r., winding and picturesque Solle heights road; from there you can reach Croix d'Augas crossroads, highest point

in forest (144 m.) and Augas cave; Reine-Amélie road (fine view at Croix-du-Calvaire) leads back to Fontainebleau; road to l. leads to Dénecourt tower, built on a pile of rocks (magnificent view). ● 'Chaos' and *Gorges d'Apremont*: forest road which leads on from Grande-Rue takes you to Bas-Bréau wood, from where you can go either to **Barbizon*** or, via Bas-Bréau crossroads, to Apremont gorges, which are extremely picturesque but accessible on foot only; Apremont 'chaos' is a weird heap of rocks (fine view); Brigands cave. ● *Gorges de Franchard*: via Round Route, Croix-de-Franchard crossroads, then St. Feuillet road, which leads to Ermitage crossroads; this hermitage, now ruined, was former place of pilgrimage and then, in 17c, a bandits' hideout; Franchard gorges, very picturesque (panoramic views from Grand-Point-de-Vue or Marie-Thérèse belvedere), are excellent for rock-climbing (marked paths).

and kitchen (imposing fireplace with three grates). 13c chapel, altered during Ren.

Fontenay (Abbey)
21 – Côte-d'Or   19 – C 2
Best-preserved of all 12c Cistercian abbeys (v.a.). Entry via main gateway; garden is surrounded by hostelry, former strangers' chapel and monks' bakery. 1652 dovecote. Mid-12c church is one of the most characteristic examples of Cistercian architecture, being both harmoniously proportioned and severe in style; it is surrounded by the chapter-house, parlour, beautiful Romanesque cloister (above, monks' dormitory), 'scriptorium' (study), calefactory, prison, etc. 17c infirmary and huge late-12c building which houses various workshops, forge, mill, etc. complete the picture, giving good idea of life of monks in Middle Ages.

Fontenay-le-Comte
85 – Vendée   23 – A 2
On borders of Bocage Vendéen and *Marais Poitevin*, capital of lower Poitou, spreading out along both banks of R. *Vendée*. Old town still has many 16 and 17c houses (Rue du Pont-aux-Chèvres, Rue Goupilleau, Place Belliard, etc.). Ren. Quatre-Tias fountain carries motto given to town by François I: 'Fountain and source of great minds'. Notre Dame church: lovely 16c belfry, Goth. Flamboyant-style doorway; Ren. Brisson chapel. Mus.: reg. hist., archaeology and

folklore. The B.C. transformer factory was designed by the artist Mathieu (b. 1921, painter and designer interested in applied arts). *Vicinity* ● 1 km W, Ch. de Terre-Neuve, charming 16c manor-house, reconstructed 19c, which belonged to poet Nicolas Rapin (1535–1608); lovely Ren. fireplaces, 16c wood panelling from Ch. de Chambord, coffered ceilings in sculpted stone, 18c furniture. ● To S, *Marais Poitevin*, between *Anse de l'Aiguillon* and **Niort***. ● 13 km S, ruins of Abbey of **Maillezais***. ● 13 km E, Abbey of **Nieul-sur-Autise***. ● 15 km N, **Vouvant***.

Fontevrault (Abbey)
49 – Maine-et-Loire   17 – B 3
Founded at end of 11c, abbey is currently being restored to its former glory; it consisted of five monasteries, of which three survive: v.a. to St. Benoît and Le Grand Moûtier; in latter, magnificent early 12c Romanesque abbey church with 84 m.-long single nave is a 'must' (interesting historiated capitals). It also contains recumbent figures of Henry II of England (d. 1189), his wife, Eleanor of Aquitaine, and their son, Richard the Lion Heart. Vast cloister and 16c chapter-house, Romanesque refectory with early 16c ribbed vaulting. The world-famed kitchens consist of a 27 m.-high octagonal tower flanked by apsidioles bristling with smoke-hoods topped by lantern turrets. Contemp. art centre. In parish church of St. Michel, numer-

ous works of art (carved wooden high altar, paintings, etc.), originally from the monastery.

Fontfroide (Abbey)
11 – Aude   42 – D 2
Important Cistercian abbey in wild valley (v.a., cl. Tues. Oct. 1–Mar. 31). Late 12c Romanesque church, severe in style, is flanked by magnificent cloister and early-13c chapter-house. Armarium, or cloister library, sacristy. In 13c lay brothers' and visitors' building, refectory and storeroom; above, monks' dormitory.

Fontgombault (Abbey)
36 – Indre   23 – D 2
Magnificent Romanesque building, occupied by Benedictines. 11–12c abbey church, 82 m. long, is unquestionably majestic (Gregorian chanting daily). 15c convent buildings, cloister and refectory. *Vicinity* ● 8.5 km NW, *Angles-sur-l'Anglin*, in amphitheatre form above R. Anglin, is dominated by ruins of 12 and 15c castle perched precariously above a ravine; very picturesque site.

Font-Romeu
66 – Pyrénées-Orientales   43 – B 3
Summer and winter health-resort at 1,800 m. alt., in magnificent setting overlooking whole of French *Cerdagne*. The sports equipment in the health school is outstanding. Hill and calvary (fine view); Font-Romeu hermitage (1,824 m.), in wooded setting, contains 18c

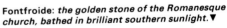

Fontevrault: *the Gothic and Renaissance grand cloister and Romanesque abbey church, with its belfry.*◄

Fontfroide: *the golden stone of the Romanesque church, bathed in brilliant southern sunlight.*▼

Fougères: *a fine example of medieval military architecture, extolled by Victor Hugo and Balzac.*

buildings and elegantly decorated chapel housing 13c miracle-working Virgin (pilgrimage).
Vicinity ● To E, Superbolquère (1,780 m.), health resort whose chalets and villas are scattered about the forest; 9 km to E, **Mont-Louis***. ● 1 km S, *Odeillo*, church with lovely Romanesque doorway and, inside, 12c Virgin; solar furnace, brought into service in 1969. ● To W, granitic rock mass of Targassonne; 8 km to SW, Angoustrine, picturesque village (11–12c Romanesque church, in granite, with 13c frescos and sevl. works of art); 3.5 km away, *Ur*, 11c church with apse in trefoil form; inside, Byzantine Christ and unusual font.

Forcalquier
04 – Alpes-de-Haute-Provence   38 – B 3
Former cathedral of Notre Dame (Romanesque and Goth., reconstructed 17c), Franciscan convent (v.a. to convent buildings and remains of church), cemetery and its astonishing topiary are main features of this little city, built in tiers on a hillside; picturesque old quarter. Municipal mus. (archaeology, 18c furniture).
Vicinity ● 6 km S, early-18c *Ch. de Sauvan*, one of most attractive buildings in upper Provence; interior is magnificently furnished (v.a. Easter–Nov. 1, cl. Mon.). ● 28 km N, via *St. Étienne-les-Orgues*: *Mt. de Lure*, wild and melancholy spot; D113 passes beside Lure

mountain refuge (1,572 m.) before climbing up to *Signal de Lure* (1,827 m.), highest point of mountain (vast panorama). ● 15.5 km NE, **Ganagobie*** priory. ● 11 km SW, **St. Michel-l'Observatoire***.

Fos-sur-Mer
13 – Bouches-du-Rhône   43 – D 2
Old town at head of *Golfe de Fos*; ruins of 14c castle, 11–12c Romanesque country church; 2 km to S, Fos-Plage. The vast industrial complex is one of Europe's most impressive technological landscapes; wide views from L'Hauture and Vigie tower. Car trip around

industrial zone, on N568 from Valin crossroads to container port. Inf. and reception centre.

Fouesnant
29S – Finistère   15 – B 1
In one of lushest parts of Brittany, covered with orchards. Noteworthy 12c Romanesque church; interior has interesting capitals.
Vicinity ● 3 km NE, *La Forêt-Fouesnant*, traditional parish church and 16c calvary; interior contains numerous examples of folk art. Port-la-Forêt marina. ● 2.5 km SE, sandy point of Cap Coz on *Baie de la Forêt*. ● 5.5 km S, *Beg-*

Fréhel: *the charming, tranquil little port of Le Guildo lies on the right bank of the Arguenon estuary.*

Meil point and village; 'Renouveau' cultural and leisure village is a most original example of contemporary architecture ● 8 km W, *Benodet*, in delightful setting: beach, large yachting centre.

Fougères
35 – Ille-et-Vilaine   9 – D 3

Castle is made up of a number of impressive 12–15c buildings, with 13 towers and remains of three perimeter walls, and is one of best-preserved examples of medieval military architecture. It is overlooked by the town, built on a promontory above Nançon valley; small footwear mus. in one of towers (v.a., hours vary, cl. Jan.). Fine views over valley, old ramparts and castle from Place aux Arbres and 15–16c church of St. Léonard, next door to 14–16c town hall. See old quarter of Place du Marchix, Rue du Nançon (16c houses), Rue des Tanneurs, Rue de la Pinterie, which links upper town to castle. Villeon mus. of painting. 15, 16 and 18c church of St. Sulpice. Notre Dame gate between two 14 and 15c towers. 18c Urbanist convent.

Vicinity ● 3 km NE, *Forêt Domaniale de Fougères* (4,150 acres), lovely beech groves, megaliths; strange alignment of 80 quartz blocks, known as 'Druids' Cordon'. ● 16 km NE, *Pontmain,* basilica of Notre Dame (pilgrimage).

Fougères-sur-Bièvre
41 – Loir-et-Cher   18 – A 2

Goth.-style stronghold is interesting example of late-15c military architecture (v.a., cl. Tues., Apr. 1– Sept. 30; cl. Tues. and Wed., Oct. 1–Mar. 31). The buildings stand in a square around picturesque internal courtyard with covered gallery. In partly Romanesque church, 16c carved choirstalls.

Vicinity ● 9.5 km SW, *Pontlevoy*, fmr. abbey (v.a.), 13–15c church choir, 17c choirstalls and retable; 17c convent buildings.

Fréhel (Cape)
22 – Côtes-du-Nord   9 – B 2

Sheer red sandstone cliffs, more than 70 m. high, rise above the sea; magnificent view. Fréhel botanical park. On E slope, below cliff, huge Grande Fauconnière rock, shaped like a leaning tower; nesting site for seabirds.

Vicinity ● 4 km SE, *Fort la Latte*, impressive reddish building on rocky headland; medieval perimeter walls surround late-12c central keep (v.a. in summer); opposite, *Pointe de St. Cast* (magnificent view over *Côte d'Emeraude*). Popular seaside resort, St. Cast has one of loveliest beaches in Brittany; from Garde point, view of town and bay; tourist path; 12 km to S, Notre Dame-du-Guildo and ruins of Guildo castle; strange mass of rocks known as 'ringing stones': the rocks make metallic sound when tapped by stone of same material.

Fréjus
83 – Var   44 – D 2

Once a flourishing Roman town, Fréjus still has many monuments to its past. In town centre, 5–14c episcopal city was originally fortified (cl. Tues.); it is grouped around fmr. early-13c Goth. cathedral of St. Léonce-et-St. Étienne: 16c outer door has Ren. carved wooden leaves; inside, *Retable de Ste. Marguerite* by J. Durandi (1450); 5c baptistry is one of most striking examples of Paleo-Christian art; staircase leads to delightful little 12c cloister (mus. of Gallo-Roman archaeology). Roman city contains many monuments, scattered throughout town: theatre (ruins of hemicycle and tiered seats), remains of aqueduct, Orée gate, quay in port and Augustus' 'lantern', amphitheatre (v.a.), etc.

Vicinity ● 2 km NE, richly decorated Buddhist pagoda. Continuing along N7 for 8 km, new quarter of Tour de Mare, chapel decorated by Jean Cocteau. ● 4 km N, Sudanese mosque in Caïs military camp; zoo park; Estérel safari park. ● 11 km W, Roquebrune-sur-Argens: picturesque village whose church contains four lovely 15–16c retables; red sandstone rocks known as *Rochers de Roquebrune* have fine views, especially of Notre Dame-de-la-Roquette. ● 3 km E, **St. Raphaël***. ● From Fréjus to **Cannes***, N7 crosses *Estérel* massif through lovely forested countryside (recommended excursion to 618 m.-high *Mt. Vinaigre*).

Fresnay-sur-Sarthe
72 – Sarthe   10 – B 3

12c Romanesque church of Notre Dame (carved leaves of Ren. doorway). Old perimeter walls of château, now public garden, are bordered by terrace from which there is superb view over R. Sarthe. Head-dress mus. (v.a. July-Aug.; Sun. only, Easter–Oct.) in one of towers in château.

Vicinity ● Excursion centre for *'Alpes Mancelles'* (see **Alençon***).

Fréjus: *from the top of Roquebrune mountain, you can see from the Gulf of Fréjus to the Alps.*

There are around 300 birds in Fréjus zoo park.

Gaillac
81 – Tarn 36 – B 3
Two interesting churches: St. Pierre, in southern Gothic style, and St. Michel, 10c former Benedictine abbey church. Early-15c mansion, Hôtel Pierre de Brens, houses mus. devoted to trade guilds, vine-growing and folklore. Philadelphe Thomas natural history mus.; also mus. of local painting and sculpture in grounds of Ch. de Foucaud. Arcaded houses and 15c Griffoul fountain, Place Thiers.
Vicinity ● 12 km SW, via *Lisle-sur-Tarn* to *Ch. de St. Géry*, lovely 18c Classical residence above R. *Tarn*. (v.a., p.m. daily, July-Aug.; otherwise, p.m. Sun. and public holidays only, Apr. 1 to Nov. 1); apartments have fine furniture; unusual dining-room. ● 11 km N, *Cahuzac*; 3 km to N, through Andillac, *Ch. du Cayla*, birthplace and home of Eugénie and Maurice de Guérin, brother and sister who had minor reputation as authors in first half 19c (v.a., cl. Fri. and Sat. a.m., apply to caretaker). ● 10 km, SE *Cadalen*, fine 12–13c church.

Gallardon
28 – Eure-et-Loir 11 – B 2
Noteworthy church, 12, 13 and 15c, with wooden vaulting painted in 18c. The 'Épaule (shoulder) de Gallardon', somewhat unusual remnant of 12c keep. 16c timbered house, with carved decoration, in Rue Porte Mouton.
Vicinity ● 5.5 km E, Ch. d'*Es-climont*, mid-16c (v.a. in summer), surrounded by lovely park; 9 km to S, *Auneau*, fine feudal keep, 13c.

Ganagobie (Priory)
04 – Alpes-de-Haute-Provence 38 – B 3
At 600 m. alt., in superb setting on plateau above R. *Durance*. Founded in 980, the priory (v.a.) is now occupied by Benedictines. The church, in late-12c Provençal Romanesque style, boasts an unusually festooned portal, framing a fairly primitive tympanum representing Christ in Glory. Romanesque mosaics in choir.

Gannat
03 – Allier 25 – A 3
Ste. Croix church, Romanesque and Gothic; unusual historiated capitals. Mus. in fmr. castle, late 12–14c, has a very fine 9c Book of the Gospels (v.a. during holiday season). St. Étienne church, 11–12c.
Vicinity ● To N, *Jenzat*: late-11c church, 15c murals known as 'Frescos of the Masters of Jenzat'. Picturesque village of *Charroux*, remains of walls, gate and belfry, 15c; also 12c Romanesque church. *Bellenaves*: 12c church of St. Martin, fine sculpted portal. *Chantelle*: St. Vincent abbey, 12c church and interesting monastic complex.

Gap
05 – Hautes-Alpes 38 – C 1
The old town is dominated by cathedral in 19c neo-Gothic style. In mus., superb 17c mausoleum of Duc de Lesdiguières (Constable of France, d. 1626), with archaeological and folklore collections.
Vicinity ● Lovely view of reg. from Ch. de Charance, 4 km NW. ● 15 km N, *St. Bonnet-en-Champsaur*, starting-point for excursions in *Champsaur* mountains: E through upper valley of R. *Drac*, dry and hot in summer, to *Orcières* (25.5 km); further 5.5 km to Orcières-Merlette (alt. 1,1850–2,650 m.), summer resort and winter sports centre. ● 19 km SE, via *La Bâtie-Neuve*, 17c church of Notre Dame-du-Laus, local pilgrimage centre.

Garabit (Viaduct)
15 – Cantal 31 – A 3
At height of 95 m. above R. Truyère, audaciously-designed railway bridge by Gustave Eiffel (constructed 1882–1884).
Vicinity ● Reservoir of *Grandval* on R. *Truyère*; excellent viewing point from belvedere of Mallet, between *Faverolles* and *Fridefont*; from there, N to Ch. d'*Alleuze* (see **St. Flour***).

Garde-Adhémar (La)
26 – Drome 37 – D 2
Old, half-ruined township; remains of château; Romanesque church

Gaillac: *the town, with its old brick houses lining the steep banks of the Tarn, is regaining its name as a wine centre.*

Garabit: *Eiffel's early masterpiece, 564 m. long, was completed three years before work began on his Paris tower.*

with two facing apses. 2 km to E, unusual Val-des-Nymphes chapel, 11c.

Gargilesse-Dampierre
36 – Indre   24 – B 2
Picturesque village where George Sand lived at one time, using it as setting for several novels; interesting mus. now installed in her country house, of which original interior has been reconstructed. 11–12c Romanesque church enclosed within remains of feudal castle; 11–15c frescos in crypt.
Vicinity ● 7.5 km S, *Éguzon* dam, on R. *Creuse* (canoes for hire on lake during summer); picturesque villages of *Éguzon*, 3 km SW (ruins of feudal castle) and *Crozant*, 10.5 km S, at foot of promontory crowned by ruins of 12–13c castle.

Gavarnie   41 – B 3
See **Luz-St. Sauveur***

Gençay 86 – Vienne   23 – C 2
Township, in superb setting at confluence of two rivers, is dominated by remains of 13–14c castle.
Outskirts ● On r. bank of R. Clouère, St. Maurice-la-Clouère, church in local version of Romanesque, with 14c murals; 1 km to S, Ch. de la Roche-Gençay, 16 and 18c (mus. of Order of Malta, v.a.).

Gérardmer
88 – Vosges   20 – D 1
In green setting on pine-covered slopes at E end of Lac de Gérardmer, largest lake in the Vosges (284 acres). The town, rebuilt after 1939–45 war, is a good base for excursions and winter sports (centred at La Schlucht, 15 km to E). Tour of lake: on foot, by car (on N417), or in motor-launch (20-min. trip, leaving from the Esplanade).
Vicinity ● To NE, via Col du Surceneux (pass at 810 m.), upper valley of R. *Meurthe*; defile of *Straiture*, with beautiful tree-covered sides; and valley of the Petite-Meurthe. ● To E, via the Saut-des-Cuves, magnificent waterfall amid enormous granite blocks, lakes of *Longemer* and *Retournemer*, also Roche du Diable (Devil's Rock – 1,000 m. alt., belvedere). The N417 climbs to *Col de la Schlucht* (1,159 m.), then descends series of hairpin bends into Alsace, in direction of **Colmar***. From *Col de la Schlucht*, you can also join the Route des **Crêtes***, road along the mountain ridges.

Germigny-des-Prés
45 – Loiret   18 – C 1
Celebrated Carolingian church (apply at presbytery), built in 806

GARDON (Gorges)
30 – Gard   37 – C 3
From *Dions* to *Collias*, the R. *Gardon* runs for 22 km between sheer walls, riddled with caves (prehistoric remains). At *Dions,* Ch. de Buissières, magnificent box-trees; 500 m. to SE, superb Dions cave, aka the Espeluques swallow-hole, a vast oval abyss, more than 400 m. round and 70 m. deep; numerous grottoes (guided tours); former oppidum of Marbacum. The *Collias* region also has many caves, notably the Bayol grotto, where what is thought to be a prehistoric place of worship, decorated with animal paintings, has been found.

GAVRINIS (Island)
56 – Morbihan   16 – A 2
Reached by boat (1 km) from *Larmor-Baden* (see **Vannes*** and Gulf of **Morbihan***). Its famed tumulus, 8 m. high and 100 m. in circumference, formed from stones piled up on a rise, is among world's most enigmatic megalithic monuments. The gallery leading to funerary chamber is covered with spiral coils carved in concentric circles, as well as figures and various symbols. Whole structure is thought to date from about 2,000 BC. Er Lannic islet has double stone circle in figure-of-eight form.

GERBIER-DE-JONC (Mt.)
07 – Ardèche   37 – C 1
The *Loire*, France's longest river, is born at the foot of this unusual sugar-loaf rock (1,551 m.). Path to top (45-min. climb); extensive view.

Gérardmer: *the lake, in a gorgeous mountain setting, is the largest in the Vosges – 2.2 km long, 6 km in circumference.*

(except for 11c nave, much restored in 19c). Only a fragment remains of mosaic in 9c apse. Notable *Arche d'Alliance* (Ark of the Covenant), supported by four angels, made from 130,000 little multi-coloured cubes.

Vicinity ● 8 km SE, abbey of **St. Benoît-sur-Loire***. ● 4 km NW, *Châteauneuf-sur-Loire*: fmr. château, 17c, now houses mus. of Loire navigation and of Old Châteauneuf, as well as town hall; magnificent rhododendrons in 100-acre

Germigny: *despite a few 'improvements', the Carolingian church is one of France's oldest places of worship.*

park. In church, 12, 13 and 16c, is monumental tomb – of theatrical baroque inspiration – of one Louis Phélypeaux de la Vrillière (d. 1681); 8 km to W, *Jargeau*, on l. bank of Loire (beach); former collegiate church, surrounded by Place du Grand Cloître and Place du Petit Cloître, has a Carolingian nave, rebuilt in 12c, and 16c Goth. choir. Oct. 18–19, picturesque annual 'Foire aux Chats' (Chestnut Fair).

Gex
01 – Ain   26 – C 2
Holiday town and centre for excursions. Summer and winter sports.
Vicinity ● To N, *Col de la Faucille* (see **Bellegarde*** and **Morez***). ● 8 km NE, *Divonne-les-Bains*, re-

nowned spa, lovely 75-acre recreational park. ● 9 km SE, *Ferney-Voltaire*, château where Voltaire lived from 1760 to 1778; room and mementoes of the great writer (v.a. Sat. only, July-Aug.).

Gien
45 – Loiret   18 – D 2
On r. bank of R. Loire; riverside quarter, destroyed in 1940, has been rebuilt in regional style. Late-15c château houses Internatnl. Mus. of the Hunt – collection of guns and many other objects to do with hunting; falconry room. Superb late-15c woodwork in main hall. Paintings by Desportes (80 works) and Oudry (both artists – d. 1743 and 1755, respectively – specialised

in pictures of royal dogs and hunting scenes). Pottery mus.
Vicinity ● 12 km NE, Ch. de **La Bussière***. ● 10 km SE, on the Loire, bridge carrying canal over river at *Briare*.

Gimel-les-Cascades
19 – Corrèze   30 – B 2
Church treasure (apply at presbytery; exhibited during summer) includes splendid late-12c reliquary of St. Étienne, adorned with Limousin enamel, and 14c silver-gilt reliquary-bust of St. Dumine.
Vicinity ● Don't miss the famed *Cascades*: the Grand Saut (45 m. waterfall), the Redole and the Queue de Cheval (horse's tail), which plunges 60 m. into the Gulf of the Inferno. ● 1.5 km NE, Ruffaud lake, in charming wooded setting; bathing.

Gisors
27 – Eure   5 – B 3
The castle, whose imposing remains cover $7\frac{1}{2}$ acres, is a remarkable example of 11–12c military architecture. Keep and ramparts, flanked by towers, survive. Interior has been turned into public garden. (Free entry; to visit keep, apply to caretaker – cl. Tues.). Church of St. Gervais and St. Protais, 13–14c, has elaborate mid-16c Ren. façade, framed by two towers; on l. side, N portal is in Goth. Flamboyant style; interior is mixture of Flamboyant and Ren. (16c stained-glass windows); mid-13c choir; elegant

Gien: *the quay, lined with houses in regional style; in the background, the château and the tower of St. Joan of Arc's church, all that remains of the original early-15c building.*

Ren. turret staircase in font chapel.
Vicinity ● 4 km E, *Trie-Château*, 12, 13 and 16c church with elegant Romanesque façade; town hall is in old court of justice (Romanesque windows); 17c château (n.v.a.).

Givet
08 – Ardennes   6 – D 1
Frontier town dominated by 16c fort of Charlemont. The Grand Givet, one-time stronghold on l. bank of R. *Meuse*, has church built by Vauban with original belfry which caught Victor Hugo's imagination. At the Petit Çivet, see early–18c church of Notre Dame (fine panelling); 11c Grégoire tower (good view) and Mt. d'Haurs.
Vicinity ● 3 km SE, Grotto of *Nichet* (v.a. during summer). ● 7 km S, Franco-Belgian *Nuclear Centre* at Chooz (group visits, by arrangement).

Gordes
84 – Vaucluse   38 – A 3
Picturesque little town, with houses stretching up rock dominated by church and château (half-Goth., half-Ren.), in which a Vasarely mus. has been installed. The mus. (cl. Tues.), opened in 1970, traces the development of the modern painter Victor Vasarely, one of the masters of 'kinetic art', by means of more than 1,500 of his works.
Vicinity ● Numerous *bories*, unusual dry-stone constructions, in surrounding countryside. ● 4 km NW, abbey of **Sénanque***.

Gisors: *the large castle, its octagonal keep flanked by a turret staircase, is a reminder of the town's warlike past.*

Gorze
57 – Moselle   13 – B 1
Ancient township. Former abbey church has Romanesque ext., but int. with Goth. nave (late 12–early 13c); on tympanum of small door to side of N arm of transept, odd late-12c representation of Last Judgment; sculpted N side door; fine 18c panelling in choir. Late-17c abbey palace in baroque style (hospice). Noteworthy courtyard.
Vicinity ● To N and NW, *Gravelotte* and *Mars-la-Tour* have two small museums devoted to 1870 Franco-Prussian war.

Goulaine (Château)
44 – Loire-Atlantique   16 – C 3
Fine 15c and Ren. construction, elegantly decorated; 17c apartments contain noteworthy furniture (v.a. daily in summer, exc. Tues.). Nearby Goulaine marshes (4,000 acres) are picturesque.

Gourdon
46 – Lot   36 – A 1
Old town is on round hill encircled by remains of ramparts. Looming above it is fortified church of St. Pierre, 14–15c, which has 17c panelling and 14c stained-glass windows. Interesting old houses, Rue de l'Hôtel-de-Ville and Rue Bertrand de Gourdon. Viewing table at top of hill.
Vicinity ● 2 km NW, *Grottoes of Cougnac* (v.a. during summer),

Gordes: *clinging to the side of a steep hill, the houses of this old Provençal town encircle the church and château, built on the site of a 13–14c fortress.*

remarkable concretions, prehistoric paintings in red and black.

Grand
88 – Vosges   13 – A 3

Remains surviving from ancient Roman town of Granum include 20,000-seat amphitheatre, a Temple of Apollo, basilica and outer walls. Mus. has sculptures and other objects recovered from excavations and a superb mosaic, covering 2,088 sq. ft., depicting a shepherd surrounded by animals (v.a.). In 15c church, shrine of St. Libaire; also chapel dedicated to the saint, from same period, in the cemetery.

Grand-Brassac
24 – Dordogne   29 – C 2

Unusual early-13c fortified church, with three domes. Above N portal, noteworthy 14c bas-relief depicting Christ, the Virgin and saints.

Grande-Chartreuse (Monastery)
38 – Isère   32 – B 2

The world-famed monastery founded in 1084 by St. Bruno, in heart of one of the most beautiful forest-clad massifs in France (n.v.a.). No cars allowed on access road, but car-park is planned in front of mus. at nearby La Correrie, devoted to Carthusian order and

Pierre-de-Chartreuse and, to W, road to La Correrie. ● From Grenoble, one way is past St. Eynard fort, *Sappey-en-Chartreuse*, the *Col de Porte* (trip rec. NNW to the *Charmant-Som*, 1,865 m.), and then *St. Pierre-de-Chartreuse*. ● Alternatively, leave Grenoble to NW through *St. Égrève, Proveysieux* and valley of the Ténaison; after Charmette pass, the road – often cut out of the surrounding rock – runs above basin of the Petite-Vache and passes near fmr. Chartreuse de Curière before reaching *St. Laurent-du-Pont* (then as before).

Grande-Motte (La)
34 – Hérault   43 – B 1

Principal holiday and residential unit in the development plan for the Languedoc-Roussillon coast. It comprises several pyramid-shaped apartment blocks, hotels, villas, holiday villages, camping and caravan sites. Large marina (52 acres).
Vicinity ● Another harbour at *Carnon-Plage*. ● Nearby, Le Ponant lake and *Étang de Mauguio*. ● Lovely coast road links *Palavas* with the *Grau-du-Roi*.

Grand-Pressigny (Château)
37 – Indre-et-Loire   23 – D 1

Little town stretches along valley of R. *Claise* under remains of castle protected by 12c square keep, 35 m. high, and 14c outer wall. The local lord's residence, or New Château, in Ren. style, houses prehist. mus., whose range of polished flint tools is among best in world (v.a.).
Vicinity ● 7 km SW, *Ch. de la Guerche*, 15c, flanked by machicolated towers (v.a.; cl. Sun. a.m.; July–Aug.; otherwise cl. Tues.); includes two basement floors, underground granaries and casemates below them.

Grands Cols (Route)
See **St. Michel-de-Maurienne*, Bourg-d'Oisans*** and **Lautaret***.

Granville
50 – Manche   9 – C 1

The upper town, ringed by early-18c ramparts, stands on steep rocky promontory high above the sea. Its old streets are lined with 18c granite houses. Walk along ramparts: superb views. 15–17c church of Notre Dame, in granite. Porte des Morts (Gate of the Dead), from 1715. Mus. of Old Granville is in royal lodgings adjoining the Grande Porte (main gate). Wonderful panorama from W tip of Rock of Granville. Oceanographic mus.: aquarium, 'fairyland of shells'. Richard Anacréon mus.: modern art, late 19–20c; hand-

GRAMAT (Causse)
46 – Lot   36 – A 1, 36 – B 1

Vast limestone plateau, largest of the causses of Quercy reg., between valley of R. *Dordogne* to N and that of R. *Lot* to S. It is crossed by two superb canyons: to N, canyon of the Ouysse and the Alzou; to S, canyon of the Célé. Between these broad, picturesque gashes stretches the Braunhie (pronounced Bron-ye), pitted with caves and gulfs. Those of Bède, the Besaces, the Vitarelles, Peureuse grotto and Crousate abyss are particularly scenic. At *Gramat*, training school for police dogs used by national Gendarmerie (demonstrations and visits to kennels on Thurs. during summer). See also **Labastide-Murat*, Rocamadour*** and Lacave grottoes, Ch. de **La Treyne*, Souillac*, Cahors***.

Grand-Bornand (Le)
74 – Haute-Savoie   32 – C 1

Summer holiday and winter sports centre (950 m.). Heaths and forests with abundant Alpine flora. Speciality: 'Reblochon' cheese.
Vicinity ● Ski centre at typically Savoyard village of Le Chinaillon. ● Via *Col de la Colombière* and Reposoir valley to *Le Reposoir*: charterhouse founded 12c, Carmelite convent; v.a. to 17c cloisters and chapel (15c portal).

illustrating monks' life over the centuries (v.a. Palm Sunday to Nov. 1).
Vicinity ● Very lovely routes to the Grande-Chartreuse from **Chambéry*** or **Grenoble***. One from Chambéry is via *Les Échelles*; at *St. Laurent-du-Pont*, the road follows the wooded Guiers-Mort gorges, dominated by impressive escarpments (aka 'route du désert' – the desert road). ● Another route from Chambéry is through *Col du Granier, St. Pierre-d'Entremont, St.*

The Grande-Chartreuse: *the slate roofs of the world-famed monastery's main buildings fit in perfectly with the austere beauty of the surrounding scenery.*

written manuscripts of contemporary writers.
Vicinity ● 3 km NE, *Donville-les-Bains*, huge sandy beach. ● 10 km NNE, near *Bréhal*, Ren. Ch. de *Chanteloup*, built within polygonal enceinte of fmr. castle in middle of lake (n.v.a.). ● To S, beaches of *St. Pair-sur-Mer* (interesting church), *Jullouville* and *Carolles-Plage* (Carolles headland, 74 m. high). ● 12 km SE, *Abbaye de la Lucerne*, abbey founded 12c; remains of its

original church, cloisters and 18c buildings (v.a.). ● 16 km out to sea, **Chausey*** islands.

Grasse
06 – Alpes-Maritimes 45 – A 1
The old town, built on a hillside, with its narrow, winding streets often broken by stairways, has hardly changed since 18c. Former cathedral of Notre Dame, in early-13c Provençal Goth. style, boasts some important pictures: the St.

Honorat retable (from 15c Nice school); 'The Washing of the Feet', one of Fragonard's rare religious works; and two Rubens. Mus. or Villa Fragonard (cl. weekends and in Nov.) has two works from his youth and paintings of his son, grandson and sister-in-law; copies of celebrated 'Fragonard de Grasse' now in Frick collection in New York. In 18c mansion of Marquise de Cabris is mus. of Provençal art and history. Admiral de Grasse

La Grande-Motte: *these bizarre pyramid-shaped apartment blocks are among the key ingredients of the tourist/holiday development along the Languedoc-Roussillon coast.*

marine mus. Internatnl. mus. of perfumery. On Place aux Aires, lined by arcaded houses, colourful open-air market.

Vicinity ● 18 km W, through *Cabris*, caves of St. Cézaire (v.a. Apr. to Oct.), concretions contrasting with reddish rocks. ● 14 km NE, *Gourdon*: very picturesque village, clinging like eagle's nest above R. *Loup*, magnificent view; mus. of medieval art in 12–14c castle; *Loup gorges*. ● 9 km SE, *Mougins*, charming Provençal village at top of isolated hill, ringed by remains of outer wall.

Gravelines
59 – Nord   1 – C 2
Former stronghold, 16 and 17c ramparts. St. Willibrod church, in Goth. Flamboyant style with Ren. portal; notable 17c woodwork (confessionals, organ-chest, etc.). Mus. of the arsenal (collection of original prints).
Vicinity ● 2 km NW, at mouth of the Aa, fishing village *Petit Fort Philippe*, good views of canal and *Grand Fort Philippe*; hinterland, intensive cultivation of endives.

Grenoble
38 – Isère   32 – B 3
Capital of the Dauphiné; has experienced considerable change since last world war, above all thanks to Winter Olympic Games of 1968. Take cable-car to Fort de la Bastille (viewing table) for fine view of town and surrounding reg.; return on foot through Guy Pape park and Garden of the Dauphins. ● The old town lies between 13c St. André church, Place de l'Étoile and Place Notre Dame. Rue Jean-Jacques Rousseau (No. 14, Stendhal's birthplace); Rue des Clercs (No. 20, lovely house of Dr. Gagnon, Stendhal's grandfather, 16c courtyard with loggias). In St. André, mausoleum of early-16c military hero Bayard (the 'knight without fear or reproach'), built about a century after his death. Oldest parts of imposing lawcourts are late 15c (entry door and chapel); interior has sumptuous panelling, carved and painted ceilings (v.a., a.m. only, apply caretaker). 12–13c cathedral of Notre Dame; to l. of entrance, huge chapel of the Sept-Douleurs, painted ribbed vaulting. St. Laurent quarter, on r. bank of R. Isère, is rich in old houses. See 11c church of St. Laurent; late-6c St. Oyend crypt is one of oldest Christian buildings in France (apply presbytery). ● Museums. (1). Mus. of painting and sculpture (cl. Tues.), among best in France for modern art (Matisse, Rouault,

Vuillard, Marquet, Bonnard, Picasso, Braque, Delaunay, Miró, Magnelli, Max Ernst, Soutine, Hartung, Soulages, Poliakoff, Gilioli, Dubuffet, etc.). Almost equally outstanding galleries for earlier artists; paintings inc. two Tintorettos, two Veronese, four Philippe de Champaigne (17c), and a Rubens which is one of museum's masterpieces, (*St. Grégoire*, surrounded by saints); also four Zurbaran (Spanish-born religious painter, d. 1664), two Jordaens (17c Flemish), two Largillière (17–18c), Canaletto, Guardi, Delacroix, Corot, Gauguin, etc. Avant-garde since 1945 also well represented. Salle Dewasne, gigantic mural, some 10,750 sq. ft. Large printroom. (2). Mus. of Dauphiné reg. in 17c convent, including baroque chapel with trompe l'oeil decoration; archaeology, ethnography, history (cl. Tues. and Feb.). (3). Stendhal mus. (cl. Mon.). (4). Natural history mus.: Alpine fauna, exceptional collection of birds. Also automobile mus. in Fort de la Bastille, and Mus. de la Résistance et de la Déportation. ● Parc Paul Mistral, 87 m.-high viewing tower in reinforced concrete (1925). For lovers of contemp. art and architecture, Maison de la Culture (1968); three superposed halls, one with revolving display inc. tapestries by Le Corbusier. Modern tapestries and sculptures as well (inc. Manessier) in 1967 town hall. Palais des Sports (12,000 seats): speed-track decorated by Vasarely. Grenoble is only town in France to display monumental works of contemp. sculpture in its streets, notably a 'stabile' by US-born sculptor Alexander Calder, in front of main station.
Vicinity ● *Chartreuse* massif **(Grande-Chartreuse*, Chambéry*)**. ● *Vercors* massif and reg. park,

Grasse: famed for its perfumes and flowers, the old town offers a marked contrast between the peace of its narrow streets and the liveliness of its markets.

either through *Sassenage* (caves, cascades, open-air restaurants) or through *St. Nizier*, **Villard-de-Lans*** and **La Chapelle-en-Vercors***. ● **Route des Grands Cols*** via **Vizille*** and *Rochetaillée*. ● L'Oisans via **Bourg-d'Oisans***.

Gréville-Hague
50 – Manche   3 – C 2
12–16c country church, often painted by Millet (born at nearby hamlet of Gruchy); int. has fine Virgin, late-13c Goth.
Vicinity ● 6 km NW, *Omonville-la-Rogue*, colourful fishing village; 13c church; Jardeheu Point (semaphore). 6 km to W, Port Racine, reputedly France's smallest port, in St. Martin cove.

Grignan
26 – Drôme   37 – D 2
Château, with many reminders of 17c author Mme. de Sévigné, stands

Grenoble: *the lawcourts, one-time seat of the local Parliament, were originally the palace of the Dauphins.*

on isolated little hill above village and is among the most beautiful in Provence (v.a., cl. Tues. and a.m. Wed.). Ren. façade, facing in direction of Mt. *Ventoux*, is particularly elegant; rising over terrace, the W façade, also 16c, adjoins main courtyard. Mme. de Sévigné's bedchamber and state rooms are decorated and furnished in 17c style. In the village, 16c church of St. Sauveur; 17c panelling and organchest; Mme. de Sévigné's tomb. Local mus., in 17c house, includes portraits and souvenirs of the redoubtable lady, 17 and 19c furniture, tapestries and pottery.

Groix (Island)
See **Lorient***   15 – C 1

Gros-Bois (Château)
94 – Val-de-Marne   11 – C 2
Built 16c, rebuilt 17c (v.a. Sun. and public holidays.). The sumptuous apartments of Marshal Berthier (one of Napoleon's principal generals) form a remarkable example of Empire decoration and furniture; 18 and early-19c paintings and sculpture; only the dining-room still has 17c décor, with stone fireplace, painted ceiling and frescos by Abraham Bosse (1602–76). Gallery devoted to Napoleonic battles.

Grottoes (Prehistoric, in Dordogne Department)
See **Eyzies-de-Tayac-Sireuil (Les)***, **Lascaux***, **Rouffignac***.

Gruissan
11 – Aude   42 – D 2
Picturesque old village on peninsula in middle of lagoons; it lies under Saracen tower known as the Tour Barberousse.

Vicinity ● 2 km SE, *Gruissan-Plage*, odd cluster of cabins on piles; nearby, group of holiday residences, built as part of development plan for Languedoc-Roussillon coast. ● 1.5 km N, Chapel of *Les Auzils*, on superb pine-covered site above the sea. ● *Mt. de la Clape*, arid limestone massif, of striking wild beauty, between **Narbonne*** and the sea; highest point is the Coffre de Pech-Redon (214 m.); 3.5 km from *Narbonne-Plage* is *St. Pierre-sur-Mer* and abyss of l'Oeil-Doux.

Guebwiller
68 – Haut-Rhin   21 – A 1
Three notable churches. (1). Late-12c St. Léger, Romanesque exterior (fine façade) but interior dating from beginnings of Rhenish Gothic. (2). 14–15c church of the Dominicans; frescos of same period in nave (used for concerts in summer); rood-screen decorated with paintings; in choir, Florival museum (medieval sculpture, headdresses, ceramics). (3). Notre Dame, mid-18c, in red sandstone; decoration in choir offers fine example of Louis XV style.
Vicinity ● 5.5 km W, *Mürbach*: late-12c abbey church in red sandstone, although partly in ruins, is one of the most majestic surviving edifices in Alsace Romanesque style. ● 5 km NW, *Lautenbach*, former abbey church, late 11c, with 15c square apse (renovated in 18 and 19c) and noteworthy Romanesque and Gothic porch. Through valley of R. *Lauch*, aka 'The Florival', to the *Lac de la Lauch* (good views); thence, at *Markstein*, join the Route des **Crêtes*** (ridge road); 7 km

farther on, route leads to the *Grand Ballon*, highest point in the Vosges (1,424 m., viewing table, magnificent panorama); the Ballon lake lies in impressive wooded setting very typical of the Vosges.

Guéméné-sur-Scorff
56 – Morbihan   8 – D 3
Central square known as Rue Bisson – long, narrow and sloping – is lined by granite houses from 16, 17 and 18c. Church of Notre Dame-de-la-Fosse, 17c.
Vicinity ● 2 km NW, 17c Crénénan chapel, surrounded by unusual drystone shelters; interior has wainscoting decorated with 17c paintings and beams carved with monsters (also 17c). 5 km to NW, *Ploërdut*:   part-Romanesque church, 11–12c; ossuary.

Gué-Péan (Château)
41 – Loir-et-Cher   18 – A 3
Among the most refined of the great Loire châteaux – and, until recently, perhaps one of the least known (v.a.; guest rooms). Former hunting lodge in quadrilateral design, flanked by four 14–15c towers (one of them a keep); incorporates Ren. and 17c portions. Interior has noteworthy decoration and furnishing (tapestries and numerous old masters). Outbuildings include headquarters of a riding club (good rides in surrounding forest).
Vicinity ● 9 km SE, *St. Aignan*: Ren. château adjoining ruins of feudal castle (v.a., ext. only, June 1–Sept. 30; int. tour of château by arrangement). Romanesque and Goth. collegiate church; crypt has unusual 12–13–14c murals.

Guérande
44 – Loire-Atlantique   16 – A 2
The town, dominating region of salt marshes, retains its medieval appearance – ringed by 15c ramparts, with eight towers and four fortified gates. Circular promenade runs along outside of the walls. Town mus. in St. Michel gate (furniture, pottery and regional costumes). St. Aubin church, 12, 13 and 15c. Many houses from 15, 16 and 18c.
Vicinity ● 4.5 km S, Saillé, whence the D99 goes NW across the salt marshes to *La Turballe* (see **La Baule***). ● 12 km NW, *Piriac-sur-Mer* and *Pointe du Castelli* (vast panorama). ● 5.5 km SE, *Ch. de Careil*, fmr. 14c castle turned into elegant aristocratic residence in Ren. period (v.a. Apr. to end of Sept.): fine apartments; 15, 16 and 18c furniture; collection of Le Croisic porcelain, 17c.

Guimiliau: *some 200 figures, in highly expressive attitudes, are used to depict the principal episodes of the Passion.*

Guerche-de-Bretagne (La)
35 – Ille-et-Vilaine   16 – D1
Old quarter has several 15–16c houses on piles. Church of same period; 16c stained-glass windows, Ren. carved stalls.
Vicinity ● 11 km W, *Roche aux Fées* (Fairy Rock): 41 blocks of purple schist forming a 22 m. prehistoric gallery tomb, one of the finest in France.

Guéret
23 – Creuse   24 – B3
Mus. in 18c Hôtel du Clos de la Senatorerie has an outstanding collection of Limousin enamel and medieval plate and a large one of ceramics (from Nevers, Moustiers, Rouen, Strasbourg, Delft, as well as Italian majolica and Ming porcelain); also 16–17–18c tapestries, plus paintings, drawings, sculpture, weapons and local archaeology.
Vicinity ● To S, Forest of Chabrières (marked paths). ● 12 km NW, *St. Vaury*, under the Trois-Cornes, ancient puy – 636 m., really lovely view. 4 km to N, Roche, panorama over mountains of La Marche,

Limousin and Auvergne. ● 20 km SE, **Le Moutier-d'Ahun***.

Guermantes (Château)
77 – Seine-et-Marne   11 – D2
Superb brick and stone construction in Louis XIII style (17c), enlarged and embellished in 18c. Admirable internal decoration includes, notably, a sumptuous state gallery, 32 m. long, with 18 big windows, known as 'La Belle Inutile' (i.e. beautiful but useless!) (v.a. weekends and public holidays., p.m., Mar. 15 to Nov. 15).

Guimiliau
29N – Finistère   8 – C2
Brittany's most beautiful calvary, dating from late 16c and adorned with more than 200 statues – some of the figures in costume of the time – representing the Life of Christ in 25 scenes, full of movement. The big cross bears four statues, the Virgin and saints, grouped two by two. 17c parish church (*enclos*), which incorporates a funerary chapel, has noteworthy Ren. porch, bedecked with statues,

from early that century, and carved oak baptistry inside.
Vicinity ● 3.5 km W, *Lampaul-Guimiliau*, another of the *enclos*: large parish church in Goth. Flamboyant style, with late-16c bell-tower and mid-16c porch adorned with statues of the Apostles and the Virgin; int. has carved wooden retables, 17c, and panelling; ossuary chapel and calvary, also 17c. 4 km to NW, *Landivisiau*, modern church in Goth. style, with mid-16c porch and bell-tower dating from 1590; St. Thivisiau fountain, 15c. From here 5 km to NW, *Bodilis*: church with Ren. sculpted porch; int. with carved beams, retables, etc.

Guingamp
22 – Côtes-du-Nord   8 – D2
The town has spread out from a feudal nucleus, of which the remains of 15c castle and part of the ramparts still survive. Notre Dame-de-Bon-Secours, Goth. and Ren., has a much-venerated Black Virgin (Breton pardon on Sat. before first Sun. in July); W façade, framed by two towers, has rich 16c portal. In Place du Centre, old houses and Ren. fountain known as the Plomée.
Vicinity ● 1 km S, former abbey of Ste. Croix, remains of 12c church, 16c abbey manor-house (v.a.). ● 3 km W, Grâces, 16–17c Notre Dame church; has magnificent beams carved with caricature-like scenes. ● 11.5 km S, *Bourbriac*: Romanesque, Goth. and Ren. church, 11c crypt, tomb and sarcophagus of St. Briac. 7 km to E, Avogour chapel, in pretty setting. ● 11 km E, *Châtelaudren*, chapel of Notre Dame-du-Tertre, 14–15–16c; choir decorated with 96 painted wood panels from 15c. (Pardon, Aug. 15.)

Guise (Castle)
02 – Aisne   6 – B2
Only military fortress in France to have preserved, on each level, all the successive constructions implemented throughout feudal era, from 11c to Ren. (v.a., June 1 to Christmas). Underground galleries; archaeology and lapidary museum. 15c church.
Vicinity ● Excursions recommended in valley of R. *Oise*, to SW: *Origny-Ste. Benoîte, Ribemont* (17c St. Germain chapel), etc.

Gy-l'Évêque
89 – Yonne   19 – A2
Rising over remains of 13–14c church is a stout 12c belfry; after church has been restored, it will house admirable *Christ aux Orties*, 16c work of art in wood, at present displayed in temporary chapel at 9 Rue St. Nicolas (v.a.).

H

Haguenau
67 – Bas-Rhin   14 – B 2

Former fortified town, with two churches worth visiting: 12–13c St. Georges (three Romanesque naves covered with Goth. vaulting); 14 and 15c St. Nicolas, which boasts an early-15c Entombment, a 14c 'Christ at the wine-press' and elegant 18c rococo panelling. Mus. of history and archaeology; Alsace mus. (folk arts). Old houses. Early 14c gate.

Vicinity ● *Haguenau forest* (52 sq. miles) has many good walks (very ancient oaks).

Hambye (Abbey)
50 – Manche   9 – D 1

Remains of Benedictine abbey,

Hambye: *in a lush green setting, the Romanesque church and part of the monastic buildings from the old Benedictine abbey.*

founded mid-12c, include notable Romanesque abbey church, 12–13c, plain and austere; see sacristy, chapterhouse (a masterpiece of Norman Goth.), the Salle des Morts (murals), calefactory, kitchen, monks' dormitory (17c tapestries, 16–17c furniture), etc. (v.a., cl. Wed. and in Jan.).

HAGUE (LA) (Cape)
50 – Manche   3 – C 2

Low, sandy point, surrounded by reefs, at the tip of the peninsula of La Hague (signal station).

Vicinity ● 1.5 km W, little port of Goury; on Gros du Raz reef, 50 m.-tall lighthouse. ● S to *Auderville*, the steep 'Corniche Road' skirts *Bay of Ecalgrain*; Hautes-Falaises signal station, on promontory 100 m. high, riddled with caves (good wide views); rocky headland known as **Nez de Jobourg***, with highly scenic sharp escarpments. From Dannery, join the D 901, which runs beside *usine atomique* (nuclear plant) to *Beaumont-Hague*. To SW, in wild country, *Vauville*, country church, Ren. manor.

The Nez (nose) of Jobourg. The steep rocky slopes of this wild headland are the haunt of innumerable sea birds.

Haroué
54 – Meurthe-et-Moselle 13 – C 3
Magnificent early-18c château of the
Princes of Beauvon-Craon, masterpiece of Classic architecture in
Lorraine (v.a. Apr. to Nov.). Its
sumptuous apartments have rich
collections of furniture, pictures,
tapestries. Lovely gardens. Unusual
little defensive fort.
Vicinity ● 8.5 km W, *Vézelise*, late-
16c timbered market halls and fine
15–16c church, with several works
of art; old houses.

Hartmannswillerkopf
(Vieil-Armand)
68 – Haut-Rhin 21 – A 1
One of Alsace's principal shrines,
scene of violent fighting in 1914–15.
Natnl. Monument is as sober as it
is grandiose; altar to La Patrie (the
fatherland) stands above crypt,
door to which is framed by two *Victoires* by sculptor Antoine Bourdelle (1861–1929). Ossuary flanked
by three chapels; in the Catholic
chapel, another Bourdelle sculpture, *Vierge à l'Enfant* (Virgin and
Child). Military cemetery with
1,260 graves. From hill above
(956 m. – 20-min. walk up path),
panorama over Alsace plain, Black
Forest and the Vosges.

Hasparren
64 – Pyrénées-Atlantiques 40 – C 1
Little Basque town. To S, the D22,
Imperial Route des Cimes
(summits) crosses the rolling
wooded country between the valleys of the Ourhandia and the *Nive*.
Vicinity ● 11 km SE, through *Isturits*, the *grottoes* of Oxocelhaya and
Isturits (v.a. Mar. to Dec.): the
former has a huge chamber, 20 m.
broad and 15 m. high, where you
can see several prehist. wall carvings; the latter include multi-coloured concretions in strange
shapes; small mus. of finds. ● 8.5 km
NE, *Labastide-Clairence*, Goth.
church renovated in 17–18c; int. has
17c decoration in Basque style;
courtyard covered with gravestones. Central square lined with
covered arcades; several old houses
in Rue de l'Église. 3 km to N, Benedictine monastery of Belloc; interesting modern church.

Hautecombe (Abbey)
73 – Savoie 32 – B 1
The abbey, former sepulchre of the
Royal House of Savoie, lies in pleasant situation on W bank of the
Lac du Bourget (see **Le-Bourget-du-
Lac***). Since 1922, it has been occupied by the Benedictines of
Solesmes*; v.a. to 12c church
(poorly restored in 19c), which has
27 funerary monuments to the
Princes of Savoie, adorned with
profusion of statues and sculpted
bas-reliefs. Mass and vespers with
Gregorian chanting.

Hautefort (Château)
24 – Dordogne 29 – D 2
One of the Périgord's most beautiful Classical châteaux, built in 17c
on site of castle owned by famed
troubadour Bertran de Born (d.
1215). The château – v.a. daily
Easter to Nov.; Sun. and public holidays only, Nov. to Easter – stands
on hill offering vast panorama; 100-
acre forest park.

Hauterives
26 – Drôme 32 – A 3
Worth visiting the celebrated 'Ideal
Palace', astonishing quasi-baroque
creation built between 1880 and
1912 by a local postman, Ferdinand
Cheval. His naive but highly
imaginative constructn. has several
galleries or grottoes and stairs
leading to flat roof. Tomb of
the postman (1836–1924), no less
original in design, is in local cemetery.

Haut-Koenigsbourg (Castle)
67 – Bas-Rhin 14 – A 3
Built at end of 15c, right at top
of rocky spur with immense sweep
over surrounding countryside, the
mighty red sandstone castle fell into
ruins and was entirely rebuilt,
between 1900 and 1908, by order of
Kaiser Wilhelm II. While the reconstruction is questionable, it does at
least give one an idea of 15c
Rhenish military architecture; int.
is characteristic of Germanic taste
in things medieval in late 19c (v.a.).
Vicinity ● 200 m. W, ruins of Ch.
d'Oedenbourg. ● To E, remains of
14c castle of *Kintzheim*, in red sandstone (v.a.); hawking, with demonstrations of eagle flying in
summer; at entrance to town, centre
for the reintroduction of storks in
Alsace (v.a. Apr. to Sept.).

Havre (Le)
76 – Seine-Maritime 4 – C 3
Ninety per cent destroyed during
last world war, the town was rebuilt
under direction of Brussels-born
architect Auguste Perret (d. 1954),
responsible notably for town hall,

Hautefort: *the majestic structure seems closer to a Loire château than one of the Dordogne's bastides.*

Haut-Koenigsbourg: *detail of the re-created feudal castle walls.*

Hendaye: *from the beach, looking towards the 'Deux Jumeaux' rocks, off Ste. Anne's Point.*

St. Joseph's church and large urban groupings, grandiose in concept but geometric in spirit. Four mus. worth visiting: (1). Mus. of Old Le Havre (cl. Mon. and Tues.), Gallo-Roman and Merovingian archae-ology, history of the town, 16 to 19c glassware. (2). André Malraux fine arts mus. (cl. Tues.); in front of it is sculpted 'beacon' in concrete; large coll. of Italian, Dutch and Spanish paintings, as well as French of 17–18c (Hubert Robert, Fragonard), 19c (Géricault, Delacroix, Courbet, Monet, Manet, Renoir, and 290 works by Boudin, born across bay at Honfleur), and 20c (inc. 70 works by Dufy, also Van Dongen, Villon, Dubuffet, etc.). (3), Mus. of natural history. (4). Mus. of Graville Priory, at Graville-Ste. Honorine (interesting lapidary collections). Depending on weather, very good views from fort of *Ste. Adresse*, the Ingouville coast or *Cape of La Hève* (lighthouse). Free access to the port (guided tours by motor-launch or organised by S.I.).
Vicinity ● To NE, *Montivilliers*, church of St. Sauveur, 11 and 15c, with two Romanesque towers and fine late-15c Flamboyant porch. ● To E, *Harfleur*, 15–16c church of St. Martin, fine Flamboyant tower topped by stone spire; mid-17c château now houses town hall. Near Gommerville, 3 km to N of *St. Romain-de-Colbosc*, late-18c Ch. de Filières (v.a., Wed., Sat. and Sun., p.m., Easter to Nov. 1): large collections of Far Eastern and 18c French art.

Hendaye
64 – Pyrénées-Atlantiques 40 – B 2
Hendaye-Plage (beach) is linked to Hendaye-Ville (town) by Blvd. du Général Leclerc, which runs above the bay of Chingoudy until reaching estuary of R. *Bidassoa*. The town, on steep little hill above the river, centres around 16–17c church of St. Vincent (which has 17c retable and 12c Crucifix inside). From the harbour, fine view over to Fon-tarabie, on other side of the bay.
Vicinity ● 2 km S, *Béhobie*; in R. *Bidassoa* downstream of frontier bridge (French and Spanish customs posts) is Isle of Pheasants, where Pyrenean peace treaty was negotiated in 1659. ● 4 km NE of Hendaye-Ville, *Urrugne*, 16c church with imposing belfry porch (Ren. portal); int. has superb 17c pulpit, sculpted with human figures.

Hennebont
56 – Morbihan 15 – D 1
Although badly damaged in the last world war, the walled town (Ville-Close) – entered through 15c Bro-Erec'h fortified gate – still has some old houses in the Grande Rue. Church of Notre Dame-du-Paradis, early-16c Goth. Flamboyant. Stud farm covers remains of abbey of La Joie, founded 13c; gatehouse, 17c, and abbot's house. Old iron well. Ironworks mus. in former lab-oratory of the Forges d'Hennebont (hist. and technology). Similarly for water and hydraulics in old gate-house of Kerglaw factory (cl. Sat. and Sun. a.m.).

Vicinity ● 14 km SW, **Port-Louis***. ● 9 km SE, *Merlevenez*, 12c Roman-esque church; 6 km farther on, *Pont-Lorois* and *R. d'Étel*, with very rugged banks. ● To NE, *Valley of the Blavet*.

Hérisson
03 – Allier 24 – D 2
Ancient little town on r. bank of R. *Aumance*, below remains of 14c feudal castle. Two town gates, 15 and 16c houses, and belfry porch as reminder of long-vanished col-legiate church of St. Sauveur.
Vicinity ● Valley of R. *Aumance*, to NW and E. ● 10 km NW, on l. bank of R. *Cher*, Vallon-en-Sully: unusual Romanesque church in grey, yellow and red sandstone; in front of it, a two-storey belfry porch. ● To N, *Forest of Tronçais* (see **St. Bonnet-Tronçais***).

Hesdin
62 – Pas-de-Calais 1 – C3
The 16c town hall boasts a richly carved bartizan (fixed wooden tower). Late-16c church of Notre Dame has sizeable amount of carved furnishings. Town museum (tapestries, furniture).
Vicinity ● Forest of Hesdin, to NW, has beautiful groves of beech and oak. ● To N, *Fressin*, ruins of feudal castle, early-16c Flamboyant church. *Azincourt* (which Henry V and Shakespeare would doubtless prefer rendered as Agincourt); a calvary serves as reminder of the deaths of 4,000 knights in the famed 1415 battle.

Hoëdic and Houat (Islands)
15 – D 2

See **Quiberon*** (Peninsula)

Honfleur
14 – Calvados   4 – C 3
The 15c Lieutenancy, with the Caen gate set into it, dominates the Old Harbour, edged by colourful quays forming a picture full of charm (as witness the many artists to be seen there in summer). Ste. Catherine church, built entirely of timber, with twin naves and two side-aisles, all wood-roofed; even the belfry, standing slightly to one side, is in timber. Mus. of Old Honfleur (hrs. vary, cl. Jan.–Mar. inc.) embraces three units: mus. of ethnology and folk art, marine mus., and proposed open-air mus. at Manoir du Désert, 2 km away. Mus. Eugène Boudin has many works by eponymous 19c marine painter, native of Honfleur, as well as impressionist and contemporary artists. Numerous old houses, particularly in Rue Haute.
Vicinity ● 1 km W, the *Côte de Grâce*, rising nearly 100 m. above Seine estuary. 17c chapel of Notre Dame-de-Grâce. Magnificent panorama; the coast road (D513) goes through Vasouy, passes St. Siméon tavern (haunt of open-air painters in 19c), and runs via *Cricquebeuf* (picturesque ivy-covered country church) and *Villerville* to **Deauville***.

Hossegor et Capbreton
40 – Landes   40 – C 1
Summer resort in superb setting, Hossegor comprises villas and hotels, in Basque style, scattered among the pines between Lake of Hossegor and sea shore, bordered by beautiful Océan beach. On the lake, five beaches, water sports facilities. Large beach also at former fishing port of Capbreton, on R. Boudigau estuary; marina.
Vicinity ● To S, on D652 to *Labenne* (4 km W, Labenne-Océan, whence 2 km SE, Irieu lake, surrounded by pines and cork-oaks). The N10 traverses Garros lake, then *Tarnos*, along 17c citadel of Bayonne and, through suburb of St. Esprit, enters **Bayonne***. ● Hossegor is base for many walks through Landes forest: *Soustons* and *Étang de Soustons*, *Étang Blanc*, *Étang de Léon*, *Étang Hardy* and *Étang Noir*, *Tosse* (Romanesque church), and *Seignosse-le-Penon*, recently established bathing centre in heart of forest.

Hérisson: *the evocative remains of the feudal castle, high above the R. Aumance, testify to this little town's former strategic importance.*

Huelgoat
29S – Finistère   8 – C 2
One of the most picturesque sites of the Breton hinterland. The magnificent forest (1,460 acres) has innumerable lively streams and paths winding through rocky wildernesses. Walks recommended to the Roche Cintrée (Curved Rock), the 'Virgin's House', the Trembling Rock, the Abyss and the Horseshoe, the grotto of Artus, the Boars' Pond (Mare aux Sangliers), the Camp d'Artus, etc. 16c chapel of Notre Dame-des-Cieux (Breton pardon, first Sun. in Aug.).
Vicinity ● 7 km SW, hamlet and chapel of *St. Herbot*, 15–16c, late-15c porch bedecked with statues of the Apostles; int. has noteworthy 16c carved wood chancel, mid-16c stained-glass windows, tomb of St Herbot; 1 km NE, former Ch. du Rusquec, 16c, and Elez dam. ● 9 km W, *Brennelis*: Mts. d'Arrée *nuclear centre* and *St. Michel reservoir*. ● Huelgoat is best departure-point for excursions to *Mts. d'Arrée* and *Montagnes Noires*.

Hyères
83 – Var   44 – C 2
Pleasant recuperation centre, in sheltered location. The old quarters, built on hillside, are crossed by steep-sloping streets (Rue Barbacane, Rue Ste. Claire, Rue Paradis, 12c house). Churches of St. Louis, early 13c, with façade in Italian Goth. style, and St. Paul, Romanesque and Goth. Interesting mus.: archaeology, 19c painting.
Vicinity ● *Hyères-Plage* and *La Capte* (sandy beach). The Giens peninsula, *Presqu'ile de Giens*, is dominated to W. by remains of feudal castle (viewing table); on S side, small harbour of Le Niel; to N, harbour of La Madrague.

Hyères: *magnificent pine forests and heathland line the beaches of Porquerolles, best known of the 'Iles d'Or'*

HYÈRES (Islands)
83 – Var   44 – C 3
Three main islands bracketed under heading of the 'Iles d'Or' (golden isles), reached by boat from **Toulon***, La Tour-Fondue, Port St. Pierre, **Le Lavandou*** or *Cavalaire*. (1). *Porquerolles* (3,099 acres): N coast is fringed by sandy beaches, backed by pine forests and heathland; S coast, much steeper, rises to height of 150 m. Superb pine forests in interior. Hamlet of *Porquerolles* lies below former fort of Ste. Agathe. Magnificent view from lighthouse (96 m.) at southernmost tip. (2). *Port-Cros* (1,580 acres): claimed as only nature reserve in world for both land and marine wildlife; marked paths; fishing village and bay of Port-Cros, base for interesting walks (Plage de la Palu, very wild Point and Bay of Port-Man, Point of La Galère, small fort of La Vigie, southern cliffs, etc.). *Ile du Levant* (2,460 acres); village of *Héliopolis*, large naturist centre. French Navy occupies NE part of island, from which public are barred.

I

Iholdy
64 – Pyrénées-Atlantiques 40 – C 2
Typical Basque village. Old houses with carved lintels. 17c church with gabled belfry and external wooden balconies (in three partitions). Sculpted portal, 1605. Traditional Basque tombs in cemetery. ● 1 km E, St. Blaise chapel, 16c. ● Ch. d'Olcé, 17c.

Ile-Bouchard (L')
37 – Indre-et-Loire 17 – C 3
Remains of former priory of St. Léonard, late 11c; notable historiated capitals in choir (Life of Christ). St. Maurice church, 14c choir, three 15c naves and hexagonal belfry. St. Gilles, on r. bank of R. *Vienne*, has two Romanesque portals with 12c geometric décor.
Vicinity ● 3 km E, **Tavant*.** ● 4.5 km E, Parçay-sur-Vienne, 12c church with fine Romanesque sculpted portal. ● 5 km N, Avon-les-Roches, church porch with noteworthy sculpted arches and historiated capitals; 2 km to NE, ruins of 15c château and former collegiate church of Roches-Tranchelion, with highly elegant Renaissance façade.

Ile Rousse (L')
2B – Corsica 45 – A 3
Little town founded at end of 18c; lovely pure sandy beach; islands linked to shore by harbour jetty.
Vicinity ● To SE, the *Balagne* (see **Calvi***); 15 km SE, *Belgodère*, old fort above village, church of St. Thomas (1269); from there, on N197 to *Ville-di-Paraso*, below mountainside village of Speloncato; *Muro* and *Lumio* (Romanesque church). From *Belgodère*, 6 km E, you can take the *Olmi-Capella* road to *Forest of Tartagine*, one of the wildest in Corsica. ● To NE, the N199 runs along narrow ledge for 4 km, offering beautiful views over coast and sea; towards **St. Florent***, the road crosses the extraordinary rocky and forest country of the *Désert des Agriates*.

Illiers-Combray
28 – Eure-et-Loir 11 – A 3
14c church, with wooden barrel-vaulting covered with paintings. The little town is Marcel Proust's 'Combray'; in his novels, the author described place where he spent his

Ile-Rousse: *formerly Paolina (from its founder, Pascal Paoli), the town now gets its name from these red granite rocks*.

childhood; direct reminders today include 'Aunt Léonie's house' (v.a.) and the 'Pré Catelan', promenade on bank of R. Loir. Small Marcel Proust mus.
Vicinity ● 13 km SE, *Dangeau*, notable early-12c Romanesque church; int. has works of folk art. ● 13 km S, *Brou*, 12 and 16c church, remains of 11c church of St. Romain (Son et Lumière in summer). 7 km to NW, *Ch. de Frazé*, 14 and 16c, formal gardens (v.a. Sat. and Sun., p.m.).

Isle-Adam (L')
95 – Val-d'Oise 11 – C 1
Charming holiday spot on R. *Oise*; river forms two shaded little islands – beach, swimming pool, water sports, etc. Ren. church of St. Martin, fine sculpted portal; int. has

Ren. furnishing, stalls carved with satirical themes. Unusual Chinese pavilion, a late-18c 'folly'.
Vicinity ● Many good walks in the forest (3,700 acres); Le Val abbey, founded 12c (n.v.a.). ● 5 km E, *Presles* (churches with 17c carved stalls – again, with caricature-like subjects).

Isle-sur-la-Sorgue (L')
84 – Vaucluse 38 – A 3
Watered by arms of R. Sorgue, its avenues are lined with magnificent plane-trees. 13c church of Notre Dame-des-Anges has superb int. decoration from 17c (panelling, pictures, sculptures, etc.). Mid-18c hospital; numerous works of art and pharmacy from same period. Still a number of old mill-wheels on some of the local canals.

Illiers-Combray: *the Château de Frazé, entered through a pavilion with sculpted corbels, is typical of the late Middle Ages.*

Vicinity ● 7.5 km E, *Fontaine-de-Vaucluse*: small Romanesque church; speleological exhibition in former town hall; small iconographic and bibliographical mus. devoted to Petrarch, who wrote his sonnets to the mysterious Laura here in 14c. Local artisan and cultural centre. 10 mins. along r. bank of R. Sorgue, rocky site of one of the world's most powerful natural springs. Remains of château of bishops of Cavaillon. 4 km to NW, *Saumane*, 15–16 and 18c château of the Marquis de Sade (n.v.a.).

Issoire
63 – Puy-de-Dôme   31 – A 2
12c St. Austremoine is one of most remarkable Romanesque churches in Auvergne; int. (see photo) was entirely repainted in 19c; from ext., the apse presents a majestic appearance – in three levels, with mosaic decoration; the crypt lies under choir, echoing its lay-out.
Vicinity ● 4 km SE, Ch. de *Paren-*

ISSARLÈS (Lake)
07 – Ardèche   37 B 1
Big stretch of water (227 acres), very deep blue in colour, lying in 108 m.-deep volcanic crater. The lake is part of the large Montpezat hydroelectric complex (beach, water sports). Traces of troglodytic dwellings; belvedere.

---

tignat, 17c (v.a. Sun. and public holidays, in May–June; p.m. daily in July–Aug.; at other periods, by arrangement); int. has 18c panelling and furnished salons, with large collection of pictures. 8 km to E, Usson: remains of château of Marguerite de Valois ('Queen Margot', d. 1615); 15c houses. 4 km to NE, *Sauxillanges*, 14–15c remains of priory.

Issoudun
36 – Indre   24 B 1
The old town is dominated by a feudal 'motte' (castle mound), on which stands the Blanche tower (v.a.), superb late-12c cylindrical

keep; extensive views. Former St. Roch hospital, early 16c; huge infirmary; the chapel, adorned with two sculpted Jesse trees from late 15c, now houses mus. (archaeological collection, medieval sculpture, religious art); in N. wing, former dispensary (v.a., cl. Tues.). Mid-19c basilica of Notre Dame-du-Sacré-Coeur, positively carpeted with ex-votos (frequent pilgrimages); Stations of the Cross and calvary.
Vicinity ● 10 km E, *St. Ambroix*, 15c church, remains of 18c priory of Semur; 4 km to S, fmr. abbey of La Prée, founded 1128, converted into château; 12c chapter-house.

Issoire: the St. Paul-St. Austremoine church, an outstanding example of Auvergne Romanesque; on right, one of the gorgeous historiated capitals in the choir, repainted in the 19th century.

J

Jaulny
54 – Meurthe-et-Moselle 13 – B 1

Picturesque village below feudal castle (v.a., Apr.–Nov.), in which 15c residential part has some fine rooms (Salle des Gardes, portrait gallery) with carved beams, furniture, wrought-iron, tapestries, etc.; museum (1878 and 1914).
Vicinity ● American and German military cemeteries near *Thiaucourt*; to SW, the *Butte de Montsec*, 375 m. hill with grandiose American memorial.

Jonte (Canyon)
48 – Lozère   37 – A 2

This superb canyon has two levels of sheer reddish cliffs; the corniche road (D 996) yields a succession of magnificent views. Unusual dolomitic rock, known as 'The Sèvres Vase'; also superb Fabié and Curvelié rocks. Splendid view along canyon from Les Terrasses belvedere. Towards *Le Rozier*, the **Tarn*** gorges.

Jausiers
04 – Alpes-de-Haute-Provence
                                        38 – D 2

In lush green basin on R. Ubaye, a tributary of R. Durance; the Ubaye valley marks N border of the *Alpes de Provence*. 14c church with 17c campanile and entry in wood; int. decorated in Louis XIV style.
Vicinity ● To N, beyond the Pas de

Grégoire, the valley narrows; *Condamine-Châtelard* (6 km W, winter sports centre of Ste. Anne). From confluence of R. *Ubaye* and *Ubayette*, the D902 climbs N up Ubaye valley and through narrow defile of the Pas de la Reyssole to *St. Paul-sur-Ubaye*, big mountaineering centre. 4 km to NNE on D25, extraordinary Pont du Châtelet, natural stone arch 97 m. above the *Ubaye*, in superb setting. 2.5 km to E, up succession of hairpin bends to mountain hamlet of Fouillouze, at mouth of wild corrie. ● To SE, a 58 km, very beautiful winding route, passing through Col de la *Bonette* (2,802 m.) to **St. Étienne-de-Tinée***; it is one of the highest roads in Europe.

Jobourg (Nez)
See **La Hague***   3 – C 2

Joigny
89 – Yonne   19 – A 1

In tiers above R. *Yonne*, the town has some lovely churches and several 15–16c timber-framed houses. St. Thibault, late 15-early 16c, possesses numerous works of art, notably a charming 'Smiling Virgin', from 14c, and highly realistic kneeling statues of donors. In St. Jean, second-half 16c, sculpted tomb with reclining figure of Adelaîs, Countess of Joigny in mid-13c. St. André church also has interesting sculptures; enclosed within the tribune, elegant Ren. funerary chapel of Ferrand family; exterior of apse is decorated with sculpted frieze depicting skeletons holding streamers with inscriptions on subject of death.
Vicinity ● To NNE, via the Côte St. Jacques (good view), *Forêt d'Othe*. ● 16 km SW, *La Ferté-Loupière*: in 12–15c church, early-16c murals inc. a 'Danse Macabre' with 42 figures; beautiful wooden stairway.

Joinville
52 – Haute-Marne   13 – A 3

Ch. du Grand-Jardin, built between 1546 and 1556, displays elegant Ren. décors on its façades; roofs are adorned with superb dormer windows; chapel with coffered

Jausiers: *the upper valley of the River Ubaye, beyond Barcelonnette, is broad and green for part of its length.*

ceiling (v.a. to ext.). 13c Notre Dame church, with Ren. portal; int. has 16c Holy Sepulchre and reliquary of 'St. Joseph's belt'. In cemetery, early-16c chapel of Ste. Anne contains sepulchre of the Ducs de Guise (royal dukes in 16c).
Vicinity ● 15 km NW, *Forêt du Val* (30 sq. miles). ● To SW, lovely excursion in upper valley of the *Blaise*, from *Doulevant-le-Château* to *Juzennecourt*.

Josselin
56 – Morbihan   16 – A 1
Castle is one of the most beautiful and historic in Brittany; 14c exterior façade and its three towers rise above R. *Oust*; inside, late-15c manor built by Jean II of the once highly-powerful de Rohan family (who still own the property); façade in refined Flamboyant style; noteworthy furniture in apartments around main courtyard (v.a. daily, June 1 to Aug. 31; Wed., Sun. and public holidays, Easter to May 31; Sept. 1 to Easter, group parties by arrangement). In stables, small mus. of dolls. Town has noteworthy Romanesque and Goth. church, Notre Dame-du-Roncier; inside it, black marble cenotaph of Olivier de Clisson (d. 1407) and Marguerite de Rohan, with white marble statues under sculpted canopies (Breton pardon, Sept. 8). On r. bank of the *Oust*: 11 and 16c chapel of Ste. Croix.
Vicinity ● 10 km SW, Guéhenno, superb mid-16c calvary; in front of it, column bearing the instruments of the Passion; ossuary and sepulchre.

Jouarre
77 – Seine-et-Marne   12 – A 1
Few traces remain of the famed Benedictine abbey founded here in 7c; present buildings are 18c. Small archaeological mus. in 12c Romanesque tower. Behind 15–16c parish church is 7c crypt (v.a., cl. Tues.); notable sculpted sarcophagi, particularly those of Ste. Telchilde and St. Agilbert; in chapel above, mus. of Brie reg.
Vicinity ● 3 km N, La Ferté-sous-Jouarre, pleasant walks on banks of R. *Marne*. ● Beautiful trip to SE through valley of the *Petit-Morin*: *St. Cyr-sur-Morin*, in green setting; *Sablonnières*, 12 and 16c church. ● To S, you can get to valley of the *Grand-Morin* and **Coulommiers***.

Jouy-en-Josas
78 – Yvelines   11 – C 2
Once a small country town, now residential and university centre, between green banks of R. Bièvre. 13–16c church; int. has unusual 12c Virgin and Child, known as 'La Diège', 16c stalls and interesting works of art. Oberkampf mus., devoted to Toile de Jouy (canvas produced locally), in Ch. de Montebello (v.a. Tues., Sat., Sun.; cl. in summer). In Ch. du Montcel and grounds, Cartier Foundation for Contemporary Art (exhibitions).
Vicinity ● In valley of the Bièvre, at hamlet of Les Metz, see house in Rue Victor Hugo where the great writer installed his mistress, Juliette Drouet, in 1835 – episode which inspired his *Tristesse d'Olympio*. Bièvres has interesting photographic mus.; Ch. des Roches (Victor Hugo stayed there several times); Vauboyen mill (various exhibitions) has modern chapel decorated by Villon, Buffet, Dufy, Lurçat, etc.

Juan-les-Pins
06 – Alpes-Maritimes   45 – A 1
Created relatively recently (1925), this highly popular seaside resort is one of the most elegant on Côte d'Azur; luxurious hotels, huge estates and villas. Joined to

Jumièges: *the imposing remains of one of Normandy's finest Romanesque abbeys, between Jumièges forest and the Seine.*

Antibes* by Blvd. du Président Wilson.
Vicinity ● 4 km W, along N559 coast road: *Golfe-Juan*, with harbour and fine sandy beach; column marks spot where Napoleon landed on his return from Elba (Mar. 1, 1815); start of the Route Napoleon; mus. devoted to him; horticultural establishments.

Jumièges
76 – Seine-Maritime   4 – D 3
The grandiose remains of the abbey, founded 7c, testify to its former importance and splendour (v.a.); façade of abbey church of Notre Dame and its two square towers, ruins of the nave (its semicircular arch still standing, as if by a miracle), and Goth. choir, make up an impressive ensemble. See also St. Pierre church, 7 and 13–14c, early 12c chapterhouse, big stillroom and, in former abbot's house, small lapidary mus. (tombstone of Agnès Sorel, beautiful royal favourite in 15c).

Kaysersberg

68 – Haut-Rhin   14 – A 3

Ringed by renowned vineyards, this picturesque old town has retained its medieval character. 12–15c church, on small square adorned with fountain, has Romanesque portal and interior with interesting works of art (magnificent 16c carved wood retable); to l., cemetery with 16c gallery and 15c chapel of St. Michel, on two floors (mus.). Town hall in Rhenish Ren. style. Late-16c Maison Brief; fortified bridge, 15–16c; birthplace of Dr. Albert Schweitzer (small mus.). Castle ruins loom over both the town and adjoining valley of R. *Weiss*. Local mus. (polychrome statues, 13–18c).

Vicinity ● Alsace wine road. ● Excursion, to S, to the Sommerberg (chapel of the Flying Man – Flieger Kapelle); lovely view.

Kerjean (Château)

29N – Finistère   8 – B 2

Magnificent mid-16c construction, half-fortress, half-Ren. palace, girdled by vast quadrilateral of fortified walls, protected by moat. Imposing main courtyard ornamented with beautiful Ren. well; timber-vaulted chapel with carved

Kaysersberg: *a typical little Alsace town, surrounded by fine vineyards and featuring old houses with wooden balconies.*

beams and cornices. Monumental fireplaces in the kitchens. Int. has exceptional collection of old Breton furniture. (V.a., cl. Tues. Floodlighting and tape-recorded commentary every evening during summer.)

Kernascléden

56 – Morbihan   8 – D 3

15c church has series of frescos, on vaulting and walls, depicting episodes from Life of the Virgin and Childhood of Christ, a 'dance macabre', Hell, etc. – together forming one of the most original groups of medieval painting.

Vicinity ● 3 km SW, *Étang* and Ch. de *Pontcallec*, 16 and 18c; château is elegantly adorned with mullioned windows and arcaded balconies (v.a. to grounds only). To S, the D 110 skirts *Forest of Pontcallec* and r. bank of R. *Scorff*.

Kerjean: *in the centre of a huge estate, this magnificent granite construction – massive, imposing, austere – was protected in olden times by a moat and a fortified wall 12 metres thick.*

L

Labastide-Murat
46 – Lot   36 – A 1
On one of highest points of Causse de **Gramat***; magnificent view. The inn in which Murat was born, virtually unchanged since 18c, has been turned into King Joachim's mus. (Joachim Murat, 1767–1815, was one of Napoleon's marshals, and, briefly, King of Naples.)
Vicinity ● La Braunhie, wildest part of Gramat causse, full of caves and swallowholes. ● 5 km NW, impressive medieval castle of Vaillac, flanked by five towers. ● 5 km N, former seminary of *Montfaucon*, 18c (sanatorium). ● 3 km SE, fmr. 14–16c priory of Soulomès; inside, 14c frescos; 5 km to SE, Caniac-du-Causse, church has lovely 12c crypt with unusual vaulting.

Labrède (Château)
33 – Gironde   35 – A 1
In heart of Graves wine reg., a picturesque château of irregular polygonal shape, a kind of medieval island surrounded by large moat filled with running water, birthplace of Montesquieu (1689) and where he wrote his major works (cl. Tues., Easter–Nov.; Sun. only, Feb. 1–Easter). 13c rectangular keep, 15c chapel, late 16c round tower with machicolations. Inside, lovely fireplaces and old furniture. Montesquieu's bedroom and library remain unchanged.

Lacaune
81 – Tarn   42 C 1
Health resort and spa town on R. Gijou. 17c church, 16c houses, picturesque late-14c Pissaïres fountain.
Vicinity ● To W, winding Gijou valley, 'Gourp Fumant' swallowhole, and, at *Viane*, ruins of medieval castle of Pierre Ségade; 8 km to W, 12 and 17c Ch. de Lacaze. ● *Mts. de Lacaune*, to S, typical landscape of granitic rocks, meadows and woods. ● 20 km S, *La Salvetat-sur-Agout*; *Barrage de la Raviège* has transformed R. *Agout* into a winding lake, 7 km long (beach, water sports); to SE, *Mts. de l'Espinouse*; after *Col du Cabaretou* (640 m.), D 907 drops down to **St. Pons*** through lush countryside.

Lagrasse
11 – Aude   42 – C 2
On r. bank of R. *Orbieu*, one-time abbey, founded 8c, contains numerous 11–18c buildings (house for holders of France's esteemed Military Medal, v.a. by arrangement only); it includes abbot's house, 11–13c cloister, 14c refectory and dormitory; an old people's home is in 18c buildings; chapel is former 14c abbey church next to rudimentary 10c church. Village, typically meridional, still has remains of its ramparts and numerous old houses. Late 14c church of St. Michel. Fine view of village and abbey from 14c Pont-Vieux.
Vicinity ● 9.5 km SW, St. Martin-des-Puits, unusual 11–12c Romanesque church, half-buried; D212 passes under ruins of Durfort castle and follows *Orbieu* gorges for 25 km; 2.5 km to S of Durfort, impressive ruins of 12c *Château Cathare de Termes* (two unusual cruciform windows).

Laguiole
12 – Aveyron   36 – D 1
Mountain town, 1,004 m. up, at foot of basaltic hill; recommended holiday and excursion centre. 16c church on platform called 'Le Fort' (wide view), reached via picturesque alleyways. Haut-Rouergue mus.
Vicinity ● 6 km SW, 15c Bousquet castle, flanked by square towers and four elbow turrets. ● 10 km E, skiing area of Puy du Roussillon (1,408 m.). ● To E, *Massif de l'Aubrac*, to SW, *Plateau de la Viadène*.

Lalouvesc
07 – Ardèche   31 – C 3
Summer resort and pilgrimage centre for St. François-Régis. 19c basilica, saint's funerary chapel and small mus. (diorama).
Vicinity ● 27 km S, via cols of Le Faux (1,025 m.) and Le Buisson (920 m.), *Lamastre*: in Macheville quarter, interesting Romanesque church. ● 11.5 km NE, *Satillieu*: old town, built in tiers; 4.5 km to NE, impressive ruins of 14c castle of St. Romain-d'Ay; chapel of Notre Dame-d'Ay.

Lamalou-les-Bains
34 – Hérault   42 – D 1
Spa town in hilly, wooded valley of R. Bitoulet; recommended excursion centre. Former Romanesque priory church of St. Pierre-de-Rèdes, early 12c, with v. unusual semicircular apse and interesting doorways.
Vicinity ● On banks of R. *Orb*, lovely Vernière park, walks, play areas, leading up to St. Michel hermitage, formerly fortified. ● To NE, 50 min. climb to Notre Dame-de-Capimont, panorama. ● To W, via *Espinouse* road, very hilly, and Col de Madale (691 m.), Mt. Caroux (1,093 m., wide view). ● Recommended excursion to Héric gorges and Forêt des Écrivains Combattants (viewing table). ● To SW, *Orb* gorges.

Labrède: *memories of Montesquieu pervade this strange château, which lends itself to study and meditation.*

Lamballe
22 – Côtes-du-Nord 9 – B 2
On St. Sauveur hill, Church of Notre Dame, in Norman Goth. style, dominates town. In lower town, 15c church of St. Jean, and interesting old houses. 15–16c St. Martin, with parts dating from 11c, has unusual porch (wooden roof with carved beams). Two mus.: local mus. in 15c Pilori mansion, and mus. devoted to Mathurin Meheut (Breton painter) in 15c Hangman's House. Natnl. stud.
Vicinity ● 15.5 km E, romantic ruins of late-14c *Ch. de la Hunau-*

to W, *Ploudiry*, mid-17c ossuary chapel, church with lovely Ren. porch dating from 1665.

Landévennec
29S – Finistère 8 – B 2
On tip of peninsula on *Aulne* estuary, at foot of magnificent rocky escarpment. 16–17c church, standing on edge of beach, is surrounded by a small cemetery. To S of town, remains of former abbey of Landévennec, founded 5c; late 11–12c abbey church's ruins are stunning (v.a., June 1–Sept. 30; small abbey mus.). Nearby are

ment, 30 m. high, topped by four pyramids, of unknown origin, date and purpose.

Langogne
48 – Lozère 37 B 1
Summer resort at 911 m. alt., on R. *Allier*, in green and airy valley. Old town, in circular layout, is flanked by six large round towers, including Clock gate. Romanesque church with 15c Goth. façade.
Vicinity ● 9 km N, *Pradelles*, rising in tiers on edge of basaltic plateau: remains of ramparts and Chambaud gate; many old houses,

Landerneau: *two specialities – early vegetables and fish – in the Place du Marché.*

Langeais: *the château still has its impressive towers and defences.*

daye (v.a.); 2 km to N, 15c Vaumadeuc manor (hôtel).

Landerneau
29N – Finistère 8 – B 2
Little old town at entrance of Elorn estuary. Ren. church of St. Houardon and 16c church of St. Thomas of Canterbury. Old houses in Place du Marché and near old bridge over R. Elorn.
Vicinity ● 3.5 km SE, *Pencran*, lovely parish enclosure, monumental gateway, calvary, ossuary (1594), 16c church with porch decorated with statues. ● 8 km SW, *La Martyre*, enclosure with Goth. triumphal gateway, surmounted by a calvary, 15c church with 13c porchbelfry and 15c carved porch; 1.5 km

buildings of new Benedictine abbey of St. Guénolé (1958).
Vicinity ● Folgoat wood; chapel of Notre Dame-du-Folgoat, in attractive setting.

Langeais (Château)
37 – Indre-et-Loire 17 – C 3
One of the rare homogenous châteaux in Loire valley, built mid-15c. Exterior, flanked by three huge towers inc. keep, is that of a fortress, while interior, exquisitely furnished, is that of an aristocratic home (cl. Mon. a.m. exc. public holidays).
Vicinity ● 5 km E, Cinq-Mars-la-Pile: ruins of 11–12c castle (fine view from top of large tower); troglodytic houses; 1 km to E, La Pile is a Gallo-Roman brick monu-

especially in Place de la Halle, surrounded by covered galleries; former hospice of pilgrims of Santiago de Compostela; N102A leads, 8.5 km to E, to Peyrebeille inn, notorious for crimes committed in 19c by the Martins (husband and wife), who were guillotined on the spot. ● 16 km S, beyond *Cheylard-L'Évêque*, abbey and forest of Mercoire; remains of 13c Cistercian abbey and 18c convent buildings stand in wild surroundings.

Langres
52 – Haute-Marne 20 A 1
This old town, surrounded by ramparts and standing on top of a rocky spur, has retained its original character. Entry from S is through

highly-fortified 17c Moulins gate. To E, late-15c St. Ferjeux tower; to W, Navarre tower. ● Rue Diderot leads to St. Mammès cathedral, an unusual amalgam of Burgundian Romanesque and Goth. styles, with late 18c neo-Classical façade; during Renaissance, inside was lavishly decorated with tapestries and wood panelling, but Romanesque choir has remained unchanged. ● Around cath. lies the old town, formerly enclosed; numerous private houses or mansions (canons' residences) give the quarter an aristocratic air; see also Place de l'Abbé-Cordier, Rues Longe-Porte, Roger, de la Charité, Abbés-Couturier, Jean-Rousseat, Cardinal-Morlot (so-called Diane de Poitiers house, No. 20). ● Breuil de Ste Germain mus. (cl. Tues.), in lovely Ren. and 18c mansion, houses interesting collection of incunabula, 17–18c emblazoned books, pottery, furniture, paintings and cutlery. Gallery devoted to Diderot, who was born in town. St. Didier mus. (also cl. Tues.): reg. Gallo-Roman antiquities, paintings by Jean and Richard Tassel, who were born in town in 17c, also by Le Brun, Delacroix, Corot, Courbet. ● Tour of ramparts recommended: fine views. *Vicinity* ● 12 km SE, between *Heuilley-Cotton* and *Chalindrey*, Ren. Ch. du *Pailly*.

Lannion
22 – Côtes-du-Nord   8 – D 1
This small, typically Breton town has a number of 15–16c houses, especially in Place Leclerc, and two interesting churches: 16–17c St. Jean-du-Baly, and 12c Romanesque church of Brélévenez, separated from town by a small valley. *Vicinity* ● The Rose Granite Coast, or Breton Corniche, from *Trebeurden* to **Perros-Guirec***, via *Trégastel-Plage* (superb chaotic mass of rose granite rocks) and *Ploumanach* (fantastically-shaped rose granite rocks, cove and beach of St. Guirec, Squewel point, etc.); this is one of the most attractive and impressive areas of Brittany. ● 7 km NW, *Pleumeur-Bodou*, fascinating space telecommunications centre, with 50 m.-high inflatable dome (v.a. in summer). ● 2.5 km W, Loguivy, parish 'enclos' with Ren. fountain and 16c church. ● To S, via D11, ruins of 14c Ch. de Coat-Frec; mid-16c *Chapelle de Kerfons* (inside, magnificent Goth. Flamboyant-style carved wooden roodscreen); ruins of 15c *Ch. de Tonquédec*, overlooking *Léguer* valley (v.a.), fine view; *Ch. de Kergrist*, famed for the great variety of styles of its façades: Goth. to N, with carved dormer windows and 14–15-

Lannion: *the strangely-shaped rocks of Ploumanac'h are one of the attractions of this tiny, typically Breton fishing-port.*

18c main building to S; Classical to W, and lovely formal gardens (v.a. p.m., July 1–Sept. 1, cl. Mon. and July 22).

Laon
02 – Aisne   6 – B 3
On promontory above the vast plain of Champagne, encircled by attractive paths along the ancient ramparts, Laon is dominated by the seven towers of late 12–early 13c cathedral of Notre Dame, one of best examples of the transition from Romanesque to Goth.; the two towers of main façade are decorated with huge bulls' heads; int., 110 m. long, and proportionately lofty, rises in four tiers; rich treasure; 13c chapter-house and elegant cloister. In former 13c hospital is Goth. infirmary, with three naves, now below ground (v.a.). Now the lawcourts, old bishop's palace has three 13 and 17c main buildings around a courtyard (view over cath. apse);

delightful late-12c two-storey chapel. In cath. quarter (Cité Notre Dame), numerous picturesque old houses, especially in Rues Sérurier and Châtelaine. Municipal archaeological mus.: outstanding collection of archaeology, prehist., Greek ceramics and sculptures, Gallo-Roman objects. In garden, 12c octagonal Templars' chapel. Fine view from citadel. W part of promontory is occupied by Bourg quarter, former 12–13c abbey church of St. Martin; 13c Soissons gate is linked by a wall to 13c Leaning Tower. *Vicinity* ● 14 km NE, *Liesse*, lovely 14–15c church of Notre Dame; noteworthy 16c white marble roodscreen; stained-glass windows by Despierre. ● To N, tour of fortified churches of *Thiérache* reg. (see **Vervins***). ● To S, *Chemin-des-Dames*, scene of violent battles in 1917–1918: cemetery and ossuary at *Cerny-en-Laonnais*; to E, Dragon's

Laon: *the sculpted tympana of the cathedral's three porches are as harmoniously proportioned as they are expressive.*

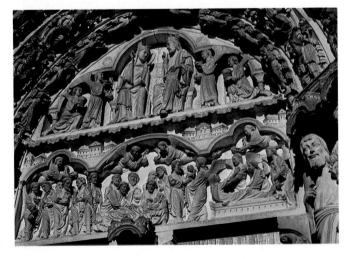

Grotto (v.a. to underground fortress and mus., Apr.–Oct.); Hurtebise farm (2 km to N, ruins of abbey of *Vauclerc*, 12–13c); *Craonne*; *Corbeny*, interesting floral park (Apr.–May: tulips and nar-cissi; July–Nov.: dahlias and gladioli), mead cellars, exhibitions.

Larressingle
32 – Gers   35 – B 3
13c fortified town whose polygonal outer precincts have retained much of their original walls, moat, square towers and imposing fortified gate reached by bridge. Ruins of 13 and 15c fortress; church now occupies ground floor of keep.
Vicinity 2 km W, 17–18c Ch. de Beaumont.

LARZAC (Causse)
34 – Hérault, 12 – Aveyron, 30 – Gard   36 – D 3 – 37 – A 3
There are various routes across this causse, the largest in France (400 sq. miles). One is from **Millau*** to *Le Caylar* via *La Cavalerie* (large military camp). *L'Hospitalet-du-Larzac* (zoo). From **Nant*** to **La Couvertoirade*** is another. ● However, much more picturesque and mountainous is route from **Roquefort-sur-Soulzon***, via Tournemire and Cougouille peak (912 m.), to *L'Hospitalet-du-Larzac*.

LAUTARET (Col)
05 – Hautes-Alpes   32 – C 3
Despite its great alt. (2,058 m.), the col (pass) has been a much-used crossing point for centuries. Its flora is one of richest and most varied in Alps. The alpine garden (Marcel Mirande botanical institute) is glorious (v.a.). Viewing table, magnificent panorama. Important crossroads: to W, towards **Bourg-d'Oisans***, **Vizille*** and **Grenoble***; to N, towards *Col du Galibier*, **St. Michel-de-Maurienne**, **St. Jean-de-Maurienne*** and **Chambéry***; to SE, towards **Briançon***.

Lascaux (Caves)
24 – Dordogne   29 – D 3
'Prehistory's Sistine Chapel', 2 km to SE of *Montignac*, contains unique coll. of prehist. wall paintings. Caves were closed to public in 1963 to save them from deterioration. Inf. centre (v.a. in summer). But nearby Lascaux II, which took 10 years to construct, is a virtually perfect replica of part of caves and their paintings (Bull Chamber and one of recesses). A fascinating prehist. art centre has been created at Le Thot, a few kms away.

Lassay-les-Châteaux
53 – Mayenne   10 – B 3
Standing on edge of a lake, this magnificent example of 15c military architecture has retained its eight towers topped by pepperpot roofs, its imposing barbican, its high walls and its main living quarters, which contain interesting 16–17c furniture and weapons (v.a. in summer. Son et Lumière).

Laval
53 – Mayenne   10 – A 3
Old town, dominated by Ren. 'New' Château (mid-16c), now law-courts, and 'Old' Château (entry via 17c porch, cl. Mon., lapidary coll.); Romanesque crypt, 13 and 15c rooms and cylindrical keep (beautiful late-12c oak timberwork) are oldest parts; Counts of Laval's main hall, 32 m. long, has numerous reg. carved monuments and magnificent wooden broken barrel-vaulting. Vieux-Chateau mus., archaeological collection, medieval sculptures, mus. of naïve art, works by Douanier Rousseau, who was born at Laval (*La Moisson au Château*, of disputed authenticity). Churches of St. Martin (11–12c), St Vénérand (15–16c, with lovely Goth. Flamboyant doorway). In old quarter, ancient houses, especially in Grande Rue (16c Master of Royal Hunt's house); some half-timbered and corbelled. 11–12c Romanesque Notre Dame-d'Avesnières has noteworthy apse with ambulatory and five Goth. Rayonnant chapels, and Trinity Church (cath.) a Romanesque nave with late-12c ribbed vaulting; see also 17c retable of high altar, 16c triptych of St. John the Baptist. Beucheresse gate still has its huge

15c towers; in Perrine garden, Douanier Rousseau's grave.
Vicinity ● 2 km N, church of Notre Dame-de-Pritz, Romanesque with some 9–10c Carolingian parts; 11, 12 and 13c murals. ● 16 km WNW, 12c Abbey at *Clermont*, lovely church in pure Cistercian style, 16c cloister. ● 18 km SSW, Cosse-le-Vivien, mus. devoted to Robert Tatin.

Lavandou (Le)
83 – Var   44 – C 2
Marina; seaside town and winter resort stretched out along sandy beach in heart of *Rade de Bormes*.
Vicinity ● To S, *Cap Bénat*, numerous private properties and villas, military areas; SW point faces *Fort de Brégançon*, French President's summer home (see **Bormes-les-Mimosas***). ● Trips to **Hyères*** islands. ● To N, *Massif des Maures*; coast road (or Maures corniche road) runs alongside sea from *Le Lavandou* to *Cavalaire-sur-Mer*, via *Cavalière*, *Cap Nègre*, Pramousquier and *Le Rayol-Canadel*: a magnificent site at foot of wooded hills; a huge flower-lined staircase links beach to terrace, 150 m. above.

Lavoûte-Chilhac
43 – Haute-Loire   31 – A 3
On peninsula in middle of R. *Allier*. Remains of Benedictine abbey; 12 and 15c church with fortified apse; unusual volcanic rocks used in buildings; to l. of nave, chapel of Notre Dame-Trouvée (Our Lady Found); interesting works of art. 15c bridge and remains of perimeter walls.
Vicinity ● 12 km SE, *Langeac* (15c church). ● To N, via *Villeneuve-d'Allier* (linked by suspension

Lessay: *the nave of the abbey church, one of Normandy's finest examples of Romanesque art.*

Laval: *the cylindrical keep of the château towers over the once-fortified Old Bridge, which spans the Mayenne.*

LERINS (Islands)
06 – Alpes-Maritimes   45 – A 1
Boat trip from **Cannes***. Island of Ste. Marguerite has imposing 17c fortress (or royal fort) (v.a.); cell occupied by Man in the Iron Mask is its principal attraction. *Ile St. Honorat* is occupied by a Cistercian monastery (v.a. to lapidary mus. and church), beside which stands castle which was converted in 11c into fortified monastery (v.a.); in pine forests are five chapels belonging to monastery: chapels of La Trinité (E point), the most unusual (with tiny conical dome), and St. Sauveur (to W) are partly 5c, remaining three date from 12c.

---

bridge to tiny medieval city of St. Ilpize), *Allier* gorges towards **Brioude***.

Lectoure
32 – Gers   35 – C 3
On promontory above *Gers* valley, town still has its 15–16c perimeter walls. From terraced Promenade du Bastion, fine view over Pyrenees. St. Gervais-et-St. Protais, in late 12–13c Goth. style. Mary Larrieu-Duler archaeological mus.: prehist., Gallo-Roman and Merovingian exhibits, 20 altars used for bull sacrifices. Catacombs; sarcophagi. Mosaics gallery (v.a.).
Vicinity ● 8 km N, at St. Avit-Frandat, 12c Lacassaigne castle; inside, main hall is copy of long-vanished High Council Chamber of Knights of St. John of Jerusalem, in Valetta, Malta (v.a. by arrangement). ● 16.5 km E, 14c Ch. de Gramont, with delicately sculpted Renaissance wing (v.a. Easter–Nov. 1, cl. Tues.).

Lescar
64 – Pyrénées-Atlantiques 41 – A 2

Romanesque former cathedral of Notre Dame, 16c façade; in apse, two unusual mosaics (dating from about 1225) representing hunting scenes. Carved Ren. choirstalls (34 figures of Apostles, prophets, etc.). Historiated capitals. 15–16c tombs of Princes of Navarre. From S end of church, fine view over Pyrenees. former bishop's palace now houses an annex of Pau's reg. mus. (archaeological collection).
Vicinity ● 18 km NW, *Lacq*: apply to public relations office if you wish to visit natural gas works, to l. of main road; 8 km to S, *Mourenx-Ville-Nouvelle*, built between 1957 and 1961 for employees of Lacq industrial complex.

Lessay
50 – Manche   3 – D 3
Late 11–early 13c former abbey church is one of most outstanding Romanesque buildings in Normandy. 18c convent buildings.
Vicinity ● To S, *Lande de Lessay* (12,500 acres), covered with rushes, wild grasses and heather; partially transformed by fields and plan-

Lille: *the Grand-Place is the lively town centre: one of its finest buildings is the Old Exchange, a superb brick and stone example of Flemish baroque architecture; on right, part of its façade.*

tations of 1,750-acre Buisson estate (now a sanatorium); huge Lessay or Ste. Croix fair, first held in 13c, takes place here each year on Sept. 10, 11 and 12.

Libourne
33 – Gironde   29 – B 3

This huge 13c bastide, a flourishing wine centre, stands on confluence of R. *Isle* and *Dordogne*. 16c town hall, on the Grande Place (aka Place Abel-Surchamp), lined by covered walks and 16–19c houses, contains Princeteau mus.: paintings by Bassano, Philippe de Champaigne, Jouvenet, and Princeteau himself (local painter of animals, who had Toulouse-Lautrec as his pupil). Contemporary works: Hartung, Picabia, Dufy, Kisling. Exotic ethnography. Port and quays on R. *Isle*, tour of 14c Grand-Port.
Vicinity ● 10 km SW, Ch. de **Vayres***. ● 6.5 km SE, **St. Emilion***.

Lichtenberg (Château)
67 – Bas-Rhin   14 – A 1

One of most evocative of Alsace's medieval fortresses. Rebuilt late 13c, castle is dominated by a keep and two towers; outer precincts were enlarged in 16–17c. Magnificent view (v.a.).

Liessies
59 – Nord   6 – B 1

In 16c church of St. Lambert, interesting folk art statues.
Vicinity ● Lovely upper valley of R. Helpe. Trip around Trélon forest towards Val-Joly lake (to E), *Trélon* (to S), then **Avesnes-sur-Helpe*** (to the W).

Lille
59 – Nord   2 – A 3

Capital of French Flanders. ●

Grand-Place and next-door Petite-Place, or Theatrical Square, are separated by former Exchange building, in 17c Flemish baroque style, covered with sculptures and decorations (lovely int. courtyard). On corner of Rue de la Bourse, 'Rang du Beau Regard', a line of 17c houses, with pilasters topped by carved scrolls. On vast Place de la République, Palace of Fine Arts, which contains one of richest mus. in France (cl. Tues.): large collection of French and Flemish early masters, 16 and 17c Flemish paintings (five Rubens, 11 Jordaens, two Van Dyck, etc.); Dutch, Italian (Veronese, Titian); Spanish (two El Greco, two Goya; 'Les Jeunes' and 'Les Vieilles', both masterpieces); and French from 18c to present day (Boucher, Quentin de La Tour, Fragonard, David, Boilly, Delacroix, Géricault, Corot, six Courbet, Van Gogh and large number of Impressionists); about 3,000 sketches; noteworthy gallery of Flemish archaeology Hospice Comtesse mus. (15–18c buildings, including huge late-15c infirmary, with panelled vaulting) contains furniture, ceramics, paintings and tapestries which evoke interior of a Flemish convent (cl. Tues.). See also Ghent Hospice, founded 1664 (sick ward), General Hospital (1739), and fmr. St. Sauveur Hospital, of which only an elegant 17c brick and stone building remains. Conclave chapel and ducal oratory are all that survive of 15c Rihour palace: natural hist. mus. (world-famed insectarium). Mus. of Egyptology. ● Interesting churches. La Madeleine (early 18c), of extremely unusual design: a rotunda surrounded by an ambulatory, topped by a cupola. St. Maurice, 14–15c 'hall-church' (Flemish paintings).

16–17c Ste. Catherine (*Martyre de Ste. Catherine*, by Rubens). St. André, elegant 18c building (magnificent baroque pulpit). 13c Notre Dame-de-la-Réconciliation, oldest religious building in town.
● Lille has many noteworthy old mansions: late-18c Bidé de la Granville mansion (1 Rue du Lombard); 17c Vieux-Hommes house (Rue de Roubaix); Louis XV-style Petitpas-de-Walle mansion (122 Rue de l'Hôpital-Militaire). Lovely 17c houses, richly sculpted and decorated, in Rue Royale, Place du Palais Rihour, etc. In St. Sauveur quarter, recently rebuilt, elegant chapel with Louis XV façade, aka 'Le Réduit St. Sauveur'.
● Numerous gates recall long-vanished perimeter walls: early 17c Gand gate; Roubaix gate (1625), in sandstone and brick; monumental Paris gate, decidedly the loveliest, constructed between 1682 and 1695, serving both as town gate and triumphal arch in honour of Louis XIV, and richly decorated. Citadel, constructed by Vauban, lapped by R. Deule, is one of best-preserved in France; its brick buildings, reached via Porte Royale, surround Place d'Armes, which is lined on one side by Governor's Mansion, chapel and Army Headquarters buildings, and on other by arsenal.
Vicinity ● Lille, *Armentières* (rebuilt post-1918), *Tourcoing* (interesting municipal mus.) and *Roubaix* form a vast industrial complex; to E of town, *Hem*, chapel of Ste. Theresa of the Infant Jesus is one of finest examples of contemp. religious art. New town of Lille-Est at Villeneuve d'Ascq has noteworthy mus. of modern art in extremely modern building (1983); works by Picasso, Braque, Modigliani, Léger, Derain, Miró, etc.

Lillebonne
76 – Seine-Maritime   4 – D 3
15c church of Notre Dame. 12c ruins, with 13c keep (v.a.), of William the Conqueror's castle. Roman theatre, 110 m. by 80 m. (v.a.), is Normandy's most notable monument of the period. Mus. of local history and ethnology.
Vicinity ● 5.5 km S, Port-Jérôme, petrol refineries; at *Quillebeuf*, on l. bank of Seine, 12–14c church with Romanesque belfry.

Lillers
62 – Pas-de-Calais   1 – C 3
Mid-12c collegiate church of St. Omer, although reconstructed between 16 and 19c, is only Romanesque church of any importance in N of France. Strange early-12c crucifix, aka 'St. Sang du Miracle', is venerated here.
Vicinity ● 3.5 km NW, *Ham-en-Artois*, former abbey of St. Sauveur, founded 11c.

Limoges
87 – Haute-Vienne
13–16c cathedral of St. Étienne has magnificent early-16c Goth. Flamboyant main doorway and 62 m.-high porch-belfry. Former episcopal palace houses mus. (cl. Tues., Oct.–June): collection of reg. enamels dating from 12c to present day; also Egyptian and Gallo-Roman archaeology, Roman sculptures, paintings by Hubert Robert, Theodore Rousseau and three Renoir, who was born in Limoges. Large collection of sculptures by Arp, works by Henri Laurens, Hajdu, Despiau, sketches and engravings. Terraced gardens of palace overlook R. *Vienne* (lovely view); early-13c hump-backed St. Étienne bridge. 13–14c St. Michel-des-Lions is dominated by 65 m.-high belfry; beautiful 15c stained-glass windows. Rue de la Boucherie, lined by old half-timbered houses, leads to late-15c chapel of St. Aure-

Limoges: the cathedral of St. Étienne, like an enormous ship in full sail. ▶

St. Michel-des-Lions owes its name to its granite lions. ▼

lien, which belongs to Butchers' Guild. Adrien Dubouche natnl. mus. (cl. Tues.), devoted to ceramics, contains more than 10,000 pieces – largest collection in France after that at Sèvres. Crypt of former abbey of St. Martial, uncovered in 1960, contains many sarcophagi; its oldest parts date from 4c; 9c polychrome mosaic (v.a., with tape commentary, in summer).
Vicinity ● 11.5 km S, *Solignac* has one of loveliest churches with cupolas in SW France (mid 12c); 17–18c abbey buildings; 3 km to SE, ruins of *Ch. de Chalusset*, 12 and late-13c. ● 22 km E, **St. Léonard-de-Noblat***. ● 23 km NW, *Oradour-sur-Glane*; ruins of village, burnt down by the Germans in 1944 after they had massacred almost all the defenceless inhabitants, have been preserved just as they were left at the time (v.a.); a new village has been built nearby; martyrs' shrine in cemetery. A gruesome but unforgettable experience.

Limoux
11 – Aude   42 – B 3
Delightful old town on R. *Aude*. 14–16c church of St. Martin. Lovely 14c bridge. Unusual Petiet Belle-Époque mus.: paintings in style of 1900, works by reg. artists.
Vicinity ● 1 km NE, 14c Notre Dame-de-Marceille; inside, lovely 18c high altar and 18c wood panelling (pilgrimage, Sept. 8); miracle-working spring in romantic setting. ● 8 km SE, St. Polycarpe, lovely Romanesque church and 17–18c abbey buildings; beautiful gold and silver plate. ● 8.5 km S, *Alet-les-Bains*, impressive ruins of former abbey church, later cathedral of Notre Dame (late-12c), in middle of cemetery; late-14c church of St. André, in S. Goth. style; Place de la République is surrounded by picturesque old houses; Cadène gate, remains of late-12c perimeter wall;

D 118 continues towards *Couiza*; on banks of Aude, imposing 16c château of Dukes of Joyeuse; 12 km to S, **Quillan***.

Lioran (Le)
15 – Cantal   30 – D 3
Summer and winter resort at 1,150 m. alt., in middle of pine forests. Road and rail tunnels run through the pass, linking **Clermont-Ferrand*** to **Aurillac***. Recommended excursion centre for Cantal massif and valleys dotted with 'burons' (shepherds' huts), where local cheese is made).
Vicinity ● 1.5 km N, Belles-Aygues 'buron' (v.a. in summer), inf. centre on shepherds' life and manufacture of Cantal cheese; many agreeable walks. ● At Super-Lioran, *Plomb du Cantal* cable-car (1,858 m.); to SE, vast panorama over Cantal and Mts. Dore. ● From *Puy Griou* (1,694 m.), to SW, exceptionally fine view over whole of Auvergne.

Lisieux
14 – Calvados   10 – C 1
The pilgrimage to Ste. Theresa of the Infant Jesus has brought great fame to this small Norman city, whose picturesque old quarters were destroyed during the last war. Unfortunately, the basilica (1933–1954) is, architecturally, as mediocre as it is pretentious (flood-lit in summer). Behind apse, monumental stations of the cross. Carmel chapel contains heavily sculpted and decorated reliquary of the saint (d. 1897). Buissonnets villa, where she spent her childhood, is still as it was in her day (v.a.). Church of St. Pierre, former 12–13c cathedral, has, to r., a lovely 12c sculpted doorway, known as Paradise Portal. To l., fmr. episcopal palace in style of Louis XIII; see 17c state reception room or Gilded Room (apply to doorkeeper). Old Lisieux mus. Mus. devoted to the wonders of the sea.

Vicinity • Lisieux is recommended excursion centre for *Pays d'Auge* to N, in lower *Touques* valley, *Ouilly-le-Vicomte*, 10–11c church, one of oldest in Normandy; 8 km to N, *Le Breuil-en-Auge*, picturesque 16c Ch. du Breuil, half-timbered, framed by two pavilions, 18c main door; 8 km to N, *Pont-L'Évêque*, 15–16c church, old houses in Rue St. Michel, early 16c Dominican manor-house; to NW, beyond *Beaumont-en-Auge*, at *St. Pierre-Azif*, interesting 12–15c church. • Via D 59, to W, abbey of *Val Richer* (turned into a château in 19c, v.a. on request); 12 km to NW, Clermont-en-Auge (from apse of church, 500 m. from village, vast panorama over Pays d'Auge), then, in direction of *Dives-sur-Mer*, *Cricqueville-en-Auge*. • To S, beyond *St. Martin-de-la-Lieue*, **St. Germain-de-Livet***, *Fervaques* (see **Vimoutiers***).

Liverdun
54 – Meurthe-et-Moselle   13 – B 2
On picturesque promontory, overlooking bend in R. *Moselle*. 16c gate, attached to part of 13c perimeter wall; late-16c Governor's mansion. Late-12c church, fine example of Romano-Gothic Cistercian architecture; inside, tomb of St. Euchaire. Good view of area from late-16c cross of St. Euchaire, on Saizerais road.

Loches
37 – Indre-et-Loire   17 – D 3
The château, a highly imposing fortress, dominates town. Entry is through 15c Royal Gate, flanked by two 13c towers, which opens on to Terroir and Lansyer mus. (in latter, 19c paintings, Far Eastern art). Rue Lansyer leads to 12c church of St. Ours, crowned by two steeples and two hollow pyramids; richly carved Romanesque doorway. 14–15c royal lodgings (v.a.; cl. Wed., Oct. 1–Mar. 14 and in Dec. and Jan.) contain Queen Anne of Brittany's oratory, finely decorated; tomb of Agnès Sorel (d. 1450, beautiful mistress of France's King Charles VII), triptych from school of Jean Fouquet. To S of walls, so-called 'Keep' fortress, with its 11c Romanesque keep, Round Tower and 15c Martelet building, is impressively fortified defensive system (v.a. to dungeons; cl. Wed., Oct. 1–Mar. 14 and in Dec. and Jan.). Recommended tour of ext. of château. Floodlighting.
Vicinity • 1.5 km E, *Beaulieu-les-Loches*; huge 11c Romanesque abbey church, partly ruined, is dominated by majestic 12c belfry; 16–17c abbot's house; so-called Agnès Sorel house (15c); via D 760, across *Forêt de Loches*, ruins of *Chartreuse du Liget*, late-12c church, 17c convent buildings (v.a.); 400 m. away, Liget chapel, a rotunda decorated with lovely 12c Romanesque frescos.

Locronan
29S – Finistère   8 – B 3
One of traditional Britanny's most characteristic towns. Central square is perfect example of architectural homogeneity, composed of 15c church, Pénity chapel, 16–17 granite Ren. houses, and an old well. Town and its 'mountain' (Plas-ar-C'horn, 289 m.) are setting for 'La Petite Troménie' (procession of St. Ronan, on second Sun. in July) and, every sixth year, 'La Grande Troménie' (next in 1989). Early-16c Pénity chapel houses St. Ronan's tomb, decorated with sculpted reliefs. Local arts and trads. mus. in 18–19c granite building. Mid.-16c chapel of Notre Dame-de-Bonne-Nouvelle.
Vicinity • 8 km NW, *Chapelle Ste. Anne-la-Palud*, in middle of heathland; its pardon on last Sun. in Aug. is one of best attended in Britanny.

Lodève
34 – Hérault   43 – A 1
14c cathedral of St. Fulcran has a fortified façade; inside, 18c choir-stalls and high altar; 15–17c cloister (fine lapidary mus.). Mus. in Cardinal de Fleury's mansion: disc-shaped stele, galleries devoted to Paul Dardé, an unusual reg. sculptor who died at Lodève in 1963. Jacques Audibert mus.: geology, paleontology, archaeology. Goth. bridge of Montifort, over R. Soulondres.
Vicinity • 6 km E, former priory of St. Michel-de-Grandmont, impressive Romanesque and Goth. monastic buildings; lovely 13c church, Romanesque cloister. • 9 km NE, picturesque Cirque de Gourgas. • 15 km N, rocky mountain gap known as *Pas de l'Escalette*: road winds precariously up face of cliffs which rise steeply to overhang valley of R. *Lergue*, 300 m. below.

Lombez
32 – Gers   41 – D 1
14c cathedral has two naves of unequal width, and a magnificent octagonal, five-tiered belfry from Toulouse school of architecture; 17c choir-stalls, 18c high altar, 15c recumbent Christ.
Vicinity • 17 km W, *Simorre*, impressive 14–15c fortified church, loveliest in Gascony; inside has numerous works of art, inc. 16 carved choir-stalls from 16c and

Viewed from the banks of the Indre, Loches is a well-preserved old town, dominated by the château, a veritable fortified city; on right, staircase leading to Anne of Brittany's oratory.

Locronan: *the impressive, lichen-covered granite steeple of Pénity church.*

magnificent 14–16c stained-glass windows. ● 9 km NE, *Cazaux-Savès*, Ch. de Caumont, impressive Ren. building in alternate lines of brick and stone, flanked by heavy, diamond-shaped towers and octagonal turrets; beautiful main courtyard (v.a., mid-July–Aug. 21, p.m.).

Longwy
54 – Meurthe-et-Moselle 7 – B 3
Industrial town made up of two distinct parts: Lower Longwy, which rises in tiers along a steep escarpment on r. bank of R. Chiers (from viewing-point of Ave. de la Liberté, vast panorama over enormous industrial complex); Upper Longwy, former fortress town built on geometrical lines within hexagonal perimeter wall fortified with bastions by Vauban (entry via France gate, town mus.). To NE, industrial quarter of Gouraincourt.
Vicinity ● 5 km N, *Mt. St. Martin*, noteworthy Romanesque church in Germanic style (deconsecrated), fine view. ● To SW, 9 km, *Cons-la-Grandville*, magnificent late-16c Ren. château (v.a., p.m., July 15–Aug. 26; for groups, a.m. on request); 9 km to SW, lovely 13c church at *Longuyon*.

Lons-le-Saunier
39 – Jura 26 B 2
Rue du Commerce, lined by 18c arcaded houses, links town hall (mus. of reg. archaeology and paintings, including four Courbet) and 18c hospital (noteworthy pharmacy with carved wood panelling, and laboratory) on Place de la Liberté. 11c St. Désiré, one of oldest buildings in Franche-Comté; lovely 11c crypt divided into three naves

with six vaulted bays each; 5c sarcophagus of St. Désiré. Spa building (salt water) and 17½-acre Parc des Bains, with two small lakes.
Vicinity ● 3 km SE, Montaigu; family home of Rouget de L'Isle (composer of the 'Marseillaise'), mus. (v.a.). ● 18 km NE, former Abbey of **Baume-les-Messieurs***
and *Cirque de Baume*.

Lorient
56 – Morbihan 15 – D 1
Important military and fishing port at end of vast bay. Centre of town, destroyed between 1940 and 1945, has been rebuilt in reg. style. R. bank of R. *Scorff* is lined by Arsenal military installations (open to French citizens only, May 15–Sept. 14); entrance is flanked by two elegant Louis XV-style pavilions. On hillock, late-18c Découverte tower (wide view) and two 17c Admiralty powder-mills, one of which houses naval mus. In town hall, mus. of reg. history and ethnography.
Vicinity ● 2 km S, Keroman, fishing port and important submarine base of *Ingénieur-Général-Stosskopf*, built by the Germans in 1941–1943 (v.a. during summer season). ● 14 km SW, out to sea, of which 6 km are within Lorient bay, excursion recommended to *Ile de Groix*, with stop at **Port-Louis***: bleak and jagged to N and W (port of *Port-Tudy*), sandy to E and S (lovely beach of Grands Sables, picturesque bay of *Locmaria*, site of Trou de l'Enfer); island contains many megaliths.

Loudun
86 – Vienne 23 – B 1
Old town, enclosed by boulevards,

has many old houses, inc. 16–17c Théophraste Renaudot house. Mid-14c church of St. Pierre, Ren. doorway. Charbonneau-Lassay mus.: local archaeology, ethnography and folklore. 14–16c church of St. Hilaire-du-Martray.
Vicinity ● 12 km SW, Ch. **d'Oiron***.
● 18 km SW, *St. Jouin-de-Marnes*, lovely 11–12c Romanesque church, notable for its vast dimensions (72 m. long, 15 m. high), its façades and its Angevin vaulting; 9 km to SW, *Airvault*, early-12c Romanesque church, large narthex leading into nave with 13c Angevin vaulting; remains of 15c cloister and 12c chapter-house of former abbey; 6.5 km to N, *St. Généroux*, church of Carolingian origin; 5 km to SW of Airvault, *St. Loup-Lamairé*, picturesque old town, many 15–16c houses in brick and half-timbering; Louis XIII-style château with 15c keep, unusual 15c court-room, three-tiered with half-timbered corbelling.

Louhans
71 – Saône-et-Loire 26 – A 2
Hospital has beautiful 17c dispensary containing earthenware jars from Lyons and Nevers. Grande-Rue is lined by 17 and 18c arcaded houses. 18c town hall.

Lourdes
65 – Hautes-Pyrénées 41 – B 2
The most famed pilgrimage site in Christendom is also a much appreciated tourist centre. The town, bathed by R. *Gave*, comprises an old part, huddled around the fortress, and the religious city. The castle, an impressive example of medieval military architecture, built on isolated 80 m.-high rock (reached by steps or a lift), houses Pyrenean mus. (v.a.), one of the

Lodève: *the tower of the old cathedral of St. Fulcran is the town's 'beacon', at confluence of R. Lergue and Soulondres.*

Lourmarin: *the château's ochre stone contrasts with the dark green of the cypresses and pines.*

most interesting and best presented reg. mus. in France; fine view from ramparts. The vast Esplanade des Processions leads to the Place du Rosaire, dominated by three shrines standing one above the other, the Rosary church, in neo-Byzantine style, the crypt and the neo-Goth. basilica (1876). Under esplanade: huge basilica of St. Pius X (1956–1959). To r. of shrines, on bank of R. *Gave*, grotto of Massabielle, where the Virgin appeared to Bernadette Soubirous in 1858. Pilgrims and tourists alike will be fascinated by Notre Dame mus., Bernadette mus. and her birthplace at the Moulin de Boly, and waxworks mus. (scenes from the lives of Christ and Bernadette). Above basilica, path winds along hillside to a monumental calvary.
Vicinity ● 3 km W, *Lac de Lourdes* (boat hire, motorboat trip round lake, pedalos, fishing, etc.). ● 15 km S, *Pic du Jer* funicular (departure every 30 min.); from upper station, path leads to top of mountain (948 m.); huge cross and viewing table. ● 7.5 km S, Pibeste cable car (1,383 m.); fine view.

Lourmarin
84 – Vaucluse   44 – A 1
The château, on small hill, consists of two parts: old, late 15 – early 16c castle to E, and, to W, main building, an elegant Ren. structure which houses Laurent Vibert foundation for artists and writers; inside

(v.a.; cl. Tues. in winter), interesting collections. Château is surrounded by terraced gardens, offering fine views. Philippe de Girard mus.
Vicinity ● To N, Lourmarin combe, a deep corrie separating large and small Lubéron mountain ranges (see **Lubéron***), leads to *Bonnieux* and **Apt***. ● 7 km NE, *Cucuron* (interesting church, belfry and keep). ● 4.5 km S, *Cadenet* ('Tambour d'Arcole' statue, 14c church).

Louveciennes
78 – Yvelines   11 – C 2
On hills overlooking l. bank of R. *Seine*. 12 and 13c church of St. Martin; interesting works of art. N.v.a. to 17 or 18c châteaux which can occasionally be glimpsed through their surrounding greenery: Ch. du Pont, Pavilions of Mme. du Barry, Voisins, etc. Remains of aqueduct which carried waters of Seine from the 'Machine de Marly' (demolished) to Versailles. Through a grille in Rue du Maréchal Joffre, you can glimpse the tiny rotunda-shaped temple in which the field-marshal is buried (d. 1931).
Vicinity ● To N, Bougival, also with many large and beautiful estates, still has some attractive rural parts; church has lovely Romanesque belfry and 13c choir.

Louviers
27 – Eure   11 – A 1
Crossed by a number of branches of R. *Eure*, town is dominated by

lovely 12–13c church of Notre Dame, ornamented with elegant profusion of 15–16c sculptures; r. side and porch, particularly elaborate, are masterpieces of Goth. Flamboyant style. In mus., interesting collection of archaeology and reg. folklore.
Vicinity ● 5 km S, *Acquigny*, lovely Ren. château on banks of *Eure*.

Lucéram
06 – Alpes-Maritimes   39 – B 3
Late-15c church, reconstructed 18c in Italian rococo style, contains important works of art, notably five 15–16c retables by Bréa family and rich church treasure. 15c chapel of St. Grat.
Vicinity ● 1.8 km, chapel of Notre Dame-de-Bon-Coeur, 15c frescos. ● 19 km SW, *Coaraze*, crafts and folk art centre huddled on a spur overlooking *Paillon* valley; to S, 'Route du Soleil' leads to *Contes*, also built on promontory; in late-16c church, one of major works of Nice school, the 'Retable de Ste. Madeleine', with two compartments (circa 1525); *Contes* is linked to Col de Nice, 14 km to NE, and to *Escarène*, by road which, to l., has one of most astonishing eyrie-like villages in reg.: Berre-les-Alpes, from which there is a really magnificent view.

Luçon
85 – Vendée   22 – D 2
13–14c Goth. cathedral of Notre Dame has late-17c Classical façade;

late-11c Romanesque gable on N transept; in choir, lovely mid-18c wood panelling, rococo stucco decoration in S transept; early-17c painted pulpit aka Richelieu's pulpit (he was Bishop of Luçon, 1608–1623). Bishop's palace surrounds Canons' cloister, which has three Goth. and Ren. galleries. Dumaine garden, typical of Napoleon III period.
Vicinity ● To S, *Marais Poitevin* (see **Niort***). ● To SW, *St. Michelen-l'Herm* (former abbey). *L'Aiguillon-sur-Mer* (centre for oyster farming and mussel breeding); to SE, *Pointe de l'Aiguillon* and to NW, *La Tranche-sur-Mer*, seaside resort among dunes planted with pines, on edge of enormous beach; centre of flowering-bulb industry (flower show in April). ● 16 km NE, *Ste. Hermine*, unusual monument to Clemenceau, depicting him at the front, surrounded by soldiers.

Lude (Le)
72 – Sarthe　　　　17 C 2
The château, one of most beautiful examples of French Renaissance, forms a square flanked by four huge round towers. Late-15c N wing has Goth. façade and S wing an elegant François I façade, decorated with sculptures and medallions. Château is surrounded by moat which has been turned into a garden. Terrace overlooking R. Loir. (V.a., p.m., Apr. 1–Sept. 30. Son et Lumière in summer.)
Vicinity ● To NE, *Champmarin* manor, Ren. (v.a. by arrangement only); *Aubigné-Racan*, 12 and 16c church.

Lunéville
54 – Meurthe-et-Moselle　13 – C 2
Early-18c château is entered through a large main courtyard; majestic main building is flanked by two small wings, separated from large wings framing courtyard by porticos; in centre of courtyard, equestrian statue of Napoleonic General de Lasalle who was killed at the Battle of Wagram; inside, mus.: Coptic art, historic souvenirs, pottery, 18–19c paintings and sculpture; interesting audio-visual display about complete works of Georges de La Tour (17c painter); Motorbike and Bicycle Mus. in annexe; elegant chapel (concert hall). Behind château, lovely formal gardens, or Promenade des Bosquets, dating from early 18c. Mid-18c church of St. Jacques is fine example of rococo style; inside, Regency-style wood panelling, carved organ-loft and organ-chest. Town hall and library now occupy buildings of former 18c abbey of St. Rémy.

LUBÉRON (Mt.)
84 – Vaucluse　　　38 – A 3 – 44 – A 1
N100, from **Apt*** in W, allows one fine view of Julien bridge across R. *Coulon*, one of best preserved Roman bridges in France; Romanesque church of *Goult* (2 km to NW, Carolingian church of St. Pantaléon surrounded by sarcophagi) and 17c Notre Dame-de-Lumière, in lovely park (well-attended pilgrimage). From there, continue SW to **Oppède-le-Vieux*** and **Ménerbes***, D109 leads, 6 km to E, to *Lacoste*: 15c château, partly ruined (v.a. by permission); 3 km to NW of *Lacoste*, via St. Véran (former Romanesque abbey of St. Hilaire), one can go to *Bonnieux*: picturesque village rising in tiers on a promontory; remains of ramparts; behind 13–15c church, on top of hill, fine view; from *Bonnieux*, to N, D36 and D943, winding and abrupt, lead to **Apt*** along a picturesque route (St. Symphorien priory, Buoux fort); to S, **Lourmarin*** via magnificent Lourmarin combe and **La Tourd'Aigues***. ● Finest route of all (magnificent panoramas) follows Peak Forest Road from **Cavaillon*** to **Bonnieux**, across high plains and Cèdres massif.

Lunéville: *the early 17c château, inspired by Versailles. In the main courtyard is a statue of General de Lasalle.*

Le Lude: *the powerful but ornate François I façade is the most impressive part of this Gothic building.*

Luxeuil-les-Bains
70 – Haute-Saône   20 – C 1

Well-known spa town. Jouffroy house is an elegant 15c building with mid-16c bartizan and unusual sculptures; inside (v.a.), lovely 16c fireplaces. Renaissance François I house, used by abbot of Luxeuil. 16–18c abbot's palace is now town hall. Basilica of St. Pierre, former 14c abbey church. 14–15c cloister in pink sandstone. 15c Tour des Echevins mus. (aka Square House, cl. Tues.). Mus.: collection of Gallo-Roman funerary steles.

Vicinity ● Except to SW, town is surrounded by forests, which offer pleasant walks. ● 15.5 km NE, *Faucogney*, one-time fortified town, in picturesque setting dominated by Mt. St. Martin, enormous sandstone rock with chapel on top; between *Faucogney* and *Le Thillot* lies Esmoulières plateau, dotted with lakes, part cultivated, part wild.

Luynes
37 – Indre-et-Loire   17 – C 2

Lovely 13–15c medieval castle, which dominates town (n.v.a.). 16c houses. 15c timber-framed market buildings. Troglodytic houses. 1.5 km to NE, ruins of Gallo-Roman aqueduct.

Luzech
46 – Lot   36 – A2

Unusual site in meandering loop of R. *Lot*, whose isthmus is only 200 m. wide at its narrowest part. Old town is most picturesque, with narrow streets crossed by arcades, and old houses. Ruins of castle, with 13c keep, on an isolated rock. 12c chapel of Pénitents Bleus. 14c church of St. Pierre. To N, remains of oppidum of Impernal. To S, Pistoule promontory.

Luz-St. Sauveur
65 – Hautes-Pyrénées   41 – B 3

Small mountain city. Luz (685 m. alt.), together with St. Sauveur – where main hotels are situated – forms a typically Pyrenean township. 12–13c church of Luz, fortified 14c, is surrounded by a crenellated perimeter wall. Romanesque side door with sculpted tympanum. Inside, small local art mus. (statues, reliquaries and objets d'art from 12 to 18c). In 17c chapel of Notre Dame-des-Sept-Douleurs, collection of local archaeology, ethnography, paintings, etc.

Vicinity ● To NW, towards *Pierrefitte-Nestalas*, N21 follows lovely *Gorge de Luz*. ● To SW, N21 crosses Napoleon bridge (1861), which rises 65 m. above Gave de Pau and enters

Luz-St. Sauveur: *'Between Luz and Gavarnie lies hell, a primitive chaos'* wrote George Sand. The Hautes-Pyrénées national park is full of such wild and beautiful landscapes. ▲

The Cirque de Gavarnie is famed for its torrents. ▼

narrow *Gorge de St. Sauveur*; beyond Pragnères (electricity power station, v.a.), *Gèdre*; to SE, N21D leads to chapel of Notre Dame-de-Héas (1,522 m.) and then to Cirque de Troumouse; from Gèdre, rejoin N21, via rocky mass of Coumély, to reach *Gavarnie*, small mountain village; 14c church contains interesting examples of folk art; excursion highly recommended to *Cirque de Gavarnie*; the immense walls of snow, rising in perpendicular tiers, and their grandiose cascades are awe-inspiring.

Lyons
69 – Rhône   31 – D 1
At confluence of R. *Rhône* and *Saône*, it is one of France's richest cities of artistic interest; its old quarters (Croix-Rousse, St. Jean) are no less impressive than its monuments. ● Place Bellecour, one of largest squares in France (310 by 200 m.), is lined on E and W sides by symmetrical Louis XVI-style façades; in middle, equestrian statue of Louis XIV. Between Place Bellecour and Place Carnot (Perrache station) lies Ainay quarter, with local decorative arts mus., Mus. Historique des Tissus and Romanesque basilica of St. Martin-d'Ainay. From Place Bellecour, Rue du Président-Herriot and Rue de la République both lead to Place des Terreaux (in centre, monumental fountain by Bartholdi), on which stand 17c town hall and fine arts mus. (St. Pierre palace).

● Croix-Rousse quarter: attractive walks from Place Tolozan along narrow alleyways known as 'traboules', which, with steep uphill streets called 'montées', afford many different views of this old silk-weavers' quarter, whose tall buildings, with myriad windows, dominate Lyons. Remains of Roman amphitheatre of Trois-Gaules in Botanic Gardens. Church of St. Bruno-des-Chartreux is interesting example of 17c baroque architecture and ornamentation. Rue d'Isly: unusual 'Canuts' museum (local term for silk-weavers).

● St. Jean quarter, or 'Old Lyons', lies along R. *Saône* below Fourvière hill. Rue St. Jean, its main street, lined by Goth. or Ren. houses, is one of most magnificent examples of 15–16c urban grouping. No. 8, Rue Juiverie, Bulliond mansion (gallery by Philibert Delorme); No. 4, Patherin mansion (masterpiece of Lyons version of Renaissance architecture); Rue de Gadagne (No. 8, Gadagne mansion, houses town hist. mus. and puppet mus., cl. Tues.). Place du Change (Loge du Change),

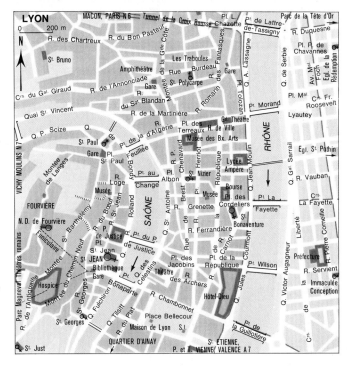

Lyons: *the old quarter is full of 'traboules' and 'montées'; street corners offer many an unusual or unexpected view.*

Places du Gouvernement and de la Baleine, Rue des Trois-Maries, etc. St. Jean cathedral is flanked to r. by wall of 11c cloister belonging to former 12c choir school ('La Manécanterie'); the bases of the façade doorways still have 350 tiny but very expressive Goth. bas-reliefs; inside, 12 and 13c stained-glass windows. To r. of cathedral, Rue Mourguet leads to picturesque Place de la Trinité.

● Fourvière hill: reached by funicular (from station on Place St. Jean) or up winding 'montées', from which there are fine views over town. Basilica of Notre Dame-de-Fourvière is typical of the architecture and decorative eclecticism of late 19c; interior's ornamentation is overpoweringly ornate; vast panorama of town from its terrace. Rue de l'Antiquaille leads to Magneval park (v.a.; cl. Sat. and Sun. in winter), where excavations have uncovered two Roman theatres, the large theatre (108 m. in diameter) and the little theatre (or Odéon), as well as a commercial quarter and the foundations of a temple of Cybele. Mus. of Gallo-Roman Civilization, built into hillside, houses largest collection of inscriptions in France.

● Principal museums: Fine arts (St. Pierre palace, or Palace of the Arts), former 17c Benedictine abbey. Large collection of sculptures (Greek, medieval and Ren.) and

paintings (Rhenish, Dutch, Italian and French, 19c Lyons school); works by Perugino, Gérard David, Pourbus, Veronese, Tintoretto, El Greco, Cranach, Rembrandt, Zurbaran, Rubens, Jordaens, Boucher, Prud'hon, Delacroix, Géricault, Corot, Courbet, Monticelli, Manet, Renoir, Van Gogh, Gauguin, Rodin, Bourdelle. Important 20c group inc. Bonnard, Matisse, Braque, Picasso, and contemporary movements. Noteworthy gallery of objets d'art. Reg. Mus. of Decorative Arts and Mus. Historique des Tissus (cl. Mon.), in two beautiful 18c mansions. Mus. des Hospices Civils in hospital (remarkable 17c dispensary). Guimet mus. (Far Eastern and natural history exhibits). Printing and Banking Mus. A visit to the Puppet Mus. (Gadagne mansion) should be rounded off by performance of French equivalent of Punch and Judy (Guignol) in Palais du Conservatoire, Rue Louis-Carrand, on Wed. and Sun. p.m. Tête-d'Or park, on r. bank of Rhône: magnificent conservatories, enormous rose garden, zoo. Also recommended: sizeable African mus., Mus. of Resistance and Deportation, Natnl. Foundation for Photography in Lumière house in aptly-named Rue du Premier-Film.

Vicinity ● 6 km NW, Barbe island, in R. *Saône*, country restaurants, shady walks, chapel and remains

of an old monastery, 16c Provost's House. ● 11 km N, Ch. de *Rochetaillée*, in huge park; Henri Malartre automobile mus. (v.a.). ● Tour of Lyons' stretch of *Mt. d'Or*, to N, via St. Cyr-au-Mt. d'Or, *Mt. Cindre* (467 m.), Mt. Thou (612 m., fine view). *Poleymieux-au-Mt. d'Or* (Ampère house: electricity mus.). ● 10 km W, *Charbonnières-les-Bains*: spa buildings, casino, park, racecourse; 17 km NW, *L'Arbresle*; Dominican convent of Ste. Marie-de-La-Tourette, one of last buildings by Le Corbusier (constructed 1957–1959). ● 10 km SW via Oullins and Yzeron valley, remains of *Aqueducs Romains* (Roman aqueducts) of Beaunant.

Lyons-la-Forêt
27 – Eure   **5 – A 3**
In middle of Lyons state forest. 18c covered market, Romanesque and Renaissance church.
Vicinity ● *Forêt Domaniale de Lyons* (41 sq. miles) is loveliest beech forest in France (hunt meetings, Sept. 15–Apr. 15). ● To S, ruins of 13c *Abbaye de Mortemer* (v.a.). ● To W, in *Andelle* valley, Vascoeuil, château (internatnl. cultural centre) and gardens (reconstructed half-timbered cottages), tiny Michelet mus.; *Fleury-sur-Andelle*; ruins of 13c abbey of Fontaine-Guérard (v.a.; p.m., Apr. 1–Oct. 31; cl. Mon.).

High over Lyons, Notre Dame-de-Fourvière was built after the 1870 war in fulfilment of a vow.

M

Mâcon
71 – Saône-et-Loire   25 – D 3
Birthplace of poet Lamartine; it has several aristocratic residences: Hôtel Senecé, early 18c (Lamartine mus.); Hôtel de la Baume-Montrevel, in Louis XVI style (town hall); Hôtel d'Ozeray, where the poet lived: Hôtel de Pierreclos (1660), etc. The municipal mus. is in former Ursuline convent, 17c; has 17–20c Dutch, Flemish and French painting, prehist. coll. In Hôtel-Dieu, Louis XV apothecary, with large collection of 18c earthenware.
Vicinity ● 12 km NW, *Milly-Lamartine*, where Lamartine spent his childhood; to W, *St. Pont*, his favourite home; Cluniac Romanesque church; the poet and his wife lie in neighbouring chapel; château, renovated in 19c, houses mementoes of the poet (v.a., a.m., March 1–Nov. 15, exc. Sun.). ● To SW, vine-growing villages of *Pouilly*, *Fuissé*, Chasselas (white wines): *Solutré*, important prehist. site (100,000 skeletons of horses found there); Cros du Charnier excavations, mus.; good views from summit of the Roche (495 m.). ● Tour of Beaujolais wine reg. (see **Villefranche-sur-Saône**).

Magny-en-Vexin
95 – Val-d'Oise   11 – B 1
Early-16c church with Ren. portal; inside, monumental 16c baptismal font. very ornate, and interesting works of art (14c Virgin; tomb statues of Villeroy family). Old quarters around church have several houses from 16 and 18c.
Vicinity ● Tour of *Aubette* valley. ● 7.5 km to SW, Ch. de Villarceaux, 18c (n.v.a.). ● 7 km to W, Ch. d'Ambleville, Ren. and 17c; fine formal gardens.

Maguelonne
34 – Hérault   43 – B 1
4 km SW of *Palavas-les-Flots*, between the sea and an inlet, fmr. cath. of St. Pierre, Romanesque, with fortifications, overlooks the Domaine de Maguelonne (vineyards and grounds). The single nave, with broken barrel-vaulting, is divided halfway up by a 16c stone gallery. In choir, 15c tombs. 5c sarcophagus and gravestones. Ruins of bishop's palace and chapterhouse.
Vicinity ● Palavas-les-Flots, fishing village and lively seaside resort, vast beach; scenic route follows the sea for 19 km, passing **La Grande-Motte***, as far as *Grau-du-Roi*; between *Carnon-Plage* and **La Grande-Motte***, enormous *Maugio lake* aka Étang de l'Or; sanctuary for multitudes of seabirds.

Maîche
25 – Doubs   20 – D 3
Summer holiday resort and winter sports centre, on plateau framed by two valleys. Old houses. Enormous 18c church; ruins of feudal castle. Clock making.
Vicinity ● Pleasant forest walks (superb pine plantations). ● To E, via *Damprichard*, the *Goumois* corniche (see **St. Hippolyte***). ● To SE, at *Fournet-Blancheroche*, the Échelles de la Mort; from belvedere (difficult climb up iron ladders), superb panorama over R. *Doubs* gorges. ● To SW, *Dessoubre* valley

Maîche: *outside the town, see the church of Bréseux with Manessier's dazzling stained-glass windows.*

(bowl of **Consolation***). Les Bréseux: in church, fine modern stained-glass windows (1950).

Maillezais
85 – Vendée   23 – A 2
In heart of the Marais Poitevin, grandiose ruins of abbey of St. Pierre (v.a.: Son et Lumière in summer): built on an island in 11c, it was visited by Rabelais and writer-warrior Agrippa d'Aubigné, who built the rectangular enceinte at end of 16c; all that remains of 11 and 14c abbey church are the narthex, two square towers and first four bays of the N wall (beautiful Romanesque capitals); floor of the Romanesque abbey and cloister foundations were excavated in 1955; two buildings, set at right angles to one another, make up the 14c Goth. abbey (v.a. to enormous vaulted cellar, fmr. kitchen, small mus., refectory and, above them, large infirmary, with timbered roof. In the town, interesting 12c church of St. Nicolas, fine portal.
Vicinity ● From abbey's quayside, boat trips around the marshes (Easter to Sept.).

Maintenon (Château)
28 – Eure-et-Loir   11 – B 2
Magnificent Ren. and 17c building,

Maillezais: *only flat-bottomed boats can negotiate the innumerable waterways of the Marais Poitevin – marshes, known as the 'Green Venice', which cover more than 37,000 acres.*

Maintenon: *In the château's main courtyard, the severe 17c façade contrasts sharply with the ornate Renaissance buildings, in brick and stone.*

Mantes: *the Gothic cathedral has three fine sculpted portals.*

surrounded by flowing water (v.a., p.m., exc. Tues., Sun. and public hols., Apr. 1–Oct. 31; Sat. and Sun., Nov. 1–Mar. 31). Apartments of Mme de Maintenon, 16c oratory (beautiful stained glass), vast gallery (portraits of the de Noailles family). The grounds, criss-crossed with waterways, have as backdrop an unfinished aqueduct, originally intended to bring water from R. *Eure* to Versailles.
Vicinity • 8 km N, *Nogent-le-Roi*, picturesque old township, 16c timbered houses, fine Goth. Flamboyant and Ren. church, with 16c stained-glass windows.

Maisons-Laffitte (Château)
78 – Yvelines   11 – C 1
One of the most beautiful châteaux in Paris region, mid-17c masterpiece by François Mansart; E façade overlooks R. *Seine* and formal flowerbeds; beautifully decorated Classical int.; chambers of the Comte d'Artois (future Charles X), on ground floor, are in Louis XVI style (circa (1780). Bedchamber of Marshal Lannes (d. 1809) yet another Napoleonic general (v.a., p.m., cl. Tues.; guided tour Sun., 15.30).

Malesherbes
45 – Loiret   11 – C 3
15c château (v.a., cl. Tues.) has chapel with François d'Entraygues's mausoleum (his statue turns its back on that of his unfaithful wife); in the outbuildings, 'Chateaubriand's House', Redevances (lit. 'dues') Tower, tithe attics and imposing dovecote.
Vicinity • To N and S, tour of green and wooded *Essonne* valley.

• Buthiers rocks (climb). • 2 km N, Ch. de Rouville, impressive Goth. building flanked by towers (v.a. to exterior). • 12 km S, *Puiseaux*, fine 13c church with unusual spiral-framed spire.

Malle (Château)
33 – Gironde   35 – A 1
At *Preignac*, one of Bordeaux reg.'s most architecturally harmonious châteaux. Charming early-17c construction, built in Italian style, in middle of vineyards. Attractive formal gardens (v.a., cl. Wed., Apr. to mid-Oct.).
Vicinity • 6 km NE, *Verdelais*, 17c basilica of Notre Dame (local pilgrimage); in graveyard, tomb of painter Toulouse-Lautrec (d. 1901). • 8 km SW of *Langon*, Ch. de *Roquetaillade* (see **Bazas***).

Manosque
04 – Alpes-de-Haute-Provence
                         38 – B 3
Small town at foot of hills covered with olive trees. It is ringed by boulevards and remains of ramparts: two gates of the old ramparts survive, Porte Saunerie and Porte Soubeyran, 14c. Church of St. Sauveur has Romanesque nave and transept, 17c side aisles. Church of Notre Dame, also of Romanesque origin, had new vaulting in 16 and 17c; inside, unusual 12c Black Virgin.
Vicinity • 1 km SW, Chapel of St. Pancrace (good view). • To S, *Cadarache* dam, *Verdon* canal. • To N, **Forcalquier***, **Ganagobie*** Priory and **St. Michel-l'Observatoire***.

Mans (Le)
72 – Sarthe   17 – C 1
St. Julien cathedral dominates town

Le Mans: *a view of the racing circuit where the famed 24-Hour race takes place every June.*

and picturesque Cité quarter; superb Goth. and Romanesque building; 13c choir is the most interesting part; fine series of stained-glass windows from 12, 13 and 15c; 16c tapestries; in Chapelle des Fonts, imposing Italian Ren. marble tombs. Old part of Le Mans is worth a long visit; in Place du Cardinal-Grente, bishop's palace is in charming Hôtel du Grabatoire (Ren.); Rue de la Reine-Bérengère has numerous old houses, inc. that of Queen Berengaria (mus., ceramics, local hist.); the Grande-Rue is lined with beautiful 15–16c houses. Main churches: Notre Dame-de-la-Couture. 11, 12 and 13c fmr. abbey church, fine late-13c portal; vast Anjou Romanesque nave; Ste. Jeanne-d'Arc (fmr. Hôpital de Coëffort), Romanesque; 12c unusual capitals inside; Notre Dame-du-Pré, late 11–12c Romanesque; 18c Visitation. Mus. de Tessé (15–19c Italian and French painting, large collection of ceramics, sculpture and objets d'art): its most prized possession is the 'Plaque d'Email Champlevé (plaque with champlevé enamelling) from Geoffrey Plantagenet's tomb, dating from 1151 (v.a.).
Vicinity ● 4 km S, *racing circuit* of the Le Mans' 24-hour race; 2 km farther on, Mus. de l'Automobile (cl. Tues.). ● 3.5 km E, fmr. *Abbaye de l'Épau*, 13c, church, chapterhouse, storeroom, kitchen, etc. (v.a.). ● Rec. trip, to NW, to the *'Alpes mancelles'* (see **Alençon***).

Mantes-la-Jolie
78 – Yvelines   11 – B 1
The late 12, early 13c church of Notre Dame is one of finest Goth. buildings in Ile-de-France; the central portal of the façade, dedicated to glorification of the Virgin, is very unusual; inside, beautiful Chapelle de Navarre, 16c. Two gates, Porte aux Prêtres and Porte de l'Étape, are interesting remains of the ramparts. At Duhamel mus., collection of ceramics. 12–13c church of *Gassicourt*.
Vicinity ● To W, *Rosny-sur-Seine* late 15, early 16c château built by Sully; handsome apartments, mementoes of Duchesse de Berry (v.a. only in Aug.); from the Rolleboise corniche, vast panorama over *Seine* valley.

Marcilhac-sur-Célé
46 – Lot   36 – B 1
Remains of abbey include the enceinte, entrance gate and postern, the Maison du Roi and Romanesque abbey church rebuilt in 15–16c (oddly archaic 10c sculpted tympanum). Present church is flanked by 12c rib-vaulted chapterhouse (unusual Romanesque capitals).

Vicinity ● 3 km NW, Bellevue grottoes aka caves of Marcilhac.

Marennes
17 – Charente-Maritime   28 – D 1
Built on fmr. island in Gulf of Saintonge, France's 'oyster capital' can be seen from a long way off, thanks to fine Goth. belfry and spire with curled leaf decoration (crockets), altogether 85 m. high. Marennes cultivates both Portugaise and Japanese oysters. Along R. *Seudre* estuary can be seen the strange grids of the oyster beds ('claires'), special basins in which the oysters are fattened, 'mature' and finally become ready to eat.
Vicinity ● 2 km W, Marennes-Plage. ● 5 km NW, *Bourcefranc*, important oyster cultivation centre; 1 km farther on, *Le Chapus*, busy harbour opposite island of **Oléron***; 13c fort, oyster-breeding exhibitions in summer. ● 6.5 km N, **Brouage***. ● 1.5 km N, Ch. de la Gataudière Louis XV style (v.a. Sun. and public hols., March 1–May 31 and Oct. 1–Nov. 30). ● On other bank of the *Seudre*, to S, *La Tremblade* oyster centre.

Marly-le-Roi
78 – Yvelines   11 – C 2
Of Louis XIV's magnificent château here, all that remains are the foundations in the centre of the grounds (v.a.), three ornamental lakes and the imposing Bassin de l'Abreuvoir; at the Grille Royale,

also in the grounds, a promenade mus. Marly-le-Roi to Louveciennes (every afternoon exc. Mon. and Tues.). Hist. of the two towns in documents, paintings, etc. Church of St. Vigor, designed by Mansart.
Vicinity ● Marly forest (8 sq. miles), pleasant walks. ● At Port-Marly, Ch. de Monte-Cristo, baroque construction by Alexandre Dumas (1848), overlooks the N13 (guided visits, Sun. p.m.).

Marmoutier
67 – Bas-Rhin   14 – A 2
Fmr. Benedictine abbey church is one of the most interesting examples of Romanesque art in Alsace, especially the mid-12c façade, in red sandstone from the Vosges; inside, rich ensemble of Louis XV panelling in choir.

Marne-la-Vallée
77 – Seine-et-Marne   11 – D 2
One of the five 'new towns' in the

Marmoutier: an archaic 'relief', below 7c vaulting, has been incorporated in the West façade of the Romanesque abbey church.

Ile-de-France; its different districts have interesting, and often original, examples of contemporary architecture, notably the Palacio d'Abrazas, a colossal and oppressive building by Ricardo Bofill, and the theatrical Place Picasso, with its two 17-storey disc-shaped apartment blocks by Manolo Nuñez. France's Disneyland is to be built next to it.
Vicinity ● 2 km to N, Ch. de **Champs***. ● 7.5 km to E, Ch. de **Guermantes***. 7.5 km farther on, Ch. de Ferrières, at Ferrières-en-

Brie, built in 1885, for Baron James de Rothschild; sumptuous Second-Empire interiors. (v.a., cl. Mon. and Tues.; but Sun. only from Oct. to May).

Marseilles: panorama of the Vieux-Port, cathedral and Joliette Basin from Notre Dame-de-la-Garde. The Fort of St. Jean, dominated by the King René Tower, guards the entrance to the Vieux-Port.

Marseilles
13 – Bouches-du-Rhône   44 – A2

The oldest of France's big cities, it is first and foremost a port. The modern docks are to NE. Take a boat trip to where the *Rove* flows underground; ferry excursions; walks on the sea wall.

● The Vieux-Port, where yachts, fishing boats and cabin cruisers are all moored together, is one of the best-known harbours in the Mediterranean; overlooked by the old town and framed by the 17c Forts of St. Nicolas and St. Jean (15c square tower), the Quai du Port runs alongside it to the E. Here stands the late-17c baroque town hall building (one of the rare survivors from a district destroyed by the Germans in 1943); next door is 16c Maison Diamantée (Mus. of Old Marseilles). Mus. of the Roman Docks (ancient commercial links; v.a., cl. Tues. and Wed. a.m.), has finds recovered in excavations carried out in this district (the imposing Roman docks of Massalia, excavated in 1947, are displayed in their original site). 17c Hôtel-Dieu and Cour des Accoules: Chapelle du Calvaire, rotunda, crowned by a cupola (inside, unusual carved scenes in artificial grottoes), large calvary and 14c Accoules Bell. 17 and 18c houses, picturesque old streets. La Major, the city's late-19c cath., in Byzan-

tine-Romanesque style, incorporates part of the original 12c cath. on its r. side, notable example of Provençal Romanesque architecture (apply to caretaker). The Panier quarter, whose tall, blackish houses seem to be linked by lines of multi-coloured washing, incorporates the Vieille-Charité, built between 1640 and 1720, designed by Puget (exhibition hall and arts centre).

● On other side of the Vieux-Port, where fish restaurants abound, old part of town with several 18c mansions (notably in Rue Sainte) as well

as fortress-like 13–14c basilica of St. Victor, built above 5c catacombs (cl. Sun.), one of oldest Gallic Christian monuments. Basilica of Notre Dame-de-la-Garde, late 19c, with wide views from its 162 m. alt., is popular place of pilgrimage. ● In city centre, the Bourse (Stock Exchange), on the famous Canebière, houses interesting naval mus. (cl. Tues. and a.m. Wed.). In commercial centre, mus. of Marseilles hist. Jardin des Vestiges (remains of the ancient city preserved in situ), leading to rooms with displays of documents, sculpture, ceramics,

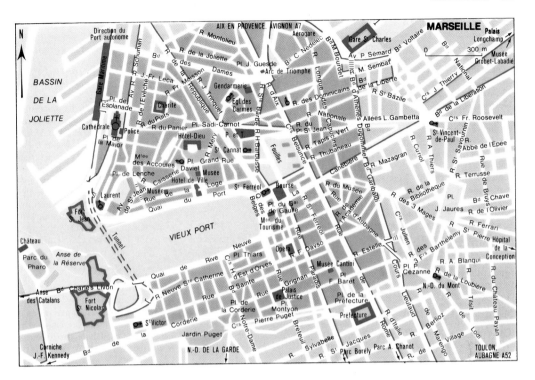

Map of MARSEILLE

glassware, etc., illustrating history of Marseilles. Rare preserved wreck of 3c merchant ship. Palais de Longchamp, enormous building in Second-Empire hyper-baroque style, overloaded with sculpture and enlivened by fountains, houses fine arts mus. in its l. wing (cl. Tues. and a.m. Wed.). Down main stairway, paintings to the glory of Marseilles; rich collection of paintings by Perugino, Rubens, Ribera, Zurbarán, Hubert Robert, Chardin, Courbet, Chassériau, Corot, Millet,

Martel: *the church and its belfry, a veritable keep, with narrow loopholes.*

etc.; large groups of work by Pierre Puget and Daumier; 18–19c Provençal painters; Pierre Guerre donation of African sculpture. Cantini mus. (cl. Tues. and a.m. Wed.): modern and contemporary art. Galerie de la Faïence: extensive range of Provençal pottery from 17–18c. Natural hist. mus. Zoo.
● Other mus. (same days as for Mus. des Beaux-Arts): Grobet-Labadié mus.: furniture, pottery, tapestries, objets d'art, 16–18c. Galerie des Transports, housed in former tram station (v.a., cl. Sun.). Borély mus.: archaeology (Roquepertuse portico, 3–2c BC), Egyptian art, 17 and 18c drawings. ● *J F Kennedy* corniche, magnificent promenade following coast from Catalans cove (beach), crossing picturesque Auffes vale, cutting across Point of Endoume (aquarium), to huge Borély park; after Prado, the route is continued by road which winds round Cap Croisette, at tip of Marseilleveyre massif, and ends (12.5 km farther on), at the Port de *Callelongue*.
● *Ch. d'If*, embark at Quai des Belges, in Vieux-Port; the island, fortified in early 17c, has mid-16c castle used as state prison. Alexandre Dumas brought it fame by using it as setting for episodes of his *Count of Monte Cristo*.
Vicinity ● To W, *Berre lake*, **Arles*** and the **Camargue***. ● To N, **Aix-en-Provence***. ● To NE, *Chaîne de l'Étoile*: ridge of limestone massif, 731 m., at its highest point; footpaths lead to the Pilon du Roi, 670 m., Signal de l'Étoile and l'Éto-

ile summit, 652 m. and Grande-Étoile, 590 m. ● To E, via *Aubagne* and *Gémenos*, **Ste. Baume***. ● To SE, Marseilleveyre massif, the *Calanques*, **Cassis***, and the Côte.

Martel
46 – Lot   **30 – A3**
This little town, which has kept its old character, has several 14, 15 and 16c houses. Fine 15c fortified church, with Romanesque portal (sculpted tympanum). 14c Hôtel de la Raymondie (mus.) has imposing 17 and 18c carved wood chimneypieces. Old covered market and remains of 13c outer walls.
Vicinity ● *Montvalent* basin (5.5 km SE) and R. *Dordogne* valley; Gluges, backed by tall cliffs: partly subterranean Romanesque church; 1 km to E, Copeyre belvedere (magnificent view); on a rise, Ch. de Mirandol (fine Ren. staircase).

Martigues
13 – Bouches-du-Rhône   **44 – A 2**
Once known as the 'Venice of Provence', its character has been radically changed, regrettably, by industrial development of the reg. Town is divided into three districts by canals. In centre, Quartier de l'Ile: picturesque quays; from St Sebastian Bridge, fine view of the multicoloured boats and brightly painted houses; Corinthian façade of 17c Madeleine church is reflected in the 'Miroir aux Oiseaux' (lit. 'The Bird Mirror'); beautiful 17c town hall. To N, Quartier de Ferrières: Chapelle de la Miséricorde, Ziem mus. (archaeology, folklore, 19–20c

Provençal paintings). To S, Quartier de Jonquières: 17c church of St-Geniès; Chapelle de l'Annonciade: wooden ceiling, with carved gilt interlacing, is decorated with three paintings.
Vicinity ● 3.5 km NW, chapel of Notre Dame-des-Marins, on a height overlooking *Martigues*; magnificent panorama. ● To SE, the D 5 crosses, then follows, the *Chaîne de l'Estaque* via *Sausset-les-Pins*, *Carry-le-Rouet* and *Le Rove*; beautiful view of the **Marseilles*** roads; the N 568B goes round the *Estaque* roads. ● To W, *Port-de-Bouc*, **Fos-sur-Mer***, and *Golfe de Fos*. ● To NE, *Berre Lake*, covering almost 58 sq. miles, in typically Provençal countryside (though much altered by industry); you can travel round the lake from *Martigues* through *St. Mitre-les-Remparts* (1 km to NNW archaeological excavations at **St. Blaise***), *Istres*, *Miramas*, **St. Chamas***, Mauran (Gallo-Roman remains), *Berre-l'Étang* and *Marignane*.

Martres-Tolosane
31 – Haute-Garonne 41 – D 2
Six Gallo-Roman villas have been excavated in the area around this little city, renowned for its potteries. The largest villa is at Chiragan, 2c; numerous works of art discovered there, among them a group of Roman busts in marble (now in St. Raymond mus. in Toulouse).
Vicinity ● 4 km E, Palaminy, many old houses and fortified gate of château astride the road. ● 10 km SW, *St. Martory*; 18c bridge is flanked by two gates of same period and a 15c cross.

Marvejols
48 – Lozère 37 – A 1
Old town with narrow streets, still huddled behind ramparts; three 14c fortified gates, flanked by machicolated towers and several 17c houses and mansions. Worth noting are two works by the sculptor Auricoste: the *Bête du Gévaudan*, Place des Cordeliers, and statue of *Henri IV* in front of the Porte de Soubeyran. Archaeology mus.
Vicinity ● To N, gorges and viaduct of the *Crueize*, via Colagne valley. ● 16 km NW, 16–17c Ch. de la Beaume in slate-covered granite (v.a.). ● To NW, cross the *Aubrac* mountains as far as the *Déroc waterfall* (30 m. high), the *Salhiens Lake* and **Aubrac***. ● 18 km SW, picturesque village of *La Canourgue* at foot of cliffs of the *Sauveterre causse*: 12 and 14c church, many old houses.

Mas-d'Azil (Grotto)
09 – Ariège 42 – A 3
One of the most interesting natural features in the Midi. Entrance to this vast tunnel, 420 m. long, is enormous arcade, 80 m. high; four floors of galleries are visitable. Their walls have many carvings and drawings of prehist. animals. In one room, exhibition of some of the finds. Gallery of the Bears (skulls of bears and bones of mammoths recovered from the caverns). 3c Christian chapel, refuge in the rocks for the Cathars, then for Protestants in 18c. In town, small mus. of prehist.

Mas Soubeyran (Le)
30 – Gard 37 – B 3
Mus. du Désert is a Protestant Mecca (v.a. March–Nov.). It is in house of Protestant, Roland, of whom there are many souvenirs. Displays illustrate history of Protestantism in France. Reconstruction of 18c Cévennes interior.

Maubeuge
59 – Nord 6 – B 1
Church of St. Pierre (1958) is interesting example of modern religious architecture. Old canonesses' chapterhouse (Henri-Boez mus.). Porte de Mons, main part of enceinte fortified by Vauban (1685). Zoo park, in wooded site.

Maule
78 – Yvelines 11 – B 1
Church of St. Nicolas: Ren. belfry and 11c crypt. Local mus. and Mus. du Vélocipède (bicycle).

Mauléon-Licharre
64 – Pyrénées-Atlantiques 40 – D 2
Little town in green valley. Hôtel d'Andurrain, fine Ren. edifice with four corner towers; interior has kept its period feel (v.a. p.m. in summer; exc. rainy days). Remains of 15c castle; fine view from parapet walk. In fmr. Trinité abbey, mus. of historical research and archaeology.
Vicinity ● 13 km S, via Saison valley or the *Gave de Mauléon* (mountain stream), *Tardets-Sorholus*; road continues across the upper Soule through *Laguinge* and *Licq-Athérey*; at the hydroelectric station, a fork in the road: to r., *Larrau*, via valley of Gave de Larrau; to SW, *Pic d'Orhy* (2,016 m.); on l., *Gorges de Kakouetta* and *Ste. Engrâce*, Romanesque church with historiated capitals.

Mauriac
15 – Cantal 30 – C 3
12c church of Notre Dame-des-Miracles, the most beautiful Romanesque church in Cantal reg. Beside it, small 14c lantern to the dead. Superb panorama from the Placette.
Vicinity ● 10 km NW, via *Chalvignac*, the *Aigle dam*, 290 m. wide and 90 m. high. ● 9 km SE, *Anglards-de-Salers*: Romanesque church with three naves and three apses topped by a cupola; 18 km SE, **Salers***. From *Anglards-de-Salers*, to E, *Vallée du Falgoux*, one of the Auvergne's most extraordinary valleys; the most impressive part is St. Vincent's Gorge; the *Falgoux* lies at entrance to natural bowl dominated by Cantal's biggest mountains; the road (D 680) climbs up to the *Puy Mary* (1,787 m.).

Mayenne
53 – Mayenne 10 – A 3
Bridge-village previously in shadow of 11c castle, ruins (vast panorama). 12–16c basilica of Notre Dame.
Vicinity ● Good base for tours of Mayenne forest, to W. ● To NE, Ch. de *Lassay**. ● To SE, *Jublains*, ruins of 3c Roman fort (entrenched camp); *Ch. du Rocher* (see **Évron***).

Mazamet
81 – Tarn 42 – C 1
Large industrial town. 'Mémoire de la Terre' mus. in Maison Fuzier.
Vicinity ● Good base for trips in and around the *Montagne Noire*, principally via D 118, which runs to **Carcassonne***, 47 km S, through Les Martys and *Cuxac-Cabardès*. (Two excursions: to W, Fontiers-Cabardès and *St. Denis*; to E, *Mas-Cabardès*, St. Pierre-de-Val, etc.). Road first traverses lush green forest scenery; then, after *Cuxac*, it descends through scrubland and pine groves to **Carcassonne*** (fine views over the Pyrenees). ● 18 km NW, **Castres***.

Meaux
77 – Seine-et-Marne 11 – D 1
St. Étienne cathedral is imposing 13c Goth. building, renovated in 15c, with Goth. Flamboyant façade and towers; it contains the tomb of Bossuet, Bishop of Meaux, famed preacher and writer (d. 1704). Bossuet Mus. (unusual 12c *Tête d'Ogier le Danois*, furniture, old paintings) is in 16–17c bishop's palace (12c chapel); the gardens, laid out by Le Nôtre (mid-17c), have pavilion that Bossuet used as a study; stairs lead to terrace laid out on 15c ramparts (fine view).
Vicinity ● Villeroy Memorial (8.5 km NW on D 129); Charles Péguy (writer), killed in Sept. 1914, is buried there. ● To N, taking the D 38, monuments of the Quatres-

Meaux: *the cathedral's huge Gothic choir, with many splendid works of art, ◀ achieves both elegance and impressive height. ▲*

Meillant: *church façade at La Celle-Bruère; among the reliefs displayed, two pre-Romanesque fighters. ▼*

Routes and (farther on) of Notre Dame-de-la-Marne, commemorating Battle of the Marne (1914). ● On the N36, American memorial overlooking *Marne* valley. ● *Trilport*, 3 km to E, on R. *Marne*, has a well-equipped beach.

Megève
74 – Haute-Savoie   32 – D 1
Large winter sports resort. Church of St. Jean-Baptiste has 15c Gothic apse; belfry dates from 1754; inside, vault is decorated with folk paintings; 18c rustic panelling.
Vicinity ● Cable-cars to summits of Jaillet (1,600 m.), Mt. d'Arbois (1,760 m.), Rochebrune (1,753 m.).

Meillant (Château)
18 – Cher   24 – C 1
This fine late-15c construction, renovated 16c, on site of castle built circa 1300, is mixture of Goth. Flamboyant and Ren. styles (v.a.). E façade displays elegant sculpted decoration, notably the Lion Tower, veritable lacework in stone. Interior has noteworthy furniture, paintings, objets d'art, tapestries, etc. In chapel, 15c Rhenish retable, depicting the Passion.
Vicinity ● 6 km SW, La Celle-Bruère, Romanesque church; unusual tomb of St. Sylvain, 16c; 1 km to W, *Bruère-Allichamps*. Gallo-Roman stone marking the geographical centre of France. ● 13 km NE, via the *Forest of Maulne* and *Dun-sur-Auron*, interesting Romanesque church with 15c Goth. vaulting, 14c stained-glass windows, 16c holy sepulchre, 16c Clock Tower, old houses.

Meilleraye-de-Bretagne (La)
44 – Loire-Atlantique   16 – C 2
2.5 km from the township, Cistercian Abbey of Meilleraye (now Trappist); 12c restored abbey church, late-18c main living quarters (v.a., p.m., exc. Sun.). In formal gardens, fine 12c pink granite portal, adorned with statues.
Vicinity ● 6 km SW, large *Vioreau* reservoir (sailing), lakes.

Melle
79 – Deux-Sèvres   23 – B 3
Its two Romanesque churches are worth visiting. 12c St. Hilaire has unusual sculpted décor; above N portal is niche containing sculpture of a knight on horseback thought to symbolise the Emperor Constantine; interior has unusual capitals. St Pierre, mid-12c, also has interesting sculptures. Early-12c church of St. Savinien has fine portal with saddle-back lintel (v.a.

to exterior). The Hôtel de Menoc, Ren., has two 15c towers.
Vicinity ● 7 km NW, *Celles-sur-Belle*, Gothic church with three naves, rebuilt in 17c; behind apse, late-17c abbey building, in Classical style.

Ménars (Château)
41 – Loir-et-Cher   18 – A 2
The 17–18c château, majestic and

Melle: *on St. Hilaire's north portal, the 12c 'cavalier' who is believed to symbolise the Emperor Constantine.*

architecturally harmonious, belonged to Mme. de Pompadour (v.a. weekends in summer). The terraced gardens, with a Temple of Love, a 'grotto' and statues, overlook the r. bank of R. *Loire*.
Vicinity ● 5 km NE, *Suèvres*, 12c church of St. Lubin, with 11c belfry, 12 and 16c church of St.-Christophe; 10c W gable has unusual ornamentation; 13–16c houses.

Menat
63 – Puy-de-Dôme   24 – D 3
The Romanesque church, fmr. 12c Benedictine abbey church, remains interesting despite having been badly restored in 19c. Sculpted capitals in nave. 14c chapterhouse and remains of 15c cloister, with timber-framed floor above.
Vicinity ● 1.5 km SE, *Le Pont-de-Menat* where the N 143 crosses R. *Sioule* in scenic country (old humpbacked bridge). Rec. trips to *Vallée de la Sioule*; to E, *Chouvigny* gorge and **Ébreuil***; to S, the D 109 follows banks of the *Sioule* (picturesque ruins of 13c Ch. Rocher) and passes through *Châteauneuf-les-Bains* to *Queuille* dam and

superb viaduct of *Les Fades*, 132 m. above the river.

Mende
48 – Lozère   37 – A2
The old town has lost none of its character. 15c bridge over R. *Lot*. Narrow streets and old houses surround St. Pierre cath., 14–16c; inside, late-17c carved stalls, panelling and eight early-18c Aubusson tapestries in choir. In mus., interesting collection of Bronze Age finds.
Vicinity ● 4 km SW, Mt. Mimat (1,060 m.) and St. Privat's Hermitage, part of which is carved out of the rock. ● 11 km. W, *Sauveterre*, pretty village of the Causses: drystone houses covered with limestone 'plaques' (skylight windows, vaulted sheep-pens, ancient oven). ● 7.5 km N, *Chastel-Nouvel*, Gévaudan zoo (v.a. in summer); 12 km N, from *Rieutort-de-Randon*, take trip E to the *Signal de Randon*, (1,544 m., vast panorama) and the *Lac de Charpal*. ● 7 km E, *Lanuejols* (Romanesque church, remains of 3c Roman mausoleum); *Bagnols-les-Bains* (black schist houses built in tiers on slopes of Mt. Pervenche; thermal springs); climb rec. up *Mt. Lozère*, with summit (1,702 m.) at the *Signal de Finiels*.

Ménerbes
84 – Vaucluse   38 – A 3
This extraordinary village, perched on spur of **Lubéron*** mountain, is dominated by ruins of picturesque

castle. Many old mansions and houses. At tip of the promontory, 14c church and graveyard. Below it is 'Le Castelet', austere 16c château shaded by pines.

Menez-Hom
29N – Finistère   8 – B 3
A peak set slightly apart from the *Montagnes Noires* (300 m.) it is one of Brittany's principal belvederes (viewing table). Chapel dedicated to Ste. Marie-du-Menez-Hom has three retables and mid-16c calvary in a shaded enclosure.

Menton
06 – Alpes-Maritimes   39 – B 3
The old town, built in tiers above the Bay of Garavan, is traversed by picturesque Rue Longue; below it lies the new town, one of largest resorts on Côte d'Azur. The church and the Place St. Michel, together with chapel of the Pénitents-Blancs and neighbouring houses, make an attractive, Italian-style picture. Winding alleys lead to fmr. cemetery on terraces above the town: strange baroque funerary monuments. In the new town, on harbour, 16c 'fortin' (bastion), housing Jean Cocteau mus. (cl. Mon. and Tues.); the great artist-writer decorated the Wedding Room in town hall. 18c Mus. du Palais Carnolès, fine Italian-style residence; 14, 15 and 16c Italian paintings; French, 17c onwards (cl. Mon. and Tues.). At Garavan, the Villa 'Val Rahmeh' has exotic botanical gardens (v.a., cl. Tues.); Domaine des Colombières (hotel-restaurant) has gorgeous gardens.
Vicinity ● 5.5 km N, late-17c Chapelle de l'Annonciade. ● 11 km N, St. Agnès: picturesque village, terrace with lovely view. 8 km N, up v. winding road, Castellar: most unusual fortified village; fmr. Palais des Lascaris; you can return to *Menton* down mule track, offering admirable view.

Metz
57 – Moselle   13 – C 1
Cath. of St. Étienne is imposing late 13, early 14c Goth. building; the nave is particularly grandiose: 123 m. long and almost 42 m. high, its stained-glass windows are among France's finest – dating from 13c (S arm of transept), 14c (façade), 15c (nave) to 16c (transept); added to this wonderful series are the windows, designed between 1957 and 1970, by the painters Villon, Bissière and Chagall; rich church treasure in sacristy (v.a.). Mus. of art and hist. (cl. Tues). has its exhibits displayed to great effect

in several old (15c Chévremont granary, 17c convent of the Petits-Carmes) and modern (19–20c) buildings: v. large Gallo-Roman collection (sculpture, objects from everyday life), Merovingian and medieval (lapidary fragments) reg. religious art; reconstruction of daily life in Metz in the past; old paintings (gallery of primitives) and French works of 18, 19 and 20c. Early-13c church of St. Martin, fine 15–19c stained-glass windows. Church of St. Vincent, in the Ile Chambière, has 18c façade in front of 13c Goth. nave. Interesting quarter around 13c church of Ste. Ségolène: late-12c Hôtel St. Livier, Rue des Trinitaires; late-14c Hôtel de la Bulette in picturesque Place Ste. Croix. The Place St. Louis is surrounded by beautiful houses built over arcades, dating from 14, 15 and 16c. 16c Maison des Têtes. Near the Esplanade, Templars chapel (octagonal, late 12c); church of St. Pierre-aux-Nonnains, one of the oldest in France – parts of the walls are from 4c Roman basilica – converted into abbey church in 7c (Ottonian nave, dated circa 1000). Below the Esplanade terrace: Lac des Cygnes – Swan Lake (Son et Lumière in summer), and the Serpenoise gate (rebuilt in 19c). The Porte des Allemands, on the Seille, is superb 13–16c fortified ensemble, flanked by towers; opposite, St. Eucaire, 14–15c; to l., Blvd. Maginot, late-12c St. Maximin (stained-glass windows by Jean

Ménars: the majestic brick and stone façade of the château rises above enormous terraced gardens overlooking the Loire.

Metz: straddling the Seille, the imposing 13–16c Porte des Allemands is a reminder of the town's warlike past.

Merveilles (Valley)
06 – Alpes-Maritimes   39 – B 3
Take the D 91 from *St-Dalmas-de-Tende* to Les Mesces, then three hours on foot to the Refuge des Merveilles, from where you can make two-day tour of the whole massif (jeeps can be hired at *St. Dalmas*). The mountainous region to W of *St. Dalmas* and **Tende*** is particularly wild; at its centre is *Mont Bego* (2,873 m.), surrounded by lakes. The Refuge des Merveilles (2,100 m.) is a good base for trips: *Mont Bego*, Grand Capelet, *Cime du Diable*, and other itineraries in direction of the Gordolasque valley. The small Merveilles valley opens out to the N, its sheer sides covered with about 45,000 graffitti – attributed to Ligurian peoples (Italian-Celtic tribe), from mid-Bronze and Iron Ages, and thought to cover period from about 3,400 to 1,400 BC. These strange schematic representations may have been some kind of symbolic language. Visits to *Vallée des Merveilles* and *Mont Bégo* should not be attempted alone; the area is accessible only during the three summer months. (Only then, too, are the carvings in the rock free of snow and visible.) For the Refuges of Les Merveilles and Valmasque, keys obtainable from the authorised holders at *St. Dalmas-de-Tende*.

Cocteau). St. Clément college has interesting Rhenish Goth. church, renovated in 17c. Metz-Plage, on R. *Moselle* (swimming pool, water sports).

Vicinity • To W, Mt. St. Quentin (357 m., panorama over *Moselle* valley), *Scy-Chazelles* (near the church, in 13c fortified chapel, tomb of Robert Schuman (d. 1963), one-time French Prime Minister and statesman who laid the groundwork for European Community. • To SW, *Moselle* valley, as far as **Pont-à-Mousson***. • To S, valley of the Seille via *Sillegny* (fine 13–14c Goth. church) and *Cheminot* (Goth. church).

Meudon
92 – Hauts-de-Seine   11 – C 2
Approached by a magnificent avenue of limes, the terrace (v.a.) of the long-vanished château commands a vast panorama over Paris. The New Château is now an observatory – the Observatoire d'Astronomie Physique (v.a. by arrangement). Mus. of art and hist. in the 'Villa Molière', 17c country house acquired by Armande Béjart Molière's actress wife, after his death in 1673. Mus. Rodin has plaster-copies of the great sculptor's main works and, in the garden, his tomb under his famed masterpiece, 'The Thinker'.
Vicinity • Meudon forest (2,840 acres), many pleasant walks.

Meyrueis
48 – Lozère   37 – A 3
Picturesque town at mouth of **Jonte*** canyon, on borders of the *Causse Noir* and *Causse Méjean*.
Vicinity • Three underground features of the causses: the **Armand*** swallow-hole, the **Bramabiau*** underground river and the *Dargilan* grotto (v.a. from Palm Sunday to end Sept.): enormous caves and galleries, very varied concretions. • Rec. trip SE to *Mt. Aigoual*, (1,567 m.) which commands one of the best panoramas in the Midi; on its summit, observatory and overnight mountain shelter; arboretum at 'Hort de Dieu'; the flora found on the Aigoual is particularly sought after by botanists.

Mézières-en-Brenne
36 – Indre   24 – A 1
In the 14c church, very elaborate Ren. Anjou chapel.
Vicinity • To S, the *Brenne*: network of small roads and footpaths provides ideal way to explore this picturesque region, dotted with ponds and marshes, which stretches between the *Claise* and the *Creuse*; many species of water-birds, gorse, heather, moors and woods. • 7 km S, the Gabrière lake, water sports centre; 7 km to S, Mer Rouge lake, dominated by *Ch. du Bouchet*, imposing medieval fortress, enlarged in 17c; v.a. to keep (panorama), terrace and ext. of château; on an island in the lake, Notre

Dame chapel (local pilgrimage site).

Millau
12 – Aveyron   36 – D 3
France's 'Capital of the Glove' has several interesting buildings: an imposing 12 and 17c belfry, 48 m. high; 16–17c church of Notre Dame and 17c Ch. de Sambucy, whose int. has both mythological and allegorical decorations (ceilings). Mus. du Gant et de la Peau (gloves and skins). In 18c Hôtel de Pégayrolles, town mus. (pottery from Graufesenque site).
Vicinity • **Le Larzac***. **Roquefort-sur-Soulzon***, **Montpellier-le-Vieux***.

Millevaches
19 – Corrèze   30 – B 1
Village in heart of the high granitic plateau to which it gives its name; 981 m. at its highest point, commanding tremendous views.
Vicinity • 3 km N, Signal d'Audouze (954 m.), vast panorama and source of R. *Vienne*; 7 km to NW, *Peyrelevade*, above lush green *Vienne* basin, surrounded by forests; 5 km to W, Lac de Servières; 5.5 km to NW of *Peyrelevade*, Chammet lake and dam on R. Chandouille. • 7.5 km SW, via *St. Merd-les-Oussines*, **Gallo-Roman remains** known as *Ch. des Cars*. • 17 km S, beyond *Mt. Bessou* (978 m., vast panorama), *Meymac*: fmr. Benedictine abbey church, 12c Romanesque and Goth. church has

Millau: *two of the main sights in the 'Glove Capital'. The unusual 12c belfry once formed part of the town hall. The old mill, on the Tarn, houses a museum with interesting Gallo-Roman pottery recovered from the Graufesenque site.*

Mirepoix: *the main square is ringed by timber 'couverts', supporting houses from 13 and 15c.*

Moissac: *money-lender tormented by a demon, detail on pier to left of portal of St. Pierre.*

an 11c porch and, inside, 10–11c very primitive historiated capitals; 17c buildings of former abbey; 15 and 16c houses; recommended trip to Merlançon lake, 2 km to SE.

Milly-la-Forêt
91 – Essonne   11 – C 3
Interesting 15c Goth. church and timbered covered market (1479). In the chapel of St. Blaise-des-Simples (v.a. cl. Tues.), is tomb of Jean Cocteau (d. 1963), who carried out its decorations. Small garden.
Vicinity ● 4 km NE, in admirable green setting, with streams, the *Ch. de Courances*, built in Louis XIII style, in stone and brick; gardens by Le Nôtre (v.a. weekends and public hols., Easter to Nov. 1).

Minerve
34 – Hérault   42 – D 2
One of the most extraordinary settings in the Midi, on a rocky platform overlooking the confluence of the Cesse and the Briant. The village, a very important Cathar centre, still evokes the siege of 1210 and the stake where almost all its inhabitants were burned as heretics. See the Romanesque church, the hollowed out cornices on the side of the cliff overlooking the gorges, and the two natural tunnels formed by the Cesse which, to the W, has worn a narrow canyon in the

Causses du Minervois. The cliffs are pitted with caves which served as dwelling places in prehist. times (human footprints have been found in the petrified clay). Small mus.
Vicinity ● To S., road goes down to *Azillanet*, then *Olonzac*, across the *Minervois* vineyards.

Miolans (Château)
73 – Savoie   32 – C 2
300 m above the *Isère* (vast panorama from the terrace), it is one of the Savoie's most famous sites. The imposing construction, whose oldest sections date back to 10c, has a 14c keep, fmr. prisons with underground cells and dungeons (v.a., cl. Sun. a.m., June 1–Sept. 15).
Vicinity ● 3.5 km, *St. Pierre-d'Albigny*, picturesque little town at foot of Baugnes mountains; in church, interesting works of art.

Mirepoix
09 – Ariège   42 – B 2
The enormous central square retains its medieval character; it is surrounded by 13–14c timbered houses, built on picturesque wooden 'couverts' (i.e. piles). Goth. nave of former 15c cath. (16c belfry) is widest in the Midi.
Vicinity ● 11 km W, *Vals*, semi-troglodytic church of Notre Dame; Carolingian crypt carved out of the rock and extended by an apse whose

vaulting is decorated with Byzantine-inspired frescos; above, a nave and connecting stairs; the church, flanked by 13c clock tower, is surrounded by a defensive wall. ●
17 km S, *Léran*, former bastide; on l. bank of R. *Touyré*, Ch. des Lévis-Mirepoix, 14–15c (n.v.a.).

Moissac
82 – Tarn-et-Garonne   35 – D 3
The portal and cloister of church of St. Pierre, fmr. Benedictine abbey church in brick and stone, consecrated at end of 12c and completed (choir and vaulting in nave) in 15c, figures amongst masterpieces of Romanesque art. Executed between 1110 and 1115, the portal, one of the first Languedoc Romanesque monumental sculptures, depicts, on the tympanum, Apocalyptic Vision of the Sovereign Judge enthroned in the Heavens, surrounded by the Evangelists and 24 old men. The lintel is decorated with rose windows of antique inspiration; the monolithic pier is sculpted with three pairs of wild animals, on their hind legs; on the side walls, fine sculpted faces of old men. St. Pierre and the prophet Isaiah are depicted on the pier. Inside, late-15c Entombment, and v. fine 12c Romanesque Christ; 16c sculpted stone choir screen. The cloisters (v.a.) owe their elegance to

delicacy of the columns and arcades, and their harmonious appearance to their multi-coloured marble (white, pink, green and grey). Noteworthy late-11c historiated capitals. On the pillars, large sculpted figures of the Apostles. In four 13c chapels, interesting monastic mus.; also mus. of folk art and traditions, and applied arts.

Molsheim
67 – Bas-Rhin   14 – A 2
Typical little Alsace town. The Metzig was headquarters of the Butchers' Guild (small mus.); cellar for tasting of local wines (Riesling). 17c church in Goth. style, with Silbermann organ. 16 and 17c houses, and old town gate.

Monastier-sur-Grazeille (Le)
43 – Haute-Loire   31 – B 3
The 11–15c abbey church of St.

MONACO and MONTE-CARLO
Principality of Monaco   45 – B 1

● Monaco, capital of the principality, is built on steep rock overlooking the sea. Prince's Palace, 13–14c, which looks like crenellated fortress, has fine main courtyard where graceful 17c horseshoe-shaped stairway in white marble leads to Galerie d'Hercule (1552), whose vaulting is decorated with 17c frescos; the main apartments are particularly sumptuous (v.a. in summer); Napoleonic mus. in SW wing of the palace. The old part of Monaco, peaceful and provincial, is criss-crossed by narrow streets lined with houses with painted façades; apart from the Chapelle des Pénitents (aka Chapelle de la Miséricorde), 17c, the buildings are late 19 or early 20c. Musée Océanographique, built in 1906, (v.a., check times) has very interesting displays of physical and chemical aspects of oceanography and marine life, as well as one of the best stocked aquariums in Europe; mus. also has a Centre d'Études Mediterranéennes and a Centre d'Acclimatation Zoologique (v.a.), inc. large collection of apes. St. Martin gardens, on terraces above the sea, have many exotic plants. The Jardin Exotique (v.a.) commands superb view and inc. rich. collection of cacti. In lower part of gardens, the Grottes de l'Observatoire, not easy to reach but picturesque: numerous different concretions.

● The harbour forms a square approx. 400 m. in length between Monaco rock and Monte-Carlo. Monte-Carlo casino is typical of architecture and Baroque decoration of second half of 19c: the theatre auditorium is particularly ornate. The Palais du Sporting-Club (1932) houses Théâtre de la Lumière. ● The principality has three museums: Musée d'Anthropologie Préhistorique (v.a., cl. May 1 and Nov. 19, hours vary); National Museum of Monaco (cl. Jan. 1, May 1, Nov. 19 and Christmas) occupies the villa Sauber, surrounded by garden with sculptures by Rodin, Maillol, Bourdelle, Zadkine, etc.; it has unusual collection of 87 clockwork toys and almost 2,000 dolls from the 18–19c (Galéa collection); the clockwork toys are set in motion daily from 15.30 to 17.30. Villa Ispahan, with collection from Prince Reza Khan, is now a museum of Iranian art.

Chaffre, built of polychromatic materials, presents mosaic-like façade, inc. arcades and columns with historiated capitals; the Romanesque nave has four bays and Goth. choir. Former abbot's château, 14c, since renovated.
Vicinity ● 25 km SE, Lac d'**Issarlès***, beach and water sports. ● 16 km N, *St. Julien-Chapteuil*: Romanesque church (capitals), ruins of Ch. de Chapteuil on a basalt hill (1,035 m.); rec. trips to volcanic massif of *Mt. Meygal*.

Monastir del Camp (Priory)
66 – Pyrénées-Orientales 43 – D 3
Founded, according to legend, by Charlemagne. Late-11c church, built of pebbles, with mid-12c white marble W portal (capitals have caricature-like sculptures), 14c grille. The cloister, finished in 1307 and extremely elegant, has 27 tri-lobate arcades supported by small columns. 13–14c monastic buildings (private property, v.a. Tues. and Fri.).

Moncley (Château)
25 – Doubs 20 – B 3
Superb Louis XVI-style construction (v.a. weekends, p.m., in July and Aug., Sun. p.m. from May 15 to Sept. 15), curved façade with, in centre, magnificent pedimented portico. Splendid vestibule and spiral stairway. Fine 18c apartments, decorated and furnished in period style. From terrace, beautiful view over *Ognon* valley.

Moncontour-de-Bretagne
22 – Côtes-du-Nord 9 – A 2
Old fortified town, built in tiers on hill between two valleys. Place Penthièvre is surrounded by 18c granite houses and church of St. Mathurin (superb 16c stained-glass windows). On small hill, 18c Ch. des Granges and 13c Moguet Tower.
Vicinity ● 2 km SE, Chapel of Notre Dame-du-Haut: int. has folk statues of the 'Saints Guérisseurs' (lit. 'holy healers'); 5 km to S, Chapel of Notre Dame-de-Bel-Air, splendidly situated at top of Mts. du Ménez (340 m., panorama). ● 7 km E, Ch. de La Touche-Trébry, late 16c but with medieval appearance (v.a., p.m. from July 1 to Aug. 31, cl. Sun. and public hols.; by arrangement out of season).

Mondoubleau
41 – Loir-et-Cher 17 – D 1
On slope overlooking l. bank of the Grenne; the imposing ruins of the feudal castle include sturdy 11c

Montal: *the château's dormer windows have richly sculpted gables.*

keep, 35 m. high, in red sandstone; the only remaining part leans dangerously.
Vicinity ● 8 km N, Ch. de *St. Agil*, 18c (v.a., ext. only); mid-16c gatehouse is flanked by towers decorated with magnificent lozenge pattern in red and brown glazed brick; 3 km NE, *Arville*, fmr. Commanderie of the Templars, late 15c gatehouse with turrets and 12c chapel behind belfry-porch. ● 6.5 km N, *Souday*, 14–15c church with pre-Romanesque nave and rib-vaulted crypt.

Monflanquin
47 – Lot-et-Garonne 35 – D 1
On hill overlooking the *Lède* valley, fmr. bastide, 13c, now a craft village (pottery), with picturesque steep alleys. Fine square with 'cornières'. Church in Goth. style typical of south of France, fortified façade, sculpted 16c portal. From ring road, fine views of surrounding countryside.

Monistrol-sur-Loire
43 – Haute-Loire 31 – C 2
The church, rebuilt in 17c, still has unusual Romanesque nave. 15 and 17c château (hospice and school), set in beautiful gardens.
Vicinity ● 7 km W, *Bas-en-Basset*: impressive ruins of 15c Ch. de Rochebaron, with three fortified walls and large towers (vast pan-

orama). ● Follow the *Loire gorges* to N, towards **St. Étienne***, and to SW, via *Retournac, Chamalières-sur-Loire* (fine Romanesque church), *Lavoûte-sur-Loire* (Romanesque church), Lavoûte-Polignac (château), to **Le Puy***.

Monpazier
24 – Dordogne 35 – D 1
This 13–14c bastide has central square with 'cornières' and timbered covered market; 14–16c church and fortified gates. Outstanding example of medieval town planning. Old houses, inc. 13c Maison du Chapitre.
Vicinity ● 8 km S, Ch. de **Biron***.

Montaigne (Château)
24 – Dordogne 29 – B 3
At *St. Michel-de-Montaigne*. The celebrated writer was born and spent most of his life here (1533–1592). Only the tower (with chapel), his room and his 'library' date from this period, the rest of the château was destroyed by fire in 19c and rebuilt afterwards. In the 'library', study where Montaigne wrote his *Essays*, the great moralist's favourite quotations in Latin and Greek are painted on beams of the ceiling (v.a., cl. Mon. and a.m. Tues.).
Vicinity ● 4 km S, *Montcaret* where large Gallo-Roman villa was uncovered in 1921; foundations of baths, traces of 5–13c necropolis on same site; small mus. displaying finds.

Montal (Château)
46 – Lot 36 – B 1
1.5 km to W of **St. Céré***. One of the greatest achievements of Romanesque architecture in the centre of France, restored and admirably refurnished (superb tapestries), from 1908 onwards, by the art collector Maurice Fenaille. The courtyard is a masterpiece of 16c decoration in the Italian style. Inside, magnificent main staircase (v.a. from Apr. to Nov. 1).
Vicinity ● 3 km SW, *Presque grotto*: beautiful concretions (v.a.). ● 3 km W, *Autoire gorge*.

Montargis
45 – Loiret 18 – D 1
Madeleine church has 12c nave and notable Ren. choir with several interesting works of art. To W, on terrace overlooking the town, fmr. 12 and 15c castle. The town hall has mus. commemorating early 19c artist Girodet: local archaeology, sculpture and paintings. In Girodet salon, 19 of his paintings.
Vicinity ● 14 km NE, *Ferrières-en-Gâtinais*, 12 and 13c church, fmr. abbey church; large series of 16c stained-glass windows; monumental tomb of Louis de Blan-

chefort, early 16c; in front of church, 15c chapel of Notre Dame-de-Bethléem, with Romanesque apse, 17c monumental retable and late-15c Black Virgin.

Montauban
82 – Tarn-et-Garonne   36 – A3
City of brick and stone, rich in art. Early-14c Pont-Vieux, once fortified, leads to bishop's palace, now housing the Ingres Mus. (opening hrs. vary); on show are several pictures by the famous painter, who was born in Montauban, and 4,000 drawings, exhibited in rotation; also galleries of early and contemp. art, large group of works by Bourdelle (sculptor, d. 1929), also native of Montauban; in the vaulted basement reg. archaeology and arts, pottery, mainly from S of France, etc. 17c Place Nationale, surrounded by double 'couverts' (arcades) in brick, is scene of v. lively market each morning. 17c Notre Dame is one of the few Classical caths. in France; inside, the *Voeu de Louis XIII* by Ingres (1824).

Montbard
21 – Côte-d'Or   19 – C 2
The Buffon Park (named after great 18c naturalist) in which lie the ruins of 14c fmr. château of Dukes of Burgundy, dominates the town; remains of town wall, 40 m. keep known as Tour de l'Aubépin, (small archaeological mus.); the Tour St. Louis (small Buffon mus.); in pavilion in the park, study where Buffon worked (v.a.). Small 12–15c church of St. Urse. Mus. of fine arts, mainly 19c paintings and sculpture. *Vicinity* ● 2.5 km NE, **Abbaye de Fontenay***. ● 16.5 km SE, **Ch. de Bussy-Rabutin***; 5 km to S, **Alise Ste. Reine*** (Alesia) and, 8 km farther to S, **Flavigny-sur-Ozerain***. ● 3 km S, 14c Ch. de Montfort; ruins clinging to hill, three octagonal towers, remains of living quarters, chapel and unusual 'Salle de la Monnaie' – 'Coin Room' (v.a.); 17 km to S, **Semur-en-Auxois***. The *Canal de Bourgogne*, many pleasant walks.

Montbéliard
25 – Doubs   20 – D 2
17–18c fmr. château of Counts of Montbéliard, with two towers, 15 and 16c, dominates the town; inside, mus. of archaeology and natural hist. In late-18c Hôtel Beurnier, mus. of hist. of Old Montbéliard. Ren. Maison des Princes. 16c covered market. *Vicinity* ● 3 km E, *Sochaux* factories (v.a.). ● 4.5 km SE, *Audincourt*: Sacred Heart church (1951), one of the more interesting examples of modern religious architecture; its façade has mosaic by Bazaine; stained-glass windows by Fernand Léger and circular stained-glass wall by Bazaine in the baptistry; the road climbs up the Doubs valley to *St. Hippolyte*, to S; at fmr. Gallo-Roman town of Mandeure, excavations of large theatre and numerous objects (digs still in progress).

Montbenoît (Abbey)
25 – Doubs   26 – C 1
12, 14 and 16c church; in the choir, magnificent 16c stalls, carved with lively, spirited satirical scenes. In the 15c cloister, unusual capital decorations (flora and fauna of the mountains).

Montbrison
42 – Loire   31 – B 2
Town is built in a circle around volcanic hill. Church of Notre Dame-d'Espérance, imposing 13–14c Goth. building, with 15c Goth. Flamboyant portal; opposite the apse, the Diana (v.a., cl. Tues.), huge late-13c hall with wooden vaulting decorated with 14c heraldic paintings; in courtyard, small lapidary mus. Mus. d'Allard: large collection of dolls and marionettes, natural hist. Around church of St. Pierre, many 15–18c mansions. *Vicinity* ● 5 km NW, *Champdieu*: 12c Romanesque church of fmr. 12 and 16c priory, all fortified in 14c. ● 8 km SE, *St. Romain-le-Puy*, at foot of basalt peak, crowned by 10–11–15c granite church of fortified priory of St. Romain; unusual sculpted décor, remains of 12 and 15c frescos and 11c crypt; 5 km SE, Ch. de *Sury-le-Comtal*, 17c: fine panelling, sculpted fireplaces and ceilings (v.a., p.m. only, Easter to Sept. 30). ● Take D 101 to WNW for tour of Forez mountains (see **Ambert***); rec. ascent of *Pierre-sur-Haute* (1,640 m.), highest of the *Mts. du Forez*, or cable-car from *Chalmazel*.

Mont Cenis   32 – D 2
See **St. Jean-de-Maurienne***.

Montbard: *the Canal de Bourgogne runs through peaceful countryside for 242 km to link the Saône and the Yonne.*

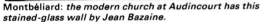

Montbéliard: *the modern church at Audincourt has this stained-glass wall by Jean Bazaine.*

Montbenoît: *capitals in the cloister, decorated with motifs of mountain flora and fauna.*

Mont-Dauphin
05 – Hautes-Alpes   38 – D 1
Small fortified town, now almost abandoned, which seems to live on in the past. Designed by Vauban and ringed by reddish marble fortifications with drawbridges, it has several military buildings. Inside, town is divided into four by two wide streets intersecting at right-angles. Church of St. Louis (only the choir is complete). Promenade called The Plantation, where shade is provided by 1,050 elms, more than 100 years old. From the Mirador, or belvedere, vast panorama.
Vicinity ● 3 km E, *Guillestre*: church, 16c Goth. style, in pink marble, has a fine porch, or 'Réal', with columns, two of which rest on couching lions, as at **Embrun***; under the porch, door with 16c panels and ornamented lock; picturesque houses and alleys in the old town; *Guillestre* is good base for excursions: petrifactive fountain at Réotier (6 km W); *Queyras*, towards **Ch. Queyras*** to NE, via the *Guil* valley; the *Vars pass*, to SE, through small Chagne valley; **Embrun***; to SW, via R. *Durance* valley; **Vallouise*** and Écrins Natnl. Park to NNW.

Mont-de-Marsan
40 – Landes   35 – A 3
Town has two interesting mus. Despiau-Wlérick mus. in 14c Lacataye keep (devoted to the two locally-born sculptors after whom the mus. is named; also other 19–20c sculpture). Mus. Dubalen, in

Romanesque chapel (archaeology and natural hist. of Landes reg.).
Vicinity ● 2 km SW, St. Pierre-du-Mont, church with Romanesque apse and fine 18c stucco work inside. ● 6 km NW, *Uchacq*, Romanesque church with 11c portal. ● 16 km SW, *St. Sever*: fmr. Benedictine abbey church, best example of Romanesque arch. in the Landes; 17c apse and six Romanesque side aisles; presbytery and town hall occupy the 17c monastic buildings; from Morlanne belvedere, magnificent panorama over the *Adour* and surrounding forest; 18 km SE, *Samadet*, pottery mus. in Ren. house.

MONT BLANC
74 – Haute-Savoie   32 – D 1
The climb to the top of the highest mountain in Europe can be made in two days, with a guide and porter, via the Bossons glacier – spending the night in the Grands-Mulets refuge, at altitude of 3,050 m. The summit (4,807 m.) is reached after about $8\frac{1}{2}$ hrs. walk through the snow. Descent during the day to **Chamonix*** (information at S.I.).

MONT-DORE (LE)
63 – Puy-de-Dôme   30 – D 2
Renowned spa and winter sports centre at alt. of 1,050 m., at foot of the Puy de Sancy; also popular base for excursions ● To S, Salon du Capucin (1,286 m. by funicular); from there in 30 mins. to the Pic du Capucin (1,465 m.), superb panorama. ● To SE, large waterfall, 30 m. drop. ● *Puy de Sancy* (4 km to S, then cable-car), via the Pied du Sancy (1,350 m.); summit of the Puy is at alt. of 1,886 m., vast panorama (viewing table). ● To N, via *Lac de Guéry* and *Col de Guéry* (1,264 m.), the *Tuilière* and *Sanadoire* rocks, gigantic dykes formed of phonolite stones, standing at entrance to a vast hemicycle constituting one of the most arresting sights in the Auvergne. ● To E and SE, rec. scenic route through *Chambon* and the impressive Chaudefour valley, overlooked by wooded heights and strangely shaped peaks; route leads, Courbanges and the Aigle Rock, to **Besse-et St. Anastaire***. ● 16 km SW, *La Tour-d'Auvergne*, built in amphitheatre form on basalt promontory at foot of prismatic 'organ-pipes': Goth. church at *Chastreix* is worth a detour; then, to SE, on to *Lac Chauvet* (133 acres), in middle of half-circle of basalt hills.

Montfort-l'Amaury: *the old quarter and its church – provincial charm and a reminder of the tranquillity of the distant past.*

Montélimar
26 – Drôme   37 – D 1
To E of the town, on hill overlooking R. *Roubion*, interesting château, 15c reinforced in 17c (v.a., cl. Tues., Wed. and in Dec.), with 12c keep and remains of Romanesque chapel.
Vicinity ● 17.5 km SE, *Trappe d'Aiguebelle*, fmr. abbey, 12c, restored in 19c; 12c church and adjoining cloister gallery, refectory, etc. (guided tours, cl. Sun.). ● 15 km NE, *Marsanne*: ruins of the medieval town (remains of Romanesque church, picturesque 15–16c houses) are worth a visit; magnificent panorama. ● 5 km NW, after crossing the Rhône, *Rochemaure*, overlooked by volcanic dykes on which the old town, now in ruins, formerly stood; *Rochemaure Dam* and Henri Poincaré hydroelectric station; follow N 86 to N for 9 km to *Cruas*, original Romanesque church, surviving from 11–12c Benedictine abbey; has two crypts; late-11c mosaic floor in choir.

Montfort-l'Amaury
78 – Yvelines   11 – B 2
Small town overlooked by ruins of 11–15c castle. The late-15c church, partly Ren., has a fine ensemble of 16c stained-glass windows. Fmr. charnel house from 16–18c, with timbered roof, surrounds the cemetery. 'Le Belvédère', home of composer Maurice Ravel (d. 1937), now a mus. Many old houses.

Montgeoffroy (Château)
49 – Maine-et-Loire   17 – B 2
Fine 18c building, well proportioned and architecturally harmonious (v.a. from Whitsun to Nov. 1). Inside, the original panelling and unusual branded Louis XVI furniture; Aubusson tapestries and 17–18c portraits.
Vicinity ● 15 km W, late 18c Ch. de Pignerolles.

Montier-en-Der
52 – Haute-Marne   12 – D 3
Church of Notre-Dame, with galleried nave and late-10c side aisles, has a choir with late-12c ambulatory, one of the best examples of early Champagne Goth. style.
Vicinity ● To N, Champaubert Reservoir and the Der forest. ● The churches in the Der region are interesting, especially to SW: *Ceffonds* (beautiful stained glass and 16c holy sepulchre); to NW, *Chavanges*, *Lentilles* (unusual timbered country church, 16c, with original wooden porch), *Outines*, Puellemontier, etc. ● To E, *Wassy-sur-Blaise* (see **St. Dizier***).

Montlhéry
91 – Essonne   11 – C 2

The tower, known as Louis le Gros, 32 m. high, is all that remains of the feudal castle. Vast panorama. At Linas, the Montlhéry motor-racing circuit.

Vicinity ● 2 km NE, *Longpont-sur-Orge*, 11c church of Notre Dame, fine 13c sculpted portal (damaged); pilgrimage, Whit Sunday; 2 km to E, *Ste. Geneviève-des-Bois*, Russian cemetery (Orthodox chapel).

Montlhéry: *the Louis-le-Gros tower, on a natural height commanding a wide view.*

Mont-Louis
66 – Pyrénées-Orientales   43 – B 3

This one-time battlefield, at alt. of 1,600 m., is a now a summer resort and winter sports centre. The ramparts, entered through the Porte de France, and Vauban's citadel are notable examples of classic military architecture. In bastion is first solar furnace ever brought into operation, in 1953 (v.a., apply S.I.).

Vicinity ● 6.5 km S, Planès, 11–12c church of Notre Dame-de-la-Merci has most unusual lay-out: a circle within an equilateral triangle crowned by a cupola, with three projecting apses; Romanesque Virgin and retables. ● 5 km SW, *La Perche* pass and Signal de la Perche, panorama over the Cerdagne; 10 km SW, *Llo*, old Catalan village in beautiful setting; to SE, lovely gorges of the *Sègre*. ● 9 km W, **Font-Romeu***. ● 10 km NW, *Les Angles*, summer and winter sports resort. ● 14 km NW, *Lac des Bouillouses*, in grandiose setting (2,013 m.), large dam and reservoir holding more than 3.3 billion gallons of water. Many excursions rec.: to the Lac d'Aude and source of R. *Aude* (2,135 m.); to dam and lake of *Lanoux* (2,176 m.); to the peaks of La Tausse, Cambras d'Aze and *Carlit* (2,921 m.), an impressive granite wilderness. ● To N, road to *Haute Vallée de l'Aude* (upper valley) (see **Quillan***).

Montluçon
03 – Allier   24 – C 2

The old town, wedged into modern urban development, lies on a height crowned by 15–16c château which now houses Mus. du Vieux-Château (noteworthy collections of ceramics and hurdy-gurdies). The steep winding streets are lined with old houses, some of them from 15 and 16c. Maison du Vieux-Montluçon (Burgundian art and customs). 15c churches of Notre Dame and St. Pierre (Romanesque) boast rare works of art.

Vicinity ● 12 km NW, *Huriel*: fmr. collegiate church of Notre Dame, superb 12c building containing interesting works of art; ruins of fmr. castle, 11–16c; 12c square keep in grey granite. ● 8 km SE, *Néris-les-Bains*, spa of repute; in old part of Néris, Romanesque church and Merovingian necropolis overlooking the spa district, ruins of Roman arenas and baths; lapidary collection at main spa building.

Montmajour (Abbey)
13 – Bouches-du-Rhône   43 – D 1

4 km NE of Arles, one of Provence's most beautiful religious buildings (v.a., cl. Tues.). The 12c abbey church, starkly majestic, is built on a crypt that is really a lower church (circa 1150). Late-12c Romanesque cloister, very harmonious lines; interesting 12 and 14c capitals. Above the monastic buildings, wrecked in 18c, is the Tour de l'Abbé, fortified keep dating from 1369, 30 m. high (good view). 10c chapel of St. Pierre, partly underground (unusual capitals). 200 m. from the keep, on rocky plateau, late-12c Ste. Croix chapel, ringed by tombs carved in the rock.

Vicinity ● 2.5 km NE, pine-shaded road to *Fontvieille*, Alphonse Daudet's famed mill (small mus.).

Montmajour: *the abbey cloister, built in purest Provençal Romanesque style.* ▼

Fontvieille: *Daudet's mill, echo of his 'Lettres de Mon Moulin'.* ►

Montmédy
55 – Meuse   7 – A 3

The Rue de Chiny, steeply sloping, leads from the Lower Town, on r. bank of R. *Chiers*, to the Upper Town – stronghold characteristic of Vauban's defensive systems, on an abrupt headland, more than 100 m. above Lower Town; extensive views; entrance through two gates with drawbridges. Walk round the ramparts is recommended.

Vicinity • 12 km SE, *Marville*: picturesque 'Spanish Houses', 16–17c; to N, the 11, 12 and 15c chapel of St. Hilaire; numerous sculptured tombs, from 16 and 17c, render it an unusual funerary mus. (Other tombs visible in neighbouring cemetery, inc. beautiful sculpted groups.)

Montoire-sur-le-Loir
41 – Loir-et-Cher   17 – D 2

In suburb on l. bank of R. Loir, 11c chapel of St. Gilles houses rare 12c Romanesque frescos, notably: in E apse, a Christ in Judgment; in the arms of the transept, Christ giving the keys to St. Peter and the Lord filling the Apostles with the Holy Spirit; on the Triumphal Arch, the Virtues triumphing over the Vices.

Vicinity • 2 km SE, *Lavardin*; in church of St. Genest, murals from 12 to 16c, illustrating the evolution of this art, from Romanesque stylisation to expressive Goth. realism. Imposing ruins of castle of the Comtes de Vendóme, 11–12 and 14c keep, 26 m. high (v.a. in summer).

Montpellier
34 – Hérault   43 – B 1

A beautiful town, capital of the Mediterranean Languedoc, with many 17–18c public buildings and mansions. The town's liveliest

MONTPELLIER-LE-VIEUX
12 – Aveyron   37 – A 3

This rocky wilderness (allow 75 mins. for short tour on foot) comprises total of 296 acres strewn with fantastically shaped dolomite blocks. Buried in the forest, it was not uncovered until 1870. Inf. on different itineraries available on spot. From here, land drops down to R. *Dourbie*.

centre is the Place de la Comédie (Fountain of the Trois-Grâces), site of the theatre; leading out of the square is the Esplanade, pleasant shaded promenade created in 18c. The Polygone, new administrative and commercial centre (with new town hall), built in resolutely 'modernist' style, is as much criticised as the 'Antigone' district to the E, whose neo-Classical design is by Catalan architect, Bofill. • The Fabre mus. (cl. Mon.) is one of France's richest; large collections of Italian painting (Veronese), Spanish (Zurbarán, Ribera), Flemish, Dutch and, above all, French 17c (Sébastien Bourdon), 18c (11 canvases by Greuze), 19c (David, Géricault, superb groups of Delacroix, 15 Courbets) and 20c; rich collection of drawings (2,000, inc. three by Raphaël). In neighbouring Hôtel de Cambrières-Sabatier-d'Espeyran, annexe of mus. has notable decorative ensembles from Louis XV, Louis XVI and Napoleon III periods; tapestries, gold and silverplate, sculptures, etc. • The old university and religious

Montpellier: *the extraordinary 17c Peyrou water-tower.*

Montrésor: *within a loop of the R. Indrois, the 17c château adjoins an earlier feudal castle.*

quarter looks much as it did in 17–18c. Place de la Canourgue (Fountain of the Unicorns, 18c). Late-18c fmr. town hall; 18c fmr. Hôtel Cambacérès-Murle, and bizarre Maison à la Coquille (circa 1700). Many 17 and 18c mansions, notably in Rue du Cannau: No. 8, Hôtel du Conseiller Jean Deydé (fine porch); No. 6, Hôtel de Beaulac, early 17c; noteworthy courtyard and staircase, sumptuous apartments. Place Aristide Briand (17c Hôtel Bonaric, beautiful courtyard); Rue de l'Aiguillerie; Place Pétrarque (Hôtel Nicolas, 18c, mus. of Old Montpellier; on 2nd floor, Mus. du Fougau). Archaeological mus. in magnificent Hôtel de Lunaret, 17c, Rue des Trésoriers-de-France. The main thoroughfare, Rue Jean Moulin, is also lined with 17–18c houses and mansions (exceptionally beautiful mid-18c Hôtel St. Côme, Chamber of Commerce); Rue des Trésoriers-de-la-Bourse (Hôtel Bonnier de la Mosson, late 17c, superb openwork staircase). ● The Promenade du Peyrou, a monumental ensemble of majestic Classical design, has terraces on two levels, below an elegant water-tower (magnificent panorama), culminating point of 18c St. Clément aqueduct, 800 m. long; in the centre, equestrian statue of Louis XIV; the Porte du Peyrou is a superb Triumphal Arch built in honour of Louis XIV (1691). The Jardin des Plantes (botanical garden) is oldest in France (1593). ● 14c cath. of St. Pierre, not completed until 19c, is approached through enormous monumental Goth. porch. Immediately adjoining cath., the Faculty of Medicine occupies the 16c buildings, renovated and enlarged, of St. Benoît's Abbey; also site of Atger mus. (v.a., cl. weekends and in Aug.), with exceptionally rich selection of 18c drawings. Mus. of natural history. *Vicinity* ● Many v. handsome 17 and 18c châteaux. To W, Ch. d'O, Ch. d'Alco, Ch. de la Piscine, Ch. de la Mosson, Ch. de L'Engarran, etc. (n.v.a.); 5 km E, early-18c Ch. de la Mogère (v.a., p.m. only from Whitsun to Sept. 30; weekends and public hols. or by appointment, from Oct 1 to Whitsun); in the grounds, splendid baroque monumental fountain. ● 10 k W, *Vignogoul*, fmr. abbey of the Assumption: 12c Cistercian church is one of the rare examples of Ile-de-France Goth. style in the Midi. ● 11.5 km S, *Palavas-les-Flots*, and **Maguelonne***. ● 23 km SE, **La Grande-Motte***.

Montpezat-de-Quercy
82 – Tarn-et-Garonne 36 – A 2
Ancient little town, built on hill overlooking the rolling valleys of the surrounding Quercy reg. The central square has 14–15c houses and covered arcades ('couverts'). The imposing 14c collegiate church of St. Martin has some valuable works of art, notably five Flemish tapestries, Goth. stone and 14c English alabaster statues.
Vicinity ● 4 km NW, small country church of Notre Dame-de-Saux, with two cupolas, 12–16c. ● 12 km NW, unusual fortified village of *Castelnau-Montratier*.

Montrésor (Château)
37 – Indre-et-Loire 18 – A 3
In a peaceful setting within a loop of the R. *Indrois*, the 15–early 16c château was built within the remains of a feudal castle (v.a., Apr. 1–Oct. 31); it has some interesting works of art and various exhibits relating to Poland.
Vicinity ● 8.5 km E, *Nouans-les-Fontaines*: 13c church has a remarkable *Descent from the Cross*, from the Jean Fouquet school (second half of 15c).

Montreuil
93 – Seine-St. Denis 11 – C 2
The Mus. d'Histoire Vivante (v.a. Tues., Thurs., Sat. and Sun.) is devoted chiefly to social struggles, from the late 18c to the present day. The venerable church of St. Pierre-St. Paul has 12c choir; nave is 15c.
Vicinity ● At Le Raincy, church of Notre Dame, in reinforced concrete, with comprehensive stained-glass walls, is by Auguste Perret (built 1922–23), one of the most imaginative examples of religious architecture from period between the two world wars.

Montreuil-Bellay
49 – Maine-et-Loire 17 – B 3
A small, fortified lodge flanked by two round towers leads to the château (v.a., from Apr. 1 to Nov. 1), built in 11c and rebuilt in 15c. In inner courtyard, to l. of entrance, kitchen with large central oven. The Petit-Château comprises four main buildings, each entered through turreted staircase. Richly decorated, the Château-Neuf has Goth. Flamboyant chapel with delicately carved ornamentation. The Porte Nouvelle and Porte St. Jean, gates surviving from the old ramparts, are at N and S ends of the Rue Nationale. Former collegiate church of Notre Dame, 15c.
Vicinity ● 8 km NW, remains of the *Abbaye d'Asnières*, 12–13c (fine church). ● 12 km NW, *Doué-la-Fontaine*, ruins of collegiate church of St. Denis, built in late-12c Anjou Goth. style; 15c church of St. Pierre; arenas of Doué (v.a.) were quarries turned into arenas in the Middle Ages. On N 160 to W, Minières Zoo (v.a.). ● 7 km SW, *Le-Puy-Notre-Dame*: collegiate church of the old priory is notable example of 13c Anjou architecture; famed relic known as 'Ceinture de la Vierge' (lit. 'The Virgin's Girdle').

Montreuil-sur-Mer
62 – Pas-de-Calais 1 – B 3
Former fortress, still with its brick ramparts and impressive 16c citadel, incorporating large remains of royal castle (v.a., walk round ramparts also recommended). Queen Berthe's Tower (panorama). St. Saulve: old abbey church, one of finest Goth. churches in the Pas-de-Calais; interior has 13c tombs and font, 17c paintings, rich treasure. Chapel of 15c Hôtel-Dieu, beautiful 17c panelling.
Vicinity ● To N, the Course valley, water-cress growing area, fish farming (trout).

Montreuil-Bellay: *the impressive fort was turned into a delightful country residence in the 15th century.*

MONT-ST. MICHEL
50 – Manche   9 – C 2

One of the most remarkable and famous places in France. The rocky island, conical in shape, is crowned by the abbey, to which access is gained through 15c Porte du Roi, fortified town gate. Lined with 15c gabled houses and souvenir stalls, the Grande-Rue leads past the 11–16c parish church and winds round mount. to stairway into abbey. The abbey church has Romanesque nave and transept, and magnificent Goth. Flamboyant choir dating from 15–early 16c, erected above 15c Gros Piliers crypt; of original early monastery, all that remains are 11–12c Romanesque rooms, virtually dug out of the rock; the 13c Goth. monastery consists largely of the 'Merveille', which dominates N side of mount. Built between 1203 and 1228, this audacious construction has three levels; from bottom to top – almoner's house and storeroom, the Salle des Hôtes and grandiose Salle des Chevaliers, with four naves, refectory and cloister. (The latter, a masterpiece of architectural harmony and refinement, has four galleries, with 227 small red granite columns, in staggered rows. To W, terraced gardens, magnificent panorama. Take parapet walk round 13–15c ramparts; also boat for better look at ext. of mount. Walking on beach is dangerous because of speed of incoming tide (check tide times). Two hist. mus. (inc. 15–18c painting on copper, weapons, sculpture). 3 km N out to sea, islet of *Tombelaine*.

Montségur (Castle)
09 – Ariège   42 – B 3

Shrine of Catharism. Ruins of the castle (difficult climb) recall the siege of 1244 and the ordeal of the Cathars who were burned at the stake at the 'Prat des Crémats'. Magnificent panorama from top. At foot, modern-day village of Montségur is starting-point for climbs of the *Pic St. Barthélemy* (2,349 m.). Archaeological mus.
Vicinity • *Lavelanet*, small industrial town. Excursions: 9 km W, to remains of Ch. de Roquefixade, 13–14c; to SE, *Bélesta* and the *Fontaine de Fontestorbes* (see **Puivert***).

Montsoreau
49 – Maine-et-Loire   17 – B 3

At foot of small hill overlooking l. bank of R. *Loire*, the 15c château – half feudal fortress, half residence – has imposing main stairway in early-16c turret on r. Inside, Mus. des Anciens Goums Mixtes Marocains (Moroccan troops in the French Army): colonial documents and exhibits (cl. Tues.). A bridge links château to old Goth. chapel of St. Michel. Beside it, fmr. residence of the Sénéschal. Many 15 and 16c houses in the town.
Vicinity • 1.5 km E, *Candes-St. Martin*, in lovely setting at confluence of the *Vienne* and the *Loire*; church of St. Martin, built in early-13c Anjou style, fortified in 15c; noteworthy façade, with sculpted 13c porch; int. has numerous statuettes in v. expressive, realist style; 2.5 km to SE, St. Germain-sur-Vienne, original Romanesque church, with sculpted portal; int. has beautiful Angevin (Anjou) vaulting in Plantagenet style. • 4 km S, abbey of **Fontevrault***.

Moret-sur-Loing
77 – Seine-et-Marne   11 – D 3

Charming small town, popular with painters, especially Sisley (his house is near the church) and Pissarro. 13–14c church of Notre Dame with fine Goth. Flamboyant portal (on the pier, Virgin with Child). Many old 15–16c houses, some of which, to r. of church, are timber-framed. So-called 'François I House' (Ren. façade with carved medallions) was removed from Paris in 1826, and reassembled in the garden of the town hall. From bridge over R. *Loing*, fine view over superb lake dominated by the church, keep of fmr. château, remains of ramparts and several old houses. Son et Lumière in summer.
Vicinity • The D 104 runs along both the *Loing* valley and the edge of the forest of **Fontainebleau***.

Morez
39 – Jura   26 – C 2

Holiday centre and winter sports resort at bottom of the Bienne valley, in narrow site with only a single street running through village. From Le Dade rock (two hrs. walk, there and back), sweeping view of whole locality.
Vicinity • 8 km SE, *Les Rousses*, summer and winter sports centre, dominated to SW by the large Fort des Rousses; 18c church, terraced cemetery; 2 km to N, Lac des Rousses, 2 km long; the N 5 follows small Dappes valley (to E, Franco-

Montségur: *now in ruins, this fortified outpost was, in 1244, the last refuge of the Cathar 'heretics'.*

Montsoreau: *in the château, a museum to the French Army's Moroccan troops.*

Swiss border) and continues through the *Faucille Pass* (1,320 m., fine view of **Mt. Blanc***) before reaching **Gex***.

Morimond (Abbey)
52 – Haute-Marne   20 – B 1
Remains of a large Cistercian abbey, founded early 12c, in heart of forest near the Morimond lake (fishing).
Vicinity ● 3 km SW, *Fresnoy-en-Bassigny*, early-16c Goth. church, interesting works of art.

Morlaix
29N – Finistère   8 – C 2
An enormous granite railway viaduct (285 m. long, 58 m. high) separates the harbour from the town. The latter has many old

MORBIHAN (Gulf)
56 – Morbihan   16 – A 2
Small inland sea, strewn with innumerable v. rocky islands, opening into the sea through a narrow bottleneck, 1 km long. Boat trips, highly rec., from **Vannes***, *Locmariaquer*, *Port-Navalo* or **Auray***. Majestically beautiful sites visited inc. the *Ile d'Arz* (12–17c church), the *Pointe d'Arradon*, the *Ile aux Moines*, *Lamor-Baden* and the **Ile de Gavrinis***.

houses, in Rue Ange-de-Guernisac, Rue Basse, Rue Haute. In Rue du Mur, late-15c building known as House of the Duchess Anne, adorned with statues of saints and grotesques; int. has carved wooden staircase. The Grande-Rue is typical of the Breton towns of old.

Fmr. church of the Jacobins, 13–15c, houses mus. (cl. Tues.): archaeology and hist., Breton religious sculptures, reg. furniture, antique and 19c paintings. St. Mathieu church has unusual opening statue of Notre Dame-du-Mur, in wood, late 15c.

Moret-sur-Loing: *the town's charm is due in great part to its situation on the River Loing. Around the fine Gothic church, many well-preserved 15–16c timber-framed houses.*

Vicinity ● The Dossen estuary, or 'Morlaix river'; *Carantec* beach (14 km NW) and Castel Bian point, bordered by white sand (see odd rock called 'The Curé's Chair').

Mortagne-au-Perche
61 – Orne   **10 – D 2**
Beautiful church of Notre Dame, 15–16c, built in Goth. Flamboyant style, with 18c panelling and choir stalls. On top of 12c Porte St. Denis are 16c living quarters, now housing small local mus. 18c fmr. mansion of the Comtes du Perche.
Vicinity ● 15 km N, *Abbaye de la Grande-Trappe*, see **Aigle* (L')**. ● 11 km NE, *Tourouvre*, interesting church and works of art. ● 17 km E, via the Forest of Réno-Valdieu: *Longny-au-Perche*, 15–16c church of St. Martin, flanked by imposing square tower decorated with canopied niches and statues. In cemetery, Ren. chapel of Notre Dame-de-Pitié, with elegant sculpted portal; 23.5 km to E, through the Forest of Longny, the *Forest of Senonches* (16 sq. miles) and *Senonches*, (15–17c château with big mid-12c decorated keep); 12 km to NW, *La Ferte-Vidame*: the 18c outbuildings of the old ruined château house the new 19c château (n.v.a.); the grounds, enclosed within a forest, have six picturesque lakes.

Mortain
50 – Manche   **10 – A 2**
In an attractive setting above the gorge of the Cance. 13c church of St. Évroult, 14c tower with Romanesque portal.
Vicinity ● 1 km N, fmr. Blanche Abbey, 12c chapel and cloister gallery, 13c chapter-house, 11c cellar, (permanent exhibition: African masks and objects); large waterfall (drops 25 m., in delightful woodland setting); small cascade (path from the Place du Château) in rocky hollow; church of St. Michel (viewing table, panorama). ● Excursions in and around the upper *Sée* valley (12 km N).

Morzine
74 – Haute-Savoie   **26 – D 3**
Large summer resort and winter sports centre, located at junction of six valleys.
Vicinity ● Cable-cars to Le Pléney (1,600 m.) and the Pointe de Nyon (2,020 m.), both offering superb views. ● Cable-car service (departing from hamlet of Les Prodains, 4.5 km to NE) climbs to new resort, *Avoriaz*, at 1,800 m.: an alternative route is by road through the Joux-Verte pass. ● To NE, the Ardent cascade and *Lac de Montriond* (1,049 m.). ● 12.5 km NW, ruins of abbey of *Notre Dame-d'Aulps*.

MORVAN
89 – Yonne – 58 – Nièvre   **19 – B2/B3**
Regional nature reserve. Rambling and horse riding; sailing, rowing and motorboat centres on the lakes; beaches. Canoeing on the rivers. also fishing and waterfowling. See **Château-Chinon***. **Quarré-les-Tombes***, **Vézelay***, and **Settons*** lake.

Moulins: *the Clock Tower, topped by a Jack-o'-the-Clock which chimes on the hour.*

Mouchamps
85 – Vendée   **22 – D 1**
Still largely Protestant since 17c, despite vicissitudes inflicted on the Huguenots at the end of that century).

Vicinity ● 4 km NE, in woods near Colombier farm, tomb of France's great World War I Prime Minister, Georges ('Tiger') Clemenceau (d. 1929), next to that of his father; tombstone depicting Pallas leaning on her lance. ● 3 km NW, Ch. du Parc-Soubise, 16–17c, burned down in 1794 and partially restored.

Mouilleron-en-Pareds
85 – Vendée   **22 – D 1**
Mus. des Deux-Victoires, mementoes and documents relating to Clemenceau and Field-Marshal de Lattre de Tassigny, both natives of Mouilleron (cl. Tues.). The Field Marshal (d. 1952) is buried in cemetery beside his son (killed in Indo-China). 15c church (13-bell carillon). Mid-16c Ren. Ch. de la Fosse.

Moulins
03 – Allier   **25 – A 2**
Cath. of Notre Dame, 15–16 and 19c, has one of the masterpieces of French painting in its sacristy; the famed late-15c *Triptych* by the Maître de Moulins, also very fine late-15 and 16c stained-glass windows. Remains of château of the Dukes of Bourbon; the Ren. Pavillon d'Anne de Beaujeu serves as entrance to mus. of art and archaeology (prehist., lapidary collections), German primitive painting, Moulins pottery, 19c academic painting. Mus. of folklore and Old Moulins in 15c house. The old quarter around cath. is picturesque, especially Rue des Orfèvres and Rue and Place de l'Ancien-Palais. In Place de l'Hôtel de Ville, 15c Clock Tower, crowned by popular mid-17c Jack-o'-the-Clock. In chapel of Lycée Banville (fmr. convent), monumental mausoleum of Henri de Montmorency, one of the key works of mid-17c French sculpture.
Vicinity ● 1.5 km E, *Yzeure*, inter

MOURÈZE (Corrie)
34 – Hérault   **43 – A 1**
Old village of Mourèze, very picturesque (narrow valleys, remains of château, Romanesque church), is ringed by a wilderness of dolomite rocks – often fantastically shaped – which form a huge corrie, or natural amphitheatre, covering more than 850 acres.

esting 12c Romanesque church, (capitals, crypt); 10 km E, late-16c Ch. de Pommay; 3.5 km farther on, *Lusigny*, 12c Romanesque church; 2 km to SSE, 16c Orvalet Manor. ● 28.5 km ESE, via *Dompierre-sur-Besbre*, the *Ch. de Thoury*: small 15c fortress in pink granite with elegant royal apartments (v.a., ext. only, in summer). ● 12 km WSW, **Souvigny***.

Moustiers-Ste. Marie   38 – C 3
04 – Alpes-de-Haute-Provence
At mouth of wide crevice, sheer walls of which are linked by the Chaîne de l'Étoile, 227 m. in length. Attractive maze of alleyways and small squares with vaulted arcades. The church, Romanesque and Goth., leads on to chapel of Notre Dame-de-Beauvoir, 12–14c, (key at presbytery), which lies directly under the Chaîne de l'Étoile. In Romanesque crypt near the church, mus. of Moustiers pottery (v.a., cl. Tues., Apr. 1 to Oct. 31). Small corniche road, to r., leads to grotto chapel of the Madeleine; wide views from terrace.

Moutier-d'Ahun (Le)
23 – Creuse   24 – B 3
12–15c fmr. abbey church has unique group of late-17c panelling and carved stalls in choir; also, in sacristy, 17c Christ, in wood, 12c painted statues and reliquaries.
Vicinity ● 1.5 km S, *Ahun*: church, part-Romanesque, 9c crypt; late-17c panelling in choir.

Moûtiers-Tarentaise
73 – Savoie   32 – D 2
Fmr. capital of *Tarentaise* reg. St. Pierre cath., 15c nave, 11c apse and crypt; rich church treasure. Mus. de l'Académie de la Val d'Isère.
Vicinity ● To S and SE, many excellent excursions in *Trois Vallées*. Also large winter sports centres: between them, *Belleville*, *Méribel* and **Courchevel*** have 300 km of maintained ski-slopes – largest single area of skiing in Europe.

Mouzon
08 – Ardennes   6 – D 2
On island formed by R. *Meuse* and the *Canal de l'Est*. Church of Notre Dame, fmr. Benedictine abbey church, 13c, is the most beautiful in the Ardennes: the façade, flanked by two towers, has a superbly sculpted 13c central portal; magnificent choir, ringed by an ambulatory with five Rayonnant chapels 14–15c. Porte de Bourgogne. Archaeological mus.
Vicinity ● To NNW, many pleasant walks along the bends of the *Meuse*.

Mouzon: *the superb sculptures on the portal of Notre Dame.*

Mulhouse
68 – Haut-Rhin   21 – A 1
Seven mus. worth visiting: (1). Mus. of Cloth Printing (cl. Tues.), only one of its kind in the world: demonstration of machine printing, unusual printing machines and materials (8 million swatches in 1,600 books), exhibited in rotation. Costumes, flower paintings, collection of preliminary sketches, handkerchiefs. (2). In Maison Steinbach, Mus. des Beaux-Arts: French and Alsatian painting, 19–20c. (3). French Railway Mus.: from 1844–1937. (4). Mus. Schlumpf, aka French Automobile Mus.: cars, in working order, from

Mulhouse: *allegorical figures on the façade of the town hall.*

1890–1974. (5). Hist. mus. in Rhenish Ren. fmr. town hall: local archaeology, hist. and pottery, toys. Gallery of folk art. 'Attic of Abundance': huge timbered room, from 1510, with objets d'art, weather vanes, shop signs, etc. (6). Lapidary mus. in chapel of St. Jean (16c murals). (7). Industrial Society of Mulhouse's mineralogical mus. ● Other sights inc.: St. Étienne temple, notable group of 14c stained-glass windows. To SE, fine zoo and botanical gardens (more than 5,000 plants). Bollwerk, Diable and Nesle Towers.
Vicinity ● *Harth Forest.*

Munster
68 – Haut-Rhin   21 – A 1
Famed above all for its cheese, but also a good base for trips. Fmr. abbot's palace, mid-16c town hall. *Vicinity* ● 'Route du Fromage' ('Cheese Road') – signposted. ● To SW, on D 10, the *Fecht* valley, or Grande Vallée; through *Muhlbach-sur-Munster* to Metzeral, centre for pleasant boat trips on two artificial lakes, Fischboedle and Schiess-rothried, at foot of the *Hohneck*. ● 7.5 km N, *Hohrodberg*, (800 m.), attractive mountain resort, magnificent panorama over the Vosges; 3.5 km to N, *Le Linge* (see **Trois-Épis***). ● 6 km E, Soultzbach-les-Bains, 14c Goth. church, interesting works of art; 18c chapel of Ste. Catherine; châteaux of Haneck and of Schrankenfels.

Murat
15 – Cantal   30 – D 3
Old town built in tiers above the Alagnon. 15 and 16c houses. 15c

Munster: *the market place evokes the past of this old Alsace city.*

church of Notre Dame-des-Oliviers; int. has a Black Virgin. *Vicinity* ● 2 km S, *Bredons*: Romanesque fortified church, late-11c Romanesque portal; noteworthy carved retables, late-17c to mid-18c. ● Recommended excursions to the *Puy Mary* and to **Le Lioran***.

Mur-de-Barrez
12 – Aveyron   36 – C 1
Old town built on hill overlooking the Bromme valley and beyond. 12c church with 14c portal; int. has interesting capitals and recumbent tomb statue of a knight. Clock Tower, fmr. town gate. Old houses. Above the town, ruins of castle. *Vicinity* ● To E, Sarrans dam, on R. *Truyère*; at Laussac, on peninsula, fine view over reservoir (swim-

ming). ● 8.5 km N, *Raulhac* (see **Vic-sur-Cère***).

Mur-de-Bretagne
22 – Côtes-du-Nord   9 – A 3
Highly rec. base for excursions. *Vicinity* ● To W, *lake-reservoir* and *barrage of Guerlédan* (988 acres, over length of 13 km, holding more than 15 billion gallons of water), in *Blavet* gorges; lovely forest of *Quénécan*; ruins of Abbey of *Bon Repos*, now enclosed within a farm (v.a.); remains of 13c chapel; majestic 18c buildings; near Les Forges-des-Salles, *Salles Lake* and remains of château, fmr. seat of the Rohan family. ● To W, the D 44 follows the wild *Daoulas* valley, which leads into the *Blavet* valley. ● To N, *Poulancre* valley, set between sheer rock faces; *St. Mayeux* and *Corlay* have interesting churches.

Mure (La)
38 – Isère   32 – B 3
Small industrial town, centre for excursions in *Valjouffrey* reg. *Vicinity* ● 12 km E, *Valbonnais*, dominating r. bank of R. *Bonne* (château dating from 1608); *Entraigues*, on terrace at confluence of the *Bonne* and the Malsane. From *La Chapelle-en-Valjouffrey*, through the wooded Béranger gorge, to the hamlet of *Valsenestre* (1,302 m.) at mouth of a v. large corrie (starting point for numerous excursions in Ecrins Natnl. Park). Alternatively, via scenic route to *Le Désert*, last hamlet in the valley (1,267 m.), below the needle and peak of *Olan*. From *Entraigues*, to N via the *Ornon Pass*, the road leads to **Bourg-d'Oisans*** (gorges and waterfalls).

Murol
63 – Puy-de-Dôme   30 – D 2
Picturesque little town, at alt. of 833 m., under a basaltic hill crowned by ruins of 12–14 and 15c feudal castle, in black and reddish lava; early 17c Ren.-style quarters and two 13–15c chapels; 15c circular keep. Splendid panoramic view. *Vicinity* ● Excursions in *Mts. Dore* (see **Mont-Dore***). ● 2 km W, *Chambon lake* (beach, fishing, water sports), at foot of the enormous Dent du Marais (1,068 m.). ● To SSW, Rocher de l'Aigle and Chaudefour valley. ● To NE, **St. Néctaire***. ● 17 km N, *Aydat* lake (fishing, canoeing), in superb surroundings.

Murat: *in the pretty Alagnon valley, the small town rises in tiers up the mountain-side.*

N

Najac
12 – Aveyron 36 – B 2
Extraordinary site on ridge of a promontory above bend in R. *Aveyron*. Ruins of 12–13c castle are dominated by a huge circular keep more than 30 m. high, which contains three vaulted rooms. Rue du Bariou, town's single street, still has numerous old houses.

Nancy
54 – Meurthe-et-Moselle 13 – C 2
Mid-18c Place Stanislas consists of a group of Classical buildings and is closed at its entrances and corners by superb wrought-iron gates and railings, with gilded decorations, by Jean Lamour; two of these frame fountains ornamented with statues: in centre, statue of King Stanislas of Poland, Duke of Lorraine; to S of square, town hall; to W, fine arts mus. (cl. Mon. a.m. and Tues.): collection of paintings from principal European schools, esp. Dutch and Flemish (Rubens), German, Spanish (Ribera), but above all French: Philippe de Champaigne, Boucher, Delacroix, Courbet, Manet, Bonnard, Modigliani. Large collection of graphic art: Callot, Grandville. 115 pieces of glassware by Daum. Rue Héré and triumphal arch to glory of Louis XV lead to long Place de la Carrière,

Najac: *the weird ruins of the castle dominate this strange village.*

with its beautiful 18c mansions and mid-18c Government Palace, ringed by colonnades. To l., huge Pépinière park, dating from 1765 (57½ acres). ● Grande-Rue contains imposing 16c ducal palace, flanked by elegantly sculpted gatehouse in Goth. Flamboyant style; it contains reg. hist. mus. (cl. Tues.) rich in archaeology, hist. souvenirs, objets d'art (five magnificent 15c Tournai tapestries), paintings (two Georges de La Tour) and reg. pottery. As annexes, it has 15c Franciscan church and convent. Former is Dukes of Lorraine's equivalent of Kings of France's St. Denis: inside, recumbent figure of Philippe de

Gueldre, second wife of Duke René II (d. 1547), one of Ligier Richier's loveliest works; to l. of choir, in octagonal ducal chapel (1607), seven black marble cenotaphs of Dukes of Lorraine. Grande-Rue, which has many old houses, leads to late-14c Craffe gate, also an annexe of reg. hist. mus. (medieval sculptures). ● 18c cath. has rich 18c decorations (screens by Jean Lamour); interesting treasure. In 18c church of Notre Dame-du-Bon-Secours, tomb of King Stanislas and queen's mausoleum; a monument contains heart of their daughter, Marie Leszcynska, wife of Louis XV. Mus. of school of Nancy (cl. Tues.): collection of Art Nouveau furniture and decorations. Zoo mus. contains lovely collection of natnl. and local fauna and enormous tropical aquarium (72 tanks).
Vicinity ● Via N4 to E, mus. of hist. of ironworking (v.a., p.m.; cl. Tues.); 17c *Bosserville* charterhouse, in purest Classical style (technical school; v.a. during school hols.); chapel, fmr. chapter-house, large cloister, etc. ● 9 km SE, Ch. de *Fléville*, Ren. with 12c keep (v.a. Sat. and Sun., Easter – Nov. 1). ● To N, Grand Couronné, scene of major battles in 1914, **Amance*** plateau and Mount Ste. Geneviève (390 m.); to E, *Champenoux*, natnl. cemetery and monument to dead of Grand Couronné.

Nant
12 – Aveyron 37 – A 3
Little old town in attractive setting at entrance to canyon of R.

Nancy: *on Place Stanislas, the magnificent 18c railings by Jean Lamour frame allegorical fountains sculpted by Barthélemy Guibal. This is the fountain of Neptune.*

The wrought-iron, gilded railings decorate the corners of the square, which is a vast rectangle, 124 m. by 106 m.

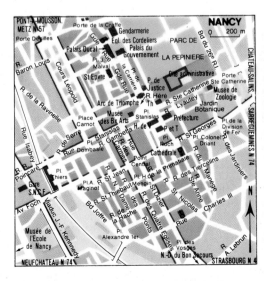

Dourbie. Late-12c fmr. Benedictine abbey is interesting example of Rouergue reg. version of Romanesque style; curious antiquated-looking porch. 17c covered market. Former church of St. Jacques, in S Goth. style (deconsecrated). Many old houses. Fine view from Promenade de Claux.
Vicinity ● Romanesque chapels of St. Martin-du-Vigan (SW) and St. Alban (S), Ch. de Castelnau (SW), village and ruins of Ch. d'Algues (SW) in magnificent setting. ● To NE, impressive *Dourbie* gorges. ● 6 km SW, Durzon spring. ● **Larzac*** causse.

Nantes
44 – Loire-Atlantique   16 – C 3
Lovely town of artistic interest; rich in monuments, of which most noteworthy is ducal castle, magnificent late-15c fortress flanked by stout towers; int. courtyard is surrounded by buildings from different periods whose elegance and rich decoration contrast with the severity of ext.; façade of main building is crowned by magnificently carved dormer windows. Three mus. occupy main building, Governor's palace and Harness building (cl. Tues., Sept. – June): decorative arts mus., reg. hist. and ethnography mus., and Salorges mus. (hist. of town's commercial and maritime activities). In 15c Horseshoe tower, exhibitions. ● 15–17c cath. of St. Pierre, completed 19c, contains one of major works of French sculpture: the early-16c tomb of François I, Duke of Brittany, and of his wife, by Michel Colombe; in N transept, lovely late-19c tomb of Lamoricière (19c general). On S side of cath., elegant 15c Psallette building. On N side, 14–15c St. Pierre door. ● Beaux-Arts mus. (cl. Tues.) is one of richest in France: Italian early masters, paintings by Flemish (Rubens) and French artists (three La Tour, Le Nain, Ingres, Courbet, Delacroix), also Impressionists. Large collection of contemp. art: Dufy, Kandinsky, Hartung, Soulages, Magnelli, Pierre Roy, Jean Gorin, Chaissac, etc. 'Domus Aureau' by Anne and Patrick Poirier. Unusual mus. devoted to Jules Verne (native of Nantes) gives highly original picture of the world-famed writer's life and work. Also rec. is reg. postal mus. and trade-guild mus. in 14–15c Hautière manor. Natural hist. mus. is one of largest in France. Dobrée mus. is devoted to medieval and Ren. art; print room (exhibitions). Next door, 15c Jean V manor (prehist., Roman and Merovingian antiquities, Greek ceramics, etc.). ● 18c town surrounds Place Royale and Cours Cambronne, while church of

Ste. Croix is heart of medieval quarter, many 15 and 16c houses. ● On fmr. Feydeau island, beautiful 18c mansions of town's shipowners. ● Town has many parks, esp. Procé park and, to E, at Doulon, Grand-Blottereau park (huge conservatories and garden with exotic plants); also botanical garden with bust of Jules Verne. Panoramic view from Brittany tower, built 1975.

Nantua
01 – Ain   26 – B 3
On E tip of *Lac de Nantua*, in narrow valley. 12c church, fmr. Benedictine abbey church (Romanesque main doorway); inside, interesting works of art. Specialities: quenelles and crayfish.
Vicinity ● Tour of lake via N84 and D74; boat trip, hire of boats and pedalos. ● From Mts. d'Ain signal point, 1 hr. 45 min. away (1,031 m.), lovely view over lake. ● To S, charterhouse of Meyriat, founded 1116 (now a forester's lodge); Meyriat forest. ● 15 km NE, *Lac Genin*. ● 8 km E, *Lac de Sylans*.

Narbonne
11 – Aude   42 – D 2
With **Béziers***, it is the capital of S of France's wine-growing region Dominated by Cath. of St. Just, of which only late 13 – early 14c choir was completed; int., with high vaults rising 40 m. from ground, is majestic; 16c stained-glass windows at end of apse, and 15c on sides; in

Narbonne: *the Archbishop's Palace and the magnificent but unfinished Cathedral of St. Just stand beside the canal.* ▲
In Sigean's African reserve: animals in the wild. ▼

ambulatory round choir, tombs of Cardinal Pierre de la Jugie (late 14c) and Cardinal Briçonnet (mid-16c); v. rich treasure (apply to sacristy). To NE of cath., St. Sébastien, in Goth. Flamboyant style, enlarged 17c. Archbishop's Palace, beside St. Just, is an imposing fortress flanked by sturdy towers between which Viollet-le-Duc built town hall. Passageway separates 12–13c old palace from 14c new palace, which houses art and hist. mus. (cl. Mon.); in fmr. archbishop's apartments, mus. interesting collections of Flemish, Dutch, Italian and French paintings; noteworthy collection of pharmacy jars. In old palace and its 13c

---

NAOURS (Caves)
80 – Somme   5 – C 1
Strange network of refuge caves, some natural, some cut into the chalk. Well-lit and with audio effects (guided tours daily), they comprise some 30 galleries, totalling 3 km in length and include 300 rooms, three chapels, stables, cowsheds, bakeries with ovens, barns, etc. Local folklore and crafts museum.

high chapel, mus. (collection of prehist., artefacts from digs at various local oppida, famed 3c marble sarcophagus, funerary stele and monumental pillars). Lapidary mus. in 13c fmr. church of Notre Dame-de-Lamourguier. Near 12–13c St. Paul-Serge, Paleo-Christian cemetery (v.a.); nearby, Trois-Nourrices house, with façade sculpted with mid-16c bare-breasted caryatids. Also rec., Maison Vigneronne (hist. of reg. wine industry) and Horreum mus. (lapidary collections).

Vicinity ● To E, between Narbonne and sea, limestone *Clape* mountain, strange, wildly beautiful area; *Narbonne-Plage*, new tourist complex at mouth of R. *Aude*. ● 14 km SE, **Gruissan***. ● 7 km S, *Bages*, old fishing village on rocky peninsula overlooking lakes of *Bages* and *Sigean* (sailing centre); near *Sigean* (small local mus.), 150-acre African reserve (enclosures with bears, rhinoceros, lions, aquatic animals, alligator farm); 5 km to E, *Port-La-Nouvelle*; to S, lakes of *Lapalme* and *Leucate*, beaches of *La Franqui* and **Port-Barcarès***. ● 14 km SW, Abbey of **Fontfroide***.

Navarreux
64 – Pyrénées-Atlantiques 40 – D 1
Once-fortified town; perimeter wall, 1.5 km long, is well preserved. 17c St. Antoine gate stands opposite 15c fortified bridge. On r. bank of torrent, 15c isolated Herrère tower.
Vicinity ● 5 km NW, imposing Louis XIII-style Ch. d'Audaux. ● 5.5 km S, *Gurs*: a deportation camp for non-French Jews was built here in 1940; memorial in cemetery; minor road leads to *Hôpital-St. Blaise*, 5.5 km away: 12c church has unusual central cupola on intersecting ribs forming an eight-pointed star; windows are closed by stone slabs with motifs of Hispano-Moorish inspiration.

Nemours
77 – Seine-et-Marne 11 – D 3
12c Goth. and Ren. church. In 12, 15 and 17c château, local mus. Modernistic reg. hist. mus. (1972), v. didactically-inclined, in wooded setting. Gréau Rocks forest park.
Vicinity ● 1.5 km and 2 km S, rocks of Chaintréauville and Beauregard (viewing-table). ● Rec. excursion in *Lunain* valley and Nanteau wood, to E. ● 8 km NW, *Larchant*: 12, 13

and 14c church of St. Mathurin, partly ruined, interesting works of art. ● 15 km S, *Château-Landon*, picturesque, once-fortified old town; Romanesque and Goth. church of Notre Dame, flanked by magnificent 13c belfry; fmr. abbey of St. Séverin (old people's home, v.a.): 11c lower church, built beneath ruins of 16c abbey church, contained 12c frescos, now on show in guardroom; lovely 13–14c convent buildings overlooking valley. ● 19 km SE, *Égreville*, 15c covered market, 13–15c church with belfry-porch on picturesque square.

Nérac
47 – Lot-et-Garonne 35 – C 2
Only N wing remains of 15–16c château which houses mus. (archaeological collections); overlooking courtyard, elegant gallery with wreathed columns and historiated capitals (cl. Mon.). Petit-Nérac has retained its medieval character, steep, winding streets and old houses, inc. lovely Ren. mansions. Magnificent Promenade de la Garenne, 2 km long, beside R. *Baïse*.
Vicinity ● 6 km NW, *Barbaste*, on R. *Gélise*, imposing 14–15c fortified mill where France's King Henri IV stayed; 8 km to NW, *Xaintrailles*, 12c castle with mid-15c square keep. ● 11 km W, at *Durance*, remains of château dating from time of Henri IV (16–early 17c); elegant 16c Lagrange chapel, unusually decorated with 60 painted figures from 15c.

Neuf-Brisach
68 – Haut-Rhin 21 – A 1
Facing citadel of Alt-Brisach (in Germany); fortified town built by Vauban, one of most noteworthy examples of 17c open-country fortifications, also the most complete. Inside octagonal perimeter wall, the town, divided into equal sections by streets which intersect at right-angles, still looks as it did originally. One of two fortified gates, Porte de Belfort, houses Vauban museum.
Vicinity ● 4 km E, hydroelectric power station of Vogelgrün on fourth level of *Grand Canal d'Alsace* (v.a.).

Neufchâteau
88 – Vosges 13 – B 3
Town is built on slopes and at foot of hill on which stand two churches, 12–15c St. Christophe, and 13c St. Nicolas, constructed above a lower Romanesque church: 14–15c chapels; inside, 15c holy sepulchre with nine figures in multi-coloured stone, of German origin.
Vicinity ● 11 km S, *Pompierre*: church has magnificent sculpted

NAVACELLES (Cwm)
34 – Hérault 37 – A 3
One of most impressive sites in the Causses, carved out of the limestone *Larzac* plateau to a depth of more than 400 m. Its whitish cliffs tower over what used to be a bend in R. *Vis*, which traces a green half-circle, only cultivable land in area, containing hamlet of Navacelles. Reached via narrow, zigzagging road (v. dangerous for cars) which winds down from *Blandas* viewing-point, crosses valley and winds up opposite side to Baume-Auriol. From road, tiny path leads along gorge to source of R. Foux and the village, built on two steep promontories.

Nevers: *the cathedral, whose 10–16c lay-out is highly unusual, towers over the old quarters and the Loire.*

Romanesque doorway with expressively realistic figures; 1.5 km before *Pompierre*, 17c chapel of Notre Dame-du-Pilar-de-Saragosse; road climbs up *Mouzon* valley to *La Motte* mountain (506 m., fine view), on which stand ruins of small town destroyed in 17c.

Neufchâtel-en-Bray
76 – Seine-Maritime   5 – A 2
Mathon-Durand mus. (cl. Mon.; Sept.–June, v.a. Sat. and Sun. only) is devoted to reg. folk arts and trads. Gallery showing how cheese is made. 13c choir and 16c nave of church of Notre Dame.
Vicinity ● To NW, Ch. de *Mesnières-en-Bray*: magnificent 16c Ren. building; lovely room with 17c painted ceiling; 16c chapel decorated with stained-glass windows and statues; late-19c chapel (v.a. Sat. and Sun. p.m., Easter–Nov. 1). ● To SW, *Forêt d'Eawy*.

Neuvic-d'Ussel
19 – Corrèze   30 – C 2
Attractive tourist centre, close to upper *Dordogne* valley (see **Bort-les-Orgues***).
Vicinity ● To ENE, *Triouzoune* reservoir (beaches, water sports). ● 19 km W on *Egletons* road, beyond Vianon gorges, ruins of *Ch. de Ventadour*, standing proudly on rocky spur dominating *Luzège* gorges, in romantic setting; fortress, one of greatest strongholds in the Limou-

sin, was built 11–12c and renovated 14–15c; lovely 12c round tower, 15c keep; famed 12c troubadour, Bernard de Ventadour, was born here.

Nevers
58 – Nièvre   25 – A 1
Town, famed for its porcelain, stands above R. *Loire*; from red sandstone bridge which crosses it (Loire bridge, N7), there is a truly lovely view of the impressive cath. which dominates old quarters. Cath. of St. Cyr and Ste. Juliette has 13c nave, 14c choir and 16c tower, while still retaining 11c Romanesque apse and transept. Late 15–16c ducal palace is elegant part-Goth., part-Ren. building, entered

via vast terraced square overlooking *Loire*. Late-16c Croux gate contains local archaeological mus. (v.a., Wed., Sat. and Sun. p.m.); in municipal mus. at 16, Rue St. Genest (cl. Tues.), fine collections of Nevers porcelain from 16 to 18c. Magnificent 13c Goth. chapterhouse. St. Étienne is noteworthy example of late-11c homogenous Romanesque style. Chapel of St. Gildard convent contains reliquary of Bernadette Soubirous, the Lourdes visionary (she died here in 1879); a small mus. is devoted to her. Church of Ste. Bernardette-du-Balnay (1966) is unusual and highly original example of contemp. religious art.
Vicinity ● To SW, picturesque site of '*Bec d'Allier*' at confluence of R. *Loire* and the *Allier*. ● 14.5 km S, *St. Parize-le-Châtel*, 12c church with noteworthy crypt, very unusual historiated capitals.

Nice
06 – Alpes-Maritimes   45 – A 1
Centre of town, in magnificent setting on famed Baie des Anges, is Place Masséna, with lovely group of neo-Classical buildings, opening on to Albert I gardens (open-air theatre), which lead in turn to Promenade des Anglais, one of world's best-known seafront avenues. ● But any visit to Nice should start in the old town, with its lively, animated streets. Place Rossetti, Cath. of Ste. Réparate, cold and unappealing 17c Classical building; Rue Droite, 17c Lascaris palace (noteworthy int. in 17 and 18c Genoese style; monumental staircase and sumptuously decorated reception rooms). Gésu church, consecrated to St. James, has exuberantly decorated baroque int. Mid-18c Miséricorde chapel also has richly decorated baroque int. and one of masterpieces of 15c Nice school: *Retable de la Vierge de Miséricorde*, by Jean Miralhet. Flower market in Cours Saleya. Old

NIAUX (Grotto)
09 – Ariège   42 – A 3
One of loveliest prehist. painted grottoes in France (v.a., July–Sept.). A succession of monumentally proportioned galleries leads, 800 m. from entrance, to huge circular chamber called the Salon Noir; walls are decorated with bison, horses, ibex, wild oxen, deer, painted in black and red in a bold but delicate realistic style. This remarkable coll., well-conserved, is one of masterpieces of Magdalenian art (12,000 B.C.).
Vicinity ● To SW, *Vallée du Vicdessos*, Capoulet-Junac; ruins of 14c castle of Miglos; Laramade. Teillet forest; *Vicdessos* (ruins of castle of Montréal); from *Auzat*, small industrial town, various excsns.: Bassiès lake, *Montcalm* (3,078 m.) and Estats peak (3,115 m.), lovely state forest of Auzat, Pradières dam and Izourt lake, etc.; from Laramade, to S, *Siguer* valley and mt. crossing.

town is dominated by castle hill (lift, magnificent view); at its foot lies port, overlooked by Boron hill; this is departure point for regular boat service to Corsica. ● Nice has 11 mus. Masséna mus. (cl. Mon. and Nov.): sumptuously decorated and furnished Empire-style reception rooms, local art and hist. (important collection of 15c early masters of Nice school). Beaux-Arts or Chéret mus. (cl. Mon.), 16–17c Italian and French canvases, Van Loo gallery, Belle Époque canvases (portraits of local personalities), Impressionists: Degas, Monet, Sisley, etc.; also galleries devoted to Jules Cheret, large Carpeaux bequest and galleries of late-19c academic and contemp. paintings (Van Dongen, Bonnard, Dufy bequest). Glorious Chagall memorial mus. (cl. Tues.): *Le Message Biblique*, works inspired by Old Testament. Vieux-Logis mus.: reconstruction of int. of 15–16c house. Mus. of human paleontology, on Terra Amata site (elephant hunters' camp, 400,000 years old). Matisse and archaeological mus. in Arènes villa at Cimiez (cl. Sun. a.m. and Mon.) Anatole Jakovksy internatnl. mus. of naive art; naval mus. in Bellanda tower (castle); natural hist. mus. (Barla mus., Blvd. Risso; malacology – study of molluscs – gallery in Cours Saleya); Franciscan mus. in Cimiez monastery. ● Archaeological digs in Cimiez have uncovered, in Arènes park, remains of 2–3c spa buildings, Roman residential quarter with paved streets, 5c Christian baptistry and basilica. Nearby 1 and 3c amphitheatre could easily hold 4,000 spectators. Church of fmr. Franciscan monastery has unusual façade in Goth. 'troubadour' style dating from 1845 (exc. porch, which dates from 1662); int. has important works of art, inc. three magnificent retables by Brea brothers, esp. *La Vierge de Pitié entre St. Martin et Ste. Catherine*, by Louis Brea (1475). Church

Nice: *the port, its tall 18c houses, and the castle hill, site of the monument to the dead.*
The modern town lies at the foot of the hill. The flower market is as colourful as it is lively.

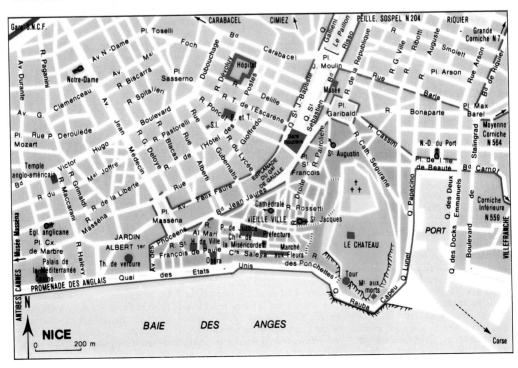

and cemetery, where Matisse and Dufy are buried, are surrounded by delightful Italian garden, which has wonderful views of town and port. To NE of Cimiez, along Blvd. Pasteur: former Benedictine abbey of St. Pons; early 18c baroque church, with elliptical nave, has Goth. Rayonnant choir and four chapels, lavishly decorated.
Vicinity • 10 km NW, *Falicon*: charming, typically reg. village (fine view of Nice from terrace), Mt. Chauve (845 m.) and *Aspremont*; v. unusual village with concentric alleys, huddled on a round hill, 13c church. • 23 km N, *Levens*: 13–14c church, view over *Var* gorges and **Vésubie***. • To NE, La Trinité, Drap. Peillon: extraordinary village perched on narrow, sheer rock (15–16c Pénitents chapel, frescos inside) and *Peille*, unusual town in magnificent setting; Romanesque and Goth. church, numerous 14–15c houses around main, arcaded square; fine view from terrace. • To E, Mt. Boron and Mt. Alban: fort on Mt. Alban is interesting example of late-16c military arch. • From Nice to Menton, the Moyenne Corniche (31 km), Corniche Inférieure (33 km) and Grande Corniche (31 km) roads lead to most impressive sites on Riviera.

Niederbronn-les-Bains
67 – Bas-Rhin   14 – A 1
Mineral-water and health resort in wooded area. Roman spring (stomach and liver afflictions, rheumatism). Celtic spring (kidneys and bladder). Small archaeological mus.
Vicinity • To W, late-13c *Ch. de Wasenbourg* (fine view) and Wasenkoepfel beacon (521 m. alt.); to NW, Ziegenberg, ruins of ovoid wall, known as 'Celtic camp'; trip recommended round Grand Win-

Nîmes: *symbol of the town's Roman past, this head of Venus belongs to the Antiquities Museum in the Maison Carrée, one of ancient Gaul's best-preserved monuments.* ▲
The Tour Magne, *main tower of the 1 BC walls, offers unsurpassed views of the town and surrounding countryside.* ▼

tersberg (581 m. alt.; marvellous view over lower Vosges range). • 10 km NW, *Ch. de Falkenstein*, whose ruins stand on top of steep red sandstone rock lined with caves: path leads to Hanau lake (45 acres)

in magnificent wooded setting; ruins of *Ch. de Waldeck*. • On plain, 3 km SE, *Reichshoffen*, which gave its name to heroic charge of mounted brigade in 1870 Franco-Prussian war.

Nieul-sur-l'Autise
85 – Vendée   23 – A 2
Former abbey, founded 11c. Abbey church, in Poitou Romanesque style, has mid-12c triple nave and interesting sculpted capitals, esp. on main doorway. On S side, 12c Romanesque cloister, only complete one in Poitou region. Chapterhouse.

Nîmes
30 – Gard   43 – C 1
'France's Rome' contains some fine monuments to its past. Amphitheatre, Maison Carrée, Temple of Diana, Magne tower, Arles gate and the 'Castellum' are open every day (single entry ticket). The amphitheatre is one of most impressive monuments of Roman Gaul; 131 m. long, 100 m. wide, it could hold around 21,000 people and was used for circus games. Maison Carrée, temple dedicated to Augustus' grandchildren, the 'Princes of Youth', houses antiquities mus. Big La Fontaine garden (open in summer and floodlit until 11 p.m.) on slopes of Mt. Cavalier; designed in 18c, it retains important elements of Roman epoch, esp. ruins of Temple of Diana (probably 1BC thermal baths), elegantly decorated; path leads to late-1BC Magne tower, which has magnificent view as far as Mt. **Ventoux***. Other Roman monuments: Arles gate, or Augustus gate, and the 'Castellum', ancient Roman watertower, at foot of 17c citadel. ● In old town, beautiful 17–18c mansions,

Niort: *the 70 m. high neo-Gothic spires of St. André dominate the old city's mass of pale-golden roofs.*

town hall (fmr. 17c Treasury building) and cath. of St. Castor (begun 1096, frequently renovated). In 17c fmr. bishop's palace, Old Nîmes mus. (cl. Tues. in winter). Archaeological mus. in 18c fmr. Jesuit college (v.a. as above): Celtic, Gallo-Roman and Roman antiquities. Beaux-Arts mus., temporarily closed. A centre of contemp. art is due to be built by architect Norman Foster.
Vicinity ● Lovely walks to N, across 'garrigues' (local heathland) between *Nîmes* and **Gardon*** gorges. ● 20 km NE, **Pont-du-**

Gard*. ● 16 km SW, then 15 min. on foot, oppidum of Nages (Neolithic and Celtic remains).

Niort
79 – Deux-Sèvres   23 – A 2
Main sights are: fmr. Ren. town hall, which contains pillory mus.; 12–13c keep, overlooking quayside along R. *Sèvre*, with ethnography mus. (arms, costumes); and late-15c church of Notre Dame. Beaux-Arts mus. occupies fmr. oratory buildings. Interesting 14–15–16c houses in old quarter (Estissac mansion, Présidial house, etc.).
Vicinity ● Sèvre marshes, or *Marais Poitevin*, so-called 'Green Venice'; boat trips along canals shaded by tall trees (departure point at *Coulon*, 11 km to W of Niort, trips last between 30 min. and 1 hr. 30. See **Maillezais***).

Nogent-le-Rotrou
28 – Eure-et-Loire   10 – D 3
Capital of Perche reg., at foot of hill dominated by imposing 12–13c castle of St. Jean, highly fortified. 15c main building and enormous 11c square keep (reg. mus.). 13–14c church of Notre Dame; in courtyard of 12–17c hospital, a chapel contains tomb of Duke and Duchess of Sully, with statues and relief sculptures (apply to caretaker). Old houses in Rues Bourgle-Comte and St. Laurent. Rec. churches are Goth. Flamboyant St. Laurent (inside, lovely Entombment) and 13–14c St. Hilaire.
Vicinity ● 14 km E, *Thiron-Gardais*; abbey church, half ruined, is an impressive 13–14c building, surrounded by 17c buildings of former Benedictine abbey.

Nogent-le-Rotrou: *the castle of St. Jean is flanked by an imposing entry fort; terracotta medallion above the entrance.*

Noirlac (Abbey)
18 – Cher   24 – C 1
Founded 12c, one of most complete examples of medieval Cistercian architecture (cl. Tues. in Oct.; flood-lighting). Late-12c church, modern stained-glass windows by J.-P. Raynaud; 13–14c cloister, chapter-house, calefactory, refectory, still-room and monks' cells give a vivid picture of medieval monastic life.

Notre Dame-de-Lorette (Ridge)
62 – Pas-de-Calais   1 – D 3
Highest point in Artois hills (166 m.), scene of big battles during 1914–1918 war. Vast national cem-etery with 18,000 graves; ossuary contains remains of 16,000 unknown soldiers (v.a.), 52 m.-high lantern-tower (small memorial museum). Diorama museum at N37 crossroads.
Vicinity ● Numerous cemeteries and memorials.

Noyers
89 – Yonne   19 – B 2
Picturesque little old town which still looks as it did in olden days. Entry, opposite bridge over R. *Serein*, is through once-fortified Painted Gate. It is well worth strol-ling around Place de l'Hôtel-de-Ville, lined by 15–16c houses with half-timbering and arcades, Place du Marché-au-Blé, also surrounded by arcaded houses, Place de la Petite-Épave-aux-Vins (timber-framed houses), Rue du Poids-du-Roy, Place du Grenier-à-Sel and Rue de la Madeleine (elegant Ren. house). Late 15–16c church of Notre Dame. 1.5 km away, at so-called Tête de Fer, Gallo-Roman site.
Vicinity ● To NW, delightful *Vallée du Serein* towards **Chablis***. ● To S, *Montréal* (see **Avallon***).

Noyon
60 – Oise   5 – D 2
Late 12–early 13c cath. of Notre Dame is lovely Goth. building, flanked by chapter-house, 13c clo-ister-gallery and chapter library in 16c half-timbered house. John Calvin museum in the world-famed religious reformer's birthplace (reconstructed). Small local museum
Vicinity ● 6.5 km S, *Abbey of Our-scamp*, founded 12c, enlarged 18c in neo-Classical style; abbey church, wrecked during French Revolution, was transformed into a 'mock ruin' during Romantic period (v.a.); 13c 'Gallery of the Dead' serves as chapel. ● 14 km SE, mid-17c Ch. de *Blérancourt*; Franco-American his-tory museum (cl. Tues.). ● To NW, (6 km S of *Roye*), majestic late-17c Ch. de *Tilloloy*, in stone and brick; large stables and half-tim-bered outbuildings (v.a., cl. Tues.); in village church, beautiful tombs of Lords of Tilloloy.

Nuits-St. Georges
21 – Côte d'Or   19 – D 3
Capital of the 'Côtes de Nuits' (red wines); late-13c church of St. Sym-phorien; Belfry Tower. Municipal museum (Maison Rodier): Merov-ingian and Gallo-Roman artefacts (from excavations of Les Bolards and Argilly); military collections.
Vicinity ● To N, Grands Crus (great wines) route (N74 then D122): *Vosne-Romanée;* ˙ *Vougeot*: Ren. château of Clos de Vougeot belongs to Confrérie des Chevaliers du Tastevin (Burgundian wine order), who hold their chapter meetings in the vast 12c cellar; huge chapter-house dating from time of Cis-tercian monks; in fermenting-room, enormous old wine-presses; Cham-bolle-Musigny; *Gevrey-Chambertin* (10c fortress, restored 13c); Brochon; at *Fixin*, Noisot park (v.a.), monument by Rude, *Napo-léon s'éveillant à l'immortalité*. Small mus. ● 13 km E, *Cîteaux*: one of best-known medieval mon-asteries (founded 1098), of which only 15c library and some 17–18c buildings remain; all the rest is modern.

Nyons
26 – Drôme   38 – A 2
Forts quarter, with its narrow alley-ways and steep steps, is dominated by chapel of Notre Dame-du-Bon-Secours, in former 13c Randonne tower. Rue des Grands-Forts is a kind of covered gallery, beneath houses backing into ramparts. Archaeological museum. Pic-turesque 14c hump-backed bridge over R. Aygues. Excellent vacation centre.

Nuits-St. Georges: *Gevrey-Chambertin's premier growth, the world-famed Chambertin, was Napoleon's favourite wine.*

NOIRMOUTIER (Island)
85 – Vendée   16 – B 3
Island can be reached by car at low tide via *Passage du Gois* (4.5 km) or at any time via viaduct-bridge of *Fromentine* (toll). *Noirmoutier-en-l'Isle*'s centre is Place d'Armes, lined by 18c mansions; 15c castle is dominated by central keep (mus.). Fmr. Benedictine abbey church, Romanesque St. Philbert, has Merovingian crypt reconstructed 11c. Island is almost bare exc. to N, where Chaize and Blanche woods (fmr. Blanche abbey) overlook rocky coast. *Bois-de-la-Chaize* (boat service to **Pornic***), lovely beaches; *L'Herbaudière*, sardine fishing port. ● 4 km out to sea, NW, island and lighthouse of *Le Pilier*.

O

Obernai
67 – Bas-Rhin   14 – A 2
Charming little town, one of most picturesque in Alsace, surrounded by part of its ramparts, alongside which runs an avenue of limes. On Place du Marché, fountain, mid-16c fmr. corn market, town hall dating from 1523, and tower and 13 and 16c belfry of long-destroyed chapel. In church, lovely 15c stained-glass windows. Many old houses. Old well. Hist. and lapidary mus.
Vicinity ● To NW, *Rosheim*, 12c 'Pagan House', one of oldest private houses in Alsace; remains of former perimeter wall; church of St. Pierre-et-St. Paul, characteristic of 12c Rhenish school, in yellow sandstone, with stout octagonal tower.

Oiron
79 – Deux-Sèvres   23 – B 1
16–17c château is one of loveliest in Ren. period (cl. Tues. and Wed.). W wing, only one storey high, is built above a gallery whose arcades are surmounted by medallions and separated by wreathed columns. Inside is a majestic gallery, 55 m. long, with painted coffered ceiling, decorated with 14 frescos depicting the *Æneid*. Ballroom, King's bed-chamber (ceiling with 17c pendentives and coffering), exquisite study (the Cabinet des Muses) whose walls are covered with ornate wood panelling decorated with paintings. Church, early 16c. former chapel of château, is harmonious mix of Goth. and Ren.; inside, sculpted tombs, with kneeling statues and recumbent figures of Gouffier family, who built the château.

Obernai: *its picturesque half-timbered, gabled houses are part of the charm of this typical Alsatian town.*

Olhain (Château)
62 – Pas-de-Calais   1 – D 3
Magnificent 13–16c fortress (v.a., p.m., Sun. and public hols. Apr.–Oct.), whose tall pepper-pot towers overlook lake formed by R. Lawe. A drawbridge links impressive gate-house to monumental main entrance flanked by huge towers. Unusual watch turret (100 steps).
Vicinity ● 3 km SE, Fresnicourt dolmen.

Oloron-Ste. Marie
64 – Pyrénées-Atlantiques 40 – D 2
Aspe and *Ossau* torrents divide Oloron into three sections, two of which are of interest. Medieval city of Ste. Croix rises in tiers on hill between the two torrents. Romanesque church of Ste. Croix has unusual cupola on intersecting ribs forming an eight-pointed star. Old houses. In lower town, Ste. Marie, 13–14c fmr. cath.; its Romanesque main doorway is ornamented with a noteworthy Descent from the Cross; inside, rich church treasure.
Vicinity ● N134, to S, follows *Vallée d'Aspe*, which is part of *Parc National des Pyrénées Occidentales*, via *Asasp* (to l., Pyrenees road towards *Eaux-Bonnes* and **Bag-**

nères-de-Luchon***, to r., 2 km to S, towards **St. Jean-de-Luz*** and **Biarritz***, *Surrance* (17c church and cloister, unusual folk-art statues), *Bedous*, *Accous*, *Etsaut*, Portalet fort, used as political prison 1941–1945, *Urdos* and *Col du Somport* (1,632 m., Franco-Spanish border), from where road continues to Jaca.
● From *Asasp*, via *Issor*, climbing up Vert d'Arette valley, road leads to *Arette-Pierre-St. Martin*, winter sports resort, and *Gouffre de la Pierre-St. Martin* (1,760 m.), a fantastic vertical abyss, 346 m. deep, explored with tragic consequences in 1952, out of which leads so-called Verna gallery at depth of 782 m. (200 m. long, 100 m. high).

Omaha Beach
See **Vierville-sur-Mer***   4 – A 3

Oppède-le-Vieux
84 – Vaucluse   44 – A 1
Unusual chaotic jumble of rocks and ruins, backing on to side of Mt. **Lubéron***; medieval houses on lower slope have been restored by writers and artists. On the summit, 16c church (traditional Christmas mass) and weirdly-shaped ruins of early-13c castle.

OLÉRON (Island)
17 – Charente-Maritime   22 – C 3 22 – D 3
Nowadays joined to mainland by toll bridge, this largest of French islands after Corsica is bordered along N coast by lines of wooded sand-dunes; to W, particularly picturesque wild coastline. D734 passes through *Le Château-d'Oléron*, former 17c fortified town whose citadel was partly destroyed by bombing in 1945, on way to *St. Pierre d'Oléron*, main town of island. In old cemetery, 13c Lantern of the Dead, 20 m. high, topped by 18c pyramid. 13, Rue Pierre Loti: 'Grandmothers' House', where the writer spent his holidays; he is buried in the garden. Museum (v.a. June 15–Sept. 15). 8 km to S of Château d'Oléron, *St. Trojan-les-Bains*, tiny port and seaside resort, bounded on W by St. Trojan state forest, a magnificent 4,395-acre expanse of sea pines. 7 km to NE of St. Pierre: *Boyardville*, beach and wooded dunes of Saumonards; boat service in summer to *Ile d'Aix* and *Fouras*; 2 km out to sea, Fort Boyard. From St. Pierre, road leads NW to *St. Georges-d'Oléron* (3 km to W, Domino beach), *St. Denis-d'Oléron* and Chassiron lighthouse, on tip of island.

Orange
84 – Vaucluse   37 – D 3
Centre of a rich and prosperous
Roman colony, Orange has many
fine monuments to its past glory,
esp. Roman theatre (v.a.), used in
summer for world-famed internatl.
festival of choral music; theatre is
only one in world to have kept its
façade, 103 m. long by 37 m. high,
and its huge stage wall, adorned

Comtat, estate belonging to ento-
mologist J. H. Fabre (1823–1915) is
worth visiting.

Orbais
51 – Marne   12 – B 1
Late-12c church contains transept
and choir of fmr. Benedictine abbey
church; latter, with Goth. Rayonnant ambulatory and chapels, is
said to be prototype of cloister at

beautiful Virgin in Majesty.
Vicinity ● 5.5 km W, *Rochefort
Montagne*, rec. trip to Rochefort
valley, which leads to *Tuilière and
Sanadoire Rocks* (see **Mont-Dore***).
● 2 km N, *Ch. de Cordès*; picturesque 15 and 17c manorhouse
(v.a.), in front of which is formal
garden whose arbours were
designed by Le Nôtre.

Orléans
45 – Loiret   18 – B 1
Town centre is Place du Martroi,
in which is statue of Joan of Arc.
Taking Rue Jeanne-d'Arc, which
branches off Rue Royale, reconstructed after 1945 in 18c style, you
come to 13–16c cath. of Ste. Croix,
with 18c neo-Goth. façade: in choir,
magnificent 18c wood panelling;
remains of 4c and 10–11c primitive
sanctuaries have been uncovered in
crypt. A number of churches are
rec.: St. Aignan, of which only choir
and 15c transept remain; 11c crypt;
12–15 and 17c St. Euverte; Romanesque St. Pierre-le-Puellier; 16c
Notre Dame-de-Recouvrance; St.
Paul, rebuilt after 1945 (chapel of
Notre Dame-des-Miracles: Joan of
Arc used to pray here). Fine-Arts
mus. (cl. Tues.), installed since 1984
in building beside cath., has magnificent paintings, mainly 17c (Le
Nain), 18c (important collection of
portraits by Perronneau, Houdon,
Nattier) and 19c (Courbet,
Gauguin, Sérusier). Contemp. art:
Soutine, Rouault, Mathieu, Sam
Francis, Hantaï. Sculptures by
Gaudier-Brzeska, Maillol, Rodin,
Zadkine, Bourdelle. Sketch and
print room. In Ren. Cabu mansion:
reg. hist. and archaeology mus.
(Neuvy-en-Sullias treasure, Roman
and Gallic bronzes). Three Ren.
houses: François I, Coquille
(Impasse de la Pierre-Percée) and
Alibert (Rue des Hôtelleries). Ren.
house, 'Maison d'Agnès Sorel', Rue
du Tabour, is now Charles Péguy
centre. Joan of Arc's house, Place
de Gaulle, in reconstructed 15c
house; large iconography,
dioramas, models. Natural science
mus. (two aquaria).
Vicinity ● 4 km S, *Olivet*, leisure
area with pleasant walks along
banks of R. *Loiret*, restaurants,
open-air taverns, fishing and water
sports; 4 km to SE, floral park of La
Source (v.a. Apr.–Oct.) and sources
of the *Loiret*.

Orly (Airport)
94 – Val-de-Marne   11 – C 2
V.a. free to terminals of Orly-Sud
and Orly-Ouest. From terraces,
panoramic views of airport installations. Organised visits by tourist
coach or plane (apply to Info.
Office, tel.: 707.85.55). On top floor
of Orly-Sud: panoramic table.

Orange: *colossal monument to all-conquering Rome, the Triumphal
Arch is sculpted with battle scenes and trophies.*

with an outsize statue of Augustus.
Old cath., in Provençal Romanesque style, was partly rebuilt (apse
and belfry) in early 17c. Municipal
mus. in 17c mansion, lapidary collections, fragments of Roman land
registers and plans. Vieil-Orange
mus. in three galleries. Triumphal
Arch is one of loveliest and best-
preserved in Roman world; it was
constructed after Caesar's victory
over the Gauls in 49 B.C.; the ornamental sculptures evoke these
battles, showing military trophies
and other decorations.
Vicinity ● 8 km N, *Sérignan-du-*

Reims; 16c carved choir-stalls.
Vicinity ● 3 km E, Mareuil-en-Brie,
church (16c wooden retable).

Orcival
63 – Puy-de-Dôme   30 – D 1
One of most noteworthy mid-
12c Romanesque churches of
Auvergne, dominated by magnificent belfry with two octagonal
tiers pierced by bays; inside, capitals
sculpted with leaf-work, occasionally historiated; on high altar,
seated statue of Notre Dame d'Orcival, 12c, in wood sheathed with
silver plate, Auvergne's most

Orbais: *the church's lovely Gothic transept has two rose windows above the triforium.*

Orléans: *the characteristic neo-Gothic towers of the cathedral of Ste. Croix.*

Ornans
25 – Doubs   **20 – C 3**
16c church containing works of art. Clear waters of R. *Loue* form the 'mirror of Ornans'. Birthplace of 19c French painter Gustave Courbet, at 2 Rue de la Froidière, has been turned into mus. containing a number of his works. He is buried in local cemetery. Interesting old houses.

Vicinity ● From promontory on which stands old castle, magnificent bird's eye view of Ornans and lovely *Loue* valley. ● 20 km SE, *Source de la Loue* in impressive rocky amphitheatre. ● 9 km SW, imposing medieval castle of *Cléron*.

Ornans: *the old houses of Courbet's native village are reflected in the 'mirror' formed by the clear waters of the Loue.*

Orthez
64 – Pyrénées-Atlantiques 40 – D 1
V. busy little town, large reg. market for poultry and foies gras. Well-known 13–14c humpbacked Old Bridge, once fortified, spans *Gave de Pau*. Interesting old houses in Rues Graverie, Bourg-Vieux (Ren. house, aka Maison de Jeanne d'Albret) and de l'Horloge. Impressive 13–14c pentagonal Moncade tower. 13–15c church.

Ottmarssheim
68 – Haut-Rhin   **8 – A 2**
On edge of v. big *Forêt de la Harth*. Unusual mid-11c octagonal church, important example of Alsace Carolingian architecture.

Ouessant (Island)
29N – Finistere   **8 – A 2**
Known in English as Ushant. Reached by boat via **Brest*** in two hrs., with stops at *Le Conquet* and *Ile Molène*. Ouessant and Molène are part of **Armorique*** reg. nature reserve. 8 km long and 3–5 km wide, Ouessant has v. jagged coasts dominated by high cliffs; tourist centre is *Lampaul* (well-sheltered beach). 1 km to NW, hamlet of Niou-Hella, heart of Ouessant ecological mus.; two houses are given over to local artisan techniques and trads. (v.a. in summer). See Créac'h lighthouse, most powerful in Brittany, and v. impressive rocks of N coast.

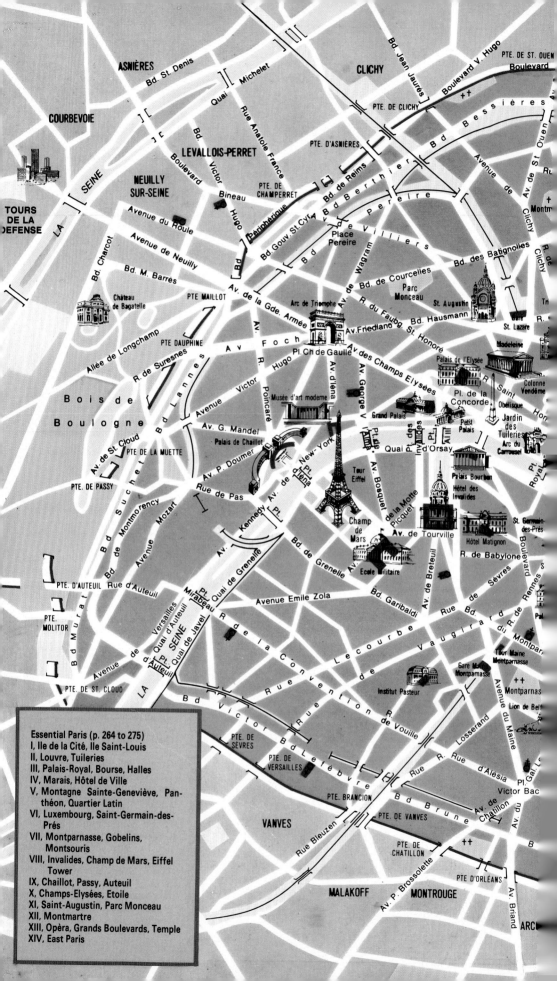

ASNIÈRES

COURBEVOIE

Bd. St. Denis

Quai Michelet

Rue Anatole France

CLICHY

Bd. Jean Jaurès

Boulevard V. Hugo

PTE. DE ST. OUEN
Boulevard

LEVALLOIS-PERRET

PTE. DE CLICHY

Bd. Bessières

NEUILLY
SUR-SEINE

Boulevard

Bineau

Hugo

PTE. D'ASNIÈRES

PTE. DE
CHAMPERRET

Bd. de Reims

Périphérique

Bd. Gouv. St.Cyr.

Bd. de Wagram

Bd. Berthier

Bd. Pereire

Avenue de

Av. de Clichy

Montm.

R. de Clichy

Tri.

TOURS
DE LA
DÉFENSE

LA SEINE

Avenue du Roule

Avenue de Neuilly

Bd. Charcot

Bd. M. Barrès

Château
de Bagatelle

PTE MAILLOT

Av. de la Gde. Armée

Arc de Triomphe

Place
Pereire

R. du Faubg. St. Honoré

Bd. de Courcelles

Parc
Monceau

St. Augustin

Bd. des Batignolles

Bd. Hausmann

Gare
St. Lazare

Madeleine

Allée de Longchamp

PTE. DAUPHINE

R. de Suresnes

Av. Foch

Pl. Ch de Gaulle

Av. Friedland

Av. des Champs Elysées

Palais de l'Elysée

R. Saint

Colonne
Vendôme

Bois de
Boulogne

Bd. Suchet

Bd. Lannes

Avenue

Victor

Hugo

Poincaré

Musée d'art moderne

Av. d'Iéna

Av. George V

Grand Palais

Petit
Palais

Pl. de la
Concorde

Obélisque

Jardin
des
Tuileries

Arc du
Carrousel

Hon.

Av. de St. Cloud

PTE. DE LA MUETTE

Av. G. Mandel

Palais de Chaillot

Av. P. Doumer

Av. de
l'Iéna

Pt.
d'Iéna

New-York

Quai
d'Orsay

Pt. des
Invalides

Pt. de
l'Alma

Pt.
d'Orsay

Palais Bourbon

Pt.
Royal

PTE. DE PASSY

de Montmorency

Mozart

Rue de Pas

Av. de Grenelle

Tour
Eiffel

Champ
de
Mars

Av. de la Motte
Picquet

Av. Bosquet

Hôtel des
Invalides

Hôtel Matignon

St. Germain-
des-Prés

Kennedy

Av.

Quai de Grenelle

Pt.

Pt.
Mirabeau

Av. de Tourville

Av. de Breteuil

R. de Babylone

Boulevard

Avenue

PTE. D'AUTEUIL

Rue d'Auteuil

Ecole Militaire

Bd. de Grenelle

Bd. Garibaldi

Rue

Bd.

de
Sèvres

Rue de Rennes

Pt.

Bd. Murat

PTE.
MOLITOR

Quai d'Auteuil

Versailles

Quai de Javel

SEINE

Avenue Emile Zola

R. de la Convention

Lecourbe

Rue

de

Vaugirard

Bd.

Montpar.

Tour Maine
Montparnasse

Av. du Maine

PTE. DE ST. CLOUD

Avenue

d'Auteuil

Pt.
d'Auteuil

LA

Bd. Victor

Bd. Lefèbvre

Rue de Vouillé

Gare Mont.
Montparnasse

Institut Pasteur

Montparnas.

Lion de Belf.

Rue

Rue

Losserand

d'Alésia

Pl.
Victor Bac.

Gal. La.

Av. du

PTE. DE
SÈVRES

PTE. DE
VERSAILLES

PTE. BRANCION

Bd. Brune

Av. de Chatillon

VANVES

Rue Bleuzen

PTE. DE VANVES

PTE. DE
CHATILLON

PTE D'ORLÉANS

Av. Briand

ARC

MALAKOFF

MONTROUGE

Av. P. Brossolette

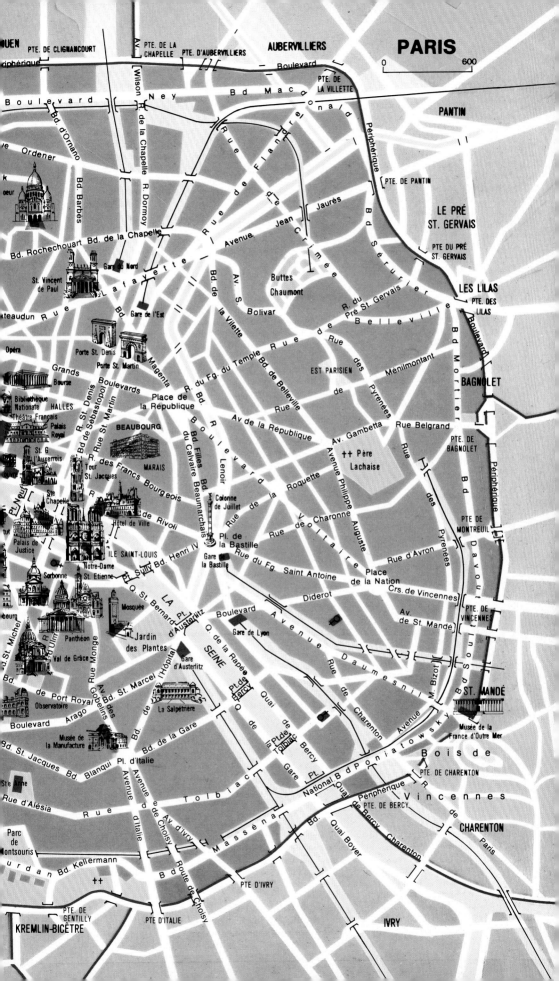

1. ILE DE LA CITÉ, ILE SAINT LOUIS

Notre Dame. The capital's cathedral, at centre of the Ile de la Cité; approached over a large square. Begun in 1163, major building work finished circa 1345. One of best examples of Gothic art. Look for fine carving on the three portals of façade: on l., Virgin's Portal; to r., Ste. Anne's Portal; in middle, Portal of the Last Judgment. On N side, the Cloister Portal (circa 1250), charming Virgin on the pier. On S side, St. Étienne's Portal (circa 1258); the apse and flying buttresses constitute an architectural achievement of great elegance. Inside, magnificent stained glass in the transept (rose windows N and S) and many works of art: choir decorated with superb early 18c panelling (114 carved stalls). Stone chancel screen is decorated with 21 14c bas-reliefs. Famous Virgin with child aka Our Lady of Paris at entrance to transept. Large collection of reliquaries associated with the Passion (v.a. 10 – 5 exc. Sun. and public holidays).
10 Rue du Cloître-Notre-Dame: *Notre Dame Mus.* Behind apse, the *Deportation Memorial* is situated at E tip of the Cité (v.a.).
Conciergerie. Former palace of the 'concierge', head of the King's Household, used as prison during French Revolution. Still has early 14c clock tower and three round towers on N side, facing R. Seine. The attractive Gothic room aka 'Salle des Gens d'Armes' (exhibitions), the defaced cells occupied by Marie Antoinette (chapel) and Robespierre, the Prisoners' Gallery, and the Girondins' Room, once a chapel and now housing small mus. of objects from the Revolution, are all open to public.
Palais de Justice. Adjoining the Conciergerie, it includes the **Ste. Chapelle,** mid-18c Gothic jewel, whose slender elegance was built to house relics of the Passion. Interior (v.a., cl. Tues.) consists of a low and a high chapel – the latter's magnificent 13c stained glass windows transforming it into an immense glass pavilion with constantly changing colours. The 1,134 scenes they depict form a 6,650 sq. ft. version of the Bible.
At W. tip of Ile de la Cité is charming *Place Dauphine* which leads on to the *Pont Neuf,* oldest bridge in Paris. Statue of Henri IV stands on a bank overlooking the *W. tip* and the *Square du Vert Galant* (excellent views of Seine, Louvre, Institut de France and Pont des Arts). Various boat trips from Pont Neuf and Square du Vert Galant.

Ile St. Louis. A pedestrian bridge joins Ile de la Cité to the Ile Saint Louis, whose quays, lined with attractive 17c mansions and planted with tall trees, are very pleasant to stroll along. Mid-17c *Hôtel Lauzun* was built by Le Vau (Louis XIV's Director of Buildings); richly decorated rooms (v.a.). *Hôtel Lambert* is also by Le Vau (n.v.a.). Church of *St Louis en l'Ile* has Jesuit-style interior, lavishly ornamented.

2. LOUVRE, TUILERIES

Louvre. Former palace of the kings of France, one of world's largest museums. Main entrance: Porte Denon (v.a., cl. Tues.; admission free on Sun.). Over next few years the Louvre is to be greatly extended, and departments relocated. At present, the Louvre houses exhibits covering everything from Ancient Orient to 19c, progressing through seven departments: Oriental, Egyptian, Greek and Roman antiquities, paintings, sculpture, objets d'art and furniture, and graphic art. Especially worth seeing are Galerie du Bord de l'Eau, with longest picture rail in the world (422 m., French 17–18c, Italian 14–15c painting), and Apollo Gallery, former ceremonial hall, restored and redecorated under Louis XIV, which now houses Crown Jewels. Renaissance and 17c parts of Louvre stand round imposing Carée courtyard, restored to its original design in 1986; the S and most noteworthy side, to l. of Clock House, is by Pierre Lescot, with mid-16c sculptures by Jean Goujon. Famed colonnade by Claude Perrault and d'Orbay in the Place St. Germain is seen at its best since a dry moat was dug round it in 1965.
St. Germain l'Auxerrois. Incorporating 13, 15 and 16c architecture, it has been the 'king's parish church' since 14c. Gothic choir and Gothic Flamboyant porch with mid-13c central portal are the most interesting features. Inside, magnificent late 17c carved pew, with a back in form of polychromatic carved wood triptych (16c). In chapel opposite, see 16c altar piece. Superb late 15c stained glass windows in transept. Particularly noteworthy is Gothic Flamboyant vaulting in right arm of transept.
Place du Carrousel. Arc de Triomphe du Carrousel (1806). Magnificent view of the Arc de Triomphe proper, looking up through the Tuileries, Place de la Concorde and Champs-Elysées, may be had from here.
Tuileries Gardens. Laid out in 16c, altered in 17c by Le Nôtre; restoration to their original design is planned for 1988–89. The Carrousel

flowerbeds are adorned with statues by Maillol. Section between Avenue Lemonier and Place de la Concorde is flanked by two long banks: on r. is the **Jeu de Paume mus.** (v.a., guided), dedicated to Impressionism and late 19c painting – collection now in Quai d'Orsay mus.; on l. is the **Orangerie des Tuileries,** where Walter Guillaume collection is housed (v.a., cl. Tues.). On ground floor, Claude Monet's *Waterlilies.*
Mus. of Decorative Arts. 107 Rue de Rivoli. Housed in the Marsan Pavilion and N wing of Louvre, reconstructed in 19c, its collection of furniture and items of everyday life, from France and abroad, covers period from Middle Ages to 20c (v.a., cl. Mon. and Tues.). Exhibitions. Library. Centre of Applied Art based here. Also Mus. of the Art of Fashion at top of Marsan Pavilion (open same days).
Place Vendôme. Designed at end of 17c by J. Hardouin-Mansart, it is lined on all sides by Classical mansions which together form an impressive illustration of Grand Siècle arch. The Colonne Vendôme (43 m.) is decorated with a spiral of bronze bas-reliefs, made from cannons captured at Battle of Austerlitz, and has statue of Napoleon at top.
St. Roch. Baroque 17c church. Corneille, Diderot and Le Nôtre are buried here.

3. PALAIS ROYAL, BOURSE, HALLES

Palais Royal. Built by Richelieu, enlarged in 18 and 19c, it houses the Conseil Economique and the Conseil d'État (n.v.a.). The rectangular garden is 225 m. long and surrounded by galleries with 18c arcades (shops). Late 18c building in SW corner is the Comédie Française.
Bibliothèque Nationale. One of world's richest libraries, it covers more than 177,000 sq. ft. and occupies several 17c mansions, extended in 18 and 19c. Exhibitions are held in mid-17c Mansart and Mazarine Galleries. Medal and Antiques Room has many ancient and medieval masterpieces (v.a.). Colbert Gallery (1826, admirably restored, Rue des Petits Champs) houses Mus. of Performing Arts and Mus. of History of the Phonograph.
Bourse. (Stock Exchange). (Entry free). Neo-classical architecture

Notre Dame seen from the tip of the Ile de la Cité. The spire above the apse, rebuilt by Viollet-le-Duc, is 90 m. high.

1

3

2

3

(1). The Pont Neuf *has 12 barrel-vaulted arches, finished in 1604.* (2). The Louvre, *former palace of kings of France (seen here, Clock House and Cour Carée), is approached* (3) *by gardens containing small* Arc de Triomphe du Carrousel. (4) *Flowerbeds adorned with statues by Maillol.*

4

(1808–1826). Particularly animated between 12.30 and 14.00 (exc. Sat. and Sun.); watching transactions taking place around entrance enclosure ('corbeille') can be amusing.

Place des Victoires. Late 17c square by J. Hardouin-Mansart, designer of many classical exteriors. In the Centre, statue of Louis XIV (1822).

Notre-Dame-des-Victoires. 17c chapel from old convent of the Barefoot Augustins or Little Fathers (no longer standing). In the choir, seven paintings by Van Loo framed by 17c panelling. More than 30,000 ex-voto.

St. Eustache. Built between 1532 and 1637, the design is Goth., the decoration Ren. It contains many paintings and works of art (Colbert's tomb); since the Halles (central markets) were pulled down, the magnificence of its nave has become clearly visible.

The Halles were moved to a site at Rungis and demolition of the 19c metal-framed halls cleared an enormous space where, above the station (metro and RER), a somewhat disparate ensemble has arisen, including two underground shopping centres, hotel, flats, offices and art galleries, separated by gardens, playgrounds and recreation spaces. Neighbouring streets, renovated to their original style, have seen rapid spread of clothes and other shops, restaurants, etc. **Centre National d'Art et de Culture Georges Pompidou** (designed by Richard Rogers and Renzo Piano). Built in resolutely contemp. style, it stands on the old Beaubourg plateau and includes Natnl. Mus. of Modern Art, exhibition halls, Centre of Applied Art and Design (C.C.I.), public reading room and library, and Institute of Research and Acoustic Coordination (I.R.C.A.M.) Above ground and over part of I.R.C.A.M. in Place Igor Stravinski is a fantasy fountain designed by sculptors Tinguely and Niki de Saint-Phalle.

Fontaine des Innocents. Square des Innocents. The mid 16c carved basreliefs depicting naiads and nymphs are by Jean Goujon. Two churches worth visiting: **St. Leu-St. Gilles,** which dates from 13 and 14c and has many interesting works of art, and **St. Merri,** early 16c Gothic Flamboyant, with many 17 and 18c paintings inside.

Tour St. Jacques. Square St. Jacques. Bell tower of early 16c St. Jacques de la Boucherie church, destroyed in 1802. Site, in 1648, of some of Pascal's experiments on atmospheric pressure.

4. MARAIS, HOTEL DE VILLE

The Marais, once an aristocratic district of Paris, still has a number of 16, 17 and 18c mansions. Most are private, but it is sometimes possible to climb stairs or look into courtyards. Of those open to public: **Hôtel de Béthune-Sully,** 62 Rue Saint Antoine, early 17c, is one of the most interesting.

Hôtel de Lamoignon, 24 Rue Pavée, Ren., houses library of Paris history (v.a., cl. Aug.), and has particularly beautiful reading room with painted ceiling, period furniture.

Hôtel Carnavalet, 23 Rue de Sévigné, houses mus. of Paris (v.a., cl. Tues.) Built in 16c (decorative sculpture by J. Goujon) and 17c (F. Mansart), its rich and extensive collections are given over to history of the capital. Reconstructions of 17 and 18c interiors. Currently being extended.

Hôtel de Marle, 11 Rue Payenne. Early 17c. Now Swedish Cultural Centre (exhibitions).

Hôtel Guénégaud, 60 Rue des Archives. Mid 17c, designed by F. Mansart, it houses *Mus. of Hunting* (v.a., cl. Tues.).

Hôtel Salé or Aubert de Fontenay, Rue de Thorigny. *Picasso Mus.,* exceptional range of the artist's work (v.a., cl. Tues.).

Archives Nationales, 60 Rue des Francs-Bourgeois. Claimed as richest archives in the world, they fill two of the most beautiful 18c mansions in the Marais:

Palais Soubise, which boasts elegant horse-shoe shaped front courtyard and superb 18c rococostyle apartments, houses *Mus. de l'Histoire de France* (v.a., cl. Tues.); and *Hôtel de Rohan,* which has famed high relief *Apollo watering his horses* by Le Lorrain (18c) in its second courtyard. Behind Palais Soubise stands entrance gate, flanked by towers, which is all that survives of late 14c manor house belonging to Olivier de Clisson, Constable of France (d. 1407).

Hôtel de Sens, 1 Rue du Figuier. This and Hôtel de Cluny are only two private residences from the Middle Ages still standing in Paris. It houses the *Bibliothèque Forney*: decorative arts, industrial techniques, various collections (v.a., cl. Sun. and Mon.).

Place des Vosges. One of the most beautiful examples of Louis XIV architecture. At No. 6: *house and mus. of Victor Hugo* (v.a., cl. Mon.).

Place de la Bastille – at its centre, the Bastille column, crowned by the Spirit of Liberty (238 steps: v.a., cl. Tues.). Huge opera house is now being built in SE corner of square.

St. Paul-St. Louis, 17c baroque. Extensive decorative carvings.

St. Jean-St. François. Early 17c, its choir has fine 18c panelling picked out in gold.

Notre-Dame-des-Blancs-Manteaux. 17c with 18c façade. In nave, magnificent mid 18c pulpit, probably of German origin.

St. Gervais-St. Protais. Late 15c-early 17c Gothic Flamboyant with classical façade (1616-1621). 16c stained glass windows. Préault's *Christ* (1840). Chancellor Le Tellier's mausoleum (1686).

Temple et Cloître des Billettes, 24 Rue des Archives. Mid 17c, former Carmelite, now Lutheran, church; it boasts only medieval (1415) cloister extant in Paris (v.a.). Memorial to Unknown Jewish Martyr is poignantly sombre (17 Rue Geoffroy l'Asnier, v.a., cl. Sat.).

Hôtel de Ville. Destroyed during the 1871 Commune, it was rebuilt in Ren. style. Sumptuously overornate interior is intriguing example of late 19c decoration and academic art (guided tour, Mon. 10.30).

5. MONTAGNE STE. GENEVIÈVE, PANTHÉON, QUARTIER LATIN

Panthéon. Formerly Ste. Geneviève church, modelled on ancient temple, built by Soufflot in second half of 18c. It was converted into civil sanctuary in 1885, dedicated to memory of great men (v.a.). The cold interior is decorated with carved monuments and academic-style decorations (*Vie de Ste. Geneviève* by Puvis de Chavannes). In crypt, tombs of Rousseau, Voltaire, Victor Hugo, Zola, Jaurès, Braille, Jean Moulin, etc.

St. Étienne-du-Mont. Late 15, 16 and 17c, houses shrine of Ste. Geneviève. Beautiful stained glass windows, elegantly carved mid 16c Ren. rood screen (only one in Paris). Numerous works of art.

Panthéon district is very picturesque, particularly Rue de la Montagne Ste. Geneviève and surrounding streets: Rues de l'Estrapade, du Pot de Fer, Lhomond and Mouffetard (shops, lively market), site of *St. Médard* church, 12 to 17c. *Blvd. St. Michel* is main artery of the Latin Quarter, traditional student haunt. At its centre is the Sorbonne, headquarters of university of Paris. Its late 19c buildings enclose 17c Sorbonne church, with Richelieu's tomb.

Mus. de Cluny, 6 Place Paul Painlevé. Late 15c Hôtel de Cluny is, with Hôtel de Sens, the only large private medieval residence still standing in Paris. Its extensive collections are devoted to life and art in the Middle Ages (v.a., cl. Tues.). Alongside it are ruins of early 3c

St. Eustache, *former parish church of the capital's central markets* (*1*).

Hôtel de Sens, *late 15c, epitomising the private homes of the medieval nobility* (*2*).

Hôtel de Béthune-Sully, *Its early 17c architecture has been superbly restored* (*3*).

Palais Soubise: *This very large 18c mansion, housing part of the National Archives, contains a museum of French history* (*4*).

Roman baths, visible from Blvd. St. Michel.

St. Séverin. 13 and 15c. One of the most beautiful Goth. churches in Paris. The ambulatory in the choir is among the most harmonious examples of Goth. Flamboyant style; it is lit by modern stained glass windows by the painter Bazaine. 15–16c galleries of old charnel house run alongside the garden.

St. Julien-le-Pauvre. Set among the trees in Square René Viviani, this venerable sanctuary from second half of 12c is now a Greek Orthodox church. Choir has interesting capitals. Natnl. Assistance Mus., 47 Quai de la Tournelle, house in 17c Hôtel des Miramiones.

Arènes de Lutèce. (Entrances, Rue Monge, Rue de Navarre or Rue des Arènes.) Built for the Roman games in mid-1c AD, with room for 16,000 spectators, the arena was excavated and restored in 19c.

New Science Faculty. Access from Rue Jussieu and Quai St. Bernard; dominated by its administrative block, it has many interesting examples of contemporary art: giant labyrinth (45 × 35 m.) by Stahly; the *Para Vista*, a lacquered aluminium floor, 32 × 20 m., by Vasarely; plus works by Beaudin, Lagrange, Gischia, Bedard, etc.

New **Institute of the Arab World,** at corner of Quai St. Barnard and Rue des Fossés St. Bernard. Below the quai, open-air *Mus. of Sculpture* with works by César, Schöffer, Ipoustéguy, Chavignier, Zadkine, Etienne-Marin, Gilioli, etc.

Jardin des Plantes. Founded 17c, it was extended and improved by the Comte de Buffon in 18c and has in its grounds the **Natural History Mus.** (v.a., cl. Tues.), a zoo and vivarium. Also a maze designed by Buffon and an Alpine garden (3,000 species from the Alps, Pyrenees, Greenland, Himalayas, etc.). Maison de Cuvier has interesting colonial hothouses. The bigger galleries and buildings house rich zoological, anatomical, palaeontological, botanical and mineralogical colls.

Paris Mosque. Built between 1923 and 1927 in Hispano-Moorish style (v.a. p.m. only), the forecourt was inspired by the Alhambra in Granada. Ornate prayer room contains magnificent carpets.

Salpêtrière Hospital. The church and other buildings reflect the austere grandeur of Louis XIV period. Designed by Le Vau, late 17c. The church, by Libéral Bruant, is unusual in having four naves, in form of a Greek cross around a rotunda, under an octagonal dome. One courtyard bears name of Manon Lescaut, who, in Abbé Pré-

vost's celebrated novel, was supposedly imprisoned here.

6. LUXEMBOURG, ST. GERMAIN-DES-PRÉS

The **Luxembourg Palace,** where the French Senate meets, was built for Marie de Médici in 1615 (v.a. Sun.). Library is adorned with paintings by Delacroix. Council chamber and ceremonial rooms were richly decorated in 19c (v.a.).

Luxembourg Gardens. Among the most attractive in Paris, though with many mediocre statues; an exception is the *Monument à Delacroix* by Dalou and beautiful 17c *Medici Fountain*, a favourite of students. Flowerbeds continue to S (on the way, Carpeaux's *Fountains From the Four Corners of The World* and, on bank to r., Rude's statue of Marshal Ney), as far as the *Observatory*, built in 17c and also surrounded by beautiful gardens (guided tours, on request, first Sat. in month; also for mus.).

Val-de-Grâce. Church built in Classical style by Mansart, with superb cupola decorated by Mignard (1663). Beautiful carved interior and 17c monumental canopy above main altar. Classical-style cloister and gate of 'Anne of Austria' pavilion are worth seeing.

St. Sulpice. Built in 17c with monumental ancient-style façade by Servandoni. Chapel to r. of entrance has magnificent Delacroix murals. In square, monumental fountain by Visconti (1844).

St. Germain des Prés district is one of liveliest on left bank. Immediately adjoining crossroads by the recently renovated church are three world-famed 'literary' cafés: Flore, Deux Magots, Lipp.

St. Germain-des-Prés. Oldest church in Paris. All that remains of 11c Romanesque abbey church are the tower above the façade and the main door, masked by a mediocre 17c porch. Inside, 12c choir and ambulatory have fine Romanesque capitals. Numerous works of art: 17c tombs of the de Castellan brothers, by Girardon; of Abbé Casimir Wasa, former king of Poland; etc. On l. of entrance, small square with Picasso's *Woman's Head* in homage to Guillaume Apollinaire (1959). In Rue de l'Abbaye, imposing abbatial palace in Louis XIII style. *Place de Fürstemberg* is one of the most appealing spots in this district; *Mus. Eugène Delacroix* is at No. 6 – in apartment where the painter lived and died (v.a., cl. Tues.).

Hôtel des Monnaies et Mus. Monétaire. (The Mint.) Imposing late 18c mansion. The mus. (v.a., cl. Mon.) has fine collection of coins and

medals, ancient and modern. (Guided visit of workshops Mon. and Wed., p.m., cl. Aug.). Exhibition galleries and displaywindows in Rue Guénégaud.

Institut de France. The Four Nations College, founded in 1661 by Cardinal Mazarin, became in 1806 the Palais de l'Institut, embracing five different academies. Instantly recognisable by famed dome of the old chapel, now a lecture theatre, it houses the *Mazarin Library.* Opposite, spanning the Seine, is Pont des Arts footbridge: superb view of W tip of Ile de la Cité and the Louvre.

École des Beaux Arts. Formerly Petits-Augustins monastery, 17c, to which were added several 18c mansions and 19c buildings. The courtyard, 14 Rue Bonaparte, has several important fragments of sculpture from demolished public buildings. Inside, charming Mulberry courtyard (Ren.). Exhibitions in chapel.

7. MONTPARNASSE, GOBELINS, MONTSOURIS

The former artists' district, once relatively tranquil, has been completely transformed by construction of the **Maine-Montparnasse** complex, with its 59-storey tower, 210 m. high (the highest building in Europe). Viewing table, telescopes and binoculars available on top floor, plus taped commentaries in six languages. New station Place Raoul-Daultry has large hall with major works by Vasarely. One of Rodin's masterpieces, the *Statue of Balzac,* stands at intersection of Carrefour Vavin and Blvd. Raspail: there, too, are Montparnasse's three most famous cafés: the Coupole, Rotonde and Dôme.

Montparnasse Cemetery. Several renowned writers and artists buried here: Baudelaire, Huysmans, Maupassant, Soutine, Zadkine, etc. Unusual tomb of married couple with surname of Pigeon. Also Brancusi's *The Kiss* (Tania Rachevskaya's tomb).

Bourdelle Mus. 16 Rue Antoine-Bourdelle (v.a., cl. Mon.) Works by the famed sculptor (d. 1929) are displayed in huge modern buildings adjoining his former studios.

Zadkine Mus. 100 bis Rue d'Assas (v.a., cl. Mon.). Studios and works of another great sculptor (d. 1967).

Postal Mus. 34 Bd. de Vaugirard. History of the post from Middle Ages to present day. Exhibitions. Square Blomet (15th arrondissement) has the *Moon Bird,* an important monumental sculpture by Miró.

Gobelins Factory. Founded in 1662, it still has several 17c buildings with an old-world charm. Varied exhi-

(1). **Luxembourg Gardens** *and Marie de Medici's Palace (Senate).* (2) **The Panthéon,** *dedicated to the memory of Great Men.* (3) **Dome of The Invalides,** *above Napoleon's tomb.* (4) **Chaillot Palace.**

bitions of tapestries. Workshops can be visited Tues., Wed., Thurs. In Rue Berbier-du-Mets, imposing building with circular peristyle belonging to the Mobilier National (Property Services Agency), 1935, and the Gobelins Gardens, Square René-Le-Gall.

Catacombs. Laid out in former quarries, they form a vast ossuary (well over 118,000 sq. ft.) containing the bones of more than six million people who had been buried in Parisian cemeteries that were deconsecrated after the French Revolution. The bones are arranged along the walls with a macabre sense of imagination. Access is via one of the pavilions built by the architect Ledoux, in Place Denfert-Rochereau, on site of old gate into Paris (v.a. Tues.–Fri. 14–16 h.; Sat. and Sun., 9–11 h and 14–16 h). Opposite, two more of the 57 pavilions built by Ledoux (aka the 'wall' of Paris).

Montsouris Park. Laid out by Alphand in 1868, covering 40 acres planted in the English style. Its

many picturesque corners include a waterfall and an artificial lake. Overlooking it is a small-size reproduction of the Bardo Palace, one-time home of the Beys of Tunis, which featured at the Paris Universal Exhibition in 1867. To r., a modern meteorological tower; to S, a surveyor's rod marks the line of the former Paris meridian. The Blvd. Jourdan separates Montsouris Park from the **Cité Universitaire,** the university's residential section – 100 acres and 37 'houses', each with architecture evocative of the different founding countries, after which they are named. In the centre the Maison Internationale (1936), with swimming pool, theatre, enormous halls, etc. The Swiss and Brazilian houses are by Le Corbusier.

8. INVALIDES, CHAMP-DE-MARS, EIFFEL TOWER

Hôtel des Invalides. Grandiose 17c

design by Libéral Bruant, built around an imposing main courtyard. (Entry free. Son et Lumière in summer). The Army Mus., one of richest in world of its kind (v.a.), is housed here (entrances at E and W sides). E side: Flag room, Vauban Room. Salons devoted to fmr. monarchy, Revolution, Empire, Restoration and Second Empire periods, and 1870 war. W side: arms and armour; 1914–1918 and 1939-1945 War Rooms. Unique scale models of French and foreign artillery. In small courtyard, replica of Napoleon's tomb at St. Helena. To W (entry, Blvd. de Latour-Maubourg), *Mus. of the Order of the Liberation.* At end of main courtyard, church of *St. Louis,* or 'Chapel of the Soldiers', in Classical style, decorated with captured enemy flags.

Dôme des Invalides. Built above and behind Hardouin-Mansart's late 17c Invalides, it rises over Napoleon I's crypt and tomb and the nearby grave of his son, the King of Rome. Chapels radiating out from centre

Architectural heights of their day: in iron, the 300 m. Eiffel Tower (1889); in aluminium, glass and concrete, the 210 m. Tour Montparnasse (1972).

contain tombs of Turenne, Vauban, Foch, Lyautey, etc. (v.a.).

Rodin Mus. 77 Rue de Varenne. Housed in 18c Hôtel Biron. Works by the famous sculptor are displayed inside and in the gardens (v.a., cl. Tues.). Varied exhibitions in former chapel.

Between Esplanade des Invalides and Bd. St. Germain runs the aristocratic *Faubourg St. Germain*, its 17–18c mansions now occupied by embassies and Ministries.

Palais de la Légion d'Honneur. In charming late 18c Hôtel de Salm, Legion of Honour Mus. (v.a. p.m., cl. Mon.).

Palais-Bourbon. Early 19c neo-Greek façade looks out over the bridge and Place de la Concorde, up to the Madeleine. Seat of the National Assembly; council chamber dates from 1832. Library decorated by Delacroix (permission needed to visit).

École Militaire. This 18c military academy (where Napoleon did part of his training), was among architect Jacques-Ange Gabriel's mas-

terpieces (v.a. on request). Opposite, statue of Joffre and the *Champ-de-Mars* (parade ground). Behind, the vast Unesco palace, built 1955–58. Among great contemporary works it contains are Picasso's *The Fall of Icarus* (860 sq. ft.) and, outside, the *Sun Wall* and *Moon Wall*, ceramic compositions by Miró and Artigas. Noguchi garden.

Eiffel Tower. Daring construction built entirely of metal (1887–1889), 320 m. high (v.a. 1000–2300 h 1st and 2nd floors; 1000–2030 h 3rd floor; post office open daily 1000–1930 h. 'Cinemax', audiovisual display. Restaurants: brasserie on 1st floor; luxury restaurant, 2nd floor; refreshment stall, 3rd floor. Wonderful panorama.

Paris Sewers. Vast network of sewers, with 2,100 km of galleries and mains drainage; each street lies above a sewer bearing its name (v.a. p.m., Mon., Wed. and 4th Sat.; entrance at corner of Alma Bridge and Quai d'Orsay). Information room is first stop before 200 m.-

long, sign-posted tour.

Bateaux-mouches. Boat trips. Boarding point: Alma Bridge (right bank). Depart. 1100, 1430, 1600. Night trips: 2100. Restaurants on board. Also Paris-Ile de France motor launches, Port de Suffren: cruises through Paris, R. Marne loop and Seine valley. Boarding points for motor launches: Eiffel Tower, Alma Bridge.

9. CHAILLOT, PASSY, AUTEUIL

Palais de Chaillot. Built in 1937, it is approached by a vast circular forecourt on which stands statue of Foch; between the two wings, spacious terrace with wide panoramic view. Palace has two concert halls (the larger completely renovated in 1975) and four museums: **Mus. of Mankind**, world-wide ethnography and anthropology, prehistory to present day, (v.a., cl. Tues.); **Mus. of French Monuments**, replicas and reproductions of masterpieces of architecture, painting and sculpture

(v.a., cl. Tues.); **Naval Mus.** (v.a., cl. Tues.); **Cinema Mus.** Aquarium in gardens. **Guimet Mus.,** 6 Place d'Iéna, Asian art (v.a., cl. Tues.).

Palais de Tokyo, 13 Avenue du Président Wilson. A Palais de l'Image will be installed in the refitted premises, comprising a French cinemathèque, Cinema Mus., Natnl. Institute for Applied Art Training and Natnl. Photographic Centre.

Paris Mus. of Modern Art. 11 Avenue du Président Wilson. Paintings and sculpture, mainly Paris School. Mus. houses the *Fée Electricité* (Electricity Fairy), largest mural in the world – more than 6,450 sq. ft. – by Dufy (due to be moved to the Palais de l'Image). Exhibitions (v.a., cl. Mon.).

Mus. Clemenceau. 8 Rue Franklin. 'Tiger' Clemenceau's apartment has been kept virtually unchanged since his death in 1929. First floor has documentary display retracing his life (v.a., p.m., Tues., Thurs., Sat., Sun., cl. Aug.).

Balzac's House. 47 Rue Raynouard. Small rustic house, surrounded by a garden, looks down on the narrow, picturesque Rue Berton (v.a., cl. Mon.). Balzac lived here from 1840–1847. Manuscripts, caricatures, furniture, documents and

other diverse objects have been used to reconstruct interior and evoke his life's work. Large library.

Maison de Radio-France. Erected between 1952–1963, by Henri Bernard, this vast crown-shaped construction, 500 m. in circumference, is dominated by a 70 m. tower. It has a radio and television mus. (v.a., cl. Mon.). Large recording studios, halls and reception rooms are decorated by contemp. artists. On l. bank of R. Seine, work is under way on one of the new districts in Paris, the **Front de Seine**, a sizeable urban development. Among more interesting buildings are Totem d'Andrault and Parat Towers; large mosaic on the pedestrian walkway.

Mus. Marmottan. 2 Rue Louis Boilly. Medieval art. Rich range of furniture and paintings from Empire and Restoration periods. Impressionist painting: important works by Monet (v.a., cl. Mon.).

Bois de Boulogne. Enormous park covering some 2,155 acres; redesigned in 19c, it contains the *Grand Lac* (27 acres, boating), the *Petit Lac* (7.5 acres), several restaurants, two race courses (*Auteuil* and *Longchamp*), and the *Jardin d'Acclimatation* (v.a.); also the *Pré Catelan* and Shakespeare Garden,

18c *Bagatelle* park (superb rose gardens), and City of Paris' floral garden at 3 Avenue de la Porte d'Auteuil. Hothouses with tropical plants (v.a.).

Mus. des Arts et Traditions Populaires. Large collections relating to rural life in France, customs and practices, entertainment, beliefs, toys, etc.; in unusual steel and glass building (1960–1972). Libraries (books, pictures and photographs) (v.a., cl. Tues.).

10. CHAMPS-ÉLYSÉES, ÉTOILE

The capital's Triumphal Way, the Champs-Élysées (1,880 m.) runs from Place de la Concorde to the Arc de Triomphe de l'Étoile; it is extended on other side of Arc by Avenue de la Grande Armée and Avenue Charles de Gaulle towards the Défense, a world of concrete, glass and steel (monumental sculptures by Calder, Agam, Philolaos, Leygue, Miró, etc.).

Place de la Concorde. Designed between 1755 and 1775 by Jacques-Ange Gabriel, also architect of two of the most imposing buildings facing over the square (Hôtel Crillon and the Ministère de la Marine [Admiralty Office]). In

centre, obelisk from Egyptian temple at Luxor (23 m. high). *Chevaux de Marly* (replicas), by Coustou, stand at entrance to Champs-Élysées.

To l. of the Place Georges Clemenceau (1932 statue of him) is Ave. Winston Churchill. To r., the **Grand Palais**, enormous building erected in 1900, used for exhibitions and similar events; also contains the *Galeries Nationales* (prestigious exhibitions) and *Palais de la Découverte* (entrance, Ave. F. D. Roosevelt, (v.a., cl. Mon.). To l., the **Petit Palais**, also built in 1900: *Mus. des Beaux Arts de la Ville de Paris* (v.a., cl. Mon.) has important collection of ancient, medieval and Ren. artefacts; also 18c painting (Boucher, Hubert Robert, Tiepolo); 19c Courbet Room; works by Corot, Degas, Cézanne, Toulouse-Lautrec. Ave. Winston Churchill runs into *Alexander III* bridge (1900). To r. of Place Clemenceau, Ave. de Marigny leads to Place Beauvau and, on r. again, to *Rue du Faubourg St. Honoré*, where most of the luxury shops are to be found. *Palais de l'Elysée*, 18c, is official residence of President of the Republic. Ave. des Champs-Élysées ends at **Arc de Triomphe de l'Étoile** (1806–1836), under which lies the grave of the Unknown Soldier (from 1914–1918 war). Opposite Champs-Élysées and to r., high relief by Rude, *The Departure of the Volunteers in 1792*, aka *The Marseillaise*. (Lift to top of the Arc.)

11. ST. AUGUSTIN, PARC MONCEAU

St. Augustin. One of the most original churches in Paris; iron framed, built between 1860 and 1871 (with 60 m. dome).

Expiatory Chapel. Noteworthy monument erected between 1815 and 1826 on place where Louis XVI and Marie Antoinette were buried. Cloister, chapel, marble sculptures of Louis XVI, Marie Antoinette and royal family, with crypt (v.a.).

Jacquemart-André Mus. 158 Blvd. Haussmann. One of richest collectors' mus. in Paris (v.a., cl. Mon. and Tues.): Italian art 15–17c; French 18c, also Flemish, Dutch and Spanish.

Cernuschi Mus. 7 Avenue Vélasquez. Art from China and Japan. Distinguished group of ancient Chinese bronzes (v.a., cl. Mon.).

Nissim de Camondo Mus. 63 Rue de Monceau. Interesting collection from 18c housed in Louis XVI-style mansion built in 1910 (v.a., cl. Mon. and Tues.).

Monceau Park. Surrounded by beautiful late 19c mansions, it houses curious 18c naumachy (arti-

4

Champs-Élysées: (1) *one of the most beautiful avenues in the world, leads to the Arc de Triomphe de l'Etoile, raised to glory of Napoleon's Grande Armée.* **(2)** *On one side, Rude's 'Departure of the Volunteers in 1792', aka 'The Marseillaise'.* **(3)** *The* Madeleine, *seen from the Place de la Concorde.*

(4) *Heights of ambition: in the foreground, the 23 m. high Luxor obelisk (13c BC), in the centre of the Place de la Concorde; a mile away, the 300 m. Eiffel Tower.*

2

1

(*1*) *The* Sacré-Coeur *basilica looms above the narrow streets on the heights of Montmartre, such as the unusual* Rue Foyatier (*2*) *with its 225 steps.*

(*3*) 'The Dance', *a group by Carpeaux (original in Louvre), on the façade of the Opéra.*

3

ficial lake) with colonnade and several statues of famous men, executed in 19c style (Maupassant, Chopin, Gounod).

12. MONTMARTRE

The old village, once famed for its windmills, has remained a popular district, both for its places of entertainment and its picturesque streets and unexpectedly rural corners. It can be reached via the Blvd. de Clichy and the Place Blanche – site of the Moulin Rouge, immortalised by Toulouse-Lautrec – or via the Place Pigalle and the Blvd. de Rochechouart (cabarets and nightclubs).

Place du Tertre. Painters' territory, the heart of Montmartre. Église St.-Pierre, 12c, lovely little rustic church, one of the oldest in Paris, in shadow of the Sacré-Coeur.

Basilique du Sacré-Coeur. Enormous Romano-Byzantine edifice, begun in 1876. With its 83 m. high dome and 84 m. campanile, it can be seen from all over the capital. The disconcertingly ornate interior provides sad proof of the mediocrity of late 19c religious art. Magnificent view from forecourt, extending up to 30 km away.

Mus. of Old Montmartre in house, Rue Cortot, where Utrillo once lived (v.a., cl. Mon.); below it is the vineyard of Montmartre and famous old cabaret, *Le Lapin Agile*. A small *Mus. of Jewish Art* is at 42 Rue des Saules (due to be transferred to Hôtel Saint-Aignan, Rue du Temple).

Moulin de la Galette, on corner of Rue Lepic and Rue Girardon. Only surviving mill in Montmartre, painted by Renoir, Toulouse-Lautrec, Van Gogh, Utrillo, Picasso, etc. Now part of an up-market residential complex. Place Emile-Goudeau: façade of the *Bateau Lavoir* (wash-shed), damaged by fire in 1970 but since restored, where such artists as Picasso, Van Dongen, Modigliani and Max Jacob lived at turn of the century. Cubism was born here.

Montmartre Cemetery has tombs of Stendhal, Degas, Giraudoux, Sacha Guitry, Louis Jouvet, Alexandre Dumas, the 'Dame aux Camélias', etc., and very fine recumbent statue of Cavaignac by Rude. In *Cemetery of St. Vincent*, tombs of Utrillo, (crowned by the '*Spirit of Painting*' by Marcel Aymé) and of Honegger, Gen. Paul, Steinlen, etc. In Rue de l'Abreuvoir, the *Allée des Brouillards* and small 18c *Ch. des Brouillards*, where Nerval and Renoir once lived; the *Ave. Junot* has several 1930s-style town houses

once occupied by artists (e.g. the cartoonist Francisque Poulbot).

13. OPÉRA, GRANDS BOULEVARDS, TEMPLE

The Grands Boulevards run from the Madeleine to the Richelieu-Drouot crossroads and on as far as the Place de la République.

Eglise de la Madeleine. Built in form of a Greek temple, from 1806 to 1842; int. is cold but imposing.

Théâtre de l'Opéra. Built in baroque style by Garnier, and sumptuously decorated from 1862 to 1875. On r. of façade, copy of renowned group of figures, *The Dance* by Carpeaux (original in Louvre). The interior is overwhelmingly ornate. Since 1964, it has had a painted ceiling by Chagall (source of much controversy). Opera museum is in Pavillon de l'Empereur, Rue Scribe (v.a., cl. Mon.).

Cognac-Jay Mus. 25 Blvd. des Capucines. Dedicated to 18c art and decorative style, it offers interesting minor works by Rembrandt, Boucher, Fragonard, Guardi, etc., plus objets d'art, furniture and panelling from time of Louis XV and XVI (v.a., cl. Mon.).

Grévin Mus. 10 Blvd. Montmartre. Popular waxworks mus. Its reconstructions of historical scenes and of contemporary celebrities have an old-fashioned charm. Also small theatre, conjuring and magic shows.

Porte St. Denis. Surviving Paris gate, erected in 1672 to celebrate Louis XIV's victories on the Rhine; it is decorated with historical scenes and sculptures of allegorical figures.

Porte St. Martin. Another old gate nearby, specifically commemorating capture of Besançon and Franche Comté by Louis XIV in 1674, with sculptures depicting scenes from the war.

Conservatoire des Arts et Métiers. Natnl. Mus. of Technology. 292 Rue Saint Martin (v.a., cl. Mon.). Installed in former church of St. Martin-des-Champs and its annexes; illustrates evolution of technology in such fields as means of locomotion (first cars, planes), physics, electricity, radio, television, cinema, etc. Library in monks' former refectory.

St. Nicolas-des-Champs. 15, 16 and 17c. On r., fine Ren. doorway, late 16c. Nave is divided into five by double row of pillars; imposing two-sided main altar, with large 17c retable in marble. Numerous paintings and works of art.

At 51 Rue de Montmorency, unusual 15c house of writer and

supposed alchemist Nicolas Flamel; at 3 Rue Volta, 14–15c timber-framed house, one of the oldest in Paris.

14. EAST PARIS

Large-scale urbanisation has transformed *Belleville* and *Ménilmontant*, although a few corners such as church of *St. Germain-de-Charonne*, with its squat 13c bell tower and rustic cemetery, remain unchanged.

Père Lachaise Cemetery. Largest and most important cemetery in Paris, with many (often bizarre) memorials to famous men (v.a.). The most picturesque section is to r. of central Monument to the Dead, here tombs are scattered over haphazard little hillocks, criss-crossed by steep paths. Among people buried here: Chopin, Champollion, Molière, La Fontaine, Corot, Ney, Masséna, David d'Angers, Murat, etc. In central alley: Musset (under his beloved willow), Colette, Baron Haussmann, Félix Faure, etc. Large columbarium. In SE corner, wall where last defenders of the 1871 Commune were killed.

Buttes-Chaumont Park. 62 acres of hilly ground, laid out around lake and belvedere crowned by a small temple. (Good views).

Mus. of African and Oceanic Art. 293 Ave. Daumesnil. Notable art exhibits from black Africa, the Maghreb (North Africa) and Oceania, all housed in huge neoclassical block built for 1931 Colonial Exhibition (v.a., cl. Tues.). In basement, tropical aquarium.

Bois de Vincennes. Vast park, covering more than 2,300 acres, laid out during last century in English garden style. Has renowned *Zoological Gardens*, among best in Europe (v.a.); two lakes (Lac des Minimes, with three islands, and Lac Daumesnil); Indo-Chinese temple and its tropical garden (v.a. Sun. p.m.). See **Vincennes***.

Paris Floral Park. (v.a.). These exceptionally beautiful 70-acre gardens include floral exhibitions, a flower valley, a large exotic flower display and a dahlia garden. Scattered throughout are statues by contemporary artists (Schöffer, Tinguely, Calder, Giacometti, Gilioli, etc.). Monumental fountain by Stahly. Permanent exhibition of rural houses of all styles.

Porte St. Ouen Flea Market. Second-hand items and antiques. Sat., Sun., Mon., 1100–1900. **Porte de Montreuil** market, same times. **Porte Didot** market, Sat. and Sun., 0800–1800.

P

Paimpol
22 – Côtes-du-Nord   9 – A 1
Agreeably situated fishing village on an enormous bay. Small maritime museum.
Vicinity • Kerroc'h Tower (2 km N, panorama). • Headland and wood at Guilben (2.5 km E). • *Loguivy-de-la-Mer*, small fishing village (4 km NW). • 6 km NE, *Pointe de l'Arcouest*, embarcation point for Ile de **Bréhat**. • 4 km SE, ruins of 13–14c *Beauport Abbey* (v.a. to exterior only, Easter Sat. to Mon.; Whit Sat. to Whit Mon.; and daily June 15–Sept. 15; on request out of season), enormous chapter-house, cloister, church, refectory, cellar, fine rib-vaulted Duke's Room. 6 km S, *Lanloup*, beautiful 16c church with granite statues of the Apostles decorating porch; 3 km S, *Kermaria-an-Isquit* chapel, 13–15c, has 15c murals including a 'danse macabre'.

Paimpont
35 – Ille-et-Vilaine   9 – B 3
The 13c abbey church houses several works of art.
Vicinity • Known in tales of chivalry as the Forest of Brocéliande, it covers some 26 sq. miles and was supposed to have belonged to the fairy Viviane and the magician Merlin. Dotted with ponds, it has many good walks: to the ruins of Telhouét Priory and the 14–15c Ch. de Comper, to the Baranton fountain, the *Tréhorenteuc* megaliths, the 'Valley of No Return', etc. • To SW, near *Campénéac*, late 14c *Ch. de Trécesson*, surrounded by moat. (n.v.a.). • To S, *Camp of the Military Academy of St. Cyr-Coëtquidan*, memorial museum.

Pamiers
09 – Ariège   42 – A 2
Notre Dame-du-Camp, 14, 17 and 18c, has large 14c crenellated brick tower. Also in brick is St. Antonin cathedral, 17c, with fine 14c Toulouse bell tower; 17c panelling. Beautiful view of Pyrenees from Promenade du Castella. The town is excellent base for excursions to Pyrenean snowfields.

Paray-le-Monial
71 – Saône-et-Loire   25 – C 2
Notre Dame church, or basilica of the Sacred Heart, characteristic of Cluniac Romanesque architecture, is important pilgrimage centre; interesting Romanesque capitals

PADIRAC (Abyss)
46 – Lot   36 – B 1
Magnificent 'aven' or swallow-hole, one of the best known in Europe. 75 m. deep, it has an underground river which has been explored over some 10 km. The Grand-Dôme chamber is 91 m. high; tours on foot and in boats (daily from Easter to 2nd Sun. in Oct.).

Paray-le-Monial: reflected in the R. Bourbince, the former abbey church of Notre Dame, now the Sacred Heart basilica.

and 15c fresco in apse. In the Parc des Chapelains is building housing relics of Ste. Marguerite-Marie Alacoque, who initiated this pilgrimage in 17c; also serves as a shelter for pilgrims and has a diorama. Shrine to the saint stands in the chapel of the Visitation, aka the Sanctuaire des Apparitions. 'Le Hiéron' Museum of Religious Art: many liturgical items and pictures, illustrating the glorification of religion through art. Of note is a Romanesque tympanum from *Anzy-le-Duc*.

Vicinity • 13 km E, *Charolles*; overlooking the town are remains of former château of the Counts of Charolais (now town hall). • 17.5 km SW, *Anzy-le-Duc*: interesting Romanesque church dating from second half of 11c; neighbouring priory has very unusual carved portal.

Paris
75 – Seine   11 – C 1/2
See pages 262 to 275.

Parthenay
79 – Deux-Sèvres   23 – B 1
Former stronghold. Picturesque old
streets, particularly Rue de la Vaux-
Saint-Jacques, lined with 15 and 16c
timbered houses, linking Place du
14-Juillet and imposing 13c St.
Jacques gate, flanked by two
machicolated towers. The citadel
quarter (mid-15c Clock Gate) is
situated at end of promontory; still
standing within ramparts are:
Romanesque church of Ste. Croix;
fine 12c sculpted portal of former
collegiate church of Notre Dame-
de-la-Couldre; and three towers of
former 13c castle.
Vicinity ● 3 km SW, Parthenay-le-
Vieux, 12c church with façade from
the Poitevin Romanesque School.
● 7 km NW, 16c Ch. du Theil, set
among woods and lakes.

Pau: *Romanesque portal of Ste-Foy at Morlaas displays the 24 Old Men of the Apocalypse and some fine friezes.*

Pau
64 – Pyrénées-Atlantiques   41 A 2
The Blvd. des Pyrénées, 1,800 m.
long, is the 'terrace' of this handsome town, whose oldest quarters
are grouped around the castle; from
it, you get matchless view of the
Pyrenees, esp. the *Pic du Midi
d'Ossau* (2,885 m.) and the *Pic du
Midi de Bigorre* (2,865 m.). ● The
castle, on a spur overlooking R.
Gave, dates back to 13–14c (Mon-
tauzer Tower, Gaston Phébus
keep); it was turned into a country-
seat in 16c (elegant Ren. main
courtyard); France's King Henri IV
was born here in 1553. In S and W
wings, the apartments form natnl.
mus. of the Château de Pau; on 3rd
floor of S wing, mus. of the Béarn
reg. ● Fine arts mus. (cl. Tues.) has
large groups of paintings: Spanish
(El Greco, Ribera), Flemish
(Rubens), French 18c (Rigaud, Largillière, Hubert Robert) and 19c
(Degas, *Le Bureau de Coton à La
Nouvelle-Orléans*, Devéria, Corot).
Also large coll. of modern art; print
room. Mus. Bernadotte is in childhood home of the field marshal who
became King of Sweden in 1818.
The castle's grounds, on banks of
the R. Gave, and the Beaumont
Park (casino) offer pleasant walks.
Vicinity ● 8 km S, via *Jurançon*
(noted vineyards), is *Gan*; 1 km to
NE, the picturesque Ch. de Tout-y-
Croît; 6 km to SE, Piétat chapel and
calvary (pilgrimage, superb view of
the Gave valley and Pyrenees); from
Gan, the road (N134 bis) continues
to *Arudy* (23 km to S): 15c church
with Goth. Flamboyant portal; the
Potz manor-house, 17c, is home of
the Mus. des Pyrénées Occidentales,
or Maison d'Ossau (v.a. in
summer). ● 7 km NW: **Lescar***. ●
11 km NE, *Morlaas*: Ste. Foy
church (handsome Romanesque
portal, restored).

PECH-MERLE (grotto)
46 – Lot   36 – A2
3 km SW of *Cabrerets*, prehist. site at foot of steep cliffs, crowned by
feudal ruins known as the 'Devil's Castle'. The cave-temple of Pech-
Merle (v.a. during summer season) has important paintings of horses,
surrounded by the imprint of hands and was without doubt a religious
centre. Mus. of prehist. and ethnography. Near *Cabrerets*, Ch. de
Gontaut-Biron, 15c, housing mus. of African prehist. and ethnography (v.a. Mar. to Nov.).

Pech-Merle: *near Cabrerets, the Ch. des Biron; a corner tower flanks the machicolated main body of the castle.*

Penne-d'Agenais
47 – Lot-et-Garonne   35 – D 2
Formerly fortified town built in eagle's nest style above R. *Lot*; one of Quercy region's most picturesque small towns; ruins of feudal castle and ramparts (three fortified gates), old houses. At top of the hill is the Notre Dame-de-Peyragude basilica, built late 19c in Romanesque-Byzantine style (pilgrimage centre); wide panorama.

Périgueux
24 – Dordogne   29 – C 3
The white cathedral of St. Front, bristling with cupolas and bell-turrets, was built in 12c and restored, controversially, in 19c; it dominates the old part of the town and the banks of R. *Isle*; on S side of cath., 12–13 and 16c cloister (small lapidary mus.) Interesting old houses; 16c Hôtel Gamanson (7 Rue de la Constitution); Gaillard House (1 Rue de la Sagesse, superb Ren. staircase); Hôtel de St. Astier (2 Rue de la Miséricorde); the so-called 'Pâtissier's (cakemaker's) House' (17 Rue Eguillerie, 15–16c decorative sculpture); also the Hôtels d'Abzac de Ladouze, 15c, and de Sallegourde, 15–16c (Rue Aubergerie), etc. To l. of Pont des Barris, colourful 'quayside' houses. The Cité quarter is situated round St. Étienne-de-la Cité, church built in Périgord-Romanesque style, originally with four cupolas (of which only two survive). Rue de l'Ancien-Évêché leads to 3c Roman arena. 150 m to SW, ruins of Ch. Barrière (fmr. 15c fortress), built on remains of Roman enceinte. Vésone Tower, remnant of 2c Roman temple. Périgord Mus. (cl. Tues.): one of the most important archaeological mus. in France, with large collections covering prehist., Mediterranean civilisation, mosaics, sculpture (antique, medieval and Ren.), 17–20c French and Italian painting. In fmr. chapel of early 17c Augustinian convent, folk art and traditions. Also Périgord military mus. (cl. Sun.).
Vicinity ● 5 km NW, Chancelade abbey; 12c church and 14–17c buildings of fmr. Augustinian abbey (15c laundry, workshops, 14c mill, 15–17c living quarters, etc.) form a v. homogenous whole (Son et Lumière in summer); small mus. of religious art. 5 km to NW, the 12–14c fmr. priory church of Merlande, fortified in 16c.

Pernes-les-Fontaines
84 – Vaucluse   38 – A 3
Attractive and lively little town which gets its name from its 33 fountains. The 13c Ferrande Tower has unusual paintings dating from 1275 (apply to Syndicat d'Initiative, summer only). 12–14c church of Notre Dame-de-Nazareth; Notre

Pernes-les-Fontaines: *Motif on the Cormoran Fountain.*

Périgueux: *the cathedral looms over the waterfront houses.* ▲
Goose liver is one of Périgord's great specialities. ▼

Dame Gate, fortified in 16c, also bridge and chapel. 18c Cormoran Fountain. Remains of three town gates, also of château of the Counts of Toulouse. Town hall is former mansion of Dukes of Brancas (17c).

Péronne
80 – Somme   5 – D 2
13c castle, where Charles the Bold imprisoned Louis XI (1468), is flanked on its W side by a brick bastion from the former ramparts, 16–17c, above a pretty lake and the Promenade de Cam. Renaissance town hall (rebuilt after 1912) houses Danicourt mus. (collection of Greek, Roman and Gallic coins). The Bretagne gate, formed by two slate-roofed brick pavilions, still has its external defences and drawbridge. Local specialities: smoked eel and eel pâté.
Vicinity ● To W, small lakes of the upper *Somme*, very picturesque (fishing and wild-fowling) ● 10 km S, near *Athies*, remains of large Gallo-Roman villa (v.a. in summer).

Pérouges
01 – Ain   32 – A 1
One of the best preserved old towns
in France. Its ramparts, winding
streets, 15 and 16c houses and 13–
15c fortified church have remained
unchanged since the Middle Ages.
Town is entered through two gates:
Porte d'En Haut (High Gate) and
Porte d'En Bas (Low Gate), from
where you get extensive views. The
main thoroughfare, Rue du Prince
(house of the Princes of Savoie),
leads to Place du Tilleul where
'Hostelry' and mus. are situated.
Rue des Rondes is lined with
corbelled or half-timbered houses.
Promenade des Terreaux for external tour of the ramparts.

Perpignan
66 – Pyrénées–Orientales 43 – D 3
Capital of French Catalonia. The
liveliest part is in the old quarter
between the Castillet: impressive
brick-fortified works, late 14c
(inside, the Casa Pairal, mus. of
Catalan folk art and traditions);
Place de la Loge, site of the Loge de
Mer (1388); 13–16–17c town hall
(patio has Maillol's *The Mediterranean*); and cath. of St. Jean, in
southern Goth. style. Large nave,
14–16c, and rich altar-pieces in
wood or marble from 15–18c.
Passage leads to much-revered 11c
chapel of Notre Dame-dels-Cor-
rechs; constructed from large river
pebbles, it is actually the S arm
of the transept and chapel of
very early church of St. Jean-le-
Vieux. Side door on S side of cath.
leads to Christ's Chapel, which contains late-13c wooden statue of the
Dévôt Christ, impressive masterpiece of realism, probably from
the Rhineland. Former 13–15c
charnel house, known as St. Jean's
Cloister. Perpignan has several
interesting churches: St. Jacques, 14
and 18c, has monumental retable
of Notre Dame-de-l'Espérance, late
15c, and 18c Sanch chapel (famed
procession of penitents on Good
Friday); see also Ste. Marie-de-la-
Réal, early 14c, southern Goth.
style. Mus. Hyacinthe Rigaud (cl.
Tues.) has noteworthy collections
of Catalan primitive art, 17–19c
paintings (inc. some by Rigaud, a
native of Perpignan). Contemp. art:
Maillol, Dufy, Clavé, Tapiès. Large
collections of Hispano-Moorish
ceramics. Mus. Joseph Puig
(unusual coins), municipal mus. of
natural hist; also an aviation mus. –
Mas Palegry, on Elne road. The
enormous, imposing Palace of the
Kings of Majorca, 13–14c, within
the 16c citadel, has regained its original appearance, thanks to extensive restoration work (v.a., cl. Tues.
and public holidays). Palace's main
courtyard and Galerie du Paradis,

**Perpignan: the Dévôt Christ,
striking example of realism from
the Middle Ages.**

its early-14c two-storeyed chapel,
royal apartments and large Salle de
Majorque (32 m. long), together
form an outstanding ensemble.
Vicinity ● 4 km SE, Cabestany;
church has priceless Romanesque
tympanum by 13c Master of Cabestany. ● 9.5 km E, *Canet-Plage*,
popular seaside resort; Blvd. de la
Méditerranée is prolonged by an
expressway as far as *St. Cyprien-
Plage* (18.5 km S); new 37-acre
marina. Resorts of *Canet-Plage, St-
Cyprien-Plage* and, to S, *Arlèges-
Plage*, together form one tourist
centre, under name of St. Cyprien.
● 18 km SW, *Thuir*; 5 km to SW,
Castelnou, fortified village dominated by 10c castle (n.v.a.). ● 28 km
NW, via Estagel, *Tautavel*, large
prehist. excavations. Notable Mus.
of Prehist., very well presented,
includes skull of 'Tautavel Man',
450,000 BC.

Perros-Guirec
22 – Côtes-du-Nord   8 – D 1
Fishing village and picturesque
seaside resort on a rocky peninsula
flanked by two beaches: Trestraou
and Trestrignel.
Vicinity ● 3 km NW, Notre Dame-
de-la Clarté, mid-15c chapel in pink
granite (Breton 'pardon' on Aug.
15); fine view; via old Customs road
to *Ploumanach* (see **Lannion***). ● In
summer, boat trips round the *Sept-
Iles*; the Ile aux Moines (Monks
Island) has a lighthouse and fort
built by Vauban; the islands of

Rouzic and Malban form a sea-bird
sanctuary unique in France.

Pesteils (Château)
15 – Cantal   30 – C 3
In Polminhac. One of the most
beautiful Auvergne châteaux, with
famed 16c square keep (v.a. July
and Aug.); on first floor of keep:
15c frescos and rooms decorated in
17c style (painted ceilings). Superb
view of *Cère* valley from terrace.
Vicinity ● To SE, Ch. de Vixouze
consists of 13c keep and imposing
18c central building: on first floor,
beautiful 17c coffered ceiling,
painted (guided tours).

Pézenas
34 – Hérault   43 – A 2
The old town offers an unusual
ensemble of 16, 17 and 18c architecture. Leading from Place du 14
Juillet, at its centre, is Rue Fran-
çois-Oustrin: at No.6 is Hôtel de
Lacoste (15c vaulted galleries and
grand staircase, 16c courtyard). In
Place Gambetta: house of the
barber, Gély, friend of Molière,
who played at Pézenas before the
Prince de Conti (1650–1651 and
1653–1656); opposite, houses of the
Consuls, mid-16c, with Ren. and
late-17c façades. From here, a sign-
posted tour of 33 sites may be followed. Mus. Vulliod-St. Germain,
housed in attractive 16 and 18c
mansion. Rue Alfred Sabatier:
Hôtel de Flottes de Sébasan, 17c
façade. Rue de la Foire has interesting houses and entrance to the
ghetto (old Jewish quarter – see the
Rues de la Juiverie and des Litan-
ies). Mid-18c church of St. Jean
(beautiful furniture); opposite:
Commanderie of St. John of Jerusalem, 16c. 17 and 18c mansions in
Cours Jean-Jaurès: at No. 28, Hôtel
de Landes de St. Palais (superb late-
15c staircase); 14c Faugères Gate.
In Rue Henri-Reboul, late-16c
Hôtel de Montmorency. Via Rue
Anatole France and Rue Denfert-
Rochereau to the Hôtel Malibran,
late-17c with fine mid-18c façade.
Rue Conti: 17c Hôtel d'Alfonce
(particularly beautiful courtyard
with loggias and open-welled spiral
staircase), where Molière performed. Former Griffon d'Or hostelry,
late-17c (interesting courtyard),
and Bât d'Argent hostelry, 16 and
17c.
Vicinity ● *Peyne* valley, 17c Ch. de
Larzac, Fondouce, St. Palais farm,
Ch. de Montpezat and Roquelune,
17c. ● To NW, near *Caux*, Ch. du
Parc, 17c, Ch. de Loubatière, 14–
16c. ● 5.5 km NE, *Montagnac*: 17c
Ch. de Lavagnac, built in Italian
villa style, above terrace and
gardens (n.v.a.). ● 13 km E, via
Montagnac, 13c Abbey of Valmagne: huge Goth. church, sizeable

Picquigny: *medieval ramparts of a former château protect a Renaissance pavilion where Mme. de Sévigné stayed.*

Pierrefonds: *the former abbey church of Notre Dame at Morienval, with towers and belfry-porch at either end of a Carolingian nave.*

remains of cloister and monastery buildings. (v.a. pm, exc. Tues., June 15 – Sept. 15; out of season, v.a., p.m. Sun. and public holidays). The abbey stands at foot of the Dentelles de Valmagne, unusual jagged rocks.

Picquigny
80 – Somme　　　　　**5 – C 2**
Impressive ruins of 14c castle (apply to caretaker), encompassing a 13, 14 and 15c church, the 'Pavillon de Sévigné' and various remains of 16–17c buildings (large Ren. kitchen);

beautiful panorama from terrace.
Vicinity ● 3.5 km NW, ruins of the *Abbaye du Gard*, 18c, (v.a.): the monks' building, 18c, and chapel are still used by a religious community; nearby leisure park (v.a. April–Oct.).

Piedicroce
2 B – Corse　　　　　**45 – B 2**
Balconied village above the bowl of Orezza. At the centre of the *Castagniccia*, chestnut tree country. *Vicinity* ● To NW, *Morosaglia*,

birthplace of the Corsican patriot Paoli; from there, S by minor roads to two villages, perched high up: *San Lorenzo* and *Sermano* (St. Nicolas chapel, 15c frescos). ● To SE, the D71 goes through magnificent countryside via *Valle-d'Alesani* (convent chapel) as far as *Cervione*, small town laid out like an amphitheatre, panorama (former cathedral of Ste. Marie-et-St. Érasme, 16c).

Pierrefonds (Château)
60 – Oise　　　　　**5 – D 3**
Enormous fortress built in early 15c but demolished and entirely rebuilt by Viollet-le-Duc, at the request and expense of Napoleon III (v.a.; cl. Tues. in summer, Tues. and Wed. in winter). Interior design is cold and impersonal; nobleman's chambers, chapel, keep, César Tower, 'Knights' Room', etc. 11–13c church.
Vicinity ● 7.5 km SW, *Morienval*, 11–12c church of Notre Dame – one of the most interesting in Ile-de-France.

Pithiviers
45 – Loiret　　　　　**11 – C 3**
St. Salomon, though with Romanesque apse, transept and belfry, is a particularly interesting example of Ren. architecture and decoration. Transport mus. in a former depot, includes 4 km trip by late-19c steam train. Municipal mus. housed in former Hôtel-Dieu (18c hospital): archaeology, pottery, paintings, large collection of Italian drawings.
Vicinity ● 6 km E, *Yèvre-le-Chatel*; huge lozenge-shaped castle, 13–14c (v.a. on request) is flanked by towers linked by a parapet walk.

Plagne (La)
73 – Savoie　　　　　**32 – D 2**
Seven winter sports resorts in one complex, founded in 1961; at 1,980 m. alt., in majestic setting surrounded by mountain peaks. 65 mechanised ski-lifts, etc., notably the Grande Rochette cable service, which climbs to height of 2,500 m. (magnificent panorama). Satellite resort, 'Aime–2000', at 2,000 m.

Plestin-les-Grèves
22 – Côtes-du-Nord　　　　　**8 – C 1**
Beautiful 16c church; 500 m. to E, St. Roch chapel, with fine views over the *Bay of Lannion*.
Vicinity ● 6 km N, *Locquirec*, small port and seaside resort; the Armorique coast road goes round Locquirec headland to *St. Efflam*, at W of the *Lieue de Grève*, immense beach stretching for 5 km along Bay of St Michel; at the E end of the

Pleyben: *last of the great Breton calvaries, with unusual 'stacking' of sculptures.*

bay, *St-Michel-en-Grève*: on terrace above the beach is 16–17c church. ● 8 km W, *Lanmeur*, modern church with Romanesque door on S side; also has pre-Romanesque crypt (unusual sculpted decorations) which is among oldest religious buildings in Brittany. Kernitron chapel, 12 and 16c.

Pleyben
29 S – Finistère   8 – C 3
The parish wall encloses a noteworthy architectural ensemble, reached through a 17c Triumphal Gate. The 16c church has a sturdy Ren. belfry, crowned with a dome and lantern, and a Goth. spire – linked by an elegant passageway, supported by two arcades, to an octagonal staired turret. Inside, the vaulted nave has 16c painted and carved panelling. Ossuary chapel in mid-16c Goth. Flamboyant style. The mid-16c calvary, one of the most impressive in Brittany, stands on a monumental base in the form of a triumphal arch; its numerous scenes from the life of Christ are portrayed with folk art realism (albeit tinged with the primitive).

Ploërmel
56 – Morbihan   16 – B 1
Small old town. The Goth. Flamboyant N portal of St-Armel church, 16c, has two sculpted doors; interior has tomb of Philippe de Montauban and his wife, early 16c, recumbent statue of Jeanne de Léhon, mid-14c, and funerary statues of Jean II and Jean III of Brittany, etc. In Rue Beaumanoir: House of the Marmousets, dec-

orated with late 16c wood carvings, and former town house of the Dukes of Brittany.
Vicinity ● 2.5 km NW, *Étang du Duc*, lake 5 km long (camping and boating centre). ● 16 km S, *Malestroit*, old township, previously fortified; many 15–16c houses in timber and stone; 15c church of St. Gilles has Romanesque parts in red sandstone.

Plougastel-Daoulas
29 N – Finistère   8 – B 2
Its early-17c calvary, in granite and ochre coloured stone, depicts 150 different figures, in a very lively way; it is one of the most original in Finistère.
Vicinity ● Plougastel peninsula is one of the best preserved traditional Breton areas; both countryside and villages have kept their old-time

Plougastel-Daoulas: *detail of The Last Supper on calvary frieze.*

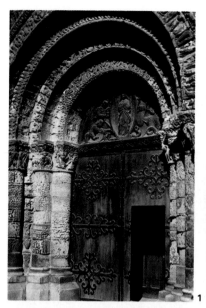

Poitiers: *Notre Dame-la-Grande* *(1)*; *central portal of St. Pierre cathedral (2); St. Jean Baptistry (3), the oldest Christian building in France*.

character. From Plougastel to SW, view of Kernisi, Caro cove, view of Kerdeniel, chapels of St. Adrien and *St. Guénolé* (panelling, painted wooden statues of saints), view of Keramenez over the cove of Auberlac. ● 12 km E, *Daoulas*; parish enclosure with 16c porch decorated with statues of Apostles; Romanesque church, late-12c; Ren. chapel of Ste. Anne; the abbey still has elegant 12c Romanesque cloister, with 14c lavatorium (washing place) in centre; 4 km to E, Irvillac, Goth. and Ren. church; 3 km to SE, unusual calvary of Notre Dame-de-Lorette.

Poissy
78 – Yvelines 11 – C 1
Notre Dame church, mainly 11–12c Romanesque, has two Romanesque belfries. The double portal on r. side is entered through elegantly decorated Goth. Flamboyant porch, 16c; int. has interesting works of art, notably the font, in which it is claimed that St. Louis was baptised. 16c St. Sepulchre. A 14c building,

with two towers, is all that remains of the abbey; now houses a toy mus., unique in France; also mus. of art and history (local life, works by Meisonnier).
Vicinity ● 4.5 km on l. bank of R. *Seine*, beach and swimming pools set in lush green surroundings; 7 km away, *Triel*, 12–13c church with Ren. porch and 16c stained-glass windows.

Poitiers
86 – Vienne 23 – C 2
One of the richest towns in France, for artistic interest. It lies on a plateau, partly encircled by the R. *Clain*. ● 12–13c cathedral of St. Pierre mixes the local Poitevin Romanesque and Angevin Goth. styles; the façade, framed by towers, has three beautiful sculpted 12c portals, above which is a fine rose window with 16 segments. Interior, 90 m. long, contains series of 19 early-13c stained-glass windows; choir has mid-13c sculpted stalls. St. Jean Baptistry, massive rectangular edifice dating from 4c,

heightened in 7c and enlarged in 11c, is without doubt the oldest Christian building in France; inside (v.a., cl. Wed. and Jan.–Feb.), it has 12 and 13c frescos and small Merovingian mus. ● Opposite, Ste. Croix Mus. (cl. Tues.) has large archaeological and lapidary collections (marble statue of Athena known as the *Minerva of Poitiers*, dating from 1c). Italian, Flemish and French painting from 18 and 19c. Impressionist and contemp. works: André Brisson, Monticelli, Boudin, Bonnard, etc. Sculptures by Constantin Meunier, Rodin, C. Claudel. Behind the cath., 11–13 and early-14c church of Ste. Radegonde, fronted by 11–12c belfry-porch; the big single nave is good example of Angevin Romanesque style; in crypt is tomb of Ste. Radegonde (d. 587). A masterpiece of Romanesque art, 11–12c church of Notre Dame-la-Grande is famed for its sculpted façade. St. Hilaire-le-Grand, 12–13c, has a central nave crowned by three cupolas, with three side aisles on each flank. St. Jean-de-Montierneuf is fmr. Benedictine abbey church dating from 11c, later extended and heightened. ● Palais de Justice (lawcourts) has large lobby from 14–15c, below magnificent late-14c gabled wall, with three monumental fireplaces and superb set of windows. 14c keep, or Maubergeon Tower. Ren. architecture is represented by: Hôtel Fumé, with late-15c façade and courtyard; Hôtel Berthelot, built 1529; Hôtel Jehan-Beaucé, etc.

Mus. de Chièvres, in 18c Hôtel Rupert de Chièvres, has archaeological and furniture collections, pottery and silverware (cl. Sun. and Mon.). ● Past Pont-Neuf, Blvd. Coligny climbs up to Dunes plateau (panorama) and to Martyrium Hypogeum (apply to caretaker), 7c underground chapel around which, at one time, spread a vast Christian necropolis; chapel is decorated with unusual symbolic sculptures.
Vicinity ● The *Clain* valley to S; at *St. Benoît*, Romanesque church and remains of Benedictine abbey. Continue to *Abbey of Ligugé*, founded in 4c; except for a few 16 and 17c parts, entirely rebuilt in 19c; renovated 16c church (interesting Gallo-Roman and pre-Romanesque remains); the abbey produces unusual enamel work; Gregorian mass every day. ● To W, Boivre valley, via the grottoes of La Norée; Ch. de Montreuil-Bonnin (cl.) in picturesque but strategic site above R. Boivre; 13–15c ruins. ● 10 km SE, *Nouaillé-Maupertuis*, remains of large Benedictine abbey, surrounded by moat and 13c fortified wall flanked by towers; the late 11–12c church has 12c belfry keep.

Poligny
39 – Jura   26 B 1
Small town – renowned for its wine and its cheese (Comté) – at entrance to a 'reculée' (local term for a blind valley). Good excursion centre. Former collegiate church of St. Hippolyte, 15c; under the porch, bas-relief of the saint's martyrdom; int. has fine coll. of statues from the Burgundian school, 15–16c; early *poutre de gloire* (beam forming a kind of triumphal arch at entrance

Poligny: *this small Jura town still has several 17c mansions with majestic portals.*

to choir), with wooden calvary. Hôtel-Dieu dating from 17c (see esp. the pharmacy).
Vicinity ● To SE, taking the **Champagnole*** road, picturesque Vaux abutment, rocky transverse valley. Fmr. Cluniac Priory of Vaux-sur-Poligny, 11c. *Poligny Forest.*

Pompadour (Château)
19 – Corrèze   30 – A 2
Begun in 11c, rebuilt in 15c and transformed in 18c. Today, though, the only bits still standing are S façade, flanked by two v. large machicolated corner towers, and an imposing entrance fort, with two towers (v.a. p.m., ext. only). Renowned stud farm, on 865-acre estate (v.a. Sun., race days and public holidays; weekdays p.m. only; cl. March to July).
Vicinity ● 6 km N, *Lubersac*, Romanesque church (lovely capitals).

Poncé-sur-le-Loir
72 – Sarthe   17 – D 1
Elegant and harmonious, the mid-16c château (v.a., cl. Sun. p.m., April–Nov. 1) houses mus. of Sarthe ethnography and folklore (cl. Sun.). Building has one of the most beautiful Ren. staircases, with six flights of stairs and coffered vaulting ornamented with delicate sculpture. In 11–12c church, 12c Romanesque murals.
Vicinity ● 3 km SE, *Couture-sur-Loir*; Goth. church has fine 17c panelling and the recumbent tomb statues of poet Ronsard's parents; 1 km to S, *Manoir de la Possonnière*, 16c where Ronsard was born in 1524 (v.a. by appointment).

Pons
17 – Charente-Maritime 29 – A 1
Crowned by a sturdy rectangular keep, dating from end of 12c, the town rises on l. bank of R. *Seugne*. Town hall occupies graceful turreted buildings, 15, 16 and 17c. Late-11c church of St. Vivien, with Romanesque façade. Former pilgrims' hospice is linked to one-time church of St. Martin by unusual 12c vaulted passage.
Vicinity ● 1.5 km SE, Ch. d'Usson: elegant construction in local Saintonge reg. version of Renaissance; the apartments (v.a. on request) are decorated with Louis XV panelling in white and gold. ● 8 km NE, *Pérignac*: the W façade of this Romanesque church is decorated with noteworthy bas-relief sculptures in superposed niches; they represent Christ and his Apostles, the Vices and Virtues, etc. ● 7.5 km E, *Echebrune*: 12c Romanesque church, fine

sculpted façade; the Saintonge Romanesque churches of Biron, *Jarnac-Champagne*, *Avy-en-Pons*, Chadenac, *Marignac*, etc, are worth visiting; 10 km S, *Jonzac*: 14–15c château with monumental fortified gate framed by towers and keep.

Pont-à-Mousson
54 – Meurthe-et-Moselle 13 – B 1
Large industrial town. The enormous Place Duroc is surrounded by 16, 17 and 18c arcaded houses. Rue Victor-Hugo has elegant House of the Seven Deadly Sins, 16c, with sculpted façade. Church of St. Laurent, 15–16c; int. has several works of art (superb Flemish retable, painted and carved, 16c). St. Martin, 15c; inside, late-15c Entombment; the organ loft is the former rood-screen, from 15c. The large Classical ensemble of town's 13c Premonstrant abbey, burned down in 1944, has been exceptionally well restored (now a cultural centre); v.a. to church, monastery buildings and three grand staircases – oval, square and round.
Vicinity ● Red Fountain, sulphur and ferruginous spring. 3.5 km E., hill of *Mousson* (382 m.) – to W, overlooking R. *Moselle* valley; and to E, the *Seille* valley (ruins, panorama). ● 13 km NW, remains of abbey of Ste. Marie-au-Bois: Romanesque church, int. with fine Ren. inlaid chimney-piece. ● 6 km S, *Dieulouard*, early-16c church in Goth. style (int. has lovely works of art, Notre Dame-des-Grottes crypt, 15c Seated Virgin); from Pont-à-Mousson to **Nancy*** following the *Moselle* valley (N57).

Pontarlier
25 – Doubs   26 – C 1
In an attractive setting, at the mouth of one of Jura's 'cluse' or transverse valleys, the town has few old buildings apart from Chapel of the Annonciades (Ren. portal with carved wooden door leaves) and an 18c Triumphal Arch. Municipal mus. (reg. painting; Courbet).
Vicinity ● 11 km E, Grand-Taureau via strategic road passing fort of Larmont-Supérieur; extensive views from the Grand-Taureau (1,328 m.) ● 5 km E, impressive Entreportes gorge, lush green 'cluse' lined with pine plantations and superb rocks. ● 5.5 km SE, cluse of *Cluse-et-Mijoux*, dominated to N by fort of Larmont-Inférieur and to S by fort of Joux, on rocky escarpment at alt. of 940 m.; built in 12–13c and later transformed by Vauban, Joux has five successive enceintes (v.a. in summer). ● 8 km S, lake of *St. Point*, 6.5 km long (water sports);

Malbuisson, pleasant summer resort on the lake.

Pont-Audemer
27 – Eure   4 – D 3
Several interesting old houses line the streets, as well as creeks of R. *Risle*. Church of St. Ouen has 11c choir, late-15c nave and façade, and handsome group of Renaissance stained-glass windows. 17c Auberge du Vieux-Puits.
Vicinity ● To N, unusual alluvial plain known as the *Marais Vernier* – crossed by the D103, along Digue des Hollandais (Dutch Dyke). ● 5 km SE, *Corneville-sur-Risle*, where the 'Cloches de Corneville' (bells of the famed musical) can be heard from Easter to Sept. at the Hostellerie des Cloches.

Pont-Aven
29 S – Finistère   15 – C 1
Welcoming little town, in attractive setting on R. Aven, much painted in late 19c by Gauguin and other artists (Pont-Aven school). Plaques show where the painters worked. Promenade du Bois de l'Amour (lit. Wood of Love) is charming; recently established municipal mus., in Place de l'Hôtel-de-Ville (town hall), has information centre about the Pont-Aven school, whose works are featured in occasional exhibitions. First Sun. in Aug. is the famous Pardon des Fleurs d'Ajoncs (annual religious procession founded in 1905). ● 1 km NW, Trémalo chapel, Goth. 17c.
Vicinity ● To N, Nizon (church and calvary) ● To S, 15–16c Ch. du Hénan; *Port-Manec'h*, in superb location; Ar-Bréchen headland; port and chapel of St. Nicolas. 16–18c Ch. de Poulguen. ● To SE, *Riec-sur-Belon*, (monument in the form of five conical concrete menhirs, dedicated to the 'Breton bards').

Pontcharra
38 – Isère   32 – C 2
1.5 km to S, early-15c Ch. Bayard (private), birthplace of the famed French soldier, Chevalier Bayard ('the knight without fear or reproach' – d. 1524). From terrace, magnificent panorama.

Pont-de-l'Arche
27 – Eure   5 – A 3
Beautiful Goth. church, 16c, with renowned 16–17c stained-glass windows; S side has noteworthy Goth. Flamboyant decoration, very rich; 18c oak stalls in choir; superb 17c retable, with statues.
Vicinity ● 1.5 km, Bonport abbey, 12–13c (n.v.a.).

Pontecoulant (Château)
14 – Calvados   10 – A 1
Fine 16–18c construction, in magnificent park. Interesting mus. (Ren. and 18c furniture, portraits, objets d'art, 18c Indo-Chinese room, etc. v.a., cl. Tues. and Oct.).

Pont-en-Royans
38 – Isère   32 – A 3
One of the most unusual sites in Dauphiné reg., at mouth of the *Bourne Gorges*, lying against a cliff above the river. The picturesque little town is built in tiers; its old houses have wooden balconies supported by lop-sided struts. Clinging to the rock dominating the *Bourne*, the town is crossed by the narrow Grande Rue. From the Place de la Porte-de-France, steep paths lead up to the Trois-Châteaux, ruins of three feudal castles, with wonderful view over whole area.
Vicinity ● 4 km N, *St. André-en-Royans*, on terrace above R. Tarze, fine panorama: 8 km to N, ruins of 13c Ch. de Beauvoir, built on an isolated crag; beautiful view over Isère valley. ● To NE, the rocks of *Presles*, State Forest of Coulmes. ● 4 km E, Châtelus; path leads to Cornouze grotto; near *Choranche*, highly picturesque grottoes in magnificent setting; *Bourne Gorges*; **Vil-**

PONT-DU-GARD
30 – Gard   37 – C 3
4 km from *Remoulins*. Magnificent piece of Roman engineering, built about 19 BC in the *Gardon* valley to bring water from the Eure spring, near **Uzès***, to Nîmes*. It has three tiers of arcades, progressively recessed (floodlit in summer). Footpaths scattered over neighbouring hills enable one to view the aqueduct from several different angles.

lard-de-Lans*. ● To SE, via the N518, the *Grands-Goulets* (see **La Chapelle-en-Vercors***).

Pontigny (Abbey)
89 – Yonne   19 – B 1
Second of the 'daughters' of Cîteaux, founded in 1114; all that now remains is one 12c building (beautiful rooms with ribbed vaulting), and the church, a masterpiece of Cistercian art from beginning of Goth. period. See the late-17c stalls in choir, 18c grilles and altar, below shrine of St Edme (d. 1240).
Vicinity ● 10 km N, *St. Florentin*, beautiful Ren. church, stained-glass windows, choir enclosure, roodscreen with three arcades and Holy Sepulchre, 16c. ● To E, *Ligny-le-Châtel*, 12c church, Romanesque portal and nave, huge Ren. choir, interesting works of art (large 15c Christ and statues); remains of ramparts; 13–16c houses known as Houses of the Queen of Sicily.

Pontivy
56 – Morbihan   9 – A 3
Town is made up of two distinct parts, linked by Place Aristide Briand; to N, the old Pontivy, around Place du Martray, lined with venerable houses and 16c basilica of Notre Dame-de-la-Joie; to S, the grid-pattern town established by Napoleon. On a height overlooking R. *Blavet*, the late-15c Ch. de Rohan, surrounded by vast moat, has preserved its outer walls intact; main façade, to W, is flanked by two huge squat towers (v.a. in summer, Wed. and Sat. p.m. out of season).
Vicinity ● 3.5 km NW, Stival, 16c Goth. chapel and fountain of St. Mériadec. ● 9.5 km E, *Ste. Noyale*, hamlet with unusual religious buildings grouped along esplanade: St. Noyale chapel, Goth. (int. has wooden ceiling adorned with 17c paintings illustrating life of the saint); oratory, ornamented cross, fountain and large calvary. ● 12 km SW, chapel of *St. Nicodème*, 16c, with sacred fountain (popular Breton pardon first Sun. in Aug.); St. Nicolas-des-Eaux, 2 km to W, worth seeing for its character and setting opposite the Couarde peninsula; vast panorama from Castennec mountain ● 11.5 km SW, Quelven, Notre Dame chapel, late-16c; interior has unusual statue (able to open up) of Notre Dame-de-Quelven (carried in pardon on Aug. 15); 8 km to SW, *Melrand*, typically Breton township, Ren. houses in granite, 17c church; the calvary is one of the most unusual in Brittany.

Pont-l'Abbé
29 S – Finistère   15 – B 1
Capital of Bigouden area and among the most characteristic towns in Brittany. Mus. devoted to the town is in 15c keep of former château, of which there also remains a huge 18c building (now the town hall). 12, 15, and 17c church of Notre Dame-des-Carmes. Embroidery festival, second Sun. in July. Ruins of 13–15c church of Lambour.
Vicinity ● Ch. de Kerazan (SE), 18c (interesting coll. of late 19–20c painting) and Ch. de Kernuz (S), 16–19c, surrounded by a fortified wall (now a hotel). ● To W, Tréminou chapel, 15c, in shady enclosure, and chapel of *Notre-Dame-de-Tronoën*, fine 15c Goth. building amid wild scenery; calvary alongside, also 15c. ● 6 km SE, *Loctudy*; church of St. Tudy is among most beautiful Romanesque sanctuaries in Brittany (early 12c – but façade and belfry 18c); opposite, the *Ile-Tudy*, water sports centre, sailing school, beach, fishing port.

Pontoise
95 – Val-d'Oise   11 – C 1
The old town, with its narrow streets and flights of steps, is built on a hill, at top of which is 12, 15 and 16c church of St. Maclou; roodscreen, sanctuary enclosure, stalls and main altar, with retable, together form remarkable 17c decorative ensemble. Late-16c church of Notre Dame. Tavet-Delacour mus., in delightful 15c mansion, Pissarro mus. The new town of Cergy-Pontoise has been under construction since 1970, around loop of R. Oise. Préfecture, administrative and commercial centres, open air and recreation areas.
Vicinity ● On left bank of the Oise, *St. Ouen-l'Aumône* has interesting 12c church with Romanesque portal and belfry; inside, unusual 13c statue (able to open up) of the Virgin; imposing 13c remains of Cistercian abbey of Maubuisson. ● 13 km W, Ch. de *Vigny*, built under Louis XII (d. 1515) and enlarged in 19c (v.a. grounds and gardens, Mar.–Nov.). ● 1 km to l. on D159, Guiry-en-Vexin, interesting Goth. and Ren. church; reg. archaeological mus., exhibits from paleolithic to end of Merovingian era.

Pont-St.-Esprit
30 – Gard   37 – D 2
Small town on R. *Rhône*, crossed by an imposing 13–14c bridge (920 m. long), from which you get splendid views of the town, its old houses and church. Baroque chapel of the Pénitents Bleus. Close by mouth of the bridge, fmr. citadel, late 16c, still has remains of 14c infirmary and of collegiate church of St. Esprit (14c choir, 15c portal). Paul Raymond mus. (regional archaeology and history).

Vicinity ● 10 km SW, *Chartreuse de Valbonne*, Carthusian monastery founded in 13c, rebuilt in 17c on the medieval model (v.a. Feb. 1–Nov. 30). ● 9.5 km NW, *St. Martin-d'Ardèche*: at mouth of the *Canyon de l'Ardèche*, boat trips along whole length of the canyon (see **Vallon-Pont-D'Arc***). ● 12 km ENE, *Bollène*: small town at gateway to Provence; panorama of Donzère-Mondragon hydro-electric works from the Pasteur belvedere, also of *Pierrelatte* and the R. *Rhône*; the *André Blondel* hydro-electric power station is one of largest in Western Europe (n.v.a. – but motorists can drive along causeway on downstream side). 9 km to E, *Suze-la-Rousse*: 12–14c château has noteworthy int. courtyard, mid 16c; fine Ren. reception rooms (v.a. p.m., July 1–Sept. 30, cl. Tues; v.a. Sun. exc. in Nov., out of season); in the grounds, old style tennis court (Jeu de Paume) dating from 1560; 17c church and Ren. town hall.

Pornic
44 – Loire-Atlantique   16 – B 3
The Gourmalon coast road, which runs round the Pointe de Gourmalon and alongside the port, offers superb views over Pornic cove and the town, built in amphitheatre form above a creek. 13–14c château dominates entrance to town. Noëveillard beach lies between two rocky outcrops. Pornic is one of embarcation points for island of **Noirmoutier***.
Vicinity ● 12 km W, *Préfailles*; 2.5 km away, *Pointe de St. Gildas*, picturesque rocky spur. ● Journey along coast from Jade and Pornic to *St. Brevin-les-Pins*.

Port-Barcarès
66 – Pyrénées-Orientales   42 – D 3
New holiday centre, 8 km long and covering nearly 1,750 acres. Leucate and Grau-Saint-Ange-Barcarès marinas. Mus. of the Sands (contemporary sculpture). The steamboat *Lydia* has been converted into a restaurant and casino.

Port-Louis
56 – Morbihan   15 – D 1
At the entrance to the roads of **Lorient***, in superb setting. Town still has impressive early-17c granite ramparts and citadel flanked by bastions (naval mus., and India Co. mus.); also retains original character as military base. Beach. Ferry for the *Gâvres peninsula*, narrow sandbank 6 km long.

Porto
2A–Corse   45 – B 3
The *Gulf of Porto*, surrounded by red porphyry cliffs, is one of Corsica's most beautiful sights, especially at sunset.

Vicinity ● Sea trips, from *Porto* to *Girolata* and to the *Calanche* (rocky inlets). ● 23 km to N, on road to **Calvi***, then one and a half hours on foot, *Gulf of Girolata.* ● To S, from *Porto* to *Piana*, the road (D81) follows the *Calanche*; it is one of the island's most extraordinary routes: the grandiose rocky escarpments, in fantastically shaped red granite, loom high over the sea (arresting view from the Chalet des Roches Bleues, base for walks around the inlets). *Piana* is a charming village, with white houses grouped around 18c church of Santa Maria; beautiful walks in Piana's forest to the E; from hamlet of Vistale, superb view over *Gulf of Porto*; the D81 continues to *Cargèse*, Corsica's 'Greek town': the Greek church houses interesting works of art (16c icon of St. John the Baptist); opposite, the Roman Catholic church (trompel'oeil decorations).

Porto-Vecchio
2A – Corse 45 – D 2
Commercial port and sailing centre at head of vast gulf. Remains of fortifications and several bastions crowning the rocks are reminder of Genoese rule.
Vicinity ● The gulf is lined with beaches and heavenly scenery: *Cala Rosa, Palombaggia*, framed by red rocks and shaded by parasol pines, San Cipriano, etc. ● Scenic route from *Porto Vecchio* to *Solenzara*, to N, over very hilly tourist route across *Forest of Ospedale*, **Zonza***, the *Col de Bavella* (1,243 m.) and *Col de Larone* (621 m.).

Port-Royal-des-Champs
78 – Yvelines 11 – B 2
In a somewhat isolated and wild valley, remains of once-famed Jansenist abbey (v.a., cl. Tues.) strike a poignant note.
Vicinity ● 2 km along the D91, the Mus. National des Granges de Port-Royal, in former 16c château which once housed the Jansenist Petites Écoles (v.a., cl. Mon. and Tues.). ● 3 km E, Magny-les-Hameaux, 12 and 15c church, with many tombstones from Port-Royal. ● 3 km S, *St. Lambert*, old country church surrounded by graveyard; a pyramid marks the communal grave of the nuns and recluses from Port-Royal; in 1944, a monument 'To the Human Being' was dedicated there.

Pouldu (Le)
29 S – Finistère 15 – C 1
Seaside resort near mouth of the *Laïta.* Grands Sables beach and port. 15–17c chapel of Notre Dame-de-la-Paix, transferred from Nizon in 1959 (modern stained-glass windows); monument to Gauguin,

Porto: *the Piana corniche looks down on extraordinary red granite rock formations rising straight out of the sea.*

Porto-Vecchio: *Palombaggia beach, in one of southern Corsica's most beautiful sites, opposite the Cerbicale islands.*

who painted at Le Pouldu from 1889 to 1894.
Vicinity ● The scenic corniche road starts at Bas-Pouldu and follows the sea as far as *Larmor-Plage*, at entry to the **Lorient*** roads: fine 15–16c church with Goth. Flamboyant porch; inside, 15c Flemish retable of the Crucifixion and other noteworthy works of art.

Pouzauges
85 – Vendée 22 – D 1
Church of St. Jacques, sturdy granite building with enormous Goth. Flamboyant choir, three lateral naves, Romanesque main nave and transept. Remains of old castle, former 13c fortress with magnificent square keep, flanked by turrets.
Vicinity ● 1 km SE, Pouzauges-le-Vieux has Romanesque church (Goth. choir) surrounded by cemetery entirely paved with gravestones; 13c murals depicting Life of the Virgin; Ch. de Puy-Papin, 15c. ● 2.5 km SE, wide view from the

Puy-Crapeau (289 m.). ● 7 km NW, **St. Michel-Mont-Mercure***. ● 7 km S, *Réaumur*, 15c fortified church; Ch. de la Haute-Cour; miraculous fountain of Ste. Marie (pilgrimage); Guichelaines vineyards on banks of R. Lay. ● To E, the *Bocage Vendéen* (characteristic local terrain of mixed woodland and pasture-land).

Prats-de-Mollo-la-Preste
66 – Pyrénées-Orientales 43 – C 3
A one-time stronghold, this small Catalan town still has its ramparts and fortified church, 17c, with 13c Goth. belfry; inside church, in Chapel of the Pietà, dating from 1427, monumental retable, gilded and sculpted. Many picturesque streets: Place Del-Rey, Rue des Marchands (house of the Kings of Aragon), Rue Nationale, etc. Behind church, vaulted underground passage leads to former fort of La Garde, 17c.
Vicinity ● Mir Tower, 13c watchtower (wide panorama); hermitage of Notre Dame-du-Coral (17c chapel and buildings; int. has 12c clothed Christ and 13c Seated Virgin with Child). ● 8 km W, *La Preste* spa.

Prémery
58 – Nièvre 19 – A 3
13 and 14c church; fine apse with two rows of windows. 14, 16 and 17c former château of bishops of Nevers, with 14c fortified door. Much of the medieval wall still stands.
Vicinity ● 10 km NE, *Montenoison*: imposing ruins of 13c castle built on isolated hill (417 m.), one of Nivernais reg.'s highest spots; Montenoison's little valleys form attractive country of woods, streams and lakes. ● 17 km SE, *St. Saulge*, interesting Goth. church; 4 km to W, Jailly, Romanesque church with sculpted portal.

Privas
07 – Ardèche 37 – C 1
Pleasantly situated, above the *Ouvèze* basin.
Vicinity ● 5 km SW, Ch. d'Entrevaux, where Richelieu once lived; 2 km farther on, Logis du Roi, Louis XIII's residence during siege of Privas (1629). ● 12 km W, *Col de l'Escrinet* (781 m.), majestic panorama; 7 km SW, impressive ruins of Ch. de Boulogne, 15–16c, superb Ren. portal. ● To NW, *Gorges de l'Eyrieux* and *Le Cheylard*,

Provins
77 – Seine-et-Marne 12 – A 2
The upper town, situated on promontory, has several historic buildings: collegiate church of St. Quiriace (beautiful late-12c choir, 17c cupola); César Tower, imposing

12c keep crowned with 16c pyramidal extension (v.a.); the Grange aux Dîmes, fine 12c house (lapidary mus.); and 12–13c St. Jean Gate. You can drive along the fine 12–13c ramparts, between the St. Jean and Jouy Gates. In the lower town, see church of Ste. Croix (12c nave, 16c choir); St. Ayoul, former Benedictine abbey church, originally 12c, renovated (beautiful Romanesque portal, int. with 16c statues and 17c panelling). In the infirmary chapel, elegant late-13c mausoleum

Provins: *the César Tower, rising high above the old citadel.*

with heart of Thibaud de Champagne (King of Navarre). Old houses, notably Hôtel de la Croix d'Or and Hôtel de Vauluisant, 13c, which houses town mus. (archaeology, ceramics).
Vicinity ● 8 km W, **St. Loup-de-Naud***. ● 18 km SW, *Donnemarie-Dontilly*, 13c church, two wooden galleries on N side and 16c gate; 3.5 km to S, ruins of the *Abbaye de Preuilly*. ● To SE, Ch. de la *Motte-Tilly*, 18c (v.a., cl. Tues. from April 1–Sept. 30, Sat. and Sun. from Oct. to Nov.).

Puget-Théniers
06 – Alpes-Maritimes 39 – A 3
This small, typically southern town has an old quarter where the houses

have picturesque porch roofs. 13c church; int. has 18c decoration, retables by Brea family (1525) and 15c Nice school, also 15 and 18c carved wood retables. On promenade, celebrated monument, *Action Enchâinée*, by Maillol, dedicated to Blanqui (much-imprisoned early Socialist, one of the leaders of France's 1848 revolution).
Vicinity ● To NE, *Gorges du Cians*, cut into rocks of different colour – the upper gorges in limestone, the lower in red schist. *Beuil*: 17c church, chapel of the Pénitents-Blancs; the *Gorges de Daluis* wild and grandiose (see **Entrevaux***) can be reached by road through the *Valberg* and *Guillaumes* passes (see **St. Sauveur-sur-Tinée***).

Puivert
11 – Aude 42 – B 3
Picturesque old township, under peak crowned by remains of 12–14c castle, with imposing keep. The keep has several rooms – including, on third floor, a musicians' room (sculpted figures).
Vicinity ● 11 km W, *Bélesta*; 1.5 km to S, *Fontaine Intermittente de Fontestorbes*; at the top of R. *Hers* valley are the impressive Frau Gorges. ● 24 km W, **Montségur***. ●

To S, through Bélesta's outstanding pine forest: the *Sault* country; via *Espezel*, excursion to *Rebenty Gorges* (see **Ax-les-Thermes***).

Puy-en-Velay (Le)
43 – Haute-Loire   31 – B 3
One of the most unusual sites in France, with the town rising in tiers at foot of volcanic peaks. ●Notre Dame cathedral, dating from second half of 12c, has six cupolas; very original polychromatic display on the façade. Grand stairway, with 102 steps, continues from picturesque Rue des Tables into huge vaulted basement, under central nave, then passes between two 12c doors with superb carved panels. Above the 18c main altar, statue of Notre Dame-du-Puy; in N arm of the transept, 12c murals; in reliquary chapel (v.a.), celebrated late-15c fresco of the Liberal Arts; interesting works of art (paintings, precious religious objects, etc.) in the sacristy. Le For porch, late 12c, leads on to terrace of Place du For, surrounded by 15–16c mansions. The St. Jean porch (notable 12c sculpted tympanum) leads to Baptistry of St. Jean, unusual 11c edifice; also cloister, masterpiece of Romanesque architecture and decoration (cl. Tues.) adjoined by Chapelle des Morts (13c Crucifixion). ● From slope up to Notre Dame-de-France, you reach the Corneille rock, on which stands colossal statue of the Virgin; panorama, viewing table. Unusual chapel of the Pénitents (17c ceiling, painted and coffered) leads to Hôtel-Dieu, whose Goth. porch has two fine Romanesque portals. ● In the old part of town surrounding the cathedral, several historic houses, notably in Rue Pannessac, Rue du Chamarlenc (des Cornards) and Place des Tables. Rue Séguret leads to the Place du Greffe, Rue du Cardinal-de-Polignac (fmr. Hôtel de Polignac, 15c), Rue Rochetaillade and Rue Chènebouterie, which runs into Place du Plot, then town hall; these streets are also lined with old houses. In 14–15c church of St. Laurent, 14c tomb containing Du Guesclin's entrails. ● At foot of town, behind the immense Place du Breuil and the Préfecture, Vinay Gardens and Crozatier mus. (v.a., cl. Tues. and Feb.): Roman and medieval archaeology, ethnography, folk art, old paintings, hist. of lace from 15c to present day. ● To N of town, chapel of St. Michel-d'Aiguilhe (v.a.), 10 and 11c, stands on top of gigantic 'needle' of lava 80 m. high, reached by stairway with 268 steps.
Vicinity ● 3 km W, bizarre basalt columns, the 'Espaly Organ-pipes'. Worth seeing Ch. de *Polignac* – its

PUY DE DÔME
63 – Puy-de-Dôme   30 – D 1
16 km W of Clermont-Ferrand, over a toll road which spirals up to 1,440 m. alt. (fine views). From end of road, short walk to summit at 1,468 m. On the top is a meteorological observatory and television tower with circular orientation balcony (v.a.). Remains of a temple of Mercury and Gallo-Roman constructions. Magnificent panorama, especially over the surrounding volcanic countryside (70 former craters). The E side may be descended on foot.

Le Puy-en-Velay: *to reach the Romanesque chapel of St Michel-d'Aiguilhe, on its volcanic 'needle', you have to climb a stairway with 268 steps.*

13–14c remains, with imposing square keep, standing on enormous basalt platform. Also 15–16c Ch. de St. Vidal (v.a. p.m., July 1 – Aug. 31). ● 15 km NNW, *Ch. de la Rochelambert*, 16c, in purple lava, flanked by turrets; apartments (v.a.) contain numerous works of art, esp. from the Haute Époque (Middle Ages and 16c); Romanesque church of *St. Paulien* also worth a visit. ● 13 km N, near *Lavoûte-sur-Loire*, Ch. de la Voûte-Polignac, 17c (v.a. in summer season); interesting works of art.

Puy-l'Evêque
46 – Lot   32 – D 2
Picturesque old town, laid out in amphitheatre form, above R. *Lot* and on isthmus of a peninsula dominated by 13c square keep. 14 and 16c church, sculpted porch. Goth. and Ren. fortified houses.
Vicinity ● 3 km N, Martignac, church decorated with noteworthy 15c murals. ● 6 km W, *Duravel*: in Romanesque church, 12c stone sarcophagus of St. Hilarion and his two companions; fine square crypt.

Q

Quarante
34 – Hérault   42 – D 2
Abbey church of Ste. Marie is one of most important examples of early Romanesque art; consecrated 1053, some parts date back to late 10c; nave has three bays, separated by arcades; transept crossing is surmounted by octagonal cupola; inside, large treasury and local mus., interesting ancient sarcophagus in white marble with two busts of women in a medallion; head reliquary of St. John Baptist in silver and silver-gilt (circa 1440). *Vicinity* ● 2 km NW, *Cruzy*, 14c fortified church, in S Goth. style.

Quarré-les-Tombes
89 – Yonne   19 – B 3
Town owes its name to numerous tombs and stone sarcophagi, of disputed origin, which surround 15c church.
Vicinity ● 2.5 km S, Fairies' Rock (Roche des Fées), strange-looking ridge of superposed blocks of granite. ● 5.5 km SSW, Les Isles Ménéfrier, in *Cure* valley; 7 km to SE, Pérouse rock (610 m., wide view). ● To NW, *Barrage du Crescent*; *Ch. de Chastellux-sur-Cure*: 13–16c fortress, remodelled 18c, tri-

QUIBERON (Peninsula)
56 – Morbihan   15 – D 3
At one time an island, 9 km long, it is now joined to coast by a narrow isthmus, 6 km long; W side, called the *Côte Sauvage*, edged by high cliffs heavily indented by lashing of waves, has a wild but grandiose beauty. *St. Pierre-Quiberon*, fishing port and seaside resort, has large number of beaches. Numerous megalithic monuments. *Quiberon* is a lively sardine-fishing port; fishermen's quarter, Port-Maria, is most picturesque. To S of peninsula, Points of Beg-er-Lan, Beg-er-Vil and *Conguel*, Fort-Neuf, Port-Haliguen, etc. Louison Bobet Thalassotherapy Institute (world-famed racing cyclist turned thalassotherapist). ● Excursions to *Ile de Houat* (red granite cliffs, beaches) and to *Ile de Hoëdic* (flat and sandy).

angular in shape, flanked by towers (n.v.a.). ● To W, late-12c *Ch. de Bazoches*, large square keep and machicolated towers, remodelled 15 and 16c; Vauban bought it in 1675 (n.v.a.). ● 5.5 km NE, *St. Léger-Vauban* (Vauban's native village); 4 km to S in lonely, wild spot, *Abbaye de la Pierre-qui-Vire*; v.a. only to chapel (service daily), exhibition hall and bookshop.

Quesnoy (Le)
59 – Nord   6 – B 1
Enclosed within a Vauban-style perimeter wall, in brick with stone facings, surrounded by water and lush greenery, town gives appearance of being both a fortress and a prosperous city. Lakes of Pont-Rouge and Fer-à-Cheval: beach, water sports, boating.
Vicinity ● To E, huge *Forêt de*

Mormal (40 sq. miles), crossed by controlled roads; picnic, camping and sports areas, etc.; arboretum; picturesque village of *Locquignol* (reg. arts and crafts).

Quilinen (Notre-Dame-de)
29S – Finistère   8 – B 3
Chapel, elegant 16c building, with two naves at right angles to each other, contains interesting works of art (wooden statues of saints). Mid-16c calvary, one of most unusual in Brittany, shaped like a pyramid with three crosses on two triangular plinths with inverted points. The rustic figures harmonise with the reddish patina of the stone.
Vicinity ● 4 km N, Goth. *Chapelle de St. Venec*, in charming leafy setting; inside, numerous statues of saints; calvary similar to that of Quilinen; 4.5 km to NE, 15, 16 and

Quarré-les-Tombes: *the Château of Chastellux has belonged to the same family for 1,000 years.*

18c *Chapelle des Trois-Fontaines*; works of art; inside is a large calvary.

Quillan
11 – Aude   42 – B 3
Good excursion centre for upper *Aude* valley, *Capcir* and Pyrenees. *Vicinity* ● 16 km NW, **Puivert***. ● To SW, *Gorges du Rebenty* and *Pays de Sault*. ● To SE, lovely Fanges forest (firs, magnificent trees). ● To S, *Haute Vallée de l'Aude* route as far as **Mont-Louis*** (68 km), is picturesque; D117 first crosses impressive *Défilé de Pierre-Lys*, 600 m. deep; after *Axat*, narrow *Gorges de St. Georges*, then *Gorge de l'Aude*, between high cliffs; *Usson-les-Bains* is dominated by ruins of castle on rocky peak (D16 leads to *Quérigut* and lonely, wild area known as Donezan); beyond *Usson* and Escouloubre-les-Bains,

road enters mountainous *Capcir* river basin: lovely state forest of Carcanet, *Barrage de Puyvalador*, *Formiguères* (1,506 m. alt.), small winter sports resort (to W, Formiguères forest, pine trees), *Barrage de Matemale*, *Col de la Quillane* (1,714 m.); road then winds down to La Llagonne (in church, 12c clothed wooden Christ in front of 13c Catalan altar) and **Mont-Louis***.

Quimper
29S – Finistère   8 – B 3
Most characterstic part of town lies along r. bank of R. *Odet* around cathedral of St. Corentin, in 13–16c Breton Goth. style; inside, 15c stained-glass windows. Fine Arts mus.: French and foreign paintings, especially 17c Flemish and Dutch. Noteworthy group of works inspired by Brittany: Boudin, Émile Bernard, Serusier, Cottet, Marquet,

Gallery devoted to Max Jacob, a a native of Quimper. In 16–17c bishop's palace, Breton reg. mus.: archaeology, furnishings, religious art, costumes from Cornouailles reg. Old houses in Rue Keréon and Place Terre-au-Duc. on l. bank of *Odet*, Locmaria: 12–13c Romanesque church. Potteries. Mus. of Quimper pottery.
Vicinity ● Boat trip down R. *Odet* from Quimper to *Bénodet* and *Loctudy* is recommended ● 1 km NE, Kerfeunteun, lovely 16c church, Goth. chapel of La-Mère-de-Dieu. ● 9 km E, Kerdévot, noteworthy 15c chapel of Notre Dame; inside, large late-15c Flemish retable in painted and gilded wood. ● Site du Stangala, 7 km to NE, rocky escarpment towering 70 m. over *Odet* in bend of the river framed by wooded slopes; picturesque hamlet of Tréouzon.

Quimperlé
29S – Finistère   15 – C 1
Little old town in lush green countryside. In upper town, 13–15c Notre Dame-de-l'Assomption; N porch and huge square tower have rich Goth. Flamboyant decorations. In lower town, rising in tiers above R. Isole, 11c church of Ste. Croix, built in rotunda shape in imitation of Jerusalem's Church of the Holy Sepulchre; inside, Ren. stone rood-screen, 11c crypt. Buildings of former abbey of Ste. Croix are 18c (Entombment; 18c cloister). Old houses in Rues Brémond-d'Ars (remains of church of St. Colomban) and Dom-Morice (timbered Archers' house contains mus. of local history and traditions).
Vicinity ● 12.5 km NE, *Roches du Diable*, enormous jumble of rocks in picturesque setting overlooking Ellé valley. ● 3.5 km S, *Forêt de Carnoët* (1,875 acres), magnificent oaks and beeches; abbey of St. Maurice-de-Carnoët, founded late 12c, 13c chapter-house (n.v.a.).

Quintin
22 – Côtes-du-Nord   9 – A 2
Small, typically Breton town. Château of Dukes of Lorges, mid-17c, enlarged late 18c, overlooking lake bordered by public garden. Nearby, Roche-Longue menhir (4.70 m. high). Delightful square dating from 1830, surrounded by old houses. Lovely Ren. canons' houses, in granite, at Nos. 5 and 7, Rue Notre Dame; opposite, 15c Notre Dame fountain. In 19c basilica of Notre Dame 14c tombstones of Dukes Geoffrey III and Jean II; highly venerated reliquary of the 'Virgin's Girdle' (Breton pardon on second Sun. in May).

Quillan: *the seething waters of the Aude rush headlong between the rocky walls of the Pierre-Lys gorge.*

R

Rambouillet (Château)
78 – Yvelines   11 – B 2
Former feudal dwelling, altered and enlarged between 16 and 18c, the château is one of the official residences of France's President. The big François I tower, in which that king died in 1547, is the only trace of previous 14c castle, and is incorporated at right-angles into the 17c buildings. V.a. to assembly rooms, decorated with superb 18c panelling, Marie-Antoinette's sumptuous bedchamber, the Duke of Penthièvre's chapel, and apartments and bathroom in the Pompeian style of Napoleon I. Also on ground floor, the Marble Room (16c). ● In addition to huge flower beds, the gardens and the park (laid out in 18c) include a water garden, formed by islands and canals, and a landscaped garden designed by Hubert Robert. In a direct line with the château is view over the Grand Canal, prolonged by the Tapis Vert. The Queen's Dairy, built by Marie-Antoinette, is pleasantly decorated with grisailles in trompe-l'oeil. The Pavillon des Coquillages (1778) is an equally charming curiosity. ● V.a. to La Ferme Nationale (natnl. farm, established by Louis XVI) and the Bergerie Nationale (shepherds' school, v.a., Sun. p.m.) built by Napoleon. Also Natnl. School of Poultry Farming. In town, House of the King of Rome, former Louis XVI mansion. Late-18c town hall (enormous 18c map discovered by Louis XVI). Rambolitain mus. (Wed. to Sat.) with toy trains and railway modelling.
Vicinity ● *Rambouillet* forest (84 sq. miles), rich in big game, affords numerous walks, notably to *Étang de St. Hubert* and to the six *Étangs de Hollande*, lakes which cover a 6 km stretch through the forest.

Rambures (Castle)
80 – Somme   5 – B 2
Noteworthy example of 15c military architecture in brick and white stone (v.a. Mar.–Nov., cl. Tues.). Its big round towers are linked by a ring of half-towers.

Rampillon
77 – Seine-et-Marne   12 – A2
Standing on its own on a rise in middle of village, the mid-18c church has magnificent sculpted portal dating from second half of 12c. On tympanum, Christ in Glory between two angels, the Virgin and St. John; on lintel, the resurrection of the dead received by Abraham and St. Michael; int. has fine 14c wooden Christ, and polychrome stone Virgin.

Rampillon: *the church portal boasts some outstanding sculpture. Above, an Apostle*

Raray (Château)
60 – Oise   5 – D 3
On each side of main courtyard, this 17–18c château has walls with arcades and niches on which hunting scenes are depicted (v.a.). Jean Cocteau filmed 'Beauty and the Beast' in this baroque setting. 15 and 16c church.

Redon
35 – Ille-et-Vilaine   16 – B 2
On R. Vilaine. St. Sauveur, fmr. abbey church with Romanesque nave and transept, the latter dominated by 12c belfry. The Grande-Rue still has 15–16c houses. Town is 'world capital' of pocket lighters.
Vicinity ● 17 km S, St. Gildas-des-Bois, 12–13c church.

RAZ (Point)
29 S – Finistère   8 – A 3
This long, thin spur, eroded by the crashing Atlantic waves, rises more than 70 m. above the sea. It is one of the most breath-taking views in France. A path runs round it, giving access to the impressive Hell of Plogoff. Beyond the point: La Vieille lighthouse, on a rock of the *Raz de Sein*. To N, *Baie des Trépassés* and *Pointe du Van*, 65 m. high (good vistas). To NE, *Pointe de Brésellec* and bird sanctuary of *Cape Sizun* (v.a., Apr.–July). Thousands of seabirds on wild site of Castel-ar-Roc'h.

Reims
51 – Marne   6 – B 3

Notre Dame cath., 13–15c masterpiece of Goth. architecture; outstanding façade crowned by two 15c towers. Central portal is consecrated to the Virgin (famed groups of the Visitation and the Presentation at the Temple); r. portal is devoted to Christ and the prophets, and l. portal to famous smiling Guardian Angel known as the *Ange au sourire*. Fine sculpted doors in N transept, notably one on l., where tympanum has a superb 'Last Judgment'. Int. of cath., almost 140 m. long, is as harmonious as it is grandiose. Back of the façade is adorned with 120 niches containing mid-13c statutes, some of which (e.g. Knight's Communion) are considered amongst finest examples of Goth. sculpture. 13c rose window, dedicated to the Virgin, and stained-glass windows in Consecration Gallery were restored after 1918; along the aisles, 17 tapestries of the Life of the Virgin (Tournai, early 16c.) are on view from Apr. to Oct. ● The Palais du Tau (13c two-storey Palatine chapel), fmr. archbishop's palace, houses mus. of sculpture and royal coronations (v.a., cl. Tues.), which has originals of the group sculptures in cath. (replaced by copies), inc. the celebrated 'Coronation of the Virgin'. Cath. treasure is exceptionally rich; several pieces were used during coronations of France's kings. Fine set of tapestries in royal banqueting hall. Mus. of fine arts, or St. Denis mus., is also one of richest in France, housed in old abbey of St. Denis (v.a., cl. Tues.): 15–16c paintings (unique); large Cranach room, Dutch and Italian painting, 17c French (Poussin, Le Nain, Philippe de Champaigne), 18 and 19c (Corot, Barbizon school, Courbet, Gauguin, Renoir), and 20c (Bonnard, Vuillard, Picasso). ● The Place Royale, notable example of 18c urbanisation, is surrounded by houses in Louis XVI style (subprefecture in one-time Hôtel des Fermes); in centre, statue of Louis XV. Interesting old houses: 30 Rue Cérès, Hôtel Ponsardin, late 18c (Chamber of Commerce); Rue Colbert; 22 Rue du Tambour (13c Gothic house attributed to Comtes de Champagne); Hôtel de La Salle, mid-16c Ren. Mus. of Old Reims (v.a., p.m., cl. Mon.) in 16c Hôtel Le Vergeur; 13c Goth. room; outstanding original Dürer engravings. See fmr. Jesuit college, with old reg. furniture 17–19c, and 17c religious painting. Planetarium, astronomical clock. ● In Place du Forum, Roman crypto-porticos have been uncovered. The Mars Gate is one of the most imposing commemorative arches from late-2c Roman Gaul. 300 m. away, neo-Romanesque chapel of Notre Dame-de-la-Paix, decorated by painter Foujita, who is buried there (d. 1963). ● To SE of the town, St. Remi basilica, formerly abbey church, Romanesque (11c transept and nave) and Goth. Int. has choir on two levels, enclosed by 17c Ren. screen in marble and stone (see St. Remi's tomb, rebuilt in 19c, with 16c statues); the periphery of the choir is the most distinctive feature. Archaeological mus. of St. Remi in former abbey: collections from prehist. to Middle Ages; tapestries of life of St. Remi (dating from circa 1525–1530); renowned 'Statues of the Musicians', adorning reconstructed façade of a 13c house. ● World-famous champagne cellars (v.a.).

Vicinity ● Champagne wine road, by way of *Montagne of Reims* (now reg. park). ● Valley of the R. *Marne* to S (**Épernay***) ● *Chemin des Dames* to NW (see **Laon***) ● *Argonne* and *Côtes de Meuse* to E.

Remiremont
88 – Vosges   20 – C 1

The main street (Rue Charles de Gaulle), lined with houses with 13c façades, is most picturesque street in the town; it includes Charles de Bruyère reg. mus. 14–16c St. Pierre church (11c crypt); Charles Friry mus. in 18c former canoness' house, Rue du General Humbert (objets d'art and mementoes of the Nobles Dames de Remiremont). Old abbey palace, mid-18c, houses town hall and law courts.

Vicinity ● Excellent walks in *Fossard* forest, to NE (climb to St. Mont, 667 m., good view); the Tête des Cuveaux (873 m. panorama); the forest of *Longegoutte* to SE; magnificent defile of the Roches valley, on D23 towards *Fougerolles*. ● 14 km SW, *Plombières-les-Bains*, large spa surrounded by parks and forests (steam room, Roman galleries and baths, v.a. during season); Louis François mus. (landscape painter of 19c Barbizon school). Tours in upper valley of Semouse, or Valley of the Forges valley, the *Val-d'Ajol*, etc.

Rennes
35 – Ille-et-Vilaine   9 – C 3

Centre of Rennes is the Place de la République (imposing Palace of Commerce), from where Rue d'Orléans leads to the Place de la Mairie, framed by theatre and 18c town hall. Place du Palais (18c houses) is overlooked by the Palais de Justice (lawcourts), fmr. Parliament of Brittany in 17c (v.a., apply to con-

---

RÉ (Island)
17 – Charente-Maritime   22 – C 3

You get to Île de Ré from *La Palice* – car ferry, 15-min. crossing – and land at Pointe de Sablanceaux. The D735 crosses whole island E to W. 3 km, Prée fort, interesting example of early-17c military architecture, in star lay-out; 1 km farther on, ruins of Cistercian abbey of St. Laurent, or Abbaye des Châteliers; 12, 13 and 14c church, remains of cloister. ● *La Flotte*: engaging little fishing and coastal shipping port, views over the Breton Pertuis (Strait). *St. Martin-de-Ré*, little white town ringed by Vauban fortifications; ramparts include two fine monumental gates, Porte Toiras to SE and Porte des Campani to SW. The narrow cobbled streets and port are well worth a leisurely stroll. Citadel is now a prison (n.v.a.). Bastions on sea-front, arresting views over Breton Straight and Vendée coast. Arsenal in former Clerjotte convent (15–16c), with courtyard lined by elegant Renaissance galleries; it houses interesting naval mus. and Cognacq mus. (history and reg. art). 15c church (interior has numerous banners captured from the English); one-time mansion of the 'gentlemen naval cadets'. ● By *La Couarde-sur Mer* and the Passe de Martray (salt-marshes) to *Ars-en-Ré*, whose narrow winding streets encircle St. Étienne, a church consisting of two contiguous buildings – 12c (fine Romanesque portal) and 15c (lovely curled-leaf spire). Seneschal's house, Renaissance. The road continues to St. Clément-des-Baleines and the *Phare de Baleines*, 55 m. tall lighthouse at W tip of island (v.a.), panorama. To N, beautiful beach called Conche des Baleines. The D101, past *Les Portes*, skirts the Fier d'Ars, oyster-beds and salt-marshes, to the Trousse-Chemise wood. Island's E coast, facing the *Pertuis* (strait) *d'Antioche*, is lined by seaside resorts with beautiful sandy beaches. *Ars, La Couarde, Le Bois-Plage, Ste. Marie*.

cierge); int. is of quite classic rich-
ness, notably the Parliament's
Grand Chamber (panelling, paint-
ing, tapestries) and the high court
(panelling, paintings by Jouvenet).
The old quarter, with interesting
old houses, lies behind town hall.
Late-18c St. Pierre cath. is in neo-
Classic style. See also 15c Porte
Mordelaise and huge Place des
Lices (17c houses and mansions).
Palais des Musées (cl. Tues.) com-
prises mus. of Brittany (archae-
ology, lapidary pieces from Middle
Ages, exceptional collection of
Breton furniture and costumes) and
fine arts mus., with large rep-
resentative collections of Italian
schools (primitives, Veronese),
Flemish, (Rubens, Jordaens), 16c
Dutch and French (Fontainebleau
school), 17c (Georges de La Tour's
Le nouveau-né, Le Nain, Philippe de
Champaigne, Jouvenet, etc.), 18c,
(Chardin) and 19c (landscape
artists, Corot, Impressionists, Pont-
Aven school). Also contemporary
art: Delaunay, Magnelli, Debré, Tal
Coat, sculpture by Germaine
Richier, César, Hajdu; 19 and 20c
reg. artists; small Egyptian section.
Notre Dame, former Romanesque
abbey church rebuilt in 14c, and
buildings of 17c St. Melaine abbey
(classical cloister) adjoin large
Thabor garden (29 acres).
Vicinity ● to NE, *Forêt de Rennes* ●
2 km E, Brittany car mus. (cl.
Tues.). 16 km SE, *Châteaugiron*,
impressive remains of 15c château
with 12–13c keep; old houses. ● To
SW, valley of R. *Vilaine*; 13 km
farther on, 17c *Ch. de Blossac*,
ringed by flowing waters; chapel
(v.a. on application).

Rennes-les-Bains
11 – Aude   42 – C 3
Pleasant spa beside torrent deep in
valley.
Vicinity ●Worth touring valleys of
the Sals and the Blanque; to SE,
Bugarach is dominated by Bugarach peak, highest point (1,231 m.)
of the *Corbières* mountains, with
superb panorama. ● 3 km N,
remains of Ch. de Blanquefort. ●
9 km NE, *Arques*, magnificent late-
13c square keep, flanked by four
turrets, 21 m. tall, and remains of
ramparts. ● To NW, *Couiza* (see
Limoux*); minor road leads to
Rennes-le-Château,   half-ruined
village, small Romanesque church
and cemetery, old château. Site
offers wonderful view of *Valley of
the Aude* and the *Corbières*.

Réole (La)
33 – Gironde   35 – B 1
On side of hill overlooking R.
Garonne. Former abbey church of
St. Pierre, 13–14c; 18c monastery

Reims: *Notre Dame, the 'Coronation Cathedral' of France's kings, has one of the world's loveliest Gothic façades, bedecked with a whole series of elegant and highly expressive statues. On left, above, Virgin on pier of the central portal; right, the 'Ange au Sourire' (smiling angel), to the left of the north portal.*

buildings (now town hall). Previous 12c town hall, with ground-floor hall. Picturesque ruins of feudal castle. Fine stretch of water on the *Garonne* (rowing competitions); municipal mus.

Vicinity ● 1.5 km E, Mirail Beacon, panorama over *Garonne* valley ● 23 km NE, *Duras*: feudal castle converted into elegant residence in 17c, still has its big round towers (v.a.). ● 6 km N, 15c fortified mill of *Bagas*.

Revel
31 – Haute-Garonne 42 – B 1
14c bastide; main square still has covered arcades. Old timbered market halls, 17c, with a belfry.

Vicinity ● Revel is good base for excursions to *Montagne Noire* and its forests (see **Mazamet*** and **Sorèze***) ● 4 km SE, *Bassin de St. Ferréol*, reservoir built in 17c to feed the Midi canal, magnificent 220–acre stretch of water surrounded by forests: beaches, sailing schools, water sports. ● 10 km W, *St. Félix Lauragais*, on ridge of scenic range of hills; 14–15c château; 14–18c church, with Toulouse-style belfry; fine vistas over the *Lauragais* and the *Montagne Noire*.

Ribeauvillé
68 – Haut-Rhin 14 – A 3
At foot of the Vosges (all-embracing view from the Gloriette). The town, famed for its wine, is overlooked by three ruined castles – Girsberg, St. Ulrich and Hoh-Rappolstein. The Porte des Bouchers (Butchers' Gate), former 13–16c belfry, straddles the Grande-Rue, which is lined with old houses. Ren. town hall (small mus.). Early-15c convent church and 13–15c parish church (sculpted tympanum on portal). Unusual Fête des Ménétriers, or Pfifferday (strolling minstrels), 1st Sun. in Sept.

Vicinity ● *Ch. de St. Ulrich*, both fortress and aristocratic residence (vast panorama); Ch. du Haut-Ribeaupierre; Notre Dame-de-Dusenbach, ancient chapel, rebuilt in 19c, in superb setting, famed pilgrimage centre. ● 19 km NW, *St. Marie-aux-Mines*: 15–16c miners' church; St. Barthélemy silver mine (v.a. to one of the galleries). In July, exhibition of minerals and precious stones. ● Magnificent pine forest of Aubure, to SW. ● Ribeauvillé is on the **Route du Vin d'Alsace*** (the Alsace wine road).

Riceys (Les)
10 – Aube 19 – C 1
Three agglomerations make up this picturesque commune: Ricey-Bas, with Ren. church, fine example of 16c Champagne reg. art, including 16–17c panelling, glassware and

sculptures, two mid-16c retables; Ricey-Haute-Rive, where 16c church has beautiful Louis XV sculpted pulpit; and Ricey-Haut, with 16c double-fronted church.

Richelieu
37 – Indre-et-Loire 17 – C 3
One of the most original towns in France, a remarkable example of 17c town planning. Founded in 1631 by Cardinal Richelieu, and designed in rectangular grid-pattern, 700 m. by 530 m., enclosed by moat and ramparts; it is crossed by the Grande-Rue, which is lined with 28 mansions of uniform style. In the Place des Religieuses is the Académie, a college founded in 1640. Place du Marché, opposite Notre Dame church, in Jesuit style, has timbered market halls with slate roofs. Municipal mus. in town hall. Of the great Cardinal's own château, all that remains is the moat, a pavilion known as the Dôme (mus.), the orangery and the cellars; also vast grounds (1,174 acres).

Vicinity ● 7 km S, Faye-la-Vineuse, interesting Romanesque church ● 6 km N, *Champigny-sur-Veude*; of the château, demolished on Richelieu's orders, only remnant is the Ste. Chapelle (v.a., cl. Tues., Apr.–Sept.), a dazzling Ren. jewel with an exceptional series of mid-16c stained-glass windows.

Rieux-Minervois
11 – Aude 42 – C 2
Mid-12c church is one of the most unusual in the Midi; it comprises two concentric circumferences and a heptagonal choir in centre, covered by a dome crowned with a tower; Romanesque capitals; in one chapel, an Entombment from 15c Burgundian school.

Vicinity ● 9 km NW, *Caunes-Minervois* has several old houses, notably mid-16c Hôtel Alibert (Italian Ren. courtyard); Romanesque and Goth. St. Pierre abbey church (int. has altars and statues in pink-veined Caunes marble); to NE, church and rustic Stations of the Cross of Notre Dame-du-Cros (pilgrimage); to N of *Caunes-Minervois*, valley and gorges of the Argentdouble (D620). ● 6 km E, *Azille*; 3 km to W, Romanesque country church of St. Étienne-de-Vaissière.

Rioux: *Romanesque church at Rétaud has a richly sculpted apse with an octagonal belfry above the transept crossing.*

Riez
04 – Alpes-de-Haute-Provence
38 – C 3

Typically Provençal little town, with its square shaded by plane-trees, its old streets and 'noble' houses (Hôtel de Maza, Ren.), and its two fortified gates, the Porte Aiguière (13–14c) and the Porte St. Sols (14c). Early-6c baptistry, with square exterior, but octagonal interior, crowned with a dome. Remains of 1c Roman temple to Apollo (columns with Corinthian capitals). Old bishop's palace, 17c, houses mus. of Nature in Provence. From Ste. Maxime hermitage – chapel (Romanesque apse) with pilgrims' shelter – splendid view over *Plateau de Valensole* and the *Alpes de Provence*.

Riom
63 – Puy-de-Dôme
31 – A 1

Notre Dame-du-Marthuret church, 14–15c, houses one of the masterpieces of medieval sculpture, 14c *Vierge à l'oiseau* (Virgin with bird). Sole remnant of Jean de Berry's castle is late-14c Ste. Chapelle, now within the Palais de Justice (lawcourts); notable 15c stained-glass windows (apply to caretaker); int. has magnificent 17c tapestries. Numerous old houses, notably the Maison des Consuls (mid-16c). Rue de l'Horloge is almost entirely lined by 16–17c mansions; 15–16c Tour de l'Horloge; Hôtel Arnoux de Maison-Rouge (early-17c courtyard); Hôtel Guimoneau (staircase and balcony ornamented with sculptures in courtyard). Mus. Francisque Mandet, in two adjoining 18c mansions (cl. Tues.); first-rate Richard donation (archaeology, Italian primitives, enamels, medieval sculpture, pottery), lapidary exhibits, old paintings, original letter from Joan of Arc. Auvergne reg. mus. (cl. Tues.), folk arts and traditions. St. Amable has Romanesque nave and transept and a Goth. choir.
Vicinity ● 1 km W, *Mozac*, one-time abbey church of St. Pierre. Romanesque historiated capitals from the former ambulatory of the nave and side-aisles are among the most unusual of their kind. The old chapterhouse, adorned with Louis XV panelling, houses rich church treasure: reliquary of St Calmin, masterpiece of 12c Limousin enamelwork; reliquary of 12c St. Austremoine, painted in 16–17c. ● 3 km SW, at Marsat, Romanesque church has one of the Auvergne's finest Black Virgins (12c, in painted wood). 4.5 km away, *Volvic*, mineral springs; big lava quarries; 11 and 12c Romanesque church. 2 km to N, remains of Ch. de Tournoël (v.a.); 12c square keep

Riquewihr: *world-famed for its Alsace wines, the town still looks much as it did in the 16th century – whole streets of timber-framed houses and picturesque merchants' signs.*

and 13c cylindrical keep, 15c aristocratic dwelling. 6 km NW, **Chât-elguyon*** ● 9 km E, **Ennezat.***

Rioux
17 – Charente-Maritime
29 – A 1

Notre Dame church is one of the jewels of Saintonge reg. version of Romanesque; façade has remarkable décor of blind arcades – one of which, in centre, holds a Virgin and Child; superb seven-sided apse, decorated with geometrical motifs; in choir, 'Mystical Marriage of Ste. Catherine', group carved in multi-coloured wood (15c).
Vicinity ● 5.5 km N, *Rétaud*: 12c Romanesque church of St. Trojan in same style as Rioux church; façade with sculpted frieze; fine octagonal apse, richly ornamented (see the corbels, in particular).

Riquewihr
68 – Haut-Rhin
14 – A 3

One of the most characteristic little towns in Alsace, beautifully situated in the middle of vineyards, this old stronghold has hardly changed since the Middle Ages – as shown by its many ancient houses and narrow streets. Delightful Place des Trois-Églises, surrounded by three old defunct churches; Liebrich house, with courtyard lined by wooden balconies (mid-17c); Preiss-Zimmer House, late 17c; the Dolder, or 'High Gate', 13c, enlarged in 15–16c, houses interesting Dolder mus. (local antiquities). Ch. des Wurtemberg-Montbéliard (v.a., cl. Tues., hours vary) has intriguing mus. of the postal service in Alsace. See also: Kiener house (late 16c); Maison Dissler, Rhenish Ren.

(1610); the Rue and the Cour des Juifs (former ghetto); Schwander house, early 17c, and its wooden balconies; the Obertor or 'Upper Gate' (1500), with portcullis.
Vicinity ● **Route du Vin d'Alsace*** (the Alsace wine road).

Roanne
42 – Loire
25 – B 3

Joseph Déchelette mus., in 18c mansion, has large prehist., Gallo-Roman and medieval collections; also 19 and 20c paintings.
Vicinity ● To S, wild, barren *Gorges of the Loire*, via D56 and *St. Maurice-sur-Loire*, on steep rock crowned by ruins of feudal castle. ● 8 km W. *Ch. de Boisy*, flanked by towers and 14c square keep (n.v.a.). ● From the Roanne hills, fine views over vineyard country (see **Ambierle***).

Rocamadour
46 – Lot
36 – A 1

Highly unusual site, in narrow gorge of the Alzou, at foot of enormous rock famed for its medieval sanctuaries (floodlit in summer). The village has only one main street, lined with old houses; several fortified gates. The grand staircase (143 steps) mounts to the Fort, or Bishop of Tulle's palace, from where you can get to the sanctuaries, built at different levels: St. Amadour crypt, mid-12c, under St. Sauveur church, 11–13c; miraculous Chapel of the Virgin (1749), containing 12c wooden statue of Notre Dame-de-Rocamadour. St. Michel chapel, 13c murals inside; 12c external tunnel and steeply winding path lead to Stations of the Cross and 14c château (n.v.a.),

from where you get magnificent view of the village and whole site. Château can be reached by car from L'Hospitalet.

Vicinity ● To W, sources of R. Ouysse and abyss of St. Sauveur. ● 5 km E, La Pucelle waterfall and abyss of Igue de Biau. ● 5 km NE, abyss of Réveillon. ● 9.5 km NW, *Grottoes of Lacave* (v.a., electric train and lifts), magnificent concretions. ● 17.5 km NE, gulf of **Padirac***. To S, causse of **Gramat***.

Rochechouart
87 – Haute-Vienne   29 – D 1
13 and 15c château (apply to caretaker) is built on promontory which offers huge panorama; now houses town hall, sub-prefecture and mus. of local antiquities; Hunting Room is decorated with unusual early 16c murals. Good view over valley from Promenade des Allées. Maisons des Consuls, 15c.

Vicinity ● 5.5 km NW, *Chassenon*: remains of Gallo-Roman town of Cassinomagus (v.a. during summer). 11c church with 14c apse. ● 12 km N, near *Étagnac*, is *Ch. de Rochebrune* – magnificent 11, 13 and 16c construction, flanked by four round towers and with moat. (v.a., Apr. to Nov. 1); apartments have fine Empire-style furniture.

Roche-Courbon (Château)
17 – Charente-Maritime   28 – D 1
One of the finest châteaux in Saintonge reg. (v.a. to château and keep,

La Roche-Courbon: *best view of this magnificent château is from beyond its terraced flower-beds and ornamental ponds.*

cl. Feb. to mid-March and cl. Thurs., Sept. 15–June 15; v.a. to gardens and grottoes daily). This superb construction – 15c (tower and keep), 16c and 17c – was saved from ruin by French author Pierre Loti (d. 1923). It rises above terraces looking over superb formal gardens. Int. retains part of its 17c décor, notably the bathroom, entirely covered with allegorical paintings or sculpted motifs.
Vicinity ● 7.5 km W, *Pont-l'Abbé-d'Arnoult*, church with Romanesque façade, renovated in 13c.

Rochefort-en-Terre
56 – Morbihan   16 – B 1
Picturesque little town much favoured by artists, perched on a spur in hilly countryside bordering the *Landes de Lanvaux*. Many old granite houses, 15, 16 and 17c, especially in Grand-Rue. Old market halls. Remains of 13c castle, fortified gate, ramparts, underground vaults, 17c outbuildings. Church of Notre Dame-de-la-Tronchaye, 14, 15 and 16c, with 17c retable (Breton pardon on first Sun. after Aug. 15). 14c calvary.

Rocamadour: *this famous pilgrimage centre enjoys a setting without equal.*

La Rochelle: *the 14th-century St. Nicholas Tower guards the Old Port.*

Rochefort-sur-Mer
17 – Charente-Maritime   22 – D 3
The Place Colbert is bordered by town hall and mid-19c church of St. Louis, with 18c belfry; in centre of square, monumental fountain dating from 1750. Former royal Corderie (rope factory), 374 m. long, masterpiece by 17c French architect Blondel, which was burned down in 1944, has been extremely well restored. Extensive Marine garden. To S, Tour aux Signaux and Porte du Soleil, sculpted with maritime trophies, monumental entrance to old arsenal (today, private works for aeronautical construction). Past glories of this one-time military port are evoked by Hôtel de Cheusses (int. has fine salons with Louis XVI and Empire panelling), which houses notable naval mus., and by Hôtel de la Marine (beautiful monumental door). Town was birthplace of author Pierre Loti. His home at 141, Rue Pierre-Loti (v.a., cl. a.m. Sun. and Mon., Apr. 1– Sept. 30) and the two neighbouring houses include a Moroccan salon, a Japanese pagoda, a mosque, Middle Ages room, Ren. room, etc. Town mus. (cl. Mon.) displays natural hist., oriental art and paintings (sketches by Rubens and *Le Port de Rochefort* by Vernet).
Vicinity ● 13 km NW, *Fouras*, seaside resort under imposing 15c château surrounded by triple fortification built by Vauban; 2 km to NW, over narrow Pointe de l'Aiguille or Pointe de la Fumée to fort of Enet, built on a rock off the coast; motor-boat service takes 20 mins. from *Fouras* to *Ile d'Aix*. Little town on the island, fortified by Vauban, still has the Emperor's House, Napoleon's last residence in France before leaving for St. Helena in July 1815. Napoleonic mus. (v.a. daily in summer); opposite it, African museum.

Roche-Guyon (La)
95 – Val-D'Oise   11 – B 1
Village is built at foot of steep slopes, crowned by 12c keep above R. *Seine*. Château of the Ducs de La Rochefoucauld (n.v.a.).
Vicinity ● 3 km W, *Gasny*, stables and troglodytic caves; spectacular views from Route des Crêtes (ridge road). ● 2 km E, Haute-Isle, troglodytic village; from there, road hugs the *Seine* at foot of lofty white cliffs; *Vetheuil*, picturesque town above a bend in the river; Goth. church, with Ren. façade and S porch; interior has fine old statues, Goth. stalls and panelling, paintings, etc.

Rochelle (La)
17 – Charente-Maritime   22 – D 3
Town still has its sea-front ramparts, with three powerful towers at entrance to the Vieux-Port (Old Port): the Tour St. Nicolas and, opposite, the Tour de la Chaîne, linked to the Tour de la Lanterne by the unusual Rue Sur-les-Murs, which follows the top of the medieval ramparts (v.a. to the three towers, cl. Tues.). In the Vieux-Port, the Porte de la Grosse-Horloge, massive square gate originally from 13c, is starting-point for Rue du Palais, which runs into Rue Chaudrier; both are lined by 17 and 18c mansions, notably Hôtel de la Bourse (noteworthy courtyard) and the Palais de Justice (lawcourts). Through Rue des Augustins (11 bis, elegant Ren. house known as Maison de Diane de Poitiers), you get to 15–16c town hall – most notable public building in La Rochelle; its courtyard, enclosed by crenellated and machicolated wall, has a fine late-16c sculpted façade, of Italian inspiration; to the l., much-adorned Ren. pavilion crowned by a bell tower with an enamelled statue of France's King Henri IV. Rue des Merciers is lined by 15–16c houses with monumental doors (No. 3, Maison de Jean Guiton; No. 8, fine 16c Maison Lechêne). Take the Rue du Minage and Rue Chaudrier to Place de Verdun and late-18c St. Louis cathedral. Rue de l'Escale, parallel with Rue du Palais, is main artery of old aristocratic quarter, where several 18c mansions can still be seen. ● La Rochelle has seven mus.: the Orbigny-Bernon mus. (fine reg. pottery and oriental art); mus. of natural hist. (cl. Sun. a.m. and Mon.), which includes Fleuriau reg. mus. (geology, paleontology, zoology); and mus. Lafaille (natural science, prehist., ethnic African) in the fmr. 16 and 19c Hôtel du Gouvernement. Fine arts mus. (French painting of 17, 18, 19 and 20c) in old bishop's palace, late 18c. Mus. of the New World in mid-18c Hôtel Fleuriau (cl. Tues.) is devoted to French settlement in America and the influence of this continent on art and literature. Protestant mus.; La Rochelle World War II mus. is in former Kriegsmarine (German Navy) bunker. Mus. of Knights Templars (Grosse-Horloge gate). ● Beach and Promenade du Mail (800 m. long), favourite leisure-spot for the Rochelais, include baths and a casino surrounded by park. To N, behind the beach, huge Charruyer park bordering W face of the Vauban walls.
Vicinity ● 2 km SW, little village and marina of Les Minimes. ● From *La Pallice*, 5 km to W, boats to Ile de Ré*. ● 12 km N, *Esnandes*, 12–14c fortified church, Romanesque Poitevin façade with sculpted frieze; beautiful views from watch-path round the top. Mussel beds in the *Anse de l'Aiguillon* ● 12 km S, *Châtelaillon-Plage*, pleasant seaside resort; unusual district of the 'boucholeurs' (mussel farmers).

Roche-Racan (Château)
37 – Indre-et-Loire   17 – C 2
17c terraced building above little valley of the Escotais, with high white façade, is flanked by an octagonal tower (v.a., Aug. to mid-Sept.; by arrangement for groups out of season).
Vicinity ● 2.5 km NW, *St. Paterne-Racan*: church has several works of art from Cistercian abbey of the Clarté-Dieu, remains of which lie 3 km to W, in a green vale – 13 and 14c vaulted rooms, cellars hollowed from the rock, foundations of church. 2 km to N, *St. Christophe-sur-le-Nais*, 14 and 16c church, covered by timber vaulting; ruins of 10–11c castle; church of *Dissay-sous-Courcillon*, 4 km to N, has fine 12c Romanesque choir; 1 km to E, remains of Ch. de Courcillon; to SE, *Bueil-en-Touraine* has late-15c church adjoining late-14c former collegiate church which has an exquisite baptistry (1521) and the tombs, with funerary statues, of Bueil family.

Roche-sur-Yon (La)
85 – Vendée   22 – C 1
Built on grid plan by Napoleon, whose statue is in Place de Napoléon in town centre. The square is bordered by St. Louis church, the town hall and the Palais de Justice (lawcourts), all in neo-Classical style. Mus. has prehist., archaeology and 19c paintings, and a Napoleonic room. The local stud farms are among largest in France.
Vicinity ● 5 km W, one-time abbey of Les Fontenelles, abbey church in Angevin Gothic style, remains of Goth. cloister and monastic buildings.

Rocroi
08 – Ardennes   6 – C 2
Its fortifications, carried out by Vauban, form a pentagonal bastioned enceinte and are among the most notable examples of 16 and 17c military architecture.
Vicinity ● Excursions from *Rocroi* to *Revin* (12 km E) through the wild Misère valley.

Rodez
12 – Aveyron   36 – C 2
Lying on a hill overlooking a wide horizon, the town is dominated by superb late-13c cathedral of Notre Dame, in red sandstone, with 87 m. tower (upper part of which is richly decorated); interior has finely worked late-15c screen, a 16c

'Entombment' in polychrome stone, and double row of late-15c sculpted stalls in the choir. The surrounding district retains its old-world character; fine Goth. and Ren. buildings. Mus. Fenaille (v.a. daily in summer), in two adjoining houses (14 and 17c), has large archaeological collections (menhirs, Graufesenque ceramics, etc.). Fine arts mus.

Vicinity ● 1 km SE, Le Monastère, remains of 13–14c abbey; 4 km to E, Ste. Radegonde: 13c church fortified in 14 and 15c, with six-storey belfry keep. ● To N, *Causse du Comtal*.

Roissy-Charles-de-Gaulle (Airport)
95 – Val-d'Oise   11 – C 1
One of Europe's most modern airports. Aérogare 1, opened in 1974, has a central ring-shaped building surrounded by seven satellites. Aérogare 2 has two facing buildings, with enormous car park between them. Terminal B was opened in

Romorantin-Lanthenay: the Ch. du Moulin, with two buildings in red and black brick, reflected in the waters of its moat.

1981 and Terminal A in 1982. The Aérogares have restaurants, bars, boutiques, conference rooms, etc. (guided tours). Roissy-Charles-de-Gaulle can be reached by car, Air-France coaches or Roissy-rail.

Romans-sur-Isère
26 – Drôme   32 – A 3
St. Barnard church, fmr. 12–13c abbey church, boasts eight superb Flemish wall hangings (mid-16c), depicting The Passion. Behind the church, old mansion of archbishops of Vienne (15–16c); in one-time convent of the Visitation, mus. devoted to shoes and reg. ethnography. Also Mus. de la Résistance and de la Déportation. In old town, houses with wooden balconies. Belfry with unusual 15c Jack o' the Clock. The Pont-Vieux, over R.

Isère, links Romans to *Bourg-de-Péage*. Local speciality: les pognes (kind of brioche).

Romorantin-Lanthenay
41 – Loir-et-Cher   18 – B 3
On the two banks of R. *Sauldre*, which forms a number of islands here, the town has several timber-framed houses in stone and brick, especially in Rue de la Résistance: the Chancellerie, the Carroir Doré (archaeological mus.) and Hôtel St. Pol. A few remaining traces of old royal château, 15–16c (now subprefecture). In town hall, mus. of Sologne reg. (ethnography and folklore). To S, Marin island with St. Étienne church, 12–13c; Rue de Venise has old houses on river bank. In Orléans district, mus. of car racing.

Vicinity ● 3 km N, *Lanthenay*, interesting works of art in 12–19c church. ● 12 km NW, near *Lassay-sur-Croisne*, *Ch. du Moulin*, elegant 15–16c manor in red and black brick, in diamond shape, surrounded by square walls and moat. (v.a., Mar. to mid-Nov.). ● To fly over the châteaux of the Loire from Romorantin, inquire at Sologne airfield, Romorantin-Pruniers.

Ronchamp
70 – Haute-Saône   20 – C D2
Chapel of Notre Dame-du-Haut, 1.5 km from the township, is one of Le Corbusier's most original creations (1951–55). For it, he abandoned his geometric discipline in favour of curved masses. Interior, very spare, receives light through asymmetrical apertures.

Roquefort-sur-Soulzon
12 – Aveyron   36 – D 3
Picturesque township backing on to the limestone cliffs of the Causse

of Combalou. See the world-famed cellars where Roquefort cheese is matured. Viewing tables on Rock of St. Pierre, wide panorama.

Rosanbo (Château)
22 – Côtes-du-Nord   8 – D 2
Superb fortified country mansion in granite, 15–17c (v.a. daily, in July–Aug.; Sat., Sun. and public holidays, Apr.–June), with succession of terraces overlooking little valley of the Bo. Apartments decorated and furnished in 17–18c style; imposing 17c wooden staircase.

Vicinity ● At Plouzélambre (to N), 15c church, calvary and elegant ossuary. ● In outskirts of *Plouaret* (to SE), several interesting 15–16c châteaux; that of *Kermanac'h*, has richly sculpted portal.

Roscoff
29 N – Finistère   8 – C 1
Seaside resort, fishing and commercial port. Important centre for thalassotherapy. University of Paris biology centre. Charles Pérez aquarium. Notre Dame-de-Kroaz-Baz, in Flamboyant style, has notable mid-16c Ren. belfry; int. has retable with seven 15c alabaster reliefs. 17c former ossuaries. 16–17c houses, Rue Amiral-Réveillère. Old Capuchin convent has renowned giant fig tree (v.a.); planted around 1625, it covers nearly 6,500 sq. ft.! To E, port and Point of Bloscon (St. Barbe chapel). Lobster and crayfish beds.

Vicinity ● 1 km NW (motorboat service), *Ile de Batz* 4 km long, fringed by sandy beaches; the harbour and village are in cove of Kernoc'h; at SE tip, colonial garden.

Rouen
76 – Seine-Maritime   5 – A 3
Capital of Upper Normandy, beautiful town of art. The best general view is from the 'Corniche de Rouen' (D95), the Côte Ste. Catherine and the belvedere of Bonsecours. Cathedral of Notre Dame, 13–14c, is one of France's finest; its grandiose façade, with pinnacle turrets, is framed by two towers, one of them the famed Tour de Beurre (77 m.). Its three portals are superbly sculpted: on S side, portal of La Calande; on N side, portal of Les Libraires; masterpieces of 14c decorative sculpture. Inside, the immense transept has a 51 m. lantern tower; choir has 15c stained-glass windows and stalls; Chapel of the Virgin shelters tomb of the Cardinals of Amboise, a splendid sculpted Ren. work, and that of the seneschal Louis de Brézé (also 16c). The ambulatory is lit by five 13c windows, in delicate colours. In l. arm of the transept,

renowned Librairie staircase. 11c crypt remains of primitive Romanesque shrine. ● The quarter around cathedral has picturesque streets and old houses (for guided tours, apply at S.I.). St. Maclou church, 15–16c, in Flamboyant style, has a magnificent porch with five bays crowned by ornate pointed gables. On l. side, Rue Martainville, with old timber-framed houses, faces the 'Aître de St. Maclou', 15–17c ossuary with four wooden galleries on stone columns, surrounded by a cemetery. St. Ouen church, 14–15c, is dominated by the Tour Couronnée, 82 m. tall, a superb Flamboyant edifice. 14c portal of the Marmousets is entered through a 15c porch; interior, big but harmonious, has lovely 14, 15 and 16c stained-glass windows. Among the historic public buildings, two 'musts' for visits are the Hôtel des Bourgtheroulde, Goth. Flamboyant and equally ornate Ren., and the Palais de Justice (lawcourts), imposing 15–16c Goth. building with marvellous sculpted decoration on façade over the main courtyard. Place du Vieux-Marché, where Joan of Arc was burned at the stake in 1431, has been updated (1979) with market halls, a new church (15–16c stained-glass windows) and a memorial. The 'Gros-Horloge' (Big Clock), best-known monument in Rouen, is flanked by an impressive late-14c belfry. Recently restored, the houses in this street are good examples of timber-framed architecture from Middle Ages to early 16c. ● Rouen's fine arts mus. (cl. Tues. and Wed. a.m.) is one of France's richest: notable collections of paintings, particularly 19c French (Ingres, Delacroix, Géricault, the Impressionists, etc.). The Northern schools, Flanders and Holland, are also well·represented, as is the Italian school, including key works by Veronese and Caravaggio; large collection of contemporary art: Dufy, Villon, Marcel Duchamp, Bissière, Vieira da Silva, Soulages, etc.; rich group of drawings. Ceramics mus. in Hôtel d'Hocqueville (same hours), Rouen pottery (16–19c). Mus. Le Secq des Tournelles, superb wrought-iron. Departmental mus., antiquities, noteworthy Middle Ages and Ren. plate, ivory, enamels, tapestries, etc. Joan of Arc mus.; Corneille mus. (in his birthplace). Mus. Flaubert. Hist. of medicine mus. in Hôtel-Dieu; mus. of natural history; Natnl. Mus. of Education. ● The port of Rouen is fourth largest in France; can be toured by motor-launch as far as La Bouille.
Vicinity ● 9 km NW, Croisset,

Rouen: *in a pedestrian precinct in the middle of the old town, below the 'Gros Horloge' and half-timbered houses.*

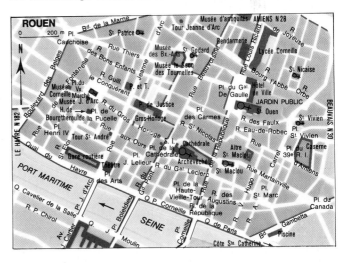

Pavillon Flaubert (small mus., cl. Tues. and Wed.) ● 8 km SW, *Petit-Couronne*, Manor of Pierre Corneille (v.a.). 7 km to SW, *Ch. de Robert le Diable*, imposing 11c feudal fortress; interior has mus. of the Vikings; leisure park; panorama over valley of the Seine. ● 16 km

E, moated *Ch. de Martainville*, late 15c. Mus. of Norman art and traditions. ● Rouen is an excellent base for visiting the (Norman) **Abbeys***.

Rouffach
68 – Haut-Rhin   21 – A 1
Picturesque little town surrounded

ROUFFIGNAC (Grotto)
24 – Dordogne   29 – D 3
5 km S of *Rouffignac*. Outstanding group of prehist. animal drawings and carvings (v.a. daily in summer, by small electric train; 50-min. journey).
Vicinity ● 4 km NW of village, remains of Ch. de l'Herm, flanked by three late-15c towers and a Flamboyant gate.

by vineyards (on **Route du Vin d'Alsace*** – the Alsace wine road). 11–12c Notre Dame church (with 13c nave and choir) is one of most interesting in Alsace. 14–15c Franciscan church (16c statues). Tour des Sorcières (Witches Tower), 13–14c, crowned with machicolations (storks' nests). Ancient houses and old town hall.

Roussillon
84 – Vaucluse   38 – A 3
One of the most striking sites in Provence. Red and yellow ochre quarries, in sheer cliffs, ring the village. The houses, also ochre, lie under plateau of the Rock, site of the church. Magnificent view (viewing table).
Vicinity ● To W, Aiguilles du Val des Fées, vertical gashes in an ochre cliff, and Chausée des Géants.

Royan
17 – Charente-Maritime   28 – D 1
Three-parts destroyed by bombardments in Jan. and Apr. 1945, Royan was rebuilt with modernist architecture, of which principal element is the sea-front. This hugs curve of Grande Conche for 600 m. Imaginatively conceived church of Notre Dame – elliptically shaped, in reinforced concrete – has 60 m. spire. Archaeological and history mus. in town hall.
Vicinity ● 2 km NW, Conche de Pontaillac; to N, *Vaux-sur-Mer*, Romanesque country church and its graveyard are worth a detour. *St. Palais-sur-Mer* (fine walks along

cliff ledge by Les Pierrières path. The *Grand Côte*, beautiful site where the dunes give way to cliffs; Grand Côte and Palmyre beaches. *Point* and *Phare* (lighthouse) of *La Coubre*; *Forêt Domaniale* (state forest) of *La Coubre* (23 sq. miles). Ragged coastline of *Arvert* peninsula is very scenic, but beware treacherous tides. ● 1.5 km SE, *St. Georges-de-Didonne*; point and beach of Suzac; *Meschers-sur-Gironde* (cliffs studded with excavations called 'Trous de Meschers'; restaurants); 6 km SE **Talmont***. ● Boat trips to lighthouse of *Cordouan*, 66 m. tall (v.a.); standing on islet at mouth of the Gironde, it was regarded as one of the 'Wonders of the World' when it was built at end of 16c. Upper part reconstructed end of 18c; on 1st floor, King's room; on 2nd, a chapel; staircase with 301 steps up to the lantern.

Royaumont (Abbey)
95 – Val-d'Oise   11 – C 1
Founded by St. Louis in 1228, now houses an international cultural centre. V.a. (cl. Wed.) to 13c cloister around monks' garden, the refectory (more than 40 m. long), the former kitchens and the chapel.

Rue
80 – Somme   5 – B 1
St. Esprit chapel, adjoining N side of St. Wulphy church, is richly ornate masterpiece of Goth. Flamboyant, 15–16c; interior has elaborate vaulting. See also the two

doors of the Treasury. Note, too, belfry above town hall.
Vicinity ● To W, *Marquenterre* park (see **Baie de Somme***).

Rueil-Malmaison
92 – Hauts-de Seine   11 – C 1
Bonaparte and Josephine left their marks on the modest Ch. de Malmaison. (She lived there until her death.) Today it is the largest Napoleonic mus. (cl. Tues.). Reception rooms, Napoleon's apartments and Josephine's quarters have superb furniture of the period, numerous objets d'art and paintings (David, Gérard, Prudhon), recapturing atmosphere and style of the Consulate and the Empire. Famous rose garden, summer house and Pavillon des Voitures. Annex of Malmaison, the Ch. de Bois-Préau, houses mus. mainly devoted to Napoleon and his family – salon of the King of Rome, Emperor's personal effects, relics from St. Helena (cl. Tues.). ● Church of Rueil-Malmaison has Josephine's tomb and that of Queen Hortense, her daughter; the late-15c Florentine organ-chest is among finest in France. Rueil-Malmaison history mus. in old town hall.
Vicinity ● Bois de St. Cucufa (lakes), Bougival, **Louveciennes***, **Marly-le-Roi***.

Ruffec
16 – Charente   23 – B 3
The church has 12c Romanesque sculpted façade and a triple nave.
Vicinity ● 7 km SW, *Courcôme*, 11–12c Poitevin Romanesque church. ● 6 km SE, *Verteuil*; 15c château with three towers: in the church, a Ren. 'Entombment' in terra cotta, with eight figures.

Ruoms
07 – Ardèche   37 – C 2
Old fortified township. Remains of its walls are flanked by seven round towers. 14–15c houses around Romanesque church.
Vicinity ● To N, the *Ardèche* winds through the strange *Défilé de Ruoms*, where marble cliffs reach almost 100 m. high. From there, see *Balazuc*; picturesque village with remains of castle (13c keep), perched on an isolated rock; fortified church and remains of ramparts. 6 km away, Ch. de *Vogüé*, imposing 16c building with towers, backing on to cliffs – atop of which are remains of another feudal castle. ● 2 km SW, near Auriolpe, *Mas de la Vignasse*, family home of Daudet (mementoes of the author, objects from country life, silk-worm farming). To SW, *Bois de Païolive*, one of the sights of the Vivarais reg. (see **Les Vans***). ● To SE, *Canyon de l'Ardèche* (see **Vallon-Pont-d'Arc***).

Ruoms: *the 16th-century Château de Vogüé still belongs to the aristocratic family from which it takes its name.*

S

Sables-d'Olonne (Les)
85 – Vendée   22 – C 2
Seaside resort and large fishing port standing on narrow sandbank between an old lagoon (now salt marshes) and the ocean. Beautiful crescent-shaped beach, more than 2 km long; running alongside it, a wide quay/terrace (Quai Wilson, Quai Georges Clémenceau, Ave. Georges Godet), with town's main hotels and villas. To W end, large casino and swimming pool, and Les Sables jetty. The corniche road, which extends the Remblai to SE, follows line of the cliff and goes as far as the Puits d'Enfer. Picturesque port, especially lively when the fishing boats return home. Notable mus. of contemp. art in abbey of Ste. Croix: 6 Magnelli, 40 Launois, 25 Chaissac, 11 Brauner, Dubuffet, Hélion, Debré. Large coll. of 19–20c lithographs (Sorlier donation). Small maritime mus. in St. Nicolas' Priory. The fishermen's quarter, La Chaume, grouped around Arundel Tower and St. Nicolas' Fort, 17c, is separated from Les Sables by the channel into the port.
Vicinity ● To NW, State *Forest of Olonne* (3,190 acres) covers the coastal dunes between *La Chaume* and the harbour at *La Gachère*, ● 13.5 km SE, *Talmont-St. Hilaire* under imposing ruins of 11c castle, rebuilt in 15 and 16c (superb keep and Romanesque chapel); 1.5 km farther on, Ch. des Granges-Cathus, early 16c. ● 5 km NE, Ch. de Pierre-Levée, charming 18c rustic 'folly' (n.v.a. exc. groups by arrangement).

Sablé-sur-Sarthe
72 – Sarthe   17 – B 1
On both banks of R. *Sarthe*, which forms several islands here. 19c church of Notre Dame has two superb 15 and 16c stained-glass windows. 18c château (n.v.a.) with 14c fortified entry.
Vicinity ● 3.5 km E, abbey of **Solesmes***.

Sabres
40 – Landes   34 – D 2
Ecological museum of Grande-Lande at Marquèze (4 km from Sabres) was first environmental mus. in France. Habitat of the Landes in 19c: vegetable garden, mill and miller's house, pond and mill race, various types of houses, etc. Exhibitions and information centre. A small steam train runs to and from the mus. (Jun. 15–Sept. 15 daily, from Sabres).
Vicinity ● 22 km NE, *Luxey*, fmr. resine distillation workshop. ● Bird sanctuary and nature centre at Le Teich (Gironde). ● 10 km NW, the 'Mexico' base at *Commensacq* supplies canoes/kayaks for the trip down the *Grande-Leyre* as far as the mouth of the Arcachon basin (120 km). ● 7 km W, *Solférino*, Napoleon III and Landes folklore mus.

St. Amand-de-Coly
24 – Dordogne   30 – A 3
The imposing Romanesque for-

Sabres: *in the Landes forest (approx. 3,670 sq. miles), resin is collected in pots hung up on the pines.*

tified church, in yellow limestone, is one of the most unusual in Périgord region.
Vicinity ● 9 km SE, *La Cassagne*: typical Périgourdin village; 12–13c Romanesque church.

St. Amand-les-Eaux
59 – Nord   2 – A 3
All that remains of the flourishing medieval abbey is, in the Grand-Place, the Flemish Ren. Pavillon de l'Echevinage (reception room decorated by Louis Watteau in 1782) and façade of the old abbey church, with a magnificent baroque tower 82 m. high, richly ornamented; the latter houses a famous carillon of 44 bells (concerts daily from 12–12.30 and in summer on Sun. from 19–20 hrs.); also small museum containing local 18c pottery.
Vicinity ● The spa is 4 km E, on edge of the *Forêt de Raismes* (1,895 acres); this, together with the Forest of St. Amand (12 sq. miles) and state forest of Wallers, makes up the Reg. Wildlife Park of St. Amand-Raismes: animal and bird reserves. Mus. of wooden barges, etc., at *Hergnies*, large water sports centre on Amaury lake; 259-acre 'parc de vision' – park in which boar, moufflon, buck and roe deer, etc., can be observed in their natural habitat.

St. Andiol
13 – Bouches-du-Rhône   37 – D 3
Impressive Romanesque church, fortified in 13c; inside, stone Goth. ciborium and 18c panelling. Mid-17c château.
Vicinity ● 2 km W, Verquières, small fortified Romanesque church, enlarged in 17c.

St. Antoine (Abbey)
38 – Isère   32 – A 3
Overlooking the town on slopes of the Furan valley, the abbey, founded at end of 11c, is one of the most interesting examples of medieval monastic architecture. Three monumental portals open on to a 17c building, in front of long rectangular courtyard surrounded by outhouses and stables; at end stands Goth. abbey church, whose façade, above a high terrace, has three sculpted portals; vast, harmonious int. has numerous works of art, notably some mid-15c frescos, the stalls, the high altar, and shrine of St. Antoine, 17c; also interesting art in the sacristy: 18c panelling, Aubusson tapestries, 17–18c sacerdotal ornaments, large collection of reliquaries.
Vicinity ● 11.5 km SE, *St. Marcellin*: 15c church, remains of town

walls and 13c castle; also ruins of 13c castles of Le Mollard and Beauvoir.

St. Avold
57 – Moselle   13 – D 1
Late-18c church, former Benedictine abbey church. Late-19c basilica of Notre Dame-du-Bon-Secours (pilgrimage centre).
Vicinity ● 2 km N, enormous American cemetery for Lorraine (16,000 graves). ● Émile-Huchet thermal power station at *Carling* is one of largest in France. ● To NE, *Freyming-Merlebach*, one of the main coal-mining centres in Europe; numerous carbo-chemical factories; the *Route des Puits* (mineshaft road), between *Carling* and *Merlebach*, runs through extraordinary industrial territory: the tall furnaces make an impressive sight at night.

St. Benoît-sur-Loire (Abbey)
45 – Loiret   18 – C 1
11–12c basilica (v.a., Gregorian chanting) is approached through a massive belfry-porch, representative of Romanesque art, with capitals alternating between stylised foliage, fantastic animals and evangelical scenes. Portal has noteworthy 13c carving. Inside, mid-12c nave, transept and choir from 1065–1108 (recumbent statue of King Philippe I, mosaic paving from 4 or 5c, early-15c stalls, interesting historiated capitals). 11c crypt has relics of St. Benoît; remains of very early sanctuary. The port district, with its old sailors' houses, is picturesque; the graceful curve of the Loire offers views of varied countryside (from the Croix-Tibi, beautiful view over the river and basilica).
Vicinity ● 5.5 km NW, **Germigny-des-Prés***. ● 8 km SE, **Sully-sur-Loire***.

St. Bertrand-de-Comminges
31 – Haute-Garonne   41 – C 3
Encircled by ramparts, the village, set on a steep slope, with narrow streets, is overlooked by the majestic nave of former cathedral of Notre Dame, built in Romanesque and Goth. styles: inside, rood-screen, choir-screen and stalls, early 16c, are carved with exceptional virtuosity; behind main altar, St. Bertrand's mausoleum, 15c, in form of gigantic reliquary; two rooms of fmr. chapterhouse hold rich church treasure. ● To S of church, fine Romanesque cloister with capitals and pillar depicting the four evangelists, from very early period; from S gallery, sweeping view down to ravine.
● Mus. de Comminges, in 18c mansion; contains finds from excavations of Gallo-Roman villa. A

19c chapel houses magnificent marble imperial Trophies, slightly damaged, from 1c. Near lower town, site of excavation of Lugdunum Convenarum (theatre, temple, basilica or market, Forum baths and Northern baths; 4c Christian basilica); v.a. – apply caretaker. 600 m. away, St. Just-de-Valcabrère, charming late-11c Romanesque church (apply to caretaker), in country graveyard; sculpted side door.
Vicinity ● 6 km NW, *Gargas Grottoes* (v.a., June to Oct.), beautiful concretions, handprints of prehistoric men. ● 7 km E, *Barbazan*; pleasant spa, in vast grounds.

St. Blaise (Excavation)
13 – Bouches-du-Rhône   44 – A 2
200 m. to S of 12c Romanesque chapel of St. Blaise, excavations have uncovered outer wall of a Greek fortress from 4c BC, as well as foundations of a 5c church and Paleo-Christian dwellings. Christian necropolis. Wide panorama.

St. Bonnet-le-Château
42 – Loire   31 – B 2
Once-fortified town, interesting group of Goth. and Ren. houses. 15–16c church in granite, with Ren. portal; in crypt, 15c frescos; burial vault for mummies. Wonderful panorama over *Forez* plain and the *Monts du Lyonnais*. Lace-making area.
Vicinity ● To N, *Lurlecq*, Goth. Flamboyant-style church, Ren. porch. ● To NW, *St. Jean-Soleymieux*: 12c church and crypt. ● To SW, *Usson-en-Forez* (15c church), *St. Pal-de-Chalençon* (fortified township). *St. Hilaire-Cusson-la-Valmitte* (church, part-Romanesque, altered in 15 and 19c).

St. Bonnet-Tronçais
03 – Allier   24 – D 2
Tourist centre on edge of the splendid *State Forest of Tronçais* (40 sq. miles), which has the most beautiful oak groves in France. Numerous good walks: in July and Aug., guided tours of the forest, departing from the Rond du Vieux-Morat. The Colbert copse has oaks believed to be more than 300 years old. Many lakes – at *St. Bonnet* (beach, water sports), *Pirot*, Saloup, etc.

St. Brieuc
22 – Côtes-du-Nord   9 – A 2
This old town has kept its Breton character, in some places almost archaic. 14–15c cath. of St. Étienne

St. Benoît-sur-Loire: *contrasting with its severe exterior, this massive belfry-porch boasts capitals of high fantasy.*

is a fortified church whose v. spare façade is framed by two loopholed towers. Mansions and old houses in Rue Fardel, Rue du Maréchal Foch, Place de la Grille, etc. Côtes-du-Nord mus.: reg. ethnography and history. To NE, beautiful views from periphery of promontory on which town stands. From the Knoll of Aubé, vast panorama.
Vicinity ● 3.5 km NE, Cesson Tower, 14c ruins overlooking mouth of the Gouët. ● 5.5 km NE, estuary of the Gouët and port of Légué; the Gouët valley is very picturesque. ● 9.5 km N, *Rosaires* beach, framed by cliffs (water sports club and sailing school); from the Pointe du Roselier, panorama. ● 14 km NW, *Binic*, fishing village and seaside resort; 6.5 km to SW, Notre Dame-de-la-Cour, 15c chapel; *Étables-sur-Mer*, *St. Quay-Portrieux*. ● 9 km S, *Plédran*, 17–19c church; Grotte-aux-Fées dolmen; 3 km to W, 17c Ch. de Graffault and 16c chapel of St. Nicolas (carved wood rood-screen and stained-glass windows, 16c); to N, *Camp de Péran*, outline of huge 600 m. development from 1c and 2c BC.

St. Calais
72 – Sarthe   17 – D 1
This unusual little town comprises two superposed rectangles crossed by two symmetrical axes parallel with the R. *Anille*. Notable church: Notre Dame, half Goth., half Ren.; architecture of its façade is of unusual geometric order. Municipal mus. includes plans and paintings by Charles Garnier, architect of Paris Opéra. Also natural history and early printed books from fmr. abbey. Quays of the *Anille* are lined with charming old houses. On l. bank, above town, ruins of 11c castle.
Vicinity ● 10.5 km S, Ch. de **Courtanvaux***. ● 7.5 km SE, *Savigny-sur-Braye*: 12, 15 and 16c church, with 15c belfry; int. has three fine 18c retables. ● 11 km E *Sargé-sur-Braye*, 11–12c church, with 14 and 16c murals; 5.5 km to N, *Baillou*, 16c church, alone on small hill, containing beautiful group of Ren. stained-glass windows. ● 25 km SW, *Le Grand-Lucé*, mid-18c château, imposing and sombre (nursing home, n.v.a.).

St. Céré
46 – Lot   36 – B 1
Important base for excursions to the *Dordogne Valley*, the *Céré gorges* etc. The town, which has several 15 and 16c houses, is dominated to N by the two 12 and 15c St. Laurent towers, where the painter

Jean Lurçat lived; permanent exhibitions of his tapestries in casino and town hall.
Vicinity ● 1.5 km W, Ch. de **Montal***. ● 9 km NW, *Ch. de Castelnau* (see **Bealieu-sur-Dordogne***).

St. Chamas
13 – Bouches-du-Rhône   44 – A 1
The Gallo-Roman Pont Flavien, 1c bridge. 17c church. The St. Chamas source of water represents final work of construction in control of R. Durance. From the turret (recorded commentaries), fine view over *Berre* lake.
Vicinity ● 4 km NE, picturesque Provençal village of Cornillon-Confoux, on promontory commanding vast panorama. ● To E, the **Aix*** road passes under *Roquefavour* aqueduct, highly complex project (1842–47) which brings Durance water to **Marseilles***.

St. Christophe-en-Oisans
38 – Isère   32 – C 3
Mountain village, in cultivated hollow under the high mountainous massifs between the Pelvoux and Meije peaks; centre for numerous excursions and climbs; in its cemetery, graves of several guides and climbers killed in the mountains.

Vicinity ● To SE, the road hugs r. bank of the *Vénéon* as far as *La Bérarde*; mountaineering centre, French skiing school, in majestic setting of high valleys with a backdrop of dazzling white glaciers; Notre Dame-des-Neiges chapel; above *La Bérarde*, impressive summits of the *Barre des Écrins* (4,100 m.) and the Meije (3,982 m.); creation of the Écrins-Pelvoux National Park (40 sq. miles) is intended to protect the land, flora and fauna of this exceptional reg.

St. Cirq-Lapopie
46 – Lot   36 – A 2
One of the Quercy's most extraordinary villages, both because of its setting and for the picturesqueness

St. Christophe-en-Oisans: *the Meije, whose highest summit, the Grand Pic, was not conquered until August 1877.*

of its old houses (some from 15–16c). 12 and 15c church. The village is dominated by the ruins of a château (panorama). Several artists and craftsmen have restored houses there and now live in them. From rocky promontory of Bancourel, view over the *Lot Valley*.

St. Claude
39 – Jura   26 – B 2
Capital of the pipe, in impressive mountain site; excellent base for

St. Cirq-Lapopie: *clustered around the church and its separate belfry-tower, the houses of this old village have corbelled façades and exposed beams.*

touring upper Jura. Good general view of the **Morez*** road. Cath. of St. Pierre, in homogeneous Goth. style, is all that remains of large 13c abbey; 38 sculpted choir stalls, from 15c; monumental Ren. retable, sculpted and painted in homage to St. Peter. Rue de la Poyat, which joined the abbey buildings to the suburbs on banks of R. *Bienne* and the Tacon, has lost none of its old character.
Vicinity ● Walks to the Combes and Font de l'Abîme torrents, to NE, to the Queue-de-Cheval falls to E; to the gorges and falls of Le Flumen and the belvedere de la Cernaise, to SE. ● *Gorges de l'Ain*: to SW, passing through the *Brienne* valley, *Dortan* and *Thoirette*; to NW, via *Moirans-en-Montagne* and the lake reservoir of Vouglans. ● To N, the *Brienne* valley.

St. Cloud
92 – Hauts-de-Seine   11 – C 2
Stella Matutina church is one of the most original achievements of contemp. religious art (1965). The 1,112-acre grounds, which cover the slopes over the *Seine*, are crossed by variegated forest paths, straight or winding, and have several especially interesting spots; from the terrace, site of château destroyed in 1870 (and now replaced by flower beds and ornamental lakes), fine view over river and **Paris***; below, on stretch along the Seine (N 187), huge 17c monumental fountains (full display on 2nd and 4th Sun., May to Sept.). In main courtyard, Mus. Historique du Domaine Nationale. Mus. Cul-

turel Ch. Oulmont in Rue du Calvaire. Follow N 187 for **Sèvres** porcelain factory.
Vicinity ● Marnes-la-Coquette; in the Villeneuve-l'Étang park, colossal La Fayette memorial dedicated to volunteer American aviators (1914–1916); crypt; beautiful gardens, romantic lakes; Vaucresson, 18c church with 12c belfry.

St. Denis
93 – Seine-St. Denis   11 – C 1
The basilica, fmr. abbey church and royal necropolis since 13c, is one of France's most impressive historic buildings; begun in 1137, the bays at the entrance to the nave (1140), the choir with ambulatory and the Rayonnant chapels (1144) are among the v. finest examples of Goth. art (v.a., cl. Sun. a.m. and during services). The tombs sum up hist. of funeral sculpture from Middle Ages (figured flagstones and recumbent statues) to the Ren. (splendid monumental tombs of Louis XII and Anne de Bretagne, François I and Claude de France, Henri II and Catherine de Médicis, with recumbent figures, kneeling statues of deceased on level above, sculpted reliefs). In the crypt, 'royal burial vault' of the Bourbons and ossuary. The 18c abbey buildings are now occupied by Légion d'Honneur educational establishment (n.v.a.). Art and history mus. in fmr. Carmelite building, 17–18c, and retaining its int. lay-out (oratory, cells), contains local archaeology, religious art and 19–20c art (Daumier room, Paul Eluard room). Extensive collection

on the Paris Commune (cl. Tues. and Sun. a.m.).

St. Dié
88 – Vosges   13 – D 3
Destroyed in 1944 and rebuilt subsequently, the town still has an excellent example of Rhenish Romanesque architecture: chapel of Notre Dame-de-Galilée (or Little Church), 12c. The cath. (or Large Church), in red sandstone, is partly in Rhenish Romanesque style (mid-12c) and partly Goth.; superb 14–16c cloister with 15c ext. pulpit. Municipal mus. (archaeology).
Vicinity ● Wooded tracts offer many good walks or excursions, especially, to NE, to the Roche du Sapin Sec (895 m.; viewing table, panorama). ● 12 km N, *Moyenmoutier*, superb 18c church, one of the most beautiful Classic religious buildings in the Vosges of Lorraine; 5 km to E, *Senones*, surrounded by dark wooded slopes; fmr. Benedictine abbey, 18c (v.a.). ● To NW, *Étival-Clairefontaine*: beautiful 12c church, fmr. abbey church, built in Cistercian and Rhenish style.

St. Dizier
52 – Haute-Marne   12 – D 2
Two churches to visit: 18c Notre Dame, 15c façade, with several 14 and 16c sculptures from Champagne school; and St. Martin-de-la-Noue, 13–14c, partly rebuilt in late-17c; inside, 17–18c folk art statues.
Vicinity ● To S, *Val Forest*; *Blaise* valley, reached via *Wassy-sur-Blaise*, whose Rhenish Romanesque church was refitted in 17c in

St. Émilion: *as befits an area producing such superb red wines, the medieval town – with its old houses, churches and innumerable other reminders of the past – is absolutely enchanting.*

Goth. style; unusual astronomical clock at town hall.

St. Émilion
33 – Gironde   29 – B 3
Built in tiers on a limestone promontory overlooking the *Dordogne* valley, its main sight is a monolithic church carved out of the rock (11–12c), the oldest building of its kind in France (v.a.). To the l., the chapel of the Trinity, early 13c, above the hermitage and 'bed of St. Émilion'; to the r., separate 12c belfry, with magnificent steeple reaching height of 67 m. The collegiate church (Romanesque nave and Goth. choir) has a 14c cloister. The Cordeliers cloister belongs, along with ruins of 14–15c church and some abbey buildings (elegant Logis de la Commanderie), to local wine interests (v.a.). Numerous old houses and traces of 12c Cardinal's Palace, with Romanesque façade.
Vicinity ● 600 m. W, unusual church of St. Martin-de-Mazerat, 11–12c. ● 4 km NE, *Montagne*, 12c Romanesque church, 14–16c Ch. des Tours. ● 21.5 km E, Ch. de **Montaigne***. ● 17 km N, St. Palais, 12c church, façade in Saintonge reg. version of Romanesque.

St. Étienne
42 – Loire   31 – C 2
This big industrial city has few important historic buildings apart from the Palais des Arts (v.a., cl. Tues.) which houses the Mus. of Art and Industry, one of the richest in France for contemporary art; Picasso, Matisse, Kupka, Magnelli, Masson, Hartung, and the post-war European and American movements (1945–1960). In former Hôtel de Villeneuve, 17c, Mus. Folklorique du Vieux-St. Étienne. Church of St. Étienne (or Grand Église), 15c, is the only really old building in the town.
Vicinity ● 7 km SE, *Rochetaillée*, old, very picturesque township, perched high above the *Furan* valley, under ruins of castle; *Gouffre d'Enfer* dam, in wooded setting. ● To E, *Massif du Pilat*, which culminates in the *Crêt de la Perdrix* (1,434 m.), Lyons TV tower, panorama. ● To SW, near *Chambon-Feugerolles*, imposing feudal castle of Feugerolles, 11–12 and 17c; to W, via *Firminy* (Maison de la Culture, stadium and housing development by Le Corbusier), to *Le Pertuiset*, in scenic site on banks of the *Loire* – which is here transformed by the *Grangent Dam* into a huge winding lake more than 25 km in length; steep corniche road (lovely views over the river). See remains of the Ch. de Cornillon, the charming village of *Chambles* and remains of Ch. d'Essalois. At *St. Rambert-sur-Loire*, 11–12c church; interesting reg. mus. in priory (v.a. daily in summer; Sat. and Sun. only, Sept. to June): archaeology and ethnography (2,000 items from every part of the world), Press cartoons (3,000 items, original lithographs by Daumier).

St. Étienne-de-Tinée
06 – Alpes-Maritimes   39 – A 2
Winter sports and mountaineering centre. 17c church with 16c Goth. choir. In chapel of the old Trinitaires convent, 17c frescos. 15c chapel of St. Sébastien, 15c frescos by Jean Canavesi and Jean Baleisoni. Chapel of St. Maur, 15c frescos.
Vicinity ● 7 km S, winter sports centre of *Auron* (1,600 m.), largest in the Alpes-Maritimes region: Ste. Érige chapel (frescos dating from 1451); Las Donnas cable-car (2,300 m., viewing table, restaurant, wide panorama). ● 14 km SE, *Isola*, in a majestic setting. Under the *Col de la Lombarde*, in beautiful mountain hollow at alt. of 2,000 m., large winter sports resort of Isola-2000; to S of Isola, the road follows the *Tinée* gorges towards **St. Sauveur-sur-Tinée***. ● To N, towards **Jausiers***, road through the *Bonette* pass (2,802 m.); this magnificent 58 km stretch, one of the highest routes in Europe, links the *Tinée* valley with valley of the *Ubaye*.

St. Florent
2B – Corsica   45 – A 2
Large seaside resort and marina, dominated by huge Genoese citadel. 1 km to E, former cathedral of *Nebbio*, in Pisan Romanesque style, early 13c; inside, unusual animal carvings on the capitals (key at the Hôtel d'Europe).
Vicinity ● 24 km E, via *Patrimonio* and the *Teghime* pass, **Bastia*** and the **Cap Corse***. ● 17 km S, *Murato*; 1 km farther on, church of San Michele (key at the Murato presbytery): the walls are dressed in the original dark green and white stone; v. detailed sculpted decoration on side windows. To NE, *défilé de*

St. Florent: *Murato's church – its dark green and white stone giving it the appearance of some kind of giant chess-board.*

Mt. Mouchet (1,465 m.): National Monument to French Underground (Maquis). ● 12 km SE, **Garabit*** viaduct. ● 12 km S, via Villedieu (Romanesque church), ruins of the Ch. d'*Alleuze* stand on a rock at bottom of desolate gorge, between two ravines. ● To W, *Roffiac*, Romanesque church with arcaded wall-belfry; to SW, *Value-jols*, interesting church, and *Paulhac*, fortified church. ● To NW, *Neussargues*, Romanesque church and 17c château.

St. François-Longchamp
73 – Savoie   32 – C 2
Winter sports resort comprising three centres, in tiers on the mountain slopes: St. François (1,400 m.), Longchamp (1,650 m.) and the *Col de la Madeleine* (2,000 m.); many ski-lifts. On edge of broad pasturages, the *Madeleine* pass affords an unusually good view of SW side of **Mont Blanc***. Three-hr. climb to the Cheval-Noir (2,837 m.).

St. Gabriel (Chapel)
13 – Bouches-du-Rhône   43 – D 1
5 km SE of **Tarascon***; one of Provence's most charming Romanesque chapels, surrounded by cypress and olive trees. Built at end of 12c, its architecture is inspired by that of antiquity; the highly elaborate sculpted decoration is charmingly archaic. Behind it, ruins of feudal castle and its outer wall.

St. Gaudens
31 – Haute-Garonne   41 – C 2
Fmr. collegiate church, St. Pierre-et-St. Gaudens is a fine 11–12c Romanesque edifice with three naves and three apses. From Blvd. Jean-Bepmale, panoramic view of the Pyrenees (viewing table). Monument to the Pyrenees' three native field marshals: Foch, Joffre and Gallieni (1951). Also mus. (Gallo-Roman ceramics, Martres-Tolosane pottery, local hist.).
Vicinity ● 16 km NW, *Montmaurin*; fascinating remains of v. big 4c Gallo-Roman villa, excavated on 44-acre site in the *Save* valley (v.a.); also mus. housing the finds; a scenic road (D 9ᴰ bis) from Montmaurin follows the *Save* gorges; important prehistoric finds have been made in its rocky caves.

St. Geniez-d'Olt
12 – Aveyron   36 – D 2
The old houses on banks of R. *Lot*, spanned by 18c bridge, make a colourful picture, under a sheer cliff (terrace, fine view). 14c church of the Pères (or Penitents) is reminder of fmr. Augustinian convent, whose 17c buildings now house town hall (inside, beautiful triptych, the Adoration of the Magi, 16c). In 18c

Lancone. Return to *St. Florent* via *Rapale* and *Santo-Pietro-di-Tenda*: unusual church in reddish stones; 800 m. from it, remains of 13c Romanesque San Pietro; its caricature-like sculptures are worth a detour.

St. Florent-le-Vieil
49 – Maine-et-Loire   16 – D 2
Picturesque village with houses of schist, on hill overlooking R. *Loire*; from the esplanade, panorama over the valley. In a chapel of the church, white marble tomb by David d'Angers of Marquis de Bonchamps, one of the leaders of Vendée's royalist uprising (mortally wounded, 1793). Mus. of local and Loire hist. in fmr. chapel of the Sacré-Coeur, early 17c (relics of the Vendéen wars).
Vicinity ● 6 km W, Ch. de la **Bourgonnière***. From St. Florent-le-Vieil to *Montjean-sur-Loire*, 15 km to E, the road follows the Loire embankment; 9 km farther E, the *Anjou*

Corniche from *Chalonnes-sur-Loire* to *Rochefort-sur-Loire* offers some v. good views over the river.

St. Flour
15 – Cantal   31 – A 3
Built on basalt plateau more than 100 m. above the Ander, this tranquil little city has an imposing cath. in 14–15c Goth. style; inside, unusual 15c 'Bon Dieu Noir'. Old houses, notably in Rue du Thuile and Rue Marchande (No. 15, Hôtel Brisson, 15–16c; No. 31, Ren. Governor's Residence). The fmr. episcopal palace houses the Haute-Auvergne Mus. (v.a. Mon.–Fri.) and the fmr. Hôtel des Consuls has the A-Douët Mus. (v.a. May 1–Oct. 15): furniture, paintings, Limousin enamel, etc. From Calvary Hill, to N, wide view.
Vicinity ● 2 km SE, Plateau de la Chaumette, fine view over St. Flour; follow the N 9 and D 4, to SE, to *Ruynes*, then forest road to

parish church, tomb of Monseigneur de Frayssinous, prelate, university chief and Government Minister (d. 1842), adorned with large bas-relief by David d'Angers. *Vicinity* ● To S, *Causse de Séverac*. ● To N, *Massif de l'Aubrac* (see **Marvejols*** and **Aubrac***).

St. Genis-des-Fontaines
66 – Pyrénées-Orientales 43 – D 3
The lintel of the church door is considered one of the best achievements of figurative Romanesque sculpture (circa 1020); it depicts Christ in Majesty, surrounded by Apostles. *Vicinity* ● 4.5 km E, St. André-de-Sorède, early-12c Romanesque Benedictine church; the portal has early-11c sculpted lintel. ● 3 km NW, *Brouilla*, 12c Romanesque church with trefoil choir. ● 9 km SE, via Sorède, remains of Ch. d'Ultera (571 m., fine view).

St. Georges-de-Commiers
38 – Isère 32 – B 3
Château with 14c tower. On a height, Romanesque chapel of Notre Dame-des-Autels (crypt) and remains of a priory. *Vicinity* ● To S, *Notre Dame-de-Commiers* (mid-16c church), overlooking causeway of same name which is part of vast hydro-electric complex (Champ and St. Georges-de-Commiers plants, Monteynard dam), belvedere; at *La-Motte-St.-Martin* take the D 116, which rises steeply to run along ledge above the *Drac* gorges, 250 m up, (at the end, *Avignonet dam and hydro-electric station*); road leads to *Marcieu* (extensive panorama from Mt. Seneppi, 1,772 m.) and *Mayres*; then it climbs N side of the Jonche valley and reaches **La Mure***.

St. Germain-de-Livet (Château)
14 – Calvados 10 – C 1
One of the most graceful châteaux of the *Pays d'Auge*. Its 15–16c dressing of white stone and brick, its tower in chequer-board pattern of pink brick and its glazed tiles make up a highly original picture (v.a., cl. Tues.). Inside, Guard Room and dining room with enormous chimney-places flanked by a turret. Traces of murals.

St. Germain-en-Laye
78 – Yvelines 11 – C 1
The château, one of the main royal residences, dates largely from the Ren.; it was restored under Napoleon III. The 14c Charles V keep and admirable Ste. Chapelle erected by St. Louis, one of the marvels of 13c Goth. art, are all that remain of previous building. The château houses Mus. des Antiquités Nationales (cl. Tues.); recently renovated, it has – excellently displayed – some

exceptional collections from prehist. to late Middle Ages. ● 18c church, Place Général de Gaulle. Municipal mus. Priory mus. (symbolist and Nabi art: Gauguin, Sérusier, Bonnard, Vuillard), in fmr. 17c home of the painter Maurice Denis, a leading member of the Nabi movement (cl. Mon. and Tues.). In the Quartier de Gramont, Général Leclerc mus. 18c mansions (Hôtel Lauzun, 1 Place André Malraux, Hôtel de Maintenon, 23 Rue du Vieil-Abreuvoir). Le Nôtre's famous terrace at St. Germain, 2,400 m. long, offers immense panorama over Seine valley. *Vicinity* ● To N stretches the *St. Germain Forest* (nearly 14 sq. miles), with many pleasant walks: Croix de Noailles, 18c; Ch. du Val (n.v.a.). Croix St. Simon, Mare aux Canards, Pavillon de la Muette, Grille Royale, Croix Pucelle, Les Lodges (Légion d'Honneur educational establishment). ● To NE, Ch. de **Maisons-Laffitte***, Conflans-Ste. Honorine (Mus. de la Batellerie – water transport), **Poissy*** and banks of *Seine*, all worth visiting.

St. Germain-Lembron
63 – Puy-de-Dôme 31 – A 2
This large township is a good base for excursions. *Vicinity* ● 5 km NE, Nonette: Romanesque and Goth. church (archaic portal), sizeable ruins of castle, one of most powerful in the Auvergne; huge panorama. ● 6 km NW, Ch. de Villeneuve-Lembron, early-16c Ren. (v.a., cl. Tues. in summer); inside, Ren. panelling and v. unusual late-15c allegorical and satiric decorative paintings, notably in N gallery of the inner courtyard, in the 'Shepherdess's Room' and on vaulting in the stables. ● 12 km SW, *Ardes-sur-Couze*, at mouth of pretty *Rentières* valley, upper valley of the *Couze* (scattered with enormous blocks of basalt). ● 9 km S, *Lempdes* (Romanesque church) and the *Alagnon Gorges*, see **Bleste***; 9 km E, **Auzon***.

St. Germer-de-Fly
60 – Oise 5 – B 3
Of abbey founded in 7c, all that remains are 14c fortified gate, 15c entrance building and pure Goth. mid-12c abbey church, the most notable religious edifice in Normandy's Bray reg.; the choir, 14 m. long, is both harmonious and imposing; a vaulted corridor links church to an elegant Ste. Chapelle, built in 13c on model of the famous one in Paris.

St. Gervais-les-Bains-Le-Fayet
74 – Haute-Savoie 32 – D 1
Twin resorts: one on the plain, *Le*

Fayet, spa; the other, *St. Gervais*, a holiday resort and winter sports centre. *Le Fayet* consists mainly of hotels and villas; the spa is set in enormous grounds (79 acres), with magnificent pines (also Bonnant torrent, Cascade des Bains and Cascade de Crépin); Notre Dame-des-Alpes is an interesting church in modern Savoyard style (1938). *St. Gervais-les-Bains* has church with fine period furniture of Italian style; excursions to Pont du Diable (Devil's Bridge) and hamlet of Les Pratz (18c chapel); remains of Ch. de la Comtesse. *Vicinity* ● *Mont Blanc* tramway (cog-rail) to the *Bionnassay Glacier*, passing across magnificent scenery. The Voza pass (1,654 m.), and ski-lift to the Prarion (1,860 m., see **Chamonix***). ● Mt. d'Arbois cable-car service, in two stages; upper station at 1,827 m., huge panorama. ● *St. Nicolas-de-Véroce*, 9 km to S, on very beautiful D 43; in church, rich collection of ecclesiastical regalia (apply at presbytery). ● Montjoie valley; 9 km to S on D 902, *Les Contamines-Montjoie* (1,200 m.), summer and winter sports resort; the road continues as far as the modern chapel of Notre Dame-de-la-Gorge, built in Savoyard baroque style, at 1,210 m.

St. Gildas-de-Rhuys
56 – Morbihan 16 – A 2
The church, fmr. Romanesque abbey church rebuilt in 18c, still has large parts dating from 11c; int. paved with tombstones, 11–18c; noteworthy 12c capitals; rich church treasure in sacristy (apply at presbytery). On S side, buildings belonging to former 18c abbey, with cloister. *Vicinity* ● 1 km W, Point of Grand-Mont (magnificent panorama). ● 6 km NE, *Sarzeau*; 4 km to SE, amazing ruins of the *Ch. de Suscinio* 13–15c. ● At tip of peninsula and mouth of the Gulf of **Morbihan***, *Port-Navalo*, harbour, beach between the headlands of Port-Navalo (lighthouse) and Ormilédec; superb view.

St. Gilles-du-Gard
30 – Gard 43 – C 1
The three sculpted portals of late-12c fmr. abbey church of St. Gilles, devoted to the life of Christ, form one of the masterpieces of Romanesque sculpture; the central portal, whose tympanum depicts Christ in Majesty surrounded by symbols of the four Evangelists, is particularly noteworthy; the crypt, an underground church in itself, has fine ribbed vaulting, (mid-12c and amongst the oldest in France). 'St. Gilles' Screw', spiral staircase in N belfry is unusual example of special

St. Gilles-du-Gard: *a masterpiece of Romanesque art, the abbey church's façade has three portals, framed by statues of the 12 Apostles and adorned with sculptures devoted to the Life of Christ.*

type of stone cutting. Archaeology mus. in unusual Romanesque house (lapidary and bird collections).
Vicinity ● 4.5 km N, on *Bellegarde* road, the Pichegru pumping station, one of the largest in Europe and key feature of the hydraulic installations in the *Rhône* valley.

St. Guénolé
29S – Finistère   15 – B 1
Large fishing village on rocky coast in midst of wild heathland.
Vicinity ● 2 km S, chapel of Notre Dame-de-la-Joie, 16c, with calvary (Breton Pardon, Aug. 15). ● 2 km NE, mus. of Finistère's prehist. ● 2.5 km E, *Penmarc'h*, unusual church of St. Nonna, Goth. Flamboyant; on the *Pointe de Penmarc'h*, very rocky and surrounded by reefs, the *Eckmühl Lighthouse* (65 m., v.a., superb panorama). 15c chapel of St. Pierre, small harbour; 5 km to SE of Penmarc'h, *Le Guilvinec*, lobster fishing village; boats return daily between 15 and 17 hrs.

St. Guilhem-le-Désert
34 – Hérault   43 – A 1
Ensconced in the Verdus gorges between two sheer escarpments, crowned by ruins of a castle, the village consists of two parallel streets linked by narrow vaulted passageways. The abbey church is all that remains of large abbey of St. Guilhem-le-Désert; the most characteristic part is, outside, the Romanesque apse framed by two apsidial chapels with 18 arched niches; the 11c nave is notably severe in design; remains of rare 12c sculpture.
Vicinity ● To W, the R. Verdus flows through the grandiose corrie of the Infernet, surrounded by

sharp cliffs of various colours. ● To S, the *Grottes de Clamouse* (v.a.), with v. varied concretions. ● To N, towards *Causse-de-la-Selle*, the *Hérault* gorges (fantastically-shaped limestone escarpments); via *St. Jean-de-Buèges*, the Buèges gorges.

St. Hippolyte
25 – Doubs   20 – D 3
In v. beautiful setting at confluence of the *Doubs* and the *Dessoubre*, below wooded escarpments. A summer holiday centre (trout fishing), the little town has managed to conserve its original character.
Vicinity ● To N, the *Doubs* valley, towards **Montbéliard***, forms a gorge, dominated by impressive

rocky escarpments. ● To SE, the *Goumois* Corniche, v. picturesque frontier route (see **Maîche***).
● To SW, *Dessoubre* valley, one of the most beautiful in the Jura (see Cirque de **Consolation***).

St. Jean-Cap-Ferrat
06 – Alpes-Maritimes   45 – B 1
Originally a small fishing village, now large residential area and seaside resort on E coast of peninsula formed by Cap Ferrat and partly occupied by magnificent private properties. The zoo and exotic garden are worth a visit. The Ile-de-France town mus., in fmr. Rothschild villa (cl. Mon. and in Nov.), overlooks superb gardens ornamented with fountain basins,

St. Guilhem-le-Désert: *this charming village, at the confluence of the Verdus and the Hérault, has a famed 11c abbey church.*

statues, pavilions, etc. (giant cacti); its exhibits are as rich as they are varied: primitives, 17–18c furniture (charming Salon des Singes – literally, Monkey Room), art from Far East, drawings and pen-and-wash drawings by Fragonard, Impressionist paintings, etc.
Vicinity ● 1.5 km N, *Beaulieu-sur-Mer*: summer and winter resort (big sailing centre). On Fourmis cove, Kérylos Villa (v.a., cl. Mon. and in Nov.): reconstruction, carried out at beginning of the century by archaeologist Théodore Reinach, of sumptuous villa from Ancient Greece. To E, coast road via Eze-sur-Mer, whence a minor road climbs to **Eze-Village***, and, still following corniche above the coast, to **La Turbie*** and **Monaco***.

St. Jean-d'Angély
17 – Charente-Maritime   23 – A 3
The old town still has its little squares and winding streets lined with 15–16c timbered houses and 17–18c mansions. The Tour de l'Horloge (Clock Tower), fmr. 14c belfry. Pilori Fountain, Ren. Old abbey; the monumental 18c façade of the abbey church, called 'Les Tours' (The Towers), was left unfinished. Interesting mus.: archaeology; exhibits from the Black and Yellow Crusades.
Vicinity ● 9 km SW, *Fenioux*, church in Saintonge reg. version of Romanesque, with open belfry and sculpted W façade; notable 12c Romanesque Lantern of the Dead; 2 km to SW: Biracq Tower, reg. folklore mus. ● 8 km NW, *Landes*, Romanesque church with 13c murals.

St. Jean-de-Luz
64 – Pyrénées-Atlantiques 40 – B 1
The port is v. lively, especially when the fishing boats return. Town centre is formed by the *Nivelle* quays, the Maison de l'Infante (red brick framed with white stone), the Place Louis XIV (site of the mid-17c town hall), and the Ch. Loho-biague, or Maison de Louis XIV (1635), flanked by turrets. 15–17c church of St. Jean-Baptiste, where Louis XIV married the Infanta Maria-Theresa, has a typically Basque int.: superb monumental sculpted retable in the choir. Blvd. de la Plage (casino) skirts the graceful curve of the bay.
Vicinity ● *Ciboure*: old town, typically Basque, a continuation of St. Jean-de-Luz on l. bank of R. *Nivelle*; many old houses and picturesque streets; 16–17c church with unusual octagonal belfry; recommended excursion to Pointe de Socoa, 17c fort (sailing club). ● 2 km W, Bordagain, chapel and observatory tower; magnificent

panorama. ● 7 km SE, *Ascain*: typical Basque church; recommended excursion to *La Rhune* (900 m.), either up footpaths (3 hr. climb) or taking rack railway from *Col de St. Ignace*, 2 km from Ascain; from the pass, the road (D 4) drops down to *Sare*, one of the villages most characteristic of the Basque region: 5.5 km to S, the grottoes of Sare.

St. Jean-de-Maurienne
73 – Savoie   32 – C 2
Old town, historic capital of the Maurienne area. 11 and 15c cath. of St. Jean-Baptiste; in the choir, unusual, v. elaborate alabaster ciborium (15c); 82 magnificent late-15c carved stalls. The original 6c church has been uncovered beneath Goth. Flamboyant cloister.
Vicinity ● Route du *Mont-Cenis*: the *Arc* valley via **St-Michel-de-Maurienne***, *Modane* internatnl. station, dominated to N by Fort de Sappey (1,723 m., panorama); accompanied cars can go by moto-rail through the *Fréjus Tunnel* between *Modane* and *Bardonnechia*. The upper Maurienne, via *Avrieux*; *Termignon* (Italian style decoration and 17c retables in the church); *Lanslebourg-Mont-Cenis*, 1,397 m., winter sports resort twinned with *Lanslevillard*, where 15c St. Sébastien chapel (key at presbytery) is worth a visit: mid-15c folk murals of impressive realism; in the parish church, early-16c monumental retable. From *Lanslebourg*, the road climbs in hairpin bends to the *Mont-Cenis Pass* (2,088 m.); new *hospice* (1967), dam (1963–67) and 1,650-acre *lake of Mont-Cenis*;

Franco-Italian frontier, in direction of *Suse*.

St. Jean-de-Monts
85 – Vendée   22 – B 1
The Grande Plage (beach) is linked to the Demoiselles Beach, to SE, by a superb embankment, 2 km long and 70 m. wide – an impressive seafront, lined with modern apartment blocks.
Vicinity ● The 'Vendéen corniche', to SE, dominates the beaches of *Sion* and *Croix-de-Vie*, fishing village on the Vie estuary, below schistous cliffs. ● To NW, coast road towards *Notre Dame-de-Monts*, *La Barre-de-Monts* and *Fromentine* (regular crossings to **Noirmoutier***).

St. Jean-du-Doigt
29N – Finistère   8 – C 1
Typically Breton village, 700 m. from the sea. The parish *enclos* has a Triumphal Gate and beautiful Ren. fountain with sculpted high relief. Mid-16c funerary chapel in Goth. Flamboyant style; very rich church treasure includes several reliquaries, among them supposed index finger of St. John the Baptist (Breton Pardon, June 23 and 24).
Vicinity ● To NW, via *Plougasnou* (16c church) and *Primel-Trégastel*, in superb setting, the Primel heath, pushing its magnificent reddish rocks in a spur out into the sea.

St. Jean-Pied-de-Port
64 – Pyrénées-Atlantiques 40 – C 2
Fmr. stronghold, one of the most picturesque Basque towns on R.

St. Jean-de-Luz: *fishing boats and yachts moored side by side in the port, at the foot of old Basque houses.*

Nive. 15 and 17c walls ring the old quarter, entered by three gates, the Porte de France, Porte de Navarre and Porte St. Jacques, linked by the Rue de la Citadelle which is lined by 16–17c houses in red sandstone (unusual 'bishops' prison'); up series of hairpin bends, road culminates at the 17c citadel, redesigned by Vauban. Church of Notre Dame-du-Pont, 18c, also in red sandstone, has a 16c portal. On other bank of the Nive is the 17c 'new quarter', likewise surrounded by ramparts; the Rue d'Espagne (many old houses) cuts across it and, continuing over the old bridge (view of the old houses above the river), prolongs the Rue de la Citadelle. Small mus. of Basque pelota in the old town hall.
Vicinity ● 8 km SE, *upper valley of the Nive*: the road mounts a savage gorge as far as Estérençuby. ● Passing through *St. Jean-le-Vieux* and *Mendive*, you get to the *Vallée du Laurhibar*, the Burdin-Curutcheta Pass (1,300 m., wide panorama), chalets and Iraty forest, with typical Pyreneen flora and fauna. ● 11 km NW, *St. Étienne-de-Baïgorry*: to S, the road again climbs *Valley of the Nive* to *Les Aldudes*, where Basque traditions are still very much in evidence; from *Les Aldudes* (367 m.), the road continues into Spain.

St. Junien
87 – Haute-Vienne 29 – D 1
The collegiate church, fine 11–12c edifice built in the Limousin Romanesque style, contains tomb of St. Junien, a masterpiece of 12c

Limousin sculpture. 14c house. 15c chapel of Notre Dame-du-Pont, delicately sculpted.
Vicinity ● To NW, banks of R. *Glane* and its picturesque rocks have often inspired artists (including a site Corot painted). ● To E, the D 32 climbs up R. *Vienne* valley towards *St. Victurnien* (12 and 14c church) and *Aixe-sur-Vienne*, whose colourful exhibitions take place every seven years (next ones in 1988); 15c fortified Romanesque church.

St. Laurent-en-Grandvaux
39 – Jura 26 – B 2
Superbly situated, on a plateau surrounded by soaring peaks.
Vicinity ● 6.5 km SW, *Lac de l'Abbaye*; Grandvaux Abbey, mid-17c church. ● 9 km NW, *Cascades du Hérisson* (see Lake of **Châlain***).

St. Léonard-de-Noblat
87 – Haute-Vienne 30 – A 1
Old town overlooking R. *Vienne*. 11–12c Romanesque church of St. Léonard has a superb Limousin-style belfry; inside, curious baptismal chapel of the Holy Sepulchre, in rotunda form, surmounted by a cupola; above the high altar, a cage with bars contains the relics of St. Léonard, patron saint of prisoners. 13, 15 and 16c houses around the church.
Vicinity ● To SE, *Maude valley* and *Mont Larron dam* (see **Eymoutiers***); very picturesque site at confluence of the *Vienne* and R. *Maulde*; remains of 12–13c Artige abbey.

St. Leu-d'Esserent
60 – Oise 11 – C 1
The church (magnificent Romanesque stone nave) built on cliff overlooking R. *Oise*, has a large Goth. choir; it is one of most notable examples of evolution of religious architecture in 12–13c; a fortified door leads to the priory, whose 12c cloister (of which only two galleries survive) affords a beautiful view of the church; vast panorama from the terrace over the *Oise* valley; ribvaulted underground room leads into several other rooms and subterranean galleries (v.a., p.m.).

St. Lizier
09 – Ariège 41 – D 3
Late-11c Romanesque fmr. cath., dominated by octagonal brick belfry in 14c Toulouse style, has rare Romanesque frescos and a charming 12 and 15c two-storey cloisters (with interlaced or historiated capitals). In fmr. episcopal palace (now a psychiatric hospital), the episcopal chapel of Ste. Marie-de-la-Sède; int. has handsome 17c panelling. Part of the Roman wall survives.
Vicinity ● 2 km S, *St. Girons*; church with Romanesque façade and crenellated wall-belfry. ● 2 km E, Montjoie: 14c fortified village; the rectangular outer wall is flanked by gates and towers; the church, too, has a fortified façade; 6 km to NE, Montesquieu-Avantès: Tuc d'Audoubert and Trois-Frères grottoes, where important prehist. discoveries have been made (visits restricted to specialists). ● Excursions recommended: to S, **Seix*** and the *Salat* and Ustou valleys; to SE, *Oust* and the *Garbet* valley as far as **Aulus-les-Bains***; to SW, the *upper valley of the Lez* and the Bethmale valley, via Audressein.

St. Lô
50 – Manche 10 – A 1
Some 80 per cent of the town was destroyed in 1944. 15–16c cath. of Notre Dame still has, on its l. side, unusual ext. sculpted pulpit. In the town hall, mus. with noteworthy late-16c tapestries, 19c paintings. Large stud farm (v.a. p.m.; horse displays, Sat. a.m. in summer). 2 km away, France-USA Memorial Hospital (1956), monumental ext. mosaic by Fernand Léger.
Vicinity ● 9 km SW, Ch. de *Canisy*, in Louis XIII style, at side of a lake (n.v.a.). ● 10 km S, *Condé-sur-Vire*, Europe's largest dairy co-operative (v.a. by arrangement); 3 km farther on, intriguing *Rocks of Ham*, a magnificent escarpment rising 80 m. above *Vire* valley, fine views. ● 13.5 km SE, *Torigni-sur-Vire*,

St. Loup-de-Naud: *squat and powerful, the old priory church has a magnificent 12c carved portal, framed by pillar-statues.*

St. Malo: *very badly damaged during the war, now restored. From the imposing, reconstructed ramparts of the walled town, you get a wonderful view of the Rance estuary.*

beautiful 16–17c château (now town hall) and two interesting churches.

St. Loup-de-Naud
77 – Seine-et-Marne   12 – A 2
The church, one of oldest in Ile-de-France (late 11c), has a v. fine carved portal (circa 1167–1170) framed by pillar-statues; the tympanum depicts Christ in Glory, surrounded by Evangelists; inside, note the progression from Romanesque to early Goth. style between the late-11c choir and the entrance to the nave, whose first two 12c bays have intersecting rib vaulting.

St. Maixent-l'École
79 – Deux-Sèvres   23 – B 2
Church of St. Maixent, fmr. cath., wrecked in 16c, was rebuilt in late 17c in Goth. Flamboyant style, but still has several parts dating from 11 and 13c. The 11c crypt has tombs of St. Maixent and St. Léger, 11c. A second, 17c crypt lies under neighbouring church of St. Léger. To r., 17c fmr. abbey (barracks). Old houses. 18c town gate and town hall.
Vicinity ● 11 km SE, *La Mothe-St.-Héray*, 15c church, remains (orangery) of fmr. 16–17c château; house called 'Maison des Rosières' (Innocent Maidens); Festival of the Rosières, second Mon. in Sept. ● 26 km E, *Lusignan*, 12c Romanesque church (15c porch); castle ruins evoke memory of the fairy Mélusine, legendary ancestress of the Lusignan family.

● 22 km NE, *Sanxay: Roman ruins* (40 acres), comprising remains of temple, a theatre, baths, etc. ● 19.5 km W, through *Breloux-la-Crèche* and *Échiré*, remains of 13c *Ch. du Couldray-Salbart*, above the *Sèvre Niortaise.*

St. Malo
35 – Ille-et-Villaine   9 – C 2
St. Malo, *St. Servan, Paramé* and *Rothéneuf* form one large commune. Rebuilt exactly as it was before its destruction in 1944, St. Malo's walled town has granite houses in 17–18c style, surrounded by ramparts. The imposing 15c castle has four corner towers and a projection flanked by two round towers, the Générale and the Quiquengrogne; they expand two earlier structures, the Little Keep (1393) and the Large Keep (1424), which houses mus. of the town's hist. (mementoes of illustrious natives of St. Malo: 16c explorer Jacques Cartier and the writer Chateaubriand). Excellent walk round top of ramparts with superb views of the sea, coast and mouth of the *Rance*. Inside the walled town, the cath. escaped damage; its exterior is Classical and Ren.; interior has Romanesque nave and Goth. choir flanked by side-aisles and 14–15c chapels; notable group of stained-glass windows by painter Le Moal (1972–1974).
Vicinity ● To S. *St. Servan*, Sablons cove, framed by the fortified Points of Le Naye and the Cité; the vast underground defence complex installed by the Germans in the Cité

peninsula between 1942 and 1944 is no longer open to the public; splendid views from the Aleth corniche. The 14c Solidor Tower, commanding mouth of the *Rance* estuary, houses Cape Horn mus.; below it, the Solidor harbour and 18–19c church of Ste. Croix. ● To E, *Paramé* stretches along broad beach, lined by embankment forming 1.5 km esplanade. *Rothéneuf*, seaside resort (rocks carved at beginning of the century by the Abbé Fouré; marine aquarium, v.a.). ● Excursions on foot: 18c Natnl. Fort on a small island, accessible at low tide, as are the islands of Grand-Bé (Chateaubriand's tomb) and Petit-Bé; 4 km to NW, by boat, the *Isle of Cézembre*, craggy and wild, has several traces of fortifications by Vauban and a large water sports centre (sailing school).

St. Martin-aux-Bois
60 – Oise   5 – D 3
Imposing 13c abbey church, entered through fortified gate of the old abbey. One of the most interesting churches in Ile-de-France; inside, the nave, almost as high (27 m.) as it is long (31 m.), is a veritable wall of light thanks to stained glass set in the elegant sweep of the apse; the choir has fine carved stalls.
Vicinity ● 5 km NW, *Maignelay Montigny* has an interesting 16c church with a polygonal vaulted porch with three arcades and Goth. Flamboyant portal; inside, unusual wooden Flemish retable, 16c, on the Passion.

St. Martin-de-Boscherville
See Abbeys (Norman)*   5 – A 3

St. Martin-de-Londres
34 – Hérault   43 – B 1
The enclosure of fmr. priory, within a ring of old houses flanked by two fortified gates, comprises an unusual early-12c Romanesque church of trefoil design.
Vicinity ● 6 km NW, *Arcs Ravine*, one of the most impressive sights in the Cévennes but difficult to get to (footpaths *must* be followed).
● 9.5 km SE, *Pic St. Loup*, 663 m., magnificent panorama.

St. Martin-du-Canigou (Abbey)
66 – Pyrénées-Orientales 43 – C 3
Situated 1,095 m. up on a rock surrounded by precipices, at foot of the **Canigou***, the abbey – founded in 1007 – was extensively restored at turn of the century (v.a.). It has an 11c upper church dedicated to St. Martin, and a crypt, Notre Dame-la-Souterraine. The (reconstructed) cloister has early-11c Romanesque capitals. Modern monastic buildings. Excursions (about 1 hr.) to St. Martin cascade.

St. Martin-Vésubie
06 – Alpes-Maritimes   39 – A 3
Capital of the 'Suisse Niçoise' (Nice's Switzerland), it has green valleys and vertiginous mountains (there are two climbing schools at Boréon and Valdeblore). Two interesting churches: that of the Assumption, richly decorated with panelling and late-17c statues, and chapel of the Pénitents Blancs, from

same period. Narrow, extremely steep Rue Droite (Rue du Dr. Cagnoli) still has central open drain.
Vicinity ● 13 km NE, *Madone de Fenestre*: country sanctuary in grandiose setting; behind the mountain shelter, a small road leads (one hr.'s. climb) to the Lake of Fenestre (2,226 m.), then to the Fenestre pass (2,474 m.) – from where, in clear weather, the view stretches as far as Mt. Cervin and Monte Rosa. ● 8 km N, *Le Boréon* (1,460 m.); high-altitude resort, good base for excursions through the 'Suisse Niçoise'; above the Boréon falls (35 m.), a reservoir-lake.

St. Maximin-la-Ste. Baume
83 – Var   44 – B 1
The abbey, in 13–15c northern Goth. style, has an enormous nave with neither ambulatory nor transept; the vaulting has fine historiated key-stones; imposing organ-chest (1773); numerous works of art inc. a retable of the Passion (1520); fine marble-work at end of apse frames three paintings and is surmounted by allegorical statues; the high altar, choir-screen and stalls are all 17c; carved pulpit is 18c; a 5c Paleo-Christian rectangular crypt, with barrel vaulting, contains four 4 and 5c sarcophagi, supposedly those of St. Maximin, Ste. Madeleine, Ste. Marcelle and Ste. Suzanne. ● In 14–18c fmr. royal convent, modern Commercial College; 15c cloister and rib-vaulted Goth. rooms.
Vicinity ● 22 km SW, via *Nans-les-Pins*, **Ste. Baume***.

St. Michel
02 – Aisne   6 – C 2
Enormous church with Ren. nave, Goth. transept and choir, and 18c façade, one of the most beautiful religious buildings in NE of France; the Classical cloister is surrounded by stone and brick buildings of fmr. early-18c abbey.
Vicinity ● The forest (nearly 12 sq. miles) has several trout rivers and abundant game.

St. Michel-de-Cuxa
66 – Pyrénées-Orientales 43 – C 3
Large Benedictine abbey (v.a.). The abbey church of St. Michel, dating largely from 10c, has somewhat excessive arches 'borrowed' from Arabic art; the square belfry is of the Lombard type. At centre of the early-11c circular crypt, the chapel of Notre Dame-de-la-Crèche. Two galleries of the demolished cloister have been reconstructed, with 12c small columns and capitals in pink marble. Fine carved Romanesque door.
Vicinity ● 3 km N, *Prades*, interesting Goth. church, with Lombard Romanesque belfry; inside, choir has a monumental 17c wooden retable, carved and gilded, with more than 40 statues. 7 km to NW, *Molitg-les-Bains*, renowned spa in picturesque Castillane gorge; baths and Grand Hotel in beautiful 37-acre grounds, lake with beach, tennis, fishing, etc. ● 13 km NE, *Vinça*: its old quarter, with narrow streets, has 18c church whose int. is a veritable museum of religious art; carved gilt retable in chapel of the

St. Martin-du-Canigou: *superbly situated, the Romanesque abbey has cloisters with early-11c capitals.*

St. Michel-de-Cuxa: *the highly detailed foliage decoration on the capitals, principal ornament of the cloisters in the old abbey.*

At Prades, the Gothic church of St. Pierre, with its beautiful Romanesque belfry.

Holy Sacrament is exuberantly sumptuous. To S, the D 13 follows the *Lentilla* gorges as far as *Valmanya* and its forest (with forest house); very bumpy and sometimes steep, road runs into the D 618 at Xatard pass, from where a picturesque route to *Amélie-les-Bains* (see **Céret***).

St. Michel-de-Frigolet (Abbey)
13 – Bouches-du-Rhône 37 – D 3
Situated in the famous 'montagnette' (small mountain) of Daudet's hunters, the disconcerting 19c neo-Goth. buildings retain some Romanesque parts and the little church of St. Michel from first half of 12c. The present 19c abbey church incorporates beautiful chapel of Notre Dame-du-Bon-Remède, in Provençal Romanesque style, adorned with magnificent 17c panelling framing 14 canvases by Mignard. Hostelry open to travellers (reservations necessary).
Vicinity ● To N, *Barbentane*, 17c château in ochre stone, above succession of terraces in beautiful grounds, 18c int. (v.a.); Romanesque and Goth. church; fmr. stronghold of Les Puget-Barbentane, 15 and 16c; keep; fortified gates. ● To SW, *Boulbon*: remains of château; Romanesque chapel in the cemetery; quaint procession on June 1.

St. Michel-de-Maurienne
73 – Savoie 32 – C 3
In the heart of an impressive hollow in the mountains, the old town has picturesque winding streets, one above the other.
Vicinity ● *Mont-Cenis* road (see **St. Jean-de-Maurienne***). ● Grands

Cols route: to S, the road is v. tortuous up to the Télégraphe pass (Fort du Télégraphe, 1,640 m.), then crosses beautiful pine forests into the lush green *Valloire* basin, summer resort and winter sports centre; 17c church at Valloire has richly decorated int. with retables, paintings and stucco in Italian style; cable-cars from Lake Thimel and La Sétaz (2,250 m.) and from Crêt Rond (2,220 m.): superb panoramas; the *Galibier* tunnel (2,556 m.) goes under the pass (2,593 m.); from the Pas du Galibier (2,645 m.), absolutely superb view over the *Meije* and the *Écrins*; the road descends in hairpin bends to the Col du **Lautaret***; via **Bourg-d'Oisans*** and *Rochetaillée* to the *Glandon* and *Croix-de-Fer* passes, then on to **St. Jean-de-Maurienne***.

St. Michel-l'Observatoire 38 – B 3
04 – Alpes-de-Haute-Provence
Two churches are worth a visit: the upper church of St. Michel, 12c, and the old Benedictine priory church of St. Paul, 12–13c, with Romanesque nave and cupola and a mid-16c apse; inside, 9c altar table.
Vicinity ● 2.5 km N, at 650 m. alt., National Astrophysical Observatory of Haute Provence (v.a. Wed. 15.00 hrs., and 1st Sun. of month, from Apr. to Sept., at 09.30).

St. Michel-Mont-Mercure
85 – Vendée 22 – D 1
One of the highest parts of the Gâtine region (286 m.). Late-19c church; at top of a tower, colossal copper statue of St. Michael (vast panorama).
Vicinity ● 2 km E, *La Flocellière*;

12 and 15–16c church, ruins of old château next to small mid-19c castle in 'troubadour' style; superb 13c keep (15c staircase). ● 5.5 km SW, *Le Boupère* priory church of St. Pierre, fortified, 13–15c.

St. Mihiel
55 – Meuse 13 – A 1
13c church of St. Mihiel, fmr. abbey church, 17c, has a Romanesque door; in the imposing 17–18c abbey, adjoining S side, are the law courts, the lycée and the library. Fine town hall with Louis XVI façade. St. Étienne, late 15c, houses celebrated *Holy Sepulchre* by Ligier Richier, a masterpiece of French sculpture (1540). Interesting Ren.-Goth. and Ren. houses.
Vicinity ● To N, unusual St. Mihiel cliffs (seven limestone blocks more than 20 m. high); panorama. ● *Meuse* valley to S, via *Sampigny* and *Lérouville* as far as **Commercy***.

St. Nazaire
44 – Loire-Atlantique 16 – B 2
Hardly anything remains of the old town, destroyed in 1943. The St. Nazaire basin is dominated by the formidable concrete submarine base built by the Germans. From the terrace, vast panorama. Beaches.
Vicinity ● To N, the **Grande-Brière***. ● The 'Côte d'Amour' route leads, via the D 292, to *St. Marc* (beach), the *Pointe de Chemoulin* and Ste. Marguerite, *Pornichet* (beach) and La Baule-les-Pins, an extension of **La Baule*** in a magnificent pine grove, part of the Bois d'Amour.

St. Nectaire
63 – Puy-de-Dôme   30 – D 2
St. Nectaire-le-Haut, terraced on a
hill, is dominated by the church,
one of the best examples of mid-12c
Auvergne Romanesque art; inside,
notable group of 103 historiated
capitals; in particular, see the six in
the apse, four of which are painted;
rich church treasure: bust of St.
Baudime, late-12c masterpiece of
Limousin plate; statue of Notre
Dame-du-Mont-Cornadore,   12c
Virgin in Majesty and several rare
works of art. St. Nectaire-le-Bas is
a spa in wooded surroundings.
Petrifactive fountain. Dolmen.
Vicinity ● To E, Puy de Mazeyres
(919 m., viewing table, wide panorama); to W, grottoes of the Puy
de Châteauneuf; to SW, the
Granges cascades. ● To NE, *Olloix*,
and the *Monne* gorges. ● Many
megalithic monuments in the
region.

St. Nicolas-de-Port
54 – Meurthe-et-Moselle 13 – C 2
Superb Goth. Flamboyant basilica,
15 and 16c, sculpted central portal;
inside, magnificent nave, 32 m. high
and 97 m. long, crossed by a transept with two bays; 16c stained-
glass windows; 17c stalls. Baptismal
chapel has 16c fonts and Ren.
retable.

St. Omer
62 – Pas-de-Calais   1 – C 2
Basilica of Notre Dame, built
between 13 and 15c (S portal is 12
and 14c), contains numerous
notable works of art: tomb with
very realistic figure of Bishop
Eustache de Croy, 16c; a 13c group
sculpture known as the 'Grand
Dieu de Thérouane'; a *Descente de
Croix* ('The taking down from the
cross'), attributed to Rubens. 13, 15
and 16c church of St. Denis;
remains of church of St. Bertin, 14–
16c. In the Henri Dupuis mus., v.
fine collection of stuffed birds,
European and exotic; also reconstruction of a Flemish kitchen. An
18c mansion houses Sandelin mus.
(cl. Mon. and Tues.): Flemish,
Dutch and French painting from 15
to 18c, ivory, tapestries, medieval
archaeology, 12c plate from Meuse
reg. (famous *Pied de Croix de St.
Bertin*, in gilded bronze and
enamel).
Vicinity ● To NE stretches the maze
of 'watergangs' (take the D209),
fmr. marshland transformed into
gardens, scattered with drainage
channels where the only means of
transport is by boat; the most picturesque one is the Romelaëre. ●
To E, Clairmarais Forest. ● Valley
of the Aa. ● To SE, after *Arques*,
see the lock at *Les Fontinettes*.

St. Papoul
11 – Aude   42 – B 2
Fmr. abbey church of Benedictine
monastery founded in 8c, later a
cath. and now parish church, has a
single wide nave, 13c, ending in a
Romanesque apse (17c mausoleum
of Bishop François de Donnadieu,
with statue and sarcophagus in
white marble); archaic capitals in
the choir; the 14c cloister has twin
historiated capitals; outside, the
Juels (jewels) Tower, 13c. Remains
of 13–14c town wall. Many old
houses.
Vicinity ● 3 km E, Ch. de Ferrais,
superb mid-17c residence (n.v.a.).

St. Paul
06 – Alpes-Maritimes   45 – A 1
One of the best known places on
the Côte d'Azur. Fortified township
on a spur above two small valleys
planted with orange and olive trees,
and with orchards and vineyards.
In the 12 and 13c church, rich
works of art, rich ecclesiastical
treasure in the sacristy. ● 800 m. to
NW, on Les Gardettes hill, Marguerite and Aimé Maeght Foundation (v.a.), notable contemp.
architecture; int. has permanent
display of contemp. works: Braque,
Bonnard, Miró, Bazaine, Tápies,
Ubac, etc.; vast courtyard by Giacometti; in the terraced grounds,
sculptures, mosaics and ceramics by
Giacometti, Miró, Tal Coat,
Chagall, Calder, etc.; contemp. art
exhibitions in the summer.
Vicinity ● Via *La Colle-sur-Loup*
(3.5 km SW), impressive *Gorges du
Loup*.

St. Paul-de-Fenouillet
66 – Pyrénées-Orientales 42 – C 3
This small town is good base for
excursions. Reg. mus.: folk art and
trads., archaeology.
Vicinity ● 15 km NE, *Ch. de Quér-
ibus*: fantastic eagle's-nest fortress,
11–12c, with vast panorama; the
keep has a beautiful Goth. room; in
sight, 10 km to NW, *Ch. de Peyrepertuse*: its grandiose ruins cover
more than 75,000 sq. ft., dominated
by v. powerful keep. Both castles
were among the last strongholds of
Cathar 'heretics' in 13c. ● 17 km W,
above Lapradelles, jagged ruins of
Ch. de Puilaurens, another 13c
Cathar castle, with v. sophisticated
defensive system. ● 9.5 km N, the
Gorges de Galamus; their dazzlingly
white escarpments loom 300 m.

St. Pol-de-Léon: *the cathedral's two spires, in a pure Norman Gothic
style, are well-known landmarks in this part of Brittany.*

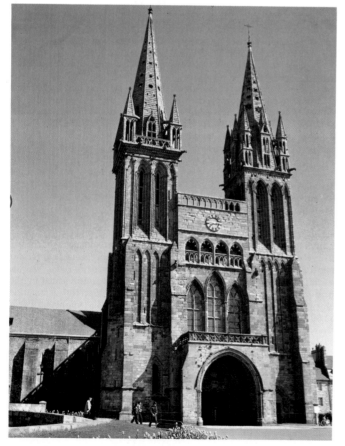

above the corniche road, itself running high above R. Agly (St. Antoine Hermitage, local place of pilgrimage). ● 23 km S, along v. winding and bumpy road, *Sournia*: interesting 14–17c château.

St. Paul-Trois-Châteaux
26 – Drôme 37 – D 2

Late-12c fmr. cath. is one of the most harmonious Romanesque churches in Provence; original decoration of W portal inspired by ancient Greece and Rome; in the apse, 13c mosaic; 17c panelling.
Vicinity ● 3 km SE, *St. Restitut*: village built on edge of limestone plateau; interesting church in Provençal Romanesque style, with 11–12c tower; 300 m. to NW, hexagonal chapel of the Holy Sepulchre, early 16c. ● 8 km E, La Baume-de-Transit: unusual Romanesque church, at one time with a cupola, had 16c nave added; ruins of feudal castle. ● 4 km NW, *Pierrelatte*: large nuclear power station (n.v.a.).

St. Philbert-de-Grand-Lieu
44 – Loire-Atlantique 16 – C 3

9c Carolingian church, one of the most venerable sanctuaries in France; in the crypt, 7c marble sarcophagus of St. Philbert. Prior's lodgings and monastic buildings, 16–17c.
Vicinity ● To N, *Lake of Grand-Lieu*, pretty setting. ● 15 km SW, *Machecoul*, ruins of 14c castle of Gilles de Rais, the legendary 'Bluebeard' (see **Tiffauges***); interesting old houses in the village; from Machecoul, NW to *Bourgneuf-en-Retz* or W to *Bouin*, road crosses the polders (reclaimed land); at *Bourgneuf*, in a 17c house, the Pays de Retz mus.

St. Pierre-sur-Dives
14 – Calvados 10 – C 1

The 12, 13 and 14c church, with lantern-tower at the transept crossing and two towers rising above the façade (one Romanesque, the other Goth.), is a good example of Norman Goth; 13c fmr. chapterhouse on S arm of the transept. Lovely timber-framed covered market, 11–12c, with three halls.

St. Pol-de-Léon
29N – Finistère 8 – C 1

Old episcopal city, famed for its magnificent belfries. Two of them, late-13c stone spires 55 m. high, dominate the cath., a superb edifice in Norman Goth. style; S arm of the transept has a 15c rose window, surmounted by an ext. pulpit.

St. Raphaël: *the dazzling contrast between its pines, clear blue sea and red rocks is a big part of its attraction.*

Inside, in the choir, 69 early-16c carved stalls; 16–17c tombs. The 14–15c Chapelle du Kreisker, where the town council used to meet (now a school chapel), also has a v. fine belfry, 77 m. high, early 15c (extensive view). Old houses in the Grande-Rue.

St. Pons
34 – Hérault 42 – D 1

St. Pons cath., late 12c once-for-tified abbey church, was transformed in 18c by a complete change of its orientation; the primitive façade, on W side, has a Romanesque portal divided into two bays, each with a sculpted tympanum; inside, superb 18c decoration in choir.
Vicinity ● 16 km N, after the Signal de St. Pons (1,033 m., panorama), Saut de Vésoles (falls), impressive site. ● 18 km NE, *Olargues*: picturesque village in a bend of R. Jaur; Goth. bridge. ● 5 km SW, at *Corniou*, Devèze *grotto* (v.a.), varied, unusual concretions.

St. Pourçain-sur-Sioule
03 – Allier 25 – A 3

Church of Ste. Croix, fmr. Benedictine abbey church, built between 11 and 19c. The abbey buildings surrounded Monks' Courtyard; 15c gatehouse and belfry. In the Benedictines' Courtyard, mus. of the vine and wine.
Vicinity ● Walks through some of France's oldest vineyards (pre-Christian era) ● 3.5 km NW, Saulcet: Romanesque church, fine octagonal belfry, 12, 13 and 14c frescos; 3 km to NW, *Verneuil-en-Bourbonnais*: typical Bourbon village, remains of château and

outer wall, 12c Romanesque church with enormous octagonal belfry.

St. Quentin
02 – Aisne 6 – A 2

Late-12 to 15c collegiate church of St. Quentin is a magnificent building of extraordinary size. Town hall, in Goth. Flamboyant style, 15–16c (peal of 37 bells). Antoine Lécuyer mus. (cl. Tues.) has 18c paintings and unique collection of 80 pastel portraits by Quentin de La Tour (18c). Also Italian, Dutch and French paintings and drawings, 17–19c, with 18c pottery and porcelain. Natural science enthusiasts should not miss mus. of entomology (v.a., p.m., days vary) which has one of the most remarkable insect collections in Europe, especially its butterflies (500,000 exhibits). Huge Champs-Elysées Park (30 acres) and Isle lake on R. *Somme*, have been adapted for recreation and sports.
Vicinity ● 12 km N, unusual underground passage for barges at *Riqueval*.

St. Quentin-en-Yvelines
78 – Yvelines 11 – B 2

One of the five 'new towns' of the Ile-de-France; among several examples of contemp. architecture see enormous neo-Classical construction of the 'Arcades du Lac' by Bofill. Fmr. Commanderie of the Templars at La Villedieu has handsome Goth. church, now an arts centre.

St. Raphaël
83 – Var 44 – D 2

Delightful seaside resort at foot of the *Esterel* massif. Commercial and

fishing port, also marina. Interesting Templars' church, in Provençal Romanesque style, early-13c, and mus. of submarine archaeology (collection of ancient amphorae, cl. Sun.).

Vicinity ● The *Esterel* road (or Golden Corniche) is one of the most beautiful routes in France; it hugs the coast (with numerous precipices above the sea); passing through *Boulouris*, the *Dramont* promontory, *Agay* (centre for excursions in the *Esterel* massif), Anthéor, *Le Trayas, La Napoule*; from *Agay* to **Cannes***, the red porphyry rocks and dense forest provide particularly striking scenery. ● 3 km N, *Valescure*, residential health resort in the middle of the pine trees.

St. Rémy-de-Provence
13 – Bouches-du-Rhône   43 – D 1
Typically Provençal little town, encircled by wide promenades. The handsome Hôtel Mistral de Montdragon, mid-16c, houses the

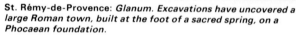

St. Rémy-de-Provence: *Glanum. Excavations have uncovered a large Roman town, built at the foot of a sacred spring, on a Phocaean foundation.*

Adjoining the Municipal Arch, the Gallo-Roman mausoleum is one of the best preserved monuments from the days of antiquity; it has four arcades and a circular colonnade, while its square base is embellished with bas-reliefs of warriors.

Pierre de Brun mus. of the Alpilles: archaeology, folk art. Chapel of Notre Dame-de-Pitié has paintings by Mario Prassinos. A passageway links it to the fmr. Hôtel de Sade, where an archaeological storehouse has been set up to house the finds made at Glanum and at **St. Blaise***. (v.a., June to Sept.).
Vicinity ● 3 km SE, Cardinal Tower, elegant 16c Ren. residence (v.a.); ● 1.5 km S, *Glanum*. Excavations have revealed traces of five successive periods, one on top of the other, shown by different construction techniques and materials. The elegant Maison des Antes, with peristyle and Doric columns, belongs to the Hellenistic town (2c BC). From the first Roman settlement (102 BC) come the baths, swimming pool, the palaestra (gymnasium) and the principal rooms around the baths, the Maison du Capricorn (interesting mosaics) and the small Maison d'Epona. From the second Roman settlement (49 BC–270 AD), the richest in buildings, date the forum (skirted by the long main street) and the temples; v. fine pieces of sculpture have been recovered, as well as remains of the Maison de Sulla (early 1c BC). Beyond the forum, the site narrows into a small valley; here, a Nymphaeum and Gallic shrine from 6c BC, cut into the rock, can be reached by steps in the mountainside. ● 200 m. to W of *Glanum*, the *Antiques* plateau. The Municipal Arch and mausoleum erected to memory of grandsons of Augustus (to whom Nîmes dedicated the Maison Carée) are among the most notable buildings surviving from Roman Gaul (1c BC). To NE of *Glanum*, fmr. St. Paul-de-Mausole priory (now a clinic); late-12c Romanesque church with v. beautiful cloister (v.a.); Van Gogh was a patient at the Maison de Santé, 1889–1890, and did numerous paintings while there.

St. Renan
29 N – Finistère   8 – A 2
Old town above the Aber-Ildut valley.
Vicinity ● 5 km W, Kerloas menhir, Finistère's tallest (12 m.). ● 10 km NW, near *Brélès*, handsome granite Ch. de *Kergroadès*, 17c; superb sculpted dormer windows (v.a. ext. only); a trip round the wild, jagged 'Côte des "Abers"' (lit. 'Coast of the River Mouths'), is highly rec.; go via *Lanildut, Porspoder* (many manor houses and menhirs in area) and *Argenton* where the corniche road rounds the Point of *Landunvez* and reaches the Point of Kersaint; impressive ruins of feudal castle of Trémazan. ● 13 km N, *Plou-*

dalmézeau, church with late-18c spire; 4 km to N, Lampaul-Ploudalmézeau, church with early-17c Ren. belfry-porch.

St. Révérien
58 – Nièvre   19 – A 3
12c church, with three naves and no transept, is one of the most interesting in Nivernais reg.: historiated capitals and carved tombstones.
Vicinity ● The small lakes of *Vaux* and Baye, separated by a dyke, are surrounded by woods, with many pleasant spots; fishing, canoeing and boating.

St. Riquier
80 – Somme   5 – B 1
All that remains of once-famous abbey, one of the most important in the Middle Ages, is 13c church, rebuilt in 16c (Goth. Flamboyant portal and tower, richly ornamented); inside, fine 16c decoration in the choir (grille, stalls, panelling, etc.); the Treasury has a 16c vaulted room, ornamented with frescos (of the Trois Morts and the Trois Vivants – The Three Dead and The Three Living); large church treasure; 17c monastic buildings. Mus. of archaeology and agrarian ethnography. 13 and 15c belfry. Early-18c Hôtel-Dieu (beautiful chapel, grilles and altar retable).

St. Sauveur-en-Puisaye
89 – Yonne   19 – A 2
12–16c church. 17c château flanked by 12c tower. House where writer Colette was born (1873); mus. planned.
Vicinity ● Good base for touring *Puisaye*. ● 11 km W, *St. Fargeau*; castle is vast 13c brick construction (v.a. in season), flanked by six large round towers. interesting inner courtyard, bordered by 17c buildings; the chapel, in one of the towers, has tombs of Le Pelletier family; in the mid-13c church, enlarged in 15 and 16c, interesting works of art; to SE, *Bourdon Reservoir*, 543 acres, water sports, 11 km scenic route round reservoir; at Boutissaint, St. Hubert wildlife park (v.a.). ● 15 km SW, *St. Amand-en-Puisaye*, Ren. château in stone and brick (n.v.a.); 7 km to SSW, picturesque fortified township of St. Vérain, remains of the outer wall and of 12–13c feudal castle. ● 10 km S, *Treigny*, church known as the 'Cathedral of the Puisaye', 15–16c; the Ch. de Ratilly, imposing 13c construction with towers, is now a well-known grès (sandstone) pottery centre (v.a., cl. Sun.); courses for beginners and exhibitions of contemp. art in summer.

● 22 km SE, *Druyes-les-Belles-Fontaines*, 12c feudal castle on top of hill above the village (v.a. Sat., Sun., and public hols., July 1 to mid-Sept.); Romanesque church (fine Romanesque portal); 15c fortified gate and traces of defensive wall; picturesque setting at sources of tiny R. Andryes.

St. Sauveur-le-Vicomte
50 – Manche   3 – D 3
Fmr. château, now an old people's home, still has remains of 12c fortress, notably an enormous keep; it houses mus. devoted to 19c French writer Barbey d'Aurevilly, a native of St. Sauveur (v.a. in summer). The 15–16c church has several fine statues. Fmr. Benedictine abbey, founded in 11c (v.a. with permission), restored in the last century; in the grounds, 18c monastic buildings.
Vicinity ● 14 km NW, *Bricquebec*: the castle (v.a.) forms an impressive architectural ensemble: 14c fortified outer wall, polygonal keep (23 m. high), Clock Tower (small local mus.), 14c rib-vaulted crypt; graceful Ren. Ch. des Galeries, renovated in 17c; 2.5 km to N, in a wooded setting, the Abbey of Notre Dame-de-Grâce, or Trappist monastery of Bricquebec (mid-19c), (Gregorian chanting in French); v.a. to church and reception building); to NW, St. Martin-le-Hébert has an early 17c manor with moat.

St. Sauveur-sur-Tinée
06 – Alpes-Maritimes   39 – A 3
Picturesque village. In 15c church, several interesting works of art.
Vicinity ● To W, extraordinary villages of Roure and *Roubion*, perched high on rocky peaks; at *Roubion*, the chapel of St. Sébastien has colourful early 16c murals. ● To S, *Tinée* gorges, heading towards **Nice***; 4.5 km farther on, a series of hairpin bends leads to village of *Rimpla*, in middle of a ridge between the mountain and a rock, site of the Ste. Madeleine chapel; the view takes in the *Tinée* valley; in the church, three large 18c retables; above the village, fort on the top of a crag.

St. Savin-sur-Gartempe
86 – Vienne   23 – D 2
The Romanesque church, fmr. abbey church, has an exceptional group of 11–12c Romanesque frescos. The most interesting, situated on the barrel vaulting of the nave, 15 m. up, cover an area of nearly 4,500 sq. ft.; they depict the story of Genesis in muted tones (pink and beige); those in the crypt

(the lives of St. Savin and St. Cyprien, and Christ in Majesty) are painted in brighter colours.

Vicinity • The *Gartempe* valley, from St. Savin to Montmorillon, makes a delightful excursion (18 km); the churches of *Antigny* and *Jouhet* have murals; *Montmorillon*, on both banks of the R. *Gartempe*: church of Notre Dame, 12–13c (crypt decorated with rare 12–13c paintings); fmr. Augustinian monastery (small seminary), 18c; within the town wall, fmr. church of St. Laurent, Romanesque (12–13c kitchen) and unusual late-12c octagonal sepulchral chapel.

St. Seine-l'Abbaye
21 – Côte-d'Or   19 – D 2
The church, fmr. Benedictine abbey church, early 13c with 15c façade, is an interesting example of Burgundian Goth.; inside, Ren. screen and carved 18c stalls.

Vicinity • 9 km N, Poncey-sur-l'Ignon, intriguing Manor of Poncey, built in 1944 by the artist Charles Huard, with stones and sculptures obtained from ruined châteaux (v.a. Sat. and Sun., p.m., or by appointment). • 10 km NW, *source of the R. Seine.* • 10.5 km SE, *Suzon valley.*

St. Sulpice-de-Favières
91 – Essonne   11 – C 2
Fine 13–14c Goth. church; interesting apse; damaged carved portal; inside, 12c chapel with relics of St. Sulpice.

Vicinity • 9 km NE, *Arpajon*, 13 and 15c church; timber-framed covered markets, 17c. • 5 km S, *Étrechy*: nearby, Ch. de *Chamarande* (to N), 17c, set in magnificent grounds irrigated by R. Juine (v.a. on request); 17c Ch. du Mesnil-Voisin, at Lardy, to NE (v.a. Sun., cl. in Aug.), and Ch. de *Villeconin* (to NW), with imposing fortified entrance and moat (v.a. in summer on request); the main part of the Henri IV living quarters is dominated by keep of former feudal castle; interesting art collections inside.

St. Thégonnec
29 N – Finistère   8 – C 2
The parish *enclos* has a late-16c Triumphal Gate and notable ossuary chapel, built in late 17c in pure Breton Ren. style and decorated like a shrine; in the crypt, Holy Sepulchre in oak with carved, painted figures, late 17c. Calvary dating from 1610. In the church, pulpit,

St. Savin: *the church and its elegant Gothic spire.* ◄

Its group of Romanesque frescos is outstanding. On the left side of the nave, Noah's Ark. ▲

masterpiece of Breton carving, late 17c; very fine 17–18c panelling.

St. Thibault
21 – Côte-d'Or   19 – C 3
This little Auxois village has a noteworthy church, built in 13c, which houses the relics of St. Thibault; the portal is one of the best examples of Burgundian Goth. sculpture; the tympanum is devoted to the Virgin, surrounded by five large statues: St. Thibault, the Duke Robert II of Burgundy, his wife, son and Bishop Hugues d'Arcy; the late-15c leaves of the doors depict the life of St. Thibault, in 30 carved panels; inside, the nave, rebuilt in the 18c is modest, but the Goth. choir has great elegance; 14c reliquary of St. Thibault, in wood.

St. Tropez
83 – Var   44 – D 2
This old Provençal village, with its narrow streets, has become one of the most fashionable places on the Côte d'Azur. On the far side of the harbour, the Chapelle de l'Annonciade, 16c, houses an excellent mus. of modern art (cl. Tues.): works by Bonnard, Braque, Dufy, Van Dongen, Matisse, Rouault, Maillol etc. On the other side of the jetty, the fishing port; v. beautiful view of the town and the Maures. The citadel (panoramic route) is a sturdy 16–17c hexagonal fort; naval museum in the keep.

Vicinity • 4.5 km E, beach of Les Salins. • 5 km E, *beach of Pampelonne.* • 10.5 km S, *Ramatuelle*: picturesque fortified village, built on a hill; from there you get to *Gassin*, typical Provençal village perched on a craggy peak (from the

belvedere, wide panorama). • 8.5 km W, via *La Foux* and *Cogolin*, to *Grimaud*, rising in tiers at foot of ruins of the Ch. des Grimaldi; 2 km N of *La Foux*, *Port-Grimaud*: modern lakeside city, Mediterranean in style (no cars allowed).

St. Valéry-sur-Somme
80 – Somme   S – B 1
Now a summer resort, it still has parts of its ramparts: 14–15c Porte de Nevers and 12c Porte Guillaume, which leads to fmr. St. Valéry abbey (remains of the church, and 18c monastic building, are private property). Chapel of the sailors, or St. Valéry's Chapel, on a hill 1 km to W, houses the saint's tomb (pilgrimage site).

Vicinity • Rec. trips to the **Baie de Somme***. • On other side of the estuary, *Le Crotoy*: fishing village and seaside resort; from the Butte aux Moulins (lit. Windmill Hill), vast panorama and a good place from which to watch the rising tide. • To NW, **Rue*** and the St. Quentin dunes.

St. Véran
05 – Hautes-Alpes   38 – D 1
Highest parish in Europe (between 1,990 and 2,042 m. alt.), this picturesque village – its houses with wooden balconies and lofts, all facing south – has a 17c church with interesting furniture.

Vicinity • 6 km SE, over a pretty poor road, chapel of Notre Dame-de-Clausis (2,390 m.); Franco-Italian pilgrimage on July 16; excursion recommended in July, when Alpine flora are in bloom.

St. Vincent-sur-Jard
85 – Vendée   22 – C 2
1 km to S, at edge of the beach of Belesbat, is 'La Bicoque' ('The Shack'), Clemenceau's fmr. home, built in the Vendéen style; unchanged since his death, it is surrounded by a garden (v.a., cl. Tues., May to Sept.).
Vicinity ● 3 km W of *Jard-sur-Mer*, former Lieu-Dieu abbey, 12–15c chapel, storerooms and chapterhouse, etc. ● 7 km NE, near Le Bernard, Frébouchère dolmen.

St. Wandrille
76 – Seine-Maritime   4 – D 3
Benedictine abbey, reoccupied by monks in 1931 (v.a.); of the 13–14c abbey church, all that remains is N arm of the transept; the cloister (women not allowed) retains three of its galleries; in its N gallery, monks' wash-room; the church (free access, Gregorian masses daily) is the former tithe barn of Canteloup, moved to this site in 1969 from La Neuville-du-Bosc (Eure). On leaving the abbey, the path alongside the cloister leads to the chapel of St. Saturnin, 10c, in trefoil design.

St. Yrieix-la-Perche
87 – Haute-Vienne   30 – A 2
The collegiate church, known as the 'Moustier', is a noteworthy 12–13c edifice, approached through a mid-12c Romanesque belfry-porch. The church's treasure includes a celebrated 15c 'chef' (head) of St. Yrieix, made of chased silver strips.
Vicinity ● 8 km NW, *Le Chalard*: Romanesque church and remains of 12–13c priory, interesting church treasure. ● 16 km SW, *Ch. de Jumilhac-le-Grand*, late 15c, enlarged in 17c: pepper-pot roofs, crowned with dormer windows, skylights and turrets (v.a. in summer; handsome apartments (inc. 'Spinner's Room', decorated with naïve paintings). ● 11 km E, *Ch. de Coussac-Bonneval*, 12, 14 and 18c; period furniture, objets d'art and fine tapestries (v.a. Thurs. and Sun., p.m.).

Ste. Anne-d'Auray
56 – Morbihan   15 – D 1
One of Brittany's principal pilgrimage centres (Grand Pardon, July 26). The basilica, built in uninspired 19c neo-Ren. style, is covered with votive offerings; the fmr. Carmelite convent surrounds a 17c Classical cloister. Rich church treasure. Gallery of popular religious art (Breton sculptures, pottery). Opposite, on the esplanade, a 'miraculous' fountain, Scala Scanta, and huge memorial to the dead of the 20c wars. To r., Nicolazic Mus. (collection of dolls in Breton costume). Nearby, Champ des Martyrs (where

---

STE. BAUME (La)
83 – Var   44 – B 2
From *Gémenos*, the road enters the *Massif de la Ste. Baume* via the Parc de St. Pons (chapel of St. Martin and remains of Romanesque abbey). Through the Espigoulier pass (727 m., big view over the sea) and Plan-d'Aups, the road leads to the International Centre of Ste. Baume (hostelry), run by Dominicans. The Thomas Gleb chapel has large tapestry (1970) by artist of that name. A path leads (45-min. walk) to the Grotto of Ste. Marie-Madeleine, aka Ste. Baume, at 886 m. alt. (altar and reliquary of the saint; a stairway leads to the place of penitence); from there, in $1\frac{1}{2}$ hrs., path to *St. Pilon* (997 m., viewing table), chapel on a rocky peak. Several possible walks through the forest and *Massif de la Ste. Baume.*

---

950 royalists were shot in 1792) and expiatory chapel. The charterhouse of Auray (institute for the deaf and dumb) has 17–18c buildings and two chapels, in one of which lie the remains of those shot.

Ste. Énimie
48 – Lozère   30 – A 2
V. picturesque village, its houses in tiers at the foot of cliffs above a bend in R. *Tarn*. Romanesque church. To W, in 25 mins., climb to Ste. Énimie hermitage (chapel and grotto).
Vicinity ● **Tarn*** gorges to SW, taking the N.107B S: *St. Chély-du-Tarn*, on l. bank, at bottom of a ring of cliffs (Romanesque church; Son et Lumière in summer). Impressive corrie of Pougnadoires; Ch. de *la Caze* (charming manorhouse, 15c, in wooded setting; hotel); *La Malène* (Romanesque church), embarcation point for boat trips down the *Tarn* (see **Tarn*** gorges); from *Les Vignes*, a winding minor road leads (13 km steep

climb) to the *Point Sublime*, above corrie of Les Baumes (magnificent view over the *Tarn* canyon and the Causses); after *Les Vignes* and as far as *Rozier*, the road continues to follow the gorges. ● To SE, **Tarn*** gorges in direction of **Florac***.

Ste. Lucie-de-Tallano
2A – Corse   45 – D 3
Superbly situated old village, under 15c fmr. Convent of St. François. The church has two fine primitive paintings, from late 15c.
Vicinity ● 5.5 km NE, the Castellu of *Cucuruzzu*, Bronze Age fortified oppidum. ● 3.5 km NE, *Levie*, (archaeological mus.); 8 km to SE, *Carbini*, interesting Romanesque church.

Ste. Maure-de-Touraine
37 – Indre-et-Loire   17 – C 3
The fortifications of the fmr. 15c château (14c square tower) has a late-12c church, Poitiers reg. version of Romanesque; central nave of crypt dates back to year 1000. Local hist. mus. in château.

Ste. Maxime: *on the north shore of the Gulf of St. Tropez, the port nestles at the foot of wooded hills.*

Vicinity ● 8 km NW, *St. Epain*, 12–16c church with 13c square tower and fortified Porte de la Prévote. ● 8 km N, *Ste. Catherine-de-Fierbois* large leisure park, covering 49 acres; lake (17 acres) with beach, water sports; fine Goth. Flamboyant church, topped by a 41 m. belfry. Maison du Dauphin (1515), and fmr. chaplain's residence (presbytery); 2 km to SE, Ch. de Commacre, strange mid-19c neo-Goth. pastiche.

Ste. Maxime
83 – Var   **44 – D 2**

Fishing village and seaside resort on the Gulf of *St. Tropez*.
Vicinity ● To NW, via the *Gratteloup pass* (225 m.), a path leads to Le Vieux-Revest (abandoned village with Romanesque church in ruins). ● 4.5 km SW, *Beauvallon*, seaside resort and residential area set among pine trees. ● 2.5 km NE, Pointe des Sardinaux (good view over the **St. Tropez*** gulf); the road continues through *Les Issambres* and *St. Aygulf* towards **Fréjus***, on a ledge above the sea (very scenic).

Ste. Menehould
51 – Marne   **12 – D 1**

The lower town's 18c architectural character is still in evidence, notably in Rue Chanzy and Place d'Austerlitz (ringed by houses in stone and brick). The upper town is on hill of the former château. This typical little Champagne township has 13c church with interesting works of art. Dom Pérignon, the 'inventor' of champagne, was born here. In a 1735 mansion, Mus. of the Argonne.
Vicinity ● 11 km W, *Valmy*: the mill, near which 1792 battle took place, has been restored (viewing table); Coeur de Kellermann pyramid. ● 6 km NW, *La Neuville-au-Pont*: fine 14–16c church. ● Rec. trips in the *Argonne Forest*: **Clermont-en-Argonne*** (NE), **Varennes-en-Argonne*** (NNE).

Ste. Mère-Eglise
50 – Manche   **3 – D 3**

On the nights of June 5 and 6, 1944, the first American airborne troops landed here. 13c church, flanked by a sturdy square tower; opposite, starting point of the *Voie de la Liberté* (literally 'Road to Liberty'). Mus. of Airborne Troops. Cotentin Farm Mus., reconstruction of old Norman rural living quarters (tourist accommodation).
Vicinity ● To S, *St. Côme-du-Mont* and *Carentan* have interesting churches. ● To SE, via *Ste. Marie-du-Mont* (imposing church with 14c square tower), you reach the D-Day landing site of **Utah Beach***.

Saintes: *a reminder of the Roman presence, Germanicus' Votive Arch, raised and re-sited in the 19th century.* ▲

St. Savinien's old houses, *reflected in the calm waters of a bend in the River Charente.* ▼

Ste. Odile (Mt.)
67 – Bas-Rhin   **14 – A 3**

The Alsace 'beacon', 761 m. high, thickly wooded. The Mount, very popular place of pilgrimage, has a convent (with hostelry) whose late-17c church has three naves and richly carved 18c confessionals. The Chapelle de la Croix, 11c, is the oldest part of the convent; it leads to the Chapelle Ste. Odile, Romanesque and Goth., where the saint's remains lie in an 8c stone sarcophagus. From the terrace (viewing tables), vast panorama; to

NW, over the *Bruche* valley; to NE, over the Alsace plain and the Black Forest; in NE corner of the terrace, Chapelle des Larmes (inside, flagstone on which Ste. Odile used to pray).
Vicinity ● Ste. Odile Fountain, Chemin de Croix and Chapelle du Rocher (1925), ruins of feudal Dreistein, 'Pagan Wall', fmr. oppidum more than 10 km in circumference; ruins of abbey of Niedermunster (late-12c Romanesque church). ● Magnificent route (1,000 m. alt.) in direction of

Hohwald, *Champ-du-Feu* (observation tower, beautiful view).

Saintes
17 – Charente-Maritime 29 – A 1
Its Roman monuments and its churches make it worth a long visit. Former cath. of St. Pierre, 15–16c Goth. Flamboyant style, has two Romanesque transept arms, covered by a cupola; the late-15c façade (sculpted portal) is crowned by a fine lantern tower. 11c church of St. Eutrope, with 14c choir, is one of the most notable Romanesque buildings in W of France; the vast crypt contains St. Eutrope's sarcophagus, 14c. Nearby, ruins of Roman amphitheatre, late 1c (apply to the caretaker). Axis of the old town is the Rue Alsace-Lorraine and Rue Clemenceau, site of former Échevinage (magistrates' house, now town hall), with 16c belfry, and the Hôtel d'Argenson, 18c. Saintes has five mus. (cl. Tues.; cl. Mon. for the Dupuy-Mestreau mus.). The fmr. Hôtel du Présidial, 17c, houses fine arts mus. (ceramics, 16, 17 and 18c paintings); Hôtel Monconseil is home of the Dupuy-Mestreau mus. of reg. art and hist. Échevinage mus. has interesting collection of 19 and 20c paintings, mainly reg. or inspired by the Saintonge area, Sèvres porcelain. On r. bank of R. *Charente* stands the Roman arch, known as Germanicus Arch, early 1c; also archaeological mus. (excellent Gallo-Roman collection), fmr. Abbaye aux Dames, founded 11c, and 12–13c church of St. Pallais. In entry courtyard, church of Ste. Marie-des-Dames, fmr. Romanesque abbey church, noteworthy 11–12c building, its façade and portal having v. beautiful sculpted ornamentation. Majestic 12c square belfry, pierced by bays and with scalloped roof.
Vicinity ● 18 km NW, *St. Savinien*, 13–14c church.

Stes. Maries-de-la-Mer (Les)
13 – Bouches-du-Rhône 43 – C 2
The church, with austere, fortified nave, machicolated and crowned by massive belfry tower, was built at end of 12c; the mid-15c crypt, under the choir, contains shrine for the relics of Sara, black servant of the three Maries, whose remains have lain since 1448 in the chapel of St. Michel, above the apse, being brought down into the nave for pilgrimages. The most colourful of these pilgrimages is that of the Gypsies, May 24 and 25; in the presbytery, rich collection of votive offerings. Baroncelli mus. (reg. hist., flora and fauna of the **Camargue***). 2 km to N, Boumian waxworks mus. (scenes of everyday life in Camargue).

Salers: *the dramatic expressionism of this famed Entombment, in painted stone, bears the stamp of Burgundian art.*

Ste. Suzanne
53 – Mayenne 10 – B 3
Built on rocky promontory above R. *Erve*, this once-fortified township still has its triangular wall, dating from 11, 13 and 15c; at tip of promontory, site of the citadel, are remains of 11c keep (v.a. in summer); good view; château in Louis XIII style (spectacles, exhibitions in summer). In 17–18c house, Mus. de l'Auditoire, folk art and trads. from the Maine reg.
Vicinity ● 1.7 km NE, the Tertre-Ganne, imposing 17c châteaux. To S, *Erve* valley is worth visiting; the grottoes and natural erosion have carved strange shapes in the cliffs.

Salers
15 – Cantal 30 – C 3
This small town, one of the strangest in the Auvergne, is built of dark volcanic rock. 15c church, with Romanesque porch; inside, a most striking Entombment, 1495, in painted stone; also 17c Aubusson tapestries. The Grand-Place (or Place Tyssandier-d'Escous) is lined by old houses and mansions with corbels, turrets and pepper-pot or timbered roofs: Maison de Bargues (v.a. with permission); Rue des Templiers, House of the Templars, with triple-windowed gable. From the Promenade de la Barouze, terraced above R. Maronne, magnificent views over the surrounding puys.
Vicinity ● *Puy Mary, Falgoux* corrie, etc. (see **Aurillac*** and **Mauriac***).

Salette (Notre Dame-de-la-)
38 – Isère 38 B 1
15 km NNE of **Corps***. Popular place of pilgrimage, in a desolate, barren mountain setting. The neo-Romanesque basilica commemorates the apparition of the Virgin to two young shepherds (1846). Fountain of the Virgin and sculpted groups evoke the event. Hostelry (telephone reservations required) and convent. Pilgrimages on Aug. 15 and Sept. 19. Ascent of Mt. Gargas (2,213 m.) is recommended (allow about 90 mins).

Salies-de-Béarn
64 – Pyrénées-Atlantiques 40 – D 1
Renowned spa, in little valley of R. Saleys, which runs through the picturesque old quarter. Winding streets, old corbelled houses on stone pillars. 15c church of St. Vincent. The spa quarter includes baths, casino and huge public park.
Vicinity ● The Pain de Sucre (sugar-loaf), the Trinité (both offering views). ● 14 km NW, **Sorde-l'Ab-baye***. ● 6 km N, *Bellocq:* 13c church, unusual carved portals; remains of 14c castle; the wall is flanked by solid towers, round and square.

Salignac-Eyvignes
24 – Dordogne 30 – A 3
Château de Salignac-Fénelon, built between 12 and 17c; the medieval defensive wall still stands (v.a. in summer).
Vicinity ● 14 km SE, Ch. de la Forge: in the grounds, prehistoric grottoes. Gouffres (abysses) of Le Boulet, Grand-Blagour and Gourguillon.

Salins-les-Bains
39 – Jura 26 – B 1
Fmr. stronghold and spa, this little town – one of the most interesting in the Franche-Comté – lies at the end of the Furieuse gorge. Its principal buildings are all to be found,

running N to S, on or near the main street. 12, 14 and 17c church of St. Maurice. 18c town hall and votive chapel of Notre Dame-Libératrice, 17c Saltworks, with 12c vaulting, (v.a.). Municipal mus. Late-17c Hôtel-Dieu (with splendid pharmacy). 13c church of St. Anatoile (Romanesque portal with carved wooden panels).
Vicinity ● To E, climb up to Belin Fort (584 m., panorama) is rec. – also to St. André Fort (586 m.), to W. ● 3.5 km E, the Bout-du-Monde (End of the World), curious half-circle of rocks; remains of Gouilles abbey. ● 9 km N, Mt. Poupet, (853 m. vast panorama). ● 15 km NE, via *Nans-sous-Ste. Anne* and the Sarrazine grotto, the *source of the Lison*; from there to the Billard Well, impressive abyss, approx. 100 m. deep. ● 18 km SE, *Joux Forest* (see **Champagnole***).

Salles-Curan
12 – Aveyron   36 – D 3
Picturesque township under remains of 15c château, former residence of the bishops of Rodez. The former collegiate church, 15c, has Goth. Flamboyant stalls and a church treasure.
Vicinity ● *Lake of Pareloup* (3,200 acres), penetrated by several jagged peninsulas; holiday boating and yachting club centre; good view from the dam, 42 m. high, in a rocky setting; tour round the lake, on pleasant minor roads, is rec.

Salon-de-Provence
13 – Bouches-du-Rhône   44 – A 1
Typically Provençal little town. Ch. de l'Emperi (of the Holy Empire), formidable 13–14c fortress built on a rock overlooking the town; large square tower, 26 m. high; charming Ren. living quarters of Queen Jeanne; 12–13c castle chapel. The premises also house the Natnl. Mus. of Military Art and Hist. (cl. Tues.), which has exceptional collections of uniforms, saddlery, weapons, decorations and flags of the French Army from Louis XIV to 1918. In a handsome late-19c house, the Mus. de Salon et de la Crau. Churches: St. Michel, first half of 13c (Romanesque carved portal); St. Laurent, 14–15c pure Provençal Goth. style (tomb of Nostradamus, born at Salon in 1503).
Vicinity ● 12 km E, imposing Ch. de la *Barben*: medieval fortress enlarged in 16–17c, interesting furnishings: fine French-style ceilings; Empire room and Pauline Borghèse's boudoir (v.a., cl. Tues. out of season); zoo and aquarium.

Salses (Fort)
66 – Pyrénées-Orientales 42 – D 3
This magnificent brick and stone military construction – early 16c, reinforced by Vauban in 17c – is one of the earliest French fortresses designed to resist artillery attack (v.a., cl. Tues.). The fort is a sectioned rectangle with four round towers and an imposing keep in the middle; to the W, two square towers previously housed the arsenal and the stores; three successive enceintes around the whole complex, which also has other advanced works.

Sancerre
18 – Cher   18 – D 3
One of the Cher's most unusual little villages, built on a high, isolated hill, on l. bank of R. *Loire*, with a v. wide view. Its ring of boulevards, tortuous streets and old houses are dominated by the Fiefs tower, a 15c cylindrical keep (viewing table) and the church of St. Jean, former 15c belfry. From the Porte de César promenade, fine view over the surrounding vineyards. Apart from its world-famed wines, another Sancerre speciality is goat's cheese.
Vicinity ● Excursions rec. to the renowned vineyards in the Sancerrois hills. ● 14.5 km NW, *Ch. de Boucard*, moated feudal construction, partially rebuilt during Ren. (v.a.); int. has fine 17c apartments; 5 km to N, *Jars* has a manorhouse and church, 15–16c, in pink sandstone and white limestone. ● 9.5 km N, via *Bannay*, *Ch. de Buranlure*, elegant 15c country seat, surrounded by flowing water (v.a.). ● 17.5 km SW, *Morogues*, 14c church; inside, 15c monumental wooden canopy; 1 km to W, *Ch. de Maupas*, 14c (v.a., p.m., Easter to mid-Oct.; a.m. Sun. and public hols., July 1– Sept. 15): inside, collection of 887 china plates from 15 to 18c, 16–17c

Salses: *under the Roussillon sun, an impressive example of medieval military architecture.*

Sarlat-la-Canéda: *few towns in France have such a homogeneous group of 15-16c houses: seen here, the Présidial.*

tapestries, souvenirs of the Duchesse de Berry and her son the Comte de Chambord (d. 1883, legitimate pretender to French throne in latter part of 19c).

Sarlat-la-Canéda
24 – Dordogne　　　　**30 – A 3**
An old town whose various picturesque quarters, with many 15–16c houses, merit a long visit. The Rue de la République, known as 'La Traverse', links the Place de la Petite-Rigaudie, to N, with the Place du 14-Juillet and the Grande-Rigaudie, to S. The oldest part of Sarlat lies around the Place du Peyrou, site of 16c fmr. bishop's palace (now a theatre) and the church of St. Sacerdos, former Romanesque abbey church and cath., rebuilt in 16–17c (Fountain Courtyard, Benedictine cemetery, Romanesque chapel of St. Benoît); also the 16c house where writer La Boétie (friend of Montaigne) was born in 1530 (now branch of natnl. savings bank). Behind the church, 12c Lantern of the Dead. Through Rue de la Liberté (on l., late-16c Hôtel de Maleville), you get to Place de le Liberté: 17c town hall (belfry) and fmr. church of Ste. Marie, 14c.

Rue de la Salamandre, lined with old houses, leads to early-17c Présidial (equivalent to present-day appeal court). Rue des Consuls is one of the town's most picturesque streets (Hôtel de Labrousse, No. 14; Hôtel de Selves du Plamon, Maison des Consuls, No.10; Hôtel de Mirandol, No. 7, etc.). In 1607 fmr. chapel of the Récollets (Augustinians), mus. of the Pénitents-Blancs. To N of the town, Temniac hill, 12c Romanesque church, remains of château of the bishops of Sarlat, in magnificent setting.

Sartène
2A – Corsica　　　　**45 – D 3**
The old town is very picturesque; its narrow streets, lined with tall black houses linked by multi-coloured lines of washing, have hardly changed since the Middle Ages. The Procession of Catenacciu, on Good Friday, is Corsica's most impressive. Prehist. and Protohist. Centre, mus. of Corsican prehist.: large archaeological collections.
Vicinity ● 21 km NW, *Propriano* and the *Gulf of Valinco*; richly coloured scenery. ● 19 km SW on the D 48, near *Tizzano*, the Palaggiu alignments (258 monoliths); from

there, 5 km along a minor road, *Cauria*, extraordinary megalithic site. ● 36 km S, Pass and Rocks of *Roccapina*, in pink granite, forming shapes of fantastic animals; beautiful beach. ● To NE, **Ste. Lucie-de-Tallano*** and oppidum of *Cucuruzzu*.

Saulieu
21 – Côte d'Or　　　　**19 – C 3**
Famous gastronomic stopping-point. ● The basilica of St. Andoche, late 11–12c, has unusual historiated capitals, amongst the most expressive in Romanesque art. In 17c mansion adjoining the basilica, the François Pompon mus. (works by Pompon, d. 1933, famed sculptor of animals, who was born at Saulieu; also Gallo-Roman archaeology, medieval religious art, rural crafts). In middle of the terraced cemetery, 15c church of St. Saturnin, surrounded by Gallo-Roman funerary stelae.
Vicinity ● 10 km E, *Thoisy-la-Berchère*: interesting 15c château with elegant Ren. façade; inside, Ren. furniture, 17–18c paintings, magnificent series of 15 and 18c tapestries; Guard Room with painted beams; vaulting in the chapel is decorated with frescos painted in the Italian style, early 17c (v.a., cl. Tues., in summer); 16c parish church is embellished with murals of the same period. ● 7.5 km to NE, *Mont-St. Jean*, an old feudal township, on top of small hill, which still has imposing ruins of 12 and 15c castle; also church with interesting works of art. ● 14 km NNW, *La Roche-en-Brénil*, moated château, 15, 17 and 18c. ● To W, some fine excursions in the **Morvan***.

Sault
84 – Vaucluse　　　　**38 – A 3**
In the heart of lavender country; good base for excursions. Small Romanesque and 14c church; 16c château; small Gallo-Roman mus.
Vicinity ● The **Ventoux***, to NW. ● The *Nesque gorges* to SW, in direction of **Carpentras***, via *Monieux*, village perched high on a hill.

Saumur
49 – Maine-et-Loire　　　　**17 – B 3**
Old town dominated by the imposing bulk of the château, which is endowed with four corner towers and machicolations. Rebuilt in 14c and since renovated several times, the château houses two mus.: one for decorative arts, with collections as rich as they are varied (15–16c tapestries, liturgical ornaments, furniture, enamel, etc.); second mus. is devoted to the horse. Three churches: Notre Dame-de-Nantilly, Romanesque, first half of 12c, renovated in 14 and 15c (inside,

fine 16–17c tapestries); Notre Dame-des-Ardilliers, 17c, with v. big rotunda in front of it; and St. Pierre, Anjou Goth. in style, with late-17c façade (16c tapestries and 15c stalls). Within the buildings of the early-16c town hall is 13c chapel of St. Jean. Around the church of St. Pierre is the old quarter described by Balzac: Rue Basse-St. Pierre, Rue Fourrier (No. 13, Maison des Anges), Rue du Fort, Place St. Pierre (Maison du Roi, fine 16c sculpted façade), Grande-Rue, etc. The Quartier des Ponts (bridges), on an island between two arms of R. *Loire*, was rebuilt after the war: elegant early-15c manor of the Queen of Sicily.
Vicinity ● 2 km SW, Bagneux dolmen, or Grand Dolmen. ● 11 km SE, Ch. de *Brézé*, imposing Ren. building with moat (v.a. by appointment). ● 10.5 km NW, *Chenehutte-les-Tuffeaux*, Romanesque church, fmr. château (hotel) incorporates remains of an 11c chapel and a 16c priory. ● On r. bank of the Loire, 9 km NW, *Ch. de Boumois*, 15, 16 and 17c (v.a., Easter to Nov. 1, cl. Tues.). ● 17.5 km NE, at *Vernantes*, 16–17c *Ch. de Jalesne* (n.v.a.); 9 km N, via *Mouliherne* (11–12c church): Ch. de la Touche (16c); inside, room with painted beams (v.a.).

Saut du Doubs (Waterfall)
25 – Doubs   20 – D 3
One of the sights of the Jura. This magnificent fall, 28 m. high, in a superb setting, can be reached by footpaths. Boat trips from *Villers-le-Lac* (90 mins. there and back), passing through *Lake Chaillexon*, then a series of basins hemmed in by sheer cliffs.
Vicinity ● To NE, the *Doubs* gorges offer some striking scenery, especially the Chatelôt dam, which spans the Franco-Swiss frontier (panorama from the belvedere); also the Échelles de la Mort (lit. 'Ladders of Death') and the *Goumois* corniche (see **St. Hippolyte*** and **Maîche***).

Sauve-Majeure (La)
33 – Gironde   35 – A 1
Imposing ruins of former abbey church of St. Gérard, 12–13c. The most interesting part is the apse: flanked by two side-aisles and pierced by three wide, sculpted bays. Rare Romanesque capitals in the choir. Remains of an early-13c Goth. cloister and 17c monastic buildings. Late-12c Goth. parish church of St. Pierre; interior has 18c frescos.

Sauveterre-de-Béarn
64 – Pyrénées-Atlantiques 40 – D 1
Small, picturesque terraced town,

above confluence of two mountain rivers, the *Mauléon* and the *Oloron*. Late-12c Romanesque church (with three naves, three apses and a sturdy square belfry) is one of the most beautiful in the Béarn region. Lovely walks along river banks.
Vicinity ● 8 km SE, Ch. de Laàs: fine 17c residence surrounded by gardens; inside, notable collection of furniture, paintings and objets d'art from 15 to 19c; 16c panelling (v.a., July–Oct.; Sat. and Sun. only from March to June).

Saverne
67 – Bas-Rhin   14 – A 2
Vast, red sandstone 18c château enlarged by Napoleon; on side facing the gardens, it has a majestic Classical façade with fluted pilasters and an eight-columned peristyle (Son et Lumière in summer); inside, archaeological and hist. mus. (large Gallo-Roman collection). In the Grande-Rue, 17c timber houses; 14–15c church, with 12c Romanesque belfry; 14c church of the Récollets (Augustinians) and cloister. The rose garden can be visited from Whitsun to Sept. 30.
Vicinity ● 5 km SW, remains of the *Ch. du Haut-Barr*, 12, 16 and 18c, aka 'the Eye of Alsace', beautiful view. ● 4.5 km N, *St. Jean-Saverne*, Romanesque fmr. abbey church, in 12c Rhenish style, aka St. Jean-des-Choix; then climb up to chapel of St. Michel, 12c, vast panorama. ● 14 km N, *Neuwiller-lès-Saverne*, former abbey church, 12–13c St. Pierre-et-St. Paul; in apse, an 11c chapel on two levels. ● 22 km N, *La Petite-Pierre*, unusual little stronghold, in middle of a forest; underground lake; inside the citadel, Mus. du Sceau Alsacien (various

local seals); pretty walk to lake of Imsthal. ● 15 km NE, *Bouxwiller*, 16–17c house, Alsatian Ren. town hall.

Sceaux
92 – Hauts-de-Seine   11 – C 2
The château, rebuilt in 1856 in Louis XIII style, houses highly varied Mus. of the Ile-de-France (cl. Tues.); its collections illustrate history and everyday life of the reg. through paintings, engravings, individual articles, folk art, ceramics and pottery. The grounds (v.a.) afford some pleasant walks: large canal, Octagon Basin and big cascades (fountain displays every Sun. from April–Oct.). Pavillon de Hanover, Pavillon de l'Aurore, Terrace of the Pintades (guinea-fowl); and big Quatre-Statues lawn. In the town, near 16c church of St. Jean-Baptiste, garden of the Félibres (writers in Provençal language) and tomb of Florian, 18c writer and playwright. Opposite here is the 'Menagerie' garden of the Duchesse du Maine, where, in an urn under two columns, her canaries and her cat are buried.
Vicinity ● Châtenay-Malabry has one of the most venerable churches in the Ile-de-France: St. Germain-l'Auxerrois, 11 and 13c. Walks rec. to: the Vallée-aux-Loups; the 'ginguettes' of Robinson (open-air taverns and restaurants, with singing and dancing), from where you get fine views of Paris; and the rose garden at Hay-les-Roses, with charming Rose Mus. (v.a. end of May to end of Sept.).

Sedan
08 – Ardennes   6 – D 2
Isolated on a rock base, the famed

Saumur: *a fortress, yet welcoming, the château is half-medieval, half-Renaissance, and houses two interesting museums.*

fortress-château dates from 15, 16 and 17c (v.a. from Palm Sunday to mid Oct.); it was birthplace of France's greatest 17c military leader, Marshal Turenne, and has interesting rooms and archaeological and military mus. The Château-Bas, fmr. residence of the Princes of Sedan, is a fine early-17c edifice.

Vicinity ● 3.5 km SE, *Bazeilles*: 18c château (v.a. in summer) and Maison des Dernières Cartouches (v.a.), scene of an heroic episode in the 1870 Franco-Prussian war; small mus. ● To S, forest of **Argonne***. ● To N, beautiful Ardennes forest and **Charleville-Mézières***.

Sées
61 – Orne   10 – C 2

13 and 14c cath. of Notre Dame is one of the finest Norman Goth. edifices; the nave is beautifully proportioned and admirably elegant; 14c choir and transept; stained-glass and rose windows, 14 and 16c; in the choir, late-18c stalls and high altar in marble adorned with sculpted reliefs. In fmr. Canon's residence, reg. mus. of sacred art (v.a. from May to Oct.).

Vicinity ● 1 km to N of *Mortrée*, the *Ch. d'O*, elegant 16–18c building in middle of a lake (v.a., cl. Tues.).

Seix
09 – Ariège   41 – D 3

Ancient little city, in tiers on l. bank of R. *Salat*. 17c church with wall-belfry; inside, huge gilt retables embellished with bas-reliefs; two-storey galleries. Old houses with wooden balconies, below remains of feudal castle.

Vicinity ● The road goes up the *Vallée du Salat*, very picturesque valley which remains narrow as far as Pont de-la-Taule, a hamlet situated at confluence of the Alet and the *Salat*; fine red marble quarries; through the Ustou valley, to SE, you get to *Bielle*; from Pont-de-la-Taule, the road continues to *Couflens* and *Salau*; excursion to *Port de Salau* (2,052 m.). To N, **St. Lizier***.

Sélestat
67 – Bas-Rhin   14 – A 3

The old part of Sélestat retains its

Semur-en-Auxois: *rising in tiers above the Armançon, it is one of the most picturesque of Burgundy's old cities.*

narrow streets, picturesque houses and imposing remains of its fortifications: Clock Tower, sturdy bulk of 14c belfry, whose lower floor was one of the gates in the old medieval wall, and Porte de Strasbourg, in sandstone, which was part of Vauban's wall. 12c church of Ste. Foy, one of Alsace's finest Romanesque churches; above transept crossing is an octagonal tower, 43 m. high. St. George's, in red sandstone and grey granite, is a handsome Goth. building, built from 13 to 16c; the main portal is surmounted by a square tower, 60 m. high. Maison Weiller, typical of Alsace, is surrounded by beautiful gardens. Maison Ziegler, 16c Ren. Mid-16c mansion of Fmr. abbey of Ebersmunster (sculpted Ren. portal). Former Ste. Barbe arsenal is an elegant 14c construction with sculpted façade; storks have built a nest in its roof. The Corn Exchange, 1843, houses Humanist Library, which has exceptional collection of early printed texts, manuscripts and old Rhenish handiwork.

Vicinity ● To NW, remains of the châteaux of Ramstein, Ortenbourg and Frankenbourg. ● *Châtenois* (5 km W), unusual Romanesque

belfry with spire and bartizans. 15c Witches' Tower (storks).

Selles-sur-Cher
41 – Loir-et-Cher   18 – A 3

On r. bank of R. *Cher*, the château, surrounded by water, still has the walls of feudal fortress, converted at the end of 16c into an aristocratic residence (v.a., Easter to Nov. 1); inside, Guard Room; Queen of Poland's bedroom, decorated and furnished in early 17c; music room, etc. 12 and 14c church of Notre Dame-la-Blanche; exterior of the apse is decorated with Romanesque sculpted friezes.

Vicinity ● 14 km S, Ch. de **Valençay***.

Semur-en-Auxois
21 – Côte-d'Or   19 – C 2

One of Burgundy's most picturesque old towns, on a steep promontory circled by a bend of the R. Armançon: above it, the enormous towers of a 13c castle. The Orle d'Or Tower houses archaeology and ethnography mus. Rues Févret and Rempart link citadel to town, which retains its provincial charm. Built in Burgundian Goth. style, the 13–14c church of Notre Dame, with 15c porch, boasts a beautiful late-15c Entombment and, in two chapels, very rare stained-glass windows depicting butchers and drapers at work; the vaulting in the apse has one of the most beautiful historiated keystones known (depicting Coronation of the Virgin). Small local mus.: archaeology, medieval collections, paintings (late-15c primi-

SEIN (Isle)
29S – Finistère   8 – A 3

Can be reached on the mail boat from **Audierne***, or from the *Port de Bestrée* and Ste. Evette. This bare, flat island consists mainly of moorland, covering 14 acres, on two islets joined by a narrow isthmus. The village and harbour are in the E part. Monument to the rallying of the islanders to Free France (1940). Megalithic remains. On NW tip: Sein lighthouse. Off the coast, *Ar Men* lighthouse.

tives and three works by Corot).
Vicinity ● 12.5 km W, **Ch. d'Époisses***. ● 3 km S, *Lac-Barrage de Pont*, on the *Armançon*, huge reservoir stretching for 6 km (beach, water sports).

Sénanque (Abbey)
84 – Vaucluse   38 – A 3

At the bottom of the Senancole canyon, which opens out on to a plateau scattered with numerous 'bories' (early dry-stone constructions) is an abbey founded in 1148 (v.a., cl. Tues.); it is one of the 'Three Cistercian Sisters of Provence' and houses several study centres: medieval, Saharan, Gregorian Chanting, Mediterranean music. The church is one of the best examples of pure Romanesque art. Early 13c cloister and chapterhouse, monks' room, old calefactory.

Senlis
60 – Oise   11 – D 1

Old town with considerable provincial charm. 12c church of Notre Dame was one of the first grandiose achievements of Goth. art; the façade, flanked by an elegant belfry and spire, 78 m. high, has a remarkable late-12c central portal, finely sculpted and consecrated to the Virgin; from the Place Notre Dame, superb view of the S side; the façade on the transept, very richly orna-

mented, provides a striking contrast with early Goth. sobriety; you can see the progression from Goth. Flamboyant to Ren. beginning here. To S. of the apse, fmr. 13 and 16c bishop's palace, 12–13c chapel of St. Frambourg, stained-glass by Miró and the 11, 15 and 16c church of St. Pierre, with Goth. Flamboyant façade. The 13c royal château includes the remains of the chapel of Louis VI and the 16c royal living quarters; it houses a remarkable mus. of hunting, Mus. de la Vénerie (cl. Tues. and Wed. a.m.), which brings together numerous works inspired by riding to hounds, from 15c to the present day. In fmr. bishop's palace, archaeology and art mus.; Mus. des Beaux-Arts in 16c Hôtel du Vermandois: 17–19c paintings. Many old houses, notably the Maison du Haubergier, 16c. To W of town, Roman arena (apply to the caretaker). To SE, fmr. abbey of St. Vincent, founded in 11c, rebuilt in 17c, Classical cloister, Romanesque belfry (now a college, v.a. during school holidays). Guided tours of the town.
Vicinity ● 2.5 km SE, remains of Victoire abbey, 13 and 15c, in an attractive setting (apply to caretaker). ● 8 km E, *Ch. de Montepilloy*: its 12c feudal ruins, on farmland (v.a.) include two powerful keeps and a few remnants of

an outer wall. ● To N, *Forest of Halatte* (more than 16 sq. miles), fmr. priory of St. Christopher, Mt. Pagnotte. ● 10 km NW, *Creil* (small pottery mus., Maison Gallé-Juillet); interesting churches at *Nogent-sur-Oise* and *Montataire*. ● 9.5 km to W, **Chantilly***.

Sens
89 – Yonne   12 – A 3

St. Étienne, the first great Gothic cathedral (circa 1140), has a late-12c façade with three sculpted portals; inside, the 12, 13 and 14c stained-glass (the earliest being to l. of choir) forms a superb ensemble. The N. door in the transept leads to the Impasse Abraham, noteworthy for an admirable Goth. Flamboyant façade on N arm of the transept, delicately carved, and for a fine, early-16c sculpted portal. Church treasure is one of the richest in France, (v.a., cl. Tues.), forming a veritable mus. of religious art: 15c tapestries, liturgical ornaments, ivory, 15–18c plate, etc. To r. of cath., 13c Officialité (ecclesiastic court); old archbishop's palace houses lapidary collections (tomb of Cardinal Duprat, 16c, embellished with notable marble bas-reliefs, fragments of 3c Roman mosaics, and many pieces of sculpture from the two abbeys of Sens); also collections from old municipal mus. (paintings, natural history). ●

Senlis: *on the cathedral portal, venerable figures from the Old Testament.*

Sens: *the Gothic Flamboyant rose window in the cathedral's south transept.*

Interesting old houses in Rue de la République, 16c Maison d'Abraham; Rue Jean Cousin, Maison du Pilier and 16c timber-framed Maison de Jean Cousin. To l. of façade of 13–15c church of St. Pierre-le-Rond, that of 13c Hôtel-Dieu (hospital) has been re-erected. To E of town, fmr. abbey church of St. Jean, now hospital chapel, has beautiful 13c apsidal chapel in Champagne-Burgundian Goth. style.

Vicinity • 15 km NNE, moated Ch. de *Fleurigny*, Ren., flanked by 14c round towers; see inner courtyard with arcaded galleries, and chapel with coffered ceiling and sculpted hanging keystones, a masterpiece of ornamentation (v.a. Sat. and Sun., p.m., from Easter to Oct.; in Aug., every afternoon exc. Wed.).

SERRE-PONÇON (Dam)
05 – Hautes-Alpes   38 – C 2
The dam (1960) on R. *Durance* is a grandiose project; it contains one of Europe's biggest artificial lakes (nearly 12 sq. miles). Above it is the French Electricity Board's belvedere (information and recorded commentaries). On the lake, water sports. From **Embrun***, the N94 crosses the reservoir at *Savines* (new village) and, after skirting the lake, reaches *Chorges* (15c church), *La Bâtie-Neuve* and **Gap***. SSW from *Savines*, the D954 follows the steep bank of the lake (beautiful views); 'Demoiselles Coiffées' of Pontis; *Le Sauze*, on terrace forming a belvedere, in very beautiful setting.

The dam, 123 m. high and 600 m. wide at the top, holds up to three billion gallons of water. The valley was flooded in 1960.

Sept-Saints (Chapel)
22 – Côtes-du-Nord   8 – D 2
Built early in 18c on a dolmen is a primitive chapel where pictures of Seven Sleeping Men of Ephesus were supposedly discovered. According to legend, they fell asleep in a grotto in year 250 and awoke only at time of Council of Ephesus in 431. The chapel is place of pilgrimage for Christians and Muslims alike (4th Sun. in July).

Serrabone (Priory)
66 – Pyrénées-Orientales   43 – C 3
Isolated in the mountains, it is one of the most interesting examples of Roussillon Romanesque art. The priory-church of Ste. Marie, 11–12c, has a richly ornamented marble gallery, supported by small columns of pink marble and the six small intersecting ribs of the vaulting; the capitals are among the masterpieces of Catalan Romanesque sculpture.
Vicinity • 10 km SE, *Fourtou Pass*; ruins of the Ch. de Belpuig, 13c, and Romanesque chapel with 12c Byzantine Christ, carved in wood, known as the 'Santa Majestat'.

Serrant (Château)
49 – Maine-et-Loire   17 – A 2
Fine Ren. building (v.a. April–Oct., cl. Tues.; daily in July and Aug.), completed in 17 and 18c, surrounded by wide moat. Chapel has superb tomb of Marquis de Vaubrun (d. 1675), by Lebrun and Coysevox. Splendid 18c apartments; the main salon is adorned with an exceptionally fine suite of 16c Brussels tapestries. Empire Room, where Napoleon slept.

Sète
34 – Hérault   43 – B 2
Port typical of the south of France, criss-crossed by canals bordered with bustling quays. From the St. Louis pier, which shelters the old 17c dock, fine view over the town, dominated by the Mt. St. Clair; stretched out on its slopes, the citadel, lighthouse and St. Pierre Fort, converted into a Theatre of the Sea. From the summit (chapel), very fine view. The writer Paul Valéry (d. 1945), a native of Sète, lies in the 'Sailors' Cemetery', which he immortalised in a famous poem. Above cemetery, Paul Valéry Mus., of very modern design (cl. Tues.): local painting; contemporary art; documents, souvenirs, drawings and watercolours by Valéry. Also born in Sète, and included in the mus., Georges Brassens (singer). Behind the station, picturesque fishing village of La Bordigue. Sète jousts, Aug. 25.
Vicinity • Trip round *Lake Thau* (27 sq. miles) via *Balaruc-les-Bains* (D129), lake of Eaux-Blanches

Serrabone: *a highly imaginative series of pictures on the capitals; here, the arcades opening out on the valley.* ◀

Silvacane: *in the Romanesque abbey, a triumph of Cistercian rigour and lack of ornamentation.* ▲

(boating centre, marina, yachting school); *Bouzigues* is a picturesque fishing village whose oysters are much sought after; *Loupian* has two interesting churches and *Mèze* a 15c Goth. church; 7 km to W. of *Mèze*, Ch. de Creyssels, birthplace of 18c adventurer, Latude; road will take you as far as **Agde***, then return via N108.

Sèvres
92 – Hauts-de-Seine   11 – C 2
Natnl. Mus. of Ceramics (cl. Tues.) is one of the best in its field; its collections cover practically the whole history of ceramics in Europe and the East. Workshops of the world-famed Natnl. Porcelain Factory here can be visited (1st and 3rd Thurs. of the month, exc. in Aug.). Villa des Jardies, where Balzac and Corot lived, and where 19c politician Léon Gambetta died, has been turned into a museum.

Seyssel   32 – B 1
74 – Haute-Savoie; 01 – Ain
The *Rhône* divides the town in two distinct parts, one belonging to the Ain Department, the other to the Haute-Savoie; they are joined by a suspension bridge.
Vicinity ● From Princes' mountain (942 m.) to E, panoramic view, especially of *Mt. Blanc* ● 3 km SSE, little valley of the *Fier*, narrow, deep gorge. ● 9 km NE, superb Ch. de *Clermont*, 16–17c, incorporating 13–14c material; main courtyard with two storeys of arcaded galler-

ies, 16c chapel (v.a. by arrangement); vast panorama.

Sézanne
51 – Marne   12 – B 2
This small town, with much provincial charm, is encircled by a ring of promenades and the remains of fortifications.

SETTONS (Lake)
58 – Nièvre   19 – B 3
In a beautiful wooded setting in the **Morvan***, at an altitude of 575 m., the lake covers 887 acres, fed by R. *Cure* and several other rivers and springs. It owes its existence to the construction of a dam across the *Cure* valley; a road follows the valley ridges (good views). Beach, water sports, regular boat trips round the lake. Fishing and waterfowling.

SIDOBRE (Le)
81 – Tarn   42 – C 1
The granite plateau of the Sidobre (56 km tour to E of **Castres***) has several natural sights, notably the rocky abysses found chiefly along the D58, which follows a corniche ledge along the *Agout* valley: Roc de Peyro-Clabado, the Trois-Fromages (lit. 'Three Cheeses'), le Chapeau du Curé (lit. 'The Curate's Hat'), Peyremoutou rocking-stone, etc. At *Burlats*, ruined Romanesque church of 12c fmr. priory; at *Ferrières*, 16c château with richly ornamented façade, Mus. of Protestantism and workshop of stringed-instrument maker (v.a.). Take N622 towards Castres: rocking-stones of Jumeaux-Bienvenu, the Sept-Faux, the Jumeaux-Valet, La Rouquette rocks, etc.

Vicinity ● To SW, *Forest of the Traconne* (more than 12 sq. miles). ● 22 km SW, *Villenauxe-la-Grande*: beautiful church.

Signy-l'Abbaye
08 – Ardennes   6 – C 2
Except for 18c monastic buildings, hardly anything survives of the Cis-

tercian abbey, founded in 12c. The *Vaux* rises within the town itself, in the Gibergeon abyss.
Vicinity ● State Forest of Signy, hilly and picturesque (13½ sq. miles), is divided by the small *Vaux* valley into the Petite Forêt to SE and Grande Forêt to NW.

Sillé-le-Guillaume
72 – Sarthe 10 – B 3
Built like an amphitheatre, this fmr. stronghold still has its beautiful 15c château, erected on the ruins of an 11c fortress (n.v.a.); a 38 m. high keep and three towers with parapet walks, machicolations and conical roofs. Church of Notre Dame with sculpted portal and crypt, 13c.
Vicinity ● To NW, *Forest of Sillé* (11 sq. miles), Defais lake (sailing, rowing and water sports) and Sillé-Plage; *Les Coëvrons*, picturesque sandstone mass, culminating at the Gros-Rochard (357 m. high).

Silvacane (Abbey)
13 – Bouches-du-Rhône 44 – A 1
In a lush setting near R. *Durance*, this Cistercian abbey was founded in 1144 (v.a., cl. Tues.); 12c church of Notre Dame – pure lines, beautifully proportioned; early-13c chapter-house, dormitory and cloister (circa 1220), whose N gallery is flanked by early-15c refectory; together, the buildings form a fine example of the austerity and pure harmony of Cistercian architecture.

Sion
54 – Meurthe-et-Moselle 13 – B 3
The *Colline Inspirée* (Inspired Hill), as it was called in book of that title by the writer Maurice Barrès (d. 1923), is one of Lorraine's shrines. Basilica of Notre Dame-de-Sion (18–19c, 14c Goth. choir) and convent of the Oblats (missionary and Gallo-Roman mus.). Extensive views.
Vicinity ● To S, the *Signal de Vaudemont* (alt. 541 m.), reached by a scenic ridge road; on the top, a 22 m. Lantern of the Dead. ● 6 km NE of Sion, *Thorey-Lyautey*, one-time home of Marshal Lyautey (military chief who established French protectorate in Morocco; also France's War Minister, 1916–17); his château now houses large collection of Moroccan art (v.a.); his mausoleum, transferred from Rabat, has been re-erected in the grounds. ● 24 km SE, *Charmes*, birthplace and tomb of Maurice Barrès.

Sisteron 38 – B 2
04 – Alpes-de-Haute-Provence
In a narrow gorge in the *Durance* valley, on the Route Napoléon, the town is dominated by an imposing citadel (v.a., Easter to Nov. 1), which houses a small hist. mus.

Citadel's oldest parts date from 13c, the fortifications in general are 16c; from the terrace, sweeping view down to the town (viewing table). 15c chapel of Notre Dame. The old quarters, along the *Durance*, have several steep streets linked by arched ramps (known as 'andronnes'). Church of Notre Dame, v. sombre inside, is in the Provençal Romanesque style. Mus. of Old Sisteron.
Vicinity ● to NE, upper valley of the Vançon and *Pierre-Écrite defile*; beyond *St. Geniez*, the strange *Dromon Rock* (chapel), *Authon*, *Fontbelle pass* and State Forest of *Mélan* (odd grotto of St. Vincent).

Sixt-Fer-à-Cheval
74 – Haute Savoie 26 – D 3
Of the abbey founded in mid-12c, all that remains are three of its main buildings (occupied in part by a hotel: the dining room is the old refectory, with 17c painted ceiling) and the 13c Goth. church; inside, interesting works of art (church treasure in the sacristy).
Vicinity ● 7.5 km NE, Plan du Lac, at the bottom of the *Cirque du Fer-à-Cheval*, the most majestic corrie in the French Alps, lying under towering cliffs, broken by several waterfalls. ● 6.5 km NW, *Samoëns*: 16c church, 7½-acre Alpine garden; 2.5 km to SW, Vercland, departure-point for cable-car to Les Saix (1,640 m.) ● 4 km S, *Rouget cascades*.

Sizun
29N – Finistère 8 – B 2
The parish *enclosure* is one of Finistère's most characteristic: monumental gate and late-16c ossuary chapel, which houses small mus. of sacred art. 16–17c church with unusual polygonal apse, decorated with canopied niches and a sculpted frieze; inside, large group of retables, altars, statues, etc.

Soissons
02 – Aisne 6 – A 3
Four churches are worth visiting: (1). St. Gervais-et-St. Protais cath., superb 13c Goth. edifice; the S arm of the transept, late 12c, is one of the masterpieces of early Goth. architecture. (2). Fmr. St. Jean-des-Vignes abbey, from which survive magnificent 13–14c Goth. cloister, sculpted with great delicacy, the late-12c refectory, the storeroom, and the abbot's living quarters, 16c (with statuary room). (3). 13c church of St. Léger, fmr. abbey church with 11c crypt; in the chapter-house and cloister, 13c, is mus. with lapidary collections, paintings. (4). Remains of fmr. Abbey of St. Médard, founded in 6c (now enclosed within a school); 13c chap-

ter-house and 9c crypt; fmr. necropolis of Merovingian kings.
Vicinity ● 18 km E, *Braine*: church of St. Yved, interesting late 12–13c building, from beginnings of Goth. style; 15c corbelled house.

Solesmes (Abbey)
72 – Sarthe 17 – B 1
This famed mother-abbey of the Benedictines in France, on site of abbey founded in 11c, now comprises mainly late-19c buildings in Goth. style, looming high over R. *Sarthe*. V.a. to church only (services with absolutely superb Gregorian chanting); within church, partly Romanesque in style, the transept contains remarkable group of Goth. sculptures known as 'The Saints of Solesmes'; 'Burial of Christ', late 15c (with renowned statue of Mary Magdalene) in r. arm of transept; in l. arm is a 16c Burial of the Virgin.

Sologne
See: **Aubigny-sur-Nère***, Ch. de **Beauregard***, Ch. de **Chambord***, the **Chapelle-d'Angillon***, Ch. de **Cheverny***, La **Ferté-St. Aubin***, **Romorantin-Lanthenay***.

Sommières
30 – Gard 43 – B 1
Unusual little town, whose tiered streets are lined with old and aristocratic dwellings. The central street, partly built on the last arches of the Roman bridge, includes – at different levels – the upper market and lower market; surrounded by arcades, they are connected by arched alleys. Ruins of a feudal castle, carved out of the rock, loom above this part of town. The Ch. de Villevieille (Ren., with fine medieval towers) stands on a steep hill; inside, Louis XIII furniture and collection of pottery (v.a. in summer).
Vicinity ● 12 km SW, on the N110, magnificent 17c Ch. de Castries (v.a.)

Sorde-l'Abbaye
40 – Landes 40 – C 1
Old, once-fortified village (remains of 13c ramparts), built around v. ancient Benedictine abbey. The church, Romanesque and Goth., was badly restored in 19c. Romanesque portal with sculpted tympanum. Inside, Romanesque historiated capitals and fragments of Gallo-Roman and Romanesque mosaics. In the 16c abbot's quarters, interesting group of Gallo-Roman mosaics. Remains of 17c monastic buildings and early-18c cloister.
Vicinity ● 8 km W, Hastingues, fmr. bastide, 16c, old houses and fortified gate. ● 6 km W, *Abbaye d'Arthous*, fmr. abbey church, 13c; the

Soissons: *St. Jean-des-Vignes, now just a façade, but still of unquestioned elegance.*

Sospel: *dramatically wild scenery in the Roya valley gorges.*

16–17c abbey buildings serve as an archaeological storehouse (interesting finds); 7 km to S, *Bidache*: imposing ruins of château of the Ducs de Gramont; monumental entrance gate and main quarters, 17c; opposite, earlier living quarters – mid-16c Ren.; 14c keep.

Sorèze
81 – Tarn   42 – B 2

A school founded by the Benedictines in 17c occupies 18c buildings in a huge park. Bedroom and tomb of Henri Lacordaire, great 19c man of religion (also politician and editor) who re-established Dominican order in France (d. 1861). Remains of 15c abbey church.

Vicinity ● Sorèze is a good base for excursions in and around *Montagne Noire*; *Arfons*; the *Cammazes dam*; the *Bassin de Lampy*, enormous expanse of water surrounded by pine forest; *Saissac*, on promontory above the Carcassonne plain (fine view of the Pyrenees); to the NW, ruins of 14c castle, etc. ● 5 km W, **Revel*** and *Bassin de St. Ferréol*. ● 9.5 km NE, *Dourgne*; 2 km to NE, *Benedictine Abbeys of En Calcat*, neo-Romanesque in style (Gregorian services).

Sospel
06 – Alpes-Maritimes   39 – B 3

Late-17c church of St. Michel has one of the masterpieces of 15c Nice school: the *Vierge Immaculée* by François Brea. Picturesque medieval bridge, with toll-gate tower.

Vicinity ● To NW, through the *Bévéra* valley (Piaon gorges and

the *Col de Turini*), round tour as far as the Pointe des Trois-Communes, highest point of the *Aution* (2,082 m., ruins of fort); from the *Turini* Pass through *La Bollène-Vésubie*: to N, **St. Martin-Vésubie***, to S, the **Vésubie** gorges. ● To SW, through the *Brouis Pass* (panorama), **Nice***. ● To NE, through the *Brouis Pass*, winding descent to the *Roya Valley* and the *Saorge* gorges, towards **Tende***; 1 km to S of dizzily perched village of *Saorge*, Romanesque Madone del Poggio sanctuary (15c frescos).

Souillac
46 – Lot   30 – A 3

Famous sculptures of the patriarch Joseph and the prophet Isaiah, masterpieces of Romanesque art, are the main focus of interest in late-12c church of Ste. Marie, fmr. abbey church with a wide nave and five cupolas; originally on the old portal, these sculptures have been re-installed on the back of the new one; the primitive pier (pilaster on r.), endowed with an extraordinary jumble of monsters, is also one of the most notable examples of Languedoc Romanesque sculpture from mid-12c.

Vicinity ● *Dordogne Valley*, **Rocamadour***, *Lacave grottoes*, *Cirque de Montvalent*, **Martel***, etc.

Soulac-sur-Mer
33 – Gironde   28 – D 2

Seaside resort, bordered by sand-dunes and surrounded by pine groves. The Romanesque Basilica of Notre Dame-de-Fin-des-Terres,

12c, was rescued from the encroaching sand in 1860. Museum of modern art.

Vicinity ● 4 km SW, *L'Amélie-sur-Mer*, set amongst pines. ● To NE, *Le Verdon* and the *Pointe de Grave*; at Port-Bloc, ferry to **Royan*** (11 km across the Gironde estuary; crossings every hour in summer, eight a day out of season; 30 mins.).

Sourches (Château)
72 – Sarthe   17 – B 1

Approached through an immense main courtyard and surrounded by

Souillac: *the prophet Isaiah seems to be dancing in this famed Romanesque sculpture.*

Strasbourg: *the Petite France quarter, the best preserved and most typical part of the old city, with its venerable houses lining the banks of the River Ill, evokes all that is colourful in Alsace tradition. Nearby, the famed spire of the red sandstone cathedral.*

a dry moat, the mid-18c château, in a lovely green setting, is imposing but elegant. The apartments are superbly furnished. The grounds were laid out by Mansart (v.a. in summer).

Souterraine (La)
23 – Creuse   24 – A 3
This little town in the upper Marche reg. has several traces of its medieval ramparts, such as the St. Jean Gate, 13–15c, and old houses. The 12–13c granite church, in Limousin style, with a belfry tower, has a harmonious Romanesque portal; in the nave, interesting capitals; 11c crypt, remains of Gallo-Roman sanctuary. Lantern of the Dead.

Souvigny
03 – Allier   25 – A 2
St. Pierre (fmr. Romanesque and Goth. priory), one of the most beautiful churches in Bourbonnais reg., is necropolis of the royal Dukes of Bourbon; the Chapelle Vieille, late 14c, to r. of the choir, houses the tomb, with recumbent statues in white marble, of Louis II of Bourbon (d. 1410) and his wife; the Chapelle Neuve, mid 12c, on l. of choir, holds that of Charles I of Bourbon (d. 1456) and his wife, adorned with a famed late-15c statue of Ste. Madeleine holding out a phial of perfume; under this chapel, large burial vault; Romanesque capitals in nave and side-aisles. To r. of church, remains of 16–18c fmr. priory (imposing neo-Classical façade). In fmr. church of St. Marc, built in Burgundian

Romanesque style, is a lapidary mus. (with renowned 'Souvigny Calendar', a 12c column of the Zodiac, richly ornamented); also a mus. of glass-making and stained-glass.

Stenay
55 – Meuse   7 – A 3
Former stronghold on R. *Meuse*. Interesting 17–18c houses with porches, lining the Place de la Republique and Place Poincaré, built at right angles to each other.
Vicinity ● To NW, *Beaumont-en-Argonne*: curious 16–17c Spanish houses. ● **Belval*** forest, to SW.

Strasbourg
67 – Bas-Rhin   14–B 2
As far as art is concerned, one of the richest towns in France. The R. *Ill*, which crosses the city, splitting into two large loops, feeds the canals of the picturesque quarter of 'Petite France'. ● The 13–15c cath. of Notre Dame, in red sandstone from the Vosges, is a magnificent Goth. edifice; towering over the W facade is a slender spire, 142 m. high, a veritable Strasbourg 'beacon' (superb panorama); famed 13–14c sculptures on the portals (now in the Mus. de l'Oeuvre Notre Dame and replaced by replicas) include in partic. The Foolish and the Wise Virgins; on r. side, the 13c Clock Portal is composed of two Romanesque doors, side by side; interesting statues (replicas) of the Church and the Synagogue; on the two tympanums, Coronation and Death of the Virgin. Inside, splen-

did group of 13–14c stained-glass windows; the transept is divided in two by the famous Pilier des Anges, surrounded by juxtaposed statues of angels, Evangelists and Christ; in the S arm, popular astronomic clock, 1571, with mechanical figures. ● In the Place de la Cathédrale, 15–16c Maison Kammerzell, typical Alsatian house (restaurant). The Mus. de l'Oeuvre Notre Dame occupies several 14, 16 and 17c houses, Hostelry du Cerf, Maison de l'Oeuvre and gardens; it contains rare-Alsatian art from Middle Ages to 17c; displayed in period room settings, it captures the 'feel' most successfully. The Ch. des Rohan, superb example of 18c Classical architecture, has three mus.: fine arts, decorative arts and archaeology. Large Cardinals' apartments include King's Bedchamber, Assembly Room, Bishops' Room, Synod Room, chapel, etc., and are decorated in a sumptuous but refined manner; the ceramics collection in Mus. des Arts Décoratifs is one of the best in Europe. The Mus. des Beaux Arts has some great works (Giotto, Botticelli, Correggio, Raphaël, Veronese, El Greco, Zurbarán, Murillo, Goya, Rubens, Van Dyck, Watteau, Delacroix) and a large group of still lifes. The late-16c Grande-Boucherie houses hist. mus. Opposite, in the old Customs House: mus. of modern art (works by Manet, Monet, Renoir, Klimt, Braque, Klee, Arp, Max Ernst and many contemp. artists; also Art Nouveau stained-glass and abstracts). On other bank of *Ill*, in three 16–17c houses, Mus.

The cathedral's astronomic clock; its mechanical figures file out at 12.30.

STRASBOURG

0   200 m

Parc de l'Orangerie
Parc de la Contade
Bd. du Pt. Wilson
R. du Fbg de Pierre
R. des Bonnes-Gens
Av. des Vosges
P. de Justice
du Gal Castelnau
R.
Palais du Rhin
Place des Halles
Pl. Clement
Q. J. Sturm
R. Schœpflin
Pl. de la République
Le Port
Bibliothèque
Conservatoire de Musique
R. de la Liberté
R. du Fbg de Saverne
[Fossé] [du] Kléber
Faux Rempart
Q. Kellermann
R. de la Fonderie
Théâtre
Préfecture
R. de la Marseillaise
Pl. et
R. Kageneck
R. Kuhn
St Pierre
Le Jeune
R. de la Nuée Bleue
R. Brûlée
R. du Dôme
R. Desaix
Q. de Paris
Pl. et R. de la Hte Montée la Mésange
Aubette
H. de Ville
R. des Juifs
R. du Parchemin
R. Marne
R. du 'Marché-aux-Vins'
St Pierre Kléber
Temple-Neuf
R. des Grandes-Arcades
St Etienne
Pl. National
St Pierre Le Vieux
R. du 22 Novembre
Grand' Rue
R. des Francs-Bourgeois
R. des Frères
R. des Veaux
LA PETITE FRANCE
R. du Bain-aux-Plantes
R. des Dentelles
Pl. Gutenberg
Maison Kammerzell
Cathédrale
Pl. du Château
Maison de l'Œuvre N-D.
Ch. des Rohan
des Bateliers
Barrage Vauban
Q. Finkwiller
St Thomas
Hôtel du Commerce
Musée historique
Ste. Madeleine
Pl. de Zurich
R. Finkwiller
R. des Glacières
L'ILL
Div. Leclerc
R. de la Douane
Musée d'Art contemp.
Musée Alsacien
Pl. d'Austerlitz
Hôpital
R. de la 1ère Armée
KEHL N 4

Alsacien. See also zoological mus., and university's Egyptology collection. Strasbourg's museums are open daily, exc. Tues. and certain holidays. Check opening times. ● The city has some outstanding churches. St. Thomas, now a Protestant church (v.a.), has magnificent monumental mausoleum of Marshal de Saxe, French military chief in first half of 18c, by sculptor Pigalle. St. Pierre-le-Jeune, also now Protestant, has fine late-13c rood-screen and 18c panelling in the choir. ● Old Strasbourg is v. picturesque; Rue de la Monnaie and Rue des Dentelles lead to Rue du Bain-aux-Plantes, lined with timbered, corbelled houses. The 'Petite France' is one of the most attractive corners in this typically Alsatian district, with its old houses reflected in the canals; the 'covered bridges', once fortified, still have four 14c towers; opposite, Vauban's dam on the *Ill* (from it, good view over 'Petite France'). Many old houses in the Grand-Rue. ● See, too, the Parc de Contades and the Synagogue de la Paix (1955), the Parc de l'Orangerie, the European Palace of the Rights of Man (1966) and the Palais de l'Europe (1977). Maison de la Radio, 1961 (broadcasting centre: in the auditorium, huge ceramic composition by Lurçat). ● Motorboat trips, run daily in summer, enable one to explore the town along the *Ill* and its canals (floodlit in summer), the port and the *Rhine*, also *Rhine* cruises, etc. (Information at S.I.).
Vicinity ● NE, Robertsau Woods, good walks, The Fuchs-am-Buckel, pleasant spot on banks of the *Rhine*

(restaurant, canoeing, etc.). ● To S, the Baggersee, small lake, water sports. ● To E, Ponts-du-Rhin on l. bank of the river; Franco-German Customs are on the Pont de l'Europe (1960); on r. bank (West Germany), *Kehl*. ● To SW, the *Bruche* valley as far as *Saales*, via **Molsheim***, *Mutzig* (famous for its beer), *Schirmeck* and *Rothau*, where the road leaves for **Struthof*** and **Ste. Odile***.

Struthof (Le)
67 – Bas-Rhin   **14 – A 3**
Site of one of the most appalling Nazi concentration camps (v.a.). Several parts have been preserved (crematorium oven, gas chamber, cells, etc.). National Deportation Necropolis and Memorial (Tomb of the Unknown Deportee).

Suippes
51 – Marne   **12 – C 1**
The picturesque reg. of the Hurlus, devastated during the 1914–18 war, unfolds to the NE. Numerous military cemeteries and commemorative monuments (mediocre for the most part); the Navarin Farm cemetery has a crypt and ossuary (tomb of General Gouraud, deputy to Marshal Lyautey in Morocco and later Governor of Paris).

Suisse Normande
See **Clécy***   **10 – B 1**

Sully-sur-Loire (Château)
45 – Loiret   **18 – C 2**
Imposing feudal fortress, surrounded by flowing water (v.a., March to mid Nov.), it has two

parts: 15c feudal keep, flanked by four small corner towers, with a high wooden roof, and the 'little château', updated in 17c by Sully (Henri IV's Minister); v.a. to his study and drawing room. In the feudal part, see the Guard Room and the upstairs room in the keep.
Vicinity ● 8 km NW, Abbey of **St. Benoît-sur-Loire***

Suresnes
92 – Hauts-de-Seine   **11 – C 1**
Memories of old vineyard and its wine harvests are preserved in René Sordes municipal mus., Ave. des Cités-Unies; also ethnography, archaeology and town hist. Mid-19c fort of Mont-Valérien rises over a magnificent panorama; in a clearing (guided tours every afternoon), the Germans shot nearly 5,000 hostages and members of the Resistance between 1940 and 1944; the chapel is covered with their graffiti; on SW ramp of the fort, imposing Natnl. Memorial to Fighting France (guided tours daily).

Surgères
17 – Charente-Maritime   **23 – A 3**
All that remains of 16c château of the Counts of Surgères is half-ruined outer wall, flanked by towers, which stretches for about 600 m. 12c church of Notre Dame has a Romanesque façade (much restored), whose architecture and sculpted subjects unite into a majestic composition. Large cooperative dairy of Surgères, 'capital' of Charentes butter region, houses Natnl. Dairy School (v.a. on request).

T

Talcy (Château)
41 – Loir-et-Cher   18 – A 2
Rebuilt in early 16c on site of a 13c dwelling, château has a square keep, flanked by turrets, which adds to its severe ext. appearance. But int. courtyard, which has beautiful covered well, is harmonious. In second courtyard, an impressive 16c dovecote, with 1,500 niches, and an interesting 17c wine press, in working order. In the apartments, superb 17 and 18c furniture: especially worth seeing are the dining room, with 18c paintings, and the Chambre de Charles IX, whose 17c furniture is upholstered in Hungarian-style embroidery (v.a., cl. Tues.). Cassandre Salviati, one of Ronsard's loves, lived here.

Tallard
05 – Hautes-Alpes   38 – C 2
An old town, with crumbling ramparts, traversed by two intersecting streets lined with old houses. 12 and 16c church. Fmr. Templars' chapel, 13c. The 14–16c château, perched on rocky outcrop above R. *Durance*, has early-16c Goth. chapel and Ren. buildings, notably inc. aristocratic apartments (n.v.a.);

TANCARVILLE (bridge)
76 – Seine-Maritime   4 – C 3
One of Europe's biggest suspension bridges (1,410 m. long, and 47 m. high mid-span), over R. *Seine* (toll). The old Ch. de *Tancarville*, built on rocky promontory 50 m. high, known as the Nez de Tancarville, has a triangular outer wall flanked by 13, 14, and 15c towers; the new château, dating from 18c, has recently been rebuilt.

inside, huge Salle des Gardes, 35 m. long.

Talmont-sur-Gironde
17 – Charente-Maritime   28 – D 1
Set apart from the flower-lined village lanes, in middle of small cemetery, the 12c church of Ste. Radegonde, built on steep rock above R. *Gironde*, is an excellent example of Saintonge Romanesque architecture; fine portal with sculpted arching. Until recently, when its foundations were strengthened, the church was threatened by sea's erosion of the chalk cliff on which it stands. From cemetery, fine view of Gironde estuary and the Meschers cliffs (see **Royan***).
Vicinity ● 4 km, Fâ mill; Gallo-Roman remains, panorama.

Tanlay (Château)
89 – Yonne   19 – C 1
Superb Ren. and 17c construction; it comprises a small château, ahead of an arcaded green courtyard, and a large château. The main body of

the building is connected to the two wings by two turret staircases, leading up to the Tour des Archives and Tour de la Chapelle (v.a., cl. Tues., Easter to Nov. 1). Sumptuous apartments. In corner turret, the Tour de la Ligue, is an interesting mythological fresco, depicting different characters from the Religious Wars, some dressed in the style of classical antiquity. Attractive grounds with canal leading to la Gloriette (526 m. long).
Vicinity ● 3 km NE, remains of fmr. Abbey of Quincy, 12, 13, and 16c buildings. ● 17.5 km SE, Ch. d'**Ancy-le-Franc***.

Tarascon
13 – Bouches-du-Rhône   43 – D 1
The majestic château of royal Counts of Provence (late 14–mid 15c) stands on banks of R. *Rhône* (v.a., cl., Tues.); there are two parts: to N, the bailey; to S, the enormous aristocratic living quarters. Inner courtyard has beautiful Goth. Flamboyant decoration, vaulted

Talmont-sur-Gironde: the Romanesque church of Ste. Radegonde overlooks the Gironde estuary from a beautiful cliff-top position. The arching of the portal is adorned with imaginary animals.

Tanlay: *built about 1550, the château is one of Burgundy's finest Renaissance buildings. A monumental portal opens on to the main courtyard.*

chapel and rooms; fmr. apartments of Provence's King René (15c) have fine views over the Rhône. 14c church of Ste. Marthe, with delicately carved late-12c portal; inside, several works of art, including tomb and recumbent statue of Jean de Cossa, Seneschal of Provence, one of the earliest pieces of Italian Ren. sculpture in France (late 15c). In crypt, fmr. tomb of Ste. Marthe, 16c; the saint's actual tomb, a 17c Genoese work, is now in the apse, holding 10c sarcophagus in which she was buried. Hôpital St. Nicolas has 15c chapel and pharmacy dating from 1742. Mus. of Old Tarascon and mus.-house of Tartarin, Alphonse Daudet's fictional hero (hist. documents, waxworks). *Vicinity* ● La Montagnette (see **St. Michel-de-Frigolet***).

Tarascon-sur-Ariège
09 – Ariège   42 – A 3
Situated at confluence of R. *Ariège* and the *Vicdessos*; consists of old upper town and modern lower town. Interesting 17c church with Gothic portal.
Vicinity ● 5 km S, **Niaux*** grotto and *Vicdessos valley*. ● To SE, the N20 climbs up the *Ariège valley* from Tarascon to **Ax-les-Thermes*** (26 km), via Notre Dame-de-Sabart (fortified Romanesque church, fmr. abbey church; pilgrimage centre); *Ussat-les-Bains* (Lombrives grotto, impressive underground site, where, it is said, Cathar 'heretics' were immured and left to die; impressive concretions (guided tours daily in summer). *Luzenac* (Ch. de *Lordat*, 13–15c, superb panorama) and finally **Ax-les-Thermes***. ● A more scenic way of getting to **Ax*** is via the Route des Corniches, from Bompas (3 km N

TARN Gorges)
48 – Lozère   37 – A 2
One of France's greatest natural wonders, with many different features over a distance of 50 km. Apart from the scenic route (107B) which follows the bottom of the gorges (see **Florac*** and **Ste. Énimie***) from *Ispagnac*, the trip down the river by boat from *La Malène* is also highly rec.; the river, broken by rapids, breasts the narrowest part of the canyon, (1 km long), then enters the bowl of Les Baumes, with its impressive reddish rocky walls, and the Pas de Soucy, marked by huge limestone blocks (see the Aiguilhe, strange monolith 80 m. high). ● Seasoned walkers are rec. to start from *Le Rozier* and follow the corniches of the *Causse Méjean* (marked paths). The main parts of the *Tarn* gorges are floodlit in summer. ● The **Jonte*** gorges at *Rozier* lead to the **Armand*** aven (swallow hole), *Dargilan grotto* and **Meyrueis***.

of Tarascon), passing through *Cazenave*, the Pas de Soulombrie and Unac, with its Romanesque church with twin-windowed, four-storey belfry.

Tarbes
65 – Hautes-Pyrénées 41 – B 2
Beautifully laid out, the Massey Gardens are amongst the finest open to the public in the Midi (35 acres). Mus. Massey (cl. Tues.) has archaeological collections and painting galleries; also houses Mus. International des Hussards (Hussars). Viewing table at top of tower (wide panorama). Restored late-14c cloister from abbey of St. Sever-de-Rustan. 18c house where Field-Marshal Foch was born is now a mus. The cath., called La Sède (The Seat), is built in modified Romanesque style. National stud farm (v.a. to grounds and stables). *Vicinity* ● 6 km W, Ibos: fortified 14c church in brick and pebbles, with circular parapet walk; vast panorama from plateau that separates the Bigorre from the Béarn (orientation guide). ● 17 km NW, *Montaner*: superb brick keep, 40 m. high, ringed by 20-sided outer wall: one of the magnificent fortresses built by Gaston Phébus, Comte de Foix, during his struggle against the Comte d'Armagnac.

Tavant
37 – Indre-et-Loire 17 – C 3
The late-11c church (apply to caretaker) houses interesting group of Romanesque paintings; in the upper church, only remaining frescos are in the choir (Christ in Majesty); in the tiny crypt, which rests on eight round pillars, the vaulted walls were once entirely covered in paintings, and those that remain are some of the best examples of Romanesque art in France (three of David: playing the harp, dancing and his fight with the lion).

Tende
06 – Alpes-Maritime 39 – B 3
Small town, built in tiers on mountain-side, whose slate-roofed houses have high blackish façades. Remains of castle. Late-15c church of Notre Dame-de-l'Assomption. Good base for excursions. *Vicinity* ● To S, *Roya valley* (see **Sospel***). ● To W, **Merveilles*** valley via *St. Dalmas-de-Tende*. ● To E, **La Brigue***.

Thann
68 – Haut-Rhin 21 – A 1
Picturesque old town, dominated by remains of Ch. d'Engelbourg. Church of St. Thiébaut is splendid example of 14–15c Gothic Flamboyant; its W portal is one of the masterpieces of late-14c Alsace

THÉUS (Demoiselles)
05 – Hautes-Alpes 38 – C 2
To NE of half-abandoned village of Théus, in picturesque setting of strangely jagged rocks, the Vallauria ravine offers the strange spectacle of pillars or needles which have been protected from erosion by a capping of rock. This 'Salle de Bal des Demoiselles Coiffées' (literally, Ballroom of the Young Ladies in Hats) is one of the more unusual sights in the Alps. Other examples of the phenomenon can be found on the E bank of the Lac de **Serre-Ponçon*** and on the **St. Véran*** and *Col de Vars* roads.

version of Gothic; in the choir, 15c stalls carved with humorous, caricature-style verve; 15c stained-glass windows. A hist. mus. has now been installed in the old Corn Exchange, 16c (archaeology, folklore etc.). *Vicinity* ● Route du **Vin d'Alsace*** (wine road). ● Routes des **Crêtes** (ridge road).

Thiers
63 – Puy-de-Dôme 31 – A 1
Small industrial town built in tiers on banks of R. *Durolle*. Many old 15–16c houses (see Maison du Pirou, Maison des Sept Péchés Capitaux and Maison de l'Homme des Bois, in particular); curious 'Coin des Hasards' (literally 'Chance Corner') and Maître Raymond Tower, etc. Churches: St. Genès is Romanesque and Gothic; Moutier, Romanesque but defaced (interesting capitals); St. Jean, 15c, perched above the *Durolle*, has fine view from its cemetery. Cutlery mus. in fmr. Hôtel des Échevins (16c magistrates' house), and Maison des Couteliers (cutlers' workshops in operation). Wide views over the Limagne, the Dôme

mountains and the Mts. Dore from the ramparts. The 'valley road' follows the *Durolle* (140 waterfalls in only 3 km). *Vicinity* ● To NE, via *St. Rémy-sur-Durolle*, cutlery centre, the *Bois-Noirs* massif, the *Puy de Montoncel* (1,292 m.), vast panorama), and, 2.5 km farther on, *Puy de Snidre*. ● 16 km W, *Lezoux*: fmr. Gallo-Roman ceramic centre; archaeological mus.; to S, *Ravel*, with 13c church and 17–18c château flanked by towers and 13c keep; inside, fine 18c apartments (v.a. in summer). *Moissat-Bas*; in church, reliquary of St. Lomer, a masterpiece of 13c plate. ● To E, the Rochers (rocks) des Margerides. ● To S, Rocher de Bordes, vast panorama.

Thines
07 – Ardèche 37 – B 2
Old, half-abandoned village, with houses of schist, in a setting of desolate grandeur. Early-12c granite church, with noteworthy ext. sculpted decoration, especially on portal on S side. Parc National des *Cévennes*'s craft centre in house typical of the region.

Thionville
57 – Moselle   7 – B 3
Fmr. stronghold on R. *Moselle*. The
market place is partly bordered by
arcaded houses. Belfry, fmr. 15c
watchtower. Fmr. Hôtel des Seig-
neurs de Raville, some of it 15c. The
Tour aux Puces, robust 14-sided
tower from 12 and 13c, houses local
hist. mus. Unique Kern organ and
baroque chest in parish church of
St. Maximin.
Vicinity ● 3 km NW, view over
town and valley from terrace of
Crève-Coeur. ● 18 km NE, *Sierck-
les-Bains*, below remains of fmr.
château of the Dukes of Lorraine;
1.5 km farther on, chapel of Mari-
enfloss, remnant of 12–13c charterhouse (13c church, pilgrimage
centre). ● The industrial landscapes
of the 'Land of Iron' have their own
peculiar beauty.

Thoiry (Château and Zoo)
78 – Yvelines   11 – B 2
The late 16c–early 17c château
(v.a.) has tastefully decorated and
furnished apartments; porcelain
collection from Far East, Gobelins
tapestries, etc. ● In the 74-acre
zoological park, follow the arrowed
route; safari park, which inc.
'African reserve' and 'Tiger Park',
must be visited in closed private cars
or by minibus.

Thônes
74 – Haute Savoie   32 – C 1
Holiday resort; excursion centre.
Vicinity ● 3 km NW, *Morette*; the
heroes of Glières, 1944 (see

*Annecy**) lie in its graveyard;
Morette waterfall, 30 m. drop. ●
8.5 km NE, *St. Jean-de-Sixt*, pleasant excursion base, particularly to
the Tête du Danay, Mt. Lachat, and
Forgeassoud ridge; 3 km to SE, *La
Clusaz*, renowned winter sports
resort, from where you can reach
the *Aravis* pass (1,498 m.).

Thonon-les-Bains
74 – Haute-Savoie   26 – C 2
Spa and holiday centre above *Lac
Léman* (Lake Geneva). The late-19c
neo-Goth. basilica of St. François-
de-Sales stands next door to the 11c
church of St. Hyppolite, altered in
17c; crypt is part-Romanesque; rich
int. decoration: stucco work and
17c paintings in the Italian style.
Mid-17c Ch. de Sonnaz houses
interesting Mus. du Chablais.
Vicinity ● 3 km NE, *Ch. de Ripaille*,
early 15c but altered in late 19c
(v.a., cl. Mon., April–Oct.) ● 6.5 km
S, ruins of the two *Ch. des Allinges*,
11–14c; within enceinte of the
Château-Neuf, late-11c chapel of
Les Allinges, wide views. ● 16.5 km
W, via *Sciez*, *Yvoire* – feudal township typical of Savoie, with narrow,
winding streets, two Goth. town
gates, old houses, an early-14c
castle and 13, 17 and 19c church.

Thor (Le)
84 – Vaucluse   38 – A 3
Superb Romanesque church of
Notre Dame-du-Lac, with Gothic
rib vaulting, ancient-style porch, an
octagonal belfry and polygonal
apse with blind arcades. Old ram-

Thoiry: *its 'African Reserve' has
giraffes, zebras, lions, ostriches
and elephants.*

parts with 14c town gate topped by
a belfry. Town is centre for trade in
(Chasselas) table grapes.
Vicinity ● 1.5 km N, Thouzon grottoes, concretions, ruins of Ch. de
Thouzon, 11c Romanesque chapel
of Ste. Croix.

Tende: *the village lies under the towers of the former Château des Lascaris (dismantled in 1692).*

Thoronet (Abbey)
83 – Var   44 – C 1
Beautifully situated in the midst of
pines, the abbey church of St.
Laurent and the late-12c monastic
buildings are a notable illustration
of the sobriety and starkness of Cistercian architecture. The simplicity
and architectural harmony of the
cloister (on a slight slope, with
monks' lavabo) is particularly
pleasing. Chapterhouse (Gothic
vaulting), dormitory, store-room
and laymen's building; tithe barn
and oil-crusher (v.a.).

Thouars
79 – Deux-Sèvres   23 – B 1
This old town, with narrow,
winding streets lined with corbelled
houses (notably in Rue St. Médard
and Rue du Château), still has a
large part of its ramparts and some
interesting churches: 12 and 15c St.
Laon, 12 and 15c St. Médard
(sculpted central portal). The
château, built in 17c on an amphitheatre of terraces linked by stairs,
has an elegant, early-16c chapel in
Goth. Flamboyant and Ren. styles.
Mus. has colls. of regional archaeology, pottery and glass.
Vicinity ● Vallée de la Cascade
(3 km W). ● Vallée de l'*Argenton*
(6 km W). ● Corrie of Missé (5 km
SE). ● 12 km E, Ch. d'**Oiron***.

Thury-Harcourt
14 – Calvados   10 – B 1
The château of the Ducs d'Harcourt, 17c, was burned down in
1944 (v.a. to grounds surrounding
its ruins).
Vicinity ● To W, Mt. Pinçon (panorama). ● 2.5 km NW, Boucle du
Hom. ● To NW, *Aunay-sur-Odon*
and *Villers-Bocage*, destroyed in
1944, provide good examples (the

churches in particular) of modern-
style reconstruction.

Tiffauges (Château)
85 – Vendée   16 – D 3
This is the château of Gilles de Rais,
alias 'Bluebeard', whose foul deeds
and turbulent life inspired the 17c
writer Charles Perrault. Its remains
cover a large area and include: 12c
keep, 15c Tour du Vidame, Guard
Room and Salle de Veille (literally
'Watch Room'; fine wooden roof)
15c chapel with 11c crypt (v.a., cl.
Tues., in summer).

Tignes-les-Boisses
73 – Savoie   32 – D 2
A new village (at alt. of 1,820 m.)
built on l. bank of R. *Isère*, replac-
ing the old one which was submerged when the *Tignes Barrage*
was built (1947–1952); 295 m. wide
and 180 m. high, the dam is linchpin
of the upper Isère's hydro-electric
complex.
Vicinity ● To SW, *Lac de Tignes*
(2,100 m.) and, on banks of the lake,
a modern winter sports resort. ● To
SE, via the impressive gorge of Isère
valley to resort of **Val d'Isère***.

Til-Châtel
21 – Côte-d'Or   20 – A 2
The mid-12c Romanesque church is
one of the most interesting in Côte-
d'Or region; it has a fine portal with
five arches and sculpted tympanum
in the façade; the tympanum on S
portal is of similar style but less
ornate; inside, noteworthy historiated capitals.
Vicinity ● 9 km SE, **Bèze***; 9 km to
SE, *Mirebeau*, once-fortified town,
with 13 and 16c church (interesting Goth. statues). ● 2 km W,
lake of Marcilly and Marcilly-sur-
Tille.

Tinténiac
35 – Ille-et-Vilaine   9 – C 3
The early 20c church retains some
interesting Goth. and Ren. parts
(mid-16c door); inside, a curious
14c font known as 'Le Beau Diable
de Tinténiac' (literally 'The Handsome Devil of Tinténiac'). 16c salt
loft.
Vicinity ● 5.5 km SW, *Les Iffs*, magnificent 15–16c Gothic Flamboyant
church; superb 16c stained-glass
inside; 1.5 km farther on, Ch. de
Montmuran, 14c (v.a.), with
machicolated towers and drawbridge; 17c main living quarters. ●
8.5 km W, *Bécherel*, 1 km to W, Ch.
de *Caradeuc*, 18c, standing in
beautiful formal gardens (v.a. daily,
Apr. to Oct. 31; Sat., Sun. and
public hols., p.m., out of season). ●
8 km N, *Pleugueneuc*: fine 16c *Ch.
de la Bourbansais*, surrounded by v.
big formal gardens (v.a. ext. only);
int. renovated in 18c; zoo, stud farm
and kennels (v.a., p.m.).

Tonnerre
89 – Yonne   19 – B 1
Former hospital, founded 1293
(v.a.); its lofty, imposing roof
(48,500 sq. ft.) covers a huge
infirmary, 101 m. long, oak-
timbered, with panelled vaulting;
the beds stood against the walls in
wooden alcoves; in the chapels,
Tomb of Louvois, by Girardon, and
holy sepulchre in stone, with seven
life-sized statues, a masterpiece of
15c Burgundian realist sculpture.
The old Hôtel d'Uzès (now natnl.
savings bank), elegant early-16c
Ren. building, was birthplace of
notorious Chevalier d'Éon (18c
secret agent, ambassador, trans-
vestite). 13 and 15c church of Notre
Dame, with Ren. façade (monumental portal) and 17c tower. The
Fosse Dionne is enormous, circular
basin, fed by a spring, serving as a
wash-house (wooden roof).
Vicinity ● 1.5 km SW, fmr. abbey
of St. Michel (now a hotel), 11 and
12c ruins in vast grounds (panorama). ● 18 km to SE, Ch. d'**Ancy-
le-Franc***. ● 9 km E, Ch. de
Tanlay*.

Toucy
89 – Yonne   19 – A 2
Unusual 16c church, flanked by two
12c towers, whose apse is fmr.
façade of a Romanesque church
(salvaged parts of which were incorporated in the later building).
Vicinity ● 8.5 km NW, *Villiers-St.
Benoît*, Ch. du Fort, 16–18c,
restored in 20c. In a 17c house, mus.
of reg. art (cl. Tues.), collection of
Puisaye sandstone and Yonne
pottery, also Burgundian sculpture;
13c church has 16c mural, 'The
Three Dead Men and The Three
Live Men'.

Le Thoronet: *the arcades of the Cistercian abbey's cloister are each
divided into two bays, resting on columns.*

Toul

54 – Meurthe-et-Moselle   13 – B 2
The town's 17c wall, with access via
four gates, still stands. Superb 13–
14c fmr. cath. of St. Étienne, with
magnificent 15c Gothic Flamboyant-style façade, framed by two
octagonal towers, 65 m. high;
beautiful Ren. chapels of Joan of
Arc (on r.) and of the Bishops, on
either side of the nave; rich marble
ornamentation in the choir; interesting 13 and 14c cloister. The
church of St. Gengoult is fine
example of Champagne reg. version
of Gothic architecture (13 and 15c);
16c cloister; to S of church, remains
of Gallo-Roman ramparts.

Toul Goulic (Gorges)

22 – Côtes-du-Nord   8 – D 2
One of Brittany's most impressive
natural features: a narrow gorge in
the upper *Vallée du Blavet*, strewn
with granite boulders; a footpath
goes as far as the Pors-Poret bridge,
1 km farther on.

Toulon

83 – Var   44 – B 2
Built at the head of superb maritime
roads, the town is overlooked by
fortifications on a succession of
steep hills behind it; the Darse
Vieille (old harbour) is lined on the
Quai de Stalingrad with houses
rebuilt since 1944. Portal of fmr.
town hall, framed by Puget's
famous mid-17c *Atlantes*, has been
incorporated in façade of the Naval
Mus. (cl. Tues.). Behind it lies the
old quarter, with picturesque small
streets. 12–17c cath. of Ste. Marie-
de-la-Sède; inside, rich baroque
decoration in chapel of the Corpus-
Domini. Lively and colourful fruit
and vegetable market every day in
Cours La Fayette. Mus. of Old
Toulon, is mainly concerned with
local hist. Mus. of Toulon, Blvd.
Maréchal Leclerc (cl. Tues.), has
many examples of contemp. art and
some old paintings; its collections
reflect principal currents of international creativity in art from 1960
on. Same building houses mus. of
nat. hist. Naval arsenal; fine monumental gateway decorated with
columns and statues (moved to ease
traffic flow).
Vicinity ● To E, the Mourillon peninsula and Cap Brun; annexe of
naval mus. is housed in early-16c
Tour de la Mitre at tip of peninsula;
vast panorama over Toulon roads.
The steep Frédéric Mistral coast
road leads to Cap Brun; beyond
there, Cap de Carqueiranne (footpath). ● To SW, via La Seyne and
the corniche of *Tamaris*, to *Les
Sablettes* at entry to isthmus of *St.
Mandrier*, fishing village, with fine
view over Toulon roads (regular
boat service between Toulon and

St. Mandrier). ● To N, *Mt. Faron*,
taking cable-car from Super-
Toulon, or by road (15 km, all one-
way); mus. and natnl. memorial to
wartime Allied landing in Provence
in Beaumont tower; chapel of Notre
Dame-du-Faron and viewing table;
Faron zoo. ● 8 km NW, after *Ollioules*, the picturesque Ollioules
gorges; at Ste. Anne, follow the
Cimail gorges to *Évenos*, an old,
half-abandoned village, under
remains of basalt château; fine view
over the Ollioules gorges.

Toulouse

31 – Haute-Garonne   42 – A 1
Capital of the Languedoc region
and, architecturally speaking, one
of France's most beautiful towns;
the weathered pink and ochre of
the brick buildings is particularly
attractive. Begin at the Capitole
(town hall) whose mid-18c main
façade overlooks the vast square of
the same name, which is lined by
brick houses; inside, Henri IV
courtyard, early 17c, and on first
floor, in the Galerie des Illustres
(62 m. long), one of the best groups
of late-19c academic painting and
decoration, lavishly ornate (v.a.);
the Théâtre du Capitole occupies
S part of the building. Behind the
Capitole, a powerful mid-15c keep.
● Take the Rue du Taur to St.
Sernin, a distinguished late 11–mid
12c basilica, one of the finest
Romanesque churches in France;
apart from main door of the
narthex, access is through the Porte
Miégeville, with statues carved in
the Romanesque style of the Midi,
or the Porte des Comtes (Romanesque capitals); brick int., 115 m.
long, characteristic of pilgrimage
churches. Seven late-11c marble
bas-reliefs adorn the ambulatory;
the choir is decorated with frescos
and the high altar incorporates the

monumental 18c tomb of St.
Sernin; rich church treasure in the
crypt and many 12–13c reliquaries.
● Opposite the basilica, Mus. St.
Raymond in an old brick college of
same name, early 16c (cl. Tues.):
prehistory, Gallo-Roman, Bar-
barian, etc. Jacobins church and
monastery provide good example
of Southern Gothic architecture
(v.a.). From there you can get to the
quays, whence superb panorama
over R. *Garonne*, Hospice de la
Grave, Hôtel-Dieu and the Pont-
Neuf. From the basilica of Notre
Dame-de-la-Daurade, 18c, go
through the old Daurade quarter to
finest Ren. building in Toulouse:
the Hôtel d'Assézat, headquarters
of many learned societies (v.a.). ●
In the Dalbade quarter, Rue de la
Dalbade and Rue de la Fonderie
have sumptuous brick mansions
whose most notable features are
sometimes in the courtyards: No. 30
(next to early-16c brick church of
La Dalbade, entirely restored after
collapse of the belfry in 1926),
mansion of the Knights of St. John
of Jerusalem; No. 25, Maison de
Pierre, aka the Hôtel Clary, early
17c; No. 22, Hôtel de Guillaume
Molinier (superb sculpted Ren.
portal), etc. The cath. of St. Étienne
is unusual in that the early-12c nave
and late 13–14c choir are not built
on the same axis. This district also
has some aristocratic residences:
Hôtel d'Ulmo, Ren., 16 Rue Ninau;
Hôtel de Mansencal, 1 Rue Espi-
nasse; Hôtel d'Espic or MacCarthy,
18c, 3 Rue Mage; Hôtel du Vieux-
Raisin, or Beringuier-Maynier, 26
Rue du Languedoc – note the rich
elegance of its sculpted decoration;
the Hôtel Dahus, or de Roquette
and the late-15c Tour de Tournoer
at 9 Rue Ozenne, etc. The Rues
(streets) of St. Rome, des Changes,
Croix-Bragnon, Malcousinat, St.

Tonnerre: *high roofs with glazed tiles add to the charm of this old
Burgundian town, famed for its ancient hospital.*

Jacques, Velane, Nazareth, etc., also have notable mansions. ● As well as Mus. St. Raymond, Toulouse has several other large mus.: that of Les Augustins (cl. Sun. a.m. and Tues.) is housed in an old Augustinian convent, whose large Goth. and small Ren. cloisters still stand. The chapterhouse, chapel and some 19c monastic buildings contain one of the richest of all groups of Romanesque and Gothic sculpture. In fmr. church of the Augustines, large group of religious paintings (Murillo, Van Dyck, Tournier, Chalette, Perugino and Rubens' superb *Christ Between The Two Thieves*); enigmatic early-16c statues of St. Sernin, in terra-cotta. In the exhibition rooms, notable collection of paintings, mainly 17–19c, inc. Philippe de Champaigne, Mignard, Ingres, Delacroix, Courbet, Corot; also works from Toulouse school (Tournier, Rivalz). Mus. Georges Labit has collections from Egypt, India and Far East. Mus. Paul-Dupuy: reg. art and ethnography. Mus. of Old Toulouse is housed in late-16c Hôtel du May. Natural hist. mus. *Vicinity* ● To NW, the Ponts-Jumeaux ('Twin Bridges'), at junction of the *Canal du Midi*, the *Canal Latéral à la Garonne* and the Canal de Brienne; late-18c bridge with large sculpted bas-relief. ● 5 km S, residential city of Toulouse-Le-Mirail, one of Europe's largest New Towns. ● 14 km W, *Pibrac*:

château is the finest example of Toulouse Ren. style (v.a. on request); 300 m. from it, triumphal arch in brick, dating from 1578; parish church contains tomb of Ste. Germaine (pilgrimage on June 15); Romanesque-Byzantine basilica (unfinished). ● 33 km SE, *Villefranche-de-Lauragais*, 14c church, with imposing wall-belfry in Toulouse Gothic style.

Touquet-Paris-Plage (Le)
62 – Pas-de-Calais   1 – B 3
One of the most attractive resorts on the *Côte d'Opale*, built during 19c, between forest and sea, and v. popular with the English. Villas and luxurious private residences within 2,000–acre forest; also airport, golf course, casinos, race-course, sports centre, marina, beach, etc. The seafront esplanade ends at large terrace (panorama).
Vicinity ● 5 km SE, *Étaples*, fishing village on r. bank of *Canche* estuary; picturesque sailors' quarter, with narrow streets lined by colourfully painted little houses. ● Excursion recommended in *Canche* valley, towards **Montreuil***, **Hesdin*** and *Frévent*.

Tour-d'Aigues (La)
84 – Vaucluse   44 – B 1
Remains of late-16c château are approached through monumental gate imitating the style of classical antiquity: two immense fluted pilasters frame a split-level triumphal

arch, separated by frieze of sculpted trophies. Church of Notre Dame has a nave built in Provençal Romanesque style.
Vicinity ● 5.5 km W, *Ansouis*: early-17c château of the Comtes de Sabran includes remains of medieval fortress; inside, Flemish tapestries and 17–18c furniture (v.a., p.m., cl. Wed.).

Tournon
07 – Ardèche   31 – D 3
Old town on r. bank of R. *Rhône*; opposite, *Tain-L'Hermitage*. In the château, rebuilt 15–16c on remains of feudal fortress, is small mus. (ethnography and hist. of the Rhône, works by sculptor Marcel Gimond, d. 1961, a native of Tournon); good view from terrace. 15c church, restored in 17c (with 16c murals in Penitents chapel). The grammar school, fmr. early-16c college rebuilt in 18c, is among the most notable educational buildings from olden times (Ren. entrance portico, chapel dating from 1721).
Vicinity ● To SW, the *Doux* gorges: from the Pont de Duzon, path leads to the 'Cuves de Duzon'. ● To S, corniche road to *St. Romain-de-Lerps*; viewing terraces; immense panorama over 13 departments.

Tournus
71 – Saône-et-Loire   25 – D 2
Church of St. Philibert – fmr. 10–12c abbey church – is outstanding example of Romanesque art; int. is in three distinct parts: the powerful,

Toulouse: *the pink brick Romanesque basilica of St. Sernin, with its extraordinary belfry.*

On the Miégeville door's capitals: *Massacre of the Innocents, Annunciation, Visitation.*

contemp. art. Mus. du Compagnonnage (cl. Tues.) is in fmr. abbey of St. Julien, whose 13c Gothic church has Romanesque belfry; vast rib-vaulted store-rooms and late-12c chapterhouse. Mus. des Vins de Touraine. The Place Foire-du-Roi is lined with 15–16c gabled houses; early-16c Ren. Hôtel Babou de la Bourdaisière. The medieval part of town, with many old houses and mansions, centres on the Place Plumereau; it embraces the Romano-Byzantine basilica of St. Martin, flanked by a Clock Tower and the Tour Charlemagne, the only 11–12c remains of old basilica burned down in 1802. Place Plumereau itself has 15c houses in timber and brick. See also: Rue Briçonnet (No. 21, fmr. Hôtel de Choiseul, 18c; No. 16, late-15c Hôtel de Pierre du Puy, in brick and stone, now a language study centre); Rue du Mûrier (No. 7, Hôtel Raimbault, early-19c: stained-glass window mus.); Place des Carmes, Rue P.-L. Courier (No. 1, Hôtel Binet, late-15c, No. 17, Hôtel Juste, 16c; No. 15, Hôtel Robin Quantin, late-16c, fine inner courtyard); Rue du Change, Rue and Place de Châteauneuf (15c Hostellerie de la Croix-Blanche), Rue des Halles, etc. 18c Hôtel Mame, at 19 Rue Émile Zola (v.a., sumptuous apartments). 15, 16 and 17c Hôtel Gouin at 25 Rue du Commerce, also archaeological mus. (cl. Wed., and in Dec.-Jan., hrs. vary).

Tournus: *entry to the old abbey church of St. Philibert is guarded by the two round towers of the Porte des Champs.*

massive narthex, (12 and 14c frescos); the nave, in pink stone; and the transept and choir, in contrasting white stone; 10c crypt decorated with 13c frescos, and, above the narthex, an upper room or Chapel of St. Michel. Still standing, on r. side of church, are N gallery of the cloister, chapterhouse and the Salle des Aumônes, or calefactory. Also several old abbey buildings around the church; 17c Logis du Trésorier, 15c abbot's living quarters and vast 12c refectory, 36 m. long. ● Mus. Greuze in fmr. Benedictine convent of Villars. Burgundian Perrin-de-Puycousin mus. in fmr. canon's house. Many old houses and mansions; in the Hôtel-Dieu (hospital), 17c pharmacy.
Vicinity ● 14 km W, *Brancion*, picturesque feudal township, perched on a sharp ridge at alt. of 400 m., below ruins of 11–14c castle. 12c Romanesque church (14c murals), 15c covered market. ● 8 km S, Uchizy, late-11c Romanesque church; unusual belfry with five offset tiers. ● 16 km SE, *Romenay*,

once fortified little town; two 14c gates stand at either end of the Grand-Rue which is lined with wooden, corbelled houses.

Tours
37 – Indre-et-Loire   17 – D 3
The capital of Touraine has two main centres of interest: the cath. of St. Gatien and mus., and medieval quarter around the Place Plumereau. The cath., an imposing 13, 14 and 15c Goth. building, has series of rare 13c stained-glass windows; charming 15–16c Psallette cloister. The Mus. des Beaux-Arts, housed in fmr. 17–18c archbishop's palace, has a sumptuous suite of rooms decorated with panelling and silk hangings (cl. Tues.); its art collections are outstanding: Italian and Flemish primitives, works by Mantegna, Magnasco, Abraham Bosse room, paintings from 17 and 18c (Rembrandt's *Flight into Egypt*, 1627, Boucher, Rubens' *Ex-voto of Virgin and Child*), neo-Classical and Romantic rooms, Delacroix, Chassériau;

Tours: *detail from carved Renaissance door.*

Troyes: *the church of St. Nizier, both Gothic and Renaissance (notable sculptures inside). On right, the narrow streets and 15–16c houses typical of the town's old quarters.*

Vicinity ● 3 km SW, *Ch. de Plessis-lès-Tours*, late 15c, houses mus. of silk weaving and local crafts. ● 3 km W, St. Cosme Priory, remains of 11, 12 and 15c church where Ronsard (Ren. poet) is buried (d. 1585); 15c Prior's House, 12c refectory. ● 3 km NW, at *St. Cyr-sur-Loire*, La Béchellerie, house in which Anatole France died (1924); mementoes of the writer. ● 10 km NE, *Ferme de Meslay*, enormous 13c barn, with remarkable chestnut-timbered roof, used for Touraine's music festivals (late June–early July). ● 4 km NE, ruins of the *Abbaye de Marmoutier* (v.a., p.m.); all that remains of the abbey are elegant early-13c Portal of the Cross and 12c bell tower; a chapel and several cells carved out of the rock serve as a reminder of 4–6c monastery, founded by St. Martin. ● 3 km E, *Rochecorbon*, at foot of cliff dominated by 15c Rochecorbon Lantern; a little 18c 'folly' houses Mus. d'Espelosin (wine mus.; cl. Tues.); intriguing troglodytic caves. ● 5 km SE, *St. Avertin*, 11 and 14–15c church; large centre for water sports, fishing and boating on R. *Cher*. ● 12 km S, *Montbazon*, below enormous, rectangular keep, 28 m. high, crowned by statue of the Virgin (v.a.)

Tréguier
22 – Côtes-du-Nord   8 – D 1
Old episcopal town, laid out in tiers above confluence of R. *Jaudy* and the Guindy. 14–15c fmr. cath. of St. Tugdual, one of Brittany's most beautiful Goth. churches, has 46 mid-17c carved oak stalls in the choir; elegant 15c cloister on N.

side. In Place du Martray, an unfortunate monument to Renan (19c scholar and critic); the 17c half-timbered house where he was born has been turned into mus. (Rue Ernest Renan). In a 17c house, Trégor hand-weaving workshop (v.a.). Many old houses, too, on the harbour, 6 km away.
Vicinity ● 2 km S, Minihy-Tréguier, 15c church; on May 19, the 'Pardon des Pauvres', lawyers and other men of the law pay tribute to St. Yves, born at the manor of Kermartin (no longer standing). ● 9 km NE, the *Pleubian* peninsula and *Sillon de Talbert* (narrow natural 'road' of sand and pebbles). ● 8 km N, Plougrescant peninsula; at *Plougrescant*, 15–16c chapel of St. Gonéry, decorated with naive paintings; granite pulpit surmounted by 16c calvary. Excursion recommended to the *Pointe du Château*, at N tip of peninsula, and to Pors-Scarff beach, with impressive jumble of rocks.

Trémolat
24 – Dordogne   29 – D 3
Interesting fortified church built in Périgord Romanesque style, with belfry-porch.
Vicinity ● To N of village, the 'Route des Crêtes' (ridge road) leads to belvedere overlooking the Cingle de Trémolat, a huge, magnificently scenic bend in the R. *Dordogne*, also famed as international watersports centre.

Tréport (Le)
76 – Seine-Maritime   5 – A 1
On l. bank of R. *Bresle*, the town is separated from *Mers-les-Bains* by

the harbour, which is dominated by 16c church of St. Jacques (sculpted Ren. portal); int. has richly sculpted keystones. On the seafront, casino and swimming pool; an 850 m.-long esplanade above the beach. Cable-car up to calvary of Les Terrasses (100 m. alt. – fine view).
Vicinity ● Many good beaches along this coast: to SW, *Criel-Plage*, *Mesnil-Val*; to NE, *Ault* and *Onival*.

Treyne (Château)
46 – Lot   36 – A 1
Near Pinsac; built in 17c on cliff overlooking R. *Dordogne*. Among château's beautifully furnished apartments (v.a.) are a large Louis XIII salon and one called Charles Quint's Room (after 16c Holy Roman Emperor). A chapel was built in the grounds to house recumbent statue of Jean de Chabannes, 15c, and a 16c Entombment.

Trois-Épis (Les)
68 – Haut-Rhin   21 – A 1
Superbly situated holiday resort. 17c convent and chapel of the Trois-Épis (popular regional place of pilgrimage); interesting modern church in reinforced concrete (1967).
Vicinity ● Belvedere, 10 mins. walk away, offers wide panorama over Alsace plain, the Black Forest and *Munster* valley. ● 30 mins. walk to NE, rocky promontory of Galz (730 m.), a place of pilgrimage, with monumental statue of Christ; vast panorama. ● From Trois-Épis, you can get to *Col du Bonhomme* via *Le Linge* (dramatic battlefield from 1914–18 war) and *Orbey*; at the

<table>
</table>

┌───┐
TRÉBOUL (Bridge)
15 – Cantal   36 – D 1
Magnificent work of art, 159 m. long and 39 m. high, above R. Truyère. It replaced a 14c Gothic bridge which, submerged by reservoir, can still be seen when water level is low. Panoramic view from the belvedere.
└───┘

Bonhomme pass, you can also join the Route des **Crêtes*** (ridge road).

Trôo
41 – Loir-et-Cher   17 – D 1
Steeply tiered, the houses of this once fortified town, built on a promontory, are linked by alleys and underground passages. See the 'caforts' (fortified cellars). Late-12c fmr. collegiate church of St. Martin, altered in 14c, and with superb Romanesque tower, is an odd mixture of Romanesque and Anjou Gothic styles; int. has Romanesque historiated capitals. In lower town, 12c Maladrerie de Ste. Catherine (hospital for lepers) and petrifactive grotto (v.a. in summer). On l. bank of R. Loir, 12c church of St. Jacques-des-Guérets, decorated with Byzantine-inspired Romanesque murals in subtle colours.
Vicinity ● 4.5 km W, Sougé (37 carved stalls, 15c, in church); 5.5 km to W, **Poncé-sur-le-Loir***.

Trouville-sur-Mer
See **Deauville***.   4 – C 3

Troyes
10 – Aube   12 – B 3
The capital of Champagne, rich in Goth. and Ren. buildings and with particularly notable churches. Cath. of St. Pierre-et-St. Paul, 13–17c, has elaborate Ren. façade, with three sculpted portals, and a fine Gothic Flamboyant rose window; the 'Beau Portail' (literally 'Beautiful Portal') of the N arm of transept is also v. ornate; inside, exceptional group of stained-glass windows – 13 and 14c (choir) and 15 and 16c (nave). Especially famed here is window on theme of The Mystic Wine-Press (1625). Gothic and Ren. church of St. Nizier; inside, rib-vaulting and elaborate keystones. Surrounding district has many 16 and 17c timbered houses. Mus. des Beaux-Arts, in fmr. abbey of St. Loup (cl. Tues.) contains archaeology, and paintings from 15 to 20c: works by Rubens, Van Dyck, Fragonard, 13 pictures by Jean Tassel de Langres, 15 Natoire, seven portraits by Boilly. Also, sculpture, from 17 and 18c (Girardon). Since 1982, fmr. bishop's palace, 16–17c, has housed fine Pierre and Denise Lévy collection of modern art (Courbet, Seurat, Gauguin, Braque, Delaunay, La Fresnaye, 80 Derain, Soutine, Wols, Balthus); also African and S Pacific art. The St. Nizier and cath. district is separated from the old town by Haute Seine Canal. ● Opposite, basilica of St. Urbain constitutes one of the masterpieces of 13c Gothic architecture: int.'s light elegance is due to the enormous number of windows, which include 13–14c stained-glass; charming 16c Virgin With Grape. Church of Ste. Madeleine has 12c nave and transept and Ren. choir with early-16c Goth. Flamboyant stone rood-screen as finely carved as lace; 16c stained-glass windows in apse; 15c statue of Ste. Marthe, major work of the 15c Troyes school. Rue de la Madeleine and very narrow Rue des Chats, lined with timbered, corbelled houses, lead to church of St. Jean, which has 14c nave and v. fine Ren. choir; inside, 17c high altar (sculptures by Girardon, painting by Pierre Mignard), 16c stained-glass. Around the church, picturesque streets and houses: Rue Champeaux, Hôtel des Ursins, Ren.; Rue Roger Salengro, Maison de l'Election, 16c; Rue des Quinze-Vingt; on corner of Rue Charbonnet, 16c Hôtel de Marisy; Rue de la Trinité, late-16c Hôtel de Mauroy (fine inner courtyard with façades that are either sculpted or decorated in the 'Champagne chess-board' style), which houses mus. of the hist. and use of implements (collection of 2,000 tools, from France and abroad, from 15c to present day). Mid-16c Hôtel de Vauluisant (v. ornate façade overlooking the courtyard) houses mus. of hist. of Troyes and Champagne reg.; also a hat mus., Mus. de la Bonneterie (cl. Tues.). Early-16c Goth. church of St. Nicolas, with Ren. additions, has original chapel of the calvary, in form of a gallery, reached up a monumental stairway (several 14–15c sculptures).
Vicinity ● Some noteworthy churches around Troyes: to N, St. Martin-ès-Vignes (Ren., with fine 17c stained-glass windows); to W, Les Noës-près-Troyes, *Ste. Savine* (16c, with 16–17c paintings); to SW, St. André-les-Vergers (16c, with fine Ren. portal and interesting statues inside); to E, *Pont-Ste. Marie* (richly decorated portals, sculpted stalls in the choir, interesting works of art), etc. ● To W, the *Forêt d'Orient*, reg. wild life park (see **Brienne-le-Château***).

Tulle
19 – Corrèze   30 – B 2
Town stretches at length along narrow Corrèze valley. 12c cath. of Notre Dame with 13c cloister and chapter-house (Mus. du Cloître André Mazeyrie: religious art and regional ethnography; also old weapons). The Enclos quarter retains its medieval appearance; numerous old houses, see in partic. the 16c Maison de Loyac (fine façade with carved decorations).
Vicinity ● 12 km NE, **Gimel***, and Ruffaud lake. ● To N, *Corrèze Valley*, picturesque drive along r. bank, then on to Vimbelle valley; in church at *Naves*, gigantic late-17c wooden retable, carved with many figures.

Turbie (La)
06 – Alpes-Maritimes   45 – B 1
Built on a rocky ridge, the village is dominated by the majestic remains of the Trophée des Alpes (aka the Trophy of Augustus), erected in 5 BC (v.a.). Monument has recently been restored and now houses small mus. From the Rondo terrace, sweeping view down to *Monte Carlo* and **Monaco***.
Vicinity ● 2 km NW, Madonna of *Laghet*: 17c church and convent, with remarkable collection of ex-voto. ● 10.5 km N, *Peille* and *Peillon* (see **Nice***). ● *Mt. Agel* (1,146 m.) looms over La Turbie to NE.

La Turbie: *the Trophée des Alpes commemorates Roman victories in Gaul.*

Ussé: *this fairytale château is said to have been the model for Sleeping Beauty's castle.* ▲

Ussel: *the granite Roman eagle – a striking, unexpected sight.* ▼

Uzerche: *St. Pierre's austere and imposing belfry.* ◄

U

Ussé (Château)
37 – Indre-et-Loire   17 – C 3
At Rigny-Ussé. Bristling with pinnacle turrets, dormer windows and chimney stacks, this elegant 15–17c building stands at top of tiers of terraces ornamented with formal gardens. Façades framing main courtyard are a blend of late Gothic and Ren. Inside, numerous works of art in the apartments, especially King's bedchamber. Lovely Gothic chapel and 15c keep (v.a., Mar. 15–Sept. 30).

Ussel
19 – Corrèze   30 – C 2
Picturesque old town of narrow streets lined by 15 and 16c turreted houses, notably in Rue du Quatre-Septembre and Place de la République, on which stands late-15c granite mansion of Dukes of Ventadour. Reg. mus. 12 and 15c church. Place Voltaire, granite Roman eagle, 1.87 m. high. 10 mins. to S, 17c Notre Dame-de-la-Chabanne, on a knoll, fine view.
Vicinity ● 9 km SW, *St. Angel*: 12 and 14c fortified granite church has Romanesque triple nave and huge 14c choir.

Utah Beach
50 – Manche   3 – D 3
'Utah Beach' stretches between Les Dunes-de-Varreville and La Madeleine. It was one of the D-Day landing beaches (June 6, 1944), and is now lined by road called the 'Route des Alliés'. Small mus. devoted to the Normandy landings (weapons, equipment, dioramas, film shows). Memorials at La Madeleine and Les Dunes-de-Varreville.

Uzerche
19 – Corrèze   30 – A 2
One of most picturesque towns in the Limousin, in magnificent setting overlooking R. *Vézère* (fine views from late-18c Turgot bridge and from the N20). 12c Romanesque church of St. Pierre is a remarkable building, with 11c crypt and Limousin-school belfry. Near church, 15c Eyssartier house with turret; main street is also lined by a number of 15–16c houses with turrets. 14c Bécharie gate, sole relic of perimeter wall's five gates, and one-time seneschal's court (flanked by three towers, police barracks).
Vicinity ● To SW, *Gorges de la*

Uzès: *its six circular offset tiers make the 12th-century Fenestrelle tower the only one of its kind in France.*

Vézère, via *Vigeois*, 11–12c former abbey church (to SW, former charterhouse of Glandier), and picturesque area known as *Le Saillant*.

Uzès
30 – Gard   37 – C 3
Château known as 'Le Duché' occupies centre of town, which is surrounded by wild heathland. The Dukes of Uzès' château, which has belonged to same family since 10c, is in the form of a huge fortified quadrilateral (v.a.); int. courtyard is dominated by Vicomté tower, with octagonal turret staircase, and Bermonde tower, an 11c square keep; elegant mid-16c Ren. façade on which are juxtaposed the three Classical orders, Doric, Ionic and Corinthian; Goth. chapel; apartments contain noteworthy 18c and Restoration furniture; ceremonial clothes belonging to Dukes of Uzès. Surrounding quarter has a number of lovely 17 and 18c Ren. mansions. 17c former cathedral of St. Théodorit is dominated by unusual 12c Romanesque Fenestrelle tower, 42 m. high, with six circular offset tiers, pierced by windows. Municipal mus. in old bishop's palace (folk ceramics). Lovely view of surrounding countryside from Promenade Jean Racine; jutting out from terrace: Racine's pavilion, where the great dramatist used to sit and daydream during his exile in Uzès (autumn 1661).
Vicinity ● 1 km N, Romanesque chapel of St. Geniès, half-ruined, in middle of pine forest. ● 4 km NW, Ch. de Montaren, rebuilt 16c on site of medieval fortress.

V W Y Z

Vaison-la-Romaine
84 – Vaucluse   38 – A 2
R. *Ouvèze* divides it in two. On l. bank, old town, dominated by ruins of late-12c castle of Counts of Toulouse, stands on a precipitous rock; its narrow streets and old houses are a delight; see 15 and 17c church, presbytery and 12–13c town marshal's house, and former episcopal palace. On r. bank, modern town stands on site of Roman city on each side of Place du 11-Novembre and Place de l'Abbé-Sautel; to E, Messii house, ancient patrician residence, Pompey portico and excavations in Puymin quarter. Archaeological mus. of Puymin hill is part of site (v.a.): among exhibits is well-known *Buste en Argent* (Roman, early 3c), and magnificent statues of emperors, numerous artefacts of Gallo-Roman daily life; to W, archaeological digs of Villasse, Buste d'Argent house and Dauphin house; to N, 1–3c Roman theatre. Church of Notre Dame, one-time cathedral, is in Provençal Romanesque style; Roman foundations and Merovingian walls have been uncovered here; 11–12c cloister houses small lapidary mus.
Vicinity ● Good departure point for climb up Mt. **Ventoux*** via *Malau-*

Vaison-la-Romaine: *statue of Empress Sabina, wife of the Emperor Hadrian (2c).*

cène, old city which once belonged to the Comtat (old county) Venaissin, 14c Romanesque fortified church.

Val (Château)
19 – Corrèze   30 – C 2
In magnificent setting, 15c château, flanked by five round towers, stands on rocky spur surrounded by waters of *Bort* reservoir, on l. bank of R. *Dordogne* (v.a.); lovely Ren. fireplaces. Beach and sailing centre.

Val-d'Isère
73 – Savoie   33 – A 2
Well-known summer and winter sports resort (1,850 m.). Cable car to Bellevarde (2,774 m.) and to Tête de Solaise (2,551 m.), magnificent views.
Vicinity ● 11 km NE and 1 hr.'s walk, Sassière lake (2,430 m.), whose green waters are overlooked by black schistous slopes of *Grande Sassière* (3,747 m.). ● To S, via *Col de l'Iseran* (2,770 m.), *Bonneval-sur-Arc*, typical Alpine village, highest in Maurienne reg. (1,734 m.); winter sports resort; arts and crafts showroom (objects in wool, wood and iron, made in winter by local residents). ● To W, **Vanoise*** natnl. park.

Valençay (Château)
36 – Indre   18 – A 3
Built on vast terraces overlooking Nahon valley, this majestic Ren. château consists of two buildings at right angles to each other, flanked by a sturdy domed round tower, called the Old Tower. 16c W building has impressive central pavilion flanked by four turrets. Mid-17c S building ends with 18c New Tower (v.a., Mar. 15–Nov. 15). In outbuildings, mus. devoted to Talleyrand, who acquired Valençay in 1803; his tomb is in Maison de la Charité, which he founded. Son et Lumière in summer. In park, Automobile du Centre mus.

Valence
26 – Drôme   31 – D 3
Late 11 and 12c Romanesque cathedral of St. Apollinaire, restored 17c, and old town which surrounds it, are worth a visit; doorway of N transept has lovely Romanesque tympanum (mutilated). The 'Pendentif' is strange Ren. funerary monument. Interesting old houses in Rue Perollerie (No. 7, Dupré-Latour house; in

courtyard, turret staircase with elegantly decorated Ren. door), Grande-Rue (1532 Têtes house, with sculpted medallions). Beaux-Arts mus., in former bishop's palace (v.a.), has noteworthy collection of 97 sketches in red chalk and drawings by Hubert Robert; lovely Roman mosaic; galleries of ethnography and local history.
Vicinity ● 4 km NW, on r. bank of R. *Rhône*, ruins of *Ch. de Crussol*: a veritable eagle's nest high above river, dominating village of *St. Péray*.

Valenciennes
59 – Nord   2 – A 3
The 'Athens of the North' has an important Fine Arts mus. rich in works from Flemish (Hieronymus Bosch, Pourbus, three Rubens, Jordaens) and French schools (Watteau, Greuze, Nattier, Boucher). Large gallery devoted to Carpeaux, born in the town, who sculpted monument to Watteau in Square Watteau: 200 sculptures, 50 paintings and several thousand sketches exhibited in rotation. Carmelite convent (by sculptor, Szekely) is highly original example of modern religious art (v.a. to chapel). See also: 13c church of St. Géry; St. Nicolas, late 18c former chapel of Jesuit college (Ren. roodscreen in white and black marble); Notre Dame-du-St. Cordon (renowned procession in Sept.). In municipal library, huge room with wood panelling and murals, fine example of 18c architecture and ornamentation.
Vicinity ● *Anzin*, bordering on *Valenciennes* (to NW), has interesting Coal-Mining and Metallurgy mus. (v.a. Wed., Sat., and Sun. a.m.). ● To NE, *Condé-sur-l'Escaut*, formerly fortified town with 15c château of Princes of Condé; remains of 17c ramparts; 18c guardroom. In Bonsecours forest, lovely 18c Ch. de l'Ermitage, with 200 windows (restored). ● To NW, St. Amand-Raisme natnl. park, towards **St. Amand-les-Eaux***.

Vallauris
06 – Alpes Maritimes   45 – A 1
This little town owes its fame to its ceramics and its reputation to Picasso, who worked in the Madoura pottery. On Place Paul Isnard, in front of town hall, is his world-famed sculpture, *L'Homme au mouton*. Former chapel of 16c

Vallon-Pont-d'Arc: *the Pont d'Arc is the Ardèche gorges' most striking natural curiosity; but the concretions in the Madeleine grotto are also impressive.*

château of Lérins monks is decorated with two important large compositions by Picasso, *La Guerre* and *La Paix* (v.a.). Château houses municipal mus. of ceramics and modern art: large group of works by Italian-born abstract painter Alberto Magnelli (d. 1971). Picasso lived and died (1973) at *Mougins*, 8 km to N.

Valloires (Abbey)
80 – Somme 1 – B 3
Founded 12c, reconstructed 18c (v.a., Apr.–Nov.). In chapel, onetime abbey church, extraordinary baroque decorations: wood panel-

ling, sculptures, choir screens, ciborium, statues, etc., all masterpieces by Austrian, Pfaff (although considered by some to be overly ornate!); reception room, chapterhouse and sacristy are decorated with elegant wood panelling; see also abbot's apartments.

Vallon-Pont-d'Arc
07 – Ardèche 37 – C 2
Best departure point for tourist circuit of *Ardèche* gorges 'or boat trip down river. In town hall, seven 17c Aubusson tapestries. Visits can be arranged to a silk farm in Mazes village (3 km NE on **Ruoms*** road).

Vicinity ● To SE, *Canyon de l'Ardèche*. ● For boat trip down river (30 km), apply to Syndicat d'Initiative at *Vallon-Pont-d'Arc*. ● By road, visit is recommended to *Pont-d'Arc*, where, from car park, there is a magnificent view over the huge natural arch, 34 m. high by 59 m. long, spanning R. *Ardèche*; footpaths lead down to its base; from *Pont-d'Arc*, scenic route which follows *Canyon de l'Ardèche* is one of loveliest in France; many well-kept viewing-points provide fine views of landscapes of wild and immense beauty, especially Madeleine grotto: three viewing points

Valençay: *the memory of Talleyrand pervades the château, where he gave magnificent parties.*

overlook Madeleine corrie, in which the *Ardèche* makes wide loop within confines of high cliffs; from narrow road between Grand and Colombier belvederes, you can reach grottoes of St. Marcel, containing a succession of galleries filled with impressive concretions: after narrow gorge, dominated to l. by rocky crag topped by medieval ruins, the river flows out of canyon and landscape changes dramatically; a cultivated valley leads to *St. Martin-d'Ardèche*. ● 21 km S, *Aven d'Orgnac* (extraordinary stalagmites). ● 18 km SE, *Aven de Marzal* (whose concretions look like fantastic animals). ● 7 km NW, **Ruoms***.

Vallouise
05 – Hautes-Alpes   38 – C 1
Old houses with balconies and weather-boarded roofs, in this typical Alpine village, surround 15c church; 16c porch has marble pillars and tympanum decorated with a fresco; door has a bolt ornamented with a chimera's head; inside, old statues (16c Pietà) and big 18c retable. Penitents chapel, decorated on outside with paintings.
Vicinity ● To N, road hugs R. Gyr, passing through scattered hamlets, then zigzags up through larch forests over which towers *Mt. Pelvoux* (3,946 m.); *Ailefroide* and Pré de Madame Carle (1,874 m.), former lake bed covered with a jumble of rocks; excursions recommeded to refuge huts of Glacier Blanc and Les Écrins.

Valognes
50 – Manche   30 – D 2
Reconstructed church of St. Malo (15c choir and side-aisles). 17c former Benedictine abbey (hospice). Numerous mansions of the nobility, especially Beaumont mansion (v.a.) in Louis XV style, one of loveliest in Normandy, remind one that this town was once 'the Versailles of Normandy'. Cider mus. in 16c house. In Alleaume quarter, Roman ruins.
Vicinity ● On road to **Ste. Mère-Église***, **Montebourg** (interesting church).

Valréas
84 – Vaucluse   37 – D 2
Tiny old town. 12c church in Provençal Romanesque style, enlarged 15c, has interesting carved doorway. Early-16c chapel of Pénitents Blancs.
Vicinity ● 9 km NW, Ch. de **Grignan***. ● 14 km SE, **Nyons***.

Vals-les-Bains
07 – Ardèche   37 – C 1
Spa town in narrow valley of R. Volane, which crosses it from N to

Vallouise: *the harshness of the Alpine landscape round this old village is softened by the Provençal sunlight.*

Vannes: *the warm ochre-coloured ramparts of the old town still have their three gates and towers, bordered by gardens.*

S. The r. bank (casino and park, church), on which lies old part of town, is dominated by ruins of medieval castle and by a calvary. On l. bank, Bains (baths) quarter, spa buildings. See unusual bottling plant of St. John's spring.
Vicinity ● Signal Ste. Marguerite (6 km to NW and 1 hr. on foot, fine view). ● 8 km N, Volane gorges. ● 21 km NW, picturesque village of *Burzet* (famed Good Friday procession), 15–16c church; *Bourges* gorges and *Cascades du Ray-Pic*. ● 19 km NW, *Montpezat-sous-Bauzon*, from which road climbs up Fontolière valley on ledge above torrent; to NW, *St. Cirgues-des-Montagnes* (Romanesque church) and lake of **Issarles***.

Vannes
56 – Morbihan   16 – A 1
13–15 and 16c St. Pierre cathedral has, in N transept, a beautiful early-16c Goth. Flamboyant doorway; to l. of nave, chapel of Holy Sacrament, Ren., houses tomb of St. Vincent Ferrier (d. 1419); 18c chapter-house. Two picturesque old streets, lined by ancient houses, run alongside cathedral, Rue St. Guenhaël and Rue des Chanoines, ending at early-15c Porte-Prison. Marle stream (old wash-houses) runs along foot of old ramparts bordered by gardens (floodlit in summer). 14c Poudrière tower. 14–15c Connétable tower. Street of covered markets, aka 'La Cohue', where the Breton high court and later the Breton Parliament used to meet. In Rue Noë, Parliament building, aka Château-Gaillard, early 15c. Vannes has several mus.: Beaux-Arts mus., in former Parliament (coll. of paintings grouped by themes); prehist. mus.; natural

VANOISE (Natnl. Park)
73 – Savoie   32 – D 2

France's first natnl. park; more than 460 sq. miles are devoted to protecting the natural environment of the Alps, on both sides of the Franco-Italian border; reached via N6 and N202, N90 and N515. Reception chalets for scientists at Col de la Madeleine, between *Lansvillard* (15c naive murals in St. Sébastien chapel) and Bessans (N202); many refuge huts and rest-houses, camping forbidden. Intnatnl. holiday centre at *Lanslébourg* (N6). Introductory nature courses at *Pralognan-la-Vanoise* (N515) and photo-safari (apply to S.I. at **Val-d'Isère***). Park's flora is among richest in Alps, while its fauna include large numbers of chamois and ibex.

VAUX DE CERNAY (Les)
78 – Yvelines   11 – B 2

Picturesque setting in valley containing watercourse of Les Vaux; lake, small cascades and strange 'Bouillons de Cernay' (bubbling whirlpools). N.v.a. to former Cistercian abbey, founded 12c, whose ruined Romanesque abbey church and convent buildings are private property.

---

science mus.; and Mus. of the Gulf and the Sea.
Vicinity ● 4 km NE, St. Avé, 15c chapel of Notre Dame-du-Loc; inside, rich 15–16c furniture. ● 4 km SW, Conleau island, beach, swimming-pool, restaurants, in wooded setting at mouth of Gulf of Morbihan. ● To SW, Port Blanc, departure point for Ile aux Moines (see **Morbihan***, Gulf). ● 14.5 km SW, *Larmor-Baden*; 1 km away (by ferry), island of **Gavrinis***.

Vans (Les)
07 – Ardèche   37 – C 2

Recommended excursion centre for surrounding region.
Vicinity ● 5 km E, *Bois de Païolive*, one of most unusual natural sights in Vivarais reg.; this fantastically-shaped limestone jumble of rocks, covered with oaks and mulberries, is such a vast maze that it is imperative to have a map (apply to Les Van S.I.); many different walks. ● To W, marked corniche road of *Chassezac* valley, over which tower medieval ruins of Casteljau, overlooks magnificent sites between high cliffs riddled with caves; beach beside R. *Chassezac*, at Mazet-Plage.

Varengeville-sur-Mer
76 – Seine-Maritime   5 – A 2

Church and its rural cemetery (graves of Georges Braque, Georges de Porto-Riche and Albert Roussel) dominate attractive countryside from top of high cliff; built 12–16c, church contains beautiful stained-glass window by Braque. Lovely

Lutyens-designed Moustiers park (v.a. Easter–Nov. 1).
Vicinity ● *Manoir d'Ango*, in Norman Ren. style (v.a. Mar.–Nov.); in centre of courtyard, overlooked by an arcaded loggia, stands dovecote, decorated with unusual patchwork of brick and stone. ● To SE, beyond *St. Aubin-sur-Scie*, 15–18c *Ch. de Miromesnil* (small mus. devoted to Guy de Maupassant, who was born here); 16c chapel (carved wood panelling); magnificent beech wood.

Varennes-en-Argonne
55 – Meuse   12 – D 1

Clocktower, where Louis XVI and his family were arrested (1791). 12 and 14c church. Large American memorial. Argonne mus. In contemporary building in Rue de Boureuilles: large collection illustrating flight and arrest of Louis XVI, folk traditions.
Vicinity ● 6.5 km SW, Haute-Chevauchée ossuary. ● To S, Lachalade, in Lachalade wood (not far from *Le Claon*), has lovely church, old Cistercian abbey church in late-13c reg. Goth. style. ● 11 km NE, American memorial of *Montfaucon*, on hill where, in Sept. 1918, there were a number of important battles; wide view. ● 17 km N, enormous American cemetery of *Romagne-sous-Montfaucon* (125 acres). ● 20 km NW, *Grandpré*: 15–16c church; reg. folklore mus.

Vassieux-en-Vercors
26 – Drôme   38 – A 1

Destroyed by the Germans during the fighting in the Vercors massif, in 1945, village has been rebuilt.

Memorial to the 'Vercors Martyrs 1944', recumbent figure by Gilioli. Vercors natnl. cemetery. Prehist. workshop devoted to flint and wood cutting, conserved in situ.
Vicinity ● Magnificent forest of *Lente*. ● To W, via *Col de la Bataille* (1,313 m., lovely view), *Léoncel*, Romanesque church. ● To N, Brudour cave; after Col de la Machine, road reaches *Combe Laval* along magnificent corniche route; after a number of tunnels, it comes out above Le Royans, permitting superb views; *St. Jean-en-Royans*, beneath towering cliffs of *Vercors*, is a good excursion centre.

Vaux-le-Vicomte (Château)
77 – Seine-et-Marne   11 – D 2

Built 1657–1661 by Le Vau for Louis XIV's finance superintendent, Fouquet, it is the most important architectural and decorative work of 17c, before Versailles (v.a. to gardens and château; ornamental fountains play on second and last Sat. of month, Apr.–Nov.). State rooms are sumptuously decorated and furnished. Gardens, designed by Le Nôtre, presage those at **Versailles***.
Vicinity ● 5.5 km E, *Blandy-les-Tours*, castle (v.a., cl. Wed., Mar. 1–Oct. 31; Sat., Sun. and public hols. only out of season), fortified 14c, altered 16 and 17c, still has its perimeter wall flanked by five towers and 32 m.-high keep (fine view); 16c chapel and remains of living quar-

Varengeville-sur-Mer: 'The Jesse Tree', Braque's famed stained-glass window.

Vaux-le-Vicomte: *the classicism of the château is echoed in the no less highly structured designs of Le Nôtre's gardens.*

ters; 2 km away, *Champeaux*, 12–14c church, one of loveliest in reg., contains numerous works of art and Ren. choirstalls whose carved figures are often surprisingly free in style.

Vayres (Château)
33 – Gironde   29 – A 3
On hill overlooking R. *Dordogne*, 13–14c château, rebuilt 16c, evokes a magnificent Italian villa (v.a., p.m., July 1–Sept. 30, cl. Tues.; Sun. p.m. only out of season). Ren. main courtyard decorated with niches, pilasters and galleries. On NE façade, elegant late-17c pavilion, which juts out from main building, crowned by a dome with eight-pillared portico. Huge formal flowerbeds.
Vicinity • To NW, interesting churches at Izon (Romanesque doorway and apse), *St. Sulpice-et-Cameyrac* (11–16c) and *St. Loubès* (Romanesque apse).

Venasque
84 – Vaucluse   38 – A 3
Tiny village, on rocky spur. Alongside 12–early 13c church of Notre Dame is late-6c baptistry, renovated 12c, one of oldest religious buildings in France.
Vicinity • 2.5 km, chapel of convent of Notre Dame-de-Vie: inside, tombstone of Bishop Boetius (d. 604), a rare example of Merovingian sculpture; 2 km W, St. Didier-les-Bains: early-16c château with Gothic Flamboyant façade overlooking courtyard; inside, painted coffered ceilings and decorative paintings by Mignard (neurological institute).

Vence
06 – Alpes-Maritimes   45 – A 1
Safely enclosed within its medieval walls, this little town has retained its original character. Main gateway, flanked by a tower, opens on to charming 15c Place du Peyra, with central fountain. In church, former 11–17c cathedral, are several works of art. From 17c chapel of Ste. Anne there is a Way of the Cross, dotted with seven chapels.
Vicinity • To SW, on Grasse road, Notre Dame-des-Fleurs château: mus. devoted to perfumery and liqueurs (cl. Tues. in winter). • To NE, on *St. Jeannet* road, Rosary chapel of Dominican convent (v.a. Tues. and Thurs.), designed and decorated by Matisse; 4.5 km to NE, *St. Jeannet*, on rocky platform at foot of well-known 'baou'; 3 km to S, near La Gaude, unusual village with steep alleys, I.B.M. study and research centre by Marcel Breuer (guided tours), important

work of contemporary architecture. • 6 km W, *Tourette-sur-Loup*, fortified village whose houses form a rampart; interesting local arts and crafts centre.

Vendôme
41 – Loir-et-Cher   17 – D 1
Built on islands lapped by waters of various branches of R. *Loir*, this little town, filled with picturesque old corners, is dominated by 12c isolated belfry, 80 m. high, of fmr. 14–16c abbey church of La Trinité; elegantly sculpted Goth. Flamboyant façade; inside, Romanesque historiated capitals; in a chapel in apse, famed 12c stained-glass window of Virgin and Child. Archaeological and folk traditions mus. in cloister of church (cl. Tues.). 14c St. Georges gate on main branch of Loir was given machicolations and sculpted décor in 16c. Late-15c Madeleine church; 15c Saillant mansion; old Oratorian college (high school), lovely Ren. chapel; abbot's lodgings, etc. Ruins of 12, 14 and 15c castle of Counts of Vendôme dominate town.
Vicinity • 3 km NE, *Areines*, 11–12c church, Romanesque murals. • 6 km NW, *Villiers-sur-Loir*; in church, early-16c murals.

Verdière (La)
83 – Var   44 – B 1
Château perched on wooded spur (v.a., p.m.); apartments include six drawing rooms decorated with plasterwork and tapestries; in main gallery, 17–18c Dutch and French paintings.

Verdun
55 – Meuse   13 – A 1
One-time fortified town, of which remains of Vauban's ramparts still stand in S and E, Verdun symbolises one of the greatest battles in history. In town centre, on Rue Mazel, huge Victory monument, over which towers a colossal, but

VENTOUX
84 – Vaucluse   38 – A 2
Best way to reach Mt. Ventoux is to take N574 from **Carpentras***. You cross rugged countryside (steep climb, magnificent views) beyond *Bédoin*; mountain road across Bédoin forest starts from hamlet of St. Estève; Reynard chalet (1,460 m., winter sports); Grave spring (1,515m.). Series of hairpin bends up to summit (1,912 m.); Met. Office observatory, Air Force radar station, radio and TV relay tower. From S platform, magnificent view as far as *Étang de Berre*, the *Mediterranean* and, on a clear day, as far as *Le Canigou*. Best way down is towards **Vaison-la-Romaine***, via Mt. Serein (summer and winter sports resort), chapel of Notre Dame-du-Grozeau and *Malaucène*.

mediocre, statue of a medieval knight; in crypt (v.a.), roll of honour. 16c Princerie mansion with 13c galleries houses mus. (medieval reg. sculptures). Notre Dame cathedral, in Rhenish Romanesque style (two apses and two transepts facing each other), with 13–14c vaulting, rebuilt 18c, has lovely Romanesque crypt; cloister is in early-16c Goth. Flamboyant style; remarkable 12c Lion doorway, sumptuously carved Romanesque décor; 18c bishop's palace. 15c Chatel gate opens on to Esplanade de la Roche, dominated by citadel (war mus. and tour of underground galleries, hrs. vary). In front of St. Paul gate, to N, remarkable monument called *L'Appel aux Armes* by Rodin.

Vicinity ● Tour of Verdun battlefield. ● On r. bank of R. *Meuse*, via Ave. de la 42e.-Division, Faubourg-Pavé and N18 to NNE, *Fort de Vaux* (v.a.); scene of horrific battles in 1916, ruins of fort of Souville (monument to Sergeant Maginot who later became Minister of War and gave his name to the Maginot Line). Near crossroads of Ste. Fine chapel, Verdun memorial and Remembrance mus. (cl. Dec.); huge *Ossuaire de Douaumont*, a vast, nondescript monument dominated by colossal lantern to the dead (v.a.), which contains 46 sarcophagi corresponding to the principal sectors of the Verdun battlefield; huge natnl. cemetery containing 15,000 graves; v.a. to *Fort de Douaumont* and Ravine of Death; a stark concrete monument covers the tragic trench which contained the Bayonet Regiments. ● On l. bank, via N64 and D38 to NNW, *Le Mort-Homme*: wooded hilltop which was bitterly fought over in 1916–1918 (monuments) and *Hill 304*, pivots of the defence of Verdun; to W, Vauquois hill; to NW, **Varennes-en-Argonne***: appalling battles took place here from 1914 to 1918; to NNW, hill of *Montfaucon*: American monument; enormous cemetery of *Romagne-sous-Montfaucon* (see **Varennes-en-Argonne***). ● *Côtes de Meuse*; via N3 and D154, SE: *Les Éparges* and Éparges ridge (memorials to battles of 1915), strategic road known as 'Calonne trench' follows ridge of *Côtes de Meuse* to SE as far as *Hattonchâtel* (14c church and two 15c cloister galleries; inside, magnificent Renaissance retable dating from 1523).

Vermenton
89 – Yonne   19 – B 2
Old town on bank of R. *Cure*, which here forms islands occupied by leisure park, beach, etc., and a port. 12–13c church of Notre Dame, with

VERDON (Canyon)
04 – Alpes-de-Haute-Provence   38 – CD 3 – 44 – C 1
Known as the 'Grand Canyon of Europe'. One of the most extraordinary sites in France, its dimensions are gigantic: 400 to 700 m. deep, 25 km long; only a few metres wide at its base, but 200–1,000 m. wide at the top. At the bottom of this gully, the river alternates between roaring torrents and still lakes. There are well-kept paths along the gully, open to all, whereas the descent of the river by canoe is only for the experienced. Tourist road, the *Corniche Sublime*, follows edge of canyon on l. bank, from its confluence with R. *Artuby*, to end of the gorges. On r. bank, N552 only follows the canyon at each extremity. *Verdon* ridge road completes these two itineraries (beginning 2 km from *La Palud*). Numerous attractive belvederes ensure impressive views of the gorges.

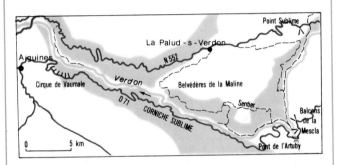

tower and Romanesque doorway. Fine view from Bétry plateau.

Vicinity ● 8 km S, *Arcy-sur-Cure*, *Grottes d'Arcy* (see **Avallon***); numerous caves, some of which are very picturesque, above R. *Cure* (St. Moré grottoes); village of St. Moré, on l. bank of Cure, has elegant 16–19c château, flanked by four round towers and 14c church; a tiny road leads to Cora camp, fortified Gallo-Roman post-station. ● 5 km NW, via *Cure* valley, *Cravant*, former fortress at confluence of *Yonne* and *Cure*, 15 and 16c church, lovely Ren. choir; 16c timber-framed houses; then follow *Yonne* valley (see **Auxerre***) to S.

Verneuil-sur-Avre
27 – Eure   10 – D 2

Little old town, previously fortified, dominated by early-16c Gothic Flamboyant tower of Madeleine church; inside, lovely 16c *Entombment*. 12c Romanesque Notre Dame, reconstructed, has 13, 14, 15 and 16c statues, a kind of regional sculpture museum. See Tour Grise, 12c round tower, 35 m. high. Numerous timbered or brick and flint houses, dating from 15 to 18c.
Vicinity ● Worth touring *Avre* valley.

Vernon
27 – Eure   11 – A 1

Sole vestige of the old castle, the 12c Archives Tower dominates the *Seine* valley (fine view). Church of Notre Dame, 14c façade and nave with 13c central tower; Ren. organ loft. A bridge links Vernon to Vernonnet on r. bank of *Seine*. Keep of 12c Tourelles castle. Alphonse-Georges Poulain mus. in four old houses (works by Monet, Bonnard, Vuillard, Steinlen, etc.).
Vicinity ● 1.5 km SW, *Ch. de Bizy*, built 18c, reconstructed 19c; magnificent drawing rooms decorated with 18c wood panelling; monumental stables, main courtyard, large pool for horses and outbuildings, all point to importance of château in 18c; the park still has numerous examples of its original decoration and its 'waters' (fountains, ornamental pools, etc.); remarkable sculptures (v.a. Easter-Nov. 1, cl. Fri.); Bizy forest lies to S and SE of château. Picturesque Valmeux area and tomb of St. Mauxe. ● 9 km SE, Notre Dame-de-la-Mer, chapel and belvedere from which there is stunning view over *Seine* valley; from Signal des Coutumes, to S, fine view of loop of *Seine* at *Bonnières* and islands in river. ● 14 km NW, *Gallion*; imposing Ren. doorway and gallery between two towers are all that remain of magnificent early-16c château of Cardinal d'Amboise. ●

1

2

3

Versailles: *statues representing French rivers recline beside the ornamental pools (1). In Louis XIV's time, the Orangery, one of Hardouin-Mansart's masterpieces, housed 200 orange trees (2). Also by Hardouin-Mansart, the marble-clad Grand Trianon contains magnificent apartments (3).*

4 km SE, *Giverny*; v.a. (cl. Mon.) to Monet's house. It has, unfortunately, been appallingly badly renovated, but there is a fine collection of Japanese prints, his studio (aka L'Atelier des Nymphéas), breathtakingly beautiful gardens and the much-painted but justly famed water-lily pool.

Versailles
78 – Yvelines   11 – C 2
Symbol of the French monarchy at its most glorious, Versailles is not just a palace and a museum – the gardens, the two Trianons and the town itself are integral with it. ● The palace of Versailles is one of France's most famed monuments (cl. Mon.); it is entered via vast Royal Courtyard, in centre of which is equestrian statue of Louis XIV; this leads into Marble Courtyard surrounded by Louis XIII's château, remodelled by Le Vau and Mansart. King's state apartments (in centre, Louis XIV's bedchamber) face on to this courtyard; behind, overlooking gardens, stretches magnificent Hall of Mirrors, masterpiece of 17c state ceremonial art. These apartments occupy N side of palace, to r. of Marble Courtyard, framed on ground-floor by recently renovated apartments (opened 1986) of royal children (Dauphin and daughters of Louis XV), and adjoin king's private apartments (Louis XV's study, superb desk by Oeben and Riesener – 18c royal cabinetmakers). S side is occupied by queen's state and private apartments; these lead to S wing, in which is famed Gallery of Battles. N wing starts with chapel and ends with late-18c Royal Opera House; mus. of French hist. occupies number of galleries on ground-floor of S wing and upper floors; excellently laid-out, they are devoted to the Revolution, the Empire and the Restoration. ● The gardens: facing palace are Basin of Latona, the Green Carpet, Basin of Apollo (in centre, Apollo's chariot) and the Grand Canal. To l. of palace, N flowerbeds, Basin of Neptune. To r., S flowerbeds and Orangery framed by the Hundred Steps. To l. of Basin of Latona: grove of Baths of Apollo, sculpture of Apollo attended by Nymphs. ● Facing Orangery, on other side of N10, enormous Swiss Lake. On each side of Grand Canal (boat hire) lies the Little Park, certain parts of which are accessible by car. (Ornamental fountains play on first and third Sun., June–Sept., at 16.30.) Late 17c Grand Trianon, with sumptuous décor of black and pink marble; entirely renovated 1963–1966, it has been decorated and furnished in Empire style. The Petit Trianon, an elegant late-18c mansion, is currently being restored; its gardens contain picturesque hamlet of Queen Marie-Antoinette. ● In town: opposite palace, on each side of Ave. de Paris, State Stables (mus. of carriages and of sculptures from park, which is under restoration), and Private Stables, monumental late-17c buildings by Mansart. Lambinet mus. in 18c mansion (v.a. p.m., cl. Mon. and Fri.). Jeu de Paume (real tennis, v.a. by request). Numerous magnificent 18c mansions, notably Mme. du Barry's mansion, in Louis XV style (Chamber of Commerce, v.a. by request). Next door, Count of Provence's stables, monumental gate and façade by Ledoux. Ave. de Paris, No. 22, former mansion of Master of the King's Revels; No. 41, home of Mme. Elisabeth, sister of Louis XVI; No. 57, dairy-dovecote, belonging to Countess of Provence, sole relic of a hamlet inspired by the Petit Trianon. Rue de l'Indépendance Américaine: No. 1, one-time Domestic Office of palace, late-18c façade and monumental gate decorated with trophies in high relief; No. 5, lovely richly sculpted doorway of former Foreign and Navy Offices (municipal library; on first floor, magnificent suite of rooms decorated with wood panelling and paintings (v.a., p.m. weekdays only). Church of Notre Dame is by Mansart (late 17c). St. Louis cathedral is in Louis XV style.

Vertus
51 – Marne   12 – B 1
This large town, crossed by lively streams, lies at end of circuit of Côte des Blancs (see **Épernay***) and has numerous old houses. 13–14c Baudet gate is part of perimeter wall. 12c church of St. Martin has noteworthy ribbed vaulting; huge square Romanesque tower.
Vicinity ● Churches of *Oger*, *Mesnil-sur-Oger* and *Bergère-lès-Vertus* are recommended (see **Épernay***).

Vervins
02 – Aisne   6 – B 2
Positioned on a hillside, it has an interesting 12 and 16c church and 16c town hall, remains of 12c perimeter wall, picturesque streets, and mus.-documentation centre of La Thiérache.
Vicinity ● Good departure point for visits to fortified churches of *Thiérache* reg., of highly unusual style. ● To S, 12c *Prisces*, square keep in brick with two diagonally-opposed turrets; *Burelles*, one of most noteworthy 16c churches: multi-coloured brick facings, stone choir, keep; upper storey of transept has been turned into a strongroom; *Hary*, Romanesque with 16c brick keep. ● To E, *Plomion*, late-16c, square keep flanked by two round towers; Jeantes, Dagny, *Morgny-en-Thiérache*, 16c Parfondeval, in brick, surrounded by houses forming a perimeter wall, with outer keep. ● To N, *Wimy*, *Origny-en-Thiérache*, *La Bouteille*, 16c, rectangular, faced with sandstone masonry.

Vesoul
70 – Haute-Saône   20 – C 2
In mid.-18c church of St. Georges, 15c stone Holy Sepulchre. Interesting old houses; 15c Thomassin mansion, Barresols house, 17–18c mansions on Place du Grand-Puits, Gothic houses on Rue Baron-Bouvier. In one-time Ursuline convent, Georges Garret mus. (archaeology, paintings).
Vicinity ● To N, La Motte (383 m. alt.); fine view. ● 4 km S, cave of La Baume.

Veules-les-Roses
76 – Seine-Maritime   4 – D 2
Delightful seaside resort in green, wooded valley. 16c Goth. church of St. Martin, flanked by square belfry, with three naves. In old cemetery of St. Nicolas, ruins of 12c church and remarkable 16c carved sandstone calvary with figures.
Vicinity ● 1.5 km SE, 12–13c Val chapel. ● 2.5 km S, *Blosseville*: 16c church with 12c belfry; inside, lovely 15c stained-glass windows. ●

VÉSUBIE (Gorges)
06 – Alpes-Maritimes   39 – A 3
From *Plan-du-Var* to *St. Jean-la-Rivière*, via D2565, road follows bottom of narrow, winding gorges bordered by sheer cliffs; at *St. Jean-de-la-Rivière*, take D32 which zigzags its way up vertiginous cliff-face to *Utelle*: 14c Gothic church of St. Véran, with three naves, restored 17c, has a *Retable de l'Annonciation* of 15c Nice school; the town, with its old houses, alleyways and tiny square, is charming; 3 km beyond, the Utelle Madonna is a place of pilgrimage (viewing-table).
Vicinity ● From *Levens* to *St. Jean-de-la-Rivière* via D19, *Vésubie* valley and *Lantosque* in direction of **St. Martin-Vésubie***.

7 km E, *Bourg-Dun*: late 11–16c church with 13c tower; in Gothic Flamboyant-style S transept, magnificent ribbed vault with finely-carved hanging keystones. ● 8 km W, *St. Valéry-en-Caux*: fishing port lying between high cliffs.

Vézelay
89 – Yonne 19 – B 2

Town, built on isolated hill overlooking miles of countryside, has as its top the basilica of Ste. Madeleine, a masterpiece of medieval architecture; most remarkable part is Romanesque narthex, a huge church porch with triple doors, 22 m. long, whose main door, which opens on to nave, is decorated with carved tympanum representing Christ in Glory, one of loveliest examples (with that at Autun) of early-12c Burgundian Romanesque sculpture; late 11–early 12c nave, in white and brown stone, has historiated capitals of highly expressive realism; late-12c choir and transept from early Goth. period; 12c chapter-house. From terrace, magnificent view of valley. Abbey mus. (v.a. during season); original fragments of 12–13c sculptures stored in building during restoration work. Tour recommended of village (old houses) and perimeter walls.

Vicinity ● 2 km E, *St. Père*: church of Notre Dame is one of most interesting Burgundian Goth. buildings, noteworthy sculpted façade (Last Judgment); reg. archaeological museum; 2 km to S, *Fouilles des Fontaines-Salées*, one of most important archaeological excavations in France; large Celtic settlements (1 BC), circular perimeter walls and covered holy pool, and Gallo-Roman (1c) spa buildings, enlarged 2c, linked to a cultic centre by 50 m.-long antichamber and portico, together stretch almost 600 m. along *Cure* valley (daily guided tours); 2 km to S, *Pierre-Perthuis*, in picturesque setting; church and ruins of castle overlook narrow *Cure* gorge; from huge bridge spanning valley, lovely view of Vézelay.

Vichy
03 – Allier 25 – A 3

Centre is Parc des Sources, surrounded by casino, main hotels and spa buildings. *Allier* park runs for 1,800 m. beside 2,200 m. sheet of water known as *Allier* lake (water sports). Old quarter has many ancient houses: Sévigné pavilion, from reign of Louis XIII (hotel), 16c Bailliage house or Chastel Franc. Valery Larbaud cultural centre, for reg. archaeological research (v.a. Sat. p.m., July to mid-Sept.).

Vicinity ● 23 km NE, 15–16c Ch. de *Lapalisse* (v.a. Palm Sun. – Nov. 1; cl. Tues. exc. June to Sept.; Son et Lumière in summer); sumptuously furnished int. has six magnificent late-15c tapestries and lovely painted ceilings. *Besbre* valley, to NNE, is dotted with interesting châteaux; medieval ruins of Chavroches (13c), châteaux of *Vieux-Chambord* (13c), *Jaligny* (Ren.), *Beauvoir* (15–17c), and *Thoury* (see **Moulins***). ● 22 km SSE, *Châteldon*, picturesque old township, 14c Clock Tower and 15–16c half-timbered houses; 13–15c castle (n.v.a.). ● 14 km S, via *Forêt Boucharde*, *Randan*: 16c château, rebuilt 19c, burnt down 1925 (n.v.a.).

Vic-le-Comte
63 – Puy-de-Dôme 31 – A 1

Absorbed into modern church, the Holy Chapel, early-16c architectural jewel, is sole relic of former Counts' castle; exterior has finely carved sculptures and cornice; inside, stained-glass windows, early-16c stone retable decorated with statues, etc.

Vicinity ● 6 km N, Busséol: ruins of late-12c castle, on rocky peak (v.a.); wide view. ● 4 km S, Buron; also perched on high rock, impressive ruins of castle; lovely view of *Allier* valley.

Vic-sur-Cère
15 – Cantal 30 – C 3

Spa town and summer resort. Old town, spread out around church, contains many lovely old houses (15c Princes of Monaco's house, 15–16c Laparra house). Spa buildings are on l. bank of R. Cère.

Vicinity ● Numerous excursions. ● To W of church, via Conche gully (cascade) and Maisonne rock, climb to St. Curial rock, curious basaltic mass (panorama). ● To NE: Salvanhac and Cère pass, impressive rocky gorge. ● 6 km NE: *Thiézac*, 15–16c church; inside, 18c retables and pulpit, 16c polychrome wood Compassionate Christ; 300 m. away, mid-17c chapel of Notre Dame-de-Consolation, vault decorated with strange paintings; Faillitoux cascade. ● To SE, via zigzagging road (fine views), Curebourse pass (997 m.) and *Rocher des Pendus*; 6 km to SE: Jou-sous-Monjou, 12–15c church; inside, unusual carved décor. Early-16c Escalmels manor. 1.5 km to S, 17c Ch. de Cropières; W wing has majestic central staircase divided into two lateral flights; a long terrace leads to state room decorated with polychrome wood panelling (v.a. by arrangement); to S, *Raulhac*, and Ch. de Messilhac, Ren., with two huge square 14c towers (v.a. in summer), richly sculpted décor. ● 5 km SW: Ch. de **Pesteils***.

Vic-sur-Seuille
57 – Moselle 13 – C 2

Old town; in 15–16c church, interesting works of art. Old houses (mid-15c Mint). Salt museum.

Vicinity ● 13.5 km NE, *Marsal*, lovely church in early-12c Rhenish Romanesque style, with 14c Gothic apse; ramparts.

Veules-les-Roses: *along the Côte d'Albâtre, park and tiny resorts are tucked among the chalk cliffs of the Pays de Caux.*

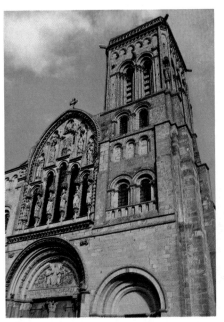

Vézelay: *the basilica of Ste. Madeleine, a Romanesque jewel. At St. Père, Gothic Notre Dame.*

Vieil-Armand
See **Hartmannswillerkopf***.
21 – A 1

Vienne
38 – Isère 31 – D 2
Ancient Roman and medieval city on banks of R. *Rhône*, full of beautiful old buildings. At St. Maurice, former 12 and 13c priory church, three Goth. Flamboyant doorways with marvellous sculpted vaulting; 90 m.-long interior has seven Romanesque bays in its Gothic nave; in choir, 16c tapestries and 18c tomb of archbishops; two side doors have had 12c sculptures added. On Place de Miremont, Beaux-Arts mus. (archaeology, ceramics, medals). St. Pierre, one of oldest monuments of Christian Gaul (4–5c), houses lapidary mus. (cl. Tues.); big collection of Roman sculptures and mosaics, medieval sculptures. ● 11–12c St. André-le-Bas has elegantly refined Romanesque cloister which leads to mus. of Christian art. ● Rue des Clercs leads to Place du Palais, on which stands Temple of Augustus and Livia (circa 25 BC), one of best preserved monuments of Roman Gaul. See also portico of the Forum, remains of Temple of Cybele and those of a theatre (excavation in progress). Roman theatre, which backs on to Mt. Pipet, crowned by ruins of Roman citadel and chapel of Notre Dame, measures 115 m. in diameter; its 46 tiers of seats could hold 13,000 spectators. ● On r.

bank of R. Rhône, at St. Romain-en-Gal, a large Gallo-Roman quarter is being excavated.
Vicinity ● Behind station, via steep Coupe-Jarret ramp and D46: excursions above *Vienne*, wide views over *Rhône* valley and the *Alps*.

Vierville-sur-Mer
14 – Calvados 4 – A 3
Seaside resort; 13c church; 500 m. to SW, delightful Renaissance manor of Vaumicel. In town hall, permanent exhibition of 'Omaha – June 6, 1944'.
Vicinity ● To W, Englesqueville-la-Percée (12–13c church); 2 km to SW, ruins of 12–13c castle of Beaumont, Romanesque chapel; late-16c Ch. d'Englesqueville, now occupied by farm, has round towers topped by stone domes. ● To SW, on N13, at *La Cambe*, huge German military cemetery. ● Beaches between Vierville and *Colleville*, aka **Omaha**

Beach*, were scene of violent battles on June 6, 1944: from Vierville to *St. Laurent-sur-Mer*, 4 km-long 'maritime boulevard'; 1 km from St. Laurent, *American cemetery*, 9,385 white crosses and an imposing mausoleum overlook the sea, the huge beach and military installations of Omaha Beach. ● To E, *Port-en-Bessin*, in a break in cliffs, picturesque fishing port; 17c Vauban tower built against cliff; excursions recommended along cliffs overlooking sea, or on foot at low tide; strange site of *Le Chaos*, 4 km to E; **Arromanches***.

Vignory
52 – Haute-Marne 13 – A 3
Romanesque church of St. Étienne has 11c nave with Carolingian-style timbered roof; archaic capitals decorated with geometric patterns or figures; chapels, added in 15 and 16c, contain some lovely sculptures

---

VIAUR (Viaduct)
12 – Aveyron 36 – C 3
This daring example of railway art (1897–1902), built of steel, 460 m. long, crosses the *Viaur* valley at height of 120 m. Huge central arch has span of 220 m.
Vicinity ● To NE, *Ch. du Bosc*, where Toulouse-Lautrec spent his childhood; souvenirs of and youthful works by the artist (v.a. Easter–Nov.11). ● 9 km N, *Naucelle-Ville*; 7 km to NW, *Sauveterre-de-Rouergue*: late-13c bastide, 14c collegiate church, fortified tower and gates, remains of ramparts.

Villandry: *the glorious terraced gardens, recreated on 16c lines, are the jewel in the crown of this château.*

Villefranche-sur-Mer: *the lively and colourful old town overlooks the port.*

of the Virgin and of saints, in 15 and 16c Champagne style.

Villandry (Château)
37 – Indre-et-Loire   17 – C 3
Built around 1530 in Ren. style, surrounded by moat, it is flanked to SW by enormous 14c keep, sole relic of former medieval castle (v.a. to château, Apr.–Nov.; to gardens, all year round). The truly magnificent gardens consist of three superposed terraces: a vegetable garden, an ornamental garden and a water garden with a beautiful lake. A visit to these extraordinary gardens, whose shapes and colours change with the seasons, is one of the

high spots of any tour of the Loire valley.

Villard-de-Lans
38 – Isère   32 – B 3
Health resort and winter sports village. Good excursion centre.
Vicinity ● For 8 km WSW, along forest road of *Valchevrière*, Way of the Cross in memory of the dead of the Vercors maquis (1944). ● Two fine climbs to NE to Col de l'Arc (1,740 m.) and to N to Pic St. Michel (1,972 m.). ● To S, via *Corençon*: cable-car, then path to *Moucherolle* (2,290 m.; climb with guide). ● To W, *Gorges de la Bourne* and **Pont-en-Royans***.

Ville-d'Avray
92 – Hauts-de-Seine   11 – C 2
Church of St. Nicolas, in Louis XVI style. Corot frequently painted beside the lakes, in delightful settings. Pleasant walks in Fausses-Reposes woods (circular Route of the Empress).

Villedieu-les-Poëles
50 – Manche   9 – D 1
16c church, old houses and unusual bell foundry (v.a.). Mus. of Norman furniture and frying-pan mus. (medieval tools and period copper utensils – town's name translates literally as 'City of God of the Frying Pans').
Vicinity ● 7.5 km W, *Champrepus* zoo (v.a.)

Villefort
48 – Lozère   37 – B 2
Good excursion centre for the *Cévennes* and lower Vivarais reg.
Vicinity ● To N, dam, enormous lake branching out of R. *Altier*; 7 km to N, *La Garde-Guérin*, unusual fortified hamlet (listed site); *Chassezac* belvedere overlooking gorges; 8 km to N, Prévenchères; 12 and 15c church. ● To S, *Mt. Lozère* road towards *Génolhac*. ● To W, *Mt. Lozère* natnl. park.

Villefranche-de-Conflent
66 – Pyrénées-Orientales 43 – C 3
Surrounded by fortified perimeter wall built 11–15c and redesigned by Vauban, old capital of Conflent reg. has scarcely changed since Middle Ages. Its narrow streets are lined by 13–14c Romanesque and Gothic Catalan houses, notably in Rue St. Jean. Wall has two late-18c gateways, France gate and Spain gate. 11c church, enlarged 12–13c, lovely Romanesque doorways in pink marble; rich furnishings, interesting works of art.
Vicinity ● To N, on Mt. de Belloch, fort built by Vauban (private property). ● 1 km SW, Canalettes grotto (v.a. Palm Sun.–Nov. 1); 2.5 km SW, Fuilla; 11c church of Beinat is one of oldest examples of early Romanesque art in Roussillon reg. ● 3 km S, Corneilla-de-Conflent, noteworthy Romanesque church with three naves and 11c square belfry; apse, in granite, is richly decorated (small marble pillars with sculpted capitals); doorway in marble with six columns and sculpted tympanum; inside, Romanesque altars, mid-14c sculpted retable.

Villefranche-de-Rouergue
12 – Aveyron   36 – B 2
Old town is dominated by imposing bulk of church of Notre Dame, in southern Gothic style, in front of

which is huge 15c belfry porch, 58 m. high; inside, late-15c carved choir-stalls. Place Notre Dame is one of most characteristic old squares in S of France, surrounded by covered arcades. Many old houses. To N of town, mid-17c chapel of Pénitents Noirs; 17c retable and 15c choir-stalls. Mus.: archaeology and lapidary fragments.

Vicinity ● 1 km S, on l. bank of R. Aveyron: 15c former charterhouse of St. Sauveur (v.a.); small visitors' chapel, high chapel (15 and 16c wood panelling), chapter-house, large and small cloisters, together form one of most remarkable Gothic ensembles in S of France; it is the only complete charterhouse open to public in France. ● 2 km N: mid-16c Ch. de Graves; inner façades elegantly decorated (v.a. by arrangement). ● To S, excursion recommended in *Gorges de l'Aveyron* (see **Najac***).

Villeneuve-lès-Avignon: *high over the town's roofs, the walls of Fort St. André are typical of medieval military architecture.*

Villefranche-sur-Mer
06 – Alpes-Maritimes   45 – B 1
Fishing port and marina. Also naval port of call. Built in tiers at end of lovely bay. Old town is unspoilt, with steep, narrow streets, often vaulted (Rue Obscure). On lively Quai des Pêcheurs, chapel of St. Pierre, decorated by Jean Cocteau (v.a.). Port is dominated to S by late-16c citadel, skirted by footpath (superb views of coast) leading to Darse marina. Volti mus. (sculptures) and Goetz-Boumeester mus. (paintings).

Villefranche-sur-Saône
69 – Rhône   25 – D 3
12–15c church of Notre Dame-des-Marais with early-16c Goth. Flamboyant façade (lovely doors in carved wood). Renaissance town hall; old houses.
Vicinity ● Tour of Beaujolais wine district: best route, NNW, through vineyards, via *Belleville-sur-Saône*, wine-making centre of the Beaujolais (from *Brouilly* hill, fine view of vineyards, chapel), Brouilly, *Beaujeu* (Mus. of Folk Traditions, church of St. Nicolas, old capital of the Beaujolais), Chiroubles, *Villié-Morgon*, *Fleurie*, Chénas (windmill), *Juliénas*, etc. ● 10 km NW, St. Julien: small mus. in birthplace of physiologist Claude Bernard (1813–1878); 3 km beyond, picturesque village of Salles, 12c Romanesque church and ruins of Cluniac priory; lovely 15c chapter-house decorated with frescos. ● 10 km W, near *Rivolet*: castle of Montmelas, ruins of two crenellated perimeter walls with gates, posterns and square towers; 14c chapel (n.v.a.).

Villemagne
34 – Hérault   42 – D 1
Little old town, built around an abbey founded by Charlemagne. Church of St. Majan, former 13–14c abbey church, fortified apse. Old parish church of St. Grégoire (deconsecrated) in pure 12c Romanesque style. Romanesque house, called the Mint. 13c ramparts.
Vicinity ● 4 km W, Taussac, dominated by strange rocks, split vertically, known as the Taussac organ-pipes. ● To E, *Bédarieux* (15–16c church) and *Orb* valley, towards Avène and dam to N. ● 5 km SW, **Lamalou-les-Bains***.

Villemaur-sur-Vanne
10 – Aube   12 – B 3
13 and 16c church, with unusual wooden belfry with three superposed and interlocking roofs, contains noteworthy Gothic and Ren. wooden rood-screen, extremely elaborate; its panels depict scenes from Life of the Virgin and from the Passion.
Vicinity ● 4 km S, *Aix-en-Othe*; in church, Ren. choir has trompe-l'oeil decorations. ● 13 km W, *Villeneuve-l'Archevêque*, 12, 13 and 16c church, 13c portal with sculpted tympanum dedicated to the Virgin; inside, 16c sculptures of Troyes school, noteworthy Holy Sepulchre dating from 1528. ● 12 km SW, *Rigny-le-Ferron*: in church, lovely early 16c Entombment, with three figures.

Villeneuve-lès-Avignon
30 – Gard   37 – D 3
Outside **Avignon*** and across R. Rhône, the road passes under 14c Philippe le Bel's tower (v.a.), 32 m. high, which dominates river 60 m. below; fine view from top. On main square, church of Notre Dame, fmr. 14c collegiate church; int. contains many works of art, ornate high altar in marble with bas-relief of Christ in the tomb; in sacristy, famed early-14c Virgin in polychrome ivory, one of masterpieces of French sculpture; Goth. cloister. Mus. (cl. Tues. and Feb.) contains another medieval masterpiece, the *Couronnement de la Vierge* (Coronation of the Virgin), painted by Enguerrand Charonton or Quarton (a local artist) in mid-15c.; also paintings by Simon de Chalon, Philippe de Champaigne and from 17c Provençal school. Rue de la République (No. 45, Conti mansion, monumental 17c door; No. 53, onetime palace of Cardinal de Thury, circa 1400) leads to charterhouse of Val de Bénédiction (v.a., cl. Tues.); in 14c church, tomb of Pope Innocent VI, with recumbent figure in white marble; chapter-house, small Gothic cloister, sacristans' courtyard (well and picturesque staircase), elegant lavatory covered by 17c dome; pontifical chapel still has large 14c frescos, damaged in parts; large St. Jean cloister with octagonal rotunda and 18c fountain. ● Follow Montée du Fort to Fort St. André, a huge building whose magnificent main gate is flanked by impressive twin towers; it encompasses Benedictine abbey of St. André, of which only an entrance porch and large 17c building remain (v.a. to gardens and terrace); charming 12c Romanesque chapel of Notre Dame-de-Belvézet (v.a.) and ruins of Bourg St. André; from main terrace, fine view over **Avignon***, Ventoux, **Alpilles*** and **Lubéron*** (v.a. 9–18 hrs).

Villers-Cotterêts: *the empty rose-window in the façade of Longpont's Cistercian abbey.*

Vitré: *the powerful defensive fort of the town's imposing medieval castle.*

Villeneuve-sur-Lot
47 – Lot-et-Garonne   35 – C 2
Former mid-13c bastide; what remains is 13 and 15c Paris gate under a square tower, Pujols gate and Place La Fayette surrounded by 'cornières'. Picturesque old houses on R. Lot, spanned by 13c Pont-Vieux. Gaston Rapin mus. has collections of archaeology, religious art and engravings by Piranesi. Plum museum (only one in world).
Vicinity ● 1 km SW, Pujols, fmr. fortified town; two churches, 16c St. Nicolas and Ste. Foy-la-Grande (deconsecrated); inside, 15–16c frescos. Old half-timbered houses.

Villeneuve-sur-Yonne
89 – Yonne   19 – A 1
Old bastide, of which only two fortified Gothic gates still stand. Church of Notre Dame, 13c (choir), 14c (nave) and 16c, with ornate Renaissance façade. Only remnant of castle is Louis-le-Gros tower, a stout 12c cylindrical keep.
Vicinity ● 4 km N, 17c Ch. de Passy; gardens designed by Le Nôtre. ● 5 km S, near Armeau, Ch. de Palteau, in Louis XIII style, where you can see room of 'Man in the Iron Mask'; 3 km to SW, *St. Julien-du-Sault*, 13–14c church, remodelled 16c; chapel of fmr. Ch. de Vauguillain (lovely view over *Yonne* valley). ● 10 km E, *Dixmont*, Romanesque and Goth. church.

Villequier
76 – Seine-Maritime   4 – D 3
Delightful little village on r. bank of R. *Seine*, in attractive setting. In cemetery of country church are graves of Léopoldine Hugo, Victor Hugo's daughter (accidentally drowned with her husband, Charles Vacquerie, while boating on river in 1843), and of Hugo's wife, Adèle; also of Vacquerie family, whose house has been turned into Victor Hugo mus. A statue of the writer stands near scene of the accident.

Villeréal
47 – Lot-et-Garonne   35 – C 1
Surviving from 13c, bastide with central square surrounded by 'cornières' and wooden balconies. Above covered market, supported by wooden pillars, is town hall. Impressive 13–14c fortified church, Gothic doorway.

Villers-Cotterêts
02 – Aisne   6 – A 3
Renaissance château is superb building (now an old people's home, v.a.), whose arcaded façade and chapel are especially noteworthy; park designed by Le Nôtre. Alexandre Dumas mus. (author of 'The Three Musketeers', etc., was born in the town).
Vicinity ● *Forêt de Villers-Cotterêts* and *Automne* valley. 7 km W, *Vez*:

12–13c church and magnificent 14c castle, built on summit of wooded hill, whose imposing 27 m.-high keep houses Valois mus. (v.a. Sun. and Wed.); 2 km to W, abbey of Lieu-Restauré, founded 12c, remains of 15c church (lovely Gothic Flamboyant rose-window). ● 11.5 km E, abbey of *Longpont*, picturesque ruins (14c fortified gate, surmounted by four turrets, and ruins of church).

Villiers-St. Benoît
See **Toucy***.   19 – A 2

Vimoutiers
61 – Orne   10 – C 1
Main commercial centre for apples and cheeses and Livarot and Camembert region.
Vicinity ● At *Camembert* (4.5 km SW), Marie Harel (statue) created the world-famed cheese. ● 3 km N, at Lisores, Fernand Léger farm-mus. (cl. Wed.); to N. 16–17c Ch. de *Fervaques*, surrounded by moat, lovely 15c fortified gate (v.a. request).

Vincennes
94 – Val-de-Marne   11 – C 2
Impressive 14 and 17c building; surrounded by an impregnable rectangular wall and huge moat, château is dominated by mag-

nificent 52 m.-square keep flanked by four turrets (cl. Tues.), history mus.; inside wall, opposite keep, is graceful Ste. Chapelle, begun 14c, finished 16c, decorated with beautiful 16c stained-glass windows; large main courtyard is framed by two parallel porticos and bordered, to r., by King's pavilion and, to l., by Queen's pavilion; entrance is through Village tower. To S, old Bois tower opens on to the esplanade.

Vicinity ● Bois de Vincennes covers 36 sq. miles (see **Paris***). To SE, *Joinville-le-Pont* (on both banks of the Marne, beaches, boating, open-air taverns); *Chennevières-sur-Marne*, on hillside, fine view from terrace; 17–18c Ch. d'Ormesson (n.v.a.); *St. Maur-des-Fossés* (11–13c church with Romanesque tower), etc.; at Charenton-le-Pont, Bread museum (auxiliary flour-millers' society).

Vire
14 – Calvados 10 – A 1

On a hill hugged by R. Vire. 13, 14 and 15c church of Notre Dame, in granite, and 15c Clock Tower, above 13c gateway, are almost the only relics of old town destroyed in 1944. Lovely view of valley from esplanade of castle.

Vicinity ● Les Vaux de Vire, narrow valleys of the *Vire* and the *Virenne*, now highly industrialised.

Vitré
35 – Ille-et-Vilaine 9 – D 3

Built on promontory above R. *Vilaine*, with magnificent feudal castle at one end, this little old town has scarcely changed since medieval times. 13–14c castle, one of the most homogenous examples of Breton medieval military architecture, is flanked by several imposing towers and entered via a defensive fort (v.a. to courtyard at any time; interior cl. Tues.). 15 and 16c church of Notre Dame, decorated with pinnacles, gables, gargoyles, etc.; late-15c external pulpit on r. side; in sacristy, triptych composed of 32 Limoges enamels from 16c. Tour of ramparts via Promenade du Val.

Vicinity ● 6 km SE, 14, 17 and 18c Ch. *des Rochers*; souvenirs of 17c author Mme. de Sévigné (v.a., cl. Sun. a.m.). ● 9 km NW, *Champeaux*, 15 and 16c church houses several Ren. works of art, notably huge two-storey polychrome stone and marble mausoleum of Guy d'Espinay, a masterpiece of 16c sculpture; 16c château.

Vitry-le-François
51 – Marne 12 – C 2

Built on grid pattern by France's King François I (16c), town was rebuilt on its original lines after its destruction in 1940. On Place d'Armes, 17–18c church of Notre Dame; town hall occupies former 17c Franciscan convent.

Vicinity ● 8 km N, *St. Amand-sur-Fion* (interesting church).

Vitteaux
21 – Côte d'Or 19 – C 3

Late 12, 13 and 14c church, lovely portal with carved leaves; interior has interesting works of art. In main street, 13c Belime house. Noteworthy 15c covered market.

Vicinity ● 3 km N, *Posanges*, mid-15c castle, flanked by four stout towers and fortified gate, still has look of forbidding medieval fortress (n.v.a.). ● 12 km NNW, *Marigny-le-Cahouët*, late 12–early 13c castle, a huge square whose corners are flanked by towers (v.a. to ext. only, Sat., Sun. and Wed., June 1–Oct. 31); in church, Ren. frescos and altar.

Vittel
88 – Vosges 13 – B 3

Spa buildings, casino and Congress Hall are adjacent to each other, on

---

VIN D'ALSACE (Road)
67 – Bas-Rhin 14 – A 2, 14 – A 3, 21 – A 1
68 – Haut-Rhin

From **Thann***, go to *Cernay* and take D5 to **Guebwiller***, *Soultzmatt*, Westhalten (picturesque village), **Rouffach***, whence follow N83 to N as far as *Pfaffenheim*, then take D1 to Husseren-les-Châteaux, highest point of Alsace vineyards (380 m.), dominated by ruins of the three towers of *Eguisheim* (one-time fortified town, still intact), Wettolsheim and **Colmar***. ● Wine Road then winds to W of N83 via *Turckheim* (old fortified town, many ancient houses); Niedermorschwihr, Ammerschwihr; **Kaysersberg***; *Mittelwihr*; *Beblenheim*, where slopes of the Sonnenglanz produce wines of great quality: Muscat, Tokay, Sylvaner and Riesling; **Riquewihr***, the 'pearl of the vineyard', produces world-famed Riesling; *Hunawihr* (fortified church); **Ribeauvillé***, equally famed for its Gewürztraminer and Riesling; *St. Hippolyte*. ● At *Kintzheim*, take D35 via *Châtenois* (see **Sélestat***) and *Dambach-la-Ville* (half-timbered houses, 15–17c chapel of St. Sébastien), as far as **Andlau***. ● D62 leads to Mittelbergheim (reputed vineyard, lovely Renaissance houses). ● At **Barr***, which produces Sylvaner, Riesling and especially Gewürztraminer, rejoin D35, which leads to **Molsheim*** via *Ottrott* (red wines; see **Obernai***) and *Rosheim*. ● Wine Road continues via Wangen, typical wine-growing village, to *Marlenheim*, where it ends.

The ancient hostelry of the Deux-Clefs at Turckheim still has its carved joists.

edge of 375-acre park which includes large leisure centre (swimming pool, tennis courts, golf course, etc.), a racecourse, Olympic swimming pool, etc. Bottling plant is most modern in Europe (v.a. during season).
Vicinity ● 5.5 km SW, *Contrexéville*, hydromineral spa. ● 19 km SE, *Darney*, small Franco-Czech mus.; to E, huge *Forêt Domaniale de Darney* (magnificent woods); ruins of abbey of *Droiteval*, founded 12c, Romanesque church.

Viviers
07 – Ardèche   37 – D 2
Old episcopal town, standing on isolated rock overlooking R. *Rhône*, *Défilé de Donzère* and Henri Poincaré hydroelectric station; its steep streets, lined by old houses, are well worth exploring. Cathedral of St. Vincent, of Romanesque origin, remodelled 14–15c, is joined by a portico to 14c bell-tower, built above 11c gateway; in choir, six Gobelins tapestries and 17c choir-stalls. From terrace behind apse, magnificent view. On Place de l'Hôtel-de-Ville, mid-16c Maisons des Chevaliers; lovely Louis XV mansions in Grande-Rue.
Vicinity ● 2 km W, Romanesque chapel and tomb of St. Ostian. ● 2 km E, Châteauneuf-du-Rhône, old village dominated by ruins of 13c castle of Montpensier and remains of perimeter wall; 16 and 17c houses. ● 3 km SW, *Défilé de Donzère*.

Vizille (Château)
38 – Isère   32 – B 3
17c building, both fortress and aristocratic residence (v.a., cl. Mon. and Tues.; Son et Lumière in summer). Pediment of main doorway is decorated with equestrian statue of the Connétable de Lesdiguières (1622). Façade overlooking park is particularly imposing. Inside, lovely main staircase and state apartments (17c fireplaces, furniture and tapestries). French Revolutionary museum.
Vicinity ● 2 km SW, unusual pre-Romanesque chapel of Notre Dame-de-Mésage, 9–10c. ● To E, *Romanche* gorges, very industrialised; to S of *Rochetaillée*, plain of Oisans and **Bourg-d'Oisans***; to N, **Grands Cols*** road and **St. Jean-de-Maurienne***. ● 9 km S, Laffrey, high-altitude resort, and *Lac de Laffrey*; equestrian statue of Napoleon evokes his 'meeting' with the troops sent to arrest him on his return from Elba (Mar. 7, 1815).

Vizzavona
2B – Corsica   45 – C 2
Well-equipped tourist resort, closed in winter despite proximity of road and Ajaccio-Bastia railway. Lovely forest of pines and beeches. Excellent excursion centre.
Vicinity ● Via *Vivario*, to N, **Corte***. ● To E, *Ghisoni*, *Défilé de l'Inzecca* and **Aleria***. ● To SW, via *Col de Vizzavona*, *Bocognano*, in heart of famed maquis, haunt of Corsican bandits, towards **Ajaccio***.

Voiron
38 – Isère   32 – B 2
Small commercial and industrial town. Huge 19c church of St. Bruno. St. Pierre-de-Sermorens, rebuilt 1920, still has 8c crypt and 14c chapels. Distillery and cellars of Grande-Chartreuse (v.a. to watch distillery process exc. Sun.).
Vicinity ● 13 km NW, **Charavines-les-Bains*** and *Lac de Paladru*. ● To E: **Grande-Chartreuse***.

Vouvant
85 – Vendée   23 – A 2
Picturesque fortified town standing on promotory in wide loop of R. Mère. Remains of medieval castle, late-12c keep, 30 m. high, known as 'Mélusine's Tower' (fine view from top). 11–12c Romanesque church; façade of N transept is remarkably finely sculpted.
Vicinity ● To S, Vouvant forest (5,720 acres), very picturesque. ● 8.5 km SE, *Foussais*, interesting 15c church with noteworthy sculpted Romanesque façade. ● 9 km S, *Mervent*, on steep escarpment in centre of Vouvant forest, in magnificent setting; *Mervent* dam, on R. *Vendée*, has created a huge lake (beach, small zoo 3 km away); from calvary overlooking Mère gorge, 4.5 km to NW, path to grotto of St. Grignion de Montfort (pilgrimage); picturesque site of Pierre-Brune, in rocky hollow.

Wissembourg
67 – Bas-Rhin   14 – B 1
A stroll in the old quarters, whose half-timbered houses and narrow streets show a Germanic influence (especially in Bruch quarter), is a 'must'. Huge 13c Gothic church of St. Pierre-et-St. Paul, Romanesque tower and 14c cloister gallery containing abbots' tombs. Westercamp mus., in two 16c houses (art, archaeology and local history). Walk around ramparts. Numerous

old houses on banks of R. Lauter and Bruch canal (16c Vogelsberger mansion).
Vicinity ● 3 km S, Gelsberg hill (243 m.). ● From *Lembach*, 15 km to SW, take trip (7 km N) to 13c *Ch. de Fleckenstein*, whose ruins occupy a remarkable strategic position; *Obersteinbach* (10 km W) is dominated by remains of Petit-Arnsbourg castle, on a rocky ridge; ruins of numerous castles.

Yeu (Island)
85 – Vendée   22 – A 1
9.5 km long, the Ile d'Yeu's Atlantic-facing coastline has been cut up into picturesque creeks and promontories. ● *Port-Joinville*, colourful fishing port and seaside resort; Luco house, in which Marshal Pétain died (in 1951) – he is buried in local cemetery. 4 km SW, strangely-shaped ruins of 11, 14 and 15c Vieux-Château, on rock battered by Atlantic Ocean. Sailors' calvary, *Châtelet* peninsula and Sabias beach. ● 4 km SE, *Port-de-la-Meule*; nearby, 'Pierre Tremblante' (trembling rock).

Yssingeaux
43 – Haute-Loire   31 – C 3
Interesting town hall in elegant late-15c manorhouse, topped by machicolations and crenellations. 5 min. away, to N, 922 m.-high hill offers magnificent view of volcanic peaks of *Meygal* massif.
Vicinity ● 13 km NW, *Retournac*; departure point for tour of *Gorges de la Loire* both up- and downstream (see **Le Puy***, **Monistrol-sur-Loire*** and **St. Étienne***). ● 19 km SE, *Tence*, picturesque town with roofs of grey lauze; 17c church contains 15c Goth. choir and carved 17c choir-stalls; 9 km to S, *Le Chambon-sur-Lignon*: summer resort, beach on R. *Lignon*.

Zonza
2A – Corsica   45 – C 2
High-altitude summer resort (764 m.), surrounded by forests, rising in tiers above Asinao valley.
Vicinity ● 9 km NE, *Col de Bavella* (1,243 m.) in grandiose setting; magnificent view dominated in N by fantastically-shaped red walls of *Aiguilles de Bavella*. ● 15.5 km W, *Serra-di-Scopamène* and Serra pass (937 m.).

Zonza: *the Ospedale forest.*

Temple of Gastronomy

No traveller's guide would be complete without touching on that most important of all aspects of visiting France, her food and wines. As the following brief summaries show, the wealth and extraordinary variety you will encounter, in each different region of the country, makes this truly a Temple of Gastronomy.

Brittany

Seafood is one of the mainstays of Breton cookery. White fish and eel, and sometimes lobster, form a rich stew known as a *cotriade*, mussels are used in a creamy soup called *mouclade*, and oysters are either eaten raw or cooked in a variety of ways. (Brittany supplies a large proportion of the oysters in France, from the rather rough and liquid-textured *Portugaise* to the more refined, firmer-fleshed, round *Belon*.) *Palourdes farçies* are clams served on half-shells with a lovely stuffing of shallots and herbs; *alose à l'oseille* is grilled shad served with a delicate sorrel sauce; and *coquilles St. Jacques à la bretonne* is a gratin of scallops presented in the half-shell. Salt-meadow lamb or mutton is served *à la bretonne*, with haricot beans. A great Breton speciality is pancakes or *crêpes*, served with either jam and/or fresh fruit as an afternoon snack, or with meat and/or eggs as a light but filling meal. The lacy, crisp *crêpe dentelle* from Quimperlé is a light, rolled biscuit which, topped with cold whipped cream, makes a mouth-watering dessert.

Normandy

This is the province of rich, cream-producing dairy herds, and of apple orchards which provide the world-famed distilled apple juice or applejack known as *Calvados*. The supreme achievement of Norman cooking is *tripes à la mode de Caen* – tripe slowly cooked with oxfeet on a bed of carrots and onions, flavoured with herbs, cider and Calvados. The next best known dish is *poulet à la crème vallée d'Auge*, cooked in cream and cider and garnished with tiny onions. *Canard à la Rouennaise* is a glorious dish, but produced under conditions which would not be tolerated by animal lovers – a wild duck is slowly strangled so that its body retains the blood, lightly roasted, flamed in Cognac, the breast meat carved, and then the carcase is pressed to squeeze out the blood which is used to flavour the accompanying sauce. *Matelote à la normande* is a fish stew flavoured with cider, the ubiquitous Calvados, butter and cream, and garnished with tiny shellfish and button mushrooms. Desserts are mainly apple-based, e.g. *bourdelots*, whole apples cooked in a delicate suet crust; *tarte normande*, a light and delicate apple flan; and *soufflé normand*, which is flavoured with Calvados and studded with apple fritters.

Pays de la Loire

The Loire's greatest contribution to French regional cookery is its exquisite butter sauce or *beurre blanc*, a reduction of shallots fused with wine vinegar and whisked up with butter – usually served with shad or pike from one of the region's numerous rivers. Among the area's other specialities are *matelote d'anguille* – eels stewed gently in wine – and *noisette de porc aux pruneaux* – a fillet of pork in a cream sauce garnished with huge juicy prunes. As an hors d'oeuvre, try *rillettes de porc*, which is shredded, seasoned, cooked, pounded and potted in its own juices and fat. Or it may be served in an open tart as a *quiche tourangelle*. Berry's *citrouillat*, a light and fluffy pumpkin tart, is justly famed, as is the rich almond-paste tart known as *gâteau de Pithiviers* from the town of that name, and the delicate apple and quince paste called *cotignac*.

Ile de France and Paris

Although Paris is the capital city and the Ile de France the centre of the country, they have actually produced few great or classic dishes. However, the market gardens around Paris do grow magnificent vegetables, so that most of the well-known regional recipes contain one or more of these, e.g. *potage Crécy* (made with carrots), *potage Soissonnais* (a purée of white beans), *soupe à l'oignon* (the ultimate late-night filler) and the ubiquitous *potage Parisienne*, which will contain every available vegetable according to season. More delicate fare includes *crème Chantilly* (sweet, whipped cream, used as a dessert or as a filling for pancakes), and *gâteau St. Honoré* (a rich choux pastry cake filled with whipped cream).

The North

Down-to-earth cookery for a down-to-earth region, based mainly on the local waterways – fish from the sea and the inland marshes and lakes, salt-meadow lamb, and migrant wild duck – such as *anguille au vert à la flamande* (sautéed eel served in an aromatic, bitter dressing), *croustade de fruits de mer* (sea-food flan), *quenelles de brochet* (slim, sausage-shaped purée of pike), *agneau à la Ste. Ménéhould*

(grilled and coated in breadcrumbs), and *pâté de caneton d'Amiens* (stuffed, boned wild duck, baked in a pastry case). Probably the area's only unusual and subtle dish is the *lapin de garenne aux pruneaux* (casseroled wild rabbit with prunes).

Alsace-Lorraine

Renowned for their solid Germanic cookery, well-suited to these provinces' long, cold winters, and based on cabbages, sausages and stews. *Choucroute garnie* is a mixture of ham, sausage and other pig products served on a bed of cooked pickled cabbage, with boiled potatoes. *Potée Lorraine* is a stew of smoked pork and bacon, sausage, beans and cabbage, while its Alsace counterpart contains potatoes and mixed vegetables along with the beans and smoked bacon. The world-famed *quiche Lorraine* is a light flan with a filling of smoked bacon, whipped cream and beaten eggs. Lorraine also serves as an elegant hors d'oeuvre a rich brawn of sucking-pig encased in a fragrant wine jelly (*porcelet en gélée*). As a breath-taking dessert, try Alsace's *vacherin glacé* (a magnificent concoction of ice-cream, meringue and glacé fruits topped with mountains of whipped cream), or a giant rum baba filled with raisins and drowned in Kirsch or rum, called a *Kugelhopf*.

The Eastern Mountains

Franche-Comté is the home of Gruyère de Comté cheese, much used in the best-famed local dish: *fondue* (which, like Gruyère itself, is by no means only Swiss!). However, the cheese is also employed in a variety of other ways, including *cancoillotte* – a kind of Welsh rarebit served hot in bowls or cold on toast – as well as *tourte comtoise*, with slices of potato and ham, and *galettes au Comté*, a kind of cheese biscuit spiced with Cayenne pepper.

The Jura has abundant fresh-water fish, wild mushrooms and fruit, found in such dishes as *mousseline d'écrevisses à la Nantua*, which is pike or perch with a creamy paste of crayfish, *morilles du Jura à la crème* (fluffy tartlets filled with morel mushrooms in a delicate cream sauce), and the light quince or apple fritters called *beignets*.

Savoie and Dauphiné are rich in potatoes, used in numerous ways in the local dishes known collectively as *gratins* – with cheese in *gratin dauphinois*, mushrooms, crayfish, or simply with seasoned stock as a *gratin savoyard*. Wild hare is used in the well-known *civet savoyard* – an extremely rich jug of highly-seasoned hare cooked with wine and cream. A fish delicacy of the Savoie is the elegant *omble chevalier* – a member of the salmon family found mainly in the region's lakes, such as Annecy, Bourget and Léman (Geneva) – cooked in myriad ways with sauces of cream, crayfish or tarragon.

Burgundy and the Lyonnais

Burgundian cookery seems to be specifically designed to exploit to the fullest the flavour of the region's many fine wines, such as the classic and deservedly world-famed *boeuf bourguignon*, slow cooked in red wine with bacon, onions and a bouquet garni, and served with sautéed mushrooms and tiny whole onions. Other examples of cooking with wine include the equally well-known *coq au vin* and its grander brother, *coq au Chambertin*, as well as *jambon persillé* (shredded ham in a jelly of ham stock, white wine and parsley) and *queue de boeuf des vignerons* (oxtail stewed with white grapes). Other dishes – especially those made with cheese – act as perfect foils for a variety of wines, such as *gougère* (a light and delicate cake of cheese-flavoured choux pastry), *petites fondues à la bourguignonne*, which make a charming hors d'oeuvre, and *escargots à la bourguignonne*, snails stuffed with garlic and parsley butter.

One speciality of the area around Lyons is *poulet demi-deuil* – chicken spiked with truffles, poached and served in a madeira sauce. Another is tripe, cooked in countless ways – the best-known of which are probably *gras double à la Lyonnaise* (with onions and seasoned with parsley) or the oddly named *tablier de sapeur* (fireman's apron), a previously-cooked slab of tripe, coated with egg and breadcrumbs, grilled until crisp and served with *sauce tartare*.

For dessert, *tourte Charollaise* – a tart filled with pears in custard – or *pruneaux au Bourgogne* – prunes poached in Burgundy.

Provence

Aromatic herbs like tarragon, rosemary, thyme and fennel; magnificent Southern vegetables such as aubergine, peppers, courgettes, artichokes and sun-ripened tomatoes; a rich variety of fish from the Mediterranean – but above all, olives, garlic and anchovies ... these are the hallmarks of Provençal cookery. At what is probably its simplest and most succulent, it is found in *aïoli* – a garlicky mayonnaise served surrounded by a mass of raw or plain-boiled vegetables and accompanied by fish and shellfish such as lobster, mussels and cod. Anchovies in a paste with olive oil, garlic and a few drops of vinegar on thick slices of bread are known as an *anchoïade*; pounded with olives, tuna fish and capers to make another paste which is served as an hors' d'oeuvre, they become a *tapenade*; and made into a pie with onions, olives and occasionally tomatoes, they are a *pissaladière*. *Bouillabaisse* is the classic fish stew of Provence – a rich mixture of Mediterranean fish liberally flavoured with

garlic and saffron; and *ratatouille* its great vegetable dish – aubergines, tomatoes, peppers and onions, sometimes with the addition of courgettes and/or potatoes, gently stewed in olive oil until soft but not mushy and then flavoured with herbs and garlic. *Ratatouille* is said to have originated from Nice, like the famed salad which bears the town's name – a mouth-watering summer hors d'oeuvre whose basis is sliced hard-boiled eggs, anchovy fillets, black olives and tomatoes in a garlic and herb dressing, to which may be added artichoke hearts, raw sliced peppers, tuna fish, diced cooked potatoes and cooked French beans. From the sea come *loup grillé au fenouil*, grilled seabass flavoured with brandy and fennel, and *morue à la provençale*, salt cod in a rich and scented sauce of tomatoes stewed with onion, black olives, saffron, garlic and herbs.

Corsica

Corsican cooking has been much influenced by that of Italy (dating from the days when Corsica was an Italian possession) and, to a lesser degree, by that of Provence. For example, it, too, has a *bouillabaisse* known as *ziminu*, although made more fiery than its Provençal cousin by the addition of a seasoning of hot red peppers; and an *anchoïade*, which is topped with slices of onion, browned under a grill and served hot. Italian origins show themselves in a spicy sauce called *pebronata* – a Corsican version of Italy's *peperonata* – or tomato, onion, pimento, juniper berries and herbs, usually poured over beef braised in wine; and in *stuffatu*, beef and pork in a scented red wine stew, served with grated cheese and noodles. A purée of chestnut flour called *polenta* can be served plain or fried as an accompaniment to blood pudding or liver sausage, or as a thick sandwich stuffed with *lonzo*, the local dried salted pork fillet, or *prizuttu*, seasoned and smoked cured ham (a Corsican cousin of Italy's *prosciutto*).

Languedoc

Pork and haricot beans dominate the cookery of this area and are found together in its best-known dish, the *cassoulet* – the most famed versions of which come from Castelnaudary, Toulouse and Carcassonne. Castelnaudary's *cassoulet* contains only pork in various forms, while in Toulouse, cooks add lamb and preserved goose and/or duck, and Carcassonne follows Toulouse in using lamb but also adds a whole partridge during the hunting season! The local snails are served in many different sauces – red peppers, ham, tomatoes, mushrooms in cherry brandy in Limoux; almond paste, warm milk and breadcrumbs mixed together and then blended with oil, garlic and an egg yolk in Narbonne – but one of the loveliest of all is in a *sauce aux noix* made with crushed walnuts, ham, shallots and parsley.

Pyrenees

Roussillon is a Catalan land and has borrowed much that is good from its other half on the opposite side of the Spanish border. Its national soup is the *ollada* – a filling combination of pork, beans, cabbage, and other vegetables such as carrots, leeks and potatoes, distinguished by the fact that the beans are cooked separately from the rest of the ingredients and added to the soup just before serving. Its national snack, in contrast, is *el pa y al*, a chunk of bread highly seasoned with garlic and soaked in olive oil. The Spanish influence is also found in the *sauce catalane*, made with tomatoes and bitter oranges, which accompanies such poultry as chicken and game birds as partridge.

Béarn is inextricably linked in most people's minds with a dish made famous by the ancient province's most heroic son, 'Henri Poule-au-Pot' or 'Le Vert Galant' – King Henri III of Navarre, who became Henri IV of France. The *poule au pot* that Henri wanted every French family to have on its table every Sunday of the year is a boiling fowl stuffed with chopped fresh pork or pork sausage meat mixed with eggs and herbs, poached gently with vegetables and a bouquet garni. Also specifically Béarnais are the thick soups called *garbures*, basically made with cabbage, bacon and preserved duck or goose, with the addition of other vegetables and meats (preserved or salted) according to the season, area and, above all, personal taste.

The Basque country has produced the label *à la basquaise* for dishes that contain pimentoes, such as potatoes stuffed with a mix of stewed pimento, diced Bayonne ham and parsley, or chicken cooked in oil with pimentoes, tomatoes and ham. The pimento appears again in the classic scrambled egg dish *piperade*, together with onions and tomatoes. From the sea coast come: *chipirones guipuzcoanes*, tiny squid stewed in their own ink, with onions, garlic and paprika; fresh oysters, often served in a startling combination with the spicy local sausage called *lou-kenkas* – the one ice-cold and raw, the other cooked till sizzling hot; and a sumptuous fricassée of fish with onions called a *ttoro*.

Aquitaine

The region around Bordeaux produces some of the most magnificent wines in France, but it is often said that its cuisine fails to live up to them. That is to ignore its rib steak cooked with beef marrow and shallots (*entrecôte à la Bordelaise* or *entrecôte marchand de vin*), its mushrooms simmered in oil with garlic and parsley (*cèpes à la Bordelaise*) and its lampreys stewed in red wine with leeks and

onions (*lamproies à la Bordelaise*). Or the succulent *agneau rôti de Pauillac* – salt-meadow lamb gently cooked with garlic and breadcrumbs and parsley and served with thin slices of fried potato and truffle. Or the delicate *foie de canard aux chasselas* – duck liver cooked with onions and carrots and served with chasselas grapes soaked in port. Or the *huîtres à la Bordelaise* – ice-cold oysters served with boiling-hot *crépinettes* (a kind of flat sausage stuffed with truffles), coated in white wine.

The Landes, the heathland and pine forest stretches to the south of Bordeaux, produce filling dishes to satisfy the huge appetites of outdoor folk – such as *épaules à la landaise* (shoulder of lamb stuffed with breadcrumbs mixed with minced veal, pork, pork liver, parsley and Cognac and served with tomatoes and potatoes), or *oeufs à la landaise* (eggs on a base of tomatoes, sausages and onions and coated with finely grated cheese), or *pommes de terre à la landaise* (thick slices of potato sautéed in goose fat with onions and local ham). There's also a nourishing soup called *potée landaise au farci* – a veritable meal in itself – in which pork, vegetables, eggs, preserved goose, sausages and slices of bacon all figure prominently.

Périgord

This is the rich country of the duck and the goose (which yield the exquisite *magrets, confits* and *foie gras* prized by true gastronomes throughout the world), the walnut tree (from which is manufactured the most glorious oil in all France, the subtly flavoured, delicate, refined *huile de noix*), and that black diamond, the truffle, which turns each dish it touches into a dish fit for a king. Every meal in the Périgord, however grand, must start with a soup, and what better than a *tourain blanchi* – golden-fried minced onions and garlic simmered in seasoned water with egg whites, to which are added, just before serving, beaten egg yolks and thin slices of bread? Then it should perhaps continue with a foie gras – or maybe *truffes sous la cendre*, whole truffles wrapped first in a thin layer of fat bacon and then in a casing of flaky pastry, coated with egg yolk, or *oeufs farcis aux cèpes*, the whites of hard-boiled eggs stuffed with their own minced yolks mixed with mushrooms, garlic and parsley. Follow this with a *filet de boeuf sauce Périgueux*, a fillet of beef spiked with bacon and truffles, cooked in white wine and brandy, served on a bed of tiny rounds of toast covered with truffles in a rich sauce of wine and madeira flavoured with shallots, truffles and the cooking juices of the meat itself. Or *poulet farci à la Périgueux*, chicken stuffed with sausage or ham, breadcrumbs, Cognac and truffles. Accompany them with *pommes de terre sautées Sarladaises* – slices of potato and truffles lightly sautéed in goose fat and served in alternating layers – and follow with the region's most exportable salad, *salade à l'huile de noix*. Then the local goat's cheese – *cabécou* – fried lightly in walnut oil with a garnish of cracked, fried walnuts, on a bed of seasonal salad vegetables. And finish with one of the local pancakes, like a *Jacques* (stuffed with apples) or a *crêpe à l'anis* (made with aniseed and served with the local jam or honey), or a *beignet* of acacia flowers or cherries.

Getting to Know French Cheeses

It has become almost a platitude to recall General de Gaulle's comment about the 'impossibility' of governing a country which has more than 400 cheeses. As it happens, he was underestimating. Any slightly prolonged drive through France will confirm that there are almost certainly well over 400 local goat's cheeses, alone ... (That only a relative handful of them can be distinguished from the rest is merely a neither-here-nor-there, of course!) The fact remains that France does produce such a great diversity of cheeses, of all kinds, that it is impossible to list them all here. However, it is useful, at least, when faced with a daunting array in a restaurant or shop, to know the basic categories, which wines to drink with them, and how to choose, store and serve them. Put at its simplest, there are three main categories:

I. Fresh cheeses
Made with pasteurised milk. Generally unfermented, easily digestible, e.g. Demi-Sel, the many and various cream cheeses, and Petit-Suisse, which can be eaten with salt or sugar as a dessert course.

II. Fermented cheeses
Far and away the largest and most diverse group, which can be subdivided into four types:
1) Soft paste cheeses.
The shapes of these vary according to their region of origin, and they come in three varieties:
  a) Cheeses with floury rinds: distinguished by the fine white mould which forms on the rind, e.g. most Bries, Camembert, mild-tasting Carré de l'Est, also Bondon de Neufchâtel, Chaource, Coulommiers and Gournay, which are all made from cow's milk; and dark-grey, pyramid-shaped Valençay and the various Pyramide cheeses from the Ile-de-France, Loire valley and Poitou-Charentes regions, which are made from goat's milk.

b) Cheeses with washed rinds: firmer in texture than the floury rind cheeses, and with a harder rind which is frequently rubbed or washed in brine during the ripening process to keep the cheese's internal moisture evenly balanced. The colour of the rind can be of any shade between yellow and red, e.g. the Boulette range (from French Flanders), Livarot, Maroilles, Munster, Pont l'Évêque, nutty-flavoured Reblochon, Vacherin.

c) Cheeses with natural rinds: soft-textured, drained and dried, mainly made from goat's milk, although some are made from cow's or ewe's milk – or any combination of the three, e.g. Cabécou or Chabichou (shaped like a large white cotton-reel), Crotin de Chavignol (small, greyish and squat), and cylinder-shaped Ste. Maure, all made from goat's milk; some Bries and St. Marcellin, made with cow's milk; Charolles, a mixture of both; and Banon de Provence, wrapped in vine or chestnut leaves (a heady mix of goat's, cow's and ewe's milk).

2) Semi-hard, pressed and uncooked cheeses.

The paste undergoes a number of fermentations and is drained by prolonged mechanical pressure. Sometimes the cheese is coated with a thin layer of wax. Shapes vary from cylindrical to round and flattened, e.g. Cantal, Port-Salut and its offspring St. Paulin, St. Nectaire and the various Tommes or Tomes de Savoie, which can be flavoured with brandy, or coated with grape-skins and pips, etc.

3) Hard pressed and cooked cheeses.

These have been cooked at a high temperature, then moulded and pressed very firmly. During maturation, holes appear in the paste, the number and size of which vary according to type, e.g. Emmenthal, Gruyère de Comté.

4) Blue-veined cheeses.

Soft paste cheeses which have been neither pressed nor cooked. The internal mould is generally a result of inoculating the curd with penicillium culture. The name 'Blue' used by itself is applied to blue-veined cheeses made from cow's milk. There are two kinds:

a) Blues with natural, dry rinds, sold under a brand name, e.g. Bleu de Bresse, Chevrotin persillé des Aravis, Fourme d'Ambert.

b) Blues with rinds made thinner by scraping, e.g. Bleu d'Auvergne, Bleu des Causses, Roquefort.

III. Fondu cheeses

These result from heating a semi-hard or hard pressed cheese to produce a soft mixture to which another variety of cheese, or even cream, is then added – with or without extra flavouring or coating such as chopped nuts, grape-skins and pips, herbs, spices, chopped vegetables or diced meat or fish, e.g. Crème de Gruyère, Fondu à tartiner, Fondu aux noix, Fondu aux raisins.

Which wines go with which cheeses

Soft paste cheeses with floury rinds – Light red wines.
Soft paste cheeses with washed rinds – Full-bodied red wines.
Soft paste cheeses with natural rinds – Dry, fruity white wines.
Semi-hard, pressed and uncooked cheeses – light, dry white, rosé or red.
Hard pressed and cooked cheeses – Dry white or rosé.
Blue-veined cheeses – Full-bodied reds, sweet and soft whites.
Fondu cheeses – Light, dry white or rosé wines.

Choosing your cheese

In a restaurant or shop, look for semi-hard or hard cheeses that show no signs of cracking or sweating (otherwise they could be mouldy inside); and never pick one with surface mould or grease, because it will be past its peak. The veins in blue cheese become more pronounced and deeper in colour as they ripen; so the darker and more noticeable the veins are, the richer flavoured the cheese will be. Brie and Camembert which you want to eat immediately should be soft and springy right through – they will then have a full, rounded flavour; if they 'give' only a little under gentle pressure from your thumb, they will need a few days longer to ripen. A chalky strip through the centre indicates a milder flavour. Avoid any soft paste cheese that is obviously runny or smells of ammonia, as it will certainly be well past its prime. Finally, never buy a film-wrapped cheese whose film is split or leaking, nor a wax-coated cheese where the wax has cracked, nor a boxed cheese in which the contents have shrunk away from the sides.

Storing

Keep cream cheese in a fridge and eat within four days or so of purchase. Wrap soft paste cheese in foil and put in a closed container at the bottom of the fridge to prevent drying out. Semi-hard and hard cheeses can likewise be loosely wrapped in foil, greaseproof paper or clingfilm and stored in the lowest part of the fridge. Blue-veined cheeses need air, but must not be allowed to lose their internal moisture, otherwise they will crack; however, their strong smell tends to pervade their surroundings – so, as a matter of self-preservation, wrap as for hard cheeses and put in a sealed container, either in a cool, well-ventilated place or in the fridge.

Serving

Cream cheese is the only variety that can be served straight from the fridge. For the rest, take all

cheeses out of the fridge at least one hour before they are to be eaten, so that they can regain their full flavour gently, at room temperature. (Brie and Camembert and the other floury rinded cheeses will need at least *two* hours for this.) Always be sure to remove wrappings before serving.

The Wines of France

Except in the far north-west and north of France, there is virtually no area of the country where you will not see a vineyard – even if, outside the actual wine regions, it is only on a roadside strip of land someone inherited from Aunt Yvonne. Broadly speaking, there are 10 principal wine-growing regions, producing wines classed in three officially-recognised categories:

Appellation d'Origine Contrôlée (AOC), also more briefly as Appellation Contrôlée (AC): the highest category, confirming that the wine comes from the exact area, town or individual vineyard specified on the label and that its production has met certain legally defined requirements (e.g. grape varieties used, maximum permitted yield per acre, and so on). Although it is not a guarantee of high quality, as such, you can take it that wines granted an Appellation are *likely* to be above average. Indeed, all France's greatest wines belong to this category.

Vins Délimités de Qualité Supérieure (VDQS): also an officially-backed guarantee as regards their stated origin, approved grape varieties, observing traditional local production methods, etc. Although one below AOC in status, VDQS is still a distinction quite difficult to obtain and the wines are anything but second-rate.

Vins de Pays: these often little-known 'country wines' are no longer just the haphazard products of individual villages but now have a formal quality category of their own and must meet stated regulations before qualifying for it. Although lower than VDQS, they are of a standard and consistency implicitly superior to the general run of inexpensive wines. To date, just over 100 have qualified, more than half of them in the southern half of the country.

In addition, there are vast quantities of *vin ordinaire*, very ordinary table wines and mass-selling branded ranges – almost certainly blended from several different wines (not all of them necessarily French). While a good number may be passable for everyday thirst-quenching purposes, their quality tends to be reflected by their cheap price. That being said, don't automatically spurn the *vin du patron* at the bottom end of a country restaurant's wine list; many local restaurateurs take a pride in offering house wines of quite reasonable standard (frequently grown locally or even by the *patron* himself).

The 10 main wine regions are:

Bordeaux. Responsible for close on one-third of all the top-grade wines in France. Roughly 250,000 acres under vine, of which about 78 per cent yield wines of AC status. (This out of a total annual production, in an average year, of around 500 million bottles!) In 1855, Bordeaux's 62 best red wines (known in English as 'clarets') were classified into five 'Grands Crus', or great growths, which still largely hold good. By universal consent, the greatest red wines in the world come from the five châteaux now classed as 'Premiers Crus': Lafite, Margaux, Latour, Haut-Brion and Mouton-Roths-child. However, although the outside spotlight tends to be turned on the 'Grands Crus', such wines probably account for less than three per cent of the whole; below them are other classifications – 'bourgeois', 'artisan' or peasant growths – which can also be of very high quality.

Among the most familiar districts within the region are: *Médoc* and *Haut-Médoc* (best-known communes are Margaux, Pauillac, St. Estèphe and St. Julien); *Graves*; *St. Émilion* (top growths are Ch. Cheval-Blanc and Ch. Ausone, followed by Ch. Figeac, Pavie, Clos-Fourtet, Trottevieille, and about half-a-dozen more); *Pomerol* (top growth, Ch. Pétrus); and, for superb sweet white wines, *Sauternes*, with *Barsac* (top growth, Ch. d'Yquem).

Other districts include Côtes de Bourg, Côtes de Blaye, Fronsac, Premières Côtes de Bordeaux, and Entre-Deux-Mers.

Burgundy. Extending in a shoulder-shaped line from Chablis to Dijon, then southerly towards Lyons, the Burgundy vineyards spread in three main strips totalling about 280 km – but sometimes less than 1 km in width. Although its acreage under vine is well under half that of Bordeaux, its best wines are equally renowned (indeed, their relative scarcity has led to increasingly high prices). Often expressed in regal terms, Burgundy's wines have Chambertin and Romanée-Conti as their king and queen, Clos de Vougeot as the regent, and about seven more recognised as 'members of the royal family' (Musigny, Corton, Richebourg, Montrachet, etc.). Other familiar names include Beaune, Pommard, Volnay, Mâcon, Meursault, Mercurey and Pouilly-Fuissé. At the far south of the region is the Beaujolais area – where, besides the fruity young generic red Beaujolais, nine individual growths have their own Appellation (e.g. Brouilly, Fleurie, Juliénas, Morgon, etc.).

Alsace. Extending along the R. Rhine in the north-east of France, its 45,000 acres stretch for some 100 km, at heights of 600 ft to 1,500 ft – assuredly the loveliest 'wine road' in the world. The vast majority of the wines are white, and around 75 per cent of production each year is of AC status.

They are 'varietal' wines, i.e. taking their name from the grape variety used, the best-known being Riesling, Sylvaner and Gewürztraminer. Other names you may meet include Muscat d'Alsace, Tokay d'Alsace (a Pinot Gris, no relation of the Hungarian dessert wine) and a blended wine under the general title of Edelzwicker. There's also an excellent sparkling wine, Crémant d'Alsace, made by the champagne method.

Champagne. True champagne can come only from this strictly-defined region spreading southwards from Reims. Its price reflects the time and skill needed to produce those precious bubbles, by means of a second fermentation of the wine, within the bottle – a painstaking process which can take a good 18 months or more to complete. Familiar places include Épernay, Ay, Mareuil, Bouzy and Cramant. However, the great champagnes are identified principally by the name of their makers (many of whom welcome visitors to their vast cellars, some dating back to Roman times). The big-name houses include Ayala, Bollinger, Veuve Clicquot, Heidsieck and Charles Heidsieck, Krug, Lanson, Laurent-Perrier, Mercier, Moët-et-Chandon, Mumm, Perrier-Jouët, Piper-Heidsieck, Pol Roger, Pommery, Louis Roederer, Ruinart and Taittinger.

Côtes-du-Rhône. In two big stretches, south from Vienne to around Avignon, with a 50 km break between. Its vineyards – which include some of the oldest in France, established by Phoenician colonists in 4 c BC – cover about 160,000 acres. Well-known wines names include Côte Rôtie, Ch. Grillet, Condrieu, Cornas, Hermitage, Crozes-Hermitage, Châteauneuf-du-Pape. Also a great rosé, Tavel, the sparkling wine Clairette de Die, and three adjoining districts mainly producing big-selling, fairly inexpensive wines: Gigondas, Tricastin and Ventoux.

Jura-Savoie. Two wines unique to this mountainous region of central eastern France are its nut-scented Vin Jaune ('yellow wine'), sold in a special bottle called a 'clavelin', and the sweet Vin de Paille ('straw wine'), for which the grapes were originally kept on straw mats to concentrate their sugar. Good sparkling and rosé wines are also made in the region.

Loire. Known above all for its whites and pinks: the dry Muscadet, Sancerre, Pouilly-Fumé, Quarts-de-Chaume, Quincy; Anjou and Cabernet Rosé. But also first-rate sparkling wines from Saumur and Vouvray. The best red wines are from Chinon and Bourgueil, plus Saumur-Champigny and fruity light young reds made with the Beaujolais region's Gamay grape (e.g. Gamay de Touraine).

Provence. Wine-making here probably dates back to about 6 c BC. Previously best known for its whites and rosés, but reds are also made – and a much higher proportion of all its wines has achieved AC status in recent years. Familiar names are Cassis, Bandol, Bellet and Palette. Habitually bracketed with Provençal wines are those of *Corsica*: whites and rosés to be drunk young, robust reds. AC wines from around Ajaccio and Patrimonio, with five more districts under the general Vin de Corse appellation.

South-West. Embraces *Bergerac* (including the famed Monbazillac dessert wine), where the quality of the wines has risen dramatically over the past decade, the dark red wines of *Cahors*, and the small district of *Gaillac* (including unusual slightly-sparkling wines). Continuing down towards the Pyrenees, others sometimes listed under the South-West heading include Jurançon, Madiran and Béarn.

Languedoc-Roussillon. The most prolific of all French wine regions, but until a generation ago was known almost solely as the main source of the country's very cheap mass-selling wines, of no distinction whatever. In recent years, strenuous efforts have been made to improve the grape varieties and production methods. Wines which have won AC status include Fitou, Corbières, Minervois and Côtes-du-Roussillon. Note also such AC dessert wines as Banyuls, Maury and Muscat-de-Frontignan, and the sparkling wine Blanquette de Limoux.

Just as a Guide

Even in a country universally acknowledged to produce the greatest wines in the world, tastes differ and assessing a wine is often bound to be a matter of subjective judgment. Because of tiny variations in local climate or other conditions, there have always been instances of individual growers making good wine in supposedly 'poor' years – and, naturally, of some unfortunate managing to produce less-than-satisfactory wine in a generally classic year. Nowadays, for the broad run of quite decent everyday wines, as distinct from the big-name growths, scientific improvements enable a reasonable product to be made almost invariably, in all but the most adverse years. A price has had to be paid, perhaps, in the form of a somewhat bland levelling-out, with less likelihood of sudden exciting peaks (or low troughs), year to year; but at least it has become increasingly rare to find a wine of any recognised status, from Vin de Pays upwards, which is completely unacceptable.

For all these reasons, tables purporting to show good, average or below-average gradings for successive vintages can sometimes be a bit of a nonsense; they should never be regarded as Tablets of the Law – merely as a rough guide. On that strict understanding, therefore, our own table sets out simply to give a general indication: it does *not* claim to be comprehensive.

Key: A = All R = Red wines. SW = Sweet whites. DW = Dry whites.			
Great Years		**Good Years**	
1945	A		
1947	A		
		1948	– for Bordeaux and Alsace
1949	A (except Loire = good)		
1950	SW	1950	– for DW, Champagne, Côtes-du-Rhône
1952	Burgundy whites	1952	All others
1953	A (except Côtes-du-Rhône = good)		
1955	Whites and Champagne (Except Burgundy whites)	1955	R
		1957	– for SW, Burgundies and Côtes-du-Rhône
1959	A (except Côtes-du-Rhône = good)		
1961	R and Alsace	1961	Other whites
1962	Burgundy whites	1962	All others
1964	Champagne and Alsace	1964	All others except Bordeaux SW
		1966	All except Alsace
1967	SW	1967	Most others
1969	Burgundies	1969	– for Champagne, Loire and Côtes-du-Rhône
		1970	A
1971	Burgundies, Alsace, Bordeaux DW	1971	All others
		1973	Burgundy whites, Loire, Alsace and Champagne
1975	Bordeaux R	1975	Bordeaux whites and Champagne
1976	SW, Alsace	1976	All others
1978	Burgundy R, Côtes-du-Rhône	1978	All others
		1979	A
		1980	Bordeaux whites
		1981	All except Burgundy R and SW
1982	Bordeaux R	1982	All others
1983	A		
		1985	All except Champagne

Prognostications for 1986 are generally good in all regions. Still much too early to be sure for 1987, but the signs are that, while average quantities may be down in some areas, late sunshine helped to save the quality.

Distanze chilometriche da città a città
Distances de quelques grandes villes entre elles
Distances between cities

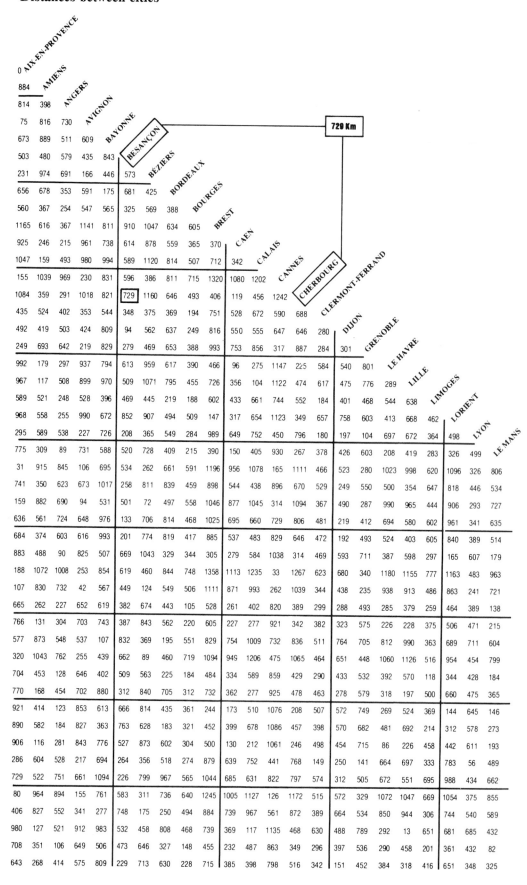

729 Km

	AIX-EN-PROVENCE	AMIENS	ANGERS	AVIGNON	BAYONNE	BESANÇON	BÉZIERS	BORDEAUX	BOURGES	BREST	CAEN	CALAIS	CANNES	CHERBOURG	CLERMONT-FERRAND	DIJON	GRENOBLE	LE HAVRE	LILLE	LIMOGES	LORIENT	LYON	LE MANS
AIX-EN-PROVENCE	0																						
AMIENS	884																						
ANGERS	814	398																					
AVIGNON	75	816	730																				
BAYONNE	673	889	511	609																			
BESANÇON	503	480	579	435	843																		
BÉZIERS	231	974	691	166	446	573																	
BORDEAUX	656	678	353	591	175	681	425																
BOURGES	560	367	254	547	565	325	569	388															
BREST	1165	616	367	1141	811	910	1047	634	605														
CAEN	925	246	215	961	738	614	878	559	365	370													
CALAIS	1047	159	493	980	994	589	1120	814	507	712	342												
CANNES	155	1039	969	230	831	596	386	811	715	1320	1080	1202											
CHERBOURG	1084	359	291	1018	821	729	1160	646	493	406	119	456	1242										
CLERMONT-FERRAND	435	524	402	353	544	348	375	369	194	751	528	672	590	688									
DIJON	492	419	503	424	809	94	562	637	249	816	550	555	647	646	280								
GRENOBLE	249	693	642	219	829	279	469	653	388	993	753	856	317	887	284	301							
LE HAVRE	992	179	297	937	794	613	959	617	390	466	96	275	1147	225	584	540	801						
LILLE	967	117	508	899	970	509	1071	795	455	726	356	104	1122	474	617	475	776	289					
LIMOGES	589	521	248	528	396	469	445	219	188	602	433	661	744	552	184	401	468	544	638				
LORIENT	968	558	255	990	672	852	907	494	509	147	317	654	1123	349	657	758	603	413	668	462			
LYON	295	589	538	227	726	208	365	549	284	989	649	752	450	796	180	197	104	697	672	364	498		
LE MANS	775	309	89	731	588	520	728	409	215	390	150	405	930	267	378	426	603	208	419	283	326	499	
	31	915	845	106	695	534	262	661	591	1196	956	1078	165	1111	466	523	280	1023	998	620	1096	326	806
	741	350	623	673	1017	258	811	839	459	898	544	438	896	670	529	249	550	500	354	647	818	446	534
	159	882	690	94	531	501	72	497	558	1046	877	1045	314	1094	367	490	287	990	965	444	906	293	727
	636	561	724	648	976	133	706	814	468	1025	695	660	729	806	481	219	412	694	580	602	961	341	635
	684	374	603	616	993	201	774	819	417	885	537	483	829	646	472	192	493	524	403	605	840	389	514
	883	488	90	825	507	669	1043	329	344	305	279	584	1038	314	469	593	711	387	598	297	165	607	179
	188	1072	1008	253	854	619	460	844	748	1358	1113	1235	33	1267	623	680	340	1180	1155	777	1163	483	963
	107	830	732	42	567	449	124	549	506	1111	871	993	262	1039	344	438	235	938	913	486	863	241	721
	665	262	227	652	619	382	674	443	105	528	261	402	820	389	299	288	493	285	379	259	464	389	138
	766	131	304	703	743	387	843	562	220	605	227	277	921	342	382	323	575	226	228	375	506	471	215
	577	873	548	537	107	832	369	195	551	829	754	1009	732	836	511	764	705	812	990	363	689	711	604
	320	1043	762	255	439	662	89	460	719	1094	949	1206	475	1065	464	651	448	1060	1126	516	954	454	799
	704	453	128	646	402	509	563	225	184	484	334	589	859	429	290	433	532	392	570	118	344	428	184
	770	168	454	702	880	312	840	705	312	732	362	277	925	478	463	278	579	318	197	500	660	475	365
	921	414	123	853	613	666	814	435	361	244	173	510	1076	208	507	572	749	269	524	369	144	645	146
	890	582	184	827	363	763	628	183	321	452	399	678	1086	457	398	570	682	481	692	214	312	578	273
	906	116	281	843	776	527	873	602	304	500	130	212	1061	246	498	454	715	86	226	458	442	611	193
	286	604	528	217	694	264	356	518	274	879	639	752	441	768	149	250	141	664	697	333	783	56	489
	729	522	751	661	1094	226	799	967	565	1044	685	631	822	797	574	312	505	672	551	695	988	434	662
	80	964	894	155	761	583	311	736	640	1245	1005	1127	126	1172	515	572	329	1072	1047	669	1054	375	855
	406	827	552	341	277	748	175	250	494	884	739	967	561	872	389	664	534	850	944	306	744	540	589
	980	127	521	912	983	532	458	808	468	739	369	117	1135	468	630	488	789	292	13	651	681	685	432
	708	351	106	649	506	473	646	327	148	455	232	487	863	349	296	397	536	290	458	201	361	432	82
	643	268	414	575	809	229	713	630	228	715	385	398	798	516	342	151	452	384	318	416	651	348	325

Le distanze riportate su questa carta sono calcolate da centro a centro secondo il percorso più agevole, non necessaria mente più breve.

Per ottenere la distanza tra due città, seguire la colonna verticale fino all'intersezione della colonna orizzontale corrispondents.

Les distances portées sur ce tableau sont calculées à partir du centre ville et en fonction du meilleur itinéraire, qui n'est pas obligatoirement le plus court.

Pour connaître la distance de deux villes entre elles, suivre les colonnes correspondantes à ces deux villes. Le kilométrage cherché se trouve à l'intersection des deux colonnes.

The distances in this chart are calculated from the city-centre and according to the best itinerary, which is not necessarily the shortest.

To find the distance between two cities, follow the columns corresponding to these cities. The distance in kilometres is found at the intersection of these two columns.

	MARSEILLE	METZ	MONTPELLIER	MULHOUSE	NANCY	NANTES	NICE	NÎMES	ORLÉANS	PARIS	PAU	PERPIGNAN	POITIERS	REIMS	RENNES	LA ROCHELLE	ROUEN	SAINT-ÉTIENNE	STRASBOURG	TOULON	TOULOUSE	TOURCOING	TOURS
METZ	772																						
MONTPELLIER	164	739																					
MULHOUSE	667	234	634																				
NANCY	715	57	682	177																			
NANTES	914	713	741	814	693																		
NICE	198	929	347	752	872	1071																	
NÎMES	138	687	52	582	630	783	295																
ORLÉANS	696	396	663	497	376	317	853	611															
PARIS	797	312	764	468	308	394	954	712	116														
PAU	582	1010	418	965	968	524	765	470	622	757													
PERPIGNAN	325	900	161	795	843	789	508	213	775	925	331												
POITIERS	735	615	562	652	594	179	892	604	218	337	420	634											
REIMS	801	182	768	383	206	544	958	716	262	154	863	929	480										
RENNES	952	680	813	781	660	106	1109	867	284	361	630	895	251	511									
LA ROCHELLE	921	773	724	789	731	147	1119	783	406	474	378	597	137	668	253								
ROUEN	937	414	904	668	438	372	1094	852	199	140	797	974	377	232	298	465							
SAINT-ÉTIENNE	317	499	284	397	442	597	474	232	379	462	635	445	418	528	635	547	578						
STRASBOURG	760	161	727	108	148	841	845	675	524	456	1058	888	742	354	808	879	586	490					
TOULON	65	821	239	716	764	963	159	187	745	846	657	400	784	850	1001	990	986	366	809				
TOULOUSE	411	913	247	881	856	579	594	299	565	681	194	210	424	806	685	387	764	441	974	486			
TOURCOING	1001	367	978	593	416	601	1168	926	392	240	1003	1139	583	210	537	705	239	710	564	1060	957		
TOURS	739	512	645	613	492	196	896	654	116	235	522	717	102	378	211	290	275	422	640	788	507	481	
TROYES	674	231	641	310	189	504	831	589	187	158	779	802	405	121	471	542	298	401	337	723	722	331	303

DOVE TROVARE GLI ENTI DEL TURISMO LOCALI ? Qualche indirizzo e numero di telefono
OÙ TROUVER LE SYNDICAT D'INITIATIVE ? Quelques adresses et numéros de téléphone
WHERE TO FIND THE LOCAL TOURIST OFFICES. Some addresses and phone numbers

01	**Bourg-en-Bresse** 6 av. Alsace-Lorraine	*74 22 49 40*
02	**Laon** place du Parvis-de-la-Cathédrale	*23 20 28 62*
03	**Moulins** place de l'Hôtel-de-Ville	*70 44 14 14*
	Vichy 19 rue du Parc	*70 98 71 94*
04	**Digne** Le Rond-Point	*92 31 42 73*
05	**Briançon** Porte de Pignerol	*92 21 08 50*
06	**Nice** 1 esplanade Kennedy	*93 92 82 82*
07	**Les Vans** place Ollier	*75 37 42 34*
08	**Charleville** 2 rue de Mantoue	*24 33 00 17*
09	**Foix** cours Gabriel-Fauré	*61 65 12 12*
10	**Troyes** 16 bd Carnot	*25 73 00 36*
11	**Carcassonne** 15 bd Camille-Pelletan	*68 25 07 04*
	Narbonne place Roger-Salengro	*68 65 15 60*
12	**Rodez** galerie Foch	*65 68 02 27*
13	**Marseille** La Canebière	*91 54 91 11*
	Aix-en-Provence 2 pl. du G.-de-Gaulle	*46 26 02 93*
	Arles 35 place de la République	*90 96 29 35*
14	**Caen** 14 place St-Pierre	*31 86 27 65*
	Bayeux 1 rue des Cuisiniers	*31 92 16 26*
	Lisieux 11 rue d'Alençon	*31 62 08 41*
15	**Aurillac** place du Square	*71 48 46 58*
16	**Angoulême** place de l'Hôtel-de-Ville	*45 95 16 84*
17	**La Rochelle** 10 rue Fleuriau	*46 41 14 68*
18	**Bourges** 21 rue Victor-Hugo	*48 24 75 33*
19	**Tulle** quai Baluze	*55 26 59 61*
2A	**Ajaccio** avenue Antoine-Serafini	*95 21 40 87*
2B	**Bastia** 33 bd Paoli	*95 31 02 04*
21	**Dijon** place Darcy	*80 43 42 12*
	Beaune face à l'Hôtel-Dieu	*80 22 24 51*
22	**Saint-Brieuc** 7 rue St-Gouéno	*96 33 32 50*
	Dinan 6 rue de l'Horloge	*96 39 75 40*
23	**Guéret** 1 avenue Charles-de-Gaulle	*55 52 14 29*
24	**Périgueux** 1 avenue d'Aquitaine	*53 53 10 63*
	Les Eyzies place de la Mairie	*53 06 97 05*
25	**Besançon** place de la 1re-Armée-Française	*81 80 92 55*
26	**Valence** place du Général-Leclerc	*75 43 04 88*
27	**Évreux** 35 rue Dr-Oursel	*32 38 21 61*
28	**Chartres** 7 cloître Notre-Dame	*37 21 54 03*
29	**Quimper** 3 rue du Roi-Gradlon	*98 95 04 69*
	Brest 1 place de la Liberté	*98 44 24 96*
30	**Nîmes** 6 rue Auguste	*66 67 29 11*
	Alès 2 rue Michelet	*66 52 21 15*
31	**Toulouse** Donjon du Capitole	*61 23 32 00*
32	**Auch** 1 rue Dessoles	*62 05 22 89*
33	**Bordeaux** 12 cours du 30-juillet	*56 44 28 41*
	Arcachon place Franklin-Roosevelt	*56 83 01 69*
34	**Montpellier** 6 rue Maguelone	*67 58 26 04*
	Béziers 27 rue du 4-septembre	*67 49 24 19*
35	**Rennes** Pont-de-Nemours	*99 79 01 98*
	Saint-Malo esplanade St-Vincent	*99 56 64 48*
36	**Châteauroux** place de la Gare	*54 34 10 74*
37	**Tours** place de la Gare	*47 05 58 08*
	Amboise quai du Général-de-Gaulle	*47 57 09 28*
	Azay-le-Rideau 26 rue Gambetta	*47 43 34 40*
	Chenonceaux 1 place de la Mairie	*47 23 94 45*
	Chinon 12 rue Voltaire	*47 93 17 85*
	Loches place de la Marne	*47 59 07 98*
38	**Grenoble** 14 rue de la République	*76 54 34 36*
39	**Lons-le-Saunier** 1 rue Pasteur	*84 24 20 63*
40	**Mont-de-Marsan** 22 rue Victor-Hugo	*58 46 40 40*
41	**Blois** 3 avenue Jean-Laigret	*54 74 06 49*
	Chaumont-s/Loire 4 rue de Lattre-De-Tassigny	*54 20 98 65*
42	**St-Étienne** 5 pl. Jean-Jaurès	*77 33 15 39*
43	**Le Puy** place du Breuil	*71 09 38 41*
44	**Nantes** place du Change	*40 47 04 51*
	La Baule 8 place de la Victoire	*40 24 34 44*
45	**Orléans** bd Aristide-Briand	*38 53 05 95*
46	**Cahors** place Aristide-Briand	*65 35 09 56*
47	**Agen** 107 bd Carnot	*53 47 36 09*
48	**Mende** 16 bd du Soubeyran	*66 65 02 69*
49	**Angers** place Kennedy	*41 88 69 93*
50	**Saint-Lô** 2 rue Havin	*33 05 02 09*
	Avranches 2 rue Général-de-Gaulle	*33 58 00 22*
	Coutances Les Unelles	*33 45 17 79*

	Le Mont-St-Michel	
	Corps de garde des Bourgeois	*33 60 14 30*
51	**Reims** 1 rue Jadart	*26 47 25 69*
52	**Langres** place Bel-Air	*25 85 03 32*
53	**Laval** place du 11-Novembre	*43 53 09 39*
54	**Nancy** 14 place Stanislas	*83 35 22 41*
	Lunéville Aile sud du Château	*83 74 06 55*
55	**Bar-le-Duc** 12 rue Lapique	*29 79 11 13*
	Verdun place de la Nation	*29 84 18 85*
56	**Lorient** place Jules-Ferry	*97 21 07 84*
57	**Metz** place d'Armes	*87 75 65 21*
58	**Nevers** 31 rue du Rempart	*86 59 07 03*
59	**Lille** Palais Rihour, place Rihour	*20 30 81 00*
	Valenciennes 1 rue Askièvre	*27 46 22 99*
60	**Beauvais** 4 rue Malherbe	*44 45 08 18*
	Compiègne place de l'Hôtel-de-Ville	*44 40 01 00*
	Chantilly avenue du Maréchal-Joffre	*44 57 08 58*
61	**Alençon** place Lamagdelaine	*33 26 11 36*
62	**Arras** 7 place du Maréchal-Foch	*21 51 26 95*
	Calais 12 bd Clemenceau	*21 96 62 40*
63	**Clermont-Ferrand** 69 bd Gergovia	*73 93 30 20*
64	**Pau** place Royale	*59 27 27 08*
	Biarritz Javalquinto, square d'Ixelles	*59 24 20 24*
65	**Tarbes** place de Verdun	*62 93 36 62*
	Lourdes place du Champ-Commun	*62 94 15 64*
66	**Perpignan** palais des Congrès	*68 34 13 13*
	Andorre 5 rue Anne-Marie-Janer Andorre-la-Vieille	*62 82 02 14*
67	**Strasbourg**	
	Pont de l'Europe	*88 61 39 23*
	Place de la Gare	*88 32 51 49*
	10 place Gutenberg	*88 32 57 07*
68	**Colmar** 4 rue d'Unterlinden	*89 41 02 29*
	Mulhouse 9 avenue du Maréchal-Foch	*89 45 68 31*
69	**Lyon** place Bellecour	*78 42 25 75*
70	**Vesoul** rue des Bains	*84 75 43 66*
71	**Mâcon** 187 rue Carnot	*85 38 06 00*
	Autun 3 avenue Charles-de-Gaulle	*85 52 20 34*
72	**Le Mans** 38 place de la République	*43 28 17 22*
73	**Chambéry** 24 bd de la Colonne	*79 33 42 47*
	Aix-les-Bains place Maurice-Mollard	*79 35 05 92*
74	**Annecy** 1 rue Jean-Jaurès	*50 45 00 33*
	Évian place d'Allinges	*50 75 04 26*
75	**Paris** Accueil de France 127 Champs-Élysées	*47 23 61 72*
76	**Rouen** 25 place de la Cathédrale	*35 71 41 77*
	Le Havre place de l'Hôtel-de-Ville	*35 21 22 88*
77	**Fontainebleau** 31 place Napoléon-Bonaparte	*64 22 25 68*
	Barbizon 41 rue Grande	*60 66 41 87*
78	**Versailles** 7 rue des Réservoirs	*39 50 36 22*
	Rambouillet place de la Libération	*34 83 11 91*
	St-Germain-en-Laye 1 bis rue de la République	*34 51 05 12*
79	**Niort** place de la Poste	*49 24 18 79*
80	**Amiens** rue Jean-Catelas	*22 91 79 28*
81	**Albi** place Ste-Cécile	*63 54 22 30*
82	**Montauban** 2 rue du Collège	*63 63 60 60*
83	**Toulon** 8 avenue Colbert	*94 22 08 22*
84	**Avignon** 41 cours Jean-Jaurès	*90 82 65 11*
85	**La Roche-s/Yon** place Napoléon	*51 36 00 85*
	Les Sables-d'Olonne rue du G.-Leclerc	*51 32 03 28*
86	**Poitiers** 8 rue des Grandes-Écoles	*49 41 21 24*
87	**Limoges** bd de Fleurus	*55 34 46 87*
88	**Épinal** 13 rue de la Comédie	*29 82 53 32*
89	**Auxerre** 1-2 quai de la République	*86 52 06 19*
	Sens place Jean-Jaurès	*86 65 19 49*
	Vézelay rue St-Pierre	*86 33 23 69*
90	**Belfort** passage de France	*84 28 12 23*
94	**Vincennes** 11 avenue de Nogent	*48 08 13 00*

Nota : il primo indirizzo indica l'ente del turismo dipartimentale. I numeri di telefono sono in corsivo.
Nota : le premier nom de la liste dans chaque département est celui du siège de la préfecture. Les numéros de téléphone sont en italique.
Note : the first name is the main one in the department. Phone numbers are in italic.

INDICE DELLE CARTE · INDEX DES CARTES · MAP INDEX

I. Indice generale di citta', cittadine e paesi
I. Index général des villes, localités et lieux-dits
I. General cities, minor towns and villages index

A

54 Azerailles 13 D2
43 Azérat 31 A2
34 Azillanet 42 D2
11 Azille 42 C2
62 Azincourt 1 C3
85 Aziré 23 A2
57 Azoudange 13 D2
40 Azur 34 C3
18 Azy 18 D3
58 Azy-le-Vif 25 A1
02 Azy-sur-Marne 12 A1

B

55 Baâlon 7 A3
54 Baccarat 13 D3
45 Baccon 18 B1
46 Bach 36 A2
24 Bachellerie (La) 29 D3
59 Bachy 2 A3
50 Bacilly 9 D2
53 Baconnière (La) 9 D1
27 Bacquepuis 11 A1
76 Bacqueville-en-Caux 5 A2
48 Badaroux 37 A2
36 Badecon-le-Pin 24 A2
24 Badefols-d'Ans 30 A2
56 Baden 16 A1
54 Badonviller 13 D2
55 Badonvilliers-
   Gérauvilliers 13 B2
57 Baerenthal 14 A1
63 Baffie 31 B2
33 Bagas 35 B1
01 Bâgé-le-Châtel 25 D3
11 Bages 42 D2
66 Bages 43 D3
46 Bagnac-sur-Célé 36 B1
65 Bagnères-de-Bigorre 41 B2
31 Bagnères-de-Luchon 41 C3
03 Bagneux 25 A2
51 Bagneux 12 B2
61 Bagnoles-de-l'Orne 10 B2
63 Bagnols 30 C2
69 Bagnols 31 C3
83 Bagnols-en-Forêt 44 D1
48 Bagnols-les-Bains 37 B2
30 Bagnols-sur-Cèze 37 D3
21 Bagnot 26 A1
35 Baguer-Pican 9 C2
28 Baigneaux 18 B1
33 Baigneaux 35 B1
41 Baigneaux 18 A1
16 Baignes-Ste-Radegonde 29 B2
21 Baigneux-les-Juifs 19 D2
40 Baigts 40 D1
64 Baigts-de-Béarn 40 D1
35 Baillé 9 D3
28 Bailleau-le-Pin 11 A3
28 Bailleau-l'Évêque 11 A2
33 Baillet 34 D1
59 Bailleul 1 D2
76 Bailleul-la-Vallée 10 C1
80 Bailleul-le-Soc 5 D3
62 Bailleul-Sir-B. 1 D3
41 Baillou 17 D1
76 Bailly-en-Rivière 5 A2
35 Bain-de-Bretagne 16 C1
62 Baincthun 1 B2
43 Bains 31 B3
11 Bains-d'Escouloubre 42 B3
88 Bains-les-Bains 20 C1
54 Bainville-sur-Madon 13 B2
35 Bais 16 D1
53 Bais 10 B3
59 Baisieux 2 A3
52 Baissey 20 A2
07 Baix 37 D1
66 Baixas 42 D3
46 Baladou 30 A3
08 Balan 6 D2
34 Balaruc-les-Bains 43 B2
35 Balazé 9 D3
42 Balbigny 31 C1
67 Balbronn 14 A2
67 Baldenheim 14 A3
68 Baldersheim 21 A1
65 Baleix 41 B2
31 Balesta 41 C2
10 Balignicourt 12 C2
33 Balizac 35 A1
91 Ballancourt-sur-
   Essonne 11 C2
37 Ballan-Miré 17 C3
14 Balleroy 4 A3
72 Ballon 10 C3
53 Ballots 16 D1
38 Balme-de-Rencurel (La) 32 A3
74 Balme-de-Sillingy (La) 32 C1
74 Balme-de-Thuy (La) 32 C1
38 Balme-les-Grottes (La) 32 A1
21 Balot 19 C1
48 Balsièges 37 A2
64 Banca 40 C2
83 Bandol 44 B2
56 Bangor 15 D2
65 Banios 41 B2
29 Bannalec 8 C3
18 Bannay 18 D3
18 Bannegon 24 D1
51 Bannes 12 B2
08 Banogne-Recouvrance 6 C3
04 Banon 38 B2
55 Bantheville 6 D3
59 Bantigny 6 A1

68 Bantzenheim 21 A1
66 Banyuls-sur-Mer 43 D3
62 Bapaume 5 D1
12 Bar 36 B2
49 Baracé 17 B2
12 Baraqueville 36 C2
81 Barat 36 B3
11 Barbaira 42 C2
13 Barbas 13 D2
85 Barbâtre 16 B3
47 Barbaste 35 B2
41 Barbazan 41 C3
65 Barbazan-Debat 41 B2
13 Barben (La) 44 A1
13 Barbentane 37 D3
10 Barbery 10 B1
16 Barbezières 29 B2
16 Barbezieux-St-Hilaire 29 B2
26 Barbières 32 A3
21 Barbirey-sur-Ouche 19 D3
77 Barbizon 11 D3
51 Barbonne-Fayet 12 B2
32 Barbotan-les-Thermes 35 B2
2B Barcaggio 45 A2
66 Barcarès (Le) 42 D3
32 Barcelonne-du-Gers 41 A1
04 Barcelonnette 38 B2
05 Barcillonnette 38 B2
64 Barcus 40 D2
77 Barcy 11 D1
82 Bardigues 35 D3
21 Bard-le-Régulier 19 C3
64 Bardos 40 C1
76 Bardouville 4 D3
65 Barèges 41 B3
76 Barentin 4 D3
10 Barenton 10 A2
50 Barfleur 3 D2
44 Bargemon 44 D1
54 Barisey-la-Côte 13 B2
63 Barisis 6 A3
37 Barjac 37 C2
48 Barjac 37 A2
83 Barjols 44 C1
55 Bar-le-Duc 13 A2
04 Barles 38 C2
08 Bar-lès-Busancy 6 D3
51 Barleux 5 D1
18 Barlieu 18 D2
62 Barlin 1 D3
05 Barly 5 C1
07 Barnas 37 C1
26 Barnave 38 A1
71 Barnay-Dessous 19 C3
50 Barneville-Carteret 3 C3
50 Barneville-Plage 3 C3
53 Baroche-Gondoin (La) 9 C2
30 Baron 11 D1
60 Baron 11 D1
57 Baronville 13 C1
12 Baroville 12 D3
67 Barr 14 A3
32 Barran 41 C1
32 Barraques (Les) 41 D1
26 Baraques-en-Vercors
   (Les) 32 A3
89 Barrault 12 A3
83 Barre (La) 44 C1
85 Barre-de-Monts (La) 22 B1
48 Barre-des-Cévennes 10 D1
27 Barre-en-Ouche (La) 10 D1
04 Barrême 38 C3
16 Barret 29 B2
81 Barrières (Les) 36 B3
37 Barrou 23 D1
33 Barsac 35 A1
13 Barst 13 C1
10 Bar-sur-Aube 12 D3
10 Bar-sur-Seine 19 C1
68 Bartenheim 21 A2
33 Barthe (La) 35 B1
65 Barthe-de-Neste (La) 41 B2
65 Bartres 41 B2
45 Barville-en-Gâtinais 18 C1
64 Barzun 41 A2
43 Bas-en-Basset 31 C2
40 Bascons 35 A3
34 Bassan 43 B2
59 Bassée (La) 1 D3
57 Basse-Ham 7 C3
57 Basse-Rive 7 C3
15 Bassignac 30 C2
19 Bassignac-le-Haut 30 B3
57 Bassing 13 D1
89 Bassou 19 A1
32 Bassoues 41 B1
51 Bassu 12 D2
64 Bastanes 40 D1
2A Bastelica 45 C3
2B Bastia 45 A2
83 Bastide (La) 44 D1
12 Bastide-Capdenac (La) 36 B2
09 Bastide-de-Boussignac
   (La) 42 B3
09 Bastide-de-Lordat (La) 42 A2
09 Bastide-de-Sérou (La) 42 A3
84 Bastide-des-Jourdans
   (La) 44 A1
09 Bastide-du-Salat (La) 42 A3
12 Bastide-l'Évêque (La) 36 B2
**48 Bastide-Puylaurent
   (La)** 37 B1
73 Bathie (La) 32 B2
38 Bâtie-Montgascon (La) 32 A2
05 Bâtie-Neuve (La) 38 C1
26 Bâtie-Rolland (La) 37 D2

70 Bâties (Les) 20 B2
05 Bâtie-Vieille (La) 38 C1
25 Battenans-Varin 20 D3
44 Batz-sur-Mer 16 A2
56 Baud 15 D1
83 Baudinard-sur-Verdon 44 C1
70 Baudoncourt 20 C2
57 Baudrecourt 13 D3
55 Baudrémont 13 A2
18 Baudres 18 A3
28 Baudreville 11 B3
83 Bauduen 44 C1
49 Baugé 17 B2
18 Baugy 18 D3
33 Baulac 35 A2
44 Baule-Escoublac (La) 16 B2
35 Baulon 16 C1
39 Baume-les-Messieurs 26 B1
25 Baume-les-Dames 20 D3
50 Baupte 3 D3
09 Baure (La) 41 D3
35 Bausaine (La) 9 C2
10 Baux-de-Breteuil (Les) 10 D1
**13 Baux-de-Provence
   (Les)** 43 D1
27 Baux-Ste-Croix (Les) 11 A1
25 Bavans 20 D2
59 Bavay 2 B3
90 Bavilliers 20 D2
59 Bavinchove 1 C2
52 Bayard 13 A2
29 Baye 15 C1
51 Baye 12 B2
10 Bayel 12 D3
14 Bayeux 4 A3
13 Bayon 13 C3
64 Bayonne 40 C1
04 Bayons 38 C2
52 Bay-sur-Aube 19 D3
51 Bazancourt 6 C3
60 Bazancourt 5 B3
33 Bazas 35 B2
17 Bazauges 23 B3
08 Bazeilles 6 D2
23 Bazelat 24 A2
65 Bazet 41 B2
60 Bazicourt 5 D3
31 Baziège 42 A1
65 Bazillac 41 B2
28 Bazoche-Gouët (La) 10 C3
58 Bazoches 19 B3
61 Bazoches-au-Houlme 10 B2
77 Bazoches-lès-Bray 12 A3
45 Bazoches-les-
   Gallérandes 11 B3
61 Bazoches-sur-Hoëne 10 C2
02 Bazoches-sur-Vesle 6 B3
72 Bazoge (La) 17 C1
85 Bazoges-en-Paillers 22 D1
85 Bazoges-en-Pareds 22 D1
58 Bazolles 19 B3
53 Bazouge-de-Chémeré
   (La) 17 C1
53 Bazouge-des-Alleux (La) 10 A3
53 Bazougers 17 A1
35 Bazouges-la-Pérouse 9 C2
72 Bazouges-sur-le-Loir 17 B2
31 Bazus 42 A1
58 Béard 25 A1
71 Beaubéry 25 C2
30 Beaucaire 43 D1
80 Beaucamps-le-Vieux 5 D3
35 Beaucé 9 D3
65 Beaucens 41 B3
31 Beauchalot 41 D2
50 Beauchamps 9 D1
80 Beauchamps 5 D2
45 Beauchamps-sur-Huillard 18 C1
07 Beauchastel 37 D1
28 Beauche 10 D2
41 Beauchêne 12 A2
77 Beauchery-St-Martin 12 A2
55 Beauclair 7 A3
90 Beaucourt 20 D2
80 Beaucourt-en-Santerre 5 D2
65 Beaudéan 41 B3
60 Beaudéduit 5 C2
59 Beaudignies 6 B1
39 Beaufort 26 A2
73 Beaufort 32 C1
49 Beaufort-en-Vallée 17 B2
26 Beaufort-sur-Gervanne 38 A1
85 Beaufou 22 C1
76 Beaufresne 5 B2
45 Beaugency 18 B1
69 Beaujeu 25 C3
70 Beaujeu-St-Vallier-
   Pierrejux-et-Quitteur 20 B2
07 Beaulieu 37 C2
21 Beaulieu 19 D2
43 Beaulieu 31 B3
45 Beaulieu 18 D2
61 Beaulieu 10 D2
55 Beaulieu-en-Argonne 12 D1
60 Beaulieu-les-Fontaines 5 D2
37 Beaulieu-lès-Loches 17 D3
79 Beaulieu-sous-Bressuire 23 A1
85 Beaulieu-sous-la-Roche 22 C1
79 Beaulieu-sous-Parthenay 23 D1
**19 Beaulieu-sur-
   Dordogne** 30 B3
49 Beaulieu-sur-Layon 17 A2
06 Beaulieu-sur-Mer 45 A1
16 Beaulieu-sur-Sonnette 29 C1
03 Beaulon 25 B2

02 Beaumé 6 C2
26 Beaume (La) 38 B1
84 Beaumes-de-Venise 38 A3
14 Beaumesnil 10 A1
27 Beaumesnil 10 D1
80 Beaumetz 5 C1
62 Beaumetz-lès-Aire 1 C2
62 Beaumetz-lès-Loges 5 D1
24 Beaumont 35 C1
54 Beaumont 13 B2
62 Beaumont 1 C2
82 Beaumont-de-Lomagne 35 D3
84 Beaumont-de-Pertuis 44 B1
77 Beaumont-du-Gâtinais 18 D1
87 Beaumont-du-Lac 30 D1
08 Beaumont-en-Argonne 6 D3
14 Beaumont-en-Auge 4 C3
50 Beaumont-Hague 3 C2
80 Beaumont-Hamel 5 D1
58 Beaumont-la-Ferrière 19 A3
37 Beaumont-la-Ronce 17 D2
27 Beaumont-le-Roger 10 D1
28 Beaumont-les-Autels 10 C3
26 Beaumont-lès-Valence 37 D1
72 Beaumont-Pied-de-Bœuf 17 C1
72 Beaumont-sur-Dême 17 C2
95 Beaumont-sur-Oise 11 C1
72 Beaumont-sur-Sarthe 10 C3
21 Beaune 25 D1
73 Beaune 32 C2
45 Beaune-la-Rolande 18 C1
21 Beaunotte 19 D2
01 Beaupont 26 A2
49 Beaupréau 16 D3
82 Beaupuy 42 A1
80 Beauquesne 5 C1
62 Beaurains 5 D1
62 Beaurainville 1 B3
01 Beauregard 25 D3
46 Beauregard 30 A3
24 Beauregard-et-Bassac 29 C3
38 Beaurepaire 32 A2
85 Beaurepaire 22 D1
71 Beaurepaire-en-Bresse 26 A2
02 Beaurevoir 6 B2
26 Beaurières 38 B2
02 Beaurieux 6 B3
79 Beaussais 23 B2
76 Beaussault 5 B2
49 Beausse 16 D3
83 Beausset (Le) 44 B2
33 Beautiran 35 A1
60 Beauvais 5 C3
17 Beauvais-sur-Matha 29 B1
80 Beauval 5 C1
83 Beauvallon 44 D2
49 Beauvau 17 B2
04 Beauvezer 38 D3
47 Beauville 35 C2
50 Beauvoir 9 C2
72 Beauvoir 10 C3
76 Beauvoir-en-Lyons 5 B3
85 Beauvoir-sur-Mer 22 B1
79 Beauvoir-sur-Niort 23 A3
10 Beauvoir-sur-Sarce 19 C1
59 Beauvois-en-Cambrésis 6 A1
02 Beauvois-en-Vermandois 6 A2
30 Beauvoisin 43 C1
31 Beaux 31 C3
43 Beauzac 31 C3
55 Beauzée-sur-Aire 13 A1
68 Beblenheim 14 A3
76 Bec-de-Mortagne 4 C2
79 Béceleuf 23 A2
35 Bécherel 9 C3
57 Béchy 13 C1
49 Bécons-les-Granits 17 A2
34 Bédarieux 43 A1
84 Bédarrides 37 D3
18 Beddes 24 D3
35 Bédée 9 C3
09 Bédeilhac-et-Aynat 42 A3
04 Bédejun 38 C3
17 Bédenac 29 C3
84 Bédoin 38 A3
64 Bedous 40 D3
46 Béduer 36 B1
39 Beffia 26 B2
57 Beftange 7 C3
33 Bégadan 28 D2
56 Béganne 16 D2
22 Bégard 8 D2
29 Beg-Meil 15 B1
88 Begnécourt 13 C3
49 Bégrolles-en-Mauges 16 D3
04 Bégude-Blanche (La) 38 C3
26 Bégude-de-Mazenc(La) 37 D2
64 Béguios 40 C2
80 Béhencourt 5 C1
49 Béhuard 17 A2
56 Béignon 16 B1
89 Beine 19 B1
51 Beine-Nauroy 6 C3
67 Beinheim 14 B1
21 Beire-le-Châtel 20 A3
36 Bélâbre 24 A3
16 Bel-Air 23 D3
64 Belair 41 A2
21 Belan-sur-Ource 19 D1
34 Bélarga 43 A1
11 Belcaire 42 B3
12 Belcastel 36 B2
09 Bélesta 42 B3
24 Beleymas 29 C3
70 Belfahy 20 D1
90 Belfort 20 D2

43 Bonneval 31 B2
73 Bonneval-les-Bains 32 D1
73 Bonneval-sur-Arc 33 A2
25 Bonnevaux 26 C1
74 Bonnevaux 26 C3
70 Bonnevent-Velloreille 20 B3
74 Bonneville 26 C3
14 Bonneville-la-Louvet 4 C3
14 Bonneville-sur-Touques 4 C3
62 Bonnières 5 C1
78 Bonnières-sur-Seine 11 B1
84 Bonnieux 38 A3
62 Bonningues-lès-Ardres 1 C2
14 Bonnœil 10 B1
44 Bonnœuvre 16 D2
45 Bonny-sur-Loire 18 D2
56 Bono (Le) 15 D1
82 Bonrepaux 36 A3
74 Bons-en-Chablais 26 C3
60 Bonvillers 5 C3
67 Boofzheim 14 B3
76 Boos 5 A3
22 Boquého 9 A2
60 Boran-sur-Oise 11 C1
33 Bordeaux 29 A3
65 Bordères-Louron 41 C3
65 Bordères-sur-l'Echez 41 B2
36 Bordes (Les) 24 B1
45 Bordes (Les) 18 C1
65 Bordes 41 B2
89 Bordes (Les) 19 A1
09 Bordes-sur-Lez (Les) 41 D3
17 Bords 22 D3
23 Bord-Saint-Georges 24 C3
07 Borée 37 C1
06 Boréon (Le) 39 A3
70 Borey 20 C2
2B Borgo 45 B2
48 Borie (La) 37 A2
83 Bormes-les-Mimosas 44 C1
47 Born 35 C1
07 Borne 37 B1
18 Borne (La) 18 C3
43 Borne 31 B3
24 Borrèze 30 A2
19 Bort-les-Orgues 30 C2
17 Boscamnant 29 B3
76 Bosc-Bordel 5 A2
76 Bosc-Hyons 5 B3
76 Bosc-le-Hard 5 A2
27 Bosguérant-de-Marcouville 4 D3
02 Bosmont 6 B2
23 Bosmoreau-les-Mines 24 D3
35 Bosse-de-Bretagne (La) 16 C1
37 Bossée 17 D3
54 Bosserville 13 C2
73 Bossons (Les) 32 D1
03 Bost 25 A3
76 Bosville 4 D2
27 Bouafles 11 A1
44 Bouaye 16 C3
64 Boucau 40 A3
03 Boucé 25 A3
61 Boucé 10 B2
38 Bouchage (Le) 32 B1
59 Bouchain 6 A1
80 Bouchavesnes-Bergen 5 D1
49 Bouchemaine 17 A2
57 Boucheporn 13 C1
74 Bouchet (Le) 26 C3
43 Bouchet-St-Nicolas (Le) 37 B1
80 Bouchoir 5 D2
39 Bouchoux (Les) 26 B3
07 Boucieu-le-Roi 31 D3
25 Bouclans 20 C3
30 Boucoiran-et-Nozières 37 C3
55 Bouconville-sur-Madt 13 B2
54 Boucq 13 B2
21 Boudreville 19 D1
53 Bouère 17 A1
53 Bouessay 17 B1
36 Bouesse 24 B2
16 Bouëx 29 C1
35 Bouëxière (La) 9 D2
85 Boufféré 16 C3
80 Bougainville 5 C2
36 Bouges-le-Château 24 B1
28 Bouglainval 11 A2
47 Bouglon 35 B2
17 Bougneau 29 A1
40 Bougue 35 A3
44 Bouguenais 16 C3
17 Bouhet 22 D3
58 Bouhy 19 A2
12 Bouillac 36 B1
82 Bouillac 35 D3
21 Bouilland 19 D3
30 Bouillargues 43 C1
76 Bouille (La) 4 D3
79 Bouillé-Loretz 17 B3
49 Bouillé-Ménard 16 D1
22 Bouillie (La) 9 B2
10 Bouilly 12 B3
79 Bouin 23 B3
85 Bouin 16 B3
21 Bouix 19 C1
26 Boujailles 26 C1
34 Boujan-sur-Libron 43 A2
12 Boulages 12 B2
32 Boulaur 41 C1
17 Boulay (Le) 17 D2
27 Boulay-Morin (Le) 11 A1
57 Boulay-Moselle 13 C1
24 Boulazac 29 D3
13 Boulbon 37 D3

26 Boulc 38 B1
66 Boule-d'Amont 43 C3
66 Bouleternère 43 C3
55 Bouligny 7 B3
28 Boullay-Mivoye (Le) 11 A2
18 Boulleret 18 D3
12 Bouloc 36 D3
31 Bouloc 42 A1
82 Bouloc 35 D2
85 Boulogne 22 C1
92 Boulogne-Billancourt 11 C1
60 Boulogne-la-Grasse 5 D2
31 Boulogne-sur-Gesse 41 C2
62 Boulogne-sur-Mer 1 B2
72 Bouloire 17 C1
66 Boulou (Le) 43 D3
83 Boulouris 44 D2
70 Boult 20 B3
51 Boult-sur-Suippe 6 C3
08 Boulzicourt 6 C2
24 Bouniagues 35 C1
85 Boupère (Le) 22 D1
27 Bouquelon 4 C3
80 Bouquemaison 5 C3
34 Bouquet-d'Orb (Le) 43 A1
11 Bouray-sur-Juine 11 C2
71 Bourbon-Lancy 25 B2
03 Bourbon-l'Archambault 24 D2
52 Bourbonne-les-Bains 20 B1
63 Bourboule (La) 30 D2
59 Bourbourg 1
22 Bourbriac 8 D2
17 Bourcefranc-le-Chapus 28 D1
08 Bourcq 6 C3
76 Bourdainville 5 A2
26 Bourdeaux 38 A1
24 Bourdeilles 29 C2
52 Bourdon-sur-Rognon 13 A3
86 Bouresse 23 C2
33 Bourg 29 A3
46 Bourg (Le) 36 B1
49 Bourg 17 A2
27 Bourg-Achard 4 D3
23 Bourganeuf 30 B1
86 Bourg-Archambault 23 D2
42 Bourg-Argental 31 C2
27 Bourg-Beaudoin 5 A3
29 Bourg-Blanc 8 B2
67 Bourg-Bruche 14 B3
26 Bourg-de-Péage 32 A3
16 Bourg-des-Comptes 16 C1
24 Bourg-des-Maisons 29 C2
82 Bourg-de-Visa 35 D2
38 Bourg-d'Oisans (Le) 32 C3
43 Bourg-d'Oueil 41 C3
24 Bourg-du-Bost 29 C2
76 Bourg-Dun 4 D2
01 Bourg-en-Bresse 26 A3
18 Bourges 18 C3
93 Bourget (Le) 11 C1
02 Bourg-et-Comin 6 B3
73 Bourget-du-Lac (Le) 32 B1
08 Bourg-Fidèle 6 C2
63 Bourg-Lastic 30 C1
71 Bourg-le-Comte 25 B3
49 Bourg-l'Évêque 16 D1
43 Bourg-Madame 43 D3
17 Bourgneuf 22 D3
49 Bourgneuf 17 B2
53 Bourgneuf-la-Forêt (Le) 10 A3
49 Bourgneuf-en-Mauges 17 A3
44 Bourgneuf-en-Retz 16 B3
51 Bourgogne 6 B3
38 Bourgoin-Jallieu 32 A2
07 Bourg-St-Andéol 37 D2
31 Bourg-St-Bernard 42 A1
61 Bourg-Saint-Léonard (Le) 10 C2
73 Bourg-St-Maurice 32 D1
53 Bourgon 9 D3
27 Bourgtheroulde-Infreville 4 D3
37 Bourgueil 17 C3
33 Bourideys 35 A2
49 Bourrière 42 B3
13 Bourmont 13 B3
17 Bournan 17 D3
86 Bournand 17 B3
85 Bourneau 23 A2
27 Bourneville 4 D3
85 Bournezeau 22 D1
47 Bourran 35 C2
82 Bourret 35 D3
40 Bourriot-Bergonce 35 A2
77 Bourron-Marlotte 11 D2
65 Bours 41 B2
41 Boursay 17 D1
22 Bourseul 9 B2
59 Boursies 6 A1
27 Bourth 10 D2
62 Bourthes 1 B3
59 Bousies 6 B1
11 Bousquet (Le) 42 B3
23 Boussac 24 C2
35 Boussac (La) 9 C2
79 Boussais 23 B1
31 Boussan 41 D2
57 Bousse 7 C3
47 Boussès 35 B2
57 Bousseviller 14 A1
25 Boussières 20 B3
02 Boustaille (La) 6 B2
16 Bouteville 29 B1
91 Boutigny-sur-Essonne 11 C3
28 Boutigny-Prouais 11 B2
26 Bouvante-le-Haut 32 A3
08 Bouvellemont 6 D2
26 Bouvières 38 A2

91 Bouville 11 C3
44 Bouvron 16 C2
14 Bouxwiller 14 A2
51 Bouy 12 C1
06 Bouyon 39 A3
52 Bouzancourt 12 D3
21 Bouze-lès-Beaune 25 D1
46 Bouziès 36 A2
34 Bouzigues 43 B2
49 Bouzillé 16 D2
80 Bouzincourt 5 D1
57 Bouzonville 7 C3
55 Bovée-sur-Barboure 13 A2
16 Bovel 16 B1
80 Boves 5 C2
02 Bovette (La) 6 A2
55 Boviolles 13 A2
17 Boyardville 22 D3
62 Boyelles 5 D1
12 Boyne 37 A2
18 Boz 18 C1
73 Bozel 32 D2
12 Bozouls 36 D2
55 Brabant-lès-Villers 12 D2
33 Brach 28 D3
12 Brachay 12 D3
76 Brachy 5 A2
18 Bracieux 18 A2
39 Bracon 26 B1
76 Bracquemont 5 A2
31 Bragayrac 41 D1
36 Brâgards (Les) 36 A3
21 Bragny 19 C2
02 Braine 6 A3
16 Brains 16 C3
49 Brain-sur-Allonnes 17 B3
49 Brain-sur-l'Authion 17 B2
49 Brain-sur-Longuenée 17 A2
16 Brains-sur-les-Marches 16 D1
11 Bram 42 B2
06 Bramafan 45 A1
32 Bramans 32 D3
02 Brancourt-en-Laonnois 6 A3
15 Brandérion 15 D1
71 Brandon 25 C2
32 Brangues 32 B1
89 Brannay-St-Sérotin 12 A3
33 Branne 35 B1
29 Brantôme 29 C2
55 Braquis 13 B1
83 Bras 44 B1
04 Bras-d'Asse 38 C3
08 Bras 8 C2
29 Brasparts 42 A3
21 Brassac 42 C1
81 Brassac 35 D2
24 Brassac 40 D1
40 Brassempouy 13 A1
13 Bras-sur-Meuse 19 B3
58 Brassy 12 D2
52 Braucourt 29 A2
33 Braud-et-St-Louis 12 C2
10 Braux 35 C2
47 Brax 1 C1
59 Bray-Dunes 11 B1
95 Bray-et-Lû 10 B1
14 Bray-la-Campagne 5 B1
80 Bray-lès-Mareuil 5 D1
77 Bray-sur-Seine 12 A3
80 Bray-sur-Somme 20 A3
21 Brazey-en-Plaine 9 C3
35 Bréal-sous-Montfort 12 C2
51 Bréban 20 A3
90 Brebotte 9 D2
50 Brécey 9 D2
56 Brech 15 D1
18 Brécy 18 C3
15 Bredons 30 D3
60 Brégy 11 D1
50 Bréhal 9 D1
22 Bréhand 9 A2
22 Bréhec 9 A1
57 Breidenbach 14 A1
49 Breil 17 C2
49 Breille-les-Pins (La) 17 B3
72 Breil-sur-Mérize (Le) 17 C1
06 Breil-sur-Roya 39 B3
67 Breitenbach 14 A3
22 Brélidy 8 D1
29 Brélès 8 A2
54 Bréménil 13 D2
25 Brémoncourt 20 D3
01 Brénaz 8 C2
29 Brennilis 26 B3
01 Brénod 37 A2
48 Brenoux 36 B3
81 Brens 12 A1
02 Breny 38 C2
04 Bréole (La) 5 C3
60 Bresles 25 A2
03 Bresnay 20 D1
88 Bresse (La) 25 D2
71 Bresse-sur-Grosne 36 A3
82 Bressols 23 A1
79 Bressuire 8 B2
29 Brest 24 B1
36 Bretagne 10 D1
27 Bretagne (La) 35 C3
32 Bretagne-d'Armagnac 35 B3
35 Breteil 20 A3
21 Bretenière 25 B3
25 Bretenière (La) 30 B3
46 Bretenoux 10 D2
27 Breteuil 5 C2
60 Breteuil 24 D2
03 Brethon (Le)

25 Brétigny-N.-Dame 20 C3
22 Brétignolles-sur-Mer 22 D2
60 Brétigny 6 A3
91 Brétigny-sur-Orge 11 C2
61 Bretoncelles 10 C3
85 Bretonnière (La) 22 D2
72 Brette-les-Pins 17 C1
14 Bretteville-le-Rabet 10 B1
14 Bretteville-l'Orgueilleuse 4 B3
50 Bretteville-sur-Ay 3 C3
14 Bretteville-sur-Laize 10 B1
14 Bretteville-sur-Odon 10 B1
70 Breuches 20 C1
03 Breuil (Le) 25 B3
41 Breuil (Le) 18 A2
12 Breuil (Le) 12 B1
85 Breuil-Barret 23 A1
14 Breuil-en-Auge (Le) 4 C3
28 Breuillet 28 D1
17 Breuil-Magné 22 D3
11 Breuillet 11 A1
63 Breuil-sur-Couze (Le) 31 A2
70 Breurey-lès-Faverney 20 C2
52 Breuvannes-en-Bassigny 20 B1
41 Brévainville 18 A1
78 Bréviaires (Les) 11 B2
10 Bréviandes 12 C3
16 Bréville 29 B1
10 Brévonnes 12 C3
49 Brézé 17 B3
05 Bréziers 38 C2
38 Brézins 32 A3
28 Brézolles 11 A2
15 Brezons 30 D3
05 Briançon 32 D3
06 Briançonnet 38 D3
36 Briantes 24 B2
45 Briare 18 D2
45 Briarres-sur-Essonne 11 C3
81 Briatexte 42 B1
52 Briaucourt 13 A3
52 Bricon 19 D1
50 Bricquebec 3 C3
14 Bricqueville 4 A3
50 Bricqueville-sur-Mer 18 B1
45 Bricy 18 B1
73 Brides-les-Bains 32 D2
09 Brie 42 A2
80 Brie 5 D1
29 Briec 8 C3
77 Brie-Comte-Robert 11 D2
10 Briel-sur-Barse 12 C3
71 Brienne 25 D2
10 Brienne-le-Château 6 B3
08 Brienne-sur-Aisne 6 B3
89 Brienon-sur-Armançon 19 B1
91 Brières-les-Scellés 11 C3
16 Brie-sous-Barbezieux 29 B2
17 Brie-sous-Matha 29 B1
08 Brieulles-sur-Bar 6 D3
55 Brieulles-sur-Meuse 7 A3
54 Briey 7 B3
63 Briffons 30 C1
19 Brignac-la-Plaine 30 A3
69 Brignais 31 D1
29 Brigneau 15 C1
29 Brignognan-Plage 8 B1
83 Brignoles 44 C2
38 Brignoud 32 B2
06 Brigue (La) 39 B3
16 Brigueil 23 D3
91 Briis-sous-Forges 11 C2
16 Brillac 23 D3
04 Brillanne (La) 38 B3
55 Brillon-en-Barrois 13 A2
69 Brindas 31 D1
58 Brinon-sur-Beuvron 19 A3
18 Brinon-sur-Sauldre 18 C2
54 Brin-sur-Seille 13 C2
49 Briollay 17 A2
36 Brion 24 B1
86 Brion 23 C2
89 Brion 19 A1
27 Brionne 10 D1
70 Brion-près-Thouet 17 B3
21 Brion-sur-Ource 19 D1
43 Brioude 31 A2
79 Brioux-sur-Boutonne 23 B2
61 Briouze 10 B2
80 Briquemesnil-Floxicourt 5 C2
08 Briquenay 6 D3
64 Briscous 40 C1
34 Brissac 37 B3
49 Brissac-Quincé 17 A2
02 Brissay-Choigny 6 A2
02 Brissy-Hamégicourt 6 A2
19 Brive-la-Gaillarde 30 A3
43 Brives-Charensac 31 B3
17 Brives-sur-Charente 29 A1
50 Brix 3 C3
17 Brizambourg 29 A1
37 Brizay 17 C3
55 Brizeaux 12 D1
06 Broc (Le) 39 A3
49 Broc 17 C3
40 Brocas 35 A3
27 Broglie 10 D1
21 Broin 20 A3
12 Brommat 36 D1
63 Bromont-Lamothe 30 D1
69 Bron 31 D1
22 Broons 9 B3
12 Broquiès 36 C3
16 Brossac 29 B2
70 Brotte-lès-Luxeuil 20 C2
28 Brou 11 A3

85 Fontaines 22 D2
72 Fontaine-Saint-Martin (La) 17 B1
41 Fontaines-en-Sologne 18 A2
21 Fontaines-les-Seches 19 C2
27 Fontaine-sous-Jouy 11 A1
77 Fontaine-sous-Montaiguillon 12 A2
80 Fontaine-ss-Montdidier 5 C2
51 Fontaine-sur-Coole 12 C2
02 Fontaine-Uterte 6 A2
33 Fontainevielle-Taussat 34 D1
46 Fontanes-du-Causse 36 A1
42 Fontanès 31 C2
11 Fontanès-de-Sault 42 B3
15 Fontanges 30 C3
21 Fontangy 19 C3
23 Fontanières 24 C3
43 Fontannes 31 A2
48 Fontans 37 A1
81 Fontasse (La) 42 C1
11 Fontcouverte 42 C2
26 Font d'Urle 38 A1
95 Fontenay-en-Parisis 11 C1
85 Fontenay-le-Comte 23 A2
14 Fontenay-le-Pesnel 4 B3
78 Fontenay-St-Père 11 B1
89 Fontenay-sous-Fouronnes 19 B2
28 Fontenay-sur-Eure 11 A3
50 Fontenay-sur-Mer 3 D2
77 Fontenay-Trésigny 11 D2
21 Fontenelle 20 A2
02 Fontenelle-en-Brie 12 A1
14 Fontenermont 9 D1
89 Fontenoy 19 A2
88 Fontenoy-le-Château 20 C1
39 Fontenu 26 B2
33 Fontet 35 B1
10 Fontette 19 C1
49 Fontevrault-l'Abbaye 17 B3
05 Fontgillarde 38 D1
36 Fontgombault 23 D2
62 Fontinettes (Les) 1 C2
57 Fontoy 7 B3
17 Fontpatour 22 D3
66 Fontpédrouse 43 B3
66 Ft-Romeu-Odeilla-Via 43 B3
10 Fontvannes 12 B3
13 Fontvieille 43 D1
57 Forbach 13 D1
83 Forcalqueiret 44 C2
04 Forcalquier 38 B3
24 Force (La) 29 C3
53 Forcé 17 A1
02 Foreste 6 A2
51 Forestière 12 B2
80 Forest-l'Abbaye 5 B1
23 Forêt-du-Temple (La) 24 B2
29 Forêt-Fouesnant (La) 8 C3
91 Forêt-le-Roi (La) 11 C3
91 Forêt-Sainte-Croix (La) 11 C3
79 Forêt-sur-Sèvre (La) 23 A1
17 Forges 22 D3
19 Forges 30 B3
56 Forges (Les) 9 A3
35 Forges-la-Forêt 16 D1
76 Forges-les-Eaux 5 B2
55 Forges-sur-Meuse 7 A3
21 Forléans 19 C2
60 Formerie 5 B2
14 Formigny 4 A3
66 Formiguères 43 B3
79 Fors 23 A3
41 Fortan 17 D1
56 Fort-Bloqué (Le) 15 C1
38 Forteresse (La) 32 A2
80 Fort-Mahon-Plage 1 B3
31 Fos 41 C3
09 Fossat (Le) 42 A2
41 Fossé 18 A2
24 Fossemagne 29 D3
13 Fos-sur-Mer 43 D2
76 Foucarmont 5 B2
80 Fourcucourt-en-Sant. 5 D2
88 Fouchécourt 20 B1
10 Fouchères 19 C1
29 Fouesnant 15 B1
54 Foug 13 B2
09 Fougax-et-Barrineuf 42 B3
49 Fougeré 17 B2
35 Fougères 9 D3
41 Fougères-sur-Bièvre 18 A2
36 Fougerolles 24 B2
70 Fougerolles 20 C1
53 Fougerolles-du-Plessis 10 A2
12 Fouillade (La) 36 B2
42 Fouillouse (La) 31 C2
60 Fouilloy 5 B2
80 Fouilloy 5 C2
52 Foulain 20 A1
27 Foulbec 4 C3
57 Fouligny 13 C1
60 Fouquerolles 5 C3
16 Fouqueure 29 B1
17 Fouras 22 D3
32 Fourcès 35 B3
58 Fourchambault 25 A1
80 Foudrinoy 5 C2
25 Fourgs (Les) 26 C1
03 Fourilles 25 A3
59 Fourmies 6 B1
73 Fourneaux 32 D3
14 Fourneaux-le-Val 10 B1
48 Fournels 37 A1
25 Fournet-Blancheroche 20 D3
60 Fournival 5 C3
63 Fournois 31 B2
66 Fourques 43 D3
31 Fourqueveaux 42 A1
04 Fours 38 D2
58 Fours 24 B1
85 Foussis-Payré 23 A2
90 Foussemagne 20 D2
31 Fousseret (Le) 41 D2
16 Foussignac 29 B1
70 Fouvent-St-Andoche 20 B2
04 Foux (La) 38 D3
83 Foux (La) 44 D2
79 Foye-Montjault (La) 23 A3
54 Fraimbois 13 C2
88 Frain 20 B1
24 Fraisse 29 C3
11 Fraissé-des-Corbières 42 D3
34 Fraisse-sur-Agout 42 D1
48 Fraissinet-Chazalais 37 A1
48 Fraissinet-de-Fourques 37 A2
88 Fraize 13 D3
25 Frambouhans 20 D3
41 Français 18 A2
57 Francaltroff 13 D1
2B Francardo 45 B2
60 Francastel 5 C2
47 Francescas 35 C3
14 Franceville-Plage 4 B3
03 Franchesse 24 D2
08 Francheval 6 D2
21 Francheville 19 D2
54 Francheville 13 B2
69 Francheville 31 D1
36 Francillon 24 A1
74 Frangy 26 B3
71 Frangy-en-Bresse 26 A1
25 Franois 20 B3
31 Franquevielle 41 C2
11 Franqui-Plage (La) 42 D3
80 Franvillers 5 C1
25 Frasne 26 C1
70 Frasne-le-Château 20 B2
39 Frasnois (Le) 26 B2
2A Frasseto 45 C3
46 Frayssinet 36 A1
46 Frayssinet-le-Gélat 35 D1
28 Frazé 11 A3
52 Frécourt 20 A1
36 Frédille 24 A1
22 Fréhel 9 B2
49 Freigné 16 D2
81 Fréjairolles 36 C3
83 Fréjus 44 D2
80 Frémontiers 5 C2
62 Frencq 1 B3
88 Frenelle-la-Grande 13 B3
38 Freney-d'Oisans (Le) 32 C3
60 Fréniches 5 D2
10 Fresnay 12 D3
44 Fresnay-en-Retz 16 B3
72 Fresnaye-sur-Chédouet (La) 10 B3
61 Fresnay-le-Samson 10 C1
28 Fresnay-l'Évêque 11 B3
72 Fresnay-sur-Sarthe 10 B3
51 Fresne (Le) 12 C1
14 Fresne-la-Mère 10 B1
50 Fresne-Poret (Le) 10 A2
89 Fresnes 19 B2
70 Fresne-St-Mamès 20 B2
55 Fresnes-en-Wœvre 13 B1
51 Fresnes-lès-Reims 6 C3
52 Fresnes-sur-Apance 20 B1
59 Fresnes-sur-l'Escaut 2 B3
80 Fresneville 5 B2
27 Fresney 11 A1
52 Fresnoy-en-Bassigny 20 B1
76 Fresnoy-Folny 5 A2
02 Fresnoy-le-Grand 6 A2
80 Fresnoy-les-Roye 5 D2
76 Fresquienne 5 A2
02 Fressancourt 6 A2
70 Fresse 20 D2
23 Fresselines 24 B2
80 Fressenneville 5 B1
62 Fressin 1 C3
79 Fressines 23 B2
05 Fressinières 38 D1
29 Fret (Le) 8 B2
41 Fréteval 18 A1
28 Frétigny 10 C3
70 Frétigney-et-Velloreille 20 B2
76 Frétis (Les) 5 B2
60 Frétoy-le-Château 5 D2
38 Frette (La) 32 A2
52 Frettes 20 B2
08 Fréty (Le) 6 C2
62 Frévent 5 C1
76 Fréville 4 D2
57 Freyming-Merlebach 13 D1
54 Friauville 13 B1
15 Fridefont 36 D1
02 Frières-Faillouel 6 A2
68 Friesen 21 A2
51 Frignicourt 12 C2
80 Friville-Escarbotin 5 B2
80 Frohen-le-Grand 5 C1
70 Froideconche 20 C1
39 Froidefontaine 26 C1
02 Froidestrées 6 B2
25 Froidevaux 20 D3
85 Froidfond 22 C1
02 Froidmont-Cohartille 6 B2
60 Froissy 5 C3
54 Frolois 13 C2
59 Fromelles 1 D3
61 Fromentel 10 B2
51 Fromentières 12 B1
85 Fromentine 22 B1
77 Fromont 11 C3
52 Froncles 13 A3
33 Fronsac 29 A3
33 Frontenac 35 B1
71 Frontenard 26 A1
38 Frontenas 32 A1
79 Frontenay-Rohan-Rohan 23 A3
34 Frontignan 43 B2
31 Frontignan-Saves 41 D2
31 Fronton 36 A3
52 Fronville 13 A3
44 Frossay 16 B3
70 Frotey-lès-Vesoul 20 C2
54 Frouard 13 B2
34 Frouzet 43 B1
62 Fruges 1 C3
25 Fuans 20 C3
04 Fugeret (Le) 38 D3
49 Fuilet (Le) 16 D3
71 Fuissé 25 D3
76 Fultot 4 D2
08 Fumay 6 D1
47 Fumel 35 D2
67 Furdenheim 14 A2
38 Fures 32 A2
13 Fuveau 44 B2
72 Fyé 10 C3
89 Fyé 19 B1

G

40 Gabarret 35 B3
64 Gabas 41 A3
34 Gabian 43 A1
12 Gabriac 36 D2
61 Gacé 10 C2
56 Gacilly (La) 16 B1
35 Gaël 9 B3
30 Gagnières 37 C2
35 Gahard 9 C3
30 Gailhan 37 B3
81 Gaillac 36 B3
31 Gaillac-Toulza 42 A2
74 Gaillard 26 C3
76 Gaillefontaine 5 B2
27 Gaillon 11 A1
11 Gaja-la-Selve 42 B2
30 Gajan 37 C3
65 Galan 41 C2
47 Galapian 35 C2
34 Galargues 43 B1
2B Galeria 45 B3
33 Galgon 29 A3
28 Gallardon 11 B2
30 Gallargue-le-Mentueux 43 C1
80 Gamaches 5 B1
27 Gamaches-en-Vexin 5 B3
40 Gamarde-les-Bains 34 D3
78 Gambais 11 B2
67 Gambsheim 14 B2
64 Gan 41 A2
04 Ganagobie 38 B3
34 Ganges 37 B3
03 Gannat 25 A3
03 Gannay-sur-Loire 25 B1
05 Gap 38 C1
78 Garancières 11 B2
64 Garaybie 40 D2
58 Garchy 19 A3
13 Gardanne 44 B2
48 Garde (La) 37 A1
83 Garde (La) 44 C2
26 Garde-Adhémar (La) 37 D2
18 Gardefort 18 D3
83 Garde-Freinet 44 D2
65 Gardères 41 B2
24 Gardonne 35 C1
31 Gardouch 42 A2
40 Garein 34 D3
27 Garennes-sur-Eure 11 A1
83 Gareoult 44 C2
82 Garganvillar 35 D3
2A Gargiaca 45 D3
36 Gargilesse-Dampierre 24 B2
18 Garigny 18 D3
31 Garin 41 C3
64 Garlin 41 A1
85 Garnache (La) 22 C1
03 Garnat-sur-Engièvre 25 B2
81 Garrigues 42 B1
28 Gas 11 B2
27 Gasny 11 B1
83 Gassin 44 D2
40 Gastes 34 C2
77 Gastins 11 D2
50 Gathemo 10 A2
50 Gatteville-le-Phare 3 D2
06 Gattières 45 A1
85 Gaubretière (La) 22 D1
40 Gaujacq 40 D1
32 Gaujan 41 C2
51 Gault-Soigny (Le) 12 B2
41 Gault-Perche (Le) 17 D1
28 Gault-Saint-Denis (Le) 11 A3
22 Gautier 8 D1
65 Gavarnie 41 B3
50 Gavray 9 D1
44 Gâvre (Le) 16 C2
56 Gâvres 15 D1
51 Gaye 12 B2
33 Gazinet 34 D1
40 Geaune 41 A1
17 Geay 29 A1
79 Geay 23 B1
65 Gèdre 41 B3
50 Geffosses 3 D3
36 Gehée 24 A1
67 Geispolsheim 14 B2
10 Gélannes 12 B3
63 Gelles 30 D1
25 Gellin 26 C1
64 Gélos 41 A2
40 Geloux 35 A3
57 Gelucourt 13 D2
21 Gemeaux 20 A2
13 Gémenos 44 B2
31 Gemil 42 A1
17 Gémozac 29 A1
16 Genac 29 B1
69 Genas 31 D1
86 Gençay 23 C2
88 Gendreville 13 B3
39 Gendrey 20 B3
82 Genébrières 36 A3
71 Génelard 25 C2
30 Générac 43 C1
61 Geneslay 10 B2
50 Genêts 9 D2
85 Genétouze (La) 22 C1
25 Geneuille 20 B3
59 Genève 6 A1
77 Genevraye (La) 11 D3
52 Genevrières 20 B2
55 Génicourt-sur-Meuse 13 A1
37 Genillé 18 A3
24 Genis 29 D2
33 Génissac 29 A3
21 Genlis 20 A3
49 Gennes 17 B3
53 Gennes-sur-Glaize 17 A1
35 Gennes-sur-Seiche 16 D1
49 Genneteil 17 B2
79 Genneton 17 A3
14 Genneville 4 C3
30 Génolhac 37 B2
31 Génos 41 C3
23 Genouillac 24 B2
17 Genouillé 23 A3
86 Genouillé 23 C3
18 Genouilly 18 B3
71 Genouilly 25 C2
33 Gensac 35 B1
23 Gentioux-Pigerolles 30 B1
60 Genvry 6 A3
50 Ger 10 A2
88 Gérardmer 20 D1
10 Géraudot 12 C3
57 Gerbécourt 13 C2
88 Gerbépal 13 D3
60 Gerberoy 5 B2
54 Gerbéviller 13 C2
02 Gercy 6 B2
71 Gercy 25 D1
21 Gerland 19 D3
51 Germaine 12 B1
52 Germay 13 A3
28 Germignonville 11 B3
89 Germiny 19 B1
45 Germiny-des-Prés 18 C1
18 Germiny-l'Exempt 24 D1
51 Germinon 12 C2
08 Germont 6 D3
67 Gerstheim 14 B3
76 Gerville 4 C2
63 Gerzat 31 A1
72 Gesnes-le-Gandelin 10 B3
08 Gespunsart 6 D2
49 Gesté 16 D3
53 Gesvres 10 B3
44 Gétigné 16 D3
74 Gets (Les) 26 D3
67 Geudertheim 14 B2
35 Gévezé 9 C3
70 Gevigney-et-Mercey 20 B1
55 Géville 13 B2
21 Gevrey-Chambertin 19 D3
21 Gevrolles 19 D1
01 Gex 26 C2
2B Ghisonaccia 45 C2
2B Ghisoni 45 C2
59 Ghyvelde 1 C1
63 Giat 30 C1
71 Gibles 25 C3
17 Gibourne 23 B3
17 Gicq (Le) 23 B3
45 Gien 18 D2
83 Giens 44 C3
21 Gien-sur-Cure 19 C3
38 Gières 32 B3
73 Giettaz (La) 32 C1
51 Giffaumont-Champaubert 12 D2
91 Gif-sur-Yvette 11 C2
34 Gigean 43 B1
34 Gignac 43 A1
46 Gignac 30 A3
39 Gigny 26 A2
89 Gigny 19 C1
51 Gigny-Bussy 12 C2
71 Gigny-sur-Saône 25 D2
84 Gigondas 37 D3
04 Gigors 38 C2
26 Gigors 38 A1
46 Gigouzac 36 A1
07 Gilhoc-sur-Ormèze 31 D3

67 Hatten 14 B1
80 Hattencourt 5 D2
57 Hattigny 13 D2
55 Hattonchâtel 13 B1
68 Hattstatt 21 A1
59 Haubourdin 1 D3
54 Haucourt-Moulaine 7 B3
55 Haudainville 13 A1
55 Haudiomont 13 A1
60 Haudivillers 5 C3
57 Haut-Clocher 13 C2
62 Haute-Avesnes 1 D3
01 Hautecourt-Romanèche 26 A3
24 Hautefort 29 D2
73 Hauteluce 32 D1
61 Hauterive 10 C2
89 Hauterive 19 B1
26 Hauterives 32 A3
08 Hautes-Rivières (Les) 6 D2
01 Hauteville-Lompnès 32 B1
40 Haut-Mauco 35 A3
59 Hautmont 6 B1
88 Hautmougey 20 C1
55 Hauts-de-Chée (Les) 13 A2
51 Hautvillers 12 B1
27 Hauville 4 D3
57 Havange 7 B3
80 Havernas 5 C1
76 Havre (Le) 4 C3
57 Hayange 7 B3
08 Haybes 6 D1
76 Haye (La) 5 A3
50 Haye-du-Puits (La) 3 D3
27 Haye-du-Teil (La) 4 D3
27 Haye-Malherbe (La) 5 A3
50 Haye-Pesnel (La) 9 D1
76 Hayons (Les) 5 A2
59 Hazebrouck 1 C2
66 Héas 41 B3
27 Hébécourt 5 B3
85 Hébergement (L') 22 C1
80 Hédauville 5 D1
35 Hédé 9 C3
67 Heidolsheim 14 A3
51 Heiltz-le-Hutier 12 D2
51 Heiltz-l'Maurupt 12 D2
68 Heimsbrunn 21 A2
55 Heippes 13 A1
68 Heiteren 21 A1
59 Hélesmes 2 A3
64 Helette 40 C2
83 Héliopolis 44 D3
57 Hellimer 13 D1
61 Héloup 10 C3
59 Hem 2 A2
57 Héming 13 D2
22 Hénanbihen 9 B2
64 Hendaye 40 B2
62 Hénin-Beaumont 1 D3
56 Hennebont 15 D1
88 Hennecourt 13 C3
88 Hennezel 20 C1
22 Hénon 9 A2
60 Hénonville 11 C1
18 Henrichemont 18 C3
29 Henvic 8 C2
85 Herbaudière (L') 16 B3
41 Herbault 18 A2
80 Herbécourt 5 D1
85 Herbiers (Les) 22 D1
10 Herbisse 12 C2
67 Herbitzheim 13 D1
67 Herbsheim 14 B3
32 Héréchou 41 C1
34 Hérépian 42 D1
59 Hergnies 2 A3
44 Héric 16 C2
70 Héricourt 20 D2
02 Hérie-la-Vieille (Le) 6 B2
25 Hérimoncourt 20 D2
03 Hérisson 24 D2
59 Herlies 1 D3
40 Herm 34 C3
48 Hermaux (Les) 37 A2
77 Hermé 12 A3
85 Hermenault (L') 22 D2
63 Herment 30 C1
60 Hermes 5 C3
62 Hermies 6 A1
35 Hermitage (L') 9 C3
22 Hermitage-Lorge (L') 9 A3
37 Hermites (Les) 17 D2
14 Hermival-les-Vaux 10 C1
51 Hermonville 6 B3
76 Héronchelles 5 A3
95 Hérouville 11 C1
51 Herpont 12 D1
67 Herrlisheim 14 B2
68 Herrlisheim-près-Colmar 21 A1
18 Herry 18 D3
62 Hersin-Coupigny 1 D3
59 Herzeele 1 C2
62 Hesdin 1 C3
62 Hesdin-l'Abbé 1 B2
68 Hésingue 21 A2
59 Hestrud 6 C1
60 Hètomesnil 5 C2
57 Hettange-Grande 7 B3
62 Heuchin 1 C3
27 Heudebouville 11 A1
13 Heudicourt-Madine 13 B1
52 Heuilley-Cotton 20 A2
55 Hévilliers 13 A2
38 Heyrieux 32 A2

38 Hières-sur-Amby 32 A1
80 Hiermont 5 C1
16 Hiersac 29 B1
16 Hiesse 23 C3
64 Higuères-Souyes 41 A2
22 Hillion 9 A2
67 Hilsenheim 14 A3
22 Hinglé (Le) 9 B2
40 Hinx 34 D3
35 Hirel 9 C2
67 Hirschland 13 D2
68 Hirsingue 21 A2
02 Hirson 6 B2
67 Hirtzfelden 21 A1
67 Hochfelden 14 A2
76 Hode (Le) 4 C3
56 Hœdic 15 D2
67 Hœrdt 14 B2
68 Hohrodberg 21 A1
67 Hohwald (Le) 14 A3
13 Holving 13 D1
80 Hombleux 5 D2
02 Homblières 6 A2
57 Hombourg-Budange 7 C3
57 Hombourg-Haut 13 D1
54 Homécourt 7 B3
57 Hommes 17 C2
11 Homps 42 D2
77 Hondevilliers 12 A1
14 Honfleur 4 C3
59 Hon-Hergies 2 B3
57 Hôpital (L') 13 D1
29 Hôpital-Camfrout 8 B2
64 Hôpital-d'Orian (L') 40 D3
25 Hôpital-du-Grosbois (L') 20 C3
64 Hôpital-Saint-Blaise (L') 40 D3
42 Hôpital-sous-Rochefort (L') 31 B1
35 Hôpitaux-Vieux (Les) 26 C1
27 Hopsores (Les) 4 C3
65 Horgues 41 B2
17 Hornoy-le-Bourg 5 B2
53 Horps (Le) 10 B3
52 Hortes 20 A1
31 Hospices-de-France 41 C3
12 Hospitalet-du-Larzac 37 A3
46 Hospitalet (L') 36 A1
09 Hospitalet-près-l'Andorre (L') 43 B3
40 Hossegor 40 C1
64 Hosta 40 C2
33 Hostens 35 A1
26 Hostun 32 A3
14 Hôtellerie (L') 10 C1
61 Hôtellerie-Farault (L') 10 C1
26 Hotonnes 26 B3
56 Houat 15 D2
74 Houches (Les) 32 D1
62 Houdain 1 C3
78 Houdan 11 B2
55 Houdelaincourt 13 A2
76 Houdetot 4 D2
88 Houécourt 13 B2
47 Houeillès 35 B2
27 Houetteville 11 A1
32 Houga (Le) 35 B3
14 Houlgate 4 B3
17 Houmeau (L') 22 D3
59 Houplines 1 D2
76 Houppeville 5 A3
64 Lahourcade 40 D2
80 Hourdel (Le) 5 B1
33 Hourtin 28 D2
33 Hourtin-Plage 28 D2
53 Houssay 10 B3
76 Houssaye-Béranger (La) 5 A2
54 Houssemont 13 B2
68 Houssen 14 A3
88 Houssière (La) 13 D3
60 Houssoye (La) 5 B3
59 Houtkerque 1 D2
28 Houville-la-Branche 11 B3
40 Huchet 34 C3
62 Hucqueliers 1 B3
29 Huelgoat 8 C2
52 Huilliécourt 13 A3
12 Huiron 12 C2
37 Huismes 17 C2
45 Huisseau-sur-Mauves 18 B1
53 Huisserie (L') 17 A1
51 Humbauville 12 C2
52 Humbécourt 12 D2
18 Humbligny 18 D3
52 Humes-Jorquenay 20 A1
62 Humières 1 C3
68 Hunawihr 14 A3
57 Hundling 13 D1
68 Huningue 21 A2
67 Hunspach 14 B1
12 Huparlac 36 D1
88 Hurbache 13 D3
03 Huriel 24 C2
54 Hussigny-Godbrange 7 B3
72 Hutte (La) 10 C3
03 Hyds 24 D3
09 Hyenville 9 D1
83 Hyères 44 C2
83 Hyères-Plage 44 C2

I

35 Iffendic 9 B3
35 Iffs (Les) 9 C3
61 Igé 10 C3
18 Ignol 24 D1

51 Igny-Comblizy 12 B1
27 Igoville 5 A3
71 Iguerande 25 B3
64 Iholdy 40 C2
37 Ile-Bouchard (L') 17 C3
17 Ile-d'Elle (L') 22 D2
85 Ile-d'Olonne (L') 22 C2
2B Ile Rousse (L') 45 A3
29 Ile-Tudy 15 B1
64 Ilharre 40 D1
35 Ilhet 41 A1
66 Ille-sur-Tet 43 C3
68 Illfurth 21 A2
68 Illhaeusern 14 A3
28 Illiers-Combray 11 A3
66 Illifaut 9 B3
67 Illkirch-Graffenstaden 14 B2
76 Illois 5 B2
21 Illzach 21 A1
67 Imbsheim 14 A2
58 Imphy 25 A1
62 Inchy-en-Artois 6 A1
25 Indevillers 20 D3
44 Indre 16 C3
68 Ingersheim 21 A1
36 Ingrandes 23 D2
49 Ingrandes 16 D2
86 Ingrandes 23 C1
37 Ingrandes-de-Touraine 17 C3
56 Inguiniel 8 D3
67 Ingwiller 14 A1
01 Injoux-Génissiat 26 B3
55 Inor 7 A3
13 Insming 13 D1
45 Intville-la-Guétard 11 C3
56 Inzinzac-Lochrist 15 D1
55 Ippécourt 13 A1
07 Iré-le-Sec 7 A3
64 Irissarry 40 C2
35 Irodouër 9 C3
29 Irvillac 8 B2
62 Isbergues 1 C3
45 Isdes 18 C2
58 Isenay 25 B1
50 Isigny-le-Buat 9 D2
14 Isigny-sur-Mer 4 B3
87 Isle 30 A1
95 Isle-Adam (L') 11 C1
32 Isle-Arné (L') 41 C1
10 Isle-Aumont 12 C3
32 Isle-Bouzon (L') 35 C3
41 Isle-de-Noé (L') 41 C1
55 Isle-en-Barrois (L') 13 A1
31 Isle-en-Dodon (L') 41 C2
32 Isle-Jourdain (L') 41 D1
86 Isle-Jourdain (L') 23 C3
84 Isle-sur-la Sorgue (L') 38 A3
25 Isle-sur-le-Doubs (L') 20 C2
89 Isle-sur-Serein (L') 19 B2
51 Isles-sur-Suippe 6 C3
55 Islettes (Les) 12 D1
06 Isola 44 A3
2B Isolaccio-di-Fiumorbo 45 C2
48 Ispagnac 37 A2
24 Issac 29 C3
33 Issac 28 D3
83 Issambres (Les) 44 D2
07 Issarlès 37 B1
44 Issé 16 C2
63 Isserteaux 31 A1
24 Issigeac 35 C1
63 Issoire 31 A2
55 Issoncourt-les-Trois D. 13 A1
64 Issor 40 D2
36 Issoudun 24 B1
21 Is-sur-Tille 20 A2
77 Issy-L'Évêque 25 B2
13 Istres 43 D1
51 Istres-et-Bury (Les) 12 B1
64 Isturitz 40 C2
02 Itancourt 6 A2
67 Ittersviller 14 A3
91 Itteville 11 C2
64 Itxassou 40 C2
77 Iverny 11 D1
02 Iviers 6 D1
27 Iville 10 D1
60 Ivors 11 D1
18 Ivoy-le-Pré 18 C3
94 Ivry-sur-Seine 11 C2
21 Ivry-en-Montagne 25 C1
27 Ivry-la-Bataille 11 A1
59 Iwuy 6 A1
31 Izaut-de-l'Hôtel 41 C3
65 Izaux 41 C2
62 Izel-les-Hameaux 1 C3
26 Izernore 26 B3

J

49 Jaille-Yvon (La) 17 A1
21 Jailly-lès-Moulins 19 C2
03 Jaligny-sur-Besbre 25 B2
49 Jallais 20 B3
25 Jallerange 18 D3
18 Jalognes 12 C1
51 Jâlons 36 B2
46 Jamblusse 36 B2
55 Jametz 7 A3
38 Janneyrias 32 A1
28 Janville 11 B3
35 Janzé 16 C3
38 Jarcieu 31 D2
86 Jardres 23 C2

85 Jard-sur-Mer 22 C2
45 Jargeau 18 C1
16 Jarnac 29 B1
17 Jarnac-Champagne 29 A2
23 Jarnages 24 B3
54 Jarny 13 B1
73 Jarrier 32 C2
18 Jars 18 D3
49 Jarzé 17 B3
70 Jasney 20 C1
01 Jassans-Riottier 31 D1
10 Jasseines 12 C2
01 Jasseron 26 A3
33 Jau-Dignac-et-Loirac 28 D2
85 Jaudonnière (La) 22 A2
28 Jaudrais 11 A2
33 Jauge 34 D1
07 Jaujac 37 C1
16 Jauldes 29 C1
02 Jaulgonne 12 A1
37 Jaulnay 23 C1
54 Jaulny 13 B1
86 Jaunay-Clan 23 C1
04 Jausiers 38 D2
24 Javerlhac-et-la-Chapelle-Saint-Robert 29 C2
04 Javie (La) 38 C2
48 Javols 37 A1
16 Javrezac 29 A1
53 Javron-les-Chapelles 10 B3
43 Jax 31 B3
64 Jaxu 40 C2
86 Jazeneuil 23 B2
17 Jazennes 29 A1
54 Jeandelaincourt 13 C2
88 Jeanménil 13 D3
02 Jeantes 6 B2
68 Jebsheim 14 A3
32 Jégun 41 C1
24 Jemave (La) 29 C3
59 Jenlain 6 B1
03 Jenzat 25 A3
68 Jettingen 21 A2
10 Jeugny 19 B1
36 Jeu-les-Bois 24 B2
36 Jeu-Maloches 24 A1
59 Jeumont 6 B1
50 Jobourg 3 C2
54 Joeuf 7 B3
89 Joigny 19 A1
52 Joinville 13 A3
94 Joinville-le-Pont 11 C2
69 Jonage 32 A1
87 Jonchère-Saint-Maurice (La) 24 A3
90 Joncherey 20 D2
52 Jonchery 20 A1
51 Jonchery-sur-Vesle 6 B3
02 Joncourt 6 A2
71 Joncy 25 C2
22 Jonquerets-de-Livet (Les) 10 D1
84 Jonquières 37 D3
30 Jonquières-et-St-Vincent 37 C3
70 Jonvelle 20 B2
17 Jonzac 29 A2
74 Jonzier-Épagny 26 B3
42 Jonzieux 31 C2
14 Jort 10 B1
63 Joserand 25 A3
41 Josnes 18 A1
40 Josse 40 C1
56 Josselin 16 A1
77 Jossigny 11 D1
77 Jouarre 12 A1
78 Jouars-Pontchartrain 11 B2
11 Joucou 42 B3
33 Joué 33 D1
61 Joué-du-Bois 10 B2
72 Joué-en-Charnie 17 B1
49 Joué-Étiau 17 A3
37 Joué-les-Tours 17 D3
44 Joué-sur-Erdre 16 C2
12 Jouels 36 C2
18 Jouet-sur-l'Aubois 24 D1
21 Jouey 19 C3
25 Jougne 26 C1
86 Jouhet 23 D2
19 Jouix 30 B2
13 Jouques 44 B1
86 Journet 23 D2
24 Journiac 29 D3
62 Journy 1 C2
21 Jours-les-Baigneux 19 C2
86 Joussé 23 C3
89 Joux-la-Ville 19 B2
28 Jouy 11 B2
89 Jouy 11 D3
78 Jouy-en-Josas 12 A1
77 Jouy-le-Châtel 12 A2
45 Jouy-le-Potier 18 B2
60 Jouy-sous-Thelle 5 C3
27 Jouy-sur-Eure 11 A1
07 Joyeuse 37 C1
33 Joze 31 A1
06 Juan-les-Pins 45 A1
53 Jublains 10 B3
22 Jugon 9 B2
44 Juigné-des-Moutiers 16 C2
49 Juigné-sur-Loire 17 A2
27 Juignettes 10 D1
19 Juillac 30 A2
65 Juillan 41 B2
77 Juilly 11 D1
69 Juliénas 25 D3

43 Julianges 31 B2
50 Jullouville 9 C2
10 Jully-sur-Sarce 19 C1
63 Jumeaux 31 A2
49 Jumelière (La) 17 A3
76 Jumièges 8 D3
24 Jumilhac-le-Grand 29 D2
65 Juncalas 41 B2
15 Junhac 36 C1
08 Juniville 6 C3
72 Jupilles 17 C1
64 Jurançon 41 A2
42 Juré 31 B1
16 Jurignac 29 B2
14 Jurques 10 A1
79 Juscorps 23 A3
15 Jussac 30 C3
70 Jussey 20 B1
02 Jussy 6 C2
18 Jussy-Champagne 24 D1
18 Jussy-le-Chaudrier 18 C1
09 Justiniac 42 A2
53 Juvigné 9 D3
51 Juvigny 12 C1
55 Juvigny-en-Perthois 13 A2
50 Juvigny-le-Tertre 10 A2
61 Juvigny-sous-Andaine 10 B2
14 Juvigny-sur-Seulles 4 B3
07 Juvinas 37 C1
02 Juvincourt-et-Damary 6 B3
91 Juvisy-sur-Orge 11 C2
10 Juzanvigny 12 C3
52 Juzennecourt 12 D3
31 Juzet-d'Izaut 41 C3
78 Juziers 11 B1

K

50 Kairon-Plage 9 C1
67 Kaltenhouse 14 B2
68 Kappelen 21 A2
57 Kappelkinger 13 D1
68 Kaysersberg 14 A3
57 Kédange-sur-Canner 7 C3
68 Kembs 21 A2
22 Kerbors 8 C1
29 Kerfani-les-Pins 15 C1
29 Kerfot 9 A1
29 Kerglintin 8 B3
29 Kergoat 8 B3
22 Kergrist-Moëlu 8 D2
22 Kerien 8 D2
22 Kérity 9 A1
29 Kerlaz 8 B3
29 Kerlouan 8 B1
29 Kermaria 9 A2
22 Kermaria-Sulard 8 D1
56 Kernascléden 3 D3
29 Kernilis 8 B2
22 Kerpert 8 D2
29 Kersaint 8 A2
56 Kervignac 15 D1
67 Keskastel 13 D1
68 Kiffis 21 A2
67 Kintzheim 14 A3
67 Klingenthal 14 A2
67 Knutange 7 B3
57 Kœnigsmacker 7 C3
68 Kœtzingue 21 A2
55 Kœur-la-Grande 13 A2
67 Kogenheim 14 A3
68 Kruth 20 D1

L

64 Laà-Mondrans 40 D1
64 Laas 40 D1
01 Labalme 26 A3
33 Labarde 29 A2
32 Labarrère 35 B3
31 Labarthe-Rivière 41 C2
64 Labastide-Clairence 40 C1
11 Labastide-d'Anjou 42 B2
40 Labastide-d'Armagnac 35 B2
07 Labastide-de-Virac 37 C2
11 Labastide-en-Val 42 C3
46 Labastide-Murat 36 A1
81 Labastide-Rouairoux 42 C1
82 Labastide-St-Pierre 36 A3
32 Labastide-Savès 41 D1
65 Labatut-Rivière 41 B1
11 Labecède-Lauragais 42 B2
31 Labège 42 A1
07 Labègude 37 C1
40 Labenne 40 C1
46 Labéraudie 36 A2
21 Labergement-Foigney 20 A3
25 Labergement-
Sainte-Marie 26 C1
15 Labesserette 36 C1
07 Lablachère 37 C2
65 Laborde 41 B3
26 Laborel 38 B2
40 Labouheyre 34 D2
81 Laboutarié 42 B1
33 Labrède 35 A1
40 Labrit 35 A2
15 Labrousse 36 C1
62 Labroye 5 C1
81 Labruguière 42 C1
21 Labruyère 26 A1
54 Labry 13 B1
46 Laburgade 36 A2
81 Lacabarède 42 C1

12 Lacalm 36 D1
33 Lacanau 28 D3
33 Lacanau-Océan 28 C3
21 Lacanche 19 C3
15 Lacapelle-Barrès 30 D3
35 Lacapelle-Biron 35 D1
15 Lacapelle-del-Fraisse 36 C1
82 Lacapelle-Livron 36 B2
46 Lacapelle-Marival 36 B1
81 Lacapelle-Pinet 36 C1
15 Lacapelle-Viescamp 30 C3
64 Lacarre 40 C2
64 Lacarry-Arhan-
Charitte-le-Haut 40 D2
81 Lacaune 42 C1
47 Lacaussade 35 D2
46 Lacave 36 A1
81 Lacaze 42 C1
73 Lac-de-Tignes 32 D2
19 Lacelle 30 B1
61 Lacelle (La) 10 B2
47 Lacépède 35 C2
16 Lachaise 29 B2
48 Lachamp 37 A1
07 Lachamp-Raphaël 37 C1
07 Lachapelle-sous-
Aubenas 37 C1
90 Lachapelle-sous-
Rougemont 20 D2
05 Lachau 38 B2
63 Lachaux 25 B3
51 Lachy 12 C2
64 Lacommande 41 A2
84 Lacoste 38 A3
81 Lacougotte-Cadoul 42 B1
09 Lacourt 41 D3
82 Lacourt-Saint-Pierre 36 A3
64 Lacq 41 A1
12 Lacroix-Barrez 36 C1
31 Lacroix-Falgarde 42 A1
60 Lacroix-Saint-Ouen 5 D3
55 Lacroix-sur-Meuse 13 A1
24 Lacropte 29 D3
81 Lacrouzette 42 C1
23 Ladapeyre 24 B3
45 Ladon 18 C1
11 Ladern-sur-Lauquet 42 C2
32 Ladevèze-Rivière 41 B1
47 Ladignac 35 D2
87 Ladignac-le-Long 29 D1
39 Ladoye-sur-Seille 26 B3
19 Lafage-sur-Sombre 30 B2
81 Lafenasse 42 C1
52 Laferté-sur-Amance 20 B1
52 Laferté-sur-Aube 19 D1
39 Lafette (La) 26 C1
15 Lafeuillade-en-Vézie 36 C1
70 Laffond 20 A2
38 Laffrey 38 B3
65 Lafitole 41 B1
82 Lafitte 35 D3
47 Lafitte-sur-Lot 35 C2
31 Lafitte-Vigordanne 42 D2
82 Lafrançaise 36 A3
34 Lagamas 43 A1
57 Lagarde 13 D2
19 Lagarde-Enval 30 B3
31 Lagardelle-sur-Lèze 42 A1
81 Lagardiolle 42 B1
32 Lagarrigue 42 C1
51 Lagery 12 B1
06 Laghet 45 B1
19 Lagleygeolle 30 B3
62 Lagnicourt-Marcel 5 D1
01 Lagnieu 32 A1
77 Lagny-sur-Marne 11 D1
64 Lagor 40 D2
07 Lagorce 37 C2
33 Lagorce 29 B3
31 Lagrâce-Dieu 42 A2
40 Lagrange 35 B3
11 Lagrasse 42 C2
31 Lagraulet-St-Nicolas 35 D3
19 Lagraulière 30 A2
19 Laguenne 30 B3
82 Laguépie 36 B3
32 Laguian-Mazous 41 B1
12 Laguiole 36 D1
47 Lagupie 35 B1
31 Laharie 34 D1
40 Laharie 34 D3
55 Laheycourt-le-Ch. 13 C2
65 Lahitte-Toupière 41 B1
64 Lahourcade 40 D2
08 Laifour 6 D2
17 Laigne (La) 23 A3
53 Laigné 17 A1
72 Laigné-en-Belin 17 C1
21 Laignes 19 C1
60 Laigneville 5 C3
45 Lailly-en-Val 18 B2
55 Laimont 12 D2
89 Lain 19 A2
39 Lains 26 A2
89 Lainsecq 19 A2
85 Lairoux 22 D2
12 Laissac 36 D2
25 Laissey 20 C3
71 Laives 25 C3
54 Laix 7 B3
71 Laizé 25 D2
14 Laize-la-Ville 10 B1
39 Lajoux 26 B2
60 Lalandelle 5 B3
67 Lalaye 14 A3

46 Lalbenque 36 A2
07 Lalevade-d'Ardèche 37 C1
24 Lalinde 35 C1
03 Lalizolle 24 D3
59 Lallaing 2 A3
35 Lalleu 16 C1
64 Lalonguette 41 A1
07 Lalouvesc 31 C3
40 Laluque 34 D3
2B Lama 45 B2
03 Lamaids 24 C3
82 Lamagistère 35 D3
34 Lamalou-les-Bains 42 D1
66 Lamanère 43 C3
13 Lamanon 44 A1
88 Lamarche 20 B1
21 Lamarche-sur-Saône 20 A3
21 Lamargelle 19 D2
33 Lamarque 28 D3
31 Lamastre 31 D3
19 Lamativie 30 B3
19 Lamazière-Basse 30 C2
29 Lambader 8 C2
13 Lambesc 44 A1
04 Lambruisse 38 C3
58 Lamenay-sur-Loire 25 A1
72 Lamnay 17 D1
22 Lamballe 9 B2
13 Lambesc 44 A1
04 Lambruisse 38 C3
58 Lamenay-sur-Loire 25 A1
72 Lamnay 17 D1
42 Lamontélarié 42 C1
63 Lamontgie 31 A2
47 Lamontjoie 35 C3
24 Lamonzie-Montastruc 29 C3
55 Lamorville 13 A1
43 Lamothe 31 A2
29 Lamothe-Montravel 29 B2
84 Lamothe-du-Rhône 37 D2
18 Lamotte-Beuvron 18 B2
26 Lamoura 26 B2
29 Lampaul 8 A2
29 Lampaul-Guimiliau 8 C2
29 Lampaul-Plouarzel 8 A2
69 Lamure-sur-Azergues 25 C3
25 Lanans 20 C3
07 Lanarce 37 B1
80 Lanchères 5 B1
22 Lancieux 9 B2
13 Lançon-Provence 44 A1
56 Landaul 15 D1
82 Lande (La) 35 D3
35 Landéan 9 D3
29 Landéda 8 B1
61 Lande-de-Goult (La) 10 B2
61 Lande-de-Lougé (La) 10 B2
29 Landeleau 8 C3
49 Landemont 16 C3
27 Landepereuse 10 D1
29 Landerneau 8 B2
33 Landerrouat 35 B1
23 Landes 23 A3
85 Landes-Génusson (Les) 16 D3
18 Landes-le-Gaulois 18 A2
14 Landes-sur-Ajon 10 A1
61 Lande-sur-Eure (La) 10 D2
56 Landevant 15 D1
29 Landévennec 8 B2
02 Landifay-et-
Bertaignemont 6 B2
61 Landigou 10 B2
33 Landiras 35 A1
61 Landisacq 10 A2
29 Landivisiau 8 C2
53 Landivy 10 A2
43 Landos 37 B1
02 Landouzy-la-Ville 6 B2
17 Landrais 22 D1
44 Landreau (Le) 16 D3
59 Landrecies 6 B1
54 Landres 7 B3
25 Landresse 20 C3
62 Landrethun-le-Nord 1 B2
10 Landreville 19 C1
57 Landroff 13 C1
73 Landry 32 D2
29 Landudec 8 B3
35 Landujan 9 B3
29 Landunvez 8 A2
56 Lanester 15 D1
52 Laneuville-à-Bayard 12 D2
54 Laneuville-devant-
Nancy 13 C2
60 Laneuvilleroy 5 D3
55 Laneuville-sur-Meuse 7 A3
22 Langast 9 A3
43 Langeac 31 A3
37 Langeais 17 C3
37 Langennerie 17 D2
28 Langey 18 A1
56 Langoëlan 8 D3
48 Langogne 37 B1
33 Langoiran 35 A1
29 Langolen 8 C3
33 Langon 35 A1
35 Langon (Le) 16 C1
85 Langon (Le) 22 D2
56 Langonnet 8 C3
22 Langourla 9 B3
52 Langres 20 A1
14 Langrune-sur-Mer 4 B3
22 Languédias 9 B2
22 Languénan 9 B2
29 Langueux 9 A2
56 Languidic 15 D1
35 Lanhélin 9 C2
29 Lanhouarneau 8 B2

29 Lanildut 8 A2
22 Laniscat 8 D3
22 Lanloup 9 A1
29 Lanmeur 8 C1
22 Lanmodez 9 A1
64 Lanne 40 D2
29 Lannéanou 8 C2
29 Lannédern 8 C2
32 Lannemaignan 35 A3
65 Lannemezan 41 C2
32 Lannepax 35 B3
28 Lanneray 18 A1
47 Lannes 35 B3
29 Lannilis 8 B2
22 Lannion 8 D1
59 Lannoy 2 A3
60 Lannoy-Cuillère 5 B2
15 Lanobre 30 C2
33 Lanot 34 D1
24 Lanouaille 29 D2
56 Lanouée 9 A3
24 Lanquais 35 C1
22 Lanrelas 9 B3
29 Lannvoaré 8 A2
38 Lans-en-Vercors 32 B3
43 Lansargues 43 B1
73 Lanslebourg-Mt-Cenis 32 D2
73 Lanslevillard 32 D2
31 Lanta 42 A1
10 Lantages 19 C1
21 Lantenay 19 D3
25 Lantenne-Vertière 20 B3
70 Lantenot 20 C2
19 Lanteuil 30 A3
18 Lanthenay 18 B3
06 Lantosque 39 A3
58 Lanty 25 B1
30 Lanuéjols 37 A3
48 Lanuéjols 37 A2
22 Lanvallay 9 B2
56 Lanvaudan 15 D1
81 Lanvellec 8 D2
29 Lanvéoc 8 B2
22 Lanvollon 9 A2
02 Laon 6 B3
28 Laons 11 A2
03 Lapalisse 25 B3
84 Lapalud 37 D2
18 Lapan 24 C1
12 Lapanouse-de-Cernon 36 D3
40 Lapeyrade 35 B3
31 Lapeyre 42 A1
24 Lapeyrouse 24 D3
30 Lapleau 30 C2
47 Laplume 35 C3
14 Lapouyade 14 A3
33 Lapouyade 29 A3
02 Lappion 6 B2
25 Laprugne 25 B3
31 Laps 31 A1
63 Laps 31 A1
63 Laqueuille 30 D1
05 Laragne-Montéglin 38 B2
40 Larceveau-Arros-Cibits 40 C2
53 Larchamp 10 A3
61 Larchamp 10 A2
77 Larchant 11 D3
04 Larche 38 D2
19 Larche 30 A3
24 Lardiers 38 C2
24 Lardin-St-Lazare (Le) 30 A3
11 Laredorte 42 C2
79 Largeasse 23 A1
37 Largentière 37 C2
56 Larmor-Baden 16 A2
56 Larmor-Plage 15 D1
36 Larnagol 36 B2
58 Larochemillay 25 B1
89 Laroche-St-Cydroine 19 A1
63 Larodde 30 C2
11 Laroque-de-Fa 42 C3
15 Laroquebrou 30 C3
66 Laroque-des-Albères 43 D3
46 Laroque-des-Arcs 36 A2
09 Laroque-d'Olmes 42 B3
47 Laroque-Timbaut 35 C2
15 Laroquevieille 30 C3
40 Larrau 40 D2
82 Larrazet 35 D3
61 Larré 10 C2
32 Larressingle 35 B3
81 Larroque 41 C2
32 Larroque 36 A3
33 Lartigue 36 B2
64 Laruns 41 A3
33 Laruscade 29 A3
33 Las 34 D1
57 Lasalle 37 B3
46 Lascabanes 36 A2
15 Lascelle 30 C3
81 Lasgraisses 36 B3
66 Las Illas 43 D3
65 Laslades 41 B2
53 Lassay-les-Châteaux 10 B3
41 Lassay-sur-Croisne 18 B3
49 Lasse 17 B2
09 Lasserre 41 D1
31 Lasserre 41 D1
47 Lasserre-de-Prouille 42 B2
64 Lasseube 41 A3
55 Lassigny 5 D3
12 Lassouts 36 D2
35 Lassy 16 C1
31 Lastic 31 A3
63 Lastic 30 D1
11 Lastours 42 C2

68 Ostheim **14** A3
2A Ota **45** B3
57 Ottange **7** B3
68 Ottmarsheim **21** A1
67 Ottrot **14** A2
58 Ouagne **19** A3
89 Ouanne **19** A2
28 Ouarville **11** B3
41 Oucques **18** A1
44 Oudon **16** D2
57 Oudry **25** C2
39 Ougney **20** B3
25 Ouhans **26** C1
14 Ouilly-le-Vicomte **4** C3
14 Ouistreham **4** B3
36 Oulches **24** A2
02 Oulchy-le-Château **12** A1
28 Oulins **11** A1
69 Oullins **31** D1
85 Oulmes **23** A2
39 Ounans **26** B1
58 Ourgneaux (Les) **25** B1
58 Ourouër **25** A1
18 Ourouer-les-Bourdelins **24** D1
69 Ouroux **25** C3
58 Ouroux-en-Morvan **19** B3
71 Ouroux-sur-Saône **25** D1
76 Ourville-en-Caux **4** D2
64 Ousse **41** A2
40 Ousse-Suzan **34** D3
45 Oussoy-en-Gâtinais **18** D1
09 Oust **41** D3
45 Outarville **11** B3
51 Outines **12** D2
11 Ouveillan **42** D2
76 Ouville-la-Rivière **5** A2
86 Ouzilly **23** C1
41 Ouzouer-le-Doyen **18** A1
28 Ouzouer-le-Marché **18** A1
45 Ouzouer-sur-Loire **18** C2
45 Ouzouer-sur-Trezée **18** D2
71 Oyé **25** C3
25 Oye-et-Pallet **26** C1
62 Oye-Plage **1** C2
01 Oyonnax **26** B3
86 Oyré **23** C1
05 Oze **38** B2
71 Ozenay **25** D2
52 Ozières **C3** A3
17 Ozillac **29** A2
77 Ozoir-la-Ferrière **11** D2
28 Ozoir-le-Breuil **18** A1
40 Ozourt **40** D1

P

42 Pacaudière (La) **25** B3
38 Pact **31** D2
27 Pacy-sur-Eure **11** A1
11 Padern **42** C3
46 Padirac **36** B1
88 Padoux **13** C3
21 Pagny-le-Château **26** A1
55 Pagny-sur-Meuse **13** B2
54 Pagny-sur-Moselle **13** B1
09 Pailhès **42** A2
60 Paillart **5** C2
33 Paillet **35** A1
26 Paillette (La) **38** A2
52 Pailly (Le) **20** A2
89 Pailly **12** A3
44 Paimbœuf **16** B2
22 Paimpol **9** A1
35 Paimpont **9** B3
79 Paizay-le-Chapt **23** B3
86 Paizay-le-Sec **23** D2
38 Pajay **32** A2
38 Paladru **32** B2
56 Palais (Le) **15** D2
91 Palaiseau **11** C2
87 Palais-sur-Vienne (Le) **30** A1
11 Palaja **42** C2
34 Palavas-les-Flots **43** B1
71 Palinges **25** C2
10 Pâlis **12** B3
19 Palisse **30** C2
63 Palladuc **31** B1
44 Pallet (Le) **16** D3
17 Pallice (La) **22** D3
85 Palluau **22** C1
16 Palluaud **29** C2
36 Palluau-sur-Indre **24** A1
12 Palmas **36** D2
2A Palneca **45** C2
2A Palombaggia **45** D2
04 Palud-sur-Verdon (La) **44** C1
09 Pamiers **42** A2
79 Pamplie **23** A2
79 Pamproux **23** B2
32 Panassac **41** C1
52 Pancey **13** A3
2B Pancheraccia **45** B2
57 Pange **13** C1
42 Panissières **31** C1
32 Panjas **35** B3
44 Pannecé **16** D2
58 Panneçot **25** B1
45 Pannes **18** D1
54 Pannes **13** B1
93 Pantin **11** C1
35 Paramé **9** C2
17 Parançay **23** A3
18 Parassy **18** C3
78 Paray-Douaville **11** B3
71 Paray-le-Monial **25** C2
49 Parçay-les-Pins **17** C2
35 Parcé **9** D3
72 Parcé-sur-Sarthe **17** B1
39 Parcey **26** A1
24 Parcoul **29** B2
62 Parcq (Le) **1** C3
64 Pardies-Piétat **41** A2
72 Parennes **10** B3
63 Parentignat **31** A2
40 Parentis-en-Born **34** D2
62 Parenty **1** B3
54 Parey-Saint-Césaire **13** B2
80 Pargny **5** D2
51 Pargny-lès-Reims **12** B1
88 Pargny-sous-Mureau **13** B3
51 Pargny-sur-Saulx **12** D2
10 Pargues **19** C1
72 Parigné-l'Évêque **17** C1
75 Paris **11** C1/2
81 Parisot **36** B3
82 Parisot **36** B2
89 Parly **19** A2
95 Parmain **11** C1
36 Parnac **24** A2
26 Parnans **32** A3
60 Parnes **11** B1
52 Parnoy-en-Bassigny **20** B1
55 Parois **13** A1
54 Parroy **13** C2
81 Parrouquial (La) **36** B3
10 Pars-lès-Romilly **12** B3
23 Parsac **24** C3
79 Parthenay **23** B2
27 Parville **11** A1
12 Pas (Le) **36** C2
53 Pas (Le) **10** A3
79 Pas-de-Jeu **23** B1
62 Pas-en-Artois **5** C1
89 Pasilly **19** B2
21 Pasques **19** D3
61 Passais **10** A2
25 Passavant **20** C3
51 Passavant-en-Argonne **12** D1
70 Passavant-la-Rochère **20** B1
38 Passins **32** A1
16 Passirac **29** B2
74 Passy **32** D1
2A Pastricciola **45** C3
45 Patay **18** B1
2B Patrimonio **45** A2
64 Pau **41** A2
45 Paucourt **18** D1
36 Paudy **24** B1
33 Pauillac **28** D2
15 Paulhac **30** D3
48 Paulhac-en-Margeride **31** A3
43 Paulhaguet **31** A3
34 Paulhan **43** A1
15 Paulhenc **36** D1
24 Paulin **30** A3
37 Paulmy **23** D1
36 Paulnay **24** A1
44 Paulx **16** C3
08 Pauvres **6** C3
42 Pavezin **31** D2
32 Pavie **41** C1
10 Pavillon-Sainte-Julie (Le) **12** B3
76 Pavilly **4** D2
46 Payrac **36** A1
07 Payzac **37** C2
24 Payzac **30** A2
11 Paziols **42** C3
38 Péage-de-Roussillon (Le) **31** D2
07 Peaugres **31** D2
56 Péaule **16** B2
43 Pébrac **31** A3
82 Pech-Bernou **36** B2
31 Pechbusque **42** A1
11 Pech-Luna **42** B2
59 Pecquencourt **2** A3
77 Pécy **12** A2
22 Pédernec **8** D2
44 Pégréac **16** B2
52 Peigney **20** A1
56 Peillac **16** B1
06 Peille **39** B3
06 Peillon **39** B3
06 Peira-Cava **39** B3
73 Peisey-Nancroix **32** D2
47 Péjouans **35** B2
46 Pélacoy **36** A1
13 Pélissanne **44** A1
38 Pellafol **38** B1
05 Pelleautier **38** C2
33 Pellegrue **35** B1
31 Pelleport **41** D1
21 Pellerey **19** D2
44 Pelierin (Le) **16** C3
49 Pellerine (La) **17** C2
53 Pellerine (La) **9** D3
36 Pellevoisin **24** A1
49 Pellouailles-les-Vignes **17** A2
48 Pelouse **37** B1
42 Pélussin **31** D2
05 Pelvoux (Commune de) **38** C1
77 Penchard **11** D1
29 Pencran **8** B2
56 Pénestin **16** A2
29 Penhors **8** B3
29 Penmarch **15** B1
81 Penne **36** B3
47 Penne-d'Agenais **35** D2
13 Pennes-Mirabeau (Les) **44** A2
13 Penne-sur-Huveaune **44** B2
38 Penol **32** A2
40 Penon (Le) **34** C3
87 Pensol **29** D1
29 Pentrez-Plage **8** B3
22 Penvénan **8** D1
56 Penvins **16** A2
29 Penzé **8** C2
06 Péone **38** D3
36 Pérassay **24** B2
50 Percy **9** D1
32 Pergain-Taillac **35** C3
38 Périer (Le) **32** B3
50 Périers **3** D3
17 Pérignac **29** A1
63 Pérignat-lès-Sarliève **31** A1
63 Pérignat-sur-Allier **31** A1
79 Périgné **23** B3
24 Périgueux **29** C3
37 Pernay **17** C2
84 Pernes-les-Fontaines **38** A3
2B Pero-Casevecchie **45** B2
34 Pérols **43** B1
80 Péronne **5** D2
28 Péronville **18** B1
19 Pérols-sur-Vézère **30** B2
01 Pérouges **32** A1
36 Pérouille (La) **24** A1
19 Perpezac-le-Blanc **30** A3
19 Perpezac-le-Noir **30** A2
66 Perpignan **43** D3
52 Perrancey-les-Vieux-Moulins **20** A1
78 Perray-en-Yvelines (Le) **11** B2
69 Perréon (Le) **25** C3
22 Perret **8** D3
89 Perreuse **19** A2
42 Perreux **25** C3
85 Perrier (Le) **22** B1
71 Perrigny-sur-Loire **25** B2
52 Perrogney-les-Fontaines **20** A1
22 Perros-Guirec **8** D1
37 Perrusson **17** D3
86 Persac **23** C2
95 Persan **11** C1
56 Persquen **8** D3
08 Perthes **6** C3
52 Perthes **12** D2
77 Perthes **11** C3
10 Perthes-lès-Brienne **12** C3
66 Perthus (Le) **43** D3
35 Pertre (Le) **16** D1
43 Pertuis (Le) **31** B3
84 Pertuis **44** B1
42 Pertuiset (Le) **31** C2
61 Pervenchères **10** C3
19 Pescher (Le) **30** B3
39 Peseux **26** A1
70 Pesmes **20** B3
33 Pessac **29** A3
32 Pessan **41** C1
17 Pessines **29** A1
67 Petersbach **14** A1
44 Petit-Auverné **16** D2
74 Petit-Bornand (Le) **26** C3
76 Petit-Couronne **5** A3
79 Petite-Boissière (La) **23** A1
67 Petite-Pierre (La) **14** A1
57 Petite-Rosselle **7** D3
76 Petites-Dalles (Les) **4** D2
51 Petites-Loges (Les) **12** C1
59 Petite-Synthe **1** C2
68 Petit-Landau **21** A2
44 Petit-Mars **16** C2
39 Petit-Noir **26** A1
33 Petit-Palais-et-Cornemps **29** B2
29 Petit-Port **8** A2
37 Petit-Pressigny (Le) **23** D1
76 Petit-Quevilly (Le) **5** A3
76 Pétiville **4** D3
85 Petosse **22** D2
2A Petreto-Bicchisano **45** C3
57 Pettoncourt **13** C2
11 Pexiora **42** B2
54 Pexonne **13** D2
23 Peyrabout **24** B3
23 Peyrat-la-Nonière **24** C3
87 Peyrat-le-Château **30** B1
46 Peyrebrune **36** A1
34 Peyrefiche **42** C2
11 Peyrefitte-du-Razès **42** B3
40 Peyrehorade **40** C1
19 Peyrehovade **30** B1
11 Peyens **42** B2
11 Peyriac-Minervois **42** C2
11 Peyriac-de-Mer **42** D2
01 Peyrieu **32** B1
87 Peyrilhac **23** D3
24 Peyrillac-et-Millac **30** A3
26 Peyrins **32** A3
19 Peyrissac **30** B2
13 Peyrolles-en-Provence **44** B1
31 Peyrouliès **36** A3
65 Peyrouse **41** B2
04 Peyruis **38** B3
26 Peyrus **38** A1
15 Peyrusse **30** D3
12 Peyrusse-le-Roc **36** B2
32 Peyrusse-Vieille **41** B1
77 Pézarches **11** D2
72 Pezé-le-Robert **10** B3
34 Pézenas **43** A2
34 Pézènes-les-Mines **43** A1
11 Pezens **42** C2
41 Pezou **18** A1
24 Pézuls **29** D3
28 Pézy **11** B3
68 Pfaffenheim **21** A1
67 Pfaffenhoffen **14** A1
68 Pfastatt **21** A1
68 Pfetterhouse **21** A2
57 Phalsbourg **14** A2
57 Philippsbourg **14** A1
66 Pia **42** D3
2A Piana **45** B3
33 Pian-Médoc (Le) **29** A3
2A Pianottoli-Caldarello **45** D3
05 Piarre (La) **38** B2
31 Pibrac **42** A1
2A Piccovagia **45** D2
63 Picherande **30** D2
80 Picquigny **5** C2
48 Pied-de-Borne **37** B2
2B Piedicorte-di-Gaggio **45** B2
2B Piedicroce **45** B2
2B Piedra-di-Verde **45** B2
24 Piégut-Pluviers **29** C1
54 Piennes **7** B3
87 Pierre-Buffière **30** A1
38 Pierre-Châtel **32** B3
70 Pierrecourt **20** B2
71 Pierre-de-Bresse **26** A1
83 Pierrefeu-du-Var **44** C2
48 Pierrefiche **37** B1
45 Pierrefitte-ès-Bois **18** D2
65 Pierrefitte-Nestalas **41** B3
55 Pierrefitte-sur-Aire **13** A1
03 Pierrefitte-sur-Loire **25** B2
41 Pierrefitte-sur-Sauldre **18** C2
60 Pierrefonds **5** D3
25 Pierrefontaine-lès-Blamont **20** D3
25 Pierrefontaine-Les-Varans **20** C3
15 Pierrefort **30** D3
26 Pierrelatte **37** D2
95 Pierrelaye **11** C1
77 Pierre-Levée **11** D1
54 Pierre-Percée **13** D2
89 Pierre-Perthuis **19** B2
02 Pierrepont **6** B2
54 Pierrepont **7** B3
80 Pierrepont-sur-Avre **5** C2
34 Pierrerue **42** D2
44 Pierric **16** C1
33 Pierroton **34** D1
51 Pierry **12** B1
2B Pietracorbara **45** A2
2B Pietralba **45** B2
2B Pietrapola **45** C2
2B Pietroso **45** C2
50 Pieux (Les) **3** C2
89 Piffonds **19** A1
23 Pigerolles **30** B1
34 Pignan **43** B1
83 Pignans **44** C2
2A Pila-Canale **45** A3
33 Pilat-Plage **34** C1
26 Pihon (Le) **38** B1
26 Pilles (Les) **38** A2
40 Pimbo **41** A1
89 Pimelles **19** C1
03 Pin (Le) **25** B2
14 Pin (Le) **4** C3
70 Pin **20** B3
77 Pin (Le) **11** D1
79 Pin (Le) **23** A1
65 Pinas **41** C2
61 Pin-au-Haras (Le) **10** C2
47 Pindères **35** B2
85 Pineaux (Les) **22** D2
49 Pin-en-Mauges (Le) **17** A3
10 Piney **12** C3
61 Pin-la-Garenne (Le) **10** C3
2B Pino **45** A2
43 Pinols **31** A3
02 Pinon **6** A3
31 Pinsaguel **42** A1
38 Pinsot **32** C2
55 Pintheville **13** B1
84 Piolenc **37** B3
23 Pionnat **24** B3
63 Pionsat **24** D3
35 Pipriac **16** B1
35 Piré-sur-Seiche **16** D1
44 Piriac-sur-Mer **16** A2
50 Pirou **3** C3
50 Pirou-Plage **3** C3
17 Pisany **28** D1
27 Piseux **10** D2
60 Pisseleu **5** C3
40 Pissos **34** D2
85 Pissotte **23** A3
45 Pithiviers **11** C3
01 Pizay **32** A1
24 Pizou (Le) **29** B3
29 Plabennec **8** B2
53 Placé **10** A3
64 Place (La) **40** C2
83 Plage de Pampelonne **44** D2
85 Plage-des-Demoiselles **22** B1
83 Plage de Tahiti **44** D2
17 Plage-du-Vert Bois **28** C1
73 Plagne (La) **32** D2
11 Plaigne **42** B2
60 Plailly **11** D1
18 Plaimpied-Givaudins **24** C1
49 Plaine (La) **17** A3
44 Plaine-sur-Mer (La) **16** B3
22 Plaintel **9** A2
12 Plaisance **36** C3
24 Plaisance **35** C1
32 Plaisance **41** B1
34 Plaisance **42** D1

Column 1

34 Pouzols-Minervois 42 D2
03 Pouzy-Mésangy 24 D2
40 Poyanne 34 D3
70 Poyans 20 A2
26 Poyols 38 A1
80 Pozières 5 D1
06 Pra (Le) 38 D2
33 Prade (La) 35 A1
43 Pradelles 37 B1
11 Pradelles-Cabardès 42 C2
09 Prades 42 B3
43 Prades 31 B3
48 Prades 37 A2
66 Prades 43 C3
81 Prades 42 B1
12 Prades-d'Aubrac 38 D2
34 Prades-le-Lez 43 B1
12 Prades-Salars 36 D2
15 Pradiers 30 D2
07 Pradons 37 C2
04 Prads 38 D3
79 Prahecq 23 A3
73 Pralognan-la-Vanoise 32 D2
04 Pra-Loup 38 D2
52 Prangey 20 A2
16 Prangey 20 A2
16 Pranzac 29 C1
52 Praslay 20 A2
28 Prasville 11 B3
09 Prat-et-Bonrepaux 41 D3
66 Prats-de-Mollo-la-Preste 43 C3
24 Prats-du-Périgord 35 D1
52 Prauthoy 20 A2
41 Pray 18 A2
54 Praye 13 B3
09 Prayols 42 A3
46 Prayssac 35 D2
47 Prayssas 35 C2
74 Praz (Les) 32 D1
74 Praz-de-Lys (Le) 32 D3
74 Praz-sur-Arly 32 D1
61 Préaux-du-Perche 10 D3
36 Préaux 24 A1
32 Préchac 35 A2
33 Préchac 35 C3
32 Préchac-sur-Adour 41 B1
72 Précigné 17 B1
18 Précy 18 D3
89 Précy-le-Sec 19 B2
10 Précy-Notre-Dame 12 C3
21 Précy-sous-Thil 19 C3
60 Précy-sur-Oise 11 C1
89 Précy-sur-Vrin 19 A1
53 Pré-en-Pail 10 B2
44 Préfailles 8 B3
45 Préfontaines 18 D1
40 Préhac-les-Bains 34 D3
33 Preignac 35 A1
70 Preigney 20 B2
11 Preixan 42 C2
38 Prélenfrey 32 B3
58 Prémery 19 A3
39 Prénovel 26 B2
28 Pré-Saint-Evroult 11 A3
59 Préseau 6 B1
38 Presles 32 A3
95 Presles 11 C1
18 Presly 18 C3
45 Presnoy 18 C1
86 Pressac 23 C3
01 Pressiat 26 A3
66 Preste (La) 43 C3
50 Prétot 9 D3
18 Preuilly 18 C3
37 Preuilly-sur-Claise 23 D1
76 Preuseville 5 B2
72 Préval 10 D3
48 Prévenchères 37 C1
18 Préveranges 24 C2
27 Prey 11 A1
52 Prez-sous-Lafauche 13 A3
52 Prez-sur-Marne 12 D2
01 Priay 26 A3
17 Prignac 29 A1
33 Prignac-et-Marcamps 28 A1
12 Primaube (La) 36 C2
29 Primel-Trégastel 8 C1
35 Princé 9 D3
51 Pringy 12 C2
44 Prinquiau 16 B2
48 Prinsuejols 37 A1
02 Prisces 6 B2
59 Prisches 6 B1
36 Prissac 24 A2
71 Prissé 25 D3
79 Prissé-La-Charrière 23 A3
07 Privas 37 C1
56 Priziac 8 D3
26 Propiac-les-Bains 38 A2
2A Propriano 45 D3
69 Propières 25 C3
51 Prosnes 12 C1
11 Prouais 11 B2
14 Proussy 10 B2
70 Provenchère 20 C2
88 Provenchères-lès-Darney 20 B1
88 Provenchères-sur-Fave 13 D2
89 Provency 19 B2
77 Provins 12 A2
80 Proyart 5 D1
10 Prugny 12 B3
72 Pruillé-l'Éguillé 17 C1
10 Prunay-Belleville 12 B3
41 Prunay-Cassereau 17 B2
2B Prunelli-di-Fiumorbo 45 C2
2B Prunete-Cervione 45 B2

Column 2

36 Pruniers 24 B1
41 Pruniers 18 B3
2B Pruno 45 A2
89 Prunoy 19 A1
21 Prusly-sur-Ource 19 D1
74 Publier 26 D2
91 Publy 26 B2
44 Puceul 16 C2
33 Puch (Le) 35 B1
27 Puchay 5 B3
80 Puchevillers 5 C1
34 Puech (Le) 43 A1
34 Puéchabon 43 B1
83 Puget-sur-Argens 44 D1
06 Puget-Théniers 39 A3
44 Puget-Ville 44 C2
25 Pugey 20 B3
33 Pugnac 29 A3
79 Puihardy 23 A2
11 Puichéric 42 C2
42 Puilaurens 42 C3
04 Puimichel 38 C3
04 Puimoisson 38 C3
65 Puio 41 B2
45 Puiseaux 11 C3
49 Puiset-Doré (Le) 16 D3
28 Puiseux 11 A2
90 Puiseux-le-Hauberger 11 C1
62 Puisieux 5 D1
29 Puisseguin 29 B3
34 Puisserguier 42 D2
34 Puits-des-Mèzes (Le) 13 A3
11 Puivert 42 B3
30 Pujaut 37 D3
42 Pujaudran 41 D1
33 Pujols 35 B1
68 Pulversheim 21 A1
65 Puntous 41 C2
74 Purgerot-Arbecey 20 B2
91 Pussay 11 B3
10 Putanges-Pont-Écrépin 10 B2
92 Puteaux 11 C2
57 Puttelange-aux-Lacs 13 D1
43 Puy (Le) 31 B3
46 Puybrun 30 B3
32 Puycasquier 41 C1
19 Puy-d'Arnac 30 B3
65 Puydarrieux 41 C2
85 Puy-de-Serre 23 A2
86 Puye (La) 23 D2
34 Puyguilhem 35 C1
63 Puy-Guillaume 31 A1
82 Puylagarde 36 B2
82 Puylaroque 36 A2
81 Puylaurens 42 B1
46 Puy-l'Évêque 35 D2
33 Puyloubier 44 B1
84 Puyméras 38 A2
47 Puymiclan 35 C1
47 Puymirol 35 D2
16 Puymoyen 29 B1
33 Puynormand 29 B3
33 Puy N.-D. (Le) 17 B3
40 Puyoô 40 D1
17 Puyrolland 23 A3
13 Puy-Ste-Réparade (Le) 44 A1
30 Puy-Saint-Gulmier 30 C1
26 Puy-Saint-Martin 37 D1
66 Py 43 C3
33 Pyla-sur-Mer 34 C1

Column 3 (Q)

34 Quarante 42 D2
89 Quarré-les-Tombes 19 B3
70 Quarte (La) 20 B2
40 Quartier-Neuf 40 C1
08 Quatre-Champs 6 D3
27 Quatremare 11 A1
19 Quatre-Routes 30 B3
46 4 Routes (Les) 30 A3
23 Queaux 23 C2
35 Quédillac 9 B3
73 Queige 32 C1
52 Quelaines-Saint-Gault 17 A1
21 Quemigny-Poisot 19 D3
21 Quemigny-sur-Seine 19 D2
22 Quemper-Guézennec 9 A1
1 Quend 1 B3
80 Quend-Plage 1 B3
50 Quenoche 20 C2
2A Quenza 45 C2
12 Quercamps 1 C2
09 Querigut 43 B2
50 Querqueville 3 C2
49 Querré 17 A2
29 Querrien 8 C3
5 Querrieu 5 C2
14 Quesnay 10 B1
80 Quesnel (Le) 5 D2
59 Quesnoy (Le) 6 B1
80 Quesnoy-sur-Airaines 5 B2
59 Quesnoy-sur-Deule 1 D2
22 Quessoy 9 A2
02 Quessy 6 A2
56 Questembert 16 A1
21 Quétigny 20 A3
50 Quettehou 3 D2
3 Quettetot 3 C2
50 Quettreville-sur-Sienne 9 D1
51 Queudes 12 B2
78 Queue-les-Yvelines (La) 11 B2
08 Queuille 30 D1
5 Quevauvillers 5 C2
56 Quéven 15 D1

Column 4

33 Queyrac 28 D2
43 Queyrières 31 C3
19 Queyssac-les-Vignes 30 B3
15 Quézac 36 C1
76 Quiberon 15 D2
4 Quiberville 4 D2
62 Quièry-la-Motte 1 D3
02 Quierzy 6 A3
33 Quiévrechain 2 B3
59 Quiévy 6 A1
11 Quillan 42 B3
27 Quilleboeuf-sur-Seine 4 D3
44 Quilly 16 B2
56 Quily 16 B1
29 Quimerch 8 B2
29 Quimper 8 B3
29 Quimperlé 15 C1
18 Quincy 18 C3
77 Quincy-Voisins 11 D1
50 Quinéville 3 D2
25 Quingey 20 B3
5 Quinquempoix 5 C3
33 Quinsac 35 A1
04 Quinson 44 C1
03 Quinssaines 24 C3
72 Quinte (La) 17 B1
07 Quintenas 31 D3
22 Quintin 9 A2
22 Quiou (Le) 9 B3
30 Quissac 37 B3
46 Quissac 36 B1
56 Quistinic 15 D1
27 Quittebeuf 11 A1

R

81 Rabastens 36 B3
65 Rabastens-de-Bigorre 41 B2
85 Rabatelière (La) 22 D1
61 Rabodanges 10 B2
59 Rabouillet 42 C3
88 Racécourt 13 C3
52 Rachecourt-sur-Marne 13 A2
59 Râches 2 A3
71 Raconnay 20 C1
70 Raddon-et-Chapendu 20 C1
61 Radon 10 C2
12 Radonvilliers 12 C3
06 Rague (La) 45 A1
29 Raguenès-Plage 15 C1
57 Rahling 14 A1
50 Rahon 20 C3
50 Raids 3 D3
05 Raille (La) 38 D1
66 Railleu 43 B3
39 Rainans 20 A3
80 Rainneville 5 C1
88 Rainville 13 B3
49 Rairies (Les) 17 B2
59 Raismes 2 A3
83 Ramatuelle 44 D2
88 Rambervillers 13 C3
78 Rambouillet 11 B2
80 Rambures 5 B2
81 Ramel (Le) 42 B1
10 Ramerupt 12 C2
31 Ramonville-Saint-Agne 42 A1
32 Ramouzens 35 B3
77 Rampillon 12 A2
69 Ranchal 25 C3
39 Ranchot 20 B3
87 Rancon 24 A3
52 Rançonnières 20 A1
55 Rancourt-sur-Ornain 12 C3
71 Rancy 26 A2
25 Randan 30 D1
63 Randanne 30 C1
61 Randonnai 10 D2
61 Rânes 10 B2
35 Rannée 16 D1
67 Ranrupt 14 A3
39 Rans 20 B3
62 Ransart 5 D1
60 Rantigny 5 C3
88 Raon-aux-Bois 20 C1
88 Raon-l'Étape 13 D3
88 Raon-sur-Plaine 13 D2
2B Rapale 45 B2
13 Raphèle-lès-Arles 43 D1
09 Rappy 42 B3
60 Raray 5 D3
71 Ratenelle 26 A2
71 Ratte 26 A2
54 Raucourt 13 C1
08 Raucourt-et-Flaba 6 D2
15 Raulhac 36 C1
50 Rauville-la-Bigot 3 C2
67 Rauwiller 13 D2
33 Rauzan 35 B1
60 Ravenel 5 C3
50 Ravenoville 3 D3
50 Ravenoville-Plage 3 D3
89 Ravières 19 C2
62 Raye-sur-Authie 5 C1
18 Raymond 24 D1
83 Rayol-Canadel-sur-Mer 44 D2
70 Ray-sur-Saône 20 B2
24 Razac-sur-l'Isle 29 C3
70 Raze 20 B2
87 Razès 24 A3
47 Razimet 35 B2
66 Réal 43 B3
76 Réalcamp 5 B2
81 Réalmont 42 B1
82 Réalville 36 A3

Column 5

77 Réau 11 D2
85 Réaumur 23 A1
47 Réaup 35 B3
26 Réauville 37 D2
17 Réaux 29 A2
77 Rebais 12 A2
64 Rébénacq 41 A2
76 Rebets 5 A3
65 Rebouc 41 B3
45 Rebréchien 18 B1
21 Recey-sur-Ource 19 D2
90 Réchésy 21 A2
54 Réchicourt-la-Petite 13 C2
57 Réchicourt-le-Château 13 D2
71 Reclesne 25 C1
26 Recologne 20 B3
26 Recoubeau-Jansac 38 A1
12 Recoules-Prévinguières 36 C1
55 Récourt-le-Creux 13 A1
30 Redessan 37 C3
35 Redon 16 B1
79 Reffannes 23 B1-2
55 Reffroy 13 A2
50 Reffuveille 9 D2
62 Regnauville 1 C3
50 Regnéville-sur-Mer 9 C1
08 Regniowez 6 C2
42 Regny 31 C1
56 Réguiny 16 A1
68 Réguisheim 21 A1
83 Régusse 44 C1
88 Rehaincourt 13 C3
54 Réhon 7 B3
67 Reichshoffen 14 B1
16 Reignac 29 B2
33 Reignac 29 A2
37 Reignac-sur-Indre 17 D3
46 Reilhac 36 B1
04 Reillanne 38 B3
60 Reilly 5 B3
51 Reims 6 B3
67 Reinhardsmunster 14 A2
68 Reiningue 21 A2
67 Reipertswiller 14 A1
32 Réjaumont 35 C3
88 Relanges 20 B1
29 Relecq (Le) 8 C2
29 Relecq-Kerhuon (Le) 8 C2
61 Rémalard 10 D3
55 Rembercourt-Sommaisne 13 A1
60 Rémérangles 5 C3
54 Réméréville 13 C2
17 Rémigeasse (La) 22 C3
71 Remigny 25 D1
57 Rémilly 13 C1
58 Rémilly 25 B1
08 Remilly-Aillicourt 6 D2
21 Remilly-sur-Tille 20 A3
56 Réminiac 16 B1
88 Remiremont 20 C1
88 Remoncourt 13 B3
41 Remonnerie (La) 18 A1
08 Rémonville 6 D3
25 Remoray-Boujeons 26 C1
44 Remouille 16 C3
30 Remoulins 37 C3
76 Remuée (La) 4 C3
56 Remungol 16 A1
26 Rémuzat 38 A2
60 Rémy 5 D3
35 Renac 16 B1
42 Renaison 25 B3
53 Renazé 16 D1
38 Rencurel 32 A3
72 René 10 C3
35 Rennes 9 C3
11 Rennes-les-Bains 42 C3
08 Renneville 6 C2
63 Rentières 31 A2
08 Renwez 6 C2
33 Réole (La) 35 B1
88 Repel 13 B3
74 Reposoir (Le) 26 D3
12 Réquista 36 C3
60 Ressons 5 C3
50 Ressons-sur-Metz 5 D2
37 Retiegné 17 C3
17 Rétaud 29 A1
08 Rethel 6 C3
60 Rethondes 5 D3
35 Retiers 16 D1
40 Retions 35 A3
43 Retournac 31 B3
62 Réty 1 B2
03 Reugny 24 C2
37 Reugny 17 D2
36 Reuilly 18 B3
60 Reuil-sur-Brèche 5 C3
51 Reuves 12 B2
31 Revel 42 B1
04 Revest-du-Bion 38 B3
83 Revest-les-Eaux 44 B2
06 Revest-les-Roches 39 A3
14 Reviers 4 B3
55 Revigny-sur-Ornain 13 A1
50 Réville 3 D2
08 Revin 6 C2
59 Rexpoède 1 C2
52 Reynel 13 A3
18 Rezay 24 C2
44 Rezé 16 C3
67 Rezonville 13 B1
67 Rhinau 14 B3
44 Riaillé 16 C2
81 Rialet (Le) 42 C1
18 Rians 18 C3

14 Saint-Aignan-de-Cramesnil 10 B1
18 Saint-Aignan-des-Noyers 24 D1
41 Saint-Aignan-sur-Cher 18 A3
53 Saint-Aignan-sur-Roë 16 D1
17 Saint-Aigulin 29 B3
71 Saint-Albain 35 D2
22 Saint-Alban 9 B2
07 Saint-Alban-Auriolles 37 C2
07 Saint-Alban-d'Ay 31 D3
73 Saint-Alban-le-Montbel 32 B2
07 Saint-Alban-sous-Sampzon 37 C2
48 Saint-Alban-sur-Limagnole 37 A1
56 Saint-Allouestre 16 A1
24 Saint-Alvère 29 D3
63 Saint-Alyre-d'Arlanc 31 B2
63 Saint-Alyre-ès-Montagne 30 D2
09 Saint-Amadou 42 A2
23 Saint-Amand 24 C3
50 Saint-Amand 10 A1
24 Saint-Amand-de-Coly 30 A3
24 Saint-Amand-de-Vergt 29 C3
58 Saint-Amand-en-Puisaye 19 A2
15 Saint-Amandin 30 D2
59 Saint-Amand-les-Eaux 2 A3
41 Saint-Amand-Longpré 17 D2
18 St-Amand-Montrond 24 C1
51 Saint-Amand-sur-Fion 51 A2
79 St-Amand-sur-Sèvre* 23 A1
48 Saint-Amans 37 A1
41 Saint-Amans-Soult 41 C1
12 Saint-Amans-des-Cots 36 C2
82 Saint-Amans-du-Pech 35 D2
81 Saint-Amans-Valtoret 42 C1
16 Saint-Amans-de-Boixe 29 B1
63 Saint-Amant-Roche-Savine 31 B2
63 Saint-Amant-Tallende 31 A1
68 Saint-Amarin 20 D1
18 Saint-Ambroix 24 C1
30 Saint-Ambroix 37 C2
88 Saint-Amé 20 D1
39 Saint-Amour 26 A2
07 Saint-Andéol-de-Vals 37 C1
69 Saint-Andéol-le-Château 31 C3
13 Saint-Andiol 37 D3
81 Saint-André 42 B1
42 Saint-André-d'Apchon 25 B3
01 Saint-André-de-Corcy 31 01
07 Saint-André-de-Cruzières 37 C2
33 Saint-André-de-Cubzac 29 A3
24 Saint-André-de-Double 25 C3
27 Saint-André-de-l'Eure 11 A1
17 Saint-André-de-Lidon 29 A1
30 Saint-André-de-Majencoules 37 B3
12 Saint-André-de-Najac 36 B2
34 Saint-André-de-Sangonis 43 A1
44 Saint-André-des-Eaux 16 B2
40 Saint-André-de-Seignanx 40 C1
30 Saint-André-de-Valborgne 37 B3
33 Saint-André-du-Bois 35 B1
38 Saint-André-en-Royans 32 A3
07 Saint-André-en-Vivarais 31 C3
01 Saint-André-le-Bouchoux 26 A3
71 Saint-André-le-Désert 25 C2
04 Saint-André-les-Alpes 38 D3
85 St-André-Treize-Voies 22 C1
01 Saint-André-sur-Vieux-Jonc 26 A3
33 Saint-Androny 29 A2
16 Saint-Angeau 29 C1
03 Saint-Angel 24 C2
19 Saint-Angel 30 C2
63 Saint-Anthème 31 B2
2B Saint-Antoine 45 C2
25 Saint-Antoine 26 C1
32 Saint-Antoine 35 C3
33 Saint-Antoine 29 A3,
38 Saint-Antoine 22 A3'
47 St-Antoine-de-Ficalba 35 C2
24 St-Antoine-de-Breuilh 35 B1
33 Saint-Antoine-sur-l'Isle 29 B3
82 Saint-Antonin-Noble-Val 36 B2
36 Saint-Août 24 B1
24 Saint-Aquilin 29 C3
32 Saint-Arailles 41 C1
56 Saint-Armel 16 A2
41 Saint-Arnoult 17 D2
76 Saint-Arnoult 4 D3
28 Saint-Arnoult-des-Bois 11 A2
78 Saint-Arnoult-en-Yvelines 11 B2
65 Saint-Arroman 41 C2
24 Saint-Astier 29 C3
04 Saint-Auban 38 D3
26 Saint-Auban-sur-l'Ouvèze 38 A2
10 Saint-Aubin 12 B3
36 Saint-Aubin 24 B1
39 Saint-Aubin 26 A1
40 Saint-Aubin 40 D1
89 Saint-Aubin 19 A1
35 Saint-Aubin-d'Aubigné 9 C3
79 Saint-Aubin-de-Baudigné 23 A1
24 St-Aubin-de-Lanquais 35 C1
28 Saint-Aubin-des-bois 11 A3
44 Saint-Aubin-des-Châteaux 16 C1
72 Saint-Aubin-des-Coudrais 10 D3
50 Saint-Aubin-de-Terregatte 9 D2
35 Saint-Aubin-du-Cormier 9 D3
50 Saint-Aubin-du-Perron 3 D3
71 Saint-Aubin-en-Charolais 25 C2
76 Saint-Aubin-le-Cauf 5 A2
79 Saint-Aubin-le-Cloud 23 A1
37 Saint-Aubin-le-Dépeint 17 C2
76 Saint-Aubin-les-Elbeuf 4 A3
58 Saint-Aubin-les-Forges 19 C3
76 Saint-Aubin-Routot 4 C3
60 Saint-Aubin-sous-Erquery 5 C3
55 Saint-Aubin-sur-Aire 13 A2
14 Saint-Aubin-sur-Mer 4 B3
76 Saint-Aubin-sur-Scie 5 A2
17 Saint-Augustin 28 D1
30 Saint-Augustin 30 B2
49 Saint-Augustin-des-Bois 17 A2
24 Saint-Aulaye 29 B2
85 Saint-Avaugourd-des-Landes 22 C2
37 Saint-Avertin 17 D3
63 Saint-Avit 30 C1
24 Saint-Avit-Rivière 35 D1
35 Saint-Avit-Sénieur 35 D1
57 Saint-Avold 13 D1
45 Saint-Ay 18 B1
83 Saint-Aygulf 44 D2
63 Saint-Babel 31 A2
30 Saint-Bard 30 C1
40 Saint-Barthélemy 40 C1
56 Saint-Barthélemy 15 D1
77 Saint-Barthélemy 12 A2
47 Saint-Barthélemy-d'Agenais 35 C1
49 Saint-Barthélemy-d'Anjou 17 A2
24 Saint-Barthélemy-de-Bellegarde 29 B3
26 Saint-Barthélemy-de-Vals 31 D3
07 St-Barthélemy-le-Meil 37 C1
07 Saint-Barthélemy-le-Plain 31 D3
42 Saint-Barthélemy-Lestra 31 C2
18 Saint-Baudel 24 C1
37 Saint-Bauld 17 D3
34 Saint-Bauzille-de-la-Sylve 43 A1
34 Saint-Bauzille-de-Montmel 43 B1
34 Saint-Bauzille-de-Putois 37 B3
31 Saint-Béat 41 C3
12 Saint-Beauzély 36 D3
43 Saint-Beauzire 31 A2
63 Saint-Beauzire 31 A1
58 Saint-Benin d'Azy 25 A1
85 Saint-Benoist-sur-Mer 22 C2
01 Saint-Benoit 32 B1
11 Saint-Benoit 42 B3
86 Saint-Benoît 23 C2
26 Saint-Benoit-en-Diois 38 A1
81 Saint-Benoît-de-Carmaux 36 B3
35 Saint-Benoît-des-Ondes 9 C2
14 Saint-Benoît-d'Hébertot 4 C3
36 Saint-Benoît-du-Sault 24 A2
55 Saint-Benoît-en-Woëvre 13 B1
88 Saint-Benoît-la-Chipotte 13 D3
45 Saint-Benoît-sur-Loire 18 C1
10 Saint-Benoît-sur-Seine 12 B3
43 Saint-Bérain 31 B3
71 Saint-Bérain-sous-Sanvignes 25 C2
71 St-Bérain-sur-Dheune 25 D1
38 Saint-Bernard 32 B2
73 Saint-Béron 32 B2
31 Saint-Bertrand-de-Comminges 41 C3
67 Saint-Blaise-la-Roche 14 A3
52 Saint-Blin-Semilly 13 A3
71 Saint-Boil 25 D2
01 Saint-Bois 32 B1
28 Saint-Bomer 10 C3
05 Saint-Bonnet 38 C1
19 Saint-Bonnet-Avalouze 30 C1
87 Saint-Bonnet-de-Bellac 23 D3
15 Saint-Bonnet-de-Condat 30 C2
71 Saint-Bonnet-de-Joux 25 C2
48 Saint-Bonnet-de-Montauroux 37 B1
03 Saint-Bonnet-de-Rochefort 25 A3
15 Saint-Bonnet-de-Salers 30 C3
42 St-Bonnet-des-Quarts 25 B3
26 Saint-Bonnet-de-Valclérieux 32 A3
30 Saint-Bonnet-du-Gard 37 D3
71 Saint-Bonnet-en-Bresse 26 A1
63 Saint-Bonnet-le-Chastel 31 B2
42 Saint-Bonnet-le-Château 31 B2
42 Saint-Bonnet-le-Courreau 31 B1
07 Saint-Bonnet-le-Froid 31 C1
63 Saint-Bonnet-près-Riom 31 A1
17 Saint-Bonnet-sur-Gironde 29 A2
03 St-Bonnet-Tronçais 24 C2
18 Saint-Bouize 18 D3
37 Saint-Branchis 17 D3
44 Saint-Brévin-les-Pins 16 B3
44 Saint-Brévin-l'Océan 16 B3
35 Saint-Briac-sur-Mer 9 B2
33 Saint-Brice 35 B1
35 Saint-Brice-en-Coglès 9 A2
22 Saint-Brieuc 9 A2
17 Saint-Bris-des-Bois 29 A1
89 Saint-Bris-le-Vineux 19 B2
58 Saint-Brisson 19 C3
45 Saint-Brisson-sur-Loire 18 C3
70 Saint-Broing 20 B2
21 Saint-Broingt-les-Moines 19 C2
35 Saint-Broladre 9 C2
38 Saint-Bueil 32 B2
72 Saint-Calais 17 D1
13 Saint-Cannat 44 A1
18 Saint-Capraise 24 C1
24 Saint-Capraise-de-Lalinde 35 C1
22 Saint-Carades-Tregomel 8 D3
22 Saint-Carreuc 9 A2
22 Saint-Cast-le-Guildo 9 B2
72 Saint-Célerin 10 C3
53 Saint-Cénéré 10 A3
61 Saint-Céneri-le-Gérei 10 B3
46 Saint-Céré 36 B1
74 Saint-Cergues 20 A1
19 Saint-Cernin-de-Larche 30 A3
46 Saint-Cevet 30 C3
06 St-Cézaire-sur-Siagne 44 D1
05 Saint-Chaffrey 32 D3
15 Saint-Chamant 30 C3
19 Saint-Chamant 30 B3
13 Saint-Chamas 44 A1
42 Saint-Chamond 31 C2
30 Saint-Chaptes 37 C3
36 Saint-Chartier 24 B2
38 Saint-Chef 32 A2
48 Saint-Chély-d'Apcher 37 A1
12 Saint-Chély-d'Aubrac 36 D1
91 Saint-Chéron 11 C2
34 Saint-Chinian 42 D2
64 Saint-Christau-Lurbe 41 A2
42 Saint-Christo-en-Jarez 31 C2
84 Saint-Christol 38 B3
30 Saint-Christol-lès-Alès 37 B3
33 Saint-Christoly-de-Blaye 29 A3
33 Saint-Christoly-Médoc 28 D2
03 Saint-Christophe 25 B3
16 Saint-Christophe 23 D3
33 Saint-Christophe-de-Double 29 B3
35 Saint-Christophe-des-Bois 9 D2
49 Saint-Christophe-du-Bois 16 D3
72 Saint-Christophe-du-Jambet 10 B3
85 Saint-Christophe-du-Ligneron 22 C1
53 Saint-Christophe-du-Luat 10 A3
36 Saint-Christophe-en-Bazelle 18 B3
71 Saint-Christophe-en-Brionnais 25 C3
38 Saint-Christophe-en-Oisans 32 C3
18 Saint-Christophe-le-Chaudry 24 C2
61 Saint-Christophe-le-Japolet 10 C2
17 Saint-Christophe-le-Nais 17 C2
12 Saint-Christophe-Vallon 36 C2
52 Saint-Ciergues 20 A1
17 Saint-Ciers-Champagne 29 A2
33 Saint-Ciers-d'Abzac 29 A3
17 Saint-Ciers-du-Taillon 29 A2
33 Saint-Ciers-s.Gironde 29 A2
46 Saint-Cirgues 36 B1
07 Saint-Cirgues-en-Montagne 37 B1
19 Saint-Cirgues-la-Loutre 30 B3
82 Saint-Cirq 36 A2
46 Saint-Cirq-Lapopie 36 A2
36 Saint-Civran 24 A2
14 Saint-Clair 10 B1
86 Saint-Clair 23 B1
61 Saint-Clair-de-Halouze 10 A2
95 Saint-Clair-sur-Epte 11 B1
14 Saint-Clair-sur-l'Elle 4 A3
32 Saint-Clar 35 C3
31 Saint-Clar-de-Rivière 41 D1
16 Saint-Claud-s.-le-Son 29 C1
39 Saint-Claude 26 B2
05 Saint-Clément 38 D1
07 Saint-Clément 31 C3
19 Saint-Clément 30 B2
54 Saint-Clément 12 A3
89 Saint-Clément 12 A3
49 Saint-Clément-de-la-Place 17 A2
17 Saint-Clément-des-Baleines 22 C2
79 Saint-Clémentin 23 A1
69 Saint-Clément-sur-Valsonne 31 C1
22 Saint-Clet 8 D2
92 Saint-Cloud 11 C2
44 Saint-Colomban 16 C3
73 Saint-Colomban-des-Villards 32 C2
47 Saint-Côme 35 D2
12 Saint-Côme-d'Olt 36 D2
50 Saint-Côme-du-Mont 3 D3
56 Saint-Congard 16 B1
15 Saint-Constant 36 C1
61 Saint-Cornier-des-Landes 10 A2
72 Saint-Cosme-en-Vairais 10 A2
11 Saint-Couat-d'Aude 42 C2
35 Saint-Coulomb 9 C2
17 Saint-Coutant-le-Grand 23 A3
05 Saint-Crépin 33 D1
17 Saint-Crépin 33 A3
60 Saint-Crépin-Ibouvillers 5 C3
40 Saint-Cricq-Chalosse 40 D1
24 Saint-Cyprien 29 D3
66 Saint-Cyprien 43 D3
66 Saint-Cyprien-Plage 43 D3
12 Saint-Cyprien-sur-Dourdou 36 C1
87 Saint-Cyr 29 D1
85 Saint-Cyr-des-Gats 22 D2
50 Saint-Cyr-du-Bailleul 10 A2
41 Saint-Cyr-du-Gault 17 D2
49 Saint-Cyr-en-Bourg 17 B3
85 Saint-Cyr-en-Talmondais 22 C2
45 Saint-Cyr-en-Val 18 B1
61 Saint-Cyr-la-Rosière 10 C3
69 Saint-Cyr-le-Chatoux 25 C3
78 Saint-Cyr-l'École 11 C2
89 Saint-Cyr-les-Colons 19 B2
42 Saint-Cyr-les-Vignes 31 C1
39 Saint-Cyr-Montmalin 26 B1
37 Saint-Cyr-sur-Loire 17 C2
01 Saint-Cyr-sur-Menthon 25 D3
83 Saint-Cyr-sur-Mer 44 B2
77 Saint-Cyr-sur-Morin 12 A1
06 St-Dalmas-de-Tende 39 B3
06 St-Dalmas-Valdeblore 39 A3
11 Saint-Denis 42 C2
93 Saint-Denis 11 C1
63 St-Denis-Combarnazat 31 A1
53 Saint-Denis-d'Anjou 17 B1
28 Saint-Denis-d'Authou 10 C3
53 Saint-Denis-de-Gastines 10 A3
45 St-Denis-de-l'Hôtel 18 C1
36 Saint-Denis-de-Jouhet 24 B2
32 Saint-Denis-de-Pile 29 B3
28 Saint-Denis-des-Puits 11 A3
17 Saint-Denis-d'Oléron 22 C3
72 Saint-Denis-d'Orques 17 B1
27 St-Denis-du-Béhélan 10 D1
72 St-Denis-du-Payré 22 D2
17 Saint-Denis-du-Pin 23 A3
01 Saint-Denis-en-Bugey 32 A1
48 St-Denis-en-Margeride 37 A1
85 St-Denis-la-Chevasse 22 C1
50 Saint-Denis-le-Gast 9 D1
61 St-Denis-sur-Sarthon 10 B2
22 Saint-Denoual 9 B2
71 Saint-Désert 24 D1
03 Saint-Désiré 24 C2
19 Saint-Dézery 30 C2
84 Saint-Didier 38 A3
01 Saint-Didier-d'Aussiat 26 A3
43 Saint-Didier-en-Velay 31 C2
03 Saint-Didier-la-Forêt 25 A3
01 Saint-Didier-sur-Chalaronne 25 D3
88 Saint-Dié 13 D3
63 St-Dier-d'Auvergne 31 A1
05 Saint-Didsier 38 B1
17 Saint-Dizant-du-Gua 29 A2
52 Saint-Dizier 12 D2
23 Saint-Dizier-Leyrenne 24 B3
56 Saint-Dolay 16 B2
35 Saint-Dominuec 9 C3
22 Saint-Donan 9 A2
30 Saint-Donat 30 D2
26 Saint-Donat-sur-l'Herbasse 31 D3
64 Saint-Dos 40 D1
34 Saint-Drézéry 43 B1
43 Saint-Eble 31 A3
22 Saint-Efflam 8 C1
38 Saint-Égrève 32 B3
11 Saint-Eliph 11 A3
31 Saint-Élix-le-Château 41 D2
32 Saint-Élix-Theux 41 C1
53 Saint-Ellier-du-Maine 9 D3
29 Saint-Éloy 8 B2
63 Saint-Éloy-la-Glacière 31 B2
63 Saint-Éloy-les-Mines 24 D3
71 Saint-Émiland 25 C1
33 Saint-Émilion 29 B3
25 Saint-Ennemond 25 A2
37 Saint-Épain 17 C3
16 Saint-Erblon 11 C1
91 Saint-Escobille 11 B3
64 Saint-Esteben 40 C2
24 Saint-Estèphe 29 C1
33 Saint-Estèphe 28 D2
66 Saint-Estève 47 D2
84 Saint-Estève 38 A3
42 Saint-Étienne 31 C2
08 Saint-Étienne-à-Arnes 6 C3
62 Saint-Étienne-au-Mont 1 B2

68 Steinsoultz 21 A2
55 Stenay 7 A3
08 Stonne 6 D3
68 Stosswihr 21 A1
67 Stotzheim 14 A3
67 Strasbourg 14 B2
59 Strazeele 1 D2
57 Sturzelbronn 14 A1
90 Suarce 21 A2
70 Suaucourt-et-Pisseloup 20 B2
37 Sublaines 17 D3
18 Subligny 18 D3
89 Subligny 12 A3
14 Subles 4 A3
09 Suc-et-Sentenac 42 A3
44 Sucé-s.-Erdre 16 C2
94 Sucy-en-Brie 11 C2
41 Suèvres 18 A2
63 Sugères 31 A1
58 Suilly-la-Tour 19 A3
51 Suippes 12 C1
01 Sulignat 25 D3
60 Sully 5 B3
71 Sully 25 C1
45 Sully-la-Chapelle 18 C1
45 Sully-sur-Loire 18 C2
30 Sumène 37 B3
31 Superbagnères 41 C3
63 Super-Besse 30 D2
05 Super-Dévoluy 38 B1
15 Super Lioran 30 D3
04 Super-Sauze 38 D2
67 Surbourg 14 B1
61 Suré 10 C3
92 Suresnes 11 C1
72 Surfonds 17 C1
02 Surfontaine 6 A2
17 Surgères 23 A3
58 Surgy 19 A2
86 Surin 23 C3
16 Suris 29 C1
14 Surrain 4 A3
50 Surtainville 3 C3
18 Sury-ès-Bois 18 D2
42 Sury-le-Comtal 31 C2
56 Surzur 16 A2
87 Sussac 30 B1
01 Sutrieu 32 B1
26 Suze-la-Rousse 37 D2
72 Suze-sur-Sarthe (La) 17 B1
02 Suzy 6 A3
39 Syam 26 B1
12 Sylvanès 36 D3
34 Sylveréal 43 C1

T

32 Tachoires 41 C1
71 Tagnière (La) 25 C1
08 Tagnon 6 C3
68 Tagsdorf 21 A2
33 Taillan-Médoc (Le) 29 A3
17 Taillant 29 A1
61 Taillebois 10 B2
33 Taillecavat 35 B1
02 Taillefontaine 6 A3
35 Taillis 9 D3
89 Tainay 19 A2
26 Tain-l'Hermitage 31 D3
80 Taisnil 5 C2
79 Taizé 23 B1
16 Taizé-Aizie 23 C3
08 Taizy 6 C3
11 Talairan 42 C3
33 Talais 28 D2
57 Talange 7 C3
21 Talant 19 D3
29 Tal-Ar-Groas 8 B2
42 Talaudière (La) 31 C2
41 Talcy 18 A2
33 Talence 35 A1
35 Talensac 9 C3
15 Talizat 30 D3
71 Tallant 25 D2
05 Tallard 38 C2
40 Taller 34 C3
74 Talloires 32 C1
2B Tallone 45 B2
80 Talmas 5 C1
21 Talmay 20 A3
17 Talmont 28 D1
85 Talmont-Saint-Hilaire 22 C2
60 Talmontiers 5 B3
83 Tamaris-sur-Mer 44 B2
34 Tamarissière (La) 43 A2
58 Tamnay-en-Bazois 25 B1
76 Tancarville 4 C3
49 Tancoigné 17 A3
39 Tancua 26 B2
62 Tangry 1 C3
74 Taninges 26 D3
89 Tanlay 19 C1
08 Tannay 6 D3
58 Tannay 19 B3
55 Tannois 13 A2
54 Tantonville 13 C3
81 Tanus 36 C3
16 Taponnat-Fleurignac 29 C1
31 Tarabel 42 A1
83 Taradeau 44 C1
69 Tarare 25 C3
13 Tarascon 43 D1
09 Tarascon-sur-Ariège 42 A3
65 Tarbes 41 B2
25 Tarcenay 20 C3

64 Tardets-Sorholus 40 D2
33 Targon 35 A1
30 Tarnac 30 B1
40 Tarnos 40 C1
19 Tarsul 19 D2
34 Tartas 34 D3
60 Tartigny 5 C2
04 Tartonne 38 C3
39 Tassenières 26 A1
31 Tassin-la-Demi-Lune 31 D1
17 Taugon 22 D2
08 Taulé 8 C2
43 Taulhac 31 B3
37 Taulignan 37 D2
66 Taulis 43 C3
56 Taupont 16 B1
12 Tauriac-de-Naucelle 36 C1
81 Tauriac 36 A3
12 Tauriac-de-Camarès 42 D1
66 Taurinya 43 C3
41 Taurignan-Castet 41 D3
66 Tautavel 42 D2
63 Tauves 30 C2
17 Tauxigny 17 D3
37 Tavant 26 A1
17 Tavaux 17 D3
02 Tavaux-et-Pontséricourt 6 B2
37 Tavel 37 D3
2A Tavera 45 C3
83 Tavernes 44 C1
11 Taverny 11 C1
39 Taxenne 20 B3
25 Tazilly 25 B1
66 Tech (Le) 43 C3
33 Teich (Le) 34 D1
07 Teil (Le) 37 D2
63 Teilhet 24 D3
35 Teillay 16 C1
44 Teillé 16 C2
81 Teillet 36 C3
03 Teillet-Argenty 24 C3
50 Teilleul (Le) 10 A2
29 Telgruc-sur-Mer 8 B2
54 Tellancourt 7 B3
21 Tellecey 20 A3
72 Téloché 17 C1
33 Temple (Le) 28 D3
41 Temple (Le) 17 D1
44 Temple-de-Bretagne (Le) 16 C2
59 Templeuve 2 A3
01 Tenay 32 A1
43 Tence 31 C3
38 Tencin 32 B2
06 Tende 39 B3
88 Tendon 20 D1
72 Tennie 10 B3
86 Tercé 23 C2
23 Tercillat 24 B2
40 Tercis-les-Bains 40 C1
02 Tergnier 6 A2
32 Termes-d'Armagnac 41 B1
73 Termignon 32 D2
28 Terminiers 18 B1
21 Ternant 19 D3
58 Ternant 25 B1
41 Ternay 17 D2
15 Ternes (Les) 30 D3
70 Ternuay-Melay-et-Saint-Hilaire 20 D1
02 Terny-Sorny 6 A3
38 Terrasse (La) 32 C2
42 Terrasse-s.-Dorlay (La) 31 C2
24 Terrasson-la-Villedieu 35 C3
32 Terraube 41 B1
52 Terre-Natale 20 B1
42 Terrenoire 31 C2
12 Terrisse (La) 36 D1
46 Terrou 36 B1
87 Tersannes 23 D3
80 Tertry 6 A2
17 Tesson 29 A1
49 Tessoualle (La) 17 A3
50 Tessy-sur-Vire 10 A1
33 Teste (La) 34 C1
57 Téterchen 7 C3
50 Teurthéville-Hague 3 C2
46 Teyssieu 30 B3
19 Thalamy 30 C2
68 Thann 21 A1
68 Thannenkirch 14 A3
67 Thanvillé 14 A3
14 Thaon 4 B3
88 Thaon-les-Vosges 13 C3
44 Tharon-Plage 16 B3
18 Thaumiers 24 D1
57 Théding 13 D1
03 Theil (Le) 25 A2
50 Theil (Le) 3 D2
61 Theil (Le) 10 D3
35 Theil-de-Bretagne (Le) 16 B3
41 Theillay 18 B3
89 Theil-sur-Vanne 12 A3
56 Theix 16 A1
54 Thélod 13 B2
46 Thémines 36 B1
17 Thénac 29 A1
41 Thenay 18 A3
03 Theneuille 24 D2
79 Thénezay 23 B1
18 Thénioux 18 B3
21 Thenissey 19 D2
24 Thenon 29 D3
06 Théoule-sur-Mer 45 A1
65 Thermes-Magnoac 41 A1
62 Thérouanne 1 C3

39 Thervay 20 B3
05 Théus 38 C2
36 Thévet-Saint-Julien 24 B2
50 Théville 3 D2
38 Theys 32 B2
28 Thézac 28 D1
11 Thézan-des-Corbières 42 D2
04 Thèze 38 B2
64 Thèze 41 A1
18 Thézée 18 A3
30 Théziers 37 D3
01 Thézillieu 32 B1
87 Thiat 23 D3
54 Thiaucourt-Regniéville 13 C1
27 Thiberville 10 C1
51 Thibie 12 C1
60 Thibivillers 5 B3
54 Thiébauménil 13 D2
51 Thiéblemont-Farémont 12 D2
12 Thieffrain 12 C3
70 Thieffrans 20 C2
03 Thiel-sur-Alcoin 25 B2
60 Thiepval 5 D1
63 Thiers 31 A1
55 Thierville-sur-Meuse 13 A1
80 Thiescourt 5 D3
80 Thieulloy-l'Abbaye 5 B2
80 Thieuloy-la-Ville 5 B2
80 Thieuloy-Saint-Antoine 5 B2
60 Thieux 5 C3
15 Thiézac 30 C3
10 Thil 12 D3
31 Thil 41 D1
27 Thilliers-en-Vexin (Les) 13 A1
55 Thillombois 13 A1
88 Thillot (Le) 20 D1
45 Thimory 18 C1
07 Thines 37 B2
08 Thin-le-Moutier 6 C2
57 Thionville 7 B3
28 Thiron 10 C3
28 Thivars 11 A3
24 Thiviers 29 D2
37 Thizay 17 D2
69 Thizy 25 C3
04 Thoard 38 C3
39 Thoirette 26 B3
73 Thoiry 32 C2
78 Thoiry 11 B2
01 Thoissey 25 D3
39 Thoissia 26 A2
21 Thoisy-la-Berchère 19 D3
86 Thollet 23 D2
74 Thollon 26 D2
13 Tholonet (Le) 44 B1
88 Tholy (Le) 20 D1
27 Thomer-la-Sogne 11 A1
77 Thomery 11 D3
24 Thonac 29 D3
55 Thonelle 7 A3
74 Thônes 32 C1
52 Thonnance-lès-Joinville 13 A3
52 Thonnance-les-Moulins 13 A3
55 Thonne-le-Thil 7 A3
74 Thonon-les-Bains 26 C2
84 Thor (Le) 38 A3
25 Thoraise 20 B3
04 Thorame-Basse 38 D3
04 Thorame-Haute 38 D3
72 Thorée-les-Pins 17 B2
06 Thorenc 38 D3
74 Thorens-Glières 26 C3
54 Thorey-Lyautey 13 B3
21 Thorey-sur-Ouche 19 D3
49 Thorigné-d'Anjou 17 A2
35 Thorigné-sur-Vilaine 16 B1
53 Thorigné-en-Charnie 17 B1
72 Thorigné-sur-Dué 17 C1
79 Thorigny 23 A3
85 Thorigny 22 C2
89 Thorigny-sur-Oreuse 12 A3
83 Thoronet (Le) 44 C1
17 Thors 29 A1
10 Thors 12 D3
21 Thoste 19 C2
17 Thou (Le) 22 D3
18 Thou 18 D2
45 Thou 17 A3
49 Thouarcé 16 C3
44 Thouaré-sur-Loire 16 C2
47 Thouars-sur-Garonne 35 C2
79 Thouars 23 B1
85 Thouarsais-Bouildroux 22 C2
06 Thouët-sur-V. 39 A3
51 Thoult-Trosnay (Le) 12 C1
08 Thour (Le) 6 B3
35 Thourie 16 B2
41 Thoury 18 B2
77 Thoury-Ferottes 11 D3
66 Thuès-entre-Valls 43 C3
07 Thueyts 37 C1
54 Thuilley-aux-Groseilles 13 B2
88 Thuillières 13 B3
66 Thuir 43 D3
27 Thuit (Le) 5 A3
86 Thurageau 23 C1
86 Thuré 23 C1
63 Thuret 31 A1
71 Thurey 26 A1
69 Thurins 31 D1
21 Thury 19 A2
89 Thury 19 A2
14 Thury-Harcourt 10 B1
61 Ticheville 11 C1
26 Tichey 26 A1
67 Tiefenbach 14 A1
49 Tiercé 17 A2

12 Tiergue 36 D3
48 Tieule (La) 37 A1
85 Tiffauges 16 D3
73 Tignes 32 D2
45 Tigy 18 C1
21 Til-Châtel 20 A2
40 Tilh 40 D1
65 Tilhouse 41 B2
32 Tillac 41 B1
28 Tillay-le-Peneux 11 B3
60 Tillé 5 C3
55 Tilleuls-Vaudoncourt 7 B3
49 Tillières 16 D3
27 Tillières-sur-Avre 11 A1
51 Tilloy-Bellay 12 C1
59 Tilloy-les-Marchiennes 2 A3
62 Tilloy-les-Mofflaines 5 D1
27 Tilly 11 B1
36 Tilly 24 A2
14 Tilly-sur-Seulles 4 A3
61 Tinchebray 10 A2
62 Tincques 1 C3
51 Tinqueux 6 B3
35 Tinténiac 9 C3
71 Tintry 25 C1
43 Tiranges 31 B2
50 Tirepied 9 D2
89 Tissey 19 B1
33 Tizac-de-Curton 35 A1
2A Tizzano 45 D3
24 Tocane-Saint-Apre 29 C2
50 Tocqueville 3 D2
76 Tocqueville-sur-Eu 5 A1
2A Tolla 45 C3
77 Tombe (La) 12 A3
47 Tombebœuf 35 C1
81 Tonnac 36 B3
17 Tonnay-Boutonne 23 A3
17 Tonnay-Charente 22 D3
47 Tonneins 35 C2
89 Tonnerre 19 B1
22 Tonquédec 8 D1
53 Torcé-Viviers-en-Charnie 10 B3
72 Torcé-en-Vallée 10 C3
52 Torcenay 20 A1
02 Torcy-en-Valois 12 A1
76 Torcy-le-Grand 5 A2
49 Torfou 16 D3
50 Torigni-sur-Vire 10 A1
16 Torsac 29 B2
18 Torteron 24 D1
10 Torvilliers 12 B3
40 Tosse 40 C1
01 Tossiat 26 A3
65 Tostat 41 B2
76 Tôtes 5 A2
14 Tôtes 10 C1
44 Touches (Les) 16 C2
17 Touches-de-Périgny (Les) 29 B1
89 Toucy 19 A2
06 Toudon 39 A3
82 Touffailles 35 D2
21 Touillon 19 C2
54 Toul 13 B2
83 Toulon 44 B2
12 Toulonjac 36 B2
51 Toulon-la-Montagne 12 C1
03 Toulon-sur-Allier 25 A2
71 Toulon-sur-Arroux 25 C1
31 Toulouse 42 A1
40 Toulouzette 34 D3
23 Toulx-Sainte-Croix 24 C3
14 Touques 4 C3
62 Touquet-Paris-Plage (Le) 1 B3
77 Touquin 11 D2
29 Tourch 8 C3
24 Tour-Blanche (La) 29 C2
59 Tourcoing 2 A2
84 Tour-d'Aigues (La) 44 B1
63 Tour-d'Auvergne (La) 30 D2
39 Tour-du-Meix (La) 26 B2
56 Tour-du-Parc (Le) 16 A2
38 Tour-du-Pin (La) 32 B2
14 Tour-en-Bessin 4 A3
06 Tourette-Levens 45 A1
06 Tourette-sur-Loup 45 A1
49 Tourlandry (La) 17 A3
50 Tourlaville 3 D2
39 Tourmont 26 B1
77 Tournan-en-Brie 11 D2
65 Tournay 41 B2
33 Tournans 35 A1
32 Tournecoupe 35 C3
31 Tournefeuille 42 A1
06 Tournefort 39 A3
15 Tournemire 30 C3
08 Tournes 6 C2
14 Tourneur (Le) 10 A1
14 Tournières 4 A3
45 Tournoisis 18 B1
07 Tournon 31 D2
47 Tournon-d'Agenais 35 D2
37 Tournon-Saint-Martin 23 D2
71 Tournus 25 D2
27 Tourny 11 B1
61 Tourouvre 10 D2
37 Tours 17 D2
73 Tours-en-Savoie 32 C2
80 Tours-en-Vimeu 5 B1
54 Tours-sur-Marne 12 C1
63 Tours-sous-Meymont 31 B1
34 Tour-sur-Orb (La) 43 A1
79 Tourtenay 17 B3
08 Tourteron 6 D3
24 Tourtoirac 29 D2

58 Vauclaix 19 B3
70 Vauconcourt-Nervezain 20 B2
76 Vaucottes 4 C2
55 Vaucouleurs 13 B2
60 Vaudancourt 5 B3
71 Vaudebarrier 25 C2
49 Vaudelnay 17 B3
54 Vaudémont 13 B3
89 Vaudeurs 19 A1
77 Vaudoy-en-Brie 12 A2
27 Vaudreuil (Le) 5 A3
14 Vaudry 10 A1
25 Vaufrey 20 D3
69 Vaugneray 31 D1
49 Vaulandry 17 B2
15 Vaulmier (Le) 30 C3
87 Vaulry 23 D2
74 Vaulx 32 B1
38 Vaulx-Milieu 32 A2
60 Vaumain (Le) 5 B3
03 Vaumas 25 B2
79 Vausseroux 23 B2
53 Vautorte 10 A3
13 Vauvenargues 44 B1
30 Vauvert 43 C1
50 Vauville 3 C2
70 Vauvillers 20 C1
31 Vaux (Le) 42 B1
86 Vaux 23 C2
02 Vaux-en-Vermandois 6 A2
25 Vaux-et-Chantegrue 26 C1
55 Vaux-la-Grande 13 A2
39 Vaux-lès-Saint-Claude 26 B2
52 Vaux-sous-Aubigny 20 A2
17 Vaux-sur-Mer 28 D1
78 Vaux-sur-Seine 11 B1
55 Vavincourt 13 A2
44 Vay 16 C2
46 Vayrac 30 B3
33 Vayres 29 A3
87 Vayres 29 D1
91 Vayres-sur-Essonne 11 C3
82 Vazerac 36 A2
42 Veauche 31 C2
18 Veaugues 18 D3
57 Veckring 7 C3
15 Védrines-Saint-Loup 31 A3
54 Vého 13 D2
21 Veilly 19 C3
55 Velaines 13 A2
70 Velesmes-Echevanne 20 B2
24 Vélines 29 B3
78 Vélizy-Villacoublay 11 C2
86 Vellèches 23 C1
70 Vellefaux 20 C2
84 Velleron 38 A3
25 Vellerot-lès-Belvoir 20 C3
36 Velles 24 B2
90 Vellescot 20 D2
25 Vellevans 20 C3
70 Vellexon-Queutey-et-Vaudey 20 B2
85 Velluire-les-Marais 22 D2
55 Velosnes 7 A3
88 Velotte-et-Tatignecourt 13 C3
62 Vélu 5 D1
15 Velzic 30 C3
95 Vémars 11 D1
27 Venables 11 A1
2B Venaco 45 B2
44 Venansault 22 C1
21 Venarey-les-Laumes 19 C2
84 Venasque 38 A3
06 Vence 45 A1
34 Vendargues 43 B1
03 Vendat 25 A3
33 Vendays-Montalivet 28 D2
34 Vendémian 43 A1
71 Vendenesse-lès-Charolles 25 C2
67 Vendenheim 14 B2
02 Vendeuil 6 A2
86 Vendeuvre-en-Poitou 23 C1
10 Vendeuvre-sur-Barse 12 C3
31 Vendine 42 B1
62 Vendin-le-Vieil 1 D3
36 Vendœuvres 24 A1
41 Vendôme 17 D1
42 Vendranges 31 C1
85 Vendrennes 22 D1
34 Vendres 43 A2
08 Vendresse 6 D2
17 Vénérand 29 A1
70 Venère 20 B3
02 Vénérolles 6 B1
31 Venerque 42 A2
81 Venès 42 B1
18 Venesmes 24 C1
77 Veneux-les-Sablons 11 D3
50 Vengeons 10 A2
70 Venisey 20 B1
69 Vénissieux 31 D1
89 Venizy 19 B1
45 Vennecy 18 B1
27 Venon 11 A1
38 Venosc 32 C3
89 Venouse 19 B1
33 Vensac 28 D2
13 Ventabren 44 A1
05 Ventavon 38 B2
51 Ventelay 6 B3
09 Ventenac 42 A3
11 Ventenac-d'Aude 42 D2
51 Venteuil 12 B1
2B Ventiseri 45 C2
88 Ventron 20 D1
16 Vents (Les) 29 C1
60 Verberie 5 D3
25 Vercel-Villedieu-le-Camp 20 C3
26 Vercheny 38 A1
49 Verchers-sur-Layon (Les) 17 B3
80 Vercourt 1 B3
04 Verdaches 38 C2
33 Verdelais 35 A1
41 Verdes 18 A1
64 Verdets 40 D2
81 Verdier (Le) 36 B3
83 Verdière (La) 44 B1
16 Verdille 29 B1
24 Verdon 35 C1
33 Verdon-sur-Mer (Le) 28 D1
21 Verdonnet 19 C2
55 Verdun 13 A1
82 Verdun-sur-Garonne 35 D3
71 Verdun-sur-le-Doubs 25 D1
18 Vereaux 24 D1
37 Véretz 17 D3
31 Verfeil 42 A1
82 Verfeil 36 B2
30 Verfeuil 37 C3
43 Vergezac 31 B3
2A Verghia 45 C3
32 Vergoignan 41 A1
04 Vergons 38 D3
83 Vérignon 44 C1
24 Vergt 29 C3
24 Vergt-de-Biron 35 D1
39 Véria 26 A2
28 Vérigny 11 A2
17 Vérines 22 D3
02 Vermand 6 A2
89 Vermenton 19 B2
49 Vern-d'Anjou 17 A2
49 Vernantes 17 B2
43 Verne 31 C3
72 Verneil-le-Chétif 17 C2
36 Vernelle (La) 18 A3
31 Vernet (Le) 42 A2
09 Vernet (Le) 42 A2
63 Vernet-la-Varenne 31 A2
66 Vernet-les-Bains 43 C3
63 Verneughéol 30 C1
51 Verneuil 12 B1
58 Verneuil 25 A1
03 Verneuil-en-Bourbonnais 25 A2
37 Verneuil-le-Château 17 C3
87 Verneuil-Moustiers 24 A2
27 Verneuil-sur-Avre 10 D2
37 Verneuil-sur-Indre 17 D3
78 Verneuil-sur-Seine 11 B1
25 Vernierfontaine 20 C3
09 Verniolle 42 A2
50 Vernix 9 D2
49 Vernoil 17 B2
21 Vernois-lès-Vesvres 20 A2
27 Vernon 11 A1
86 Vernon 23 C2
10 Vernonvilliers 12 D3
21 Vernot 19 D2
37 Vernou-s.-Brenne 17 D2
41 Vernou-en-Sologne 18 B2
28 Vernouillet 11 A2
79 Vernoux-en-Gâtine 23 A1
07 Vernoux-en-Vivarais 37 D1
35 Vern-sur-Seiche 9 C3
57 Verny 13 C1
2A Vero 45 C3
89 Véron 19 A1
71 Verosvres 25 C2
38 Verpillière (La) 32 A2
21 Verrey-sous-Salmaise 19 D2
49 Verrie 17 B3
10 Verrières 12 C3
51 Verrières 12 D1
61 Verrières 10 C3
86 Verrières 23 C2
25 Verrières-du-Grosbois 20 C3
79 Verrines-sous-Celles 23 B3
46 Vers 36 A2
78 Versailles 11 C2
01 Versailleux 32 A1
39 Vers-en-Montagne 26 B1
12 Versols-et-Lapeyre 36 D3
14 Verson 10 B1
39 Vers-sous-Sellières 26 B1
60 Ver-sur-Launette 11 D1
14 Ver-sur-Mer 4 B3
40 Vert 35 A3
78 Vert 11 B1
17 Vert-Bois (Le) 28 C1
24 Verteillac 29 C2
47 Verteuil-d'Agenais 35 C2
16 Verteuil-sur-Charente 23 C3
33 Vertheuil 28 D2
89 Vertilly 12 A3
91 Vert-le-Grand 11 C2
62 Verton 1 B3
44 Vertou 16 C3
51 Vertus 12 B1
55 Vertuzey 13 B2
02 Vervins 6 B2
71 Verzé 25 D2
51 Verzenay 12 C1
51 Verzy 12 C1
39 Vescles 26 B2
2B Vescovato 45 B2
18 Vesdun 24 C2
78 Vésinet (Le) 11 C1
27 Vesly 5 B3
70 Vesoul 20 C2
07 Vesseaux 37 C1
50 Vessey 9 D2
91 Vétheuil 11 B1
76 Veules-les-Roses 4 D2
76 Veulettes-sur-Mer 4 D2
03 Veurdre (Le) 24 D1
38 Veurey-Voroize 32 B2
51 Veuve (La) 12 C1
41 Veuves 18 A2
21 Veuvey-sur-Ouche 19 D3
05 Veynes 38 B2
12 Veyreau 37 A2
63 Veyre-Monton 31 A1
74 Veyrier-du-Lac 32 C1
19 Veyrières 30 C2
38 Veyrins-Thuellin 32 B2
60 Vez 5 D3
15 Vezac 36 C1
89 Vézannes 19 B1
02 Vezaponin 6 A3
15 Vèze 30 D3
89 Vézelay 19 B2
54 Vézelise 13 B3
30 Vézenobres 37 C3
51 Vézier (Le) 12 A2
02 Vézilly 12 B1
49 Vezins 17 A3
12 Vézins-de-Lévézou 36 D2
2B Vezzani 45 B2
28 Viabon 11 B3
48 Vialas 37 B2
19 Viam 30 B2
81 Viane 42 C1
47 Vianne 35 C2
95 Viarmes 11 C1
12 Viarouge 36 D2
34 Vias 43 A2
12 Vibal (Le) 36 D2
16 Vibrac 29 B1
72 Vibraye 17 D1
09 Vicdessos 42 A3
65 Vic-en-Bigorre 41 B2
32 Vic-Fezensac 35 B3
03 Vichy 25 A3
63 Vic-le-Comte 31 A1
2A Vico 45 C3
80 Vicogne (La) 5 C1
22 Vicomté-s.-Rance (La) 9 C2
03 Vicq 25 A3
36 Vicq-Exemplet 24 B2
86 Vicq-sur-Gartempe 23 D1
36 Vicq-sur-Nahon 18 A3
15 Vic-sur-Cère 30 C3
57 Vic-sur-Seille 13 C2
83 Vidauban 44 C2
60 Viefvillers 5 C2
43 Vieille-Brioude 31 A3
39 Vieille-Loye (La) 26 B1
27 Vieille-Lyre (La) 10 D1
15 Vieillespesse 31 A3
15 Vieillevie 36 C1
44 Vieillevigne 16 C3
62 Vieil-Moutier 1 B2
02 Viel-Arcy 6 B3
32 Viella 41 B1
65 Vielle-Aure 41 B3
64 Viellepinte 41 B2
40 Vielle-Saint-Girons 34 C3
64 Vielleségure 40 D1
40 Vielle-Soubiran 35 B3
81 Vielmur-sur-Agout 42 B1
02 Viels-Maisons 12 A1
21 Vielverge 20 A3
48 Vielvic 37 B2
38 Vienne 31 D2
45 Vienne-en-Val 18 C1
51 Vienne-la-Ville 12 D1
51 Vienne-le-Château 12 D1
84 Viens 38 B3
23 Viersat 24 C3
14 Vierville-sur-Mer 4 A3
18 Vierzon 18 B3
18 Vierzon-Forges 18 C3
02 Vierzy 6 A3
14 Viessoix 10 A1
03 Vieure 24 D2
34 Vieussan 42 D1
59 Vieux-Berquin 1 D2
40 Vieux-Boucau-les-Bains 34 C3
35 Vieux-Bourg (Le) 9 C2
56 Vieux-Bourg 16 B1
59 Vieux-Condé 2 B3
77 Vieux-Maisons 12 A2
60 Vieux-Moulin 5 D3
27 Vieux-Port 4 D3
59 Vieux-Reng 2 B3
80 Vieux-Rouen-sur-Bresle 5 B2
27 Vieux-Villez 11 A1
06 Vievola 39 B3
21 Viévigne 20 A2
21 Viévy 25 C1
38 Vif 32 B3
02 Viffort 12 A1
15 Vigean (Le) 30 C3
30 Vigan (Le) 37 B3
46 Vigan (Le) 36 A1
86 Vigeant (Le) 23 C3
19 Vigeois 30 A2
45 Viglain 18 C2
80 Vignacourt 5 C1
2A Vignalella 45 D2
31 Vignaux 41 D1
05 Vigneaux (Les) 38 D1
48 Vignes (Les) 37 A2
55 Vigneulles-lès-Hattonchâtel 13 B1
44 Vigneux-de-Bretagne 16 C2
02 Vigneux-Hocquet 6 B2
11 Vignevieille 42 C3
52 Vignory 13 A3
18 Vignoux-sur-Barangeon 18 C3
95 Vigny 11 B1
36 Vigoux 24 A2
57 Vigy 13 B3
49 Vihiers 17 A3
36 Vijon 24 B2
22 Vildé-Guingalan 9 B2
03 Vilhain (Le) 24 D2
18 Villabon 18 D3
24 Villac 30 A3
10 Villacerf 12 B3
10 Villadin 12 B3
33 Villagrains 35 A1
21 Villaines-en-Duesmois 19 C2
53 Villaines-la-Juhel 10 B3
37 Villaines-les-Rochers 17 C3
95 Villaines-sous-Bois 11 C1
24 Villamblard 29 C3
33 Villandraut 35 A2
37 Villandry 17 C3
05 Villard (Le) 38 C1
74 Villard 26 C3
38 Villard-Bonnot 32 B3
11 Villardebelle 42 C3
38 Villard-de-Lans 32 B3
73 Villard-Léger 32 C2
38 Villard-N.D. 32 C3
38 Villard-Reymond 32 C3
73 Villard-sur-Doron 32 D1
74 Villards-sur-Thônes (Les) 32 C1
05 Villar-Loubière 38 C1
24 Villars 29 C2
84 Villars 38 A3
52 Villars-en-Azois 19 D1
25 Villars-lès-Blamont 20 D3
01 Villars-les-Dombes 26 A3
06 Villars-sur-Var 39 A3
11 Villasavary 42 B2
31 Villaudric 36 A3
67 Villé 14 A3
41 Ville-aux-Clercs (La) 18 A1
50 Villebaudon 9 D1
77 Villebéon 11 D3
21 Villebichot 19 D3
01 Villebois 32 A1
16 Villebois-Lavalette 29 C2
37 Villebourg 17 C2
03 Villebret 24 C3
82 Villebrumier 36 A3
77 Villecerf 11 D3
41 Villechauve 17 D2
69 Villechenève 31 C1
89 Villechétive 19 A1
12 Villecomtal 36 C2
32 Villecomtal-sur-Arros 41 B2
91 Villeconin 11 C2
83 Villecroze 44 C1
11 Villedaigne 42 D2
92 Ville-d'Avray 11 C2
55 Ville-devant-Chaumont 7 A3
17 Villedieu (La) 23 A3
21 Villedieu 19 C1
23 Villedieu (La) 30 B1
48 Villedieu (La) 37 A1
86 Villedieu-du-Clain (La) 23 C2
82 Ville-Dieu-du-Temple (La) 35 D1
70 Villedieu-en-Fontenette (La) 20 C2
49 Villedieu-la-Blouère 16 D3
61 Villedieu-les-Bailleul 10 C2
50 Villedieu-les-Poêles 9 D1
36 Villedieu-sur-Indre 24 A1
2B Ville-di-Paraso 45 B3
37 Villedômain 18 A3
51 Ville-Dommange 12 B1
17 Villedoux 22 D2
51 Ville-en-Tardenois 12 B1
16 Villefagnan 23 B3
89 Villefargeau 19 A2
11 Villefloure 42 C2
48 Villefort 37 B2
89 Villefranche 19 A1
81 Villefranche-d'Albigeois 36 C3
03 Villefranche-d'Allier 24 D2
66 Villefranche-de-Conflent 43 C3
31 Villefranche-de-Lauragais 42 A2
24 Villefranche-de-Lonchat 29 B3
12 Villefranche-de-Panat 36 D3
12 Villefranche-de-Rouergue 36 B2
24 Villefranche-du-Périgord 35 D1
47 Villefranche-du-Queyran 35 B2
41 Villefranche-sur-Cher 18 B3
06 Villefranche-sur-Mer 45 B1
69 Villefranche-sur-Saône 25 D3
11 Villegailhenc 42 C2
18 Villegenon 18 C2
11 Villegly 42 C2
36 Villegongis 24 A1
33 Villegouge 29 A3
36 Villegouin 24 A1
52 Villegusien-le-Lac 20 A2
94 Villejuif 11 C2
84 Villelaure 44 A1
82 Villemade 36 A3
34 Villemagne 42 D1
45 Villemandeur 18 D1
10 Villemaur-sur-Vanne 12 B3
60 Villembray 5 B3
77 Villemer 11 D3
49 Villemoisan 17 A2
66 Villemolaque 43 D3

II. Indice generale di luoghi geografici, curiosità turistiche e naturali
II. Index général des noms géographiques et des noms de curiosités touristiques et naturelles
II. General geographic areas and natural tourist attractions index

Achevé d'imprimer en fevrier 1988 par Printer Industria Gráfica, S.A., Barcelona, Espagne
Dépôt légal: mars 1988. Dépôt légal 1ʳᵉ édition: 2ᵉ trimestre 1976
Imprimé en Espagne